Management of Physical Education and Sport   Thirteenth Edition

March L. Krotee
North Carolina State University

Charles A. Bucher
(deceased)
University of Nevada, Las Vegas

Boston   Burr Ridge, IL   Dubuque, IA   Madison, WI   New York   San Francisco   St. Louis
Bangkok   Bogotá   Caracas   Kuala Lumpur   Lisbon   London   Madrid   Mexico City
Milan   Montreal   New Delhi   Santiago   Seoul   Singapore   Sydney   Taipei   Toronto

The McGraw-Hill Companies

Higher Education

*To my wife Leslie,
my two sons Chip and Rob,
my daughter-in-laws Kim and Margot,
granddaughter Katie and grandsons Will and Lee,
without whose love and support
such an undertaking would be impossible.
I love you.*

MANAGEMENT OF PHYSICAL EDUCATION AND SPORT
THIRTEENTH EDITION
Published by McGraw-Hill, a business unit of The McGraw-Hill Companies, Inc., 1221 Avenue of the Americas, New York, NY 10020. Copyright 2007, 2002, 1998, 1993, 1987, 1983, 1979, 1975, 1971, 1967, 1963, 1958, 1955 by The McGraw-Hill Companies, Inc. All rights reserved. No part of this publication may be reproduced or distributed in any form or by any means, or stored in a database or retrieval system, without the prior written consent of The McGraw-Hill Companies, Inc., including, but not limited to, in any network or other electronic storage of transmission, or broadcast for distance learning.

Some ancillaries, including electronic and print components, may not be available to customers outside the United States.

This book is printed on recycled, acid-free paper.

1 2 3 4 5 6 7 8 9 0 DOC/DOC 0 9 8 7 6

ISBN-13: 978-0-07-297292-4
ISBN-10: 0-07-297292-0

Vice president and editor-in-chief: *Emily Barrosse*
Publisher: *William R. Glass*
Senior sponsoring editor: *Christopher Johnson*
Executive marketing manager: *Pamela S. Cooper*
Director of development: *Kathleen Engelberg*
Developmental editor for technology: *Julia D. Ersery*
Media producer: *Michelle Borrelli*
Project manager: *Valerie Heffernan, Carlisle Publishing Services*
Compositor: *Carlisle Publishing Services*
Typeface: *10/12 Times Roman*
Printer: *R. R. Donnelley & Sons Company, Crawfordsville, IN*

Library of Congress Cataloging-in-Publication Data
Krotee, March Lee, 1943-
    Management of physical education and sport March L. Krotee, Charles A. Bucher
    13th ed.
        p. cm.
    Includes bibliographical references and index.
    ISBN 0-07-297292-0
    1. Physical education and training—Administration. 2. Sports administration. 3. Leisure.
I. Krotee, March L. II. Title.

GV343.5.B787 2007
613.7'068—dc22

                                                                        2005057690

www.mhhe.com

BRIEF CONTENTS

CONTENTS

v

Part 2   Management of Physical Education and Sport Programs   63

3   Physical Education Instructional Programs 64

Part 3 Management of Physical Education and Sport Programs in the Public and Private Sector 195

6

Physical Education and Sport Programs in the Public and Private Sector 196

Part 4　Management Functions 233

7　Human Resource Management and Supervision 234

The thirteenth edition of *Management of Physical Education and Sport* is designed to provide a comprehensive, contemporary text for management and administration courses dealing with physical education, sport, and recreation. The text has been carefully revised based on developments and trends that have taken place within our dynamic profession and reflects the most current thinking and research available. As in past editions, seminal works have been maintained and referenced to provide a solid foundation on which newer management concepts, skills, and techniques may be built.

NEW TO THIS EDITION

This thirteenth edition has maintained the conceptual framework of the previous edition; however, the content has been revised and shaped to reflect the most current trends affecting the organization and management of physical education, sport, and recreation in both the public and private domains. Where appropriate, crucial issues such as race, ethnicity, gender, age, and disability are discussed, and contemporary educational initiatives concerning multiculturalism and internationalization have been included.

Changes in the text include an expansion of the leadership and management foundations components in Chapter 1, The Management Process. Chapter 2, Management Organization to Achieve Objectives of Physical Education and Sport, has been revised and incorporates new physical education and sport objectives as well as enriched content concerning assessment.

Chapter 3, Physical Education Instructional Programs, includes the most current information on content standards, as well as updated information about public laws and programs for individuals with disabilities. New participatory information is included in Chapter 4 and 5, as are expanded discussions of gender equity, substance abuse, and risk management and security, along with the effects of these issues on physical education, sport, and recreation programs.

The chapters covering public and private sector physical education and sport programs, human resource management and supervision, and program development (Chapters 6, 7, and 8) have been extended in scope. Expanded coverage concerning various sport organizations, including the Women's Sports Foundation, and the Atlantic Coast Conference, are presented in these chapters, along with additional material concerning group dynamics and team building, professional growth, and potential employment opportunities. Chapter 9, Facility Management, includes an upgraded total facility management package (TFMP) as well as the latest information on joint partnering ventures. Chapters 10 and 11 offer the most up-to-date information about fiscal management, budget design, and purchase and care of supplies and equipment. Chapter 12, Management and the Athletic Training Program, expands its previous coverage concerning the important role that athletic training and sports medicine play for the teacher, coach, and sport administrator, and includes new NATA guidelines. Chapter 13, Legal Liability, Risk, and Insurance Management, has been reshaped and revised and includes new representative court cases concerning Title IX and product liability as well as risk management tips and guidelines for safe and effective teaching, coaching, and supervision. Chapter 14, Public Relations and Marketing, includes expanded guidelines concerning public relations and the media, as well as updated sections concerning advocacy, consumer involvement, and technology. Chapter 15, Office Management, includes updated information on record management systems as well as expanded material on office management objectives and tasks. The new edition also features a thoroughly revised illustration program, including many new photographs and reference diagrams, making the thirteenth edition of *Management of Physical Education and Sport* the most up-to-date and authoritative text in this regard in the profession.

PEDAGOGICAL FEATURES

To facilitate the text's use by students and instructors, several pedagogical aids have been incorporated into this edition. These include the following:

- Instructional Objectives and Competencies. Each chapter begins with instructional objectives and competencies that introduce the main points of the chapter. Attaining these objectives and competencies indicates fulfillment of the chapter's intent.
- Introductory Paragraphs. A short introduction begins each chapter. This provides students with a transition when progressing from the previous chapter.
- Chapter Summary. Each chapter ends with a brief review of the critical material presented in the chapter. These summaries assist students in focusing, understanding, and retaining the most important concepts covered in the chapter.
- Self-Assessment Activities. Each chapter includes a set of activities that enables students to determine whether they understand the main points in the chapter. These activities also serve as a means for students to place theory into practice and may be used as take-home or group assignments by instructors.
- References. Each chapter provides both foundational and contemporary references that may be used to acquire further information about the content presented.
- Suggested Readings. Additional readings have been selected and, where appropriate, annotated to enable students to further explore chapter topics.

- Internet Resources. Each chapter concludes with Take It To the Net! a feature containing useful Web sites pertaining to the chapter's content and assessment activities.

INSTRUCTOR'S RESOURCES

Instructor's resources to accompany the thirteenth edition of *Management of Physical Education and Sport* include an Instructor's Manual, a Computerized Test Bank, and PowerPoint slides. These resources may be downloaded from the Instructor's Resource Web site (www.mhhe.com/krotee13e).

ACKNOWLEDGMENTS

I would like to thank Paul F. Blair, Leslie L. Krotee, and Edie Ridgeway for their assistance in the preparation of the manuscript. Special thanks are also accorded to Senior Sponsoring Editor Christopher Johnson and Developmental Editor Melissa Mashburn of McGraw-Hill for their confidence, patience, and diligence while bringing this project to completion. In addition, I would like to personally thank the reviewers of this and previous editions who provided invaluable input in order to ensure the integrity of the text:

FOR THIS EDITION

Dianne Busch
Southwestern Oklahoma State University

Brady Gaskins
Bowling Green State University

Ray Schneider
Bowling Green State University

Michael Smucker
Texas Tech University

Suzanne C. Willey
University of Indianapolis

FOR THE PREVIOUS EDITIONS

Robin Ammon, Jr.
Slippery Rock University

Frank Ashley
Texas A&M University

Charles Chase
West Texas A&M University

Maureen Fitzgerald
University of Missouri

Mark Fohl
University of Minnesota—Morris

Dennis D. Francois
Idaho State University

Diana Gray
Indiana University

Graham Hatcher
University of North Carolina—Wilmington

Susan E. Keith
Angelo State University

Keith Lambrecht
Northern Illinois University

James D. LaPoint
University of Kansas

Kathleen McCann
University of North Dakota

Rick W. Nelson
Northland Community College

James Reynolds
Jacksonville State University

Ralph Sabock
Pennsylvania State University

Vernon Vrandenburg
University of Wisconsin—Platteville

Victor Wallace
Lambuth University

Jim Wasem
Eastern Washington University

I would like to acknowledge Gerry Vuchetich, Wendell Vandersluis, Michelle King, Jerry Lee, and Andrew J. Hill; The Department of Intercollegiate Athletics, University of Minnesota; The School of Kinesiology and Leisure Studies, University of Minnesota; Anthony Brown and Al Gronhovd, The Department of Recreational Sports, University of Minnesota; Department of Dance, University of Minnesota; The University of Nevada at Las Vegas; The Minnesota State High School League; USOC; AAHPERD; AAPAR; NASPE; NFHS; PCPFS; The Cooper Institute for Aerobics Research, Dallas, TX; Alan Blum, University of Alabama School of Medicine; Bradley Arnett, University of Arizona; Eric Solberg, MD Anderson Cancer Center, University of Texas, Houston, TX; Special Olympics International, Washington, D.C.; Donald Krotee Partnership, Planning, and Architecture, Santa Ana, CA; Joanne Lombardo, Comprehensive Planning Services, Newport Beach, CA; Hellmuth, Obata, and Kassabaum, Inc., Sports Facilities Group, Kansas City, MO; Bill Beyer, Stageberg Beyer Sachs, Inc., Architects and Planners, Minneapolis, MN; Grafton Adams, Fotograf, Columbia, Maryland; Images by Lawrence, Lawrence Bestmann, Ph.D., Fairhope, AL; Mike Mularkey, Miami Dolphins; P. A. Rull, Leisure Policy Division, Urban Services Division, Hong Kong; Trina Tinti, Department of Intercollegiate Athletics, University of California at Berkeley; Jerry Yeagley, Department of Intercollegiate Athletics, Indiana University; Deborah Yow, Director of Intercollegiate Athletics, University of Maryland, College Park, MD; Lee Fowler, David Horning, Jon Fagg, Carrie Leger, Jody Moylon, Charlie Rozanski, Bruce Winkworth and Wayne Wright, Department of Athletics, North Carolina State University; Larry Brown, Nikki Faison, and Ann Young, Department of Physical Education, North Carolina State University; Tommy Holden, Bittu Ali and Andrew Delisle, Outdoor Leadership Program, North Carolina State University; Mary and Casper Holroyd, NCSU Adult Fitness Group, North Carolina State University; Chris Corchiani, DNJ Mortgage, LLC, Raleigh, NC; Carla Stoddard, Barton College; Rick A. Kolopzies/ the f-stop; USA Basketball; David Anderson, Schroeder YMCA, Browndeer, WI; Vanessa Booth, Multi-Sport Director, SPORTTIME at Syosset, Syosset, NY; Robert Q. Krotee, Director of Aquatics, St. Joseph's University, Philadelphia, PA; Peter W. Vacho, Charlotte Panthers; Garth Weiss, United States Tennis Association; Tom Snicker and Heidi Martin, Wayzata School District, Wayzata, MN; and Dr. Thomas C. Slettehaugh, Commissioner, Minneapolis Arts Commission, for their assistance in securing photographs and materials for this thirteenth edition.

A special thanks to Annie Clement, Ph.D., J.D., Berry University, Miami, FL, and Bob Kaufer, General Counsel, Athletics, Management, and Consulting, St. Paul, MN, for their legal advice and significant contribution to the manuscript.

I would also like to thank the many friends and professional colleagues who helped in many ways with the revision of the thirteenth edition—from answering crucial questions to proofing to loaning reference materials. Thus, the thirteenth edition is truly a team effort by professionals who continue to pursue excellence and strive to provide a quality educational experience for both students and teachers.

This past year the text was also selected by McGraw-Hill to be published in Chinese, Korean, and Turkish and thus the global community will continue to be drawn closer together by the profession of physical education, sport, and recreation. It is indeed an honor to be a full participant in this transnational enterprise.

Finally, as you know, this text once again will go to press without a good friend, mentor, and colleague, Charles Bucher. Charlie did much to shape the roots of the profession, specifically, management and administration of physical education and sport. Through his dedicated career, he touched the lives of many young, aspiring professionals. I hope that our text continues to reflect the spirit, sensitivity, and dedication of this truly great man.

March L. Krotee Ph.D.
Professor and Head
Department of Physical Education
North Carolina State University

ABOUT THE AUTHORS

March L. Krotee is a Professor and Head of the Department of Physical Education at North Carolina State University. He received a B.S. in Health, Recreation, and Physical Education from West Chester University; an M.A. in Physical Education from the University of Maryland; and a Ph.D. in Education, with a minor from the School of Medicine, from the University of Pittsburgh. Dr. Krotee has served on the faculties of the University of Maryland, Carnegie-Mellon University, George Mason University, and served for over twenty-five years at the University of Minnesota. His professional recognition includes: Fellow in the Research Consortium of AAHPERD, Kellogg/Partners of the Americas Fellow, Sports Ethics Fellow of the Institute for International Sport, past Chair of the Sports Sociology Academy and the International Relations Council of AAHPERD, Co-Director of the Sports Management Commission of ICHPER-SD, and Senior Fulbright Scholar. Dr. Krotee has received numerous recognitions and awards including the Ray Ciszek International Scholar Award and the Distinguished Service Award from AAHPERD. He has presented papers and serves on university and journal review boards throughout the world. He has consulted with the USOC, Special Olympics International, and the President's Council on Physical Fitness and Sport.

Charles A. Bucher, now deceased, was a professor of physical education at the University of Nevada, Las Vegas, where he helped form the School of Health, Physical Education, Recreation, and Dance. A pioneer in the field, Dr. Bucher devoted himself to administering programs in physical education, physical fitness, sports, health, and recreation at universities across the nation. He was one of the first recipients of the Healthy American Fitness Leaders Award, served as president of the National Fitness Leaders Council, and was a consultant to the President's Council on Fitness and Sports. He was also the author of numerous textbooks, professional articles, and a syndicated news column on health and fitness. Like Professor Krotee, he lectured and presented papers worldwide. In a career spanning more than four decades, Dr. Bucher helped shape the development of physical education, health, recreation, and fitness throughout the global community.

PART 1

The Management Process

CHAPTER 1

The Management Process

INSTRUCTIONAL OBJECTIVES AND COMPETENCIES TO BE ACHIEVED

After reading this chapter the student should be able to

- Outline the Physical Activity and Sport Continuum (PASC) and define sport management.
- Explain why the study of management is important to the physical educator, athletic and activities director, coach, or sport and leisure services manager.
- Identify the skills, functions, and qualifications essential for effective physical education and sport management.

- Enumerate the major roles and tasks of a manager in a physical education and sport setting.
- Outline the decision-making/problem-solving process.
- Describe and contrast the traditional and modern views of leadership.
- Discuss Total Quality Management (TQM).
- Appreciate the advantages, challenges, and problems associated with a democratic and participatory management.
- Identify issues relevant to contemporary physical education and sport management.

This text is concerned with the study of management as it is applied to the domain of physical education and sport.* Like other professions, the way organizations are managed is continuously changing or being reframed. Information technology, globalization, workplace diversity, and the building of

---

*For the purposes of this text, the terms *physical education* and *sport* include a comprehensive spectrum of movement as adapted from the Physical Activity and Sport Continuum (PASC) developed by Krotee in 1980. The PASC, illustrated here, ranges from play and leisure pursuit to professional and performing sport and dance.

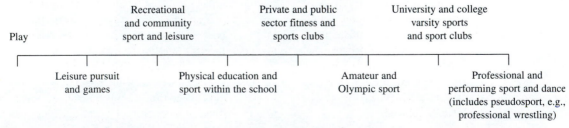

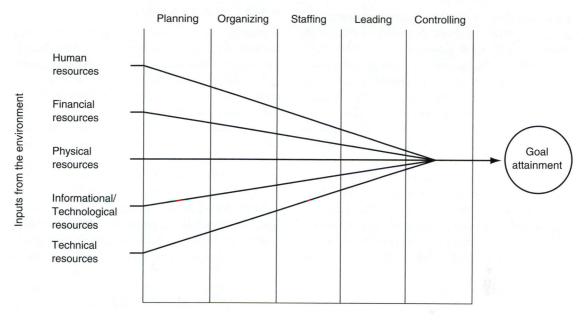

Figure 1-1. The management process.

strategic partnerships are just some of the change agents affecting contemporary management. Management theories, concepts, skills, functions, roles, programs, and principles, however, still cut across the expansive arena of the Physical Activity and Sport Continuum (PASC), and thus the primary focus of the text remains the management of the delivery systems of school physical education, interscholastic, intercollegiate, and recreational sports, and sport and recreation programs in the public and private domain. Management is a crucial ingredient in any physical education or sports program and must be soundly implemented if that program is to be conducted in an effective, efficient, and meaningful fashion. Management involves the interaction between those who administer and those who participate in the physical education and sporting processes. It involves, but is not limited to, such important matters as human resources, long-range and strategic planning, programming, facility management, budget, legal liability and risk management, public relations, and marketing. This text explores these managerial dimensions and examines ways in which they can be effectively and efficiently employed.

WHAT IS MANAGEMENT?

Daft and Marcic (2004) refer to management as the attainment of organizational goals in an effective and efficient manner through planning, organizing, leading, and controlling organizational resources. DuBrin (2003) defines management as the coordinated and integrated process of utilizing an organization's resources (e.g., human, financial, physical, informational/technological, technical) to achieve specific objectives through the functions of planning, organizing, leading, controlling, and staffing (see figure 1-1).

Hersey, Blanchard, and Johnson (2001), DeCenzo and Robbins (1999), and Williams (2005) note that management is working with and through individuals and groups to effectively accomplish organizational goals. Educational administrators (1955) have long described management as "the total of the processes through which appropriate human and material resources are made available and made effective for accomplishing the purpose of an enterprise." The Sport Management Program Review Council (SMPRC), a representative council of the National Association of Sport and Physical

Education (NASPE) and the North American Society of Sport Management (NASSM) (1993, 2000) further identify sport management as "the field of study offering the specialized training and education necessary for individuals seeking careers in any of the many segments of the industry." Regardless of its definition, Drucker (1980) believes that management, its competence, its integrity, and its performance, is decisive and paramount as we move forward in the new millennium.

The antecedents of the theory and practice of management as we think of it today have their roots in the ancient civilizations of humankind. Leakey's diggings of the hand-axe man (predating 3000 B.C.) of Olorgesailie (Kenya) and Olduvai Gorge (Tanzania), the cuneiform tablets of the Sumerian society (circa 2500 B.C.), the physical evidence of Angkor Wat (Cambodia), Machu Picchu, and Vilcabamba, the last refuge of the Incas (Peru), the pyramids and the tombs of Beni Hasan (Egypt), and the Great Wall each serve as testimony to the management processes requisite to accomplish various societies' sociocultural objectives. Other often-cited examples of early management mastery include the ancient Olympic Games (circa 776 B.C. to A.D. 493), Roman Empire (circa 753 B.C. to A.D. 476), the Chinese civil service system (circa 165 B.C.), the Roman Catholic Church (circa A.D. 110), and the trading cities of Amsterdam and Venice (circa A.D. 1300). Thus management is recognized as a fundamental integrating process designed to achieve organized, purposeful, and meaningful results.

The term *management* was derived from the French word *menager,* meaning "to use carefully" and the Italian word *maneggiare,* meaning "to handle." The term was originally applied to the training of horses and later was extended to the operations of war and the reorganization of the military, referring to the general notion of taking charge or control. Contemporary management implies an ongoing process by which managers create, direct, maintain, operate, and service purposive organizations through coordinated, cooperative human effort to ensure that organizational resources are appropriately used to attain high levels of performance and productivity.

WHAT IS A MANAGER?

A manager is someone whose primary activities are part of the management process. Specifically, a manager is someone who plans, organizes, leads, staffs, makes decisions, motivates, assesses, and controls organizational resources. They are the organization's members who coordinate, integrate, oversee, and direct the work of the other members (Robbins and Coulter 1999). A manager is the person responsible for the work performance of group members and holds the formal authority to commit organizational resources to the enterprise (DuBrin 2003). Managers may be physical education teachers or department chairs; athletic coaches and directors; commissioners of leagues; general managers of professional teams; directors of health, golf, or racquet clubs, managers of country clubs, corporate or community fitness centers, Ys, or ski areas; managers may be involved in any number of positions of responsibility within a traditional education system or the multi-billion-dollar sporting industry.

More than six million individuals in the United States hold managerial positions, and the U.S. Bureau of Labor Statistics estimates a 17 percent growth in the administrative and management sectors in the next decade. As technology and information continue to expand and packaging, promoting, and marketing become more sophisticated, even more well-trained and prepared individuals will be called on to perform the myriad administrative duties required to effectively and efficiently manage successful physical education, sport, and leisure operations. The art of management has indeed also become a science.

There are many different kinds of managers. They range from first-line to top management in position and status. Some possess warm, friendly personalities that foster a relaxed working environment and are popular with their staffs, whereas others are cold and unresponsive to human needs. Managers carry out their responsibilities in various ways. Some will shape members of their staffs; others are known for their inaction (seemingly waiting for problems to solve themselves); some are despots and authority figures; and others believe in

Table 1-1. Examples of Resources Employed by Sports Organizations

Organization	Human	Financial	Physical	Informational	Technical
Minneapolis Public Schools	Athletic and activities director Coaches Municipal employees	Tax revenue Gate receipts	Municipal building Stadiums and Grounds	Scheduling Transportation Minnesota State High School League	Open enrollment PL 94-142
University of Minnesota Athletic Department	Student-athletes Faculty athletic representatives Academic counseling Sport psychology	Corporate sponsorship Alumni product contributions Fund-raising Signage, licensing, and naming rights	Williams Arena Golf course Training complex Mariucci Ice Arena Baseball and softball complex	Sports information Public relations Publications Media guides Outreach programs	Lexicon system Drug testing protocol Web site development
Eden Prairie Community Center	Director Aquatics coordinator	Rental of ice time Bond issues	Ice arena Aquatic center Racquetball courts	Shared utilization Senior programs	Energy cost Pool operation and maintenance
Clark Hatch Fitness Centers	Fitness director Business manager Staff	Corporate memberships Guest fees Rentals	Strength training equipment Pools and courts	Promotional packages Nutritional programs	Computers Equipment repair and maintenance
Minnesota Vikings	Owners Corporate executives and board members Player personnel and staff players	Television profits Stockholder investments Skyboxes Parking and concessions	Metrodome Training complex Strength training and rehabilitation center	Sales forecasts Playoff revenue Television commercials Community service	NFL Players Association Contracts Internet Cybercasts

providing democratic and situational leadership for their organization. Each manager is different, influenced by such characteristics as professional preparation, training, personality, experience, beliefs, and values. These managerial characteristics often play a significant role in determining how managers utilize the resources at their disposal (see table 1-1).

In today's marketplace, some managers are not sufficiently trained to assume managerial roles. Although this trend seems to be reversing itself within the profession, it is still apparent that contemporary managers need to equip themselves with the necessary technical, human, conceptual, political, and leadership skills that are required for

what Peter Drucker (1980) noted as a most "crucial resource" for developed nations, as well as one of the most needed resources in countries that are struggling to develop.

WHY PURSUE A MANAGEMENT CAREER?

Many reasons motivate individuals to pursue a career in management. Some persons like the recognition and prestige that frequently accompany a person who is a chairperson, athletic director, coach, or corporate fitness manager. The fact that management positions usually carry a higher salary than other positions in the organization can be a strong motivating factor for some. Authority and power may also be reasons for seeking a management position.

The manager usually controls functions such as recommending salary increases and promotions, making human resource decisions, and determining workloads and travel, all of which appeal to some individuals. Some persons prefer management duties to those of teaching and coaching. Others seek to create, build, and put into operation their own ideas and vision for helping the organization grow and gain a better identity. Clearly, individuals enter management and become managers for many different reasons.

Whether individuals are successful in getting into the field of management (e.g., department chair, principal, head coach, athletic and activities director, aquatic or leisure services director) depends on the particular situation and other factors. A physical education teacher who is experienced, respected by students and faculty, and a leader in the school or a coach who is experienced, popular with players and staff, and active in the community may be selected. People are selected for managerial positions based on such factors as academic and professional preparation and certification for the position, maintaining a thorough knowledge of the position, experience in the field, management skills, and philosophy. Other valuable managerial commodities that may assist one in gaining a managerial position might include social and communication skills, problem-solving and decision-making skills, poise and self-discipline, self-confidence, a cooperative demeanor, motivational skills, in-house political savvy, and technical skills (e.g., computer, financial, or legal).

THE IMPORTANCE OF MANAGEMENT

How well an organization such as a school, college, community center, fitness or racquet club, or aquatic complex charts its course and achieves its objectives depends on how well managers outline and perform their jobs. Therefore it is imperative that all physical educators and sports personnel thoroughly understand the importance of effective and efficient management. Some of management's important contributions follow.

The way in which organizations are managed determines the course of human lives. Human beings are affected by management. It influences the type of program offered (e.g., consumer oriented, rehabilitative), the climate, culture, or environment in which the program takes place, the goals and objectives that are sought, and the health, wellness, and happiness of members of the organization as well as those being served.

Management provides an understanding and appreciation of the underlying principles of the science of this field. Methods, techniques, strategies, and procedures employed by the manager can be evaluated more accurately and objectively by staff members if they possess managerial understanding. Also, sound management will be better appreciated and unsound practices more easily recognized.

Studying management will help a person decide whether to select this field as a career. Increased understanding and appreciation of the management process and its growing body of knowledge will help individuals evaluate their personal qualifications and potential within the field.

Most physical educators perform some type of management work; therefore an understanding of management will contribute to better performance. Management is not restricted to one group of individuals. Most staff members have reports to complete, equipment to order, assessments to make, and other duties to perform that are managerial in nature. An understanding of management will help in efficiently carrying out these assignments.

Management is fundamental to associated effort. Goals and objectives are created, stated, and reached, ideas are implemented, and esprit de corps is developed with planning and cooperative action. A knowledge of management facilitates the shared responsibility and achievement of such aims.

An understanding of management helps ensure continuity. A fundamental purpose of

Teachers and coaches should be well skilled in managing group dynamics and team building.

significantly contribute to the shrinking global community. Every individual belongs to formal organizations. Through a democratic and cooperative approach to management, the individual can aid in carrying on what has proved to be successful in the past.

MANAGEMENT IN TRANSITION

The role of management has changed markedly in recent years. The role of the manager has evolved from where "the manager" most often possessed the only voice in the governance of the organization (including such key decision making as hiring, salary, assignment, and advancement) to today's team-oriented management approach. The contemporary manager has become keenly aware of the importance of the individual within the organizational framework. This awareness has developed because of the complexity of the tasks involved in managing a classroom, gymnasium, sport club, or team or in successfully operating a ski area, aquatic complex, or community or fitness center. Physical education and sport have become a "shared" or team-related phenomenon, one that is gradually becoming multicultural in nature, requiring increased consciousness and appreciation concerning race, ethnicity, and gender. The manager is part of that team whose job might be to facilitate, implement, or remove constraints to help other team members within the organizational framework achieve their respective goals and develop to their full potential. In this respect, today's manager has become a coach. Today's manager must be thoroughly informed and an expert in communication, group dynamics, role differentiation, motivation, goal setting, decision making, consensus building, and positive reinforcement. These types of interpersonal processes must be masterfully exercised if the individual, the organization, and management are to be successful.

Despite the perpetual state of transition and adaptation of managerial roles, some work characteristics remain somewhat stable. Managers often work long hours at an unrelenting pace. Some

management is to carry on what has proved successful rather than destroy the old and attempt a new and untried path. An appreciation of this concept by all members of an organization will help ensure the preservation of the organization's best traditional practices while embracing paradigm shifts and new challenges of change.

A knowledge of management helps further good human relations. An understanding of sound management principles will ensure the cooperation of the members of the organization and produce optimal efficiency and productivity.

Managers contribute to the realization of a better society. Because managers influence productivity, performance, and establish organizational policies and goals, they collectively influence a nation's standard of living, physical environment, and quality of life.

The study of the art and science of management is essential to everyone. It can result in a better-ordered, more healthy, vibrant, and inclusive society where all may take ownership and

Dynamic leaders help shape the direction of physical education and sport.

seem to never catch up! Their day is broken up into a large number of brief, diverse, and fragmented managerial activities. Managers meet, interact, network, and maintain contact with a large number of people. They often have little time for reflective thinking or planning, and many seem to prefer oral to written or electronic communication. Much of the manager's work is initiated by others, and oftentimes managers do not control their own destiny.

If prospective managers of physical education and sport programs are thinking about being in a position to possess power over other individuals, force personal ideas on other members of the organization, or provide opportunities for making unilateral decisions, then they should not go into management because they are doomed to failure. The formula for success is to be creative, adapt ideas, set goals, motivate, promote social justice and equality, and make shared decisions with members of the organization. The power of the *organization* is crucial, not the power of the *individual*.

MANAGERIAL FRAMEWORK, FUNCTIONS, AND TASKS

The conceptual framework for the study of management has evolved since classical school management pioneers such as Frederick W. Taylor (1856–1915), Henri Fayol (1841–1925), and Mary Parker Follett (1868–1933) proposed various ingredients, possessions, duties, and responsibilities that served to shape the management process. Thus the modern manager's makeup, which may be characterized as dynamic, continuous, fluid, and controlling in nature, has grown into a complex interrelated spectrum of duties and responsibilities influenced and tempered by the manager's personality, capability, training, and experience as well as the environment and culture in which the organization must function (see table 1-2).

Within this framework, some of the commonly identified functions of management follow.

Planning

Planning defines where the organization wants to be in the future and how to arrive there. Planning is the process of logically and purposefully outlining the work to be performed, together with the methods to be used and the time allotted for the performance of this work. The total plan including setting goals, will result in the accomplishment of the purposes for which the organization is established. Of course this planning requires a clear conception of the mission, objectives, and aims of the total organization. To accomplish this planning, the manager must have vision to look into the future and prepare a strategy for what is forecast. He or she must recoganize the influences that will affect the organization in order to

Table 1-2.	A Framework for Shaping the Management Process	
Planning	**Organizing**	**Staffing**

Mission statement
Objectives and aims
Goal setting
Develop plans to coordinate and
  implement work
Cast and frame decisions
	Develop formal structure
	Determine what is needed, who will
	  do it, and how it will be effectively
	  accomplished
		Ensuring human resources to get
		  job done
		Training and professional
		  development
		Appropriate assignment
		Establishing an ideal work
		  environment
		Recruiting
		Selection
		Retention

Leading	**Controlling**	
Directing Influencing Motivating Nurturing Mentoring Conflict resolution Role modeling Communications Creating a shared culture	Monitoring Assessment Evaluation Feedback Accountibility Reengineering Reframing Rewarding	

arrive at prudent decisions concerning future organizational challenges.

Organizing

Organizing refers to the development of the formal structure of the organization whereby the various management coordinating centers and subdivisions of work are arranged in a synergistic manner with clearly defined lines of authority. The purpose behind this structure is the effective accomplishment of established objectives through a coordinated and integrated marshalling of human and physical resources.

The structure should be set up to avoid red tape and provide for the clear assignment of every necessary duty to a responsible individual or cooperative work unit. Whenever possible, stan-

dards should be established for acceptable performance for each assigned duty.

The coordinating centers of authority are developed and organized primarily on the basis of the work to be done by the organization, the services performed, the individuals available in light of incentives offered, and the efficiency of operation. A single manager cannot perform all the functions necessary except in the smallest organizations. Hence responsibility must be logically assigned to others. These individuals occupy positions along the line, each position being broken down in terms of its own area of specialization. The higher up the line an individual goes, the more general the responsibility; the lower down the line the individual, the more specific or focused the task and responsibility (see figure 1-2).

Management functions of organizing, controlling, staffing, and communication are crucial to physical education, sport, and recreational activities.

Staffing

The management function of staffing refers to the entire personnel duty of selection, assignment, training, and staff development and of providing and maintaining favorable working conditions for all members of the organization. The manager must have thorough knowledge of staff members. He or she must select employees with care and ensure that each subdivision in the organization has a competent leader and that all employees are assigned to jobs in which they can be of greatest service. Personnel should possess talent, energy, initiative, and loyalty. The duties of each position must be clearly outlined. All members of the organization must be encouraged to use their own initiative. They should be praised and rewarded fairly for their services and informed (and perhaps reprimanded) if performance is not up to standards. Vested interests of individual

employees must not be allowed to endanger the general interests of the majority. Work environment and conditions should be made as pleasant and as ideal as possible. Physical, social, and multicultural factors should be provided for. Personnel who feel good about themselves and their work environment usually produce significant and meaningful results.

Leading

Leading is a responsibility that falls to the manager as head of the organization. The manager must lead, positively motivate, influence, and empower the individuals who make up the organization and therefore will affect the operations and conduct of the program. This means implementing and carrying out approved plans through work of employees and staff to achieve or exceed the organization's objectives. Leading means creating a vision as well as a shared culture and commitment. It means communicating goals, values, and shared resposibility, and instilling desire to perform at a high level. A good leader is influenced by the nature of organizational plans and structures as he or she elicits behavior that will support the achievement of the organization's objectives. A good leader maintains sound interpersonal relationships while developing systems and structures that motivate employees and satisfy their needs.

The ability to motivate is an integral part of leadership in order for the employee, organization, and manager to develop to their fullest potential. Motivation is associated with the "why" of human endeavor. Motivation in physical education and sport involves effort, persistence, and purposeful and goal-directed behavior as they relate to governing choices that affect achievement and productivity. Factors such as discipline, satisfaction, achievement, recognition, and advancement may all contribute to the enhancement of human potential.

Managerial effectiveness is determined by the ability to influence, guide, assist, mentor, and direct others successfully toward established goals. Managers who are good leaders receive high marks in determination, persistence, endurance, and courage. Good leaders affirm values, create options, explain and clarify, inspire, unify, and serve as role models. They clearly understand the organization's purposes and keep them in mind while guiding the way. Through leadership, managers maximize communication, cooperation, creativity, innovation, and shared decision making to ensure the integrity, success, and "culture of quality" of the organization.

Controlling

Controlling ensures the proper execution of plans and consists of several factors. Job standards or expectations should be set, and methods and procedures for monitoring and assessing whether standards are met should be established. Controlling and resulting assessment should be performed in light of the goals of the organization. Corrective action should be taken when goals are not met or if they may not be met. Controlling also means interrelating all the various phases of work within an

organization; therefore the organization's structure must clearly provide close relationships and competent leadership in the coordinating centers of activity. The manager should meet regularly with chief assistants to make arrangements for unity of effort to eliminate obstacles to coordinated work.

Coordination should also take place with management units outside the organization when such outsourcing responsibilities are necessary. Controlling means that subordinates must be kept informed through regular reports, research, monitoring, and evaluation concerning performance and accountibility measures in relation to expected standards and outcomes. In this respect the manager is a point of intercommunication. In addition to accepting the responsibility for reporting to a higher authority, managers must continually know what is going on in the area under their jurisdiction. Members of the organization must be

Talent, education, energy, initiative, innovation, and leadership yield Hall of Famer's such as North Carolina State's Kay Yow.

informed on many topics of general interest, such as goal achievement, progress, strong and weak points, and new areas proposed for development.

OTHER MANAGEMENT FUNCTIONS

There are myriad other interrelated and associated managerial functions found throughout the literature. Those functions most often mentioned include the following:

- *Decision making:* the sequence of steps completed to select a course of action from two or more alternatives. This may include various interpretive phases by the management team.
- *Problem solving:* approaching a problem in a systematic way in order to enhance the probability of arriving at the proper decision.
- *Budgeting:* strategic planning to allocate resources required to support institutional objectives. The budget is most frequently associated with the control function.
- *Evaluating/assessment:* the process of measuring progress, comparing it with objectives and outcomes, and taking needed corrective or reframing action.
- *Communicating:* the ability to articulate a clear and concise viewpoint or message to others. Effective communication leads to respect, trust, and increased performance outcome.
- *Reporting:* the ability to provide meaningful feedback, including analysis of data, in a clear and concise fashion in order to determine if organizational goals are being met.
- *Delegating:* the process by which authority is distributed by the manager downward (vertically) in the organization. Delegating should be a form of positive motivation if planned and properly executed.
- *Innovating:* the ability to introduce a new idea, technique, method, or purpose into the management process.
- *Coordinating:* the ability to interconnect the aims of the organization with the aspirations and needs of the participants.

- *Representing:* serving as the spokesperson, figurehead, or liaison for the organization or team to various outside organizations, groups, or individuals.
- *Creating:* the ability to originate, envisage, fashion, devise, or design a new system or strategy concerning the management process.
- *Motivating:* the process by which behavior is mobilized and sustained in the interest of achieving organizational objectives.

MANAGERIAL TASKS

The functions of management all integratively serve to assist in the attainment of organizational goals in an efficient and effective way. Throughout the various levels and types of management (top-level, midlevel, front-line, team leaders, general and functional) certain key tasks have been identified in the literature (Kraut et al. 1989; Pearson 1989). These include, but are not limited to, the following:

- Shaping, defining, and setting standards for the work environment
- Crafting a strategic vision—where the organization is headed
- Allocating resources to work groups and managers
- Developing future managers and leaders
- Building, growing, and moving the organization forward
- Overseeing operations—identifying, diagnosing, and solving problems

The tasks of management are intimately involved with many topics salient to the study of management. These tasks will be reintroduced throughout the text.

FUNCTIONAL, EFFECTIVE, AND EFFICIENT MANAGEMENT
Qualifications

The qualifications of physical education and sport managers are many and varied. Sound health and fitness for the job is requisite for any physical education or sport position. It is not uncommon, because of the stress of managerial positions, to find health (including burnout) to be a contributing factor to resignation. A thorough knowledge and understanding of the functions, tasks, and associated risks of the position are also keys not only to job qualification but also job satisfaction. Clearly, possession and command of the managerial skills, tasks, and competencies associated with the position and the willingness to accept responsibility are crucial qualifications at any managerial level, including teaching, coaching, or directing a sport, recreation, or activities program.

Other associated qualifications include, but are not limited to, the following:

Experience

- Teaching skill
- Previous and continued involvement in physical education and sport
- Coaching, event management, or sport administrative duties at various levels or other managerial, practicum, or internship experience
- Community, public relations, and fund-raising

Education

- College or university preparation and degree
- Communication skills, computer skills, and coursework related to the job position, including child development, finance, legal issues, and human relations
- Certification (e.g. first aid, CPR, AED, WSI, NATA, ACSM, NSCA, CSCS, CAPE, lifeguard training, pool operator's license, teaching and coaching license or certification)
- Attendance and active participation at clinics, staff development workshops, and appropriate professional job-related conventions, conferences, congresses, and seminars

Personal traits

- Honest, trustworthy, fair, ethical, cooperative, confident, intelligent, creative, original, personable, dedicated, professional, ethical, and decisive, among others

Just as the qualifications and abilities of managers vary, so do the tasks and responsibilities. To complete managerial tasks successfully, certain skills are required, whether from a top, middle, or front-line manager. The primary skill areas deemed crucial to effective and efficient management practice are technical, human (interpersonal), conceptual, political and leadership (Katz 1974; DuBrin 2003).

Skills, Leadership, and Roles
Technical Skills

Technical skills involve the ability to understand and employ specialized knowledge and expertise with various equipment, procedures, methods, tools, and techniques to perform a specific task. The manager must understand the product (e.g., physical education, interscholastic ice hockey, or Special Olympics) or service that is being managed and the processes involved by which the product is created, packaged, marketed, and delivered. Front-line managers often rely heavily on operational and technical skills (e.g., Web site development, financial and statistical analysis, and video integration) to make certain the organization provides its services as effectively and efficiently as possible.

Human Skill

Human or interpersonal skill deals with the ability and judgment to work with and through people. Communication, attitude shaping, cooperative effort (teamwork), consensus building, conflict resolution, facilitating, and motivation are key ingredients that a manager must master to achieve the organization's mission, goals, and objectives. Knowledge and understanding, character, ethics, sound judgment (predicting, diagnosing, and attributing), common sense, social and intercultural sensitivity, multicultural skills, and ability to influence behavior (behavior modification and stress management) are just some of the skills especially critical to middle managers as they attempt to integrate the work of first-level employees and staff with the desires of top management.

Conceptual Skill

Conceptual skill implies the cognitive ability to see the "whole picture," or "total view," of the organization and the environment or culture in which the organization must function. It means

Qualifications such as experience, professional preparation, communication skills, and personal integrity are requisite to good leaders.

the ability to "think strategically"—to take the broad, long-term view. It entails the ability to think in the abstract and analyze and understand the cause-and-effect relationship of the various interrelated organizational interests and interdependent functions. Conceptual skills are used to formulate and implement an organization's strategic plans and are most often associated with top-level management where responsibilities such as decision making, resource allocation, and innovation require the ability to see the organization as a total entity.

Political Skill

Political skill is the ability to acquire or assume the requisite power necessary to reach objectives. Part of political skill is networking and impressing the right people in order to gain an appropri-ate share of power as well as prevent others from taking power away from you. Mastery of the skill often reduces stress and enables the manager to operate at a high level of effectiveness. Political skill should be regarded as a supplement to job competence and the other basic skills and should not be an all-consuming investment of time or distraction from primary job functions, roles, and tasks.

Leadership

Another often-mentioned management skill, trait, or process is leadership. Leadership is the skill of influencing the activities, situation, perceptions, and expectations of an individual or group in an ef-fort to have them willingly strive for a common purpose or organizational goal in a given situation. It is an influence relationship among leaders and followers who intend real changes and outcomes that reflect their shared purposes. Thus, leadership involves the influence of people to bring about change toward a desirable future (Daft 2005). Avolio (1999) suggests that the most important leaders in society are parents, followed by teachers, and then managers.

Northouse (2001) identifies two forms of leadership. These include assigned and emergent. Assigned or formal leadership is based on having a formal title, position, or status within the organization whereas emergent leadership is more functional in nature and results from what one does and how one acquires support from followers. There is little doubt that the ability to lead is proportional to managerial effectiveness. What remains at issue are whether leaders are born (i.e., Churchill, Roosevelt) or can be schooled in leadership skill acquisition.

Leadership is a social process that involves activating, influencing, and working with people. Personality traits and attributes such as charisma and optimism will not in themselves result in leadership. Furthermore, conferring a title does not necessarily induce leadership. Instead, the existing situation and the ability of the person to lead in that situation are critical. Leaders embed and transmit their message or culture through building trust and instilling values and standards, paying attention to and rewarding the people around them, allocating resources, performing role modeling, handling crises, and attending to recruitment, selection, promotion, and retention. Characteristics and traits often associated with leadership are classified under general headings of capacity, achievement, responsibility, participation, and status (Pierce and Newstrom 2000; Daft 2005).

1. Capacity (intelligence, alertness, communication, originality, judgment)
2. Achievement (knowledge, understanding, scholarship, extracurricular, service)
3. Responsibility (dependability, initiative, persistence, aggressiveness, self-confidence, desire to excel)
4. Participation (activity, socialability, cooperation, humor, humility, adaptability)
5. Status (socioeconomic, popularity, following)

Other leadership guidelines dealing with developing a culture of trust may also be helpful. These include, but are not limited to, the following:

- Practice openness, share ideas, knowledge, and information
- Be fair, honest, ethical, and truthful (integrity)
- Show consistency, reliability, shared purpose, and sound judgment
- Follow through on promises
- Maintain self-confidence and know yourself
- Demonstrate competence, knowledge, and inclusiveness (diversity)
- Drive for responsibility, tact, and diplomacy
- Know and support your team
- Delegate, but do not abdicate
- Be loyal

Leaders are individuals who are inventive, who take risks, and who are entrepreneurial. They provide vision of potential and promise, and possess the ability to attract, mobilize, energize, and empower others. People usually function best under leadership that is creative, dynamic, and imaginative. Leadership cuts across all levels of management and is present in any situation in which someone is trying to influence the behavior of another, especially when attempting to build a culture of performance, trust and integrity. Leadership helps shape personal philosophies of management, management style and decision making, and is crucial in charting a successful course for any program or organization.

The management domain is structured in a number of ways and consists of various interrelated systems, stages, and levels. Figure 1-2 is a dual schematic that reflects various managerial levels (top, middle, and front-line), the amount of time (in percentage) that a manager at a particular level might engage in technical and conceptual skill functioning, and the decrease in managerial opportunity as the management ladder is climbed.

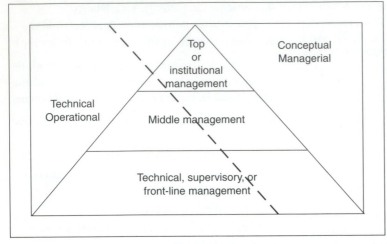

University presidents, provosts, corporate directors and vice presidents, superintendents of schools, owners of sports teams and fitness complexes

Deans of college faculties, general managers, principals, athletic and activities directors, head, regional, and national team coaches

Department chairs, area coordinators, curriculum supervisors, directors of elementary and secondary education, heads of special and adapted physical education, teachers, and coaches

0%   Time   100%

Figure 1-2.   Management skill schematic. A dual schematic reflecting managerial levels (top, middle, and front-line), the amount of time (in percentage) of managerial skill functioning (human skills held constant and crucial at each level), and the decrease in managerial positions as the educational, sporting, or corporate ladder is climbed.

Roles

The roles that managers play in physical education and sport organizations are varied and multidimensional in nature. A role is a set of expectations for a manager's behavior. Mintzberg (1973) offers ten distinct roles of an effective administrator, which have been adapted to the physical education and sporting process (see table 1-3). These roles are divided into three categories: informational, interpersonal, and decisional (managing action). It is important to remember that although each role is presented independently, in reality the roles interact with each other and are intimately related to managerial functions so that managers can carry out their duties.

Other Considerations

Regardless of where physical education and sport is delivered (e.g., schools, private clubs, community), the need for the development of a functional, effective, and efficient management scheme is required. This means developing an organizational structure that lends itself to delegating authority,

resolving organizational conflict, making meaningful decisions, and forming sound policies and procedures for safe and efficient conduct of the programs set forth by the organization.

Delegating Authority

The effective manager delegates tasks and responsibilities and with them the authority to make the necessary decisions for carrying out such duties.

Many managers are overwhelmed with their assigned duties. In many cases it is impossible for one person to discharge all these duties. Therefore it is important to delegate responsibilities to well-trained and qualified people who can perform effectively on behalf of the organization.

A clear understanding should exist between the manager and the people to whom the duties are being delegated. The latter must be willing to assume such responsibilities and must know exactly what their tasks and expected outcomes are. Successful delegation includes information about the what, when, where, who, and how. It is a good idea to place these in writing.

Table 1-3. Key Physical Education and Sport Managerial Roles

Role	Description	Management Activities of Teachers, Coaches, Athletic Directors, Officials, Sport and Leisure Managers, and Administrators
Interpersonal Roles		
Figurehead	Symbolic head; obliged to perform a number of routine duties of a legal or social nature	Ceremonies receptions, official visits, and banquets, fund-raising solicitations, alumni outings, workshops, conferences
Leader	Responsible for the motivation and activation of subordinates; responsible for staffing, training, professional development, mentoring, and associated duties	Virtually all managerial activities involving subordinates; organizes and explains policies, rules and procedures
Liaison	Maintains self-developed network of internal and external contacts who provide resources, support, and information	Acknowledgment of correspondence; internal and external work; other activities involving external sources such as conferences, media, and local, state, regional, and international visitations
Informational Roles		
Monitor	Seeks and receives wide variety of special information (much of it current) to develop a thorough understanding of other organizations and environments; emerges as nerve center of internal and external information of the organization	Handling all correspondence; monitors unit performance, cost, and productivity; oversees equipment and facilities
Disseminator	Transmits information received from outsiders or from other subordinates to members of the organization; some information factual, some involving interpretation and integration of diverse value positions of organizational influencers and shapers	Forwarding correspondence into the organization for informational purposes, verbal contacts involving information flow to subordinates (e.g., review sessions, instant communication, construction of web sites, flow of facts and information)
Spokesperson	Transmits information to outsiders on organization's plans, policies, actions, performance, etc.; serves as expert on organization's industry, posture, and culture	Staff meetings; handling correspondence and contacts involving transmission of information to external sources such as the community and involving speeches and printed and electronic media
Decisional Roles		
Entrepreneur	Searches organization and its environment for opportunities and initiates "improvement projects" to bring about change; supervises and designs certain projects	Strategy and review sessions involving initiation or design of enhancement projects (e.g., facilities, programs, media production)
Disturbance Handler/Problem Solver	Responsible for corrective action when organization faces important, unexpected disturbances or problems; resolves conflicts and problems	Strategy and review sessions involving disturbances and crises (e.g., eligibility, harassment charges, lawsuits)
Resource Allocator	Responsible for the allocation of organizational resources of all kinds; sets priorities and assigns tasks	Scheduling; requests for authorization; any activity involving budgeting and the programming of subordinates' work
Negotiator	Responsible for representing the organization at major negotiations	Negotiation (e.g., facility rental, travel, purchasing, and staff, union, and media contracts)

Adapted from Mintzberg, H. 1973. *The nature of managerial work.* New York: Harper & Row.

In physical education programs, the director or chair of physical education often delegates to others the responsibilities for the physical activity program, recreational sports, and curriculum development. The director of athletics and activities frequently delegates authority to coaches, certified athletic trainers, and equipment and facility supervisors. The manager should recognize that in delegating responsibilities, he or she is still responsible for the conceptual and overall functioning of the unit, whether it is a school division, department, or program.

Resolving Organizational Conflicts

Wherever human beings and the variant of social change or development are involved, conflicts may develop. Conflict refers to the antagonistic interaction in which one party attempts to obstruct the intentions or goals of another. Conflicts may arise around such human needs as security, status, esteem, or self-actualization, especially when these needs are not satisfied. People have physical needs, such as the need for physical comfort; psychological needs, such as a feeling of belonging and recognition; or social needs, such as the desire to work with a certain group of people. Organizational conflict might occur when employees perceive a lack of consistent supervisory practice or fail to see how they fit into their assigned roles. Reward, recognition, status, job assignment input, and job task equity (money, information, supplies) are other trouble spots for managers. Conflict often results in poor performance, absence, frequent turnover, and organizational dissociation.

Organizational conflicts, as far as possible, should be solved swiftly and effectively by the manager. This means creating an environment in which employees want to work and can achieve self-esteem, respect, and self-actualization. It means providing opportunities for personal growth and opening channels of communication to improve both situational and employee relations. It means making work as interesting and challenging as possible to ensure positive and productive performance. It also means involving employees in decisions that affect their well-being, morale, pride, and job effectiveness.

Organizational conflicts are kept to a minimum if the management is aware of human needs and tries to satisfy these needs in the best interest of all concerned. The manager often handles conflict by employing various behavior intervention strategies such as avoiding, accommodating, compromising, competing, and collaborating depending on the situation. It is mandatory that the manager be a master of conflict resolution.

DECISION MAKING

Decision making in the management process requires that certain steps be followed to bring about meaningful action. This problem-solving approach usually includes recognizing a problem, defining/diagnosing the problem, gathering relevant data, analyzing the data, identifying alternative solutions, and finally arriving at a decision. Management, however, must not stop at the point of arriving at a decision. Figure 1-3 presents a model of sequential phases that extend the problem-solving and decision-making processes to ensure that effective and meaningful decisions are being implemented. The model includes the following phases:

Perceiving. The process of recognizing that a problem exists is the starting point of successful decision making/problem solving.

Defining/diagnosing. Defining and diagnosing the problem is sometimes not an easy task. Conflicting facts requiring skillful interpretation, as well as personal reluctance to address a delicate problem, often arise. Managers need an understanding of norms, standards, and ethics that govern the selection, definition, and diagnosis of problems. They need to know what the critical factor is.

Gathering relevant data. This may be accomplished by observation, interviewing, production of special reports by task forces or committees, and distributing questionnaires, surveys, personnel evaluations, or other appropriate sources. Information close to the source is desirable even though such sources may contain bias.

Analyzing data. After the significant and relevant information is gathered, the data is evaluated using either an objective or a qualitative

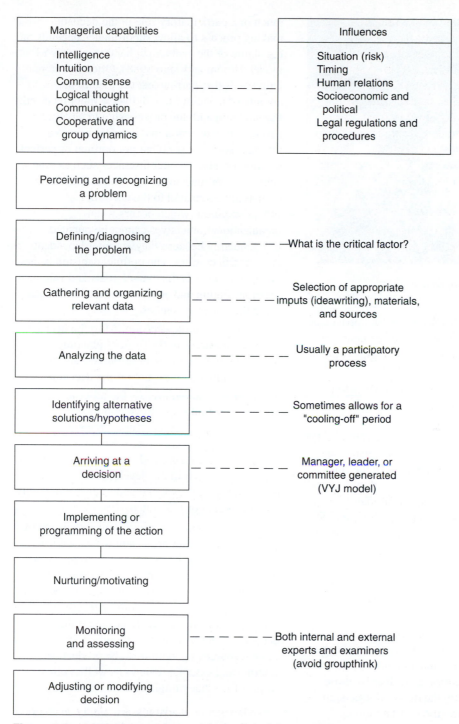

Figure 1-3. Model for problem solving and decision making.

Decision making is a cooperative effort.

approach. Decisions that are made for appearance or for the enhancement of the management record rather than for inherent validity or logic should be avoided.

Identifying alternative solutions. Decision alternatives can be thought of as the tools for reducing the difference between the organization's current and desired performance. A set of solutions should be developed, listed, and studied, if possible, before arriving at the final decision. This is necessary because of the ramifications that the decision itself may generate. This process should allow for creativity, brainstorming, ideawriting and group interaction, especially when developing new projects, programs, and proposals. This synergistic approach may yield a large number of creative solutions to seemingly complex decision situations.

Making the decision. Decisions are often affected by the environment, culture, information, personalities of decision makers, timing, situation status, and communication as well as by those who will be affected by the decision. Decisions are sometimes made by the manager alone; however, ad hoc, advisory, or standing committees may play a significant role. How

much of a participatory role in the decision-making process to allow subordinates depends on the nature of the problem at hand (see the VYJ model, Vroom and Jago 1988). Often the more individuals that participate, the greater the amount of meaningful and diverse input received. Participation and due process should always be part of sound decision making. Oftentimes a manager selects a good but not optimal or perfect solution because of circumstances such as time constraints or inaccuracy of information. Such "satisfying" is related to the need for suboptimization, which occurs when organizational objectives cannot be pursued independently because they are interdependent and often in conflict. The optimal decision is the one which best fits the overall goals and values of the organization and achieves the desired results using the fewest resources.

Implementing the decision. After the decision is made, resources in the form of planning, budget, equipment, human resources, and so on should be mobilized to support the decision.

Nurturing/motivating. As the program or position is set into operation, continued motivational support (i.e., funds, reward structures, increased commitment) should be visible. This nurturing and continued interest and support will assist in the development of proper organizational attitude and add to the productivity of the program or individual.

Monitoring and assessing. This dimension of the problem-solving process may be established over a prescribed time period (e.g., monthly or quarterly) and is an attempt to determine whether the decision was effective. This input in the form of monthly or quarterly reports will serve as a primary source of data to determine if the decision might be adjusted, modified, or allocated more resources to continue to be productive. Internal and external reviews as well as other forms of feedback might also be employed.

Managerial decisions are rarely as rational and calculated as managers like to believe. Most decisions are a result of bounded rationality because of the myriad influences that pervade the decision-making process (e.g., conflicting goals, ill-defined problems, missing facts, laws, regulations, contracts). Managers become effective decision makers through exercise (trial and error), and sometimes less than desirable results will occur. The manager must accept the reality and learn from past omissions or errors, yet not become too cautious because this might lead to lost opportunities for both the organization and the decision maker.

Tips for Decision Makers

1. Prudent planning should minimize the number of decisions with which the manager must contend.
2. Insist that subordinates (e.g., division heads of physical education, coaches, aquatics directors, recreation leaders) assume responsibility for their programs and line staff.
3. Assess the impact of organizational politics, biases, and attitudes when others are invited into the decision-making process.
4. View problems as opportunities to demonstrate problem-solving and decision-making prowess.
5. Seek out the best alternatives rather than the most convenient. Be creative when generating alternative solutions and do not critically analyze while the generation process is underway. (Avoid group think!)
6. Decision making involves risk, and a manager who never makes a wrong decision is often short-changing the organization as well as the decision maker.

Forming Sound Policies

The efficient management of a physical education, athletic, or recreation department requires the establishment of sound policies if it is to achieve its goals. Policies serve as a standing plan or guide in general terms of how the sports organization will run and how its activities are to be implemented and conducted. They are also an important means of training, socializing, and informing personnel as to their roles and conduct within the organization. Policies shape the procedures (specific actions), rules, and regulations (what and how an action must be done) of an organization. Without policies, there is little to guide the activities and conduct of the organization in the pursuit of its goals. With well-reasoned policies the organization and its members will better understand what is expected of them and as such may serve to head off potential behavior and legal problems. Policy making is decision making that restricts managers' discretion and provides limits within which acceptable and ethical decisions and behavior must fall. Policies often come as part of a "policy manual" or in the form of group meetings, orientation, or training sessions.

They are guides to action that reflect procedures that, when adhered to, fulfill the best interests of the organization and the purposes for which it exists and communicate the organization's culture and philosophy. If properly selected and developed, policies enable each member of the organization to know what duties are to be performed, the type of behavior that will result in the greatest productivity for the enterprise, the best way the departmental goals can be accomplished, and the procedure by which accountability will be established, maintained, and evaluated.

Management policies are statements of procedures that represent the legalistic framework under which the organization operates. In some instances policy manuals have been held to be legally binding. Management policies are not developed on short notice or hastily drafted without the input of the management team and those charged with organizational and legal compliance. Wording of any policy must be sensitive to the culture, language, and diversity differences in the workplace or user group.

Although policies are carefully and thoughtfully considered and formulated, they should be reviewed periodically in light of any new developments that occur. For example, at present some high schools are involved with open enrollment. This new freedom for students makes some existing policies concerning student-athlete participation outdated and obsolete. Therefore, policy review and change are needed.

How Policy Is Developed

Policy emanates as a result of many phenomena. For example, the Constitution of the United States sets forth various conditions that affect policy development in organizations throughout the country. Educators, for example, must comply with such conditions as equal rights for all in the public schools and separation of church and state. Other conditions educators must comply with are the various conditions inherent in the democratic process and those included in such legislation as Title IX and the Individuals with Disabilities Education Act (IDEA).

Because education is a state responsibility, the state government also issues policies that must be adhered to by local education authorities. These policies include such items as the number of days schools must be in session, certification qualifications, core subject requirements, and salary schedules for teachers and coaches. Within the framework of these policies or guidelines established by federal and state agencies, however, local education authorities, such as school boards, are permitted freedom to develop their own policies. Thus they establish policies pertaining to students' driving to school, attendance, substance abuse, physical education requirements, student-athlete eligibility, and many other crucial factors. Sometimes local policies conflict with state policies, in which case the local policies are declared invalid. In other instances, local policy (e.g., core class content or status) might conflict with institutions such as the state high school league or the NCAA (NCAA Initial-Eligibility Clearinghouse). These conflicts may be negotiated.

Policy is developed in many ways in physical education, athletic, and recreation departments. In some organizations it is done autocratically, with a manager establishing policy unilaterally. The process is devoid of deliberations and creative input from the members of the organization. The trend now, however, is toward greater involvement of staff members in developing policy.

As a general rule, the expression "many heads are better than one" is true of policy development. Policies must be carefully researched and thought through before they are drafted and presented to authorities. Only those areas that specifically need guidance should be addressed. There is no need for proliferation. Therefore it is usually better to involve people who look at problems affecting policies from many different angles. Although staff members may participate in policy development, it should be recognized that the formulation and development of policy is different from the execution of the policy. Execution of policy is usually a management responsibility and should be recognized as such.

Writing Policy

Before a policy is written, much research must be done to determine what goes into the substance of that policy. This research can be accomplished in several ways. One method is for the director of physical education or athletics and activities to appoint a committee to research or strategically plan and to recommend policy to the management. When the committee to recommend policy has been formed, the members will want to gather and investigate the facts thoroughly. They may decide to research the status of policies regarding this problem; what other similar organizations are doing; what policies already exist; the stand taken by selected national professional and athletic associations; views of other managers; the position of the American Civil Liberties Union, teachers' unions, and school board lawyers; and other specialized sources of information. After gathering the data, the committee will want to deliberate carefully and then make a recommendation. If the recommendation is approved, the director of physical education or athletics and activities may then recommend it to his or her superior for approval, who in turn may recommend it to the school board, regents, or other responsible group for the final approval as the policy governing the organization.

The policy that finally emanates from the committee should be written clearly and concisely.

There should be no ambiguities or possibilities for misinterpretation of what is intended. The statement of policy formulated by the committee should be reviewed carefully by staff members and management, as well as legal compliance experts to further determine that the statement clearly says what the organization's position is on this particular topic or issue.

When Policy Is Needed

Only the most important items facing the department or organization should have policy statements. Policies on trivial matters should not be carried on the books, because confusion and failure to adhere to many of the policies can result when policies are not known or understood. Furthermore, too many policies may cause the important ones to be obscured by the proliferation of those less important. It is usually better to have only a few carefully researched and crafted policies that cover major management functions. The other matters, if they need attention, can be covered by rules and regulations or in some other manner.

PHILOSOPHICAL AND THEORETICAL DIMENSIONS OF MANAGEMENT

One of the fundamental components of management, and one that is often neglected, is the establishment of a sound philosophy concerning physical education and sport. Philosophy is the process of critical examination, reasoning, and insight undertaken in an effort to arrive at truth and reality. It promotes the development and clarification of beliefs and values that serve as a foundation for the behavior and, ultimately, the performance outcome of the management team and organization.

Critical to the multidimensional management process are philosophical and theoretical questions that might be raised by a master manager. These might include the following:

- Does the present management process positively affect the manager and others involved?

- Does the process include meaningful integration and interaction between the individuals involved and the environment?
- Are management actions based on accomplishing the most good for the majority of those involved?
- Do management's actions positively contribute to the improvement of the quality of life of humankind and society?
- Does management strive for inclusion and fair and equitable opportunity, or for exclusion?

Of course these questions and the whole management process are strongly tempered by contemporary philosophical and theoretical constructs, values, ethics, politics, economics, nationalism, education, diversity, religion, ecology, and numerous other sociocultural forces that play a significant role in not only shaping the management process, but also in building a personal philosophy of management.

Management has traditionally been divided along a bipolar authoritarian-democratic continuum (see figure 1-4). Managers, for the most part, acquired their management style or orientation from prior experience, former mentors, schooling or formal training, and/or environmental or situational circumstance. Traditional management evolved from its initial stages of classical and scientific management where the employee was technically trained and required to improve task and outcome performance to the behavioral or human relations phase. This behavioral approach focuses on staff feelings, attitudes, communication, teamwork, social interaction, and needs and on a more integrative approach in which philosophical and theoretical constructs forge a new multileveled and eclectic approach to organizational behavior.

Traditional theories of philosophical and theoretical managerial orientation include authoritarian, democratic, and laissez-faire. From these as well as from the more recent systems and eclectic approaches, such as Total Quality Management (TQM), future managers can adopt, develop, and refine their own personalized management orientation or style.

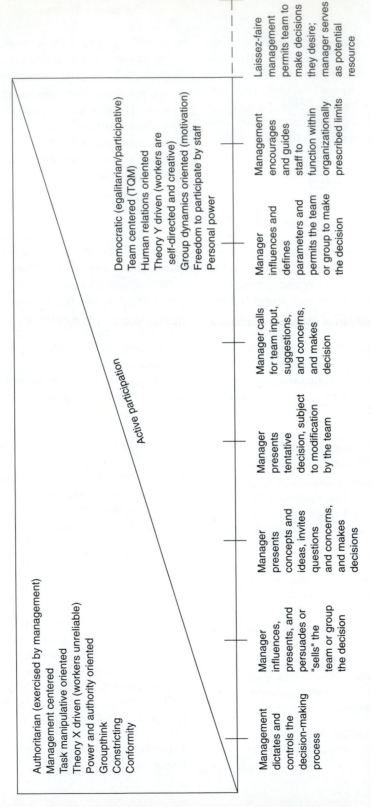

Authoritarian (exercised by management)
Management centered
Task manipulative oriented
Theory X driven (workers unreliable)
Power and authority oriented
Groupthink
Constricting
Conformity

Democratic (egalitarian/participative)
Team centered (TQM)
Human relations oriented
Theory Y driven (workers are self-directed and creative)
Group dynamics oriented (motivation)
Freedom to participate by staff
Personal power

Active participation

Management dictates and controls the decision-making process

Manager influences, presents, and persuades or "sells" the team or group the decision

Manager presents concepts and ideas, invites questions and concerns, and makes decisions

Manager presents tentative decision, subject to modification by the team

Manager calls for team input, suggestions, and concerns, and makes decision

Manager influences and defines parameters and permits the team or group to make the decision

Management encourages and guides staff to function within organizationally prescribed limits

Laissez-faire management permits team to make decisions they desire; manager serves as potential resource

Figure 1-4. Management philosophical and theoretical orientation and leadership continuum.

Authoritarian

The authoritarian orientation implies one-person leadership with decision making imposed on group members by the manager. An example of this orientation is the chairperson of a physical education department who seldom holds a staff meeting. Instead, directives are issued from the office dictating the policy and procedures that each staff member is expected to follow. This style is often associated with McGregor's Theory X, in which employees often dislike their assigned tasks or tend to shun responsibility. Authority seems to reside in the position as the head of the administrative unit. As a result, staff members frequently hesitate to disagree, and their creativity and ambition are often stifled.

Democratic

The democratic or egalitarian philosophy implies a manager who submits or delegates important matters to group discussion and involves group members in both the input and output (decision-making) process. This follows McGregor's Theory Y, in which employees are assumed to be committed to the task at hand and seeking responsibility and ownership.

An example of this orientation is the intercollegiate athletic director who holds regular staff meetings in which items that affect the department and student-athletes are discussed. Each member of the staff is respected as a person as well as for his or her expertise, creative suggestions, and ideas. The staff helps in formulating goals and procedures that influence the operation of the department. The athletic director realizes that for the organization to achieve its goals, the staff (i.e., coaches, sports medicine, compliance, academic support, marketing, facilities) must cooperate and feel like an integral part of the organization.

Laissez-faire

The laissez-faire orientation is an extension of the democratic approach in which little guidance is provided and decision making is frequently left to group members.

An example of this orientation is the physical education chairperson who does not provide active leadership. He or she believes that problems will solve themselves if given time. This individual frequently spends much time in activities that are personal in nature or that do not have significant importance in the management of the organization. To a great degree, staff members function on their own because of the absence of leadership in the organization. This fragmentation often leads to low morale and ineffectiveness.

Systems

The systems theory is an extension of the humanistic perspective that describes organizations as open, synergistic, and interdependent. It has stemmed from the rapid growth of technology and management in recent years. By borrowing techniques from the business world, managers have constructed models that bring together in a unified fashion the many parts or facets of an organization. The systems theory is a method designed to collect data on interrelated and interacting components that, when working in an integrated manner, help accomplish a predetermined goal or goals. The systems approach provides a conceptual framework for integrating the various components within an organization and for linking, for example, human resource management (recruitment, selection, development, assessment, adjustment) with larger organizational needs. Input or information from the organization (i.e., human, financial) is used to transform (using teamwork) the system into an end product, outcome, or service. Feedback both internal and external (the environment) is then employed to keep the system and its synergistic parts fresh and on the cutting edge.

Total Quality Management

Total Quality Management (TQM) is one of the most pervasive approaches to the total management process. Total Quality Management has its philosophical foundations rooted in W. E. Deming's (circa 1950) international work in Japan concerning the transformation of organizations. Deming placed great value on respect for individuals and work teams that were committed to continuous improvement while meeting the needs of

Total quality management leads to success, as evidenced by USA basketball team. Courtesy of USA Basketball.

the customer (e.g., user groups, consumers, children, student-athletes, fans) who use or benefit from the service or product provided. Total Quality Management has expanded beyond its early definition to include anyone who interacts with the organization either internally or externally. TQM managers assign or empower more responsibility and decision making to those who are carrying out the process (such as an aquatics director or sport court specialist) and who should possess greater knowledge for the quality, conduct, and improvement of their programs. TQM includes teamwork, better communication between employees and management, more attention to customer relations, and statistical analysis of outcomes and problems as a measure of quality and continuous improvement. It requires changing the system, letting go of authority, and instilling self-confidence in a well-trained and committed staff. It also provides staff with appropriate technological and informational resources, support staff, equipment and facilities to efficiently and effectively accomplish their tasks. These organizational changes lead to open, team-centered behavior in which employees seek out and share new concepts, ideas, and linkages. TQM encourages people to look outside traditional boundaries that formerly tended to shackle thinking and restrict vision. Total Quality

Management has been credited with increasing productivity, profitability, safety, and, most crucial, satisfied staff, students, and user groups.

Eclectic

The eclectic approach might be considered the offspring of management's traditional philosophical and theoretical constructs and orientations. In this regard, the eclectic approach is adaptable, fluid, and situational in nature (similar to the contingency theory approach where there is no single best way to manage people or work in every situation) and might build on any number of the best and most appropriate management orientations (i.e., a mixture of democratic and laissez-faire). The manager must therefore be aware of the spectrum of contemporary management theoretical orientations in order to ensure that the eclectic approach functions at full effectiveness. This spectrum might range from Ouchi's Theory Z (in which the design of the organization serves to motivate and develop employees who are deemed as keys to productivity and quality) to Management Science (in which the quantitative orientation focuses on mathematical and network modeling as well as on computer and information systems to increase workers productivity). It certainly may also include Contingency Theory (which is situational in nature) and Drucker's Management by Objectives (where management and subordinates at all levels collectively set goals, discuss strategy, and regularly review progress toward their goals). It may be a composite of many orientations that are implemented to support management's decisions and infuse best management practices. Knowledge, understanding, and appreciation of the systems approach, in which the organization is viewed as an interrelated set of subsystems working synergistically; the contingency theory, which suggests that organizational behavior cannot always be generalized or extrapolated from the apparent situation; and TQM, in which teamwork is the cornerstone, should all be an integral part of the manager's philosophical and theoretical repertoire.

Box 1-1   Key Points for Management Orientation

1. Create an environment for constant improvement and to provide quality service.
2. Constantly prepare and provide leadership for change.
3. Focus on improvement of the process, building trust in those included to enhance quality.
4. Be financially responsible while ensuring quality organizational resources.
5. Continually strive to improve productivity and service to improve quality outcomes.
6. Plan and institute on-the-job training and development.
7. Promote leadership in supervisory personnel to improve productivity.
8. Drive out fear so all feel part of the team to promote effective work patterns.
9. Promote "boundarylessness" between work units to break down barriers and foster teamwork and cooperative effort.
10. Instead of demanding perfection and targets for employees, improve the system that will enable the workers to improve quality.
11. Eliminate management by numbers and quotas. Substitute leadership!
12. Encourage pride and quality in work rather than merit ratings based on management numbers and quotas.
13. Institute a vigorous program of education, professional development, mentoring, and self-improvement.
14. Promote teamwork and cooperative cultural environment, so all in the organization contribute to its success, change, and viability.

Adapted from Deming (1986).

Regardless of the type of philosophical or theoretical approach to management employed, certain key points should be considered as you develop your management philosophy, style, and orientations (see box 1-1).

A PHILOSOPHY OF MANAGEMENT FOR PHYSICAL EDUCATION AND SPORT

Humankind and the environment in which we live represent the most important considerations in the world. The real worth of a field of endeavor, organization, or idea is found in what it does for people. The most important and worthwhile statement that can be made about a particular vocation, organization, or movement is that it contributes to the betterment of humankind.

Individuals possess goals that represent a variety of human objectives. Those goals include the need for health, wellness, and security for oneself and one's family, the desire to obtain an education and to be employed in a worthwhile, meaningful, and gainful occupation, and the right to engage in a free society and to enjoy leisure pursuit.

People do not miraculously work together. They do not spontaneously band together and strive to accomplish common objectives. Because many groups and individuals possess common goals, however, through associated effort they help each other achieve goals that would be impossible for someone to accomplish alone. No one person, for example, can establish a comprehensive school for his or her children's education, but through cooperative effort and support many people join together to make quality education possible.

Organizations, to function effectively, need machinery to help them run efficiently, to organize and execute their affairs, and to keep them operating smoothly, so that the goals for which they have been created will be achieved. This machinery is management—the framework of organizations and the part that helps organizations implement the purposes for which they have been established.

Management, therefore, exists to help individuals achieve the goals they have set to live happy, productive, healthful, and meaningful lives. Management is not an end in itself; rather, it is a means to an end—the welfare of the people for whom the organization exists. Management exists for people, not people for management. Management can justify itself only while it serves

Effective management leads to positive outcomes.

TAKE IT TO THE NET!

American Alliance for Health, Physical Education, Recreation and Dance (AAHPERD)
www.aahperd.org

American Management Association
www.amanet.org

Journal of Sport Management
www.humankinetics.com

North American Society for Sport Management (NASSM)
www.nassm.org

Sport Management Information Center—European Association for Sport Management
www.unb.ca/web/sportmanagement

the individuals who make up the organization, helping them achieve the goals they possess as human beings and as members of society.

SUMMARY

Management is the process by which key personnel provide leadership so that an organization functions efficiently and effectively in achieving the goals for which the organization exists. Management involves such functions as planning, organizing, leading and motivating, controlling, and staffing. Problem solving and decision making are also important facets of the management process. A philosophy of management for physical education, sport, and recreation should recognize that the needs and welfare of the human beings who make up the organization are paramount to success. The contemporary manager also needs special qualifications, as well as skills (technical, human, conceptual, political, and leadership qualities) that take into account various philosophical and theoretical underpinnings of management. These skills, combined with the appropriate measure of knowledge, sound judgment, experience, political savvy, and training, will prepare the contemporary manager to effectively lead any program or organization as well as to achieve success and satisfaction.

SELF-ASSESSMENT ACTIVITIES

These activities will assist students in determining if material and competencies presented in this chapter have been mastered.

1. Take a sheet of paper and divide it into two halves as indicated here. On the left side, list the skills and functions of a manager, and on

the right side, list specific preparation you would undertake to acquire these skills.

Skills and Functions of a Manager	Preparation for Skill Acquisition

2. Assume you are a manager who believes in TQM or participatory management. Describe how you would implement this orientation as the manager of a program of physical education.

3. Discuss your philosophy of management.

4. You are superintendent of schools of a large school system and are interviewing applicants for the position of director of athletics and activities. Construct a job description for the position.

5. List and describe what you consider to be the major roles performed by a manager of a physical education, sport, or recreation program.

6. You aspire to be the manager of a community fitness center. Briefly describe the steps in the decision-making process that you would employ to solve a major conflict.

7. Construct a meaningful policy concerning participation in physical education for all levels (K–12) of a public school.

8. Interview a manager of a sport organization. Find out which roles and tasks the manager thinks are most important.

REFERENCES

1. American Association of School Administrators. 1955. *Staff relations in school administration.* Washington, D.C.: American Association of School Administrators.
2. Avolio, B. J.1999. *Full leadership development.* Thousand Oaks, CA: Sage.
3. Daft, R. L. 2005. *The leadership experience.* Mason, OH: South-Western.
4. Daft, R. L., and D. Marcic. 2004. *Understanding management.* Mason, OH: South-Western.
5. DeCenzo, D. A., and S. P. Robbins. 1999. *Human resource management.* New York: Wiley.
6. Deming, W. E. 1986. *Out of the crisis.* Cambridge, MA: Center for Advanced Educational Services.
7. Drucker, P. F. 1980. *Managing in turbulent times.* New York: Harper & Row.
8. DuBrin, A. J. 2003. *Essentials of management.* Mason, OH: South-Western
9. Hersey, P., K. H. Blanchard and D. E. Johnson. 2001. *Management of organizational behavior: Utilizing human resources.* Old Tappan, NJ: Prentice Hall.
10. Katz, R. L. 1974. Skills of an effective administrator. *Harvard Business Review,* September–October, 90–102.
11. Kraut, A. I., et al. 1989. The role of the manager: What's really important in different management jobs. *The Academy of Management Executive,* November, 286–293.
12. Mintzberg, H. 1973. *The nature of managerial work.* New York: Harper & Row.
13. NASPE-NASSM. 2000. *NASPE-NASSM sport management program standards and review protocol.* Reston, VA: AAHPERD Publications.
14. NASPE-NASSM Joint Task Force on Sport Management Curriculum and Accreditation. 1993. Standards for curriculum and voluntary accreditation of sport management education. *Journal of Sport Management* 7:159–170.
15. Northouse, P. G. 2001. *Leadership: Theory and practice.* Thousand Oaks, CA: Sage.
16. Pearson, A. E. 1989. Six basics of general managers. *Harvard Business Review,* July–August, 94–101.
17. Pierce, J. L., and J. W. Newstrom. 2000. *Leadership and the leadership process.* New York: McGraw-Hill.
18. Robbins, S. P., and M. Coulter. 1999. *Management.* Upper Saddle River, NJ: Prentice Hall.
19. Vroom, V. H., and A. G. Jago. 1988. *The new leadership: Managing participation in organizations.* Englewood Cliffs, NJ: Prentice Hall.
20. Williams, J. C. 2005. *Management.* Mason, OH: South-Western.

SUGGESTED READINGS

Blanchard, K., and S. Johnson. 1982. *The one minute manager.* New York: William Morrow.
Presents a compilation of findings and management implications from medicine and behavioral science.

Bolman, L. G., and T. E. Deal. 1997. *Reframing organizations.* San Francisco: Jossey-Bass.
Presents a thorough overview of the converging forces that play a significant role in reframing the management process. Power, conflict, and other psychological concerns are well represented.

Calip, L. 1995. Policy analysis in sport management. *Journal of Sport Management* 9:1–13.

Conner, D. 1992. *Managing at the speed of change*. New York: Villard Books.
Focuses on organizational and human behavior issues and concerns in management.

Crosby, B. C. 1999. *Leadership for global citizenship*. Thousand Oaks, CA: Sage.
Discusses new challenges and opportunities for leaders in the twenty-first century.

Daft, R. L. 2005. *The leadership experience*. Mason, OH: South-Western.

Danylchuk, K., and R. Boucher. 2003. The future of sport management as an academic discipline. *International Journal of Sport Management* 4:281–300.

DeSensi, J. T. 1994. Multiculturalism as an issue in sport management. *Journal of Sport Management* 8:63–74.

Drucker, P. F. 1980. *The frontiers of management*. New York: Harper & Row.

Kraus, R. G., and J. E. Curtis. 2000. 6th ed. *Creative management of recreation, parks and leisure services*. New York: McGraw-Hill.

Maxwell, J. C. 1998. *The 21 irrefutable laws of leadership*. Nashville: Thomas Nelson Publishers.
Reviews the essential laws of leadership and suggests a balanced approach to the art of management. Offers interesting case studies.

McClean, D. D., A. R. Hurd, and N. B. Rogers. 2005. *Kraus' recreation and leisure in modern society*. Boston: Jones and Bartlett Publishers.

Roberts, K. H., and D. M. Hunt. 1991. *Organizational behavior*. Boston: PWS-KENT Publishing.
Discusses resources and views of such theorists as Peter Drucker, Abraham Maslow, and Max Weber as applied to leadership at the department level.

CHAPTER 2

Management Organization to Achieve Objectives of Physical Education and Sport

INSTRUCTIONAL OBJECTIVES AND COMPETENCIES TO BE ACHIEVED

After reading this chapter the student should be able to

- Discuss how and why management organization and structure are important to the effectiveness of physical education and sport programs.
- Define an efficient and effective organization.
- Identify the objectives of physical education and sport for which the organization and structure exist.
- Describe a physically educated person.
- Outline the principles that should be followed in establishing an effective organization for physical education and sport programs.
- Define assessment and identify the characteristics of a good assessment program.

- Describe a formal and an informal type of organization and structure and provide rationale for each.
- Outline the factors that need to be considered to develop a functional organization.
- Describe the organization and structure of physical education and sport programs that exist in elementary and secondary schools, colleges and universities, and other representative organizations responsible for the delivery of physical education and sport.
- Prepare a management organizational chart for a physical education and sport program.

The first chapter covered the nature and scope of the management process. Such things as managerial functions, skills, tasks, roles, qualifications, and philosophy were presented. This chapter discusses the objectives of physical education and sport and the management organization (a social entity that is goal directed and deliberately structured) and structure needed to accomplish these goals.

31

Schools, colleges, and other organizations do not function efficiently without some element that holds them together and gives them direction so that they can achieve the goals for which they exist. This element is management. Management is the glue that bonds the various units and provides the control, accountibility, communication, motivation, nurturing, and leadership needed to achieve success. To accomplish these functions, a structure is needed that provides an efficient (i.e., the amount of resources used to achieve an organization's goal) and effective (the degree to which the organization achieves a stated goal) way of operating and carrying out the various duties and responsibilities existing within the organization. The structure illustrates the roles various members of the organization play in achieving established goals. The structure indicates to whom each member reports and who is responsible for carrying out duties. It presents a blueprint or plan of action for getting the job done.

The primary purpose of structure in physical education and sport is to make it possible to achieve goals and objectives. Unless the organization and structure perform this function as efficiently and effectively as possible, it is headed for failure and should be abandoned. The structure is a means to an end, not an end in itself. Because this is true, it follows management must possess a clear understanding of its goals and accompanying objectives.

Organizational goals represent general broad-based statements of purposes, intent, and aims that reflect the derived outcomes to be achieved by participants in its programs over time. An example of such a goal may be for every student K–12 to become "a physically educated person" (see box 2-1). Objectives, on the other hand, are usually derived from goals and may vary from general to specific in form. Objectives describe specifically what an individual should know, understand, or be able to accomplish or demonstrate as a result of instruction in the K–12 program as participants challenge themselves to become physically educated. An example of an objective closely associated with the goal to become physically educated may be to demonstrate safety skills and techniques while performing in a fifteen-minute continuous swim. As we move fur-

---

Box 2-1   National Standards for Physical Education

Physical activity is critical to the development and maintenance of good health. The goal of physical education is to develop physically educated individuals who have the knowledge, skills, and confidence to enjoy a lifetime of healthful physical activity.

A physically educated person

- Demonstrates competency in motor skills and movement patterns needed to perform a variety of physical activities.
- Demonstrates understanding of movement concepts, principles, strategies, and tactics as they apply to the learning and performance of physical activities.
- Participates regularly in physical activity.
- Achieves and maintains a health-enhancing level of physical fitness.
- Exhibits responsible personal and social behavior that respects self and others in physical activity settings.
- Values physical activity for health, enjoyment, challenge, self-expression, and/or social interaction.

NASPE, 2004.

---

ther into the twenty-first century, management and the profession of physical education, sport, and recreation will have new challenges and must always be able to articulate clear goals and objectives for their ever-changing programs.

PHYSICAL EDUCATION OBJECTIVES TO BE ACHIEVED

The objectives of physical education discussed here pertain, in general, to all educational levels—elementary, junior high or middle school, secondary, college, and university—although there could be further delineation of goals for each level, age, or developmental stage. In addition, the objectives also relate to most other agency and institutional physical education, recreation, and physical activity programs.

Effective teachers and coaches guide students to ensure that objectives are being realized. Trina Tinti, head coach of gymnastics, University of California at Berkeley.

Traditional physical education objectives have their roots in Bloom (1974), Krathwohl, Bloom, and Masia (1973), and Harrow's (1972) taxonomies of educational objectives. These were divided into three distinct learning domains: cognitive (intellectual/thinking); affective (social-emotional); and psychomotor (motor behavior). Further studies by professionals in the field (Kirchner and Fishburne 1996; Gallahue and Ozmun 2006; and Estes and Mechikoff 1999) have served to split the psychomotor domain into physical fitness development and motor skill development revealing the four general phases in which growth and development within the physical education context take place. These objectives are in line with the Year 2010 Objectives for the Nation, the National Association of Sport and Physical Education's (NASPE) definition of a physically educated person, and UNESCO's International Charter of Physical Education and Sport (see appendix A). They also fit well within NASPE's (2004) National Standards for Physical Education. Well-managed, safe, systematic, progressive, purposeful, and informative physical education can significantly contribute to each of these phases and ultimately to the enhancement of health and well-being for all those who actively participate.

Physical Fitness Development Objective

The physical fitness development objective deals with the program of activities that builds and maintains power in an individual through the development of the various organic systems of the body. It results in the ability to sustain adaptive effort, to recover, and to resist fatigue. The value of this objective is based on the fact that an individual will be more active, perform better, and be healthier if the organic systems of the body are adequately developed and functioning properly.

Muscular activity plays a major role in the development of the organic systems of the body, including the digestive, circulatory, excretory, heat regulatory, respiratory, and other body systems. Participating in activities such as hanging, climbing, balancing, running, throwing, leaping, striking, carrying, kicking, and lifting helps these systems function more efficiently. Health status is also intimately related to muscular activity.

Vigorous muscular activity also produces several other beneficial results. Krotee and Hatfield (1979) point out that the various aspects of health-related fitness—cardiovascular and cardiorespiratory efficiency and endurance; appropriate body composition; muscular strength, endurance, and power; and flexibility and relaxation—represent basic elements essential to proper functioning. Research overwhelmingly supports the fact that these physical activity and health-related fitness components, when safely and progressively developed, can significantly improve quality of life. The trained heart provides better nourishment to the entire body. It beats more slowly and pumps more blood per stroke, delivering more food to the cells and more efficiently removing waste products. During exercise, the trained heart's speed increases more slowly and has a longer rest period between beats, and after exercise, it returns to normal much more rapidly. The end result of this state is that the physically fit or trained individual can perform work for a longer period of time, expend less energy, and operate more efficiently than can the untrained or unfit individual. The physically fit individual also decreases his or her risk for cardiovascular heart disease as well as other illnesses related to a sedentary lifestyle (e.g., diabetes, depression, obesity, osteoporosis). Whether participating in physical education class, performing routine tasks, or responding to emergencies, this trained or fit condition facilitates a vigorous and active quality of life. Therefore, physical education should aid in the development of the physically fit individual so that he or she will be able to live a healthful, happy, and productive life. The profession is being challenged to revitalize and recommit to this crucial "healthy person" objective (USDHSS 2000). Properly addressed this will result in making health-related physical fitness a national priority as well as lifelong pursuit.

Motor Skill Development Objective

The motor skill development objective (Gallahue and Ozmun 2006) is concerned with developing body awareness, making purposeful physical movement with as little expenditure of energy as possible, and being proficient, graceful, and aesthetic in this movement. This objective has implications for work (human factors), play, and other activities that require physical movement.

Effective motor behavior results in aesthetic qualities of movement and in the development of a movement sense, which in essence is the development of motor skill together with appropriate knowledge and understanding about the skill and a positive attitude toward its development and use. In other words, proper control of movement during life's patterns and routines takes place in the physically educated person (see box 2-1 and appendix A).

Effective movement or motor behavior depends on a harmonious working relationship of the muscular and nervous systems. Effective movement results in greater distance between fatigue and peak performance; it is found in activities involving running, hanging, jumping, dodging, tumbling, lifting, kicking, striking, bending, twisting, carrying, and throwing, among others; and it will enable one to perform daily work efficiently without reaching the point of exhaustion too quickly.

In physical education activities, the function, form, and flow of efficient body movement or mo-

Motor skill development is evident in many forms and begins at an early age.

tor skill is to provide the individual with the ability to perform with a degree of proficiency, which results in greater enjoyment of participation. Most individuals enjoy doing those particular things in which they have acquired some degree of mastery or skill. For example, if a person has mastered the ability to throw a ball consistently at a designated target and has developed batting and fielding prowess, he or she will be likely to choose to play baseball or softball. If the person can strike a ball with some degree of effectiveness, then golf or tennis might provide the challenge. Few individuals enjoy participating in activities in which they have little skill. Students are also reluctant to engage in activites (e.g., swimming, golf, soccer, aerobics, dance) where comfort and confidence levels, both psychosocially and culturally, may be perceived as a barrier. Therefore, the objective of physical education is to develop in all individuals as many physical skills as possible so that the participants' interests will be wide and varied. This development will not only result in more enjoyment for the participant, but at the same time will allow for better adjustment to the group situation. Other values of motor skill are that it reduces expenditure of energy, contributes to confidence, promotes affiliation and recognition, enhances physical and mental health, makes participation more enjoyable and safer, and contributes to the aesthetic sense.

The motor skill development objective also has implications for the health-related and recreational outcomes of the program. The skills and functional motor patterns that are acquired during physical education will help determine how leisure time will be spent. If a person excels in swimming, much leisure time may be spent in a pool or lake, or pursuing another aquatic endeavor. If the person is successful in racquet sports, he or she may be found frequently on the courts. Physical educators should develop in all individuals an understanding and appreciation of human movement while taking into account each individual's unique needs, circumstances, and movement potential.

Young people who are in school should obtain fundamental skills that will afford them maximal satisfaction and happiness throughout life. To achieve these skills and behaviors, a balance should exist in any physical education program between team, dual, individual, and lifetime sports. Team sports such as football, basketball, soccer, volleyball, and softball perform a great service by providing an opportunity for students to develop physical prowess and enjoy exhilarating competition. In many school physical education programs, however, team sports dominate the curriculum at the expense of individual and dual sports such as tennis, badminton, swimming, weight training, and golf, not to mention dance. In such cases, students are being deprived of the opportunity to develop skills in activities in which they can participate throughout their life span. It has been estimated that only 1 out of every 1,000 students who play organized football, for example, will ever play the game again after leaving school, whereas many will swim, jog, skate, ski, canoe, dance, and play tennis, rac-

Golf instruction provides insight into motor skill development and neuromuscular control.

quetball, or golf well into their older years. Another challenge in the domain of motor skill development that has often been missing in physical education, sport, and recreational programs is that of "global games/dance." Too often the profession shies away from both the movement and "content" of activities such as squash, net ball, field hockey, archery, table tennis, martial arts, dance, and other forms of grassroots, traditional or indigenous sports, games, and dance. Only through a well-balanced and inclusive program of fitness and team, dual, individual, lifetime, and global sports and dance will it be possible to develop a well-rounded individual, not to mention an informed global citizen of the twenty-first century.

Physical educators can and should be proud of the contribution they make to humankind. It is within their power to help many individuals learn physical skills and thus help them lead healthier, happier, and more meaningful and productive lives. The world is a better place to live in as a result of the work of competent and committed physical educators, because the development, mastery, and understanding of motor skill has significant and lifelong value (see box 2-2).

Box 2-2   Definition of the Physically Educated Person

A physically educated person:

HAS learned skills necessary to perform a variety of physical activities.

- Moves using concepts of body awareness, space awareness, effort, and relationships
- Demonstrates competence in a variety of manipulative, locomotor, and nonlocomotor skills
- Demonstrates competence in combinations of manipulative, locomotor, and nonlocomotor skills performed individually and with others
- Demonstrates competence in many different forms of physical activity
- Demonstrates proficiency in a few forms of physical activity
- Has learned how to learn new skills

IS physically fit.

- Assesses, achieves, and maintains physical fitness
- Designs safe personal fitness programs in accordance with principles of training and conditioning

DOES participate regularly in physical activity.

- Participates in health-enhancing physical activity at least three times a week
- Selects and regularly participates in lifetime physical activities

KNOWS the implications of and the benefits from involvement in physical activities.

- Identifies the benefits, costs, and obligations associated with regular participation in physical activity
- Recognizes the risk and safety factors associated with regular participation in physical activity
- Applies concepts and principles to the development of motor skills
- Understands that wellness involves more than being physically fit
- Knows the rules, strategies, and appropriate behaviors for selected physical activities
- Recognizes that participation in physical activity can lead to multicultural and international understanding
- Understands that physical activity provides the opportunity for enjoyment self-expression, and communication

VALUES physical activity and its contributions to a healthful lifestyle.

- Appreciates the relationships with others that result from participation in physical activity
- Respects the role that regular physical activity plays in the pursuit of lifelong health and well-being
- Cherishes the feelings that result from regular participation in physical activity

Reprinted by permission of National Association for Sport and Physical Education. Physical Education Outcomes Committee: *Definition of the physically educated person; outcomes of quality physical education programs.* Reston, Va., 1990, AAHPERD.

Cognitive Development Objective

The cognitive development objective (Barrow and Brown 1988) involves the accumulation of knowledge and the ability to think and interpret this knowledge. It involves the functional relationship between mind and body.

Physical education is about human movement. Physical education's body of knowledge has its roots in the sciences, humanities—including a rich history and cultural context—and other domains that interpret the nature of human movement and the impact of movement on the growth and development of the individual and on his or her culture. Scientific principles regarding movement—including those that relate to such factors as time, space, flow, and how humankind interfaces with machines—should be considered. The study of human movement should be part of the education of each individual who comes in contact with a physical education program. Indeed it is the "basic stuff" (AAHPERD 1987) of the profession.

Leadership, problem solving, courage, and cooperation are requisite to climbing the wall.

Physical activities must be learned, hence, the necessity of thinking by the intellectual mechanism. The techniques and coordinations involved in various movements must be mastered, understood, and adapted to the environment in which the individual lives, whether it be fitness walking, running, driving an automobile, snow boarding, playing Arachnophobia, Dance Dance Revolution, NBA Live 2005, or stroking a crosscourt forehand with topspin in tennis. These movements require the participant to think, analyze, synthesize, and coordinate the muscular and nervous systems into an outcome-based motor behavior or performance. Furthermore, this type of knowledge is acquired through trial and error, practice, cooperative effort, affordance, and opportunity and then, as a result of this experience, meaning and sophistication in the

movement situation (for example, pattern or performance outcome) changes and is applied to a new situation.

The individual should not only learn to move, but should also acquire a knowledge of rules, techniques, safety, ethics, and strategies involved in physical activities. In basketball, for example, the participant should know the rules; the strategies for offense and defense; the tactics involved in the transition game; the various types of passes; the difference between screening, blocking, and blocking out; and finally, the values that may be derived from participation. Techniques learned through experience result in knowledge and understanding that should also be acquired. A ball travels faster and more accurately if one steps in the direction of the pass, for example, in basketball, and time is saved when the pass or shot is made from the same position in which it was received. Individuals should also gain knowledge and understanding of frequency, intensity, and duration as they apply to health-related self-prescribed exercise schedules. Furthermore, a knowledge of followership, leadership, courage, cooperation, self-reliance, assistance to others, interdependence, safety, etiquette, history, multiculturalism, global context, and adaptation to group patterns should be transmitted or transferred in each class meeting.

Knowledge about health should also play an important part in the program. All individuals should know about their bodies, the importance of cleanliness; factors in disease prevention; the importance of sound nutritional practices; the merits of exercise and fitness; the importance of adequate rest; values of sound health-related attitudes and habits; facts concerning smoking, alcohol, and substance abuse; cardiovasular risk factors, obesity and stress; and which community and school agencies provide health service and counsel. With the accumulation of knowledge of these and other relevant facts, participation in physical education activities acquires a new meaning, and health practices and behavior are associated with definite purposes.

Physical educators can and should intellectualize their activities more. They should impart more "basic stuff." Physical activities are not performed in a vacuum. Physical educators should continually provide appropriate knowledge and information for participants and encourage them to ask "Why?" *Why* is it important to participate in this activity? *Why* should an hour be devoted to physical education each day? *Why* are exercise and fitness important? *Why* is it important to play by the rules? *Why* do I warm up? *Why* should I cooperate? Physical educators should also provide participants more opportunities to think and take ownership and responsibility, that is, allow participants to make choices, plan strategies, and select appropriate activities instead of usurping all this responsibility themselves. Whereas the decade of the 1990s saw gains in a healthier nation primarily because of a decrease in smoking, the twenty-first century has been labeled "fragile" by the American Public Health Association due to the high prevalence of obesity. Clearly, the profession must promote "doing" and not just "thinking" about our health-related physical education objectives.

Affective Development Objective

The affective (social-emotional) development objective is concerned with assisting an individual in making personal and group adjustments, including attitude and value formation, as well as adjustments as a member of society. Physical education activities can offer valuable opportunities for making these adjustments and provide unique opportunities to enhance social and emotional development if proper management is provided.

Physical educators should find as many ways as possible to positively influence human behavior. The rules of the game often reflect the standard of the democratic way of life. In games, one sees democracy in action and an individual is evaluated on the basis of ability and performance. Ethnicity, economic status, cultural background, race, gender, or other characteristics should not play a role, but differences should be recognized, understood, and appreciated. Performance and participation are the criteria of success.

Another aspect of the affective objective of physical education is the need for each individual to develop an appropriate self-concept. Partici-

Physical education contributes to affective and social-emotional development. Crest View Elementary School, Brooklyn Park, Minn.

pants need to develop wholesome attitudes toward themselves as maturing persons. During the various stages of physical growth and development that young people experience, they are often accepted or rejected by classmates because of physical characteristics and/or physical prowess. It is therefore important for individuals to develop themselves physically not only for reasons of their own self-awareness, but also because of the implications that their physique and physical skills have for their psychosocial image.

Each individual has certain basic social needs that must be met. These include a feeling of belonging (affiliation), recognition, self-respect, and love. When these needs are met, the individual becomes well adjusted socially. When they are not met, antisocial characteristics and negative behavior may develop. For example, the aggressive bully may be seeking self-respect, the gang member may be seeking affiliation, and the substance abuser may be seeking recognition. The needs theory has implications for the manner in which physical education programs are conducted. The desire to win, for example, should be subordinated to meeting the needs of the participants. Students today "need" more support, more success, and more positive experiences than at any other time in history. Physical education *must* contribute its fair share.

All human beings should experience success. This factor can be realized through physical education. Through successful encounters in physical activities, people develop a positive self-concept and satisfaction in their achievements. They also become less isolated as in the case of special needs students or the elderly. Physical education can provide for this successful experience by offering a variety of challenges and invigorating activities as well as developing the skills, values, attitudes, and appreciation necessary for successful participation in these activities. These attitudes can and should last a lifetime.

In a democratic society all individuals must develop a sense of cooperative consciousness and shared responsibility. This should be one of the most important objectives of the program. Therefore in various activities the following factors should be stressed: assistance for the less skilled participant, respect for the rights of others, subordination of one's desires to the will of the group, and realization of cooperative living as essential to the success of society. Individuals should be made to feel that they belong to the group and have the responsibility of directing and contributing their actions in the group's behalf. The rules of fair play, followership, and leadership should be developed and practiced in all activities offered in the program. Qualities such as courtesy, sympathy, fairness, ethical behavior, honesty, respect for authority, and abiding by the rules will help considerably in the promotion of social efficiency.

Another factor that should not be overlooked is the plus factor of affective development. Physical educators cannot be content once they have developed the physical body, mapped the skills in the nervous system, and developed the amenities of social behavior. Something else still remains—affective development—and this represents one of the greatest challenges to the field in which so many young people have a drive to engage.

Affective development is about attitudes, appreciations, values, and beliefs. Therefore physical education should be concerned with such things as helping individuals develop a healthy response to physical activity and recognize the contribution that physical education can make to health, to performance, and to the worthy pursuit of leisure. The individual should develop a positive attitude toward physical education, respect for others, self-discipline, and a wholesome attitude toward cooperative group work and play. In sum, the adoption of a healthy lifestyle for all is the ultimate goal of the profession.

Members of the physical education profession should help young people set goals and clarify and think through their value judgments, appreciations, and attitudes. Although physical educators should not indoctrinate students with the educators' own value systems, they should recognize their position as role models and realize that much can be done to motivate and facilitate learners of all ages in formulating, analyzing, reevaluating, and renewing values, attitudes, and personal responsibility.

THE OBJECTIVES OF SPORT

Although the theoretical relationship between physical education and sport in the educational setting becomes increasingly complex as we move through the Physical Activity and Sport Continuum (PASC), each maintains many of the same general objectives already presented. At the same time, sport has additional goals that relate directly to the achievement of a high degree of skill and sporting success; not to mention maintenance of sustainable financial competitive advantage. Some physical educators believe that in certain situations the goals of sport programs are not compatible with the goals of physical education. Furthermore, the goals of highly competitive sport differ in various respects for each educational level and each specific institutionalized sport program.

Sport in the Elementary School

The sports program in the elementary school should stress what is good for the child and provide opportunities for a variety of positive experiences. All sport activities should be geared to the developmental level of each child and not just to his or her grade level, chronological age, or weight. Children at this stage vary greatly in physical and psychosocial development; therefore both an informal program and policies that recognize individual differences and needs should be initiated.

The sports program should provide a wide variety of developmental (physical, motor, intellectual, and psychosocial) experiences and should focus on lower organizational and lead-up games involving large muscle activity (e.g., running and jumping). Sports offerings that are selected should be broad based and diverse, and opportunity for all to participate should be encouraged. There should not be undue concentration on developing skill in just a few sports or sport-specific positions; nor should children be pressured into conforming to adult standards in a rigid, authoritarian, highly organized, and highly competitive sports program. Contact or collision sports, particularly tackle football, are considered by many experts to be injurious for children of this age. Indeed, many football programs have been phased out of elementary school environs and picked up by myriad community-based organizations.

Sport activities—including play days, traditional sport and dance days, clubs, and field trips—should be part of an overall well-organized and integrated school and community education program. Competent personnel, medical supervision, and safety and risk management procedures should be emphasized.

Sport in the Junior High or Middle School

The junior high or middle school sports program should be adapted to the needs of boys and girls in grades 6, 7, 8, and 9. This is a period of transition from elementary to senior high school and from childhood to adolescence. It is a time when students are trying to understand their bodies, gain independence, achieve social status, acquire self-confidence, and establish a system of values. It is a time when a sport program is needed to challenge the abilities and broadening interests of the student.

Interscholastic sport of a varsity type, if offered, should be provided only after the prerequisites of sound physical education (including adapted) and recreational sport programs have been developed and implemented. Selected varsity sports should be permitted only after the assurance of special controls in regard to such items as qualified management (coaches and officials), medical and athletic training supervision, health status, safety, facilities, game adaptations, and appropriate classification of players. Some worthy goals at this level are to build team spirit; nurture the competitive drive; teach self-discipline, self-assessment, and self-control; and develop pride in accomplishment and hard work. There should be room for everyone on the team, playing time should be planned and programmed for maximal participation, and, yes, fun is permitted! The governance of the sport programs should also lie within the same educational and goal structure as that of physical education. It is crucial to have well-trained physical educators intimately involved in managing and coaching school sport programs.

Sport in the Senior High School

Representative goals of sport at the senior high school level are usually articulated by each school district. Common goals often espoused by high school officials include promoting physical excellence; engendering an appreciation of competition and the will to win; instilling morale, honesty, fair play, and self-discipline; achieving goals such as self-assurance, group loyalty, and responsibility; providing a wholesome channel for expression of emotions; integrating various aspects of the self (social, emotional, physical, and intellectual) into action; and developing qualities of good citizenship and other valuable personal qualities such as leadership and empowerment. Other goals include providing an outlet for the release of personal energies in constructive ways, using sports as a unifying force for school, home, and community, and providing activities that will help students live a healthy, productive, and balanced life.

Sport in College, University, and Associated Programs

The objectives of highly organized and competitive sport programs in many junior colleges and colleges, universities, and associated programs include developing excellence in sports competition; providing a program that is financially self-sufficient; establishing a leadership position in sports among peer institutions; satisfying needs of the spectators, athletes, alumni, community, and coaches; and providing sport programs for the gifted student-athlete. In some instances (NCAA Division III), sports may take on a lower profile. Programs at this level often focus on student participation and campus community building and for the most part do not depend on spectators and gate receipts for their existence.

At the NCAA Division I and II scholarship level where sport programs are expected to raise millions of dollars, there seems to be a rather continuous conflict between not only the objectives of sport, but also the outcome, time, academics, institutional control, and numerous other issues (Coakley 2004; Mertzman 2000) that have become growing concerns for athletic administrators. For the most part, however, sport at the college and university level provides tremendous opportunity for student-athletes to develop to their fullest potential.

Overall Objectives of Physical Education and Sport

It is crucial to realize that the overall objectives of physical education and sport across the totality of the Physical Activity and Sport Continuum (PASC) have traditionally been embodied in the goals of education as set forth in 1918 by the Commission on the Reorganization of Secondary Education. The commission's Seven Cardinal Principles include (1) health, (2) command of fundamental processes, (3) worthy home membership, (4) vocational competence, (5) effective citizenship, (6) worthy use of leisure, and (7) ethical character.

These principles, together with the 1938 *Purposes of Education in American Democracy* tenets of self-realization, human relationships, economic efficiency, and civic responsibility, have set the tone for physical education and sport in the United States. This tone has been more recently conceptualized and globalized by organizations such as UNESCO (International Charter of Physical Education and Sport 1993), NASPE (The Physically Educated Person 2004), USDHSS/CDC (Guidelines for School and Community Programs to Promote Lifelong Physical Activity Among Young People 1997), and the North American Regional Forum (AAHPERD 1995). The latter, a joint statement by the American Alliance and Canadian Association for Health, Physical Education, Recreation and Dance, summarized that physical education and sport has a vital role in the design of education for the future. It empowers individuals to learn about their world and be active participants within it. In doing so, human and social values are nurtured, and human rights and freedoms are encouraged; in these ways, our humanity can be most profoundly expressed. (See appendix A for UNESCO's International Charter and the AAHPERD/CAHPERD Global Vision for School Physical Education statement, which also includes The Physically Educated Person).

The aim of organized physical education and sport programs remains constant and is to create an environment that stimulates selected movement experiences resulting in desirable responses that contribute to the optimal development of the individual's potentialities in all phases of life.

Education should be available to, and meet the needs of, all citizens. It should furthermore be delivered in a dynamic, diverse, ethical, and professional fashion, and should be continually assessed to insure continuous quality improvement (CQI).

ASSESSMENT OF PHYSICAL EDUCATION AND SPORT: GOALS, OBJECTIVES AND PROGRAMS

Assessment is a process that is intimately linked to an organization's mission, program, or learning goals and objectives. It may be defined as the careful and systematic collection, review, discussion, and use of information about programs for the purpose of improving or enhancing participant learning, development, or performance (Palomba and Banta, 1999). The assessment process can take place at all levels—institutional, program, course, or "authentic" individual. Assessment at one level is interrelated to the process at another. Assessment helps educators—coaches or sports managers and leaders—to determine, for instance, how successful they have been at what they are trying to accomplish. How well are objectives being met? What exactly do their students or athletes know, what can they do, and what do they value? How can they better motivate participants to get engaged and persist? What changes or modifications can be made in their programs/courses to be more effective, and how can they, as professionals, better meet the needs of those individuals entrusted to them in their programs, classes, playing fields, and gymnasiums?

Assessment, however, is more than a collection of data (e.g., numerical, visual, verbal, descriptive, comparative). It is a critical component of continuous quality improvement (CQI). It is an information and synthesizing process for the purpose of making decisions about participants' learning, development, and instructional needs as well as about the individual and the environment. Assessment, including measurement and evaluation, can be used in numerous ways within physical activity specific environs. Examples may include the following:

- Making decisions concerning day to day instructional strategies and delivery
- Determining participant status and progress
- Providing feedback/knowledge of results to the participant/public
- Classification of physical activity, prowess, and capability
- Making decisions about inclusion including divisioning for special needs populations
- Screening and referral in special situations
- Determining transitioning and life span needs

To make assessment more meaningful and valuable, educators, coaches, and sports leaders must be prudent, careful, purposeful, and inclusive in their actions. The following represents some characteristics that make up sound assessment practice:

- Asks important questions
- Reflects institutional mission
- Reflects programmatic goals, objectives, and learning outcomes
- Contains a thoughtful approach to assessment planning
- Is linked to decision making about the curriculum
- Is linked to processes such as planning, programming, and budgeting
- Encourages involvement of individuals from on and off campus
- Creates experiences leading to learning outcomes
- Develops and employs relevant assessment techniques
- Includes direct evidence of learning
- Reflects what is known about how students learn
- Shares information with multiple stakeholders to improve learning
- Leads to reflection and action by faculty, staff, and students
- Allows for continuity, flexibility and improvement in the assessment process

Sound assessment practices enable the professional to gain and develop a deeper understanding of what students know, understand, and can do as a result of their educational experience whether in the classroom, gymnasium, pool, fitness center, or on an outdoor field trip. In order to be meaningful and valuable, assessment must be ongoing and dynamic, and it may be embedded into lessons and practices (formative) or applied at the conclusion of a unit, semester, or season (summative). In special instances alternative assessment may be employed when regular assessment strategies are not to be accommodated. Traditionally, most assessment (tests) is classified as norm-referenced, criterion-referenced or content-referenced. Norm-referenced refers comparing assessment outcomes to established standards most often across age, gender, or developmental level; for example, a female student scores at the eighty-fifth percentile in executing a certain number of push-ups in a thirty second time frame. Criteria-referenced assessment, on the other hand, reflects tests designed to indicate mastery or pass/fail status on various tasks ranging from fitness assessment where the student scores in the "healthy fitness zone" of the FITNESSGRAM to shooting par in golf. Content-referenced typically infers teacher-made assessment tests, tasks, or challenges that continually serve to guide student progress during the instructional process; for example, a student returns service to within two feet of the opponent's baseline 75 percent of the time in tennis match play.

Regardless of the topic, mode, or style of assessment, it must be grounded in sound, careful, accurate, and purposeful practice. Requisite to the process are clear (S.M.A.R.T.) goals—Specific, Measurable, Attainable, Realistic, Timely; meaningful and accurate assessment measures; concise statements of outcomes; sound interpretation and discussion of results; and expert application of results as the process culminates in subsequent improvement of program, learning, or performance (see figure 2-1) (Huba and Freed 2000; Williams 2005).

Successful assessment practice requires carefully laid groundwork and is a challenging task for all professionals. The call and accompanying pressures to reexamine program outcomes and student learning have arrived and will continue to play an integral role in all physical education and sport programs. Professionals need to tap into the potential of assessment not only to improve existing programs and help shape "innovative" initiatives but also to better communicate to our publics (i.e., students, parents, alumni, community, funding sources) the value and integrity of our programs.

Figure 2-1. The assessment process.

DEVELOPING A MANAGEMENT STRUCTURE THAT WILL ENABLE OBJECTIVES OF PHYSICAL EDUCATION AND SPORT TO BE ACCOMPLISHED

After the goals and objectives for physical education and sport programs have been identified, a management or organizational structure (an arrangement of people and tasks) that will contribute to the achievement of these goals should be developed.

The structure refers to the framework whereby such things as titles of positions, role assignments, task allocations, functions, and relationships are graphically illustrated. The structure implies hierarchy of authority, lines of communication, coordination, cooperation, and decision making.

Planning, developing, organizing, and reengineering the structure for a physical education, sport, or leisure program are important management responsibilities. Efficient organization and structure result in proper delegation of authority, effective assignment of responsibilities to staff members, adequate communication among the various units of the organization, clarification of the tasks assigned, and a high degree of morale among line and staff members. All these factors determine whether the organization's goals are achieved.

Management experts such as Donnelly, Gibson, and Ivancevich (1998) and Williams (2005) have suggested the following guidelines for developing a management blueprint that is organized around activities rather than around people. Their suggestions include the following:

- Review the program and its objectives at least twice a year because realignments in duties and responsibilities may be necessary.
- Design each position so that a short label describes its primary responsibilities. Each title should be descriptive yet short enough to use in normal conversation.
- Assign each person clear-cut duties, responsibility, and authority, so that each position holder will possess freedom to act. When people know exactly what they are responsible for and to whom to report, they can concentrate on getting things accomplished rather than wondering if they are infringing on someone else's prerogatives.
- Establish line and staff positions that will enable management to realize the advantages of functional departmentalization as well as centralization and decentralization. The term *line* refers to those people who are involved in the primary purpose of the sports organization (i.e., athletic director, head coach, assistant coaches, and players) whereas *staff* refers to individuals, for example, in marketing, group ticket sales, or athletic compliance, and do not, per se, directly contribute to on-field performance. Line managers maintain authority over their line personnel; however, they usually only consult and advise with those in staff positions.
- Design each position so that the position holder can make maximal use of his or her knowledge, understanding, talents, and skills.
- Design positions so that decision-making authority is as close as possible to the scene of the action. Routine decisions should be made by the individuals or team leaders "on the line."
- Give managerial staff responsibility for as many positions as possible. This is both economically and organizationally efficient and effective.

PRINCIPLES FOR MANAGEMENT ORGANIZATION AND STRUCTURE

Experts in many areas have also developed principles to aid in effective management organization. Some of the most significant principles include the following:

The management structure of an organization should clarify the delegation of authority and responsibility. For the goals of the organization to be met efficiently and successfully, management must delegate some of its powers to responsible individuals. These powers and the associated tasks should be clearly defined to avoid overlapping authority. Most formal authority is concentrated at the top and tends to decrease as one moves down the ladder.

Management work may be most effectively organized by function. The doctrine of unity or unity of command maintains that all personnel engaged in a particular type of work should function under a single authority or supervisor.

Span of control should be considered in organizational structure. The number of subordinates who can be supervised adequately by one individual determines the span of control.

Successful management depends on communication. Communication is essential to effective management because it saves time, helps avoid waste and duplication, and promotes cooperation among departments and staff.

Coordination and cooperation among various departments in an organization are necessary for effective management. Coordination among departments keeps each subsystem well informed and working together in a complementary and synergistic manner.

The manager must be an effective leader. An effective leader appreciates both the goals of the organization and the personnel working for the organization. Both are essential for the success of the organization.

Staff or task specialization assists effective management. To achieve objectives, organizations must perform many different tasks that require the

Organization, coordination, and communication are necessary for every physical education staff.

abilities of various area specialists (i.e., marketing, sports information, fund-raising, photography).

Duties and rights of personnel. Each employee should have a precise job description and a current policy and procedure manual or have guidelines readily accessible. In this way all know their duties and responsibilities and job overlapping is minimized.

Authority must be commensurate with responsibilities, and lines of authority must be clearly drawn. An organizational chart is useful to illustrate the lines of authority. These lines should be well defined and unambiguous.

Organization and social purpose cannot be separated. The structure of an organization is a means to an end, and not an end in itself.

There is no single correct form of organization. Such factors as size, human resources, and economic constraints often determine the most appropriate organizational structure for a particular situation.

TRANSLATING THE MANAGEMENT STRUCTURE INTO GRAPHIC FORM (ORGANIZATIONAL CHARTS)

Once the desired type of management structure has been determined, the next step is to prepare it in graphic form so that it can be easily understood by members of the organization and by other interested individuals.

Organizational charts are frequently used to illustrate and clarify the structure of an organization. These charts clearly depict the management setup of an organization and the key management positions and their functions. Management uses these organizational graphic representations to orient new staff members to their roles, responsibilities, and place in the total structure of the organization. These charts also serve as a public relations instrument to show the community and other publics how they are intimately linked to the physical education and sport process.

Petersen, Plowman, and Trickett (1962) set a standard when they outlined a six-step procedure for the development of organizational charts.

1. *Identify the objectives of the organization.* These objectives are designed to meet the mission and goals of the organization, which in turn determine the structure that must be developed.

2. *Arrange objectives into meaningful functional units.* This step requires assessing the organization with its differentiated parts and units and organizing it to bring about a harmonious and integrated whole. If this step is successfully accomplished, it reduces friction and fragmentation and brings about a closely coordinated, smoothly functioning organization.

3. *Arrange the identified functional units into appropriate management units, such as departments.* This step varies in each organization, but it should represent the most effective and meaningful relationships for achieving the goals of the organization.

4. *Prepare a model of the structure of the organization and perform a trial run.* To make sure that the model represents the best

management structure for the organization, it should be implemented initially on a trial basis.

5. *Revise the model in light of input received.* Views from personnel and participants within and outside the organization should be sought and the model revisited and modified where necessary to achieve the most satisfactory, efficient, and effective structure possible.

6. *Evaluate the final design and assign staff who work within the organization to appropriate functional units.* As a result of this final step, each member of the organization can see where and how he or she fits into the total organizational structure.

Line and Staff Organization

The most common type of organizational chart is a line and staff chart (see figure 2-2). A person in a line position has direct responsibility and authority for a specific objective or objectives of the organization. For example, a senior associate director of athletics would be in a line position, with direct responsibility for duties assigned by the director, and in turn would report directly to the director. A person in a staff position has an indirect relationship to a specific objective or objectives of an organization. Staff personnel often have advisory positions or are in positions that are not responsible for carrying out the central mission of the organization. An example would be a facilities coordinator in the athletic department of a university or college program. Staff personnel do not have authority over line personnel. Line positions are related to, and derive authority from, the management head. In charts, staff positions are usually indicated by broken lines and line positions by solid lines. Line personnel are depicted in a vertical line in an organizational chart reflecting the hierarchy of power, whereas staff personnel are often depicted in a horizontal line.

Small management units with limited staff, such as interscholastic departments of physical education or athletics, frequently have little distinction between line and staff personnel because very few, if any, staff positions per se exist.

FORMAL AND INFORMAL ORGANIZATION AND STRUCTURE

Organizational theory and structure require that first, there must be a need for an organization to exist, and second, the organization must know the goals it is trying to achieve. To accomplish these goals and associated objectives, a structure should be provided that enables the management to plan and make decisions, organize, staff, lead, motivate, control, and evaluate. These tasks can be performed through either a formal or an informal organization.

Formal Organization

A formal organization is based on a hierarchical job structure, with tasks assigned by managers to subordinates, concomitant with their job-task hierarchy and communications network. Figure 2-3 illustrates an interscholastic athletic and activities department and its formal relationship within a public school setting. Such an organizational structure is concerned first with the positions to be filled (coaches) and tasks to be accomplished (the conduct of sport programs), and then with the persons to be assigned to these positions and tasks. Clearly delineated lines of authority and formal rules and regulations are earmarks of traditional formal organization, as are dependence, obedience, discipline, reward, and chain of command.

A formal organizational structure depicting a vertical hierarchy is still employed in most educational and sport conceptual frameworks because it provides a clear picture of the positions that exist and the tasks to be performed. It represents a way to get things done by the use of authority and chain of command. It places subordinates in positions where they must perform as instructed; thus things get done. It assumes that control of behavior is accomplished through rational judgment and that the manager is the person most qualified to make decisions and solve problems. It assumes that people should be instruments of production and is authoritarian by nature and design.

The shift by some organizations toward a more flat or horizontal structure or "learning organization" to improve communication flow, share more information, empower staff, and team build has

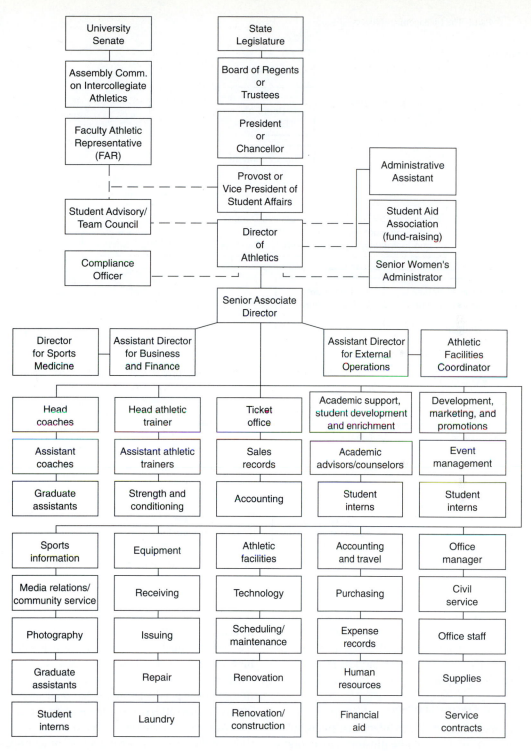

Figure 2-2. Organizational structure of an athletic department at a large college or university.

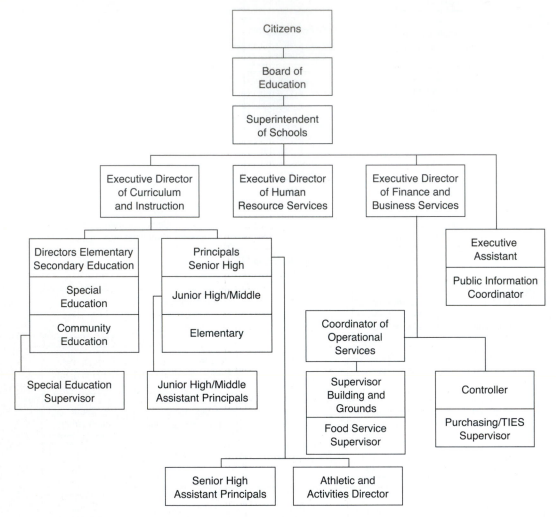

Figure 2-3. Formal organizational structure of a public school system athletic and activities department.

been slow to develop in the traditional education and sport systems, models, and culture. Today's professional is challenged and charged to change and encourage openness, boundarylessness, equality, trust, and continuous quality improvement.

Informal Organization

An informal organization realizes that many relationships exist that cannot be illustrated in an organizational chart. In other words, things get done outside the formal relationships that a chart re-

flects. It assumes that relationships occur in many informal settings where ideas are generated; productivity is enhanced; and cooperation, loyalty, and high morale are developed. Figure 2-4 represents such an informal structure concerning the articulation of physical education, recreational sports, and intercollegiate athletics at a large university.

Advocates of informal organization similar to those of the "learning organization" or team-based model contend that this structure reflects how tasks are actually accomplished and thus oppose

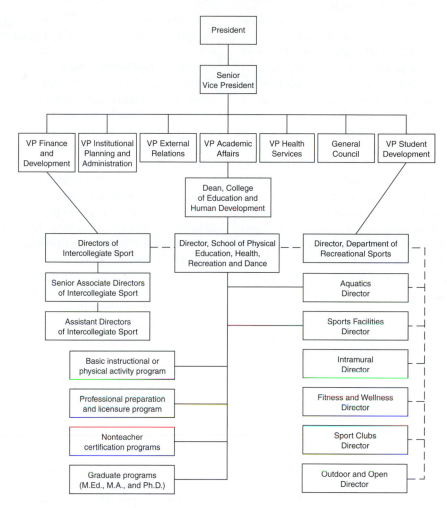

Figure 2-4. Informal organizational structure for physical education at a large college or university.

the formal, authoritarian type of organization. They also maintain that people who hold rank in an organization do not always behave rationally nor do they have complete access to reliable information at all times. Advocates of informal organization also believe that members of an organization are not merely instruments of production, but instead have desires, values, needs, and aspirations that must be taken into consideration.

Modern theories of organization and structure indicate a shift away from the formal organizational structure (vertical) toward an informal orientation recognizing the value of the human relations perspective. These modern theories and approaches (e.g., behavioral management, team-based TQM, contingency, Ouchi's Theory) are based on the fact that although most persons agree that some type of organizational framework is usually needed, most individuals are capable of some self-direction and self-motivation to perform admirably on the job.

One aspect of informal organization is the formation of subgroups or teams that do not appear on organizational charts. For example, employee unions represent an important group with whom managers must interact. In some organizations committees, commissions, councils, and task forces also represent influential subgroups. Therefore management must understand and appreciate what a staff member wants or desires and needs from his or her position, whether it is increased wages or benefits, job security, improved working conditions, a share in the decision-making process, or some other condition.

Modern theories of management are moving more and more toward an eclectic and participatory, or more horizontal, approach in which staff members and managers both are involved in many organizational decisions. Employees will better identify with an organization if they are involved in the decision-making process, and research suggests that performance outcome may also be significantly enhanced.

MANAGEMENT STRUCTURES FOR PHYSICAL EDUCATION AND SPORT PROGRAMS

The management structures currently employed for physical education and sport programs in elementary, junior high or middle school, secondary schools, colleges and universities, and community organizations are presented and discussed on the following pages. The examples offered are models and may be adapted, modified, and reengineered to better serve each individual physical education and sport-specific circumstance.

The Organization and Structure of Physical Education and Sport in Elementary, Junior High or Middle Schools, and Secondary Schools

The school district is the basic management unit for the operation of elementary, junior high or middle schools, and secondary schools, and is a quasi-municipal corporation established by the state. In the United States, this basic educational unit ranges from a one-teacher rural system to a large metropolitan system serving thousands of students. A system may be an independent governmental unit or part of a state or county government or other local administrative unit. The governing body of the system is the school board.* The chief administrative officer is the superintendent of schools.

The school board is the legal management authority created by the state legislature for each school district and usually consists of a chair, vice chair, clerk of the board, and treasurer. The chair works intimately with the superintendent and is responsible for conducting school board meetings. The vice chair serves in this capacity in the absence of the chair. The clerk of the board is legally responsible for the board's records and documents, and the treasurer works closely with the executive director of finance and business. The responsibility of the elected board is to act on behalf of the residents of the district. It has the duty of appraising, planning, and initiating state-mandated educational programs (i.e., graduation standards, special education, birth-through-age-21, assurance-of-mastery, etc.). It selects executive personnel and performs duties essential to the successful operation of the schools within the district. The board develops policies that are legal and in the interest of the people it serves. It devises financial means within its legal framework to support the cost of education. It keeps its constituents informed about the effectiveness and needs of the total program, and it solicits citizen input, advice, and counsel.

An example of a mission statement for a school board would be to prepare all students for the future by providing a challenging education that builds academic competence, encourages creativity, promotes lifelong learning, advances critical thinking skills, instills commitment to personal wellness, and fosters respect for self and others.

The key management personnel charged with carrying out the mission of the school district within each school system usually consist of the superintendent of schools, executive directors or assistant superintendents, principals, and directors.

---

*The term *school board* is used throughout the text although *board of education, school committee, community-school board*, and *board of directors* are used in some regions of the United States.

Superintendent of Schools

Within a large school system, a superintendent has management responsibility of the school program. Executive directors or assistant superintendents are in charge of curriculum and instruction, human resource services, business and finance, and various other phases of the program, such as elementary and secondary education. There is also usually a superintendent's position associated with smaller schools. These managers are known as district superintendents; they are often responsible for many schools within a wide geographical area.

The superintendent's job is to carry out the educational policies of the state and the school board. The superintendent acts as the leader in educational matters in the community and provides the board of education with the professional advice it needs as a lay organization. The superintendent also supervises the executive assistant, who manages the daily functions of the superintendent's office. The executive assistant attends all meetings, functions, and retreats of the school board and serves to ensure that the operations of the school board are in compliance with the legal requirements, policies, and procedures set forth by the school board and the state.

Executive Director of Curriculum and Instruction

The executive director of curriculum and instruction supervises the divisions of elementary education, secondary education, special education, athletics, community education, and summer school education, and is responsible for the staff development of teachers and all district employees. The principals of elementary, junior high or middle schools, and secondary schools, as well as directors of physical education and directors of athletics and activities, fall within the curriculum and instruction director's domain. The executive director of curriculum and instruction is also involved in the development and evaluation of curriculum and the organization and supervision of instruction and preservice and in-service teacher training. The executive director of curriculum and

Impact skills course offerings such as kayaking make physical education an attractive curriculum elective.

instruction is first in line to perform the duties of the superintendent of schools in the event of the superintendent's absence.

Executive Director of Human Resource Services or Director of Personnel Services

The executive director of human resource services is the chief personnel officer of the district and, as such, manages the personnel functions for all licensed (teachers, coaches, administrators, etc.) and classified (secretaries, clerks, etc.) staff. The executive director also assists the superintendent in district management and represents the district in assigned school-community relations. In addition, aspects of employee relations such as negotiations of union contracts, fringe benefit packages, and insurance coverage for teachers and coaches also fall within the human resource manager's domain. In the absence of the executive director of curriculum and instruction, the human resource director represents the superintendent.

Executive Director for Finance and Business Services or School Business Manager

The finance and business manager serves as head of business affairs and supervises the controller, purchasing, operations, and the total information educational systems (district technology consortium for record keeping, grading, athletic eligibility, etc.) employed by the district. Buildings and grounds, food service, and the business office staff also usually fall under the domain of the finance and business manager. The executive director of finance and business is last in line to assume duties during the superintendent's absence.

Principal

The position of principal is similar to that of the superintendent; it differs mainly in the extent of responsibility. Whereas the superintendent is usually in charge of all the schools within a particular community, the principal is in charge of one particular school. The duties of the principal include executing educational policy as outlined by the superintendent, appraising educational offerings, making periodic reports on various aspects of the program, directing the instructional program, promoting positive relationships between the community and the school, and supervising the maintenance of the physical plant.

Supervisor

The supervisor is generally responsible for improving instruction in a specific subject area, although sometimes a supervisor is responsible for an entire elementary or secondary instructional program.

Director

The director is responsible for functions of a specific subject matter area, such as physical education or athletics and activities or a particular educational level (i.e., elementary or secondary). The responsibilities have administrative and supervisory implications.

At some secondary schools, the positions of *director of physical education* and *director of athletics and activities* are consolidated into one position. Other school districts, however, separate the two responsibilities into two positions.

The *director of physical education* provides leadership, programs, facilities, and other essentials concerning the conduct of the program, which includes grades K–12. Specific responsibilities include the following: providing coordination between physical education and athletics; supervising inside and outside physical education facilities; overseeing equipment and supplies for special areas (includes maintenance, safety, replacement, and accounting operations); maintaining liaison with community groups (includes holding educational meetings to interpret and improve the program and serving on various community committees); preparing periodic reports regarding areas of activity; and supervising the total physical education program (classroom, gymnasium, adapted, aquatic, intramural, and extramural programs). The director of physical education provides leadership for other staff members, evaluates personnel, and is responsible for long-range planning, including curriculum and program development.

A *director of athletics and activities* assumes many duties similar to those of the director of physical education. There is, however, little organized, competitive sport (e.g., Spring Track and Field Day) at the K–6 level. Many junior high or middle schools also maintain minimal competitive sport programs (sometimes limited to football, soccer, volleyball, and basketball). In many parts of the United States, community youth and recreation and park board sport programs have filled this competitive sport void.

The director of athletics and activities serves to provide leadership, sport programs, and facilities in a coordinated and cooperative effort with the physical education department and community education or recreation and parks department of the district as well as with other community youth sporting groups and potential shared facilities opportunities. The athletic director monitors and evaluates coaches and attends to the health status, eligibility, and behavior (e.g., awards or misconduct) of the student-athlete. The director must also budget, plan, purchase, allocate, and oversee maintenance of programs and equipment. It is necessary for the athletic director to keep up with the latest safety codes concerning equipment and facilities. Scheduling of games and officials, coordination of special game events (e.g., bands, dance lines, cheerleaders, etc.), insurance, and medical supervision also fall under the jurisdiction of the athletic director. Public relations (e.g., television, radio, and print media), marketing, production and sales, fund-raising, booster clubs, and accounting for finances provide the athletic director with a full-time position that has become an integral part of our educational system. In many communities, the term *activities* has been added to the athletic director title, thus enlarging the managerial scope to include most extracurricular school activities ranging from debate to dance line to one act play.

High School Sport Councils

In some high schools, sport councils or leadership teams are formed to serve in an advisory capacity to the school board and the administrative officers of the school. Membership might include principals, athletic and activities directors, physical education directors, students, physicians, athletic trainers, coaches, parents, and community leaders. The sport council performs such functions as recommending policy, awards, eligibility, and budgets, and making sure that the athletic program is managed according to acceptable educational standards. Many state high school leagues/associations provide additional guidelines for these standards.

The Organization and Structure of Physical Education in Colleges and Universities

A college or university is characterized by a governing board, usually known as a board of regents or trustees, which is granted extensive powers of control by legislative enactment or by its charter. The governing board of a college usually delegates many of its powers of management to the administration and faculty of the institution. The chief management officers, usually headed by a president and several vice presidents, are commonly organized into such principal areas of management as academic affairs, student development, finance, planning, and public or external relations. The members of the faculty are usually organized into colleges, schools, divisions, and departments of instruction and research. Large institutions frequently incorporate a university or faculty senate or assembly committee that is the voice of the faculty and serves as a liaison between faculty and administration.

Physical education (also referred to as kinesiology, exercise science, sport studies, etc.) is organized as one management unit for men and women in almost all colleges and universities in the United States. The management unit may be either a college, school, division, or department. The manager in charge of the physical education program may be called a director; chair; or division, department, or area head (see figure 2-4). In most institutions of higher education, these managers are responsible directly to a dean, but they may also be responsible to the director of athletics. In some institutions, recreational sport is included as a part of the physical education program. However, in many larger institutions, recreational sport programs maintain a separate identity and often report to a vice president of student affairs or development, whereas physical education reports to an academic dean, provost, or vice president.

The duties of the head of a physical education department (depending on the size of the institution) may include coordinating the activities and facilities within the particular unit, requisitioning supplies and equipment, preparing schedules and budgets, conducting meetings, teaching classes, coaching, making human resource decisions, developing community relations, supervising recreational sports and intercollegiate athletic programs, overseeing and assessing the required or basic physical activity program, representing the department at meetings, facilitating the raising of external funds, and reporting to superiors.

Physical education or kinesiology in colleges and universities is commonly organized in four components: (1) the basic instructional or physical activity program; (2) the teacher preparation and licensure program; (3) the nonteacher certification programs such as exercise science, athletic training, sport studies, and sport management; and (4) graduate programs (see figure 2-5). The basic instructional or physical activity program provides physical education instruction for all students, including people with varying disabilities. Basic

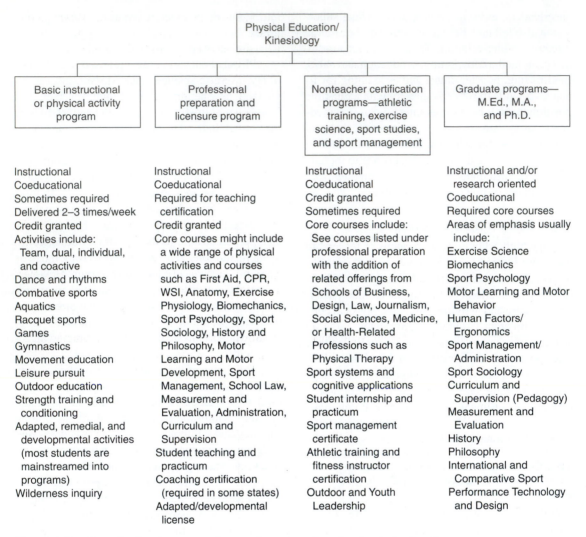

Physical Education/
Kinesiology

Basic instructional or physical activity program	Professional preparation and licensure program	Nonteacher certification programs—athletic training, exercise science, sport studies, and sport management	Graduate programs— M.Ed., M.A., and Ph.D.
Instructional	Instructional	Instructional	Instructional and/or
Coeducational	Coeducational	Coeducational	research oriented
Sometimes required	Required for teaching	Credit granted	Coeducational
Delivered 2–3 times/week	certification	Sometimes required	Required core courses
Credit granted	Credit granted	Core courses include:	Areas of emphasis usually
Activities include:	Core courses might include	See courses listed under	include:
Team, dual, individual,	a wide range of physical	professional preparation	Exercise Science
and coactive	activities and courses	with the addition of	Biomechanics
Dance and rhythms	such as First Aid, CPR,	related offerings from	Sport Psychology
Combative sports	WSI, Anatomy, Exercise	Schools of Business,	Motor Learning and Motor
Aquatics	Physiology, Biomechanics,	Design, Law, Journalism,	Behavior
Racquet sports	Sport Psychology, Sport	Social Sciences, Medicine,	Human Factors/
Games	Sociology, History and	or Health-Related	Ergonomics
Gymnastics	Philosophy, Motor	Professions such as	Sport Management/
Movement education	Learning and Motor	Physical Therapy	Administration
Leisure pursuit	Development, Sport	Sport systems and	Sport Sociology
Outdoor education	Management, School Law,	cognitive applications	Curriculum and
Strength training and	Measurement and	Student internship and	Supervision (Pedagogy)
conditioning	Evaluation, Administration,	practicum	Measurement and
Adapted, remedial, and	Curriculum and	Sport management	Evaluation
developmental activities	Supervision	certificate	History
(most students are	Student teaching and	Athletic training and	Philosophy
mainstreamed into	practicum	fitness instructor	International and
programs)	Coaching certification	certification	Comparative Sport
Wilderness inquiry	(required in some states)	Outdoor and Youth	Performance Technology
	Adapted/developmental	Leadership	and Design
	license		

Figure 2-5.   Organizational structure for a college or university physical education program.

skills, movement patterns, rules, strategies, and enjoyment of mastery are the prime focus. Surveys indicate that basic physical activity programs remain a high priority not only because of their cost effectiveness but also because of their popularity among students, staff, and faculty. Many institutions have discontinued their physical activity requirements and have infused their curriculum with attractive and creative "impact" courses, ranging from aerobic dance to kayaking.

The teacher-professional preparation program is for students interested in pursuing a teaching career and includes basic skill courses, physical education major activity and pedagogy courses, and various physical education content courses, such as applied physiology, biomechanics, history and philosophy, school law, motor behavior, organization and management, sport psychology, and sport sociology. The experience usually culminates in a student teaching and practicum setting. Also associated, and often integrated, with the professional preparation program are certification and licensure programs (e.g., adapted/developmental education or coaching). These programs usually reflect current state mandates and remain integral parts of most college programs. Some colleges are in fact moving to five-year professional training programs leading to a master's degree in teaching.

The nonteacher certification component of physical education is rapidly expanding in many colleges. These programs provide a basic core of traditional physical education/kinesiology content courses integrated with appropriate core courses from schools of business, law, journalism, management, medicine, and health-related professions such as physical and occupational therapy. An internship (e.g., cardiac rehabilitation center, corporate fitness center, YMCA/YWCA, professional sports organization) usually serves as the culminating experience in this nontraditional physical education delivery system. Certifications in athletic training, sport management, fitness instruction, strength and conditioning, and adapted physical education are often awarded in conjunction with associations such as the National Athletic Trainers Association (NATA), National Association for Sport and Physical Education (NASPE), American College of Sports Medicine (ACSM), National Strength and Conditioning Association (NSCA), IDEA Health & Fitness Association (IDEA), and the National Consortium for Physical Education and Recreation for Individuals with Disabilities (NCPERID).

The fourth component of many college and university physical education departments is the graduate program. For the most part, advanced and concentrated work in physical education major content areas (e.g., sport psychology, sport sociology, sport history and philosophy, sport management, international and comparative sport, biomechanics, human factors, motor learning and development, exercise physiology) is prescribed with statistical methods and computer application techniques forming a research foundation or core. A minor or supporting area (e.g., law, business, marketing, international relations, counseling, special education, child development, school adminis-

tration) is usually required, thus providing the potential graduate with an increased scope of the domain of human movement.

The Organization and Structure of Sport in Colleges and Universities

Because athletic programs are organized and administratively structured differently in colleges and universities than in high schools, the organization of sport in colleges and universities (see figure 2-2) requires further elaboration and discussion.

The Director of Athletics

The athletic director in colleges and universities is responsible for the management of the intercollegiate athletic program. In large institutions, this is a full-time position (usually with several associates or assistants), whereas in smaller institutions, it may include other responsibilities involved with teaching or coaching.

Some of the key duties of many athletic directors include scheduling contests and preparing contracts; arranging for team travel; appointing, supervising, and evaluating the coaching staff; making arrangements for home sports contests; representing the institution at athletic association and league meetings; securing officials; checking and preparing player eligibility and insurance lists; preparing the budget; fund-raising; marketing; and overseeing facility supervision and maintenance.

Faculty Athletic Committee

Most colleges and universities with sport programs of significant size have a faculty athletic committee. This committee serves in an advisory capacity to the president of the institution or, in most instances, a vice president. The membership of such committees frequently includes appointed and elected faculty representatives, students, coaches, student-athletes, community leaders, and alumni. The athletic director and faculty athletic representative (FAR) are usually ex officio and nonvoting members. The faculty athletic committee is involved in functions such as approving budgets, developing eligibility standards, approving financial awards, authorizing schedules, acting on problems that arise, developing policies,

Directors of athletic and activities programs should promote their programs and their student-athletes.

investigating infractions, reviewing scholarship decisions and compliance issues, and deciding to what extent certain sports might be added or eliminated.

Faculty Athletic Representative

Many colleges and universities have a faculty athletic representative (FAR). The athletic representative is a member of the faculty who represents the college or university at national association meetings such as the National Collegiate Athletic Association (NCAA) and the National Association of Intercollegiate Athletics (NAIA), as well as the conference to which the institution belongs (e.g., ACC, Big Ten, Pac-Ten, Big East, Big Twelve, SEC.). The faculty athletic representative usually conducts faculty athletic committee meetings as a nonvoting member and presents periodic reports and updates to the faculty athletic committee and faculty senate. The FAR serves at the behest of the president or chancellor and usually votes according to institutional policy.

Structure of the College or University Athletic Department

The structure of athletic departments on college and university campuses usually depends on institutional enrollment, tradition, budget, funding sources, and focus of each specific institution of higher education. Figure 2-2 reflects the structure necessary for the

conduct of a Division I NCAA sport program that provides balanced offerings for both men and women. The roles, duties, responsibilities, and support service personnel, of course, would have to be modified, adapted, or collapsed somewhat for institutions offering fewer sports or less revenue driven sports programs. Regardless, sport participation opportunity and their associated support systems and services should be equitable across gender lines.

The Organization and Structure of Physical Education and Sport in the Private and Public Sector

Physical education and sport programs exist in settings other than school systems and institutions of higher education. Because of the current interest in health and physical fitness, a variety of delivery structures have evolved. From executive, corporate, and medical center fitness programs to community-service-oriented programs such as community centers and Ys, not to mention the booming fitness club industry, the quest for enhanced physical activity and sport opportunities has developed into a multibillion-dollar enterprise. The organization and structure for such enterprises range from being operated by a private owner to being accountable to a community board of directors. Some structures are motivated by profit, whereas others might be community-service or even family oriented, and still others might exist as part of a health-related employee fringe benefit package or referral system.

Regardless of the situational circumstances, the need to provide well-trained managers and personnel to meet the consumer demand is apparent and provides yet another attractive professional marketplace for those who are well-prepared, skilled, schooled, and certified in the delivery of physical education and sport-related services. The physical education personnel involved in these programs include people trained in physical education specialties such as exercise science, biomechanics, sport management, sport psychology, coaching, nutrition, athletic and fitness training, dance, sports journalism, public relations, and marketing. Figures 2-6 and 2-7 represent organizational structuring of various private-sector enterprises.

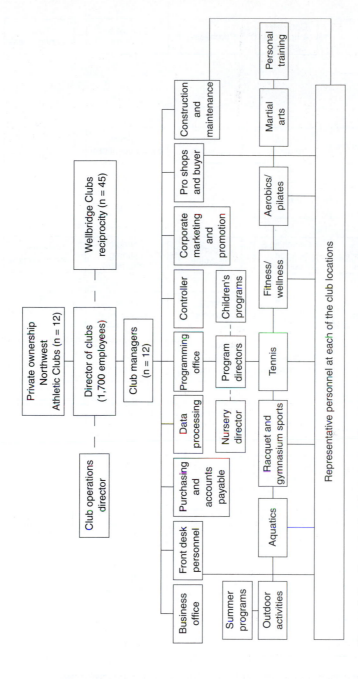

Figure 2-6. Organizational structure of a private-sector, owner-operated enterprise.

The figure shows the following organizational structure:

- Private ownership Northwest Athletic Clubs (n = 12)
  - Club operations director
  - Director of clubs (1,700 employees)
    - Wellbridge Clubs reciprocity (n = 45)
    - Club managers (n = 12)
      - Business office
      - Front desk personnel
      - Purchasing and accounts payable
      - Data processing
      - Programming office
      - Controller
      - Corporate marketing and promotion
      - Pro shops and buyer
      - Construction and maintenance
      - Nursery director
      - Program directors
      - Children's programs
        - Summer programs
        - Outdoor activities
        - Aquatics
        - Racquet and gymnasium sports
        - Tennis
        - Fitness/wellness
        - Aerobics/pilates
        - Martial arts
        - Personal training

Representative personnel at each of the club locations

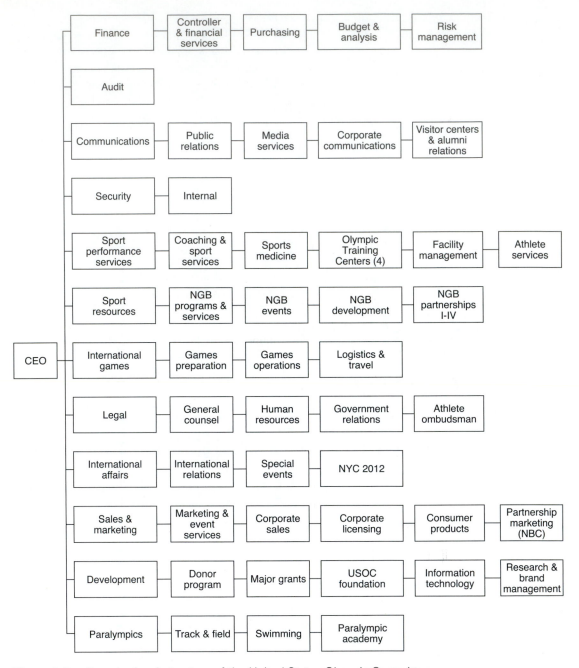

Figure 2-7. Organizational structure of the United States Olympic Committee.

TAKE IT TO THE NET!

American Association for Physical Activity and Recreation (AAPAR)
www.aahperd.org/lrpaf

Canadian Association for Health, Physical Education, Recreation and Dance (CAHPERD)
www.cahperd.ca

National Association of Sport and Physical Education (NASPE)
www.aahperd.org/naspe

National Collegiate Athletic Association (NCAA)
www.ncaa.org

Public Health Service (Healthy People 2010)
www.health.gov/healthypeople

Surgeon General's Report on Physical Activity
www.cdc.gov/nccdphp/sgr/sgr.htm

United Nations Educational, Scientific, and Cultural Organization (UNESCO)
www.unesco.org

United States Olympic Committee (USOC)
www.usoc.org

WHAT DETERMINES AN EFFECTIVE ORGANIZATION

Whether in the public school environment or the private sector, an organization at any level must possess certain ingredients to be effective. The effective organization needs a well-trained, skilled, and dynamic leader who can formulate sound aims and objectives and set goals in order to achieve the mission of the organization. The organization must also possess a functional, integrated infrastructure, staffed by motivated team members who work cooperatively to meet the goals and challenges of the organization. The end result will be a job well done with a high degree of satisfaction achieved by all involved.

SUMMARY

One of the functions of management is to develop an organizational structure through which the goals of physical education and sport can be ac-

complished in an effective and efficient manner. The physical education and sport objectives to be achieved include physical fitness, motor skills, cognitive, and affective (social-emotional) development. Physical education and sport objectives (through the physical) are vital and unique to education and must be present to truly "educate" the whole individual. To meet the needs of all students, including those with varying disabilities, the objectives of physical education and sport will vary at each educational and institutional level. One thing that remains constant, however, is the need to insure continuous quality improvement not only of the organization itself, but also of its programs and participants. This is accomplished through the dynamic process of assessment that enables the manager/professional to develop a deep understanding of his or her sphere of responsibility.

Management structures for physical education and sport are organized differently for elementary, junior high or middle schools, secondary schools, and colleges and universities. Fitness centers, Ys, and organizations other than schools and colleges also maintain their own organizational schemata. Furthermore, it is important to recognize that a formal as well as an informal management organization and structure affects most programs. It's imperative that today's organizations are adaptable because they are continually changing. It is therefore crucial in developing organizational structures that management principles and guidelines be incorporated.

SELF-ASSESSMENT ACTIVITIES

These activities will assist students in determining if material and competencies presented in this chapter have been mastered.

1. You have been asked by the head of a governmental organization to identify the objectives that physical education will be able to achieve for the citizens of that country and to show what management structure you would recommend to help achieve these objectives. Prepare a written statement for presentation before the country's legislative body.

2. Write an essay on the topic "Developing and organizing the structure for a sports program is an important management responsibility."

3. Cite at least six principles that should be observed in developing an effective management organization.

4. Describe the various characteristics of sound assessment practice and how learning outcomes may be employed as motivational tools in a classroom, physical activity, and sport-specific setting.

5. Form a three-member writing team and construct a mission statement with accompanying goals, objectives, and learning outcomes for your newly formed Community Fitness and Wellness Center.

6. Form a team from your class and attend a local school board meeting. Interview at least one board member concerning his or her perception of the role of physical education and sport in the school district. Report back to the class.

7. Draw a structural organizational chart for each of your college physical education, athletic, and recreational sports departments, showing the various management components; discuss their responsibilities and relationships.

REFERENCES

1. American Alliance for Health, Physical Education, Recreation and Dance (AAHPERD). 1987. *Basic stuff series I and II*. Reston, VA: AAHPERD.

2. ——— 1995. A global vision for school physical education. *Update,* September/October, 1, 6.

3. Barrow, H. M., and J. P. Brown.1988. *Man and movement: Principles of physical education*. Philadelphia: Lea and Febiger.

4. Bloom, B. S.1974. *Taxonomy of educational objectives*. Handbook I: *Cognitive domain*. New York: David McKay.

5. Coakley, J. J.2004. *Sport in society: Issues and controversies*. 8th ed. Dubuque, IA: McGraw-Hill.

6. Donnelly, J. H., J. L. Gibson, and J. M. Ivancevich. 1998. *Fundamentals for management*. New York: Irwin-McGraw-Hill.

7. Estes, S. G., and R. A. Mechikoff. 1999. *Knowing human movement*. Boston: Allyn and Bacon.

8. Gallahue, D. L., and J. C. Ozmun. 2006. *Understanding motor development: Infants, children, adolescents, adults*. New York: WCB/McGraw-Hill.

9. Harrow, A. J. 1972. *A taxonomy of the psychomotor domain*. New York: David McKay.

10. Huba, M. E., and J. E. Freed. 2000. *Learner-centered assessment on college campuses*. Boston: Allyn and Bacon.

11. Kirchner, G., and G. J. Fishburne.1996. *Physical education for elementary school children*. New York: WCB/McGraw-Hill.

12. Krathwohl, D. R., B. S. Bloom, and B. B. Masia. 1973. *A taxonomy of educational objectives*. Handbook II: *Affective domain*. New York: David McKay.

13. Krotee, M. L., and F. C. Hatfield. 1979. *The theory and practice of physical activity*. Dubuque, IA: Kendall/Hunt.

14. Mertzman, R. A. 2000. *Voices in sports and society*. Dubuque, IA: Kendall/Hunt.

15. National Association for Sports and Physical Education (NASPE). 1990. *Definition of the physical education person: Outcomes of quality physical education programs*. Reston, VA: AAHPERD.

16. National Association for Sport and Physical Education (NASPE). 2004. *Moving into the future: National standards for physical education*. Reston, VA: NASPE.

17. Petersen, E., E. G. Plowman, and J. M. Trickett. 1962. *Business organization and management*. Homewood, IL: Richard D Irwin.

18. Palomba, C. A., and T. W. Banta. 1999. *Assessment essentials: Planning, implementing, and improving assessment in higher education*. San Francisco, CA: Jossey-Bass.

19. USDHHS. 2000. *Promoting better health through physical activity and sports: A report to the President from the Secretary of Health and Human Services and the Secretary of Education*. Washington, DC: U.S. Government Printing Office.

20. USDHHS/CDC. 1999. *Promoting physical activity: A guide for community action*. Champaign, IL: Human Kinetics.

21. Williams, C. 2005. *Management*. Mason, OH: South-Western.

SUGGESTED READINGS

American Alliance for Health, Physical Education, Recreation and Dance (AAHPERD). 1987. *Basic stuff series I and II*. Reston, VA: AAHPERD.
   Presents the views of the profession concerning application of physical education to the curriculum.

Kelly, L. E., and V. J. Melograno. 2004. *Developing the physical education curriculum*. Champaign, IL: Human Kinetics.
   Contains theoretical and practical considerations for the implementation of achievement-based physical education programs.

Midura, D. W., and D. R. Glover. 1995. *More team building challenges*. Champaign, IL: Human Kinetics.

Peters, T. 1987. *Thriving on chaos*. New York: Knopf.
A guide on goal setting, power, accelerated change, and leadership. The author also delves into creativity and innovation.

Recreational Sports and Fitness. 2004. *Associations*. Westbury, NY: NIRSA.
A guide to certification associations and organizations in the physical education and sport profession.

Slack, T. 1997. *Understanding sport organizations*. Champaign, IL: Human Kinetics.
Provides a significant overview of many dimensions involved in sport organizations. Discusses sport-related issues and problems in relation to organizational theory. Case studies are presented.

Thoma, J. E., and L. Chalip. 1996. *Sport governance in the global community*. Morgantown, WV: Fitness Information Technology.
Delves into governance issues ranging from national sports policies and the Olympic Movement to politics in sport. The book also includes treatment of bidding and hosting large events.

United Nations Educational, Scientific, and Cultural Organization (UNESCO). 1993. *International charter of physical education and sport*. Paris: UNESCO.

Vroom, V. H., and E. L. Deci. 1981. *Management and motivation*. New York: Penguin.
Presents an overview of motivation including theoretical constructs concerning attitude formation, job satisfaction, and performance. Organizational change is also covered.

Wuest, D. A., and C. A. Bucher. 2003. *Foundations of physical education, exercise science, and sport*. New York: McGraw-Hill.
Provides an overview of physical education and sport including philosophy, history, and core content. Career patterning and issues in the profession are also explored.

PART 2

Management of Physical Education and Sport Programs

CHAPTER 3

Physical Education Instructional Programs

INSTRUCTIONAL OBJECTIVES AND COMPETENCIES TO BE ACHIEVED

After reading this chapter the student should be able to:

- Provide a description of the nature, scope, purpose, and value of instructional programs in physical education.
- Outline management guidelines for preschool, elementary school, secondary school, and college and university physical education instructional programs.
- Describe management instructional strategies for physical education programs resulting from Title IX legislation.
- Justify the need for certain management procedures, such as scheduling, time allotment for classes, size of classes, instructional loads, class and locker-room management, uniforms, taking roll, selecting physical education activities, grouping, and area of student involvement.

- Understand the professional nature of selected management problems in instructional programs such as required or elective physical education, substitutions, credit, class attendance, excuses, instruction by specialist or classroom teacher, dressing and showering, record keeping, and grading.
- Discuss what is meant by an adapted/developmental program of physical education.
- Describe the various elements that make up an individualized education program (IEP).
- Describe administrative procedures to comply with and implement Public Laws 94-142; 99-457; 101-336 (ADA); 101-476 and 105-17 (IDEA), and P.L. 107-110 (NCLB).
- Discuss various motives that individuals have for participating in physical education programs.

Thus far in this text we have concerned ourselves with the nature and scope of management as they relate to physical education and sport. We have also discussed the goals and objectives these programs are designed to achieve, the organizational structure needed to efficiently and effectively pursue and accomplish these goals, and the importance of a sound assessment process to ensure program and participant improvement. This chapter delves into the instructional physical education program and identifies associated guidelines, variables, issues, and concerns.

By tradition, the basic instructional physical education program was graphically represented at the base of an isosceles triangle. The part immediately above the instructional base was the recreational sports program, and at the apex of the triangle was the varsity athletic program. What the isosceles triangle symbolized in the past is still true to the effect that a sound physical education program should serve as a solid base for all other school and community physical activity and sport programs (see figure 3-1). The instructional program in physical education is the place to teach skills, strategies, concepts, and essential knowledge concerning the relationship of physical activity to physical fitness, motor skill, cognitive, and affective development. It is a place to challenge, build competence, encourage creativity, promote lifelong activity, advance critical action skills, instill commitment to personal wellness and responsibility, and foster respect for others. It is also a

place to introduce an awareness of the development and maintenance of optimal levels of health-related physical fitness.

Skills should be taught from a scientific, theoretical, and progressive approach so that the various mediators and human factors that affect human movement are clearly understood by the participant (see figure 3-2). Demonstration, videotapes, clips and DVDs, handheld computers, heart rate monitors, posters, journals and logs, and other audiovisual aids and materials enhance instruction and are useful for optimal learning.

The physical education program presented throughout the school years should be sequential in development and progressive in application. A physical fitness program should also be developmental and progressive in nature, as well as personalized, starting with the individual's present state of mental and physical fitness and gradually moving to higher levels.

Performance objectives and strategies should be established and targeted for individual student progress, achievements, and accountability. When boys and girls advance from one grade to another, they should have achieved certain objectives in various physical education activities, just as they achieve various levels of skills, knowledge, and competencies in other school subjects. A plan for assurance of mastery or graduation standards in physical education must be developed and implemented. In this fashion, physical education should keep pace with the No Child Left Behind Act (NCLB) of 2001.

Physical education should involve more than physical activity. As the participant understands more fully the importance of human movement; what happens to the human body during exercise and stress; the relationship of physical activity to one's biological, psychological, and sociocultural development; the history of various activities; and the role of physical activity in the interdependent global community, physical education will take on a new meaning, grow in intellectual respectability, and contribute to building a more healthy and productive society.

Just as textbooks, handouts, and resource materials are employed within other courses in the educational system, so should they be used in

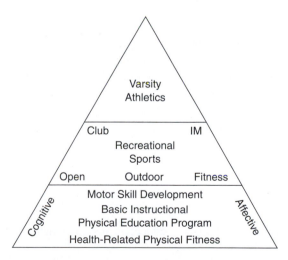

Figure 3-1. A traditional view of the relationship between the basic instructional or physical activity program, recreational sports, and varsity athletics.

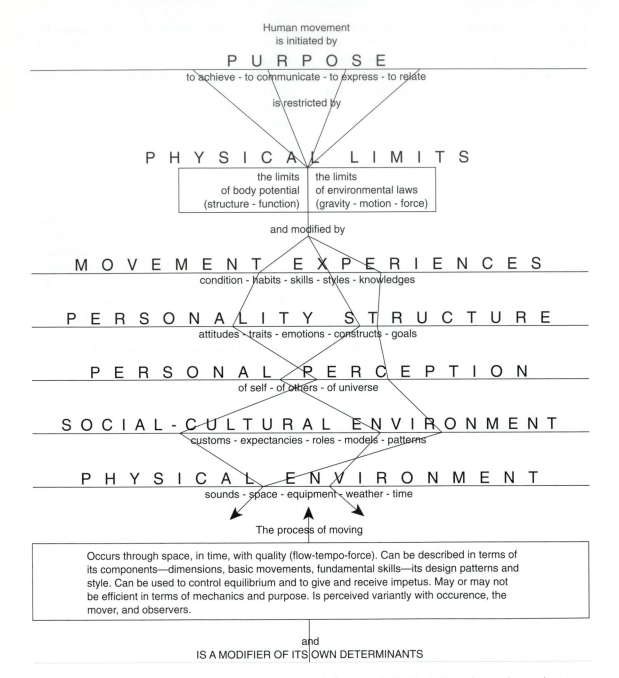

Figure 3-2. Mediators of human movement serve to influence all physical education and sport instructional programs.

the physical education program. Textbooks should not only contain material pertaining to physical skills, but should also explore the totality of the subject matter of physical education (e.g., health-related fitness, nutrition, risk factors, stress management, etc.).

Meaningful assessment and developmental records that follow a student from grade to grade should be maintained throughout his or her school life. These records will indicate the degree to which the objectives of the program have been achieved by the student. The level and degree of physical skill and fitness achievement, involvement in outside activity, health status, and social conduct may all serve to interpret what role physical education has played for the students as they meet the challenges of an ever-growing and complex society.

The basic instructional physical education program cannot be conducted in a hit-or-miss fashion. It must be planned in accordance with the needs and interests of the individuals it serves as well as the society in which they will become contributing members. Regardless of the individual's motives for participation (e.g., to pursue pleasure and satisfaction, to gain affiliation, to master skills, to attain or maintain fitness and health, to seek excellence), physical education class is where the process of a healthy lifestyle begins and where sound management is requisite. In this regard, physical education instructional programs may be guided by the AAHPERD/NASPE's Content Standards in Physical Education (see chapter 2), the Council for Physical Education for Children (COPEC), and Guidelines for the Physically Educated Person (see chapter 2 and appendix A).

MANAGEMENT GUIDELINES FOR SCHOOL AND COLLEGE PHYSICAL EDUCATION PROGRAMS

Physical education programs in schools and colleges have played a prominent role in educational systems since the turn of the twentieth century. Physical education programs exist at the preschool,

elementary, junior high, middle, and senior high school levels as well as at the college and university educational level.

The state of physical education, however, is not as solid as it should be. It is evident that an active child can accrue tremendous benefits (Leon 1997, USDHHS 2000), yet 36 percent of our youth and 40 percent of our adults do not engage in vigorous physical activity, and our overweight student population has tripled since the 1980s. The Centers for Disease Control and Prevention (CDC) reports that over nine million children are overweight, and estimates associated obesity sick care costs at $100 billion per year or 8 percent of the national health-care budget (NASPE 2004). The number of high school students in daily physical education classes decreased from 42 percent to 29 percent during the last decade. More problematic is that less than half of the nation's schools offer daily physical education and the trend of less participation as students increase in age is well documented (Kann et al. 1998). The challenge as we move into the future is to construct a more sound multidimensional (knowledge, skills, attitudes) path to lifetime health and fitness.

Preschool Physical Education Programs

The concept of early schooling is no longer regarded as a custodial or compensatory undertaking. Instead it is viewed as a necessary provision for the normal growth and development of children. Research by psychologists, child development specialists, and sociologists has indicated that the early years are crucial for the child intellectually, physically, socially, and emotionally. In light of such findings, as well as the return of many mothers to the workforce, nursery schools and child day-care centers have gained wide popularity.

Preschool educational programs should involve indoor and outdoor play-learning activities. Physical education activities should include the development of fundamental movement skills, fitness, self-testing and team-building activities, music and rhythmic activities, creative free play, and rhymes and story plays. A sound program of selected physical activities helps the child develop a positive self-concept; develop, practice, and test social skills; enhance physical fitness; and improve cognitive and sensorimotor skills. Research maintains that a relationship exists between perception and motor development and that perception is related to cognition; therefore physical movement experiences play a crucial role in cognitive development.

Preschool programs are becoming an integral part of educational systems in this country, and physical education should play an important role in such programs.

Elementary School Physical Education Programs

Contemporary elementary physical education programs continue to focus on the foundation of the profession—human movement. Physical education takes on an important part of the schools' instructional program and is designed to foster development of fundamental motor skills, health-related fitness, and knowledge and attitude relative to physical activity through a carefully planned curriculum that includes, for example, movement skills (running, jumping, skipping/fitness), nonlocomotor skills (stretching, balance), manipulative skills (throwing, kicking/ball skills), and rhythms and dance. These learning experiences help students understand how to move and to become more aware of their body within the environmental framework of force, time, space, and flow. The experiences of, through, and about physicalness are managed in such a fashion that exploration, problem solving, decision making, cooperation, and challenge contribute to the development of positive feelings toward oneself and others as well as of physical activity as a valuable contribution to a wholesome and healthy quality of life.

Physical education at this level should promote the individual child's standard of motor performance and establish a physical activity comfort level so that each child develops an appreciation and enjoyment of movement.

Elementary schools also combine the essential movement skills and perceptual motor development, and in some schools, an interdisciplinary approach is utilized, whereby the subject matter of physical education is integrated with certain other subjects such as health, music, science, history, and art.

Here are some management guidelines for elementary school physical education programs. The program should meet the needs of all children, including those with learning or physical disabilities, the culturally or environmentally deprived, and the gifted. The program should include a variety of developmental experiences that will help the child form a sound foundation on which to build more complex skills, techniques, strategies, and concepts. The program (ranging from basic motor skills to low-organized and beginning-related games) should provide developmental and progressive experiences in a safe and wholesome environment. Children should accumulate at least 60 to 150 minutes of age-appropriate physical activity on most days including several bouts of sustained physical activity lasting at least 15 minutes in duration. Physical education should also foster creativity, challenge, self-expression, social development, team building, positive self-concepts, and appreciation for the importance and value of lifetime health-related fitness.

Secondary School Physical Education Programs

The junior high, middle, and senior high schools of the nation should build on the physical education foundation provided at the elementary school level. Here are some management guidelines that represent important considerations in secondary school physical education programs. Most of the guidelines set for the elementary school also have merit in developing programs for secondary schools. The secondary program should be based on the developmental tasks of secondary school students. The program should consist of a variety of age-appropriate activities, including gymnastics, self-testing activities, rhythm and dance, movement skills, aquatics, physical fitness activities, outdoor

Movement exploration is a key ingredient in elementary physical education.

education, and individual, dual, and team sports. The program should provide a thorough understanding of the human body and the impact of physical activity on its various organic systems. The *Basic Stuff Series I and II* (1987) developed by the National Association for Sport and Physical Education (NASPE) of the American Alliance for Health, Physical Education, Recreation and Dance (AAHPERD) contains concepts, principles, and developmental ideas extracted from physical education's body of knowledge and might serve as a valuable K–12 programmatic guide. The American College of Sports Medicine (ACSM), COPEC, and NASPE also offer sound guidelines. The program should teach a variety of skills progressively, eliminate excessive repetition of activities, and ensure the inclusion of lifetime sports and health-related fitness concepts. The program should be open to all students, including those with varying disabilities, who should be provided an opportunity to function in the least restrictive environment. The program should encourage at least 30 minutes of daily vigorous physical activity in and outside of class, including individual fitness and participation in community, recreational, and varsity interscholastic sport.

In addition, to these management guidelines, the following points should be stressed:

The physical education class provides the student with a safe and wholesome environment in which to learn the skills, strategy, appreciation, understanding, knowledge, rules, regulations, and other material and information that are part of the program. It is not a place for free play, intramurals, or varsity practice. It is a place for proactive and dynamic instruction. The class period should be devoted to teaching students the skills and content matter of physical education, sport, and leisure activity.

Instruction should be fundamental, dynamic, and interesting. Skills should be broken down into basic components and presented so that each individual may understand clearly what is expected to be accomplished and how it is to be done. Use of demonstrations, computer simulations, digital media, handheld computers (PDAs), online interactive material and other audiovisual aids and materials can help make the instruction more meaningful and interesting; however, dynamic and functional instruction is requisite.

Instruction should be progressive. There should be a definite progression from basic to complex skills. Just as a student progresses in mathematics from basic arithmetic to algebra, geometry, and calculus, so the physical education student should progress from basic skills and materials to more complex and involved skills, techniques, and problem-solving strategies.

Instruction should involve definite standards. Students should be expected to reach individualized standards of achievement (assurance of mastery) in the class program. A reasonable amount of skill—whether it is in swimming, tennis, dance, or another activity— should be mastered, keeping in mind individual differences. Upon graduation from high school, students should have met definite assurance-of-mastery standards and goals that indicate that they are *physically educated.*

Instruction should involve more than physical activity. All physical education classes do not have to be conducted in the gymnasium, where physical activity predominates. A reasonable proportion of class time, perhaps as much as 10 percent to 20 percent, can be devoted to class interaction and discussion, guest lecturers, independent study, cooperative projects, field trips (e.g., skiing, backpacking, bowling, sailing, skating, or golf), and working on individualized fitness and learning packages. Physical activity should not be conducted in a vacuum; if it is, it has no meaning and will not be applied when the student leaves the class and school setting. As the student understands more fully the importance of physical activity and sport, what happens to the body during exercise, how to cooperate to succeed, the roots of the various activities in which he or she engages, and the role of physical activity across cultures (such as the breaking of racial, ethnic, and gender barriers), physical

education will take on a new meaning and perhaps play a significant role throughout the life span of each individual.

There should be assessment and records. The instructor should keep accurate daily records to provide tangible evidence concerning the degree to which student objectives are being met. This means that data concerning skill achievement, physical fitness level, critical knowledge, and other information, including social conduct— such as fair play, cooperative effort, and out-of-class participation—should be a part of the database. Assessment should be employed with the notion to enhance and improve both program and individual performance.

There should be homework. It is just as reasonable to assign homework in physical education as in biology or math. Much subject matter is to be learned, many skills are to be mastered, and fitness levels must be improved or maintained. Teachers who require their students to work on various skills (physical and mental), endurance activities, and knowledge acquisition outside of class will find more time for meaningful, functional, and targeted physical activity instruction during class.

Each student should have a thorough medical examination before participating in the physical education program. An annual health examination should be regarded as a minimum, essential not only to ensure the student's safety but to effectively prescribe the frequency, duration, and intensity of the physical activity to best meet each student's needs.

The teaching load of physical educators should be determined not only by the number of instructional class periods assigned, but also by the total number of activities handled by the teacher both in class and outside of class. For teachers to be effective, their normal daily workload should consist of not more than five hours of instruction, or five class periods. In addition, provisions should be made to ensure one hour of class-preparation time. Attached to the teaching load will be requests for active

Individual lifetime sport foundations and fundamentals are promoted in secondary schools.

involvement in extracurricular activities (e.g., coaching, intramurals, clubs, etc.). Regardless of assignments, a teacher's time management skills will be put to good use.

Trends and Innovative Ideas in Secondary School Physical Education

Many innovative instructional programs are being employed in physical education at the secondary school level. This is a result of programs such as AAHPERD's Lifetime Sports Education Project (LSEP) and of the President's Council on Physical Fitness and Sports (PCPFS) Active Lifestyle Model School and President's Challenge Programs. It is estimated that 75 percent of the nation's secondary schools emphasize lifetime sports. These include programs that stress personalized, individualized, and cooperative learning; that emphasize performance objectives, competency and responsibility packages, and goal setting (Hellison 2003; Cooper Institute 2004); that concern career and leadership opportunities; that stress flexibility in scheduling; and that concentrate on specialized electives and group experiences such as camping, sailing, skiing, backpacking, and outdoor and wilderness leadership activities during which the student interacts with the environment as well as with other cultures.

College and University Physical Education Programs

Colleges and universities should provide instruction in physical education that meets the following management criteria:

■ The program should be available to all students.

■ The program should not be a repetition of the high school program, but should offer more advanced work in physical education and health-related fitness (e.g., yoga, aerobic boxing, BOSE, pilates, spinning). However, instruction in the development of basic skills should continue to be an integral part of the program.

■ The program should include innovative features to meet the needs of students and at the same time be interesting and challenging.

■ Management should prelude athletics, marching band, ROTC, recreational sports, or other activities from serving as a substitute for physical education.

■ The program should provide a wide range of course selection including individual, dual, and team activities as well as aquatics, health-related fitness, dance, and outdoor pursuits.

■ The program should stress knowledge and understanding of the value of physical activity and its relationship to the environment.

■ The program should stress the study as well as the practice of the science and art of human movement.

■ The program should focus on lifetime activities.

■ The program should be conducted by well-trained and fully certified faculty and staff.

In the 1970s, some U.S. colleges and universities moved physical education from a mandatory to an elective status. The current trend, however, is to maintain physical education typically for a one- to two-year period. Classes usually meet two or three times per week, with some colleges still requiring standards of achievement (most often swimming and basic fitness and wellness). Today's physical activity programs also place more emphasis on lifetime sports, outdoor pursuits, and health-related fitness and wellness activities, including aerobics, conditioning, and strength training.

The growth of community and junior colleges has been significant. In many respects, the activities for these institutions are the same as those for colleges and universities. Many community and junior colleges require students to take at least one year of physical education. Most of the programs require two hours each week and stress the successful completion of physical education as a requirement for awarding of the associate degree.

The college and university physical education program is the end of formal physical education for many students. Student age range in colleges and universities is wide, incorporating participants from age sixteen to sixty and beyond. However, most college students are in their late teens or early twenties and have matured in many ways. Many hold part-time jobs. They are entering the period of greatest physical efficiency and possess many interests, including physical activity and sport. Many want to prepare themselves for successful vocations, an objective that requires the physical educator to show how an active lifestyle can contribute to success in their future profession. College students are also interested in developing socially, and coeducational activities help provide a training ground for gender-free experiences in a wide variety of settings. In addition, students are interested in developing skills that they can use and enjoy throughout life as well as in becoming physically fit and looking good.

In formulating a program at the college and university level, one needs to remember that many students enter with limited physical activity backgrounds. Therefore the program should be broadly based and varied at the start, with opportunities to elect more advanced activities later. Considerable opportunity should exist for instruction, feedback, and practice in those activities in which a student desires to specialize. As much individual attention as possible should be given to ensure necessary safety as well as skill or technique, fitness, and attitude development.

The program of activities should be based on the interests and needs of students as well as on the availability of facilities and staff. Some colleges have introduced foundation courses, which cover basic subject matter ranging from nutrition and weight control perspectives to the philosophical underpinnings of physical education (Corbin and Lindsey 2005).

In college physical education programs, physical skill and fitness achievement tests should be employed to assess student status, set reasonable goals, and ensure progress. Special assistance, systematic feedback, and individually prescribed programs should be offered to help all students develop to their fullest potential. Technology is becoming more user friendly and functional in this pursuit.

MANAGEMENT VARIABLES RELATING TO ONE OR MORE EDUCATIONAL LEVELS

Certain management variables relate to one or more educational levels (elementary, secondary, college and university). Some of the more pertinent variables include interrelationships of elementary, secondary, and college and university programs; instructional aids and materials; class management; interpretation of Title IX regulations for instructional strategies; and implications of the Individuals with Disabilities Education Act (IDEA) for adapted/developmental physical education programs for persons with varying disabilities.

Interrelationships of Elementary, Secondary, and College and University Programs

The physical education programs from the K–12 levels through the college and university level should be interrelated. Continuity and progression should characterize the program from the time the student enters kindergarten until graduation.

Program content and its delivery should be based on current research and best practices. Overall planning is essential to ensure that each student becomes physically educated and to guarantee that duplication of effort and time, curricular omissions, and content shortages do not occur.

Continuity and progression do not exist today in many of the school systems in the United States. Instead, to a great degree, each institutional level is autonomous, setting up its own program with curriculum-writing teams and consultants responsible for course content and development. If the focus of attention is on the student—the consumer of the product—then curriculum planning will provide the student with a continuous program, developed to meet the dynamic needs and interests from the beginning to the end of the formal educational process (kindergarten through college or university and beyond).

Consideration and cooperative planning should also exist for the entire community to ensure that each child's needs are met and that no child is left behind. Many communities have school and community physical education directors and recreation program managers who regularly meet to ensure an integrated, coordinated, inclusive, and continuous program of physical activity for the entire community.

In some communities, shared partnerships involving both physical and human resources ranging from aquatics to ice hockey arenas are commonplace. Computer software, tracking, and information retrieval make it easier to construct a physical education profile for each student to not only accommodate, for example, K–12 developmental fitness level status, but also track each student's use and preference of community fitness resources as well. In this way, school and community should develop even stronger interconnectedness.

Management Guidelines for Selecting Instructional Aids and Materials

When selecting audiovisual aids or other instructional resources and materials, physical educators should consider the following principles that make using these aids effective, meaningful, and valuable.

Selection and screening of materials. The teacher should preview the materials to determine if they are appropriate for the unit and age level of the students and to ensure that they present information in an interesting, progressive, and stimulating manner.

Proper preparation of materials should be made. The teacher or responsible school official should check all equipment that may be necessary for the presentation of materials to make sure that it is in operating condition and has backup. Computers, camcorders, videotape and DVD players, and overhead and multimedia projectors, in particular, need to be carefully checked before each use. Maintenance schedules and records should also be maintained on equipment.

Presentation of materials should be planned and integrated into the lesson. Students should be properly introduced to the topic, and materials strategically placed so that they positively influence the learning process and the student understands their relationship to the unit of study.

Materials should be presented to the students in a proper learning environment. Students should be prepared and positioned so that all may hear, see, and learn from the material being offered. They should realize that they will be held responsible for the information being presented.

Materials should be diverse and varied. Different types of materials should be selected for presentation to stimulate and motivate the students. A teacher using videotapes, DVDs, or slides exclusively does not take full advantage of other supplementary materials such as PowerPoint and Web-based materials that may have widespread appeal.

Use of supplementary materials should be limited. The teacher should place a reasonable limit on the use of supplementary teaching materials in order to maintain an appropriate balance between time involved in physical activity and time engaged in, for example, viewing the serving technique of a professional tennis player via computer clip.

Care should be taken to be fiscally responsible. A reasonable part of the instructional budget should be set aside for supplementary materials. This amount should be in accordance with the emphasis placed on this phase of the teaching program, and items selected should possess long-term redeeming value.

Records and evaluations should be maintained and backed up. All supplementary materials should be carefully cataloged and kept on computer file for future reference. This should save the unnecessary time and expense involved in reordering or duplicating materials and in culling outdated materials.

By following these principles, the teacher is able to optimize the learning environment with materials that are interesting, meaningful, and valuable to the students. Here are various types of materials, activities, and human resources that can be used in the instructional process.

- *Reading materials:* textbooks, trade books, magazines, rulebooks, pamphlets, journals, news clippings, handouts
- *Audiovisual aids:* motion pictures, slides, learning loops, television, videotapes, and videoclips, DVD players, audiotapes, disks
- *Special aids:* computers, handheld devices, charts, photographic materials, bulletin boards, magnetic boards
- *Professional personnel:* presenters from professional associations and organizations
- *Community activities:* recreational activities, PTA/PTO-sponsored events, Special Olympics, events sponsored by Red Cross, Partners of the Americas, Senior Games, and other private volunteer organizations (PVOs)
- *Clinics:* special games and programs conducted by visiting teams, professional teaching organizations, community organizations, foundations such as the Women's Sport Foundation, sports federations such as the United States Tennis Association (USTA), and state high school leagues/associations

- *Computers:* computer-assisted learning and digital media feedback, Web site and home page information

Class Management

Sound management does not just happen. It requires careful thought, good judgment, and planning before the class begins. Management practices help to ensure that the class functions as a coordinated group in order to effectively and efficiently accomplish the goals and tasks that have been established. Quality management leads to enjoyable, satisfying, safe, and worthwhile experiences. The teacher who is in charge of a class where optimal learning conditions exist has spent considerable time planning the details of the class from start to finish.

The following reasons for good organization should be recognized by every teacher and administrator:

- It ensures the participant's health, safety, and maximal performance outcome.
- It helps eliminate discipline problems.
- It gives meaning and purpose to instruction and to the assigned activities.
- It results in efficiency, provides proper focus, and allows the best use of precious time.
- It more fully ensures that the needs and interests of the participants will be protected and satisfied.
- It ensures meaningful progression and continuity in the program.
- It provides for measurement, assessment, and evaluation of objectives as well as timely feedback concerning knowledge of results.
- It encourages program adaptations to meet each individual's needs and interests.
- It reduces errors and omissions.
- It helps conserve the teacher's time and energy and provides the teacher with a sense of accomplishment.

Management Guidelines

- The classroom environment should be one that is safe yet unrestricted, and creative movement should be encouraged. Equipment should be in proper condition, thoroughly inspected, and placed appropriately for safe activity. Field and gymnasium markings, equipment arrangements, logistics for activities, and other essential details should be attended to well before class.

- A risk management walkabout before class is highly recommended.
- Strategic and long-term planning for the semester and the year should be prepared as well as daily, weekly, and seasonal planning.
- A definite time schedule should be planned for each period, considering learning objectives and the priorities concerning dressing for class, taking roll, safety, warm-up, class activity, cooldown, and other pedagogical essentials.
- The activity should be carefully planned so that class proceeds with precision and dispatch, with a minimal amount of standing around, and a maximal amount of student activity.
- Procedures to be followed in the locker room should be clearly established to provide for traffic, valuables, clothes, showering, and dressing.
- The instructor should always be early for class and last to depart.
- Participants should be encouraged and motivated to do their best at all times.
- A planned program of assessment and evaluation should be provided to determine progress and improvement being made by participants. The effectiveness of teaching strategies and programs may also be determined.
- Students should be made aware of the rules and consequences for failing to comply or participate in class activities.
- The instructor should wear appropriate clothing.
- The instructor should possess a thorough command of the subject, recognizing the value of demonstrations, visual aids, cooperative goal structuring, and other techniques and instructional strategies that promote learning.

Behavior modification through physical activity presentation to physical educators at the International Special Olympic Games Symposium, University of Minnesota.

- Desirable attitudes toward and understanding of physical fitness, learning skills, fair play, respect, responsibility, inclusiveness, safety, vigorous participation, and other concepts inherent in physical education should be continually stressed.
- Procedures for emergencies should be established, disseminated to all involved in class (students, classroom teachers who sometimes deliver physical education classes, paraprofessionals, nurses, principals, etc.) and maintained on file. Students' identity and health status should also be known to school personnel involved with the delivery of physical education and of all activity.

TITLE IX

On May 27, 1975, President Gerald Ford signed into law Title IX of the Education Amendments Act of 1972 (Clement 2004), which states that no person, on the basis of sex, be excluded from participation in, be denied the benefits of, or be subjected to discrimination under any educational program or activity receiving federal assistance. Title IX clearly established a mandate for educational institutions that received federal financial assistance to eliminate gender discrimination within their programs, including physical education and sport. The effective date of the regulation was July 21, 1975. Title IX affects nearly all the nation's 16,000 public school systems and nearly 2,700 postsecondary institutions. As a first step, the regulation provides that educators (including physical educators) should perform a searching self-examination of policies and practices in their schools and institutions and take whatever remedial action is needed to bring them into compliance with federal law.

Reason for Title IX

The primary reason for the enactment of Title IX was testimony before congressional and other committees to the effect that females were frequently denied enrollment in traditionally male courses and activities and that girls and women were continually denied equal participatory opportunity. A national survey conducted by the National Education Association showed that although women constituted a majority of all public school teachers, they accounted for only 3.5 percent of the junior high school and middle school principals and 3 percent of the senior high school principals. It was believed that by instilling and perpetuating traditional gender roles and sexual differentiation, educational institutions have, over time, denied women equal educational and employment opportunity and therefore equal participation in the sociocultural process. Title IX was legislated to correct this fundamental problem.

Implications of Title IX for Physical Education Teachers and Their Instructional Strategies

Physical education classes must be organized on a coeducational basis. Teachers and staff should ensure that instructional offerings and opportunities are coeducational or gender-balanced. Most activities should be coeducational in nature, and equal opportunity for participation and equal time must be afforded to all students.

This regulation does not mean that activities must be taught coeducationally. Within classes, students may be grouped by gender for such contact sports as wrestling, basketball, ice hockey, rugby, and football. Also, within physical education classes, students may be grouped on an ability basis even though such grouping may result in a single-sex grouping. However, gender must *not* be the criterion for grouping. Furthermore, if an evaluation standard has an adverse impact on one gender, such as a standard of accomplishment in a physical fitness test, different evaluation requirements must be utilized.

Schools and colleges must provide equal opportunities for both genders. Equal opportunity in this respect means that the activities offered must reflect the interests and abilities of students of both genders. Adequate course offerings, facilities, and equipment must be available for both sexes in physical education and sport programs. Furthermore, one gender cannot dominate the facilities or the most popular or new equipment. In addition, adequate time for practice and instructional assistance must be provided for both genders. Again, one gender cannot dominate.

Schools and colleges must spend funds in an equitable manner. Although equal aggregate expenditures are not required, an educational institution cannot discriminate on the basis of gender in providing proper equipment, supplies, and associated services.

Title IX takes precedence over all state and local laws and conference regulations that might be in conflict with this federal regulation.

If an institution receives federal aid, it must be in compliance with Title IX, even though its physical education or athletic program does not directly receive any of this aid.

There can be no discrimination in respect to personnel standards. No discrimination can exist in respect to personnel standards by gender, including marital or parental status, for employment, promotion, retention, salary, recruitment, job classification, or fringe benefits.

Financial aid must be awarded equitably. The regulations require an institution to select students to be awarded financial aid on the basis of criteria other than a student's gender.

Interpretation of Title IX Regulations

Some interpretations of Title IX regulations that affect physical education instructional strategies are listed here. Interpretations such as the following have come from various sources. Gender designations associated with class schedules, activities, and budgets are not permitted. The term *girls' gymnasium* can be used; however, the scheduling of this facility must be nondiscriminatory in respect to each gender. Policies and procedures in regard to items such as uniforms and attendance must apply to both genders. Gender-segregated administrative units, such as departments, do not necessarily have to be merged, although having faculty men and women in integrated offices in newly combined administrative units is encouraged. If a significantly greater number of one gender is enrolled in a particular physical education class, the administration, if called on, should be prepared to provide the rationale for such organization. Supervision of locker rooms may be assigned to teacher aides, paraprofessionals, or teachers in other departments. Marks or grades given in physical education classes should reflect individual growth and performance and not compare genders with one another. Standards of performance that provide an unfair comparison for one gender should not be employed. In some cases, separate standards might be used for each gender; for example, on a physical fitness rating, such as number of push-ups or chin-ups in sixty seconds.

Coeducational Physical Education Classes

Because the provision for coeducational classes is one of the key implications of Title IX regulations, this topic is discussed further here.

Problems in physical education classes concerning Title IX have been cited in the professional literature. Clement (2004) indicates that problems such as the following have developed as a result of Title IX: the teacher is not professionally prepared to teach various activities in a coeducational setting; male and female teachers who traditionally made decisions on their own are finding it difficult to function as a team and share the decision-making process; students are also finding problems such as being unable to perform some activities satisfactorily in front of members of the opposite sex; and those with poor skills are excluded from participation on highly skilled coeducational teams.

Many of these problems can be solved by such means as teachers eliminating their personal gender biases, employing new instructional strategies and techniques, and reexamining philosophies concerning the teaching of physical education. The main consideration in establishing coeducational programs is to respond to the interests and ability levels of the participants. When conducting activities on a coeducational basis, appropriate modifications may be made in the rules and conduct of the activities to equalize competition between genders.

Coeducational physical education. Birchview Elementary School, Wayzata, Minn.

Other problems that have arisen in physical education classes as a result of Title IX include assignment of office space, scheduling of gymnasiums for various activities, supervision of locker rooms, dressing standards, potential for sexual impropriety, and the teaching of combative or contact activities such as wrestling or self defense.

Compliance with Title IX   Title IX is being enforced by the Department of Education of the federal government. The first step seeks to have voluntary compliance. This process should be the job of the physical education teacher, physical education department, and school administration. If violations are found, federal financial support may be cut off and other legal measures taken, such as referring the violation to the Department of Justice for appropriate court action.

In 1992, the U.S. Supreme Court ruled that if schools intentionally violate Title IX, the plaintiff could sue for damages. Typically most complaints have been about athletics, not physical education. Further information about Title IX may be found in chapter 5.

Coeducational dance instruction. University of Minnesota.

THE ADAPTED/DEVELOPMENTAL PHYSICAL EDUCATION PROGRAM

The adapted/developmental program refers to the phase of physical education that meets the needs of the individual who, because of some physical inadequacy, functional defect capable of being improved through physical activity, or other deficiency, is temporarily or permanently unable to take part in the regular physical education program or the phase in which special provisions are made for students with disabilities in regular physical education classes. It also refers to students of a school or college population who do not fall into the "average" or "normal" classification for their age or grade. These students deviate from their peers in physical, mental, emotional, or social characteristics or in a combination of these traits.

The principle of individual differences that applies to education as a whole also applies to physi-

cal education. Most administrators believe that as long as a student can attend school or college, he or she should be required to participate in physical education. If this tenet is adhered to, it means that programs may have to be adapted to meet individual needs. Many children and young adults who are recuperating from long illnesses or surgery or who are suffering from other physical or emotional conditions require special consideration concerning their full and vigorous participation in physical activity programs.

It cannot be assumed that all individuals in physical education classes do not possess some type of disability. It is unfortunate that many programs are administered on this basis. An estimate has been made that 11 percent of the children in our schools have disabilities that require special provision in the educational program (Auxter, Pyfer, and Huettig 2005).

Physical education teachers instructing students with severe disabilities.

Schools and colleges will always have students who, because of many factors such as heredity, environment, disease, accident, drugs, or some other circumstance, have physical or other major disabilities. Many of these students have difficulty adjusting to the demands that society places on them. The responsibility of the physical educator is to help each individual enrolled in the school to be engaged in appropriate physical education. Even though a person may possess various disabilities, this is not cause for neglect. In fact, by legal mandate and professional challenge, it is required that each child enjoy the benefits of participating in physical activities adapted to his or her needs. Provision for a sound adapted/developmental program has been a shortcoming of physical education throughout the nation because of a lack of properly trained teachers, because of the financial cost of remedial instruction, and because many administra-

tors and teachers are not aware of their responsibility and the contribution they can make in this phase of physical education. These obstacles should be overcome as the public becomes aware of the mandate to educate *all* individuals in *all* phases of the total educational process and leave no child behind.

People with Varying Disabilities

The nation's estimated fifty million people with disabilities have engaged in an aggressive civil rights movement. These actions were aimed at obtaining the equal protection promised under the Fourteenth Amendment to the Constitution of the United States.

As a result of the actions on the part of persons with disabilities, the nation is finally awakening to their needs as well as to their human potentialities. Until recently, persons with disabilities were viewed as nonproductive, functionally disruptive, and draining on society. As a result, persons with disabilities have often become discouraged. Today, however, the picture has changed. Persons with disabilities are achieving their rights under the Constitution, under public laws such as the November 29, 1975, Education for All Handicapped Children Act (P.L. 94-142). This law provided the first legal basis for adapted/developmental physical education. It specified physical education as a direct service and, therefore, it was required (Sherrill 2004). P.L. 94-142 was followed by its upgrades, the 1986 Education for All Handicapped Children Act Amendments (P.L. 99-457) and in 1990 consolidated and became the Individuals with Disabilities Education Act (IDEA) (P.L. 101-476). These significant federal funding statutes and their subsequent reauthorizations in 1997 and 2003, combined with the American with Disabilities Act of January 26, 1992 (P.L. 101-336), a civil rights law mandating that all public facilities or accommodations (school gymnasiums, community centers, pools, playgrounds, bowling alleys) permit equal access, use, and services for all individuals regardless of capacity, have served to build a bridge between public school delivery of adapted physical education and community recreational services for students with disabilities. Combined, these mandates have served to enlarge the rights of people with disabilities, freeing them from discrimination in schools, community recreation environments, and beyond. Persons with disabilities are gaining accessibility, receiving more educational opportunities, gaining meaningful employment in the public workforce, and taking their rightful place in an accessible and inclusive society.

Definitions Relating to the Adapted/Developmental Program

Many terms have been used to define and classify persons with disabilities. These terms vary from publication to publication. Categories of children designated by the U.S. Congress in relation to legislation for persons with disabilities, Section 504 of the Rehabilitation Act of 1973 (P.L. 93-112),

will be the primary classifications used in this text; however, these terms will be modified to reflect the changing view concerning persons with disabilities, such as those infected with Human Immunodeficiency Virus (HIV), Attention Deficit Hyperactivity Disorder (ADHD), or Fetal Alcohol Syndrome (FAS). These classifications include the mentally disabled, hearing impaired, speech impaired, visually impaired, emotionally and behaviorally disordered, learning disabled, physically disabled, and other health-impaired individuals who may require educational services out of the ordinary. In effect any school-age person who has a physical or mental impairment that substantially limits major life activities (i.e., learning, walking, seeing, hearing) is included. Students falling under P.L. 93-112 Section 504 are required to have an educational accommodation plan comparable to the education of students who are not disabled. Many times these students are mainstreamed or participate in the same classes as their classmates. Students who are eligible to be placed under IDEA, on the other hand, are required to have on file Individualized Educational Plans (IEPs) specifying adequate educational programs and outlining their respective learning outcomes and benefits.

Special Education

Under federal law, special education includes physical education instruction as a direct service. The direct service must be provided to meet the unique needs of students with disabilities and may take place in the classroom, gymnasium, pool, home, hospital, or institution. These services are to be free, appropriate, and they are to take place in the least restrictive environment.

Physical Education

Physical education as it relates to the persons with disabilities under federal law is the development and delivery of (1) physical and motor fitness, (2) fundamental motor skills and patterns, and (3) skills in aquatics, dance, and individual and group games and sports (including recreational and lifetime sports). Physical educators must serve as part of the adapted student's resource team and be prepared to design specific and appropriate programs of physical activity for each student.

Individualized Education Program

The individualized education program (IEP) is the program or prescription written for each child in relation to his or her specific disability. It is required by law and specifies the service that the student must receive in each school subject in which he or she is declared disabled. This IEP might range from full mainstreaming or inclusion in regular physical education classes (sometimes with a paraprofessional) to a specialized physical education setting under the direction of a licensed adapted physical educator. The IEP determines the least restrictive environment in which the student will receive instruction. The IEP will be discussed in more detail later in this chapter (also see appendix B).

Least Restrictive Environment

In essence, the *least restrictive environment* (see figure 3-3) means that individuals with disabilities are placed in a class or setting that is as similar to a normal class as possible and in which the child can function safely. This location ranges from a full-time regular physical education class (inclusion), to a regular physical education class with consultation from specialists in adapted physical education, to part-time regular physical education and part-time adapted physical education, to adapted physical education with regular physical education only for specific activities, to full-time adapted physical education in a regular school, to adapted physical education in a special school. The current trend is to include the special student (inclusion), if possible, within the regular physical education instructional class, where appropriate and safe activities may be enjoyed.

Functional Physical Education Goals for Individuals with Disabilities

Selected goals that provide direction to the physical education program for the student with disabilities and that translate into objectives for each

participant, as outlined by AAHPERD, are presented here in an updated and modified format:

- Inform each student of his or her capacities, limitations, and potentials.
- Provide each student within his or her capabilities the opportunities to develop organic vigor, muscular strength and endurance, joint function and flexibility, and cardiovascular endurance.
- Provide each student with opportunities for social development in recreational sports and games.
- Provide each student with opportunities to develop skills in recreational sports and games.
- Help students meet demands of day-to-day living.
- Help students with disabilities in their social development.
- Help students develop personal pride in overcoming disabilities or other forms of impairment.
- Help students develop an appreciation for individual differences and an ability to accept limitations and still be an integral part of the group.

The Adapted Physical Education Council of AAHPERD and the National Consortium for Physical Education and Recreation for Individuals with Disabilities (NCPERID) also provide specific recommendations concerning national standards and competencies as well as national certification for people working in this enriching and challenging arena (NCPERID 1995).

Public Law 94-142/Public Law 101-476 (IDEA) and Public Law 105-17 (IDEA 97)

A milestone in legislative proposals providing for persons with disabilities was the passage of the Education for All Handicapped Children Act (EAHCA) of 1975, which was signed into law by the president of the United States as P.L. 94-142. The act has been upgraded and consolidated via

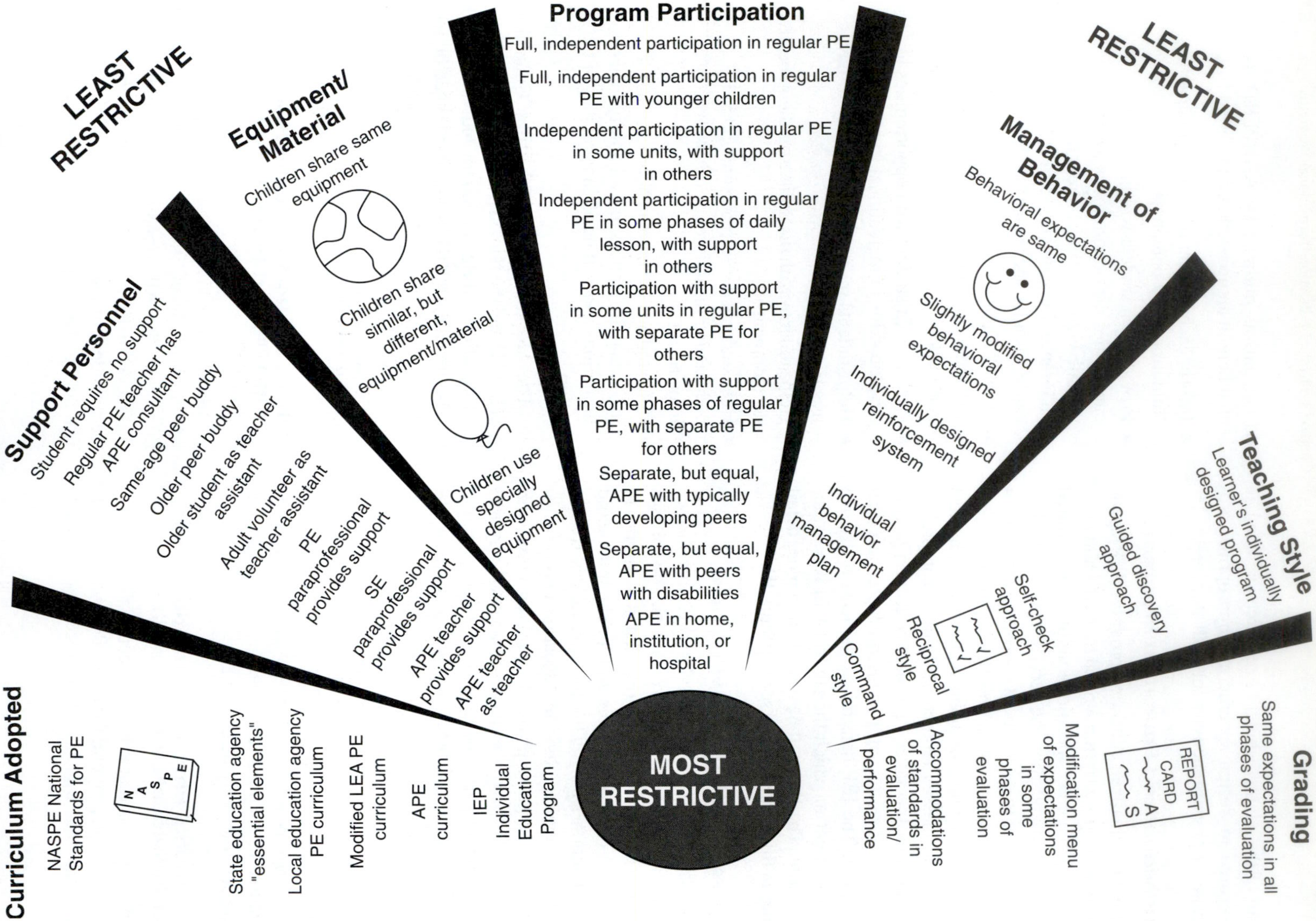

Figure 3-3. Least restrictive environment continuum (LREC). (Adapted from Auxter, Pyfer, and Huettig, 1997).

P.L. 101-476, the Individuals with Disabilities Education Act of 1990 (IDEA), and has been reauthorized in 1997 and 2004 (the Individuals with Disabilities Improvement Act, November 19, 2004.). This legislation spells out the federal government's commitment to educating children with disabilities and provides for annual funding on a sliding scale for this purpose. It provides educational services to children with disabilities who are not receiving a free and appropriate public education as well as assistance for those children receiving inadequate help. IDEA mandates that physical education services, specially designed if necessary (IEP), must be made available to every child with a disability receiving a free and appropriate education.

These services have now been extended from birth through age twenty-one. Children with disabilities, as defined in IDEA-Part B or Subchapter H are those who require some type of special education and related services. Related services, under the act, are defined as "transportation and developmental, corrective, and other supportive services, including but not limited to, occupational, speech, and physical therapy, recreation, and social, medical, and counseling services." Although gifted children might need special education and related services, they are not covered under the law.

Other specific stipulations of IDEA require the following:

- That state and local educational agencies initiate policies to ensure all children the right to a free and appropriate education in the least restrictive environment.

- The planning of individualized educational programs, including health and physical status and motoric ability, and the scheduling of conferences that include parents, teachers (including physical education and special education teachers), case managers, administrators, representatives of local educational agencies, and where appropriate, the children themselves. These conferences must be held at least once a year.

- Due process for parents and children to ensure that their rights are not abrogated.

- A per-student expenditure that is at least equal to the amount spent on each nondisabled child in the state or local school district.

- That the state and local educational agency carry out the mandates of the law according to specific timetables provided therein.

- The development of a comprehensive system of personnel training, including preservice and inservice training for teachers.

- That students with disabilities will be educated in the least restrictive environment. This means that they will be placed in the regular class whenever possible.

Aspects of IDEA related to physical education. The following requirements are stipulated for physical education: (a) *General.* Physical education services, specially designed if necessary, must be made available to every child with disabilities receiving a free appropriate public education. (b) *Regular physical education.* Each child must be afforded the opportunity to participate in the regular physical education program unless

1. The child is enrolled full-time in a separate facility, or
2. The child needs specially designed physical education, as prescribed in the child's IEP.

(c) *Special physical education.* If specially designed physical education is prescribed in a child's IEP, the public agency responsible for the education of that child shall provide the services directly or make arrangements for services to be provided through other public or private programs. (d) *Education in separate facilities.* The public agency responsible for the education of a child with disabilities who is enrolled in a separate facility shall ensure that the child receives appropriate physical education services in compliance with paragraphs (a) and (c) of this section.

Individualized Education Programs for People with Disabilities

After identification and eligibility have been determined for students with disabilities, an IEP must be developed for each individual. IDEA specifies the requirements and guidelines for the development of such programs (also see appendix B):

> The term *individualized education program (IEP)* means a written statement for each child with disabilities developed in any meeting by a representative of the local educational agency or an intermediate educational unit who shall be qualified to provide or supervise the provision of specially designed instruction to meet the unique needs of children with disabilities. The design of an IEP shall include:
>
> A. An assessment of the present levels of educational performance of the child;
> B. A statement of annual goals, including short-term instructional objectives;
> C. A statement of the specific educational services to be provided, and the extent to which the child will be able to participate in regular educational programs;
> D. The projected date for initiation and anticipated duration of the services; and
> E. An outline of appropriate objective criteria and evaluation procedures and schedules for determining, on at least an annual basis, whether instructional objectives are being achieved.

The comprehensive IEP is developed using the team approach. The following persons may be included on the team: parent, teacher (classroom, adapted physical education, and special education), administrator, case manager, student, and—when appropriate—the people responsible for supervising special education, related services such as school psychologist (diagnostic evaluation), and other agency representatives (e.g., social worker, physical therapist, etc.).

Adapted/Developmental Physical Education Facilities

Appropriate and adequate facilities, equipment, and supplies are important to successful programs of physical education for persons with disabilities.

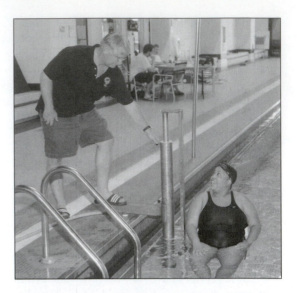

Accessible facilities provide learning, exercise and fitness opportunities for all. St. Joseph's University, Philadelphia, Penn.

However, these items must be modified for special or adapted physical education students because facilities and equipment are usually designed for students in the regular class. Adaptations are often necessary when students are mainstreamed or included into regular programs.

The passage of the Americans with Disabilities Act (ADA), P.L. 101-336 in 1990, and the results of various legal decisions have prompted school districts to make available and accessible the necessary facilities, equipment, assistive technology, supplies, and services including transportation and telecommunications to ensure a quality and equal education for all students. There is some question, however, about whether students with disabilities are being provided with adequate facilities, equipment, and supplies, as well as highly trained personnel to deliver their physical education. The types of facilities and equipment needed for adapted/developmental physical education will vary according to the nature of the program (adapted or unified sports; remedial or corrective exercises; or rest, rehabilitation, and relaxation), the student's disability, and the school level at which the program is conducted. For example, the elementary school program in adapted physical education may be taught in the regular gymnasium or, in less desirable circumstances, in the classroom. In some secondary schools and colleges, however, a special facility or gymnasium for adapted physical education may be provided. However, with the movement to inclusion regular facilities will provide most of the instructional forums.

The following provide a few of the facilities and public accommodation considerations (see appendix F for others) physical educators should be concerned with when providing an optimal learning environment for students with disabilities:

Within Building

- Doors easy to open (automatically activated), at least forty-eight inches in width, and two-way in design.
- Nonslip ramps, properly sloped and maintained, with handrails on both sides.
- Elevators or chair lifts when necessary with properly placed operating mechanisms (closing door, starting, assistance button in braille, etc.).
- Floors with nonslip surfaces.
- Restrooms with toilets at proper height (twenty inches), with rails provided, and with properly designed doors.

Outside Building

- Loading and parking areas convenient to accessible entrances. These areas should be properly lighted, barrier- and curb-free and, if possible, covered.
- Parking spaces at least twelve feet wide.
- Ramps suitable for wheelchairs and accessible to all building levels.
- Doorways and sidewalks wide enough for two passing wheelchairs.
- Emergency exits for wheelchairs.

Other Considerations

Certainly many other considerations are crucial in order for persons with disabilities to be able to function within the operating codes. Other considerations are listed below:

- Telephone (height, length of cord forty-two inches, raised numerals for visually impaired).
- Aquatic facilities (accessible dressing and changing facilities and hair dryer at proper height).
- Safety doors at exits.
- Water fountains (height thirty-three inches above the floor and accessibility).
- Restrooms (accessibility).

All physical education, athletic, and recreational sport programs must operate with sensitivity to provide every student with the opportunity to equal access. Such areas as site location of facility, parking, access ramps, locker rooms, stairs, pools, restrooms, and safety and emergency codes must be attended to in a professional manner. The author refers the reader to Auxter, Pyfer and Huettig (2005), Dunn (1997), and Sherrill (2004) for a more comprehensive treatment of adapted facilities and inclusive programs. This is one area in which we must strive to do a better job.

Adapted/Developmental Physical Education Equipment and Supplies

For the most part, equipment and supplies that are used in the regular classroom can be modified to meet adaptive needs, and certainly equipment that already exists at regular playgrounds can and should be employed. Special care and safety measures must be taken, however, to prevent children from getting struck by such items as moving swings, teeter-totters, and ropes. Of course specialized equipment can be purchased or constructed by creative school personnel. Programmatic needs can be met now by myriad supplies, information, and organizations, ranging from the Courage Center and the National Beep Baseball Association to the Minnesota Outward Bound School for the Handicapped and the International Sports Organization for the Disabled (ISOD). The U.S. Consumer Product Safety Commission (CPSC) also is a valuable resource for safety guidelines for both facilities and equipment.

MANAGEMENT ISSUES RELATED TO PHYSICAL EDUCATION INSTRUCTIONAL PROGRAMS

Scheduling

The status and role that physical education plays in the educational curriculum reflect the mission and goals of the school as well as the physical education leadership and its relationship with central administration. Physical education is more meaningful for participants when the schedule reflects their interests rather than administrative convenience.

Physical education instruction is usually scheduled within a six- or seven-period structure, block, flexible, or modular fashion. Scheduling should be done according to a well-conceived plan. Physical education should not be inserted in the overall master scheduling plan whenever there is time left over after all the other subjects have been scheduled. This important responsibility cannot be handled on a hit-or-miss basis because that basis disregards the interests and needs of the students. Instead, physical education should be scheduled early on the master plan, along with other crucial subjects that are required of all students. This allows for progression and for grouping according to the interests and needs of the individual participants. The three important items to consider in scheduling classes are (1) the number of qualified teachers available, (2) the number of teaching stations available, and (3) the number of students who must be scheduled. This formula should be applied to all subjects on an equitable basis.

When appropriate, all students should be scheduled. If the student is able to attend school or college, he or she should be encouraged to enroll in physical education. Special attention should be provided, however, to those with disabilities or to gifted individuals to ensure that they are included in a program suited to their individual needs. Also, attention should be accorded those students who need extra help developing physical skills, strength, and endurance and who are searching to find their way in the psychosocial realm.

Physical educators should make a point of presenting to central administration their plans for scheduling physical education classes. Facility availability, equipment, supplies, weather, and student interest and attention span should be taken into consideration when preparing a master scheduling plan. The need for equitable consideration should also be discussed with the principal and the scheduling committee. Through persistent action, progress will be made. The logic and reasoning behind the formula of scheduling classes according to the number of teachers and teaching stations available and the number of students who must be scheduled should not be denied. The program should be planned according to these guidelines to ensure progression and safe, meaningful instruction.

Period and Block Scheduling

Many physical education programs have schedules based on a six- or seven-period day. In this system, the teacher might teach five or six forty-five- or fifty-minute classes with one preparation period. Some primary or elementary schools limit their scheduled class periods to thirty or thirty-five minutes, in which the teacher may teach from eight to ten class periods daily. In many schools classroom teachers instruct the classes if licensed physical education teachers are not available.

Many junior high, middle, and senior high schools have moved to block scheduling. Block scheduling divides the school year into terms (usually four nine-week terms per year); a student might enroll in four or five classes during each term that meet daily and are each ninety minutes in duration. The advantage of block scheduling is that it is more economical and easier to set up and administer. Students are in the same class at the same time for the same amount of time each day, thus creating a more stable environment. Research indicates that block scheduling tends to maintain or increase academic performance, student retention, higher-order thinking and problem solving, while reducing drop-out rates and suspension (Carroll 1994). The block system is demanding on human resources, but more and more progressive school systems seem to be adopting this scheduling system.

Flexible and Modular Scheduling

The introduction of flexible scheduling into school programs has implications for the management of school physical education programs. Flexible scheduling assumes that the traditional system of having all subjects meet the same number of times each week for the same amount of time each period is not always possible. Flexible scheduling provides class periods of varying lengths, depending on the course content being covered by the students, methods of instruction, and other factors pertinent to such a system. Whereas the traditional master plan makes it difficult to promote flexible scheduling, the advent of the computer has made this innovation a potential.

Flexible scheduling also makes it possible to schedule activities for students of varying abilities at different times so that all students are not required to have a similar schedule based on a standard format of the school day. It also might permit physical education students to go bowling, rockclimbing, skiing, or skating in a three-hour block during the week. Under the traditional system, all students who were academically at risk, for example, took as many courses as the brightest. Under flexible scheduling, some students may take as few as four courses and some as many as eight. In either case, physical education should be a part of every student's schedule.

Modular scheduling breaks the school day into periods of time called modules. In a high school in Illinois, for example, the school day comprises twenty-minute modules, and classes may vary from one to five modules depending on the purpose of the course. The school is on a six-day cycle and operates by day one, two, or three rather than the traditional days of the week. In physical education, each grade level meets for three modules per day, four days each week. Each grade level also has a two-module group meeting once every cycle. In this meeting, guest speakers and classroom lectures provide students with physical education content standard concepts.

In other schools employing modular scheduling, students frequently have unscheduled modules that can be used for elective aquatics or gymnasium activities. Recreational sports, open lab facilities, sport clubs, and school demonstrations or exhibitions also provide opportunities for students to actively and regularly utilize the skills they have learned in physical education class.

Dress

Dress does not have to be elaborate, but it should be comfortable, safe, and appropriate. An important concern is that the clothing ensures safety when students are engaged in physical activity. For both males and females, simple washable shorts and T-shirts or sweatshirts are suitable and most comfortable. Some schools still require uniforms, especially where laundry service is provided. Of course, appropriate footwear should be worn. It is important to keep the uniform clean. The instructor or physical education department should establish a policy concerning safe, clean, and appropriate attire and work diligently to see that hygienic standards are met by all. Students who do not dress for class should not be permitted to fully participate in activities at the time, however, they should be engaged and accountable for the class time missed.

Time Allotment

Just as scheduling practices vary from school to school, district to district, college to college, and state to state, so does the time allotment for physical education. Some states have laws that require a certain amount of time each day or week be devoted to physical education, whereas in other states, permissive legislation exists. For the most part, however, school districts set their own K–12 schedules. Some require twenty minutes daily and others, thirty minutes daily. Some districts also specify the time by the week, ranging from 50 minutes to 300 minutes. Colleges and universities do not usually require as much time in physical education as do elementary, junior high, middle, or senior high schools. At the college level, requirements take the form of semesters or quarters of physical education that are usually delivered in one-hour blocks two to three times per week. The general consensus among physical education leaders is that for physical education to be of value, it must be offered with regularity. For most individuals, this means daily or at least three times per week. An accumulated physical activity time from 60 to 150 minutes daily has been recommended by NASPE.

Some individuals believe that, especially in elementary schools, a program cannot be adapted to a fixed time schedule. However, as a standard, there seems to be agreement that a daily experience in physical education is needed as well as laboratory periods during which students can exercise and practice the skills they have acquired.

On the secondary level, it is recommended that sufficient time be allotted for dressing and showering in addition to the time needed for participation in physical education activities. Some leaders in physical education have suggested a double period every other day rather than a single period each day. This arrangement would assist in encouraging students to shower, which has long been a problematic issue. However, the importance of daily periods should be recognized and achieved wherever possible. Administrators should work toward providing adequate staff members and facilities to allow for a daily period of physical education or NASPE's target of 225 minutes of physical activity per week. This remains a challenge in times of fiscal constraint.

The amount of time suggested for adults to spend in physical activity programs is a minimum of three times a week (not on consecutive days). However, a daily physical education regimen is considered optimal and should be the goal of every professional physical educator.

Class Size

Some school and college administrators contend that physical education activity classes can accommodate more students than so-called academic content classes. This is a misconception that has developed over the years and needs to be corrected.

The problem of class size seems to be more pronounced at the secondary level than at other educational levels. At the elementary level, for example, the classroom situation represents a unit for activity assignment, and the number of students in this teaching unit is usually reasonable (fifteen to twenty-five). However, some schools combine various units or classrooms for physical education, resulting in large classes that are not safe and provide a less than desirable teaching and learning environment.

Classes in physical education should be approximately the same size as classes in other subjects offered in the school. Such a class size is just as essential for effective teaching, individualized instruction, and optimal performance in physical education as it is in other content subjects. Physical education contributes to educational objectives on an equal basis with other subjects in the curriculum. Therefore, the class size should be comparable so that educational objectives can be attained.

After much research, many committees established a standard for an acceptable size of physical education classes. They recommend that thirty students make up a class, with enrollment never exceeding thirty-five for one instructor. A lecture or other activity adaptable to greater numbers may make it possible to have more persons in the class, especially if an assistant or paraprofessional is on hand. For remedial work, a suitable class size is from one-on-one to ten and should never exceed twenty in order to optimize individual attention. Aquatics, gymnastics, and other high-risk activities also call for reduced student-to-teacher ratio with 20:1 being the upper limit for older students and less for elementary school-age children. With flexible scheduling, the size of classes can be varied to meet the needs of the teacher, facilities, and type of activity being offered. Creative managers should employ this technique when higher-risk units such as beginning swimming, gymnastics, or rock climbing are introduced.

Instructional Loads and Staffing

The instructional load of the physical educator should be of prime concern to management. To maintain a high level of enthusiasm, vigor, and morale, it is important that the load be fair and equitable so that physical educators can perform to their fullest potential.

Some professional guidelines recommended that one full-time physical education teacher should be provided for every 240 elementary or 190 secondary students enrolled. Such a requirement would provide adequate professional staffing and avoid an overload for many of the teachers. This arrangement might also keep more physical education teachers involved in after-school extracurricular activities, especially coaching and intramurals.

Professional recommendations regarding teaching loads at K–12 educational levels have been made that would limit class instruction per teacher to five hours or the equivalent in class periods per day, or 1,500 minutes per week. The maximum would be six hours per day or 1,800 minutes a week, including after-school responsibilities. A daily load of 200 students per teacher is recommended, and this number should never exceed 250. Finally, each teacher should have at least one preparation period daily and other scheduled time for consultation and conferences with students.

It is generally agreed that the normal teaching load in colleges and universities should not exceed twelve to sixteen contact hours per week. At research universities, however, the load of the physical education (kinesiology, sports studies, etc.) professor is accommodated to take into account research, publishing, and service requirements. In many institutions, including K–12 levels, professional organizations, teachers' associations, and unions prescribe the length of the workday, including the instructional workload and number of contact hours.

The workload in a physical fitness center, which typically might open at 5:30 A.M. and close at 11 P.M. seven days per week, is often forty to fifty hours per week. Corporate fitness centers usually maintain an eight-hour working day. Some, however, stay open at night, so the staff may have to work "off-hour" shifts (see chapter 6). Regardless of position, the profession of physical education is a full-time labor of love.

Differentiated Staffing

Many innovations, such as differentiated staffing, are directed toward aiding teachers in the performance of their duties. Paraprofessionals, contracted professionals, qualified undergraduate interns, volunteers, teaching assistants, and student teachers provide many schools with valuable support staff.

Differentiated staffing relates to increased responsibilities or differentiation of functions among staff members. For example, in team teaching, higher salaries may be awarded to team leaders or head teachers. Staff members who assume such roles as heads of departments or staff supervisors or assistants are usually compensated accordingly. In some school systems, highly competent staff members with expertise in certain areas are often assigned to special projects such as curriculum-writing teams and may also receive extra compensation for these duties.

The benefits derived from differentiated staffing are obvious from the responsibilities assigned to various staff members. In schools, for example, teachers are able to devote more time to helping individual students and to working with small groups to assist students in mastering learning tasks. Differentiated staffing allows the teacher to focus on teaching and not be directly involved in time-consuming clerical and physical responsibilities.

Paraprofessionals

Responsibilities include (1) supervised instructional assistance, (2) assisting with the swimming pool, (3) clerical duties, (4) student conduct supervision, and (5) preparation of learning materials.

Contracted Specialists

In some instances a local specialist in instructional activities such as swimming, scuba, skiing, skating, or rock climbing is employed. Contacts and partnering with community recreational centers or YMCAs, for example, have made this a growing trend. Checks should be made as to philosophical and instructional approaches, as well as to the ethical character and background of such potential hires.

Qualified Undergraduate Interns

Responsibilities include (1) clerical assistance, (2) record keeping, (3) preparation of learning materials, (4) conduct supervision in noninstructional areas, (5) individual assistance, and (6) observation.

Volunteers

Volunteer assistance programs are becoming more active in the public and private schools. Volunteers are made up of talented and interested parents and community residents. Special in-service training is needed to train the volunteers in specific targeted areas (e.g., fitness testing, track and field).

Teaching Assistants

Responsibilities may be the same as those of an instructor at the college or university level. Physical activity programs at many larger universities are staffed primarily by teaching or research assistants.

Student Teachers

Responsibilities include (1) observation, (2) supervised clinical teaching experience, (3) assistance to supervising teachers, (4) preparation of learning materials, (5) individual assistance, and (6) extracurricular guidance.

Taking Roll

There are many methods of taking roll. If a method satisfies the following three criteria, it is usually satisfactory. (1) It is efficient—roll taking should not consume too much time. (2) It is accurate—after class, it is important to know who was present and who was not, as well as who came late or left early. (3) It is uncomplicated—any system that is used should be easy to manage. The following provides some methods for roll taking:

1. *Having numbers on the floor.* Each member of the class is assigned a number that he or she must stand on when the signal for "fall in" is given. The person taking attendance records the numbers not covered.

2. *Reciting numbers orally.* Each member of the class is assigned a number that he or she must say out loud at the time the "fall in" signal is given. The person taking attendance then records the numbers omitted.

3. *Using a tag board.* Each member of the class has a number recorded on a cardboard or metal tag that hangs on a peg on a board in a central place. Each member of the class who is present removes his or her tag from the board and places it in a box. The person taking attendance records the absentees from the tags remaining on the board.

4. *Using the Delaney system.* This system uses a folder with cards that are turned over when a person is absent. It is a cumulative system that records the attendance of students over time.

5. *Using the squad system.* The class is divided into squads and the squad leader takes the roll for his or her squad and in turn reports to the instructor. Squad leaders should be rotated on a monthly basis.

6. *Signing a book or register.* Students are required to write their names in a book or register at the beginning of the class. Some systems require the writing of a name at the beginning of a period and crossing it out at the end. The person taking attendance records the names not entered from the master roll.

7. *Calling the roll.* This is the most frequently observed method; it may appear tedious, yet it is effective.

Selecting Physical Education Activities

Physical education activities represent the core of the program. They are the means for accomplishing objectives and achieving educational goals. Because activities are so important to the physical education program, they must be selected with considerable care.

Physical education class incorporating fundamental movement. Crest View Elementary School, Brooklyn Park, Minn.

Criteria for Selection

Activities should be selected in terms of the values they have in achieving the objectives of physical education and, of course, the mission or vision of the school. This means that activities should serve to promote and develop not only body awareness, movement fundamentals, and physical fitness, but also the cognitive, affective, and socioemotional makeup of the individual.

Activities should be interesting and challenging. Activities should appeal to the participants and present them with problem-solving activities and situations that challenge their skill, ability, and creativity. Activities should be appropriate and adaptable to the growth and developmental needs and interests of children, youth, and adults. The needs of individuals vary from age to age. As a consequence, movement activities, the pattern of organization, and instructional delivery strategies must also change. The activity must be suited to the person, not the person to the activity. Wherever possible, participants should be permitted some choice and input into their physical education program and class.

Activities should be modifications of fundamental movements such as running, jumping, throwing, walking, striking, kicking, and climbing.

Activities must be selected in light of the facilities, supplies, equipment, and other human and physical resources available in the school, college, or community. An extensive tennis program, for example, cannot be carried out if only one court is available.

Activities should be selected not only with a view to their present value while the child is in school, but also with a view to adopting a postschool healthy lifestyle. Skills learned during school and college can be used throughout life, thus contributing to enriched living. Patterns for many skills used in adult leisure hours are developed while the individual is in the formative years of childhood.

Health and safety factors must be considered when selecting activities. High-risk activities should be kept to a minimum and should be prudently delivered and monitored.

The local education philosophy, mission, policies, codes of conduct, and school or college organization must be considered.

School activities should provide situations similar to those that children experience in natural play and competitive physical activity situations outside school.

Activities should provide the participant with opportunities for creative self-expression.

Activities selected should elicit appropriate social and moral responses through high-quality leadership and role modeling.

Activities should reflect the democratic way of life (i.e., inclusion, equity, fairness, respect).

Physical education activities are frequently classified into myriad categories or instructional/learning units (i.e., locomotor skills, exercises, sports, games, low-organized games, cooperative games, dance and rhythmic movement, fitness activities, gymnastic activities, stunts and manipulative skills, combatives, and large apparatus activities, just to mention a few). The following list of physical activities represents a core of offerings or mediums from which literally hundreds of activities can be summoned, depending on age, developmental or grade level, and/or physical education objective (motor skills, physical fitness, cognitive, affective):

CORE PHYSICAL ACTIVITY LIST (CPAL)

Team games
Baseball
Basketball
Codeball
Field hockey
Flag football
Floor hockey
Football
Ice hockey
Kickball
Soccer
Softball
Speedball
Team handball
Touch football
Volleyball

Outdoor winter sports
Broomball
Ice hockey
Ringette
Roller-skating
Skating
Skiing (Alpine and Nordic)
Snow-boarding
Snow games
Snowshoeing
Tobogganing

Other activities
Camping and outdoor
  activities
Combatives (judo, karate, Tai
  Kwon Doe)
Correctives (breathing,
  posture control)
Fly-fishing
Fly-tying
Games of low organization
In-line skating
Jogging
Mountaineering
Movement education

Orienteering
Pilates
Progressive relaxation
Relays
Rock climbing
Self-testing activities
Tag games
Tai Chi
Yoga

Rhythmic movement and dance
Aerobic dancing
Ballroom dancing
Folk dancing
Modern dancing
Movement fundamentals
Rhythms
Square dancing
Social dancing
Tap dancing

Formal activities
Calisthenics
Marching

Water activities
Canoeing
Diving
Kayaking
Lifeguarding
Rowing
Sailing
Scuba diving
Swimming
Water games
Water polo
Water safety instructor
Windsurfing

Gymnastics
Acrobatics
Apparatus
Obstacle course
Pyramid building

Rhythmic gymnastics
Rope climbing
Stunts
Tumbling

Dual and individual sports
Archery
Badminton
Beach volleyball
Bocce
Bowling
Checkers
Cycling
Darts
Deck tennis
Fencing
Fishing
Golf
Handball
Horseback riding
Horseshoes
Paddleball
Paddle tennis
Platform tennis
Racquetball
Rifle
Rope skipping
Shuffleboard
Skeet shooting
Skish
Squash
Table tennis
Tennis
Tetherball
Track and field
Trapshooting
Volleyball
Walking (fitness)
Wallyball
Weight training
Wrestling

Grouping Participants

Proper grouping of students in physical education classes is crucial to both obtaining desired results and complying with guidelines such as Title IX and IDEA. Because of considerations such as these, the physical educator needs to develop a broad spectrum of organizational strategies concerning grouping procedures.

By tradition, physical educators have tended to favor homogeneous grouping. The theory behind this strategy is that placing individuals with similar capacities and characteristics in the same class makes it possible to better meet the needs of each student. Grouping individuals with similar skill, ability, and other factors (e.g., age, height, weight, maturity) also aids in equalizing competition.

Current trends toward grouping students, however, take more of a heterogeneous approach. Research indicates that heterogeneous grouping promotes positive social interaction between students of differing ability, skill level, and other characteristics (e.g., race, gender, socioeconomic level, physical or mental disability) and enhances overall performance (Johnson, Bjorkland, and Krotee 1984). Moreover, heterogeneous grouping means that compliance with governmental mandates is easily accomplished.

Because of scheduling considerations, many schools group students by grade, which has inherent advantages as well as disadvantages. Grouping by grade provides many students with a sense of security since they are comfortable with their cohorts. On the other hand, height, weight and other developmental variations must be taken into account.

Perhaps the preferable class organizational structure is a combination of homogeneous and heterogeneous grouping. Grouping boys and girls into physical education classes by grade meets Title IX regulations and presents the physical educator with limitless possibilities for grouping strategies within the class. These grouping methods might range from having captains (with instructor guidance) self-select teams to counting off in twos, fours, or fives to using birth dates, dividing circles into segments, or randomly drawing

Skill and ability dictate some instructional groupings. North Carolina State University.

colored cards or sticks out of a hat. This, in turn, allows a variety of goal structures ranging from competitive to cooperative, with combinations thereof, to be utilized. In competitive situations in which height and weight are factors or in which it is inappropriate for boys to compete against girls (and vice versa), homogeneous groups can compete against others within their group. In other circumstances, teams formed homogeneously can be pitted against other teams from within the same skill division; on still other occasions, teams that are developed heterogeneously can compete against like teams.

Heterogeneous grouping provides unique opportunities for students to develop physically as well as cognitively and affectively or socially. For example, within a heterogeneous tennis class of thirty students, the instructor, can assign six captains to choose their own heterogeneous teams of five students. Each group practices as a team, teaching and coaching teammates, and when the competition round begins, the team plays against other teams so that number 1 players compete against other number 1s, number 2s play number 2s, and so on. This approach allows all players in the class to compete at their own level and to work toward a common goal (learning and improving their tennis skills) with students who are at different levels. This fosters leadership, team loyalty, and cooperative spirit. It also enables the less skilled students in the class to make a meaningful contribution toward their team's success.

Many schools offer elective courses in physical education, which often is a very effective way of grouping students. Electives permit students to self-select, which usually serves to group students with similar interests and abilities in the class. Elective coursework gives the innovative physical educator many opportunities for structuring task and goal interdependence in order to stimulate students physically, cognitively, and affectively or psychosocially.

STUDENT LEADERSHIP AND INVOLVEMENT

In recent years students have been demanding greater involvement in the educational process, and in most cases, this increased involvement has been satisfactory to students, teachers, and administrators. Some of these areas of involvement are discussed briefly here.

General Planning

Students should be involved in planning meetings that discuss scheduling, curriculum innovations, and recent changes in educational methods and instructional strategies. Students might be invited to join community task forces, attend school board and parent association meetings, and also accompany teachers and administrators to other schools at which certain innovations may be directly observed. Some schools and colleges have instituted student advisory boards that meet with staff members to discuss problems, recommend changes, and participate in future strategic planning.

Curriculum Planning

Student surveys sometimes reveal the extent of curriculum changes desired by the student body. Administrators, teachers, and students should carefully weigh this information in light of current literature, Title IX implications, research, and cur-

Heterogeneous grouping promotes positive social interaction. Crest View Elementary School, Brooklyn Park, Minn.

riculum innovations in similar schools and colleges. Student participation and feedback are essential; however, students do have limited experience in educational matters, and this must also be considered. Frequently the limited use of experimental programs can help evaluate the change before it is implemented on a larger scale.

In a high school in Massachusetts, students take an active role in curriculum planning. Students, for example, plan what and how they are going to learn in a gymnastics unit. Several days are set aside for students to set goals, plan the steps needed to reach a specific goal, outline the evaluation requirements, and make a commitment to learning and improvement. The students put their goals in writing and then strive to achieve them. Instruction is provided, and grading is a cooperative venture between students and teacher.

Establishing the Student Leader

Student leaders may be used in the physical education program in several capacities.

Class Leaders

Opportunities abound in the physical education instructional class period for student leaders to be of great assistance. These duties include acting as squad leader; serving as captain of a team; being a leader for warm-up exercises; demonstrating skills, games, and tactics to be performed; taking attendance; serving as an official or referee, time or scorekeeper assisting with locker-room supervision; and providing risk management and safety measures for class participation such as serving as a spotter, checking equipment and play areas, or assisting as an outdoor peer leader or buddy.

These class leadership experiences can and should carry over into after-school activities (e.g., recreational sports, varsity sports), as well as within various community-based physical education and sport programs (e.g., Special Olympics, Wilderness Inquiry).

Committee Members

A physical education student committee should be formed, so student leaders can gain valuable experience. These positions include being a member of a *rules committee,* by which rules are established and interpreted for games and sports; serving on an *equipment and grounds committee,* at which standards are established for the storage, maintenance, and use of these facilities and equipment; participating on a *committee for planning and coordinating special events* in the physical education program, such as play, sports, or field days; and joining a task force on long-range strategic planning for the building or sharing of new or existing facilities.

Supply and Equipment Manager

Supplies and special equipment ranging from basketballs and floor hockey equipment to audiovisual aids and assistive technology are among the items continually used in the conduct of the physical education program. The equipment must be removed

Student leaders assist the teacher in taking roll. Birchview Elementary School, Wayzata, Minn.

from the storage areas, transported to where the activity will be conducted, safely set up, and then safely returned. The student leader can help immeasurably in this process and profit from the cognitive, technical, and logistical experience.

Program Planner

Various aspects of the physical education program need to be planned, and students should be involved. Student leaders, because of their special qualifications and interest, are logical choices to participate in such planning and curriculum development. Their knowledge and input can ensure that the program more fully meets the needs and interests of all students who participate in the program.

Record Keeper and Office Manager

Attendance records, test scores, and inventories must be taken, recorded, and filed; bulletin boards kept up-to-date; visitors greeted; and other responsibilities effectively met. These necessary functions provide worthwhile experiences for the student leader to develop human and technical skills as well as to assist the teacher.

Special Events Coordinator

A multitude of details are always involved in play days, sports days, demonstrations, and exhibitions, as well as other partnered community events. Student leaders should help plan and conduct these events. This participation is a great way to experience sport management up close.

It is important to keep in mind that student leaders are to be accorded respect and rewarded for their work. They are invaluable volunteers whom the teacher wants to encourage, involve, and offer responsibility. Student leadership experiences, however, should not detract from or substitute for their physical education classroom learning experience. Student leaders or any staff members are not substitute teachers; safety, risk management, and legal responsibility must always remain with the teacher.

SELECTED MANAGEMENT CONCERNS IN INSTRUCTIONAL PROGRAMS

The manager of any physical education program is continually confronted with questions such as the following: Should physical education be required or elective? Should other activities be substituted for physical education? How much credit should be awarded? What is the policy on class attendance? How should an instructor deal with excuses? What grading system should the physical educator utilize? Who should deliver physical education at the elementary school level? These questions and other issues, including dressing and showering, record keeping, and safety considerations, are addressed in this section.

Should Physical Education Be Required or Elective?

General agreement is that physical education should be required at the elementary, junior high, and middle school levels. However, there are many advocates on both sides of the question of whether it should be required or elective at the secondary and college levels. Most professionals believe physical education should be required, whereas some school administrators and parents believe elective offerings are the order of the day. Following are some of the arguments presented by each side.

Required

Physical education is a basic need of every student. Students need regular and vigorous physical activity to develop to their fullest potential and to release tension from the rigors of not only the academic setting, but also daily life as well.

The student considers required subjects most important, and if physical education is not required, many individuals who could benefit from active participation may choose not to do so.

Various subjects in the curriculum would not be selected by some unless they were required. This is probably true of physical education. Until mandated by state legislatures and school districts, physical education was ignored by many school administrators. This noncommittal administrative philosophy might cause physical education to suffer curtailment or possible elimination when the country is faced with its highest "sedentary lifestyle rate" in its history.

Even if physical education was required, it does not seem to be meeting all the physical, cognitive, psychomotor, and socioemotional needs of students. Therefore, reduction to an elective program may only further inhibit student growth and development.

Elective

Physical education "carries its own drive." If a good basic instructional physical education program is developed in the elementary and middle schools, with students acquiring the necessary skills and attitudes, the drive for such meaningful activity will carry through to the secondary school and college. There should be no need to require physical education because students will want to take it voluntarily.

The objectives of physical education are focused on acquiring skills and learning activities that have carryover value, on assisting in the establishment of a healthful lifestyle, and on recognizing the importance of developing and maintaining one's body in its best possible condition. These goals cannot be legislated. They must become a part of each individual's attitudes and desires if they are to be realized.

Some children and young adults do not like physical education. This dislike is indicated in their manner, attitude, and desire to get excused from the program and to substitute something else for the experience. Under such circumstances, the values that accrue to these individuals are not great. Therefore it would be best to place physical education on an elective basis so that those students who choose to participate actually desire to do so. In the day and age of freedom of expression and individual choice, it seems antithetical that requirements are a part of the educational curriculum.

Should Substitutions Be Permitted for Physical Education?

A practice exists in some school and college systems that permits students to substitute some other activity for their physical education requirement. This practice should be scrutinized and resisted aggressively by every educator.

Some of the activities often used as substitutions for physical education are athletic participation, Reserve Officers' Training Corps, driver education, and marching band. There is no substitute for a sound program of physical education. In addition to the healthful physical activity, physical education also develops an individual socially, emotionally, and mentally. Furthermore, the individual learns many skills in a gender-free environment that can be applied throughout life. These essentials are lost if a student is permitted to substitute some other activity for physical education.

Should Credit Be Awarded for Physical Education?

Whether credit should be awarded for physical education is another controversy with which the profession is continually confronted. Here again advocates can be found on both sides. Some think the joy of the activity and the values derived from participation are sufficient in themselves without awarding credit. On the other hand, some believe that physical education is no different than any other subject in the curriculum, and therefore credit should be granted.

The general consensus among physical education leaders is that if physical education is required for graduation and if it enriches a person's education, credit should be awarded.

What Policy Should Be Established on Class Attendance?

It is important for every department of physical education to have a clear-cut policy concerning class attendance that covers absenteeism and lateness. These regulations should be concise and clearly stated in writing so that they are recognized and understood. They should allow for a reasonable number of absences and "lates." Perfect attendance at school or college should not be stressed. Many harmful results can develop if students feel obligated to attend classes when they are ill and should be at home. There should be some provision for independent study and out-of-class activity as well as makeup work when important experiences are missed. Makeup work should be planned and conducted so that the student derives essential values from such participation rather than perceiving it as a disciplinary measure. There should also be written provisions for the readmission of students who have been ill or injured.

The current movement in physical education is to break away from the "chop" system or point-deduction system for missing class and focus on the values and positives of physical education. Students then can earn points and privileges for full participation in class activities. Try it; it works!

A final point to remember is the importance of keeping accurate, daily attendance and risk management records to minimize administrative problems and maximize student accountability and safety.

What about Excuses?

The principal, nurse, or physical educator frequently receives a note from a parent or family physician requesting that a student be excused from participating in physical education. Many times, for various reasons, the student does not want to participate and obtains the parent's or family physician's support.

Most schools permit a student to be excused from daily physical education on the basis of a parental note, a memorandum from the family physician, or at the discretion of the physical education teacher. Although some schools accept the recommendation of any of these three persons, other schools might accept only an excuse from the school physician. At the college level, most programs accept the college physician's excuse or permit the instructors to use their own discretion in granting excuses to students.

At the school level, it is recommended that all medical and home excuses be presented to the school nurse or appropriate school administrator before school or class. The nurse will make the class participation decision and forward this decision to the teacher. In this way, valuable instructional time is saved.

Some prevalent reasons for granting daily excuses in physical education have prevailed over time. Secondary schools grant most of their excuses for participation in sports, school band, choir, debate, or some other school-sponsored activity. Some schools excuse athletes from physical education on game days, whereas others grant a blanket exemption from physical education for the entire sport season. Other reasons for excuses include makeup examinations, driver training, counseling, and medical considerations. Students who are excused usually are required to attend study halls or to score, officiate, or assist with the conduct of physical education class or assist the department in some meaningful task. Failure in the class usually results when too many absences accumulate.

Some school systems have attempted to control the indiscriminate granting of requests for excuses from physical education. Policies have been established, with the support of the board of education, requiring that all excuses be reviewed and approved by the school physician or nurse before they are granted. Furthermore, family physicians have been asked to state specific reasons for requesting excuses from physical education. This procedure has worked satisfactorily in some communities. In other places, physical educators have taken particular pains to work closely with physicians. They have established a physical education program in collaboration with the school physician so that the needs of each individual are met regardless of his or her physical condition. They have met with the local medical society in an attempt to gain support for the purpose and conduct of the program. Family

physicians have been brought into the planning process. As a result of such planning, problems with excessive excuses have been reduced. In such communities, the values derived from participation in the program are clearly recognized, and because most parents and physicians want children to have worthwhile and healthy experiences, they encourage rather than limit such participation.

Cooperative effort between physical educators and physicians has resulted in the formulation of a list of statements with respect to this problem:

- Orient the student, parent, and physician at an early date in regard to the objectives of the physical education program.
- Route all excuse requests through the school physician, nurse, or on-site administrator.
- Discard permanent and blanket excuses. Instead of being categorically excused, students can be assigned an appropriate physical activity in keeping with their special needs.
- Students involved in excuse requests should be periodically monitored as to their school performance. Parents, students, and appropriate school officials should be involved.
- Cooperation between the school physician, nurse, counselor, and the head of the physical education department needs to be emphasized, especially in the case of continuous and excessive excuse requests.

Grading and Assessment of Students

To determine whether students are meeting the objectives of the physical education instructional program, it is requisite that each instructor develop meaningful, effective, and efficient methods for assessment. Assessment is the continuous process of determining student gain and program effectiveness. This assessment will also assist in determining a grade or mark for each student that may be reported by semester, term, trimester, or quarter, and usually becomes a part of the student's permanent record. Grades are a serious matter and not only serve to inform students about their class progress but also may be used to gain admission to college, for employment, to qualify for a scholarship, or to receive preferred automobile insurance rates. Students are proud of their grades!

For grades or marks to be meaningful, they should be based on established criteria (e.g., school or national norms), which are clearly presented to the student and class. A grade should reflect the student's progress toward these prescribed criteria as well as others designed by the student and the instructor. Grading is both a science and an art and should possess the following characteristics: (1) grades should be valid—they should reflect that which is intended (e.g., improvement in muscular strength or endurance, cardiovascular endurance, the defensive clear in badminton), (2) grades should be reliable—they should be a true reflection of the student's prowess and capability to perform, (3) grades should be objective—they should be based on well-defined criteria (e.g., making six out of ten foul shots reflects free throw proficiency), and (4) grades should be fair, equitable, and consistent—students performing at similar levels, for the most part, should receive similar grades.

Many different philosophies and methods are employed when it comes to the grading and assessment of students in a physical education class. Skill acquisition, motor performance, fitness level, effort, participation, fair play, knowledge of the subject, and an understanding of the rules are typical criteria for grading. In some forms of assessment, gender and disability may also serve as determinants.

Assessment is crucial to the evaluation process.

Other guidelines for assessment include NASPE's benchmarks, which consider whether the child

- HAS learned skills necessary to perform a variety of physical activities.
- IS physically fit.
- DOES participate regularly in physical activity.
- KNOWS the implications of and the benefits from involvement in physical activities.
- VALUES physical activity and its contributions to a healthful lifestyle.

The teacher usually assigns a pass or fail, satisfactory or unsatisfactory, a grade from A through F, or sometimes a percentage. Regardless of the grading system employed, it is important to meet with each student in order to personalize grading. Finally, it is crucial to keep a record of each student's yearly objectives and performance outcomes and the teacher's and student's written assessments on file.

Who Should Conduct the Elementary School Physical Education Class?

The question of who should conduct elementary school physical education class has been discussed and debated for many years. Some educators suggest that the elementary classroom teacher instruct physical education classes, whereas physical education advocates prefer that a physical education specialist assume this responsibility. The regular classroom teacher usually possesses limited professional training in physical education. Most classroom teachers are not interested in teaching physical education and of course legal concerns are also raised. Furthermore, the renewed interest in physical education and the return to mainstreaming children with disabilities into the gym implies that qualified and certified physical education teaching specialists should conduct these classes. The trend is toward more emphasis on motor skill development, physical fitness, lifetime skill acquisition, and other aspects of education (e.g., weight loss, nutrition, stress management) with which the profession is concerned. There is an increased emphasis on looking to the physical education specialist for help and advice in planning and conducting the elementary school program, including both the regular and self-contained classroom. These developments have implications for sound in-service programs to assist the classroom teacher in doing a better job of delivering physical education.

In light of the present status of physical education in the elementary schools of this country, such recommendations as the following should be very carefully considered. Each elementary school should be staffed with a specialist in physical education. Although the classroom teacher may significantly contribute to the physical education program in primary school, factors such as the growth and developmental changes and interests taking place in boys and girls and the more complex specialized program that exists at this level make it imperative to seek the help of a specialist who possesses the ability, experience, training, and licences required to meet the needs of the students, school district, and state. The physical education specialist and the classroom teacher should pool their experience to provide the student with an optimal learning environment. Professionals have much to contribute and should be encouraged to cooperatively work together so that the students can develop to their fullest potential.

Dressing and Showering

The problem of dressing and showering is not so pertinent at the elementary level where the age of the participants and type of activities usually do not require special dress and showering. Some junior high, middle, and senior high schools still require physical education uniforms. Reasons for this include safety, uniformity, and name identification. Programs that do not require physical education uniforms typically request that students wear comfortable, safe clothing without zippers and buttons, as well as appropriate footwear.

Controversy over uniforms and dress codes should not develop into an issue. If no uniform is required, high school–age students should be able to choose appropriate and safe attire and footwear that should not be detrimental to the accomplishment of a program or specific activity objectives. Appropriate clothing can usually be purchased at a local sporting goods store. With greater variety of activity offerings (e.g., aerobics, yoga, martial arts, weight training, outdoor pursuit, etc.) dress codes are becoming more informal in nature.

In the interests of comfort and good hygiene practices, ample time and provisions should be made for showering, drying off, and dressing. At the junior and senior high levels where no towel service is provided, many students choose not to shower. At this age, choices are important, and although showering may not be mandatory, it should be encouraged and its healthy benefits reinforced. Therefore schools should make special provisions for secure, clean, attractive places to dress and shower. Such places should be convenient to the physical education areas, be comfortable, and afford privacy. Although boys and girls are becoming increasingly accustomed to using group showers, many still prefer private showers. In the interests of these individuals as well as those students with disabilities, such facilities should be provided. When possible, there should also be a towel laundering service and hair drying facilities for the convenience of the students. Attractive and convenient locker room and showering facilities will lead more students to take advantage of this healthful practice.

Record Keeping

Records are essential in keeping valuable information regarding the participants' welfare and progress. Records also are essential to efficient program planning and management. They should, however, be kept to a minimum and should be practical and functional. They should not be maintained merely as busy work and for the sake of filling files.

Some of the records should be concerned directly with the welfare of the participant and others with certain programmatic and administrative variables.

- Records that concern the health status, the cumulative physical education record, attendance reports, grades, and accident reports are of prime value.

- Health records are essential. They contain information on the most current medical examination, health appraisal, health counseling, and any other data pertaining to the person's health and medical status. These should be protected by HIPAA.

- The cumulative physical education record should contain information about activity participation, physical fitness appraisals, growth and development status, and other pertinent information concerning the student's participation in the physical education program. If a student has a disability, the student's IEPs should be on file.

- There should be special records for attendance, grades, and any other unique occurrences bearing on the participant that are not a part of other records.

- A year-end assessment for each student should be maintained.

- If a student is involved in a physical education class accident or incident, a full account of the circumstances surrounding the accident or incident should be recorded. Usually special forms are provided for such purposes.

- Management records should provide general information, including a list of the year's events, activities, records of teams, play days, sports days, recreational sports, events of special interest, techniques that have been helpful, budget information, and any other data that would be helpful in planning for succeeding years. Memory often fails over time, with the result that many good ideas are lost and many activities and techniques of special value are not employed because they are forgotten. The computer is extremely valuable for this function.

- There should be records of equipment, facilities, and supplies that show the current status, repair, maintenance, and replacement dates, inventory (type, make, ID number), new materials needed and ordering timeline, and the location of various equipment and materials so that they can be easily found. Records of such items as locker or basket assignments, lock combinations, and equipment checkout are essential to the efficient and effective running of a physical education program.

The computer is becoming more and more essential to not only record keeping but high quality program delivery.

Technology in the Gymnasium

The use of computers and online information retrieval and delivery in the physical education and sport setting can serve to greatly enhance the programs. Software continues to develop for data management, ranging from Physical Best and AC-TIVITYGRAM personalized fitness reports to individualized exercise and nutrition prescriptions to digital video simulation and palm pilots. Attendance reports, schedules, equipment status and inventory, facility usage, normative comparisons of fitness levels, and most record keeping and administrative functions can be facilitated with today's technology. Computer-assisted instruction can also enhance student learning, from rules and safety to digital performance analysis, and from heart rate monitors to self-designed CD-ROM training and tracking programs such as Nutri Wellness. Educational technology is a tool and its use in the classroom and gymnasium must be prudently employed and managed (e.g., size and makeup of groups, type of feedback, task persistence) to ensure its effective implementation (Becker 1988).

Other uses of "computers in the gym" include scoreboard and message center operations. Software packages are also available to publish classroom data and statistics (i.e., fitness, health-related data) in "real time" on the Internet, so the student and parent/guardian have immediate access. Class schedules, assignments, and associated events (e.g., TV, Olympic Games, school sporting event Webcasts) can be published on the school district or departmental home page. The instructor and student alike now have the Internet to surf information concerning the latest research on topics such as nutrition, stress, drugs, eating disorders, as well as the benefits of participating in physical education activities. The Net is here, and the Take It to the Net section at the conclusion of each chapter will help guide the way.

Safety Considerations

The teacher of the instructional physical education program is responsible for the basic conduct of the program. This responsibility ensures that each class is operated in a safe, progressive, and prudent fashion. Teachers must provide a safe environment in terms of facilities, equipment, supervision, se-lection of age- and ability-appropriate activities, and an outline of proper procedures if an emergency should arise.

The teacher is also responsible for thoroughly explaining and demonstrating each activity, warning students of potential risks and hazards, employing proper and progressive skill

Physical educators must be aware of safety and liability considerations.

techniques, requiring appropriate and safe dress, and providing prudent supervision.

The teacher should be licensed and hold current certification (e.g., first aid, CPR/AED, lifeguard training, coaching, adapted physical education) to ensure safety and provide the optimal learning environment for the students.

Each student should have a thorough medical examination by a qualified physician on file with the school or institution, and the physical education teacher should be aware of this health status (e.g., activity restrictions, medications, allergies).

Safety policies and procedures should be posted in several accessible and appropriate areas, and all students and their parents or guardians should be informed of these procedures and what is expected under emergency circumstances. Activity release and modified program forms, accident forms, and return-to-activity clearance forms should all be standardized and maintained in departmental records.

The teacher should also be encouraged to join the appropriate professional organizations of his or her choice. Such organizations provide not only up-to-date professional information and ideas but also insurance that covers potential professional injury and disability as well as legal liability.

Most legal issues develop concerning the method and mode of instruction, supervision, and facilities and equipment (see chapter 13). It is requisite to be a very prudent physical education teacher.

CRITERIA FOR ASSESSING PHYSICAL EDUCATION INSTRUCTIONAL PROGRAMS

The checklist in box 3-1 on the next three pages has evolved and has been adapted for assessing physical education instructional programs. This checklist can serve to evaluate the instructional units or modules as well as the people who use (student) and deliver (teacher) the learning package. The checklist results can also guide curriculum modification as well as development of new instructional strategies.

SUMMARY

The instructional program in physical education is the place to teach such foundational elements as skills, strategies, and understanding concerning the contribution of physical activity to total well-being.

Physical education instructional programs exist at all educational levels and in various community agencies and private volunteer organizations.

Management guidelines exist for teaching physical education in all these settings as well as for selecting instructional aids, guides, materials, and appropriate educational technology.

Effective class operation facilitates successful management of a physical education organization.

Title IX affects the implementation of physical education instructional programs in all educational institutions receiving federal assistance. To ensure compliance, all physical educators should be familiar with Title IX guidelines.

The adapted/developmental physical education program is designed to meet the needs of all individuals with disabilities. Public Law 101-476/105-17 (IDEA 97 and IDIA 2004) mandates educational services for all students, usually in either the adapted physical education setting or in the regular physical education program and P.L. 101-336 (ADA) assures equal accessibility to appropriate facilities and services.

Management variables that relate to physical education instructional programs include scheduling, grading and assessment, class size, differentiated staffing, selection of appropriate activities, grouping of and instructional strategies for participants, and student involvement.

Selected management problems related to the instructional programs involve whether physical education should be required, who should deliver physical education at the elementary level, whether to permit the substitution of other activities for physical education, and the awarding of credit. Other elements and issues to be addressed include the development of policies concerning class attendance, excused absences, grading and assessment, dressing and showering, record keeping, technology enhancement, emergency, risk management, and safety considerations.

Box 3-1 Criteria for Assessing Physical Education Instructional Programs

	Poor (1)	Fair (2)	Good (3)	Very Good (4)	Excellent (5)
Meeting Physical Education Objectives					
1. Does the class activity contribute to the development of physical fitness?	☐	☐	☐	☐	☐
2. Does the class activity foster the growth of ethical character and desirable emotional and psychosocial characteristics?	☐	☐	☐	☐	☐
3. Are the class activity objectives clearly stated?	☐	☐	☐	☐	☐
4. Does the class activity contain lifetime carryover value?	☐	☐	☐	☐	☐
5. Is the class activity accepted as a regular part of the curriculum?	☐	☐	☐	☐	☐
6. Does the class activity meet the needs of *all* participants in the group?	☐	☐	☐	☐	☐
7. Does the class activity encourage the development of leadership?	☐	☐	☐	☐	☐
8. Does the class activity fulfill the safety objective in physical education?	☐	☐	☐	☐	☐
9. Does the class activity cultivate a better understanding of and appreciation for physical activity and sport?	☐	☐	☐	☐	☐
10. Does the class activity foster a better understanding of fairness and equity?	☐	☐	☐	☐	☐

PERFECT SCORE: 50   ACTUAL SCORE: _____

	Poor (1)	Fair (2)	Good (3)	Very Good (4)	Excellent (5)
Leadership (Teaching Conduct)					
1. Is the teacher appropriately dressed for the class activity?	☐	☐	☐	☐	☐
2. Does the teacher know the activity thoroughly?	☐	☐	☐	☐	☐
3. Does the teacher possess adequate communication skills?	☐	☐	☐	☐	☐
4. Does the teacher project an enthusiastic and dynamic attitude in class presentation?	☐	☐	☐	☐	☐
5. Does the teacher maintain discipline?	☐	☐	☐	☐	☐
6. Does the teacher identify, analyze, and correct faulty performance in guiding students?	☐	☐	☐	☐	☐
7. Does the teacher present a sound, logical method of teaching motor skills, for example, explanation, demonstration, participation, and assessment?	☐	☐	☐	☐	☐
8. Does the teacher avoid the use of destructive criticism, sarcasm, and ridicule with students?	☐	☐	☐	☐	☐
9. Does the teacher encourage a positive class mood?	☐	☐	☐	☐	☐
10. Does the teacher possess high standards and ideals concerning his or her work?	☐	☐	☐	☐	☐

PERFECT SCORE: 50 ACTUAL SCORE: _____

Box 3-1 Criteria for Assessing Physical Education Instructional Programs—cont'd

	Poor (1)	Fair (2)	Good (3)	Very Good (4)	Excellent (5)
General Class Procedures, Methods, and Techniques					
1. Does class conduct demonstrate evidence of prior planning?	☐	☐	☐	☐	☐
2. Does the organization of the class allow for individual differences?	☐	☐	☐	☐	☐
3. Does the class exhibit maximal activity and minimal teacher participation (e.g., proper emphasis or explanation and/or demonstration)?	☐	☐	☐	☐	☐
4. Are adequate motivational devices such as audiovisual aids and computer-assisted instruction effectively utilized?	☐	☐	☐	☐	☐
5. Are student leaders effectively employed when appropriate?	☐	☐	☐	☐	☐
6. Does the class start promptly at the scheduled time?	☐	☐	☐	☐	☐
7. Are students with medical excuses from regular class supervised and channeled into appropriate activities?	☐	☐	☐	☐	☐
8. Is the class roll taken quickly and accurately?	☐	☐	☐	☐	☐
9. Are accurate records of progress and achievements maintained?	☐	☐	☐	☐	☐
10. Is equipment quickly issued and properly stored?	☐	☐	☐	☐	☐

PERFECT SCORE: 50   ACTUAL SCORE: _____

Student Conduct

	Poor (1)	Fair (2)	Good (3)	Very Good (4)	Excellent (5)
1. Are the objectives of the activity clearly known to the learner?	☐	☐	☐	☐	☐
2. Are the students interested in the class activities?	☐	☐	☐	☐	☐
3. Do the student enjoy their physical education class?	☐	☐	☐	☐	☐
4. Are the students familiar with organizational procedures such as those for taking roll and missing class?	☐	☐	☐	☐	☐
5. Are the students appropriately dressed for the class activity?	☐	☐	☐	☐	☐
6. Does the class exhibit a spirit of cooperation in learning new skills?	☐	☐	☐	☐	☐
7. Do students avoid mischief and stay on task?	☐	☐	☐	☐	☐
8. Do students shower when the nature of the activity requires it?	☐	☐	☐	☐	☐
9. Do lesser-skilled students receive as much opportunity to participate as higher-skilled classmates?	☐	☐	☐	☐	☐
10. Do students show respect for the teacher?	☐	☐	☐	☐	☐

PERFECT SCORE: 50   ACTUAL SCORE: _____

	Poor (1)	Fair (2)	Good (3)	Very Good (4)	Excellent (5)
Safe and Healthful Environment					
1. Is the area large enough for the activity and number of participants in the class?	☐	☐	☐	☐	☐
2. Does the class possess adequate equipment and/or supplies?	☐	☐	☐	☐	☐
3. Are adequate locker and shower facilities available and readily accessible?	☐	☐	☐	☐	☐
4. Is the equipment and/or apparatus clean and in good working order?	☐	☐	☐	☐	☐
5. Does the activity area contain good lighting and ventilation?	☐	☐	☐	☐	☐
6. Are all safety hazards eliminated or reduced where possible?	☐	☐	☐	☐	☐
7. Is first aid and safety equipment readily accessible?	☐	☐	☐	☐	☐
8. Is the storage area adequate for supplies and equipment?	☐	☐	☐	☐	☐
9. Does the activity area contain a properly equipped room for use in injury or illness or for rest periods?	☐	☐	☐	☐	☐
10. Does the activity area contain accessible toilet facilities?	☐	☐	☐	☐	☐

PERFECT SCORE: 50   ACTUAL SCORE: _____

Criteria	Perfect Score	Actual Score
Meeting physical education objectives	50	_____
Leadership (teacher conduct)	50	_____
General class procedures, methods, and techniques	50	_____
Student conduct	50	_____
Safe and healthful environment	50	_____
TOTAL	250	_____

TAKE IT TO THE NET!

American Dance Association (ADA)
www.aahperd.org/nda

Council for Exceptional Children
www.cec.sped.org

National Association for Health and Fitness
www.physicalfitness.org

National Mental Health Services Knowledge
Exchange Network
www.mentalhealth.org/

Physical Education Links 4 U
www.pelinks4u.org

President's Council on Physical Fitness and Sports
(PCPFS)
www.fitness.gov

Society of State Directors of Health, Physical
Education & Recreation
www.thesociety.org

Special Olympics International
www.specialolympics.org

SELF-ASSESSMENT ACTIVITIES

*These activities will assist students in determining
if material and competencies presented in this
chapter have been mastered:*

1. You are a member of a physical education staff
   in a high school in which the instructional program is under attack by the faculty. It has been
   suggested that the program be abolished. Prepare a brief defense of the instructional physical education program that describes its nature,
   scope, and worth in the educational process.

2. You have been invited to speak to the PTO in
   your community on the topic "The role of physical education in the community." Prepare a
   speech that describes the role of physical education and present it to your class.

3. Develop a model for a high school instructional
   physical education program and discuss how Title IX legislation has influenced your model.

4. Compare how traditional physical education instructional programs have been conducted with
   respect to students with disabilities and how
   they should be conducted as a result of inclusion
   or mainstreaming and IDEA.

5. Develop a list of policies for physical education
   instructional programs that would serve as
   guides for each of the following: scheduling,
   time allotment for classes, class size, instructional loads, uniforms, taking roll, activity offerings, grouping, and student involvement.

6. You are a director of a school physical education program and have been assigned by the superintendent of schools to plan an adapted
   physical education program for the entire
   school system. Prepare the plan you will submit
   to the superintendent, including the objectives
   you will strive to achieve, the guidelines you
   will follow, and the activities to be offered.

7. Develop an emergency policy for the conduct of
   a junior high physical education program.

8. Select a partner and travel around the school as
   if one of you were blind or in a wheelchair.
   Keep a log and report back to class.

REFERENCES

1. American Alliance for Health, Physical Education,
   Recreation and Dance (AAHPERD). 1987. *Basic
   Stuff Series I and II*. Reston, VA: AAHPERD.
2. Auxter, D., J. Pyfer, and C. Huettig. 1997, 2005.
   *Principles and methods of adapted physical
   education and recreation*. New York: McGraw-Hill.
3. Becker, H. 1988. *The impact of computer use on
   children's learning: What research has shown and
   what it has not*. Baltimore: Center on Elementary
   Schools, Johns Hopkins University.
4. Carroll, J. M. 1994. The Copernican plan
   evaluated; The evolution of a revolution. *Phi Delta
   Kappen* 76 (20), 105–113.
5. Clement, A. 2004. *Law in sport and physical
   activity*. Dania, FL: Sport and Law Press.
6. Cooper Institute. 2004. *FITNESSGRAM/
   ACTIVITYGRAM test administration manual*.
   Champaign, IL: Human Kinetics.
7. Corbin, C. B., and R. Lindsey. 2005. *Fitness for
   life*. Champaign, IL: Human Kinetics.
8. Dunn, J. M. 1997. *Special physical education*.
   New York: McGraw-Hill.
9. Hellison, D. 2003. *Teaching responsibility through
   physical activity*. Champaign, IL: Human Kinetics.

10. Johnson, R. T., R. Bjorkland, and M. L. Krotee. 1984. The effects of cooperative, competitive, and individualistic student interaction patterns on achievement and attitudes of the golf skill of putting. *Research Quarterly for Sport and Exercise* 55:129–134.

11. Kann, L. et al. 1998. Youth risk behavior surveillance—United States. In *CDC Surveillance Summaries,* August 14, 1998. Morbidity and Mortality Weekly Report 47 (No. SS-3): 1–89.

12. Leon, A. 1997. *Physical activity and cardiovascular health: A national consensus.* Champaign, IL: Human Kinetics.

13. National Consortium for Physical Education and Recreation for Individuals with Disabilities (NCPERID). 1995. *Adapted physical education standards, 1995.* Champaign, IL: Human Kinetics.

14. National Association for Sport and Physical Education (NASPE). 2004. Moving into the Future: National Standards for Physical Education. Reston, VA: NASPE.

15. Sherrill, C. 2004. *Adapted physical activity, recreation and sport: Crossdisciplinary and lifespan.* New York: McGraw-Hill.

16. USDHHS. 2000. *Promoting better health for young people through physical activity and sports: A report to the President from the Secretary of Health and Human Service and the Secretary of Education.* Washington, DC: U.S. Government Printing Service.

SUGGESTED READINGS

Chepko, S., and R. K. Arnold. 2000. *Guidelines for physical education programs.* Boston: Allyn and Bacon. Provides coverage concerning standards, objectives, and assessments divided by K–5, grades 6–8, and grades 9–12.

Dunn, J. M. 1997. *Special physical education.* New York: McGraw-Hill. Presents valuable information about managing the learning environment, learning developmental patterns, and understanding the myriad disabilities that physical educators will be involved with. It also includes lists, guidelines, and organizations and associations for physical education and recreational and competitive sports.

Gallahue, D. L., and J. C. Ozmun. 2006. *Understanding motor development: Infants, children, adolescents, adults.* New York: McGraw-Hill. Presents a conceptual view of motor development throughout the life span. Provides various assessment suggestions as well as managerial considerations regarding curriculum, computer utilization, and instructional strategies.

Glover, D. R., and D. W. Midura. 1992. *Team building through physical challenge.* Champaign, IL: Human Kinetics.

Glover, D. R., and L. A. Anderson. 2003. *Character education.* Champaign, IL: Human Kinetics.

IMPACT II/The Teachers Network. 1996. *Teachers' guide to cyberspace.* New York: IMPACT II/The Teachers Network. Provides information concerning innovative classroom projects as well as using the Internet and creating home pages.

Pangrazi, R. P. 2004. *Dynamic physical education for elementary school children.* San Francisco, CA: Benjamin Cummings. Provides a thorough view of elementary skills and activities for both physical education and recreational sports. Also offers curriculum and management concepts.

Rink, J. E. 2002. *Teaching physical education for learning.* New York: WCB/McGraw-Hill. Promotes teaching practices that make a difference in the learning of students. Guidelines and suggestions offered will help preservice and experienced teachers in their instructional roles. Task complexity and difficulty, learner readiness, and relatedness of sequential learning experiences are considered. Helps students become competent teachers by improving their skills and effectiveness in achieving desirable goals. Identifies the major components of the instructional process and describes, analyzes, and interprets the instructional process in light of the teacher's role.

Singer, J. D. 1985. 10th anniversary of P.L. 94–142: A visionary law that has worked. *Education Week,* February, 27.

U.S. Consumer Product Safety Commission. 1992. *Handbook for public playground safety.* Washington, DC: U.S. Consumer Product Safety Commission. Provides a resource guide for playground areas, facilities, equipment, and maintenance. Includes a section concerning parks and recreation for persons with disabilities.

U.S. Department of Education. 1994. *The goals 2000: Educate America Act—Launching a new era in education.* Washington, DC: U.S. Government Printing Office.

CHAPTER 4

Recreational Sports: Intramural, Fitness, Open, and Sport Club Programs

INSTRUCTIONAL OBJECTIVES AND COMPETENCIES TO BE ACHIEVED

After reading this chapter the student should be able to:

- Define *intramural, fitness, open,* and *sport club programs* and name the objectives each is designed to achieve.
- Prepare a list of policies that, if followed, will enable a person to organize and manage intramural, fitness, open, and sport club programs.
- Understand the roles played by various managerial personnel in conducting intramural, fitness, open, and sport club programs.
- Discuss how intramural, fitness, open, and sport club programs are administered in elementary schools, junior high or middle schools, secondary schools, colleges and universities, and other representative organizations.
- Organize various types of competition for intramural and extramural activities.
- Show the importance of and the procedures for managing sport clubs, corecreation, and programs for faculty and for persons with varying disabilities.
- Discuss the importance of open or self-directed recreational activities.

Chapter 3 discussed basic instructional physical education programs, one of the triad of components of a well-rounded offering for students in schools and for members of other representative organizations. This chapter discusses the second component, the intramural, fitness, open, and sport club programs, which are often referred to collectively as recreational sports. By tradition, the term *intramural* denotes programming and competition "within" the institution, whereas the term *extramural* depicts competition with "outside" schools. Sport clubs fall in-between the two definitions offering both instructional and social, as well as competitive experiences for their members. Recreational sports offer competition and other types of physical activities for individuals of all levels of skill and ability. A 1999 recreational sports student interest survey at a Big Ten institution revealed that 82 percent of the students participated in recreational sports activities. The survey indicated heavy interest in fitness activities (50 percent), and in intramurals and open play (28 percent each), whereas sport clubs attracted about 10 percent of the students polled. In universities and colleges, as discussed in chapter 2, recreational sports is usually organized into a department separate from physical education. This separation is also the case in some elementary and secondary schools. However, for many schools recreational sports programs are considered an extension of the physical education program.

Recreational sports make up that phase of an activities program in a school, college, corporate, or other representative organization that is geared to the abilities and skills of the entire student body or all the members of the organization. Recreational sports consist of voluntary participation in games, sports, fitness, open, outdoor, self-directed, and other activities. Recreational sports offer intramural activities within a single school or institution as well as extramural activities such as play days, festivals, sports days, and extravaganzas that bring together participants from several institutions.

Each club within a sports club program is usually devoted to one activity, such as handball, rock climbing, sailing, skiing, squash, or volleyball, and it encourages students and other individuals to participate at all levels of skill. Sometimes two or more clubs combine (cross-training club) for more effective management. Clubs compete within their own ranks as well as with other outside clubs. Sport clubs may be managed by members of the organization, such as students in schools and colleges, or by the central management of the organization. Members, advisors, or community volunteers usually provide instruction and coaching. Clubs are popular in schools and colleges as well as in other organizations. Many communities have tennis, golf, swimming, running, hiking, racquetball, riding, rowing, and other types of clubs.

Recreational sports in the form of intramurals were started many years ago (circa 1850s–1870s; Princeton's Nassace Baseball Club, Yale's Boat Club, and Minnesota Football) as a result of student initiative in schools and colleges. At first they received little central administrative notice or support and were poorly organized. However, as student interest grew, the demand for departmental control kept pace. In 1913, intramural sports came under faculty control and was departmentalized at the University of Michigan and Ohio State University. Dr. Elmer D. Mitchell of the University of Michigan is considered the "father of intramurals." The University of Michigan opened its Intramural Sports Building (IMSB) in 1928. Since that time, intramurals, extramurals, and sport club programs have continued to grow and develop and in most educational institutions today are under the management and direction of fully trained professional personnel (see figure 4-1). The National Intramural-Recreational Sports Association (NIRSA) (formerly the National Intramural Association founded by Dr. William N. Wasson at Dillard University in New Orleans) was formed in 1950 and is considered the major professional organization concerning the conduct of recreational sports. Its *Recreational Sports Journal* is published twice a year and its official magazine is *Recreational Sports & Fitness.*

RECREATIONAL SPORTS PROGRAMS
Objectives

Recreational sports programs (school, university, industry, public and private sector) have evolved and expanded tremendously throughout the country. This may be directly attributed to the fact that properly managed recreational sports programs meet the many important needs of the participant. In order to meet these needs, recreational sports programs should strive to satisfy the following objectives.

The objectives of the programs may be classified under four headings: (1) health and fitness, (2) skill, (3) psychosocial development, and (4) recreation.

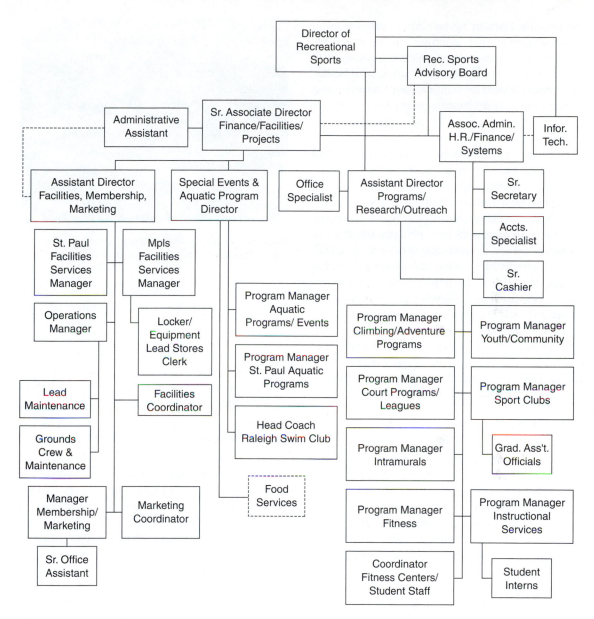

Figure 4-1. Organizational structure of a large university recreational sports department.

Health and Fitness

Recreational sports activities contribute to the physical, social, and emotional health of the individual. They contribute to physical health through participation in activities offering healthful exercise. Such fitness components as muscular strength and endurance, agility, flexibility, cardiovascular endurance, speed, and body control and composition are developed and enhanced. Recreational sports contribute to psychosocial health through group participation and working toward achievement of group goals. Participation also contributes to emotional health by helping a person achieve self-confidence and improve his or her self-concept. It is estimated that over half the students at colleges and universities are involved with health- and fitness-related recreational sports activities that range from aerobics to strength training.

Skill

Recreational sports activities allow every individual to develop and display his or her skills in various physical activities settings. Through specialization, instructional programs, and voluntary participation, recreational sports offer individuals the opportunity to excel and to experience the thrill of competition and the satisfaction of open or self-directed activity. Most individuals enjoy activities in which they have developed skill. Recreational sports help participants develop proficiency in both individualized and group activities in which each person is grouped according to skill, thus providing for equality of programming or competition, which helps guarantee greater success and enjoyment. These programs also enable many persons to spend leisure time profitably and happily.

Psychosocial Development

Opportunities for psychosocial development are numerous in recreational sport activities. Through many social contacts, coeducational experiences, and playing on and against other teams, desirable qualities are developed. Individuals learn to subordinate their desires to the will of the group; they also learn fair play, courage, cooperation, group loyalty, social poise, discipline, and other desirable traits. Participation in such a program is voluntary, and people who desire to participate under such conditions will do so by group codes of conduct. These experiences offer training for lifelong learning, citizenship, and human relations.

Recreation

Recreational sports programs help participants develop an interest in many sports and physical education activities. They also serve to develop and enhance appreciation, attitudes, and habits that help lay the foundation to an active, healthy

Participation in recreational sports activities offers many opportunities for psychosocial development.

lifestyle that will last a lifetime. Besides the physical, skill, and psychosocial development benefits derived from participation in recreational sports programs, the mental process through a continuous "re-creation" of beliefs, values, and attitudes assure the fun, enjoyment, and social meaningfulness of active participation. It is crucial that recreation opportunities be accessible and "inclusive" for all.

Relation to Basic Instructional and Highly Organized Athletic Programs

Recreational sports activities and interscholastic and intercollegiate sports are integral phases of the total sport program in a school or college. This total sporting package includes the intramural and extramural programs, sport clubs, and varsity sport as well as the basic instructional physical education program. Each makes an important contribution to the achievement of educational principles and physical education objectives. It is crucial to maintain a proper balance so that each program phase enhances and does not restrict the others.

The basic instructional program in physical education is viewed by many physical educators as the foundation for recreational and competitive sports programs. The instructional program includes teaching such fundamentals as sport skills, concepts, rules, and strategies. Recreational sports programs provide opportunities for all students and

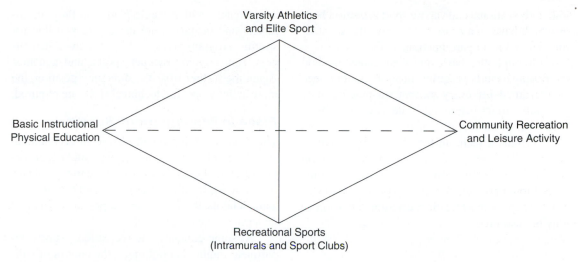

Figure 4-2.   A modern conceptualization of the interaction of school and community physical education and sport.

others to employ these basic skills, concepts, and strategies in games and contests that are usually competitive. This part of the total Physical Activity and Sport Continuum is sometimes referred to as the laboratory, where the individual has an opportunity to experiment and test what has been learned in the physical education program.

Whereas recreational sports are for everyone, varsity sports are for those individuals who are highly skilled in sport-specific activities. The intramural phase of the recreational sports program is conducted on an intrainstitutional basis, whereas sport club and varsity sports are conducted on an interinstitutional basis.

Very little conflict should exist among the three phases of the total sports program. However, shared facilities and equipment, land and space, time, personnel, and finance, among others, offer managers a creative challenge so that all those involved can share equitably in the benefits of physical activity and sport.

If conducted properly, each phase of the total sports program should contribute to the other, and through an overall, well-balanced sports program, the entire student body or all members of an organization will gain appreciation for physical activity

and sport and the great potential it has for improving physical, mental, psychosocial, and emotional growth (Espinosa 1994).

The philosophical model that was shown in figure 3-1 illustrated the placement of recreational sports within the province of physical activity. This triangular-shaped model depicted an interdependence and a building of skills from the basic instructional physical education level to the recreational sports level and, finally, to the level of varsity and elite competition. This model conveyed the philosophy that instruction and opportunity in school and community recreation programs are basic to the other programs and that recreational sports skills are essential to producing the high-level skills found in varsity and elite play.

The diamond-shaped model in figure 4-2 is presented because of its implications for viewing the phases of the physical education program as both interdependent and equal. It establishes each phase as independent of the others. Recreational and varsity sports are placed close to each other because each is related to the other more closely than are leisure activity and basic physical education instruction. Community recreation is included in the model because of its contribution and conceptual link to recreational and varsity sport activities, both of which have as a primary objective the satisfaction derived from participation.

Although the basic physical education and recreational sports programs in a school or college are designed for every student, in practice they generally attract beginning students or those with moderate levels of skill. The highly skilled person usually finds a niche in the club sport or varsity program. This system has its benefits in that it is an equalizer for competitive structuring. In some cases further recreational sport skill divisions (e.g., "Jag" leagues, co-rec, first division, Division I) may be instituted.

MANAGEMENT PERSONNEL

Many management personnel are needed if a recreational sports program is to be a success. Some key persons involved are the director, associate and assistant directors, program managers, student leaders, recreational sports council members, and officials.

The Director and Management Team

Many larger schools, colleges, corporations, and other organizations have established the position of director of recreational sports. In some cases other titles are used. The director is responsible for establishing programs, securing adequate funding, involving the community, and assessing program outcomes. Some of the more specific duties of the director include planning programs; organizing tournaments and other forms of competition; supervising the maintenance of facilities, equipment, and supplies; attending and planning sports council meetings; interpreting the program to the membership, the administration, and the public in general; supervising the program in action; preparing budgets; and evaluating the needs and worth of the program.

In larger institutions (see figure 4-1) besides a director, there may be an associate, assistant, and program directors or managers. The associate and assistant directors work closely with the director on responsibilities such as budgeting, facility

maintenance, and strategic planning. Program directors and managers are usually responsible for specific program areas such as health-related fitness, sports clubs, racquet sports, and aquatics. Again the further from the director's position, the more activity-specific technical skills are required.

Place in Management Structure

The director or person in charge of recreational sports in an elementary, junior high, middle, or secondary school is usually responsible to the director of physical education or athletics and activities. In some schools, these various components are not all under the same department.

At some colleges, the recreational sports department might also fall under the control of a director of physical education or athletics and in some instances, a student activities director. These program administrators usually appoint one person to manage the entire campus recreational sports program of which intramurals, fitness, open, and sports club activities are integral parts. In many schools, partial responsibility for recreational sports activities is delegated to students themselves.

In some larger colleges and universities, recreational sports departments maintain separate divisions, similar to the physical education or athletic divisions, and receive the same considerations concerning staff members, finances, facilities, equipment, supplies, and other departmental essentials. The department is usually headed by a director well schooled in physical education and sport or recreation management. Working with the director (when conditions warrant) should be associate and assistant directors, program managers, graduate assistants, supervisors, student managers and assistants, and other staff members as needed, depending on the size of the organization. There should also be an adequate number of trained officials and support staff.

Student Leaders/Employees

Student involvement in all phases of education has been steadily increasing. Involvement in the management of recreational sports has been happening in high schools and on college campuses since the 1850s. Student leader roles may range from serving as board members to being managers, office assistants, team or sport-specific unit leaders, coaches, and officials. For example, many colleges have drop-in or information centers where student supervisors are available to establish programs, reserve equipment, answer questions, and arrange additional usage hours for the gymnasium, multipurpose areas, or swimming pool. In addition to student leaders, many larger colleges have outstanding opportunities for well-schooled graduate assistants to help in nearly all phases of program delivery, control, and assessment. It's vital that student leaders, graduate assistants, and other employees be carefully screened and selected, thoroughly trained, and appropriately certified (i.e., first aid, CPR/AED, NSCA-CPT, WSI, CRSS). This has serious implications concerning safety, legal liability, and risk management (see chapter 13).

Recreational Sports Council Members

An important feature of the overall management of a recreational sports program is a recreational sports council, which is usually an elected body with representatives from the participants, central administration, and recreational sports staff. The council is influential in establishing policy and practices for a comprehensive recreational sports program. The council assists and advises the person in charge as well as the staff members. In some cases, the council plays an important role in the decision-making process. The council also helps make decisions about program operation and policy, financial allocation, and fee structures and serves as a sounding board for ways in which the program may be improved.

Officials

Excellent officials are necessary for a quality recreational sports program. They should have special qualifications, including a knowledge of the

Information and drop-in centers are crucial in well-managed recreational sports programs.

activity, the participants, the goals of the program, and the organization's philosophy of competition. Some of the responsibilities of the managers of the recreational sports program are to find sources for competent officials and then to recruit, select, and train them so that they enhance the program. Some of the duties performed by officials are to have game equipment ready before the contest, see that accurate score sheets are prepared, check for any safety hazards, prepare accident reports if needed, and officiate the game or activity objectively and impartially. Some institutions put officials through training sessions, supervise them during the playing season, and evaluate their performance after the season (Schuh 1999). Whereas most colleges pay their officials, elementary and secondary schools usually do not have the budget to provide compensation. Many schools seek voluntary help from students, staff, parents, and the community; these volunteers need close supervision, should be offered high-quality in-service training, and in some instances go through background checks.

POLICIES AND PROCEDURES FOR ORGANIZATION AND MANAGEMENT

A list of policies and procedures governing the various features of the program should be in writing and well publicized, perhaps in handbook form. NIRSA possesses a large database and serves as an excellent resource for this undertaking (NIRSA 1996).

Policies and procedures for recreational sports should be developed in at least the following areas: student involvement in program organization and management, health and welfare of all participants, activities that meet the interests and needs of the participants, officiating, coaching, protests, eligibility standards, fees, forfeits, postponements, point systems, and awards. Policies and procedures concerning user groups, guest fees, rental structure, noise, food consumption, key control, equipment control, travel, and facility use should also be on record. The health and safety of the participants

must be a top priority, and policies concerning emergency and disaster procedures should be well publicized.

MANAGEMENT CONCERNS IN K–12 SCHOOLS

The management of recreational sports at the elementary, junior high, middle, and secondary school levels presents some problems that are peculiar to these programs. In many colleges and universities, students live in dormitories and on campus, but students in K–12 systems do not have such living arrangements. Some students in K–12 systems have after-school jobs or need to catch a bus to take them home and cannot stay after school to participate in recreational sports. College students are more often able to participate because they are not faced with such problems, at least in institutions with dormitory living. Also, many times the parents of elementary, junior high, middle, and secondary school students do not see the value of recreational sports and so do not encourage their children to participate after school. College students, on the other hand, usually make their own decisions. Another problem faced by managers of K–12 recreational programs is the lack of facilities. Most schools have limited gymnasium and outdoor space. Varsity sports are often given priority in the use of these facilities, which causes a hardship on the recreational sports program. The question of financial and human resource support also exists in many schools, but recreational sports, especially at the junior high, middle, and high school levels, are clearly on the "most needed" list for many school districts.

In light of these problems, managers of school recreational sport programs need to be creative when trying to initiate such programs. Some schools, for example, form partnerships with other schools, private fitness clubs, community centers and parks, YWCA/YMCA swimming pools, and Boys' and Girls' Clubs to provide facilities that meet the programmatic needs of their students (Miller 1997).

Recreational sport provides students opportunities to participate and promote fair play through officiating.

MANAGEMENT CONCERNS FOR COLLEGES AND UNIVERSITIES

Recreational sports have grown so large on the college campus that they present a different pattern of concerns and challenges than recreational sports in the K–12 school setting. It is estimated that 40 percent to 80 percent of college students participate in recreational sports. Despite this increase in participation, finances remain a prime concern. Most programs' primary sources of revenue are institutional funds and student fees. A trend toward decreasing institutional funding has challenged many programs to create alternative sources of funding (e.g., opening facilities to the public, providing instructional classes, operating sport camps).

Although recreational sport has mushroomed in the last decade, there is still a tremendous need to attract and retain students with various disabilities. Professionals clearly need to take the initiative to become more inclusive.

Facility development and renovation, however, remains alive and well—one just has to visit Georgia State, Haverford College, Johns Hopkins, Pittsburgh, Ohio State University, or the Universities of Houston, North Texas, South Carolina, Tulsa, or Wisconsin-Madison, to mention a few that have invested in architectural showcase facilities. Furthermore, with the development of new and refurbished facilities, myriad opportunities exist for qualified and well-trained professionals to provide leadership in recreational sport management.

ORGANIZATIONAL CONSIDERATIONS

The organization of a recreational sports program involves selecting activities, scheduling, determining eligibility, establishing awards and point systems, maintaining records, planning health and fitness assessments, financing, and directing publicity and promotion.

Activities

The activities constituting the recreational sports program determine the amount of resulting participation. It is therefore important to select the most appropriate activities. The following are recommended management guidelines that will help in selecting activities:

- Activities should reflect the needs and interests of the students or the members of the organization. These may include faculty, staff, and alumni. Annual institutional needs assessments should be initiated.

- Activities should be selected in accordance with the season of the year and local conditions, culture, and influences.

- Coeducational recreational activities and recreational activities for students with varying disabilities should be provided.

- The activities included in the school physical education program should be coordinated with the activities included in the recreational sports program, which could serve as a laboratory experience for physical education.

- Activities offered should require little special equipment and not require long periods of training to prepare the participant for appropriate playing condition.

- Consideration should be given to such recreational activities as field trips, rock climbing, camping, canoeing, backpacking, hiking, road racing, bicycling, orienteering, and other outdoor and adventure pursuit activities.

- Activities should be selected with special attention to the ability, safety, and risk management of the participant as well as the provider.

Open, self-directed, or informal recreational sports activities should play a primary role when organizing a program. Indeed, this phase of recreational sports programming is the most popular and rapidly growing phase. Opportunities should be provided for students to come to a well-kept facility and work out without having to enter a competitive environment, particularly in light of the physical fitness and wellness movement and of today's stressful lifestyle. Box 4-1 illustrates some offerings that have been employed successfully in various recreational sports programs throughout the nation.

Scheduling

Recreational sports activities schedules will depend on student needs, student and faculty availability, facilities, season of year, community culture and support, and budget constraints.

One of the most popular and convenient scheduling times for schools is late afternoon, especially in the fall and spring. This time has proved best for many elementary, junior high, middle, and senior high schools. It is an economical time because lighting is not required, outdoor space is available, and faculty, staff, and adult supervision is readily available.

Evenings have been used quite extensively at colleges, and this trend has been followed in many high schools. This time is not recommended for elementary, junior high, or middle schools. Some schools that have flexible or block scheduling use selected hours during the school day. Physical education classes, however, should have priority and use of this period for intramurals or extramurals does not conform to the standards set by the profession. Some schools have satisfactorily used free periods, activity periods, club periods, and even before-school hours for recreational sports programs when facilities were available.

The noon hour has also been utilized in some schools, especially in elementary, junior high, middle, and secondary schools and particularly in rural schools in which students do not go home or off campus for lunch. Because students will be active

Safety is always a concern in any sporting activity, especially those involving slippery conditions.

anyway, the lunch period offers possibilities in selected situations if moderately strenuous activities are offered.

Saturdays have also been used for recreational sports programs. On occasion, special weekend days are set aside in many schools for track and field days, on May Day, for example, when all the students participate in a day or a half day devoted entirely to the program's activities. These traditional sports days remain quite popular, especially at the K–6 level. For the most part, however, recreational sports programs, especially at the school level, have remained subdued in their weekend sports activity programming.

Recreational sports activities in the corporate setting, youth-serving agencies, senior communities, and other organizations are scheduled

Box 4-1 Recreational Sports Composite Activities

Selected Individual Activities

Aerobics	Orienteering	Alpine)
Archery	Paddle tennis	Snowboarding
Badminton	Physical	Squash
Ballroom dance	fitness	Swimming
Billiards	Pilates	Table tennis
Bowling	Racquetball	Tai Chi
Curling	Rock	Tennis
Cycling	climbing	Track and
Deck tennis	Rodeo	field
Fencing	Rope	Triathlon
Golf	climbing	Tumbling
Gymnastics	Scuba diving	Strength
Handball	Shooting	training
Horseshoes	Shuffleboard	Wrestling
Karate	Skiing	Yoga
Judo	(Nordic and	

Selected Recreational Activities

Backpacking	Horseback	Rifle
Camping and	riding	Roller
cookouts	Hosteling	blading
Canoeing	Ice skating	Rowing
Cycling	In-line	Sailing
Dance	skating	Whitewater
Figure skating	Kayaking	rafting
Fishing	Mountain	
Hiking	biking	

Selected Team Sport Activities

Baseball	Roller	Touch
Basketball	hockey	football
Broomball	Rugby	Track and
Dodgeball	Soccer	field
Field hockey	Softball	Volleyball
Flag football	Speedball	Water polo
Gymnastics	Swimming	
Ice hockey	Team	
Lacrosse	handball	

at various times to meet the convenience of the members. Activities might be scheduled at any time during the day or night. With more single parents and more dual working-parent households, after-school activities have become standard rather than an experiment.

Eligibility

A few simple eligibility rules are needed. These should be kept to a minimum, because the recreational sports programs should offer something for all students.

It is generally agreed that in schools and colleges players should not be allowed to participate in like activities when they are on the varsity team or squad. A student should be allowed to participate on only one team in a given activity during the season. Students, of course, are eligible to participate in more than one activity during a season (e.g., flag football, coeducational soccer) and should be enrolled in or affiliated with the school and conform to the institutional and NIRSA rules for participation.

Unbecoming conduct should be handled in a manner that is in the best interests of the individual concerned, the program, and the established code of student conduct. On occasion a student's eligibility may be forfeited for serious or repeated rules infractions.

Certain activities by their very nature are not appropriate for individuals with certain health problems. Therefore such individuals should be cleared by their personal physician or the school health service or department before being permitted to participate.

Several states have instituted policies linking academic achievement (GPA) and attendance of students with their eligibility to participate in extracurricular activities. However, some controversy has developed about whether a student should be denied the right to participate in such activities because of poor grades. In some cases, state officials have threatened to challenge such action in the courts. It is important to have written policies in place concerning all phases of one's total sports program and eligibility.

Awards

There are arguments for and against granting awards for recreational sports involvement. Some recreational sport administrators argue that awards stimulate interest, serve as extrinsic incentive for participation, and recognize achievement. Some

Recreational sports activities range from beach volleyball to broomball and from group exercise to outdoor pursuit.

argue that awards make the program more expensive and that typically a few individuals or special interest groups capture most of the awards. Leaders who oppose awards also stress that there should be no expectation of awards for voluntary, leisure-time participation and that it is difficult to present awards on the basis of all factors that should be considered. Their belief is that the intrinsic joy and satisfaction received through participation are reward enough.

Research indicates that approximately four out of five recreational sports programs give awards. Awards, if presented, should be appropriate, such as trophies, medals, ribbons, certificates, plaques, cups, wall posters, or letters. Letters, pins, cups, and medals have been used most frequently in K–12 schools, whereas trophies and plaques are awarded more extensively at colleges, universities, and in other organizations. A popular practice is

the giving of T-shirts as awards. T-shirts can be imprinted with a school or recreational sports logo and provide excellent and cost-effective publicity for the program.

Point Systems

Many recreational sports programs have a cumulative point system figured on an all-year basis, which maintains interest and enthusiasm over the course of the school year and encourages greater participation in a wide range of programming initiatives.

An optimal point system should stimulate wholesome competition, sustain interest, and conform with the goals and objectives of the total program. The point system should be readily understood by all and easy to manage. Under such conditions, points should be awarded on the basis

Trophies and awards play an integral part in many recreational sport programs.

of contests won, championships gained, standing in a league or order of finishing, participation, fair play, and contribution to the objectives of the program.

A point system might be based on the following items:

Each entry, 10 points

Each win, 2 points

Each loss, 1 point

Forfeit, -5 points

Each team championship, 10 points

Second-place team championship, 6 points

Third-place team championship, 3 points

Each individual championship, 6 points

Second-place individual championship, 4 points

Third-place individual championship, 3 points

Being homeroom or team representative, 10 points

Each meeting attended by homeroom or team representative, 2 points

It is common practice for officials to "grade" team or group behavior during competition. These grades are converted into points which may be applied to the overall point/award system or for separate recognition, such as for "good sportsmanship." Similar community engagement and service learning projects' points may also factor in.

Protests and Forfeitures

Procedures and policies should be established in advance so that all participants involved know what the rules are when a protest is made and when forfeitures of contests take place. The circumstances under which protests and forfeitures will be acted upon, the decision-making process, and the penalties that will be assessed should be clearly set forth. An attempt should be made to have established policies that help prevent and discourage protests and forfeitures, because a great deal of time and effort are involved in such actions, and they also frequently result in ill will and negative public relations (Mueller and Reznik 1979).

Some programs will not permit individuals or teams who have forfeited during the season to participate in postseason championship play.

Records

Efficient management of the program will necessitate keeping records. These records should not be extensive but should contain the information needed to effectively conduct the program. Supervisors are typically assigned such site-based management record keeping tasks as checking equipment in and out, validating and collecting officials work/time and game forms, verifying team rosters, score sheets, and protest forms, and recording any injuries or incidents. A facility maintenance/repair exit (postgame) form should also be part of daily and weekly record keeping.

Additionally, program records concerning critical numbers and demographics, as well as assessment outcomes determining the worth, value and progress of program units, should be key components of the annual reporting process.

Such records allow for comparison with other similar organizations. They show the degree to which the program is providing for the needs of the entire membership, the extent of participation, and retention and adherence rates. They track the activities that are popular as well as those that are struggling. They focus attention on the best units of competition, needs of the program, effective management procedures, and leadership strengths and weaknesses. Record keeping is an important phase of the program that should not be overlooked.

Computer Utilization in Recreational Sports

Contemporary recreational sports managers rely on computers and the latest software (i.e., Active.com, EZ Score Promotions, Rec WAre PRO, Overtime, Tournament Builder, Schedule Editor, League Link, Club One, iFit.com, icetime.com) to operate their programs with the greatest possible efficiency. Virtually all data relating to recreational sports, including names, addresses, telephone numbers, e-mail addresses, student I.D. numbers, health status, and medical information, can be managed more effectively with computer technology. Many programs also maintain their own Web sites and use the Internet to provide current and potential participants with registration and eligibility notices, game schedules and locations, results and standings, and other program and special events information. Some offer the service of online registration to make it easier for potential participants to sign up for leagues, tournaments, and other activities. The high-tech trend of Internet use has recently led to a proliferation in the number of ".com" companies competing to offer registration, scheduling, tournament management, personal training, and other services to recreational sports managers. Computer literacy and Internet skills are requisite for all future managers to ensure maximal efficiency, accuracy, risk management, and effective use of time, thereby rendering better service to students and other clientele (Ross and Forrester 2001).

Medical Examinations

Medical examinations should be required of all participants as a safeguard to their health as well as legal protection for the program. In some schools, this requirement is handled through annual school or health services medical examinations and, at other schools, through personal medical examinations given before a seasonal activity starts. The Health Insurance Portability and Accountability Act (HIPAA) of 1996 established and legislated national standards to provide security and protect the privacy of such health and medical information. Recreational sports programs and all employers must adhere to this privacy law, which went into effect on April 14, 2001, and provided a two year implementation compliance window. The health status and protection of health-related data of all participants is of crucial importance for all managers of recreational sports programs.

Finances

The monies involved in recreational sports programs are raised in various ways at the school level. Because these programs often make significant contributions to educational objectives as do other parts of the educational program, they should be financed out of board of education and central administration funds just as other phases of the school are financed.

At the university level the traditional practice has been to share in equal mixture of central administration funding (50 percent) and student fees (50 percent). This trend, however, is being tested as central funding is being reduced and departments are being asked to generate money (20 percent to 30 percent) to supplement their budgets in order to support, sustain, or grow their programs.

Alternative methods of financing used by some schools, universities, and organizations include the use of varsity sport gate receipts, facility and equipment rental, required participant or user entry fee, and special fund-raising projects such as sports nights, carnivals, clinics, and corporate sponsorship drives. Some argue that such practices discourage persons from participating and that relying on special projects to raise money should not be necessary for such a valuable phase of the institution. As mentioned previously, however, revenue generation and self-sufficiency have become vital in the conduct of recreational sport programs especially at the college and university level (see appendix G for sample budget summary).

Publicity and Promotion

Members of an organization and the general public must understand the role of recreational sport programs, the individuals they service, the activities offered, and their vision, mission, goals and objectives. Such information should be disseminated to the appropriate individuals through a well-planned and properly timed and framed publicity and promotion campaign.

Newspapers and newsletters (local and school) and other print and electronic media should be used to provide appropriate space and publicity to "sell" the program and its activities. Brochures, print and electronic bulletin boards, posters, e-mail, Web sites, and Webcasts can provide additional impetus for the program. Notices can be prepared and sent home to K–12 parents. A handbook should be prepared that explains the various aspects of the total program and can be distributed to all who are interested. Record boards and display cases can be constructed and placed in conspicuous settings. Clinics, workshops, and demonstrations can be conducted on various activities and sports. Orientation talks and discussions can be held in school and college assemblies and at other gatherings. Special days can be slated with considerable publicity, and catchy slogans such as "It Pays to Play" can be adopted.

Other public relations ideas include a *Weekly Intramural Report,* T-shirts for champions, team uniforms paid for by local merchants, pictures of winners on the Recreational Sport Bulletin Board, community-oriented events such as the IM mile, and an annual Intramural Champions Pizza Party.

Good publicity and promotion will result in greater student participation and better parental and public understanding and support.

PATTERNS OF ORGANIZATION
Recreational Sports Programs in the Elementary School

The recreational sports programs in the elementary school should be outgrowths of the physical education program. They should consist of a wide variety of activities including stunts, rhythmic activities, relays, and tumbling. They should

Elementary school recreational sports should be fun and well supervised. Crest View Elementary School, Brooklyn Park, Minn.

be suited to the developmental ages and interests of children at this level and should be carefully supervised (Humphrey 1994). The younger children in the primary grades probably will benefit most from simple games, lead-up activities, and low-organizational and cooperative games. In the upper elementary grades, more advanced activities can take place on both intragrade and intergrade basis (see Box 4-2). These programs should also be broadly based, varied, and progressive. Special field days and theme days, such as the Olympic and the Pan-American Games, can add an international/global educational component to the program as well as contribute to cross-curricular learning.

Guidelines for recreational sports programs in the elementary school follow.

- A basic instructional offering geared to the needs, interests, and growth and developmental levels of primary school children is prerequisite to and foundational for recreational sport programs.

Box 4-2   Suggested Program of Activities for Elementary Schools

Fall and Spring

Beat the runner	Longball
Bicycle distance race	Play days
Bocce	Prisoner out
Capture-the-flag	Relays
Cosom hockey	Rope jumping
Cooperative games	Soccer
Endball	Softball
Fitness day	Speedball
Flag football	Stealing sticks
Foursquare	Tetherball
Hopscotch	Track and field
Kickball	Wiffleball

Winter

Badminton	Martial arts
Basket shooting	Newcomb
Basketball	Parachute
Battleball	Relays
Bowling	Rhythms
Cageball	Rock climbing
Cooperative games	Rope climbing
Cosom bowling	Shuffleboard
Cosom hockey	Tug-of-war
Floor hockey	Tumbling
Frisbee	Volleyball
Gym scooters	Wiffleball
Gymnastics	Wrestling
Ice skating	

Canoeing is a popular seasonal recreational pursuit at the middle school level and above.

- Qualified leadership should be provided, characterized by competencies involving understanding the physical, mental, emotional, and social needs of the child.
- Cooperative and team-building games and large-muscle activities should be integral parts of the program.
- Competition should involve only those children who are developmentally compatible (e.g., maturity, size, and ability).
- In the elementary school, recreational sports competitions should be limited to grades 4 through 6. Grades kindergarten through 3

should focus on the basic instructional physical education program, which should provide sufficient organized activity.

- Desirable health, physical, social, and emotional outcomes for students should be the goal of recreational sport programs.
- Tackle football and other dangerous contact/collision activities should not be encouraged.
- Program planning should involve students, parents, administrators, and the community.

Recreational Sports Programs in the Junior High or Middle School

The junior high and middle schools provide a setting in which many students develop a keen interest in sport and physical activity. This is a time of limitless energy, physiological change, and immense psychosocial challenge. A full concentration of challenging recreational sports activities should be made available for all students who are not involved in seasonal interscholastic competition. In fact, many professional groups favor recreational sports programs at this level and are opposed to high degrees of competition. Activities conducted after school (see Box 4-3) should provide the student with the opportunity to develop skills, gain self-confidence, have fun, socialize, gain recognition, develop self-worth, and serve to break down cliques as well as racial and gender stereotypes.

Box 4-3　Suggested Activities for Junior or Middle and High Schools

Team Sports

A	Basketball	W	Gymnastics	A	Speedball
S	Baseball	W	Ice hockey	FS	Team handball
FS	Bocce	FS	Kickball	F	Touch (or flag) football
W	Broomball	W	Ringette	S	Track and field
S	Fieldball	A	Soccer	F	Tug-of-war
FS	Field hockey	S	Softball	W	Volleyball

Individual and Dual Sports

A	Aerobic exercise (varying levels of impact)	W	Gymnastics	A	Rope climbing
FS	Archery	A	Handball (1-wall)	F	Rowing
A	Badminton	FS	Horseshoes	A	Shuffleboard
A	Basketball free throw and field goal shooting	A	Jogging	A	Table tennis
A	Bounce ball	A	Paddleball	FS	Tennis
A	Bowling	FS	Paddle tennis	A	Tetherball
FS	Cross-country	FS	Paddle tetherball	FS	Track and field
W	Deck tennis	A	Quoits	AW	Tumbling
		A	Racquetball	W	Wrestling
		W	Squash		

Corecreational Activities

A	Badminton	FS	Golf	W	Snow-boarding
A	Bicycling	FS	Horseshoes	W	Swimming
A	Bowling	W	Ice skating	A	Table tennis
FS	Canoeing	FS	Kayaking	FS	Tennis
A	Dance (social and folk)	FS	In-line skating	FS	Track and field
W	Deck tennis	A	Shuffleboard	AW	Volleyball
F	Flag football	W	Skiing (Alpine, Nordic)		

Club Activities

A	Bicycling	FS	Golf	FS	Roller skating
S	Canoeing	A	Hiking	FS	Sailing
A	Dance (social, folk, square, modern)	W	Ice skating	A	Tumbling
FS	Fishing	A	Karate		
		FS	Rock climbing		

Special Events

S	Baseball	FS	5K Fun Run	S	Triathlon
WA	Basketball skills contest	WS	Relay carnival		
FS	Field day	FS	Softball		
A	Fitness day	FS	Track and field meet		

F, fall; W, winter; S, spring; A, all seasons

The program should be well structured, properly supervised and managed by the school's physical education teachers, and student-run. Challenges by homeroom, grade, neighborhood, academic interest area, or school club are often used as motivators for maximal student participation. Weekends, lunch hours, and special event days featuring faculty and community challenges should not be overlooked as a means of building school and community pride as well as healthful, wholesome, physically active lifestyles that, it is hoped, will carry over into adulthood. The program should be open to all students with any type of special need regardless of disability or physical limitation, and provision should be made for inclusion versus exclusion.

Recreational Sports Programs in the High School

At the senior high level, recreational sports should continue the pattern that has been laid down at the junior high or middle school level (Farrell and Thompson 1999). Recreational sport activities should be varied and should focus on skill development, fun, building positive self-images, cooperation, and friendly challenges and competition as well as setting a positive tone for lifetime participation. At this level, activities can be conducted not only at noon, during prescribed activity hours during the day, and in the afternoon, but also in the evenings. The activities should cut across age, grade, and gender barriers, although wholesome rivalries by grade still seem to permeate the high school environs.

Personnel for the conduct of recreational sports programs should be well-trained professionals. Sound, creative leadership is needed if the programs are to prosper. Each school should be concerned with developing a plan in which proper supervision and guidance are available for after-school hours. Recreational sport clubs may be initiated to help train students and community volunteers to take an active role in the planning and conduct of the high school program. Qualified officials are also a

Intramural inner tube water polo. Lyons Township High School, La Grange, Ill.

necessity to ensure safe, equal, and wholesome competition. Facilities, equipment, and supplies should be apportioned equitably for the entire recreational sports program. No part of any group or any program should monopolize facilities and equipment, and a cooperative effort of the school and community is crucial to having a first-class high school recreational sports program.

Recreational Sports Programs in Colleges and Universities

College and university recreational sports programs offer an ideal setting for both men and women to participate in a wide range of physical activity (Edginton, Hudson, Dieser, and Edginton 2004; Haines 2001). These programs range from individualized activity such as strength training or Tai Chi to a full complement of team and individual sports, from corecreational endeavors to carnival or special event days, and from group exercise to outdoor pursuit. The recreational sports center on a college or university campus is a place to gather, work out, and socialize and should offer a wide range of physical activity for the entire university community. It is a place that can and should bring a sense of community to the institution.

An example of one recreational sports department's mission statement reflects its commitment to the total educational process. They serve universities and colleges by

- Providing facilities for academic units and intercollegiate athletics
- Offering abundant opportunities for student employment and student development
- Cultivating interest and opportunity in active leisure pursuits
- Increasing knowledge of wellness and health-related physical fitness
- Promoting healthy lifestyle behaviors
- Providing facilities and programs that encourage interaction among members of the university community
- Introducing members of the public to university facilities and programs

- Hosting state, national, and international sports competitions and special events
- Making the university more attractive to both prospective and current students, faculty, and staff

One of the core areas of growth in recreational sports programming is sports clubs. These organizations provide participants with opportunities for high-level competition in many different activities. Universities offer a wide range of sport club (intercollegiate/recreational/instructional) opportunities that may be available for the college sport club participant (see table 4-1). Many club sports, ranging from flag football to soccer and volleyball, sponsor national championship competitions, while others offer state or regional titles. Championships and corporate sponsorships seem to be the wave of the future.

Sport clubs, however, are only one component of the college and university recreational sport program. Intramurals (e.g., competitive A, B, and C leagues; recreational and corecreational leagues), outdoor pursuit activities, extramurals, fitness (e.g., aerobics, core, BOSU, pilates, spinning, lap swimming, cardio and strength training, running), faculty and staff leagues, and even summer sport camps are integral parts of the contemporary college recreational sports scene.

Open or self-directed recreation, in which individuals choose to play tennis, racquetball, squash, pick-up basketball, cycle, and so forth, on their own is also growing in popularity and deserves the attention of recreational sport managers. Activities for men, women, graduate students, staff, faculty, family, and guests as well as corecreational sports, fitness assessments, counseling, and outdoor and instructional activities are all delicately woven into the collegiate recreational sports endeavor (see table 4-2). Safety, health status, eligibility, responsibility for the conduct of the program, funding, facilities, and space continue to be the salient issues to be addressed by sound management.

At many colleges and universities, student involvement in the management process is integral and ranges from the formulation of recreational

Table 4-1. Examples of University Sport Clubs

Team	Men's	Women's	Corec	Club Intercollegiate	Recreational Instructional
Aikido			✓		✓
Aikido, Yoshinaki			✓		✓
Archery			✓	✓	✓
Badminton			✓	✓	✓
Ballroom dance		✓	✓		✓
Bowling	✓	✓		✓	✓
Crew		✓		✓	
Cricket	✓	✓		✓	✓
Cycling		✓	✓	✓	✓
Fencing	✓	✓		✓	✓
Gymnastics			✓		✓
Ice hockey	✓	✓		✓	✓
Judo	✓	✓		✓	✓
Juggling					✓
Karate, int'l league			✓		✓
Karate, Japanese			✓		✓
Karate			✓	✓	✓
Kung Fu, Chinese			✓	✓	✓
Kung Fu, Vo Lam			✓		✓
Lacrosse	✓	✓		✓	✓
Marlinettes (synchro)		✓		✓	✓
Rodeo	✓	✓		✓	✓
Rugby	✓	✓		✓	
Sailing	✓	✓		✓	✓
Scuba	✓	✓	✓		✓
Ski, Alpine	✓	✓	✓	✓	
Ski, Nordic	✓	✓	✓	✓	
Skydiving	✓	✓	✓	✓	✓
Soccer	✓	✓	✓	✓	
Squash	✓	✓	✓	✓	✓
Swim club			✓		✓
Synchronized swimming		✓	✓	✓	✓
Tai Chi		✓			✓
Tai Kwon Do		✓			✓
Team handball	✓	✓	✓	✓	✓
Tennis	✓	✓	✓	✓	✓
Triathlon	✓	✓	✓	✓	✓
Ultimate frisbee			✓	✓	✓
Volleyball	✓	✓		✓	
Water polo	✓	✓		✓	
Water ski			✓		✓
White-water kayak/canoe	✓	✓		✓	✓

Table 4-2. University of Tennessee Recreational Sports

Men	Women	Faculty/staff	Corecreation
Fall			
Team			
Flag football	Flag football	Flag football	
Bowling	Bowling	Bowling	
Volleyball	Volleyball	Volleyball	Volleyball
Golf		Golf	Softball
Indoor soccer	Indoor soccer	Racquetball	
Outdoor soccer	Outdoor soccer	Tennis	
3-on-3 basketball	3-on-3 basketball	Turkey trot	
Wally ball	Wally ball	Free-throw shooting	
3-on-3 football	3-on-3 football	Sand volleyball	
Individual and Dual			
Racquetball	Racquetball		
Tennis	Tennis		
Golf	Golf		
Pass, punt, and kick	Pass, punt, and kick		
Turkey trot	Turkey trot		
Free-throw shooting	Free-throw shooting		
Table tennis	Table tennis		
Tennis classic	Tennis classic		
Spring			
Team			
Softball	Softball	Softball	Softball (5 male/5 female)
Tennis	Tennis		Tennis (2 male/2 female)
Track and field			
Racquetball	Racquetball		
3-point shoot-out	3-point shoot-out		
Basketball	Basketball		
Floor hockey	Floor hockey		
3-on-3 basketball	3-on-3 basketball	3-on-3 basketball	
Tug-of-war	Tug-of-war		
Sand volleyball	Sand volleyball	Sand volleyball	Volleyball (3 male/3 female)
Mud volleyball	Mud volleyball		
Individual and Dual			
Golf	Golf	Golf	Golf
Racquetball	Racquetball		
Bowling	Bowling		
Summer			
Team			
Softball	Softball	Softball	Softball (5 male/5 female)
3-on-3 basketball	3-on-3 basketball	3-on-3 basketball	
Sand volleyball	Sand volleyball	Sand volleyball	Sand volleyball (3 male/3 female)
		Golf (2 players)	Tennis (2 male/2 female)
		Golf (2 players)	Tennis (2 male/2 female)
Individual and Dual			
Tennis	Tennis		
Golf (2 players)	Golf (2 players)		

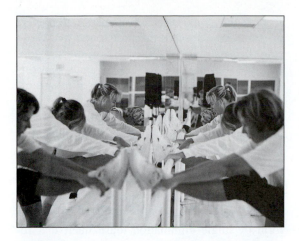

Open fitness is an important ingredient for many fitness and wellness centers, including hotels and convention centers.

sport policy to officiating. Many colleges still structure much of their recreational sport programming around units such as residence halls, living and learning centers, the Greek system (fraternities and sororities), or academic departments, although the traditional practice of competitions between teams that are arbitrarily formed at registration under labels ranging from the Nerds to The Simpsons still seems to permeate recreational sports programs.

Recreational Sports Programs in Other Organizations

Recreational sports programs play a major role in many organizations outside the educational domain. For example, the corporate setting offers a wide range of health-related physical activities and recreational sport leagues for their employees. In many instances, softball diamonds, basketball and volleyball courts, jogging areas, platform and lawn tennis courts, swimming pools, fitness centers, and even golf courses are provided. Some companies compensate employees for joining nearby public-sector fitness clubs, and in other situations, businesses subcontract their recreational sports commitment to a private-sector enterprise. Employees usually take an active role in these programs, which contributes much to their morale,

health, and physical and mental well-being. Research attests to the increased work productivity and reduction of absenteeism.

The military establishment also offers a full complement of recreational sports programming to their men, women, and dependents sometimes under civilian management. These services fall under morale, welfare, and recreation and offer another job opportunity for those who wish to serve their country.

Recreational sports programs may also be found in YWCAs/YMCAs, Boys' Clubs, Boy Scouts, Girl Scouts, Girls Inc., community centers, park and recreation districts, religious organizations, military installations, and other youth- and adult-serving agencies. In addition to the organizations mentioned here, the NCAA and many sports federations and associations, such as those of golf and tennis, are also beginning to sponsor inner-city youth programs. Recreational sports represent an important part of many organizations' curricular and educational offerings (see chapter 6).

The same types of formats for structuring multidimensional and creative physical activity and sport competition employed in schools and colleges are used by these nonschool organizations.

COMPETITIVE STRUCTURING

There are several different ways of structuring competition within most recreational sports programs. Three of the most common are leagues, tournaments, and special events. These modes of structuring take many forms, with league play popular in the domain of club and team sports, elimination tournaments used to a great extent after culmination of league play, and special events held to recognize the closure of a season or year of sports activity.

Various types of tournament competition have been employed extensively in recreational sports; descriptions of some competitive tournament structures will be included here.

The round-robin tournament is probably one of the most widely used and one of the best types of competitive structures, because it allows for maximal play. It is frequently used in leagues, where it works best with no more than eight teams. Each team plays every other team at least once during the tournament. Each team continues to play to the completion of the tournament, and the winner is the one who has the highest percentage, based on wins and losses, at the end of scheduled play (see figure 4-3A).

The single, or straight, elimination tournament is set up so that one defeat eliminates a player or team (see figure 4-3B and C). This structure does not allow for maximal play; the winners continue to play, but the losers drop out. A team or individual is automatically out when it or he or she loses. However, this form of organization is the most economical from the standpoint of time in determining the winning player or team. Usually a drawing for positions takes place, with provisions for seeding the better players or teams on the basis of past performance. Such seeding provides more intense competition as the tournament moves toward the finals. Under such a structure, byes are awarded in the first round of play whenever the number of entrants does not fall into units to the power of two (i.e., 2, 4, 8, 16, 32, 64, etc.). The number of byes is determined by subtracting the number of entrants from the next higher power of two. Figure 4-3B has thirteen entrants ($16 - 13 = 3$ byes). Although such a tournament is a timesaver, it possesses a flaw because it does not adequately select the second- and third-place winners. The second or third best player may meet the best player, and eventual winner, in the first round of play, which often dampens the enthusiasm for the remaining games or matches in the tournament. Another weakness is that the majority of participants play only once or twice in the tournament.

The double elimination tournament (see figure 4-4A) avoids some of the weaknesses of the single elimination because it is necessary for a team or individual to lose twice before being eliminated. This is also characteristic of various types of consolation elimination tournaments that permit the player or team to play more than once (see figure 4-4B).

In some consolation tournaments, all players or teams who lose in the first round and those who, because they received a bye, did not lose until the second round get to play again to determine a consolation winner. In other similar tournaments, any player or team who loses once, regardless of the round in which the loss occurs, is allowed to play again. Other tournaments include the Mueller-Anderson playback, in which the competitors continue to play until all places of finish have been determined in the tournament (see figure 4-4C), and the Bagnall-Wild elimination tournament (see figure 4-4D), which is a form of single elimination tournament that focuses on more accurately selecting the second- and third-place finishers. As was mentioned, the single elimination tournament sets up the possibility that the second or third best player is eliminated in an early round by the eventual winner. In the Bagnall-Wild, the players eliminated by each finalist participate in separate consolation tournaments.

The ladder tournament (see figure 4-4E) adapts well to individual competition. Here the contestants are arranged in a ladder, or vertical, formation, with rankings established arbitrarily or on the basis of previous performance. Each contestant may challenge the one directly above or in some cases two above, and if he or she wins, the names change place on the ladder. When a contestant loses to a challenger from below, he or she may not immediately rechallenge the winner, but must accept another challenge from below. This is a continuous type of tournament that does not eliminate any participants. However, it is not ideal because it may drag and interest may wane.

The pyramid tournament (see figure 4-5) is similar to the ladder variation. Instead of having one name on a rung or step, several names are on the lower steps, gradually pyramiding to the top-ranking individual. A player may challenge anyone in the same horizontal row, and then the winner may challenge anyone in the row above.

The spider web tournament takes its name from the bracket design, which is the shape of a spi-

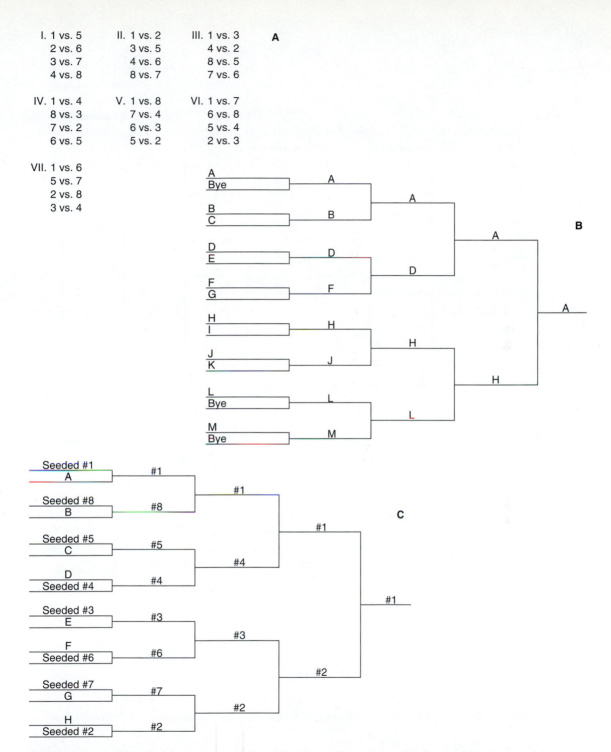

Figure 4-3. A, Round-robin tournament for eight teams. Team 1 remains fixed while the remaining teams rotate clockwise. B, Single elimination tournament with 13 entrants. C, Single elimination tournament with seedings.

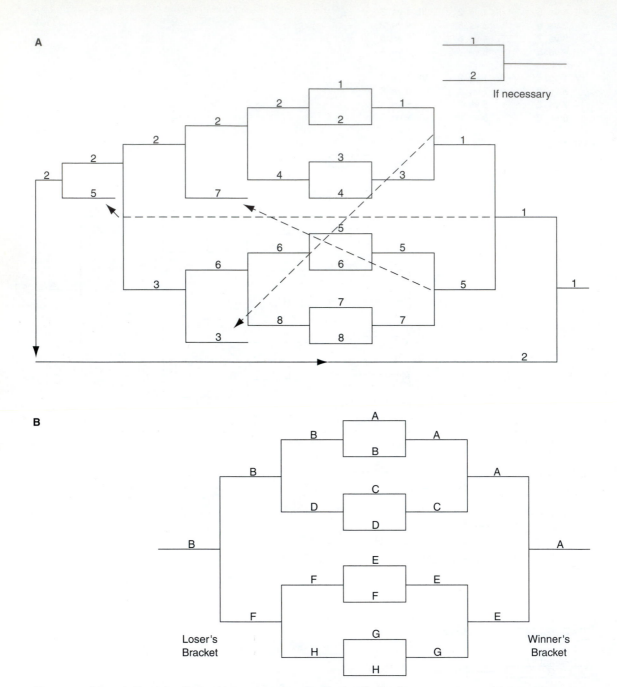

Figure 4-4AB. A, Double elimination tournament. B, Single elimination tournament with consolation bracket.

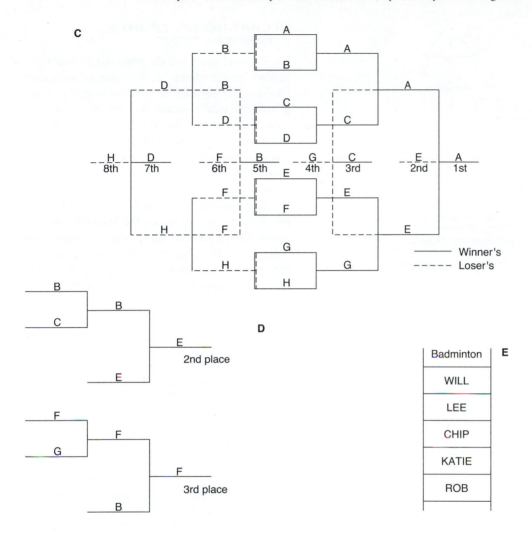

Figure 4-4C–E. C, Mueller-Anderson playback. D, Bagnall-Wild brackets of a single elimination tournament. E, Ladder tournament.

der's web (see figure 4-6). The championship position is at the center of the web. The bracket consists of five (or any other selected number) lines drawn radially from the center, and the participants' names are placed on concentric lines crossing these radial lines. Challenges may be made by persons on any concentric line to any person on the next line closer to the center. A player must defeat someone on his or her own level after losing a challenge in the immediate inner tier of the web. This tournament provides more opportunity for competitive activity.

The type of tournament structure adopted should be the one deemed best for the unit, user, group, activity, or local interests and culture. The

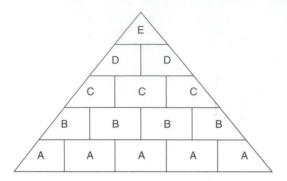

Any A may challenge any B.
Any B may challenge any C.
Any C may challenge either D.
Either D may challenge E.

Figure 4-5. Pyramid tournament.

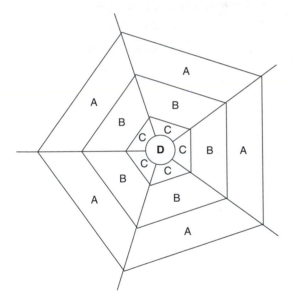

Figure 4-6. Spider web tournament.

goal should be maximal participation within facility and time constraints. Tournaments encourage participant interest and enthusiasm and are an important part of the recreational sports experience.

RECREATIONAL SPORTS CONSIDERATIONS

Recreational sport has the potential to make significant contributions to all levels of education (K–12 and college and university) as well as to the private and public sectors. In light of recent legislation, such as Title IX, IDEA, and ADA, special sensitivity is warranted and effort mandated to include opportunities for women and persons with varying disabilities as well as for other diverse populations.

Recreational sports and physical education professionals must provide the leadership to outsource their combined talents and expertise to our more active than ever senior population. We must extend our professional reach to what will soon be our largest population in the nation—citizens over sixty-five, many of whom live in extended-care environments and are in need of wholesome physical activity experiences. This is a great challenge that must be addressed!

Recreational sports has led the way in opportunity for corecreational activities, and now recreational sports' overall objectives must be further extended. Objectives should include provisions for (1) opportunities for both genders as well as our older citizens and persons with disabilities (in the least restrictive environment) to participate in wholesome physical activity experiences, (2) cooperative experience through physical activity for all in order to enhance self-esteem and develop interdependence, (3) participants to enjoy themselves, develop friendships, improve personal skills, and gain and maintain mutual respect through both traditional and new activities, and (4) participants to gain the skills, understanding, information, and the support network needed for spending leisure hours constructively in wholesome physical activity and leisure pursuits.

The goal of having persons with disabilities participate in the least restrictive environment and to join the regular recreational sports program is challenging, to say the least. Programs such as "Special Friends" and "Unified Sports" (a program instituted by Special Olympics International)

Chess as a recreational activity. Division of Municipal Recreation and Adult Education, Milwaukee, Wis.

should be included. Special populations' participation in sports days, play days, and invitational days—which have long been traditional intramural and extramural recreational sports activities endorsed by AAHPERD, NIRSA, and the National Association of Girls and Women in Sport—should also be encouraged.

The goal of providing our senior population with meaningful recreation and leisure pursuit activities must be addressed. This is a wonderful opportunity to contribute to the health and welfare of a significant portion of our population and immediate community who are in need of quality recreational activities.

At the college and university level, recreational sports managers should not forget graduate students (many older students are now returning to school), faculty and staff, and those individuals' families and significant others. The immediate

community should also be included. Research suggests that an attractive recreational sport program assists in recruiting and retaining both faculty and students. Inclusion of significant others will contribute to sustained participation in physical activity throughout the life span. Certainly all managers of both physical education and recreational sport should continually strive to improve the quality of life for the populations they serve. For some guideposts to assist in this venture, see boxes 4-4, 4-5, and 4-6.

Strategic Program Planning in Recreational Sports

One of the most important functions of the recreational sports manager (or any manager) is the continuous crafting of the strategic plan concerning programs. In today's highly competitive climate, a program must not only meet the needs of

Preamble

An outstanding characteristic of a profession is that its members are continually striving to improve the quality of life for the population they serve. In making the choice to affiliate with a professional association, individuals assume the responsibility to conduct themselves in accordance with the ideals and standards set by the organization. For NIRSA members this means they will strive to uphold the Bylaws in a manner illustrated in the Code of Ethics.

Article I

The NIRSA member in fulfilling professional obligations shall

1. Seek to extend public awareness of the profession and its achievements.
2. Be true in writing, reporting, and duplicating information and give proper credit to the contributions of others.
3. Encourage integrity by avoiding involvement or condoning activities that may degrade the Association, its members, or any affiliate agency.
4. Perform dutifully the responsibilities of professional membership and of any offices or assignments to which appointed or elected.
5. Encourage cooperation with other professional associations, educational institutions, and agencies.
6. Practice nondiscrimination on the basis of diversity related to age, disability, ethnicity, gender, national origin, race, religion, and sexual orientation.

Article II

The NIRSA member in relations with employers and employees shall do the following:

1. Practice and implement the concept of equal opportunity and fairness in employment practices and program administration.
2. Refrain from exploiting individuals, institutions, or agencies for personal or professional gain.
3. Secure the trust of employees by maintaining, in confidence, privileged information until properly released.
4. Support the contributions of fellow employees by properly crediting their achievements.
5. Assist and encourage the education of employees in the area of professional development.

Article III

The NIRSA member in providing programs and services shall do the following:

1. Endeavor to offer the safest and highest quality program achievable with available resources.
2. Take responsibility for employing qualified individuals in positions that require special credentials or experience.
3. Strive to keep abreast of current skills and knowledge and encourage innovation in programming and administration.
4. Promote integrity by accepting gratuities for service of no more than normal value.
5. Encourage promotion of the ideals of recreational sport by incorporating such values as fair play, participation, and an atmosphere that promotes equitable opportunity for all.

NIRSA National Center
4185 SW Research Way, Corvallis, OR 97333
541-766-8211
www.nirsa.org

Box 4-5 Checklist for Recreational Sports Programs

	Yes	No
1. Is the recreational sports program an outgrowth of the regular school physical education program?	____	____
2. Does the program have clearly stated objectives?	____	____
3. Does the program supplement the formal curriculum (cross-curricular learning) by increasing knowledge and skills?	____	____
4. Are recreational sports activities, including clubs, organized in terms of educational value rather than administrative convenience?	____	____
5. Does the administration set adequate policies to guide the program?	____	____
6. Have the aims and objectives of the program been determined?	____	____
7. Can any student participate?	____	____
8. Is a student limited in the number of recreational sports activities he or she may join?	____	____
9. Does each club have a constitution and bylaws that can guide students in the conduct of the organization?	____	____
10. Does recreational sports participation prepare the student for democratic living?	____	____
11. Do the activities help develop school, organization and community spirit?	____	____
12. Are recreational sports activities scheduled so that they do not conflict with regularly scheduled school activities?	____	____
13. Does the school administrator support the program with adequate space, staff, and funds?	____	____
14. Can a student discover and develop valuable attitudes and abilities through the recreational sports program?	____	____
15. Does the program offer opportunities for vocational exploration?	____	____
16. Is the individual student able to develop socially acceptable attitudes and ideals through the program?	____	____
17. Does the recreational sports experience provide situations that will contribute to the formation of improved student behavior?	____	____
18. Do participants actively participate in program planning?	____	____
19. Are the activities and projects of the program student driven?	____	____
20. Do all the activities performed pertain to the program objectives?	____	____
21. Are the students allowed to select recreational sport activities according to interests?	____	____
22. Are students issued a calendar or schedule of events?	____	____
23. Does the school library make available books and periodicals needed by the program's participants?	____	____
24. Does the director enlist the confidence of all students?	____	____
25. Is the director willing to give time and thought to make the recreational sport, fitness, open, outdoor, or club program a success?	____	____
26. Is a faculty supervisor on hand for all events?	____	____
27. Does the school administration assess the program periodically?	____	____
28. Does the recreational sport program allow time for the evaluation of activities?	____	____

Box 4-6   Recreational Sports Program Assessment Checklist

A program can be evaluated in terms of the stated principles and objectives or according to prevalent acceptable standards.

   How does the recreational sports program measure up to the acceptable minimum standards? By taking a few minutes to check off the items listed below, a quick evaluation can be made of the present status of the quality of the program.

	Yes	No
Philosophy and Objectives		
1. Is a written mission philosophy statement, or a set of program objectives available to the participants?	____	____
Organization and Management		
1. Is the director professionally qualified to manage the program?	____	____
2. Does the director devote sufficient time per week to managing the program?	____	____
3. Are participants included in the management and decision making of the program?	____	____
4. Is there an advisory committee?	____	____
Units of Competition		
1. Are participants classified according to ability, age, height, or weight within the competitive unit?	____	____
2. Within the basic unit, are participants permitted to select the members of their teams?	____	____
Program Activities		
1. Does the director consult with the participants to make sure that their interests are of prime consideration in the selection of programmatic activities?	____	____
2. Are there both fitness and open or self-directed activities in the program?	____	____
3. Are there both team and individual sports in the program?	____	____
4. Are there at least five different sports making up the program?	____	____
5. Do corecreational activities make up part of the program?	____	____
6. Are there programs for persons with disabilities?	____	____
Time Periods		
1. Do the hours when participants are free receive top priority for scheduling?	____	____
2. Is the noon hour used for programming?	____	____
Methods of Organizing Competition		
1. Is the round-robin tournament used whenever possible in preference to others?	____	____
Point System of Awards		
1. Is recognition of any kind given to the participants for their achievements?	____	____
2. Is the award primarily for achievement instead of incentive for participants?	____	____

---

its users/clients, but also be cost effective or risk the possibility of being phased out. In order to accomplish the above and serve its participants, the manager must plan a strategy (a specific pattern of action to achieve organizational goals) to take advantage of the planning process.

   The strategic planning process involves a number of steps or phases that can be modified for most management circumstances. The following planning process phases or guideposts are offered for consideration.

A Mission or Vision of Accomplishment

This statement explains what the program should accomplish and how it fits into the conceptual and

Box 4-6 **Recreational Sports Program Assessment Checklist—cont'd**		

Rules and Regulations   Yes   No

1. Are the rules defining such things as eligibility, health, safety, forfeits, postponements, and team membership distributed to all participants? _____ _____
2. Is the lack of fair play regarded as a rule violation? _____ _____
3. Is equipment provided for all activities offered? _____ _____
4. Is proper supervision required for all activities offered? _____ _____

Publicity

1. Is there a special bulletin board for recreational sports news and information? _____ _____
2. Does a newsletter or Web site exist that carries recreational sports news and information? _____ _____

Finances

1. Does the organization provide funds for the operation of the program? _____ _____

Rating Scale

At least one "Yes" answer must be given in each category if a program is to be considered good or excellent. Each "Yes" counts as 1 point.

Excellent	17 to 25
Good	14 to 16
Fair	11 to 13
Poor	10 or fewer

philosophical view of the organization. It is important to set the tone and infuse the organization with a sense of purposeful action.

Overview/Analysis of the Situation

A managerial analysis of the conditions, climate, timing, and complexities of the task serves as a guide to set realistic goals. This analysis should include the organization's strengths, weaknesses, opportunities, and threats (SWOT) (Pitts and Lei 2003).

Specification of Goals

Goals and objectives are needed to provide a series of direct measurable tasks that contribute to the organization's visions. Goals must be realistic, reasonable, challenging, achievable, and quantifiable when possible (e.g., to increase the number of students with disabilities in the program from sixteen to thirty-two participants; to generate 15 percent more funding from corporate sponsors). Goals may be long range, intermediate, or short-term in nature. Growth, profitability, client satisfaction, retention, and social aware-

ness are examples of areas in which organizational goals might be established.

Identification of Constraints

A description of the conditions and barriers that may hinder goal attainment, including alternative pathways toward goal attainment, should be outlined. Constraints may be human, technical, environmental, economic, geographic, informational, or sociopolitical.

Identification of Resources

Closely linked to the development of any plan of action is the establishment of information-gathering criteria to assist in the generation of sound ideas. Vital to this phase is research and input from consultants, students, staff, and community.

Formulation of the Plan

For any plan to be effective, the manager needs to involve all the individuals (human resources) who are necessary for its implementation. The plan that must be formulated should match the external and

Recreational sport programs continue to attract sponsors such as Schick, Enterprize Rent-A-Car, Kwik Goal, Molton, Nestlé, Nutri-Grain (Kellogg), Cosmopolitan magazine, Target, and the United States Tennis Association.

internal opportunities with the program's strength, so it has the potential to be successful and sustained. Clearly defined tasks and roles, job descriptions and expectations, how the parts relate to the whole, timetables, cost, individual values and beliefs, and direct input and inclusiveness are vital to the plan.

Implementation

An important aspect of an organization's mission is its commitment to the strategic planning process. This includes hiring, staffing, and training of human resources and providing the necessary budgetary support, including rewards, professional development, and incentives, to fully implement a plan of action.

Assessment

Assessment techniques concerning recreational sports will differ but generally should include (1) the program goals and objectives; (2) data collection (e.g., number of participants, number of teams, games played); (3) an appraisal of players, coaches, officials, game scores, facility utilization, and so on; (4) recommendations from internal and external review groups; (5) consultant visitation; and (6) participant opinion and rating forms concerning the overall conduct of the program.

On completion of the assessment phase of the planning process, the recreational sports director and the program staff (the management team) may want to revise, modify, make corrective adjustments to, or institute new programs to further meet the cognitive, psychomotor, sociocultural, and affective demands of the user group being served.

TAKE IT TO THE NET!

The American Association for Physical Activity and Recreation (AAPAR)
www.aahperd.org/aalr

IDEA Health and Fitness Association (IDEA)
www.ideafit.com

National Association for Health & Fitness
www.physicalfitness.org

National Coalition for Promoting Physical Activity (NCPPA)
www.ncppa.org

National Intramural-Recreational Sports Association (NIRSA)
www.nirsa.org

President's Council on Physical Fitness and Sport (PCPFS)
www.fitness.gov

Recreation Management
www.recmanagement.com

Recreational Sports & Fitness Magazine
www.recsportsandfitness.com

The realization of the need for careful and prudent strategic planning, as well as the total involvement of all recreational sports program participants, leads to sustained and successful programs.

SUMMARY

Recreational sports programs represent a very important component of the total educational process. They contribute to important qualities such as health and wellness, fitness, feelings of self-worth, skill, and social development. In addition, these programs provide an opportunity for all students to participate and interact on a voluntary basis. Activities should be selected that reflect and extend the basic physical education instructional program as well as student interests and needs. The activities should be in consort with the laws of the land. The management of recreational sports programs at lower education levels is sometimes difficult because of a lack of transportation for students during after-school hours as well as a lack of facilities, finances, staffing, and parental support. To have a well-run program and to serve the best interests of the students, the management of recreational sports should be concerned with items such as safety, risk management, supervision, health of participants, scheduling, awards, point systems, eligibility requirements, and officials. Many different types of tournaments can be employed in the recreational sports setting to increase the flavor of and interest in the competition. Programs should be carefully and strategically planned and evaluated periodically to determine if they meet the mission, vision, and goals of the organization and how they can be improved and marketed to better serve the clientele for which they have been established.

SELF-ASSESSMENT ACTIVITIES

These activities will assist students in determining if material and competencies presented in this chapter have been mastered.

1. Justify the role of intramural, fitness, open, outdoor, and sport club programs, in terms of their objectives and activities, in the total educational plan of a school, college, or other organization.

2. You are the director of physical education in a high school, college, or other organization. You have been requested by your superior to develop a list of topics for a new recreational sports handbook for your organization. Prepare the topics in a table of contents format and submit them to your class for their critical evaluation.

3. Conduct a job analysis of the roles played by various management personnel involved with the recreational sports program of the college you are attending. Compare it with the personnel roles discussed in this chapter.

4. Develop what you consider to be a model sports club for an elementary school, high school, college, or large corporation.

5. Identify a list the strengths and weaknesses of the following: round-robin tournament, straight elimination tournament, ladder tournament, pyramid tournament, and double elimination tournament. Using one of these tournaments, prepare a hypothetical competitive league for sixteen volleyball teams.

6. Develop a strategic plan for organizing a sailing club in your school.

7. Divide into teams of three and construct a weekly recreational sports service-learning project that could be implemented to a targeted special group in your community. Be creative!

REFERENCES

1. Edginton, C. R., S. R. Hudson, R. B. Dieser, and S.R. Edginton. 2004. *Leisure programming: Service-centered and benefits approach*. New York: McGraw-Hill.

2. Espinosa, C. 1994. Recrafting programs: IM-rec sports and TQM (Total Quality Management). *NIRSA Journal* 18 (Winter): 18–20.

3. Farrell, A., and S. Thompson. 1999. The Intramural program: A comprehensive analysis. *NIRSA Journal* 23(2):32–38.

4. Haines, D. J. 2001. Undergraduate student benefits from university recreation. *NIRSA Journal* 25(1):25–33.

5. Humphrey, J. H. 1994. *Physical Education for the Elementary School*. Springfield, IL: Charles C Thomas.

6. Miller, L. 1997. *Sport business management*. Gaithersburg, MD: Aspen Publishers.

7. Mueller, C. E., and J. W. Reznik. 1979. *Intramural-recreational sports: Programming and administration.* New York: Wiley.

8. NIRSA. 1996. *General and specialty standards for collegiate recreational sports.* Corvallis, OR: NIRSA.

9. Pitts, R. A., and D. Lei. 2003. *Strategic management.* Mason, OH: South-Western.

10. Ross, C. M., and S, Forrester. 2001. Web technology in recreational sports. *NIRSA Journal* 25(2):25–33.

11. Schuh, J. H. 1999. Student learning and growth resulting from service as an intramural official. *NIRSA Journal* 23(2):51–61.

SUGGESTED READINGS

Beede, M., and D. Burnett. 1999. *Planning for student services: Best practices for the 21st century.* Ann Arbor, MI: Society for College and University Planning.

Byl, J. 2002. Intramural recreation: A step-by-step guide to creating an effective program. Champaign, IL: Human Kinetics.

———.1999. *Organizing successful tournaments.* Champaign, IL: Human Kinetics.

Davis, K. L. 1996. *The art of sports officiating.* Needham Heights, MA: Allyn and Bacon.
Offers views on how to select, train, and maintain quality officials for your interscholastic, intercollegiate, and recreational sports programs.

Gibbs, R. 1995. The NIRSA natural high: An alcohol and other drug prevention program with promise. *NIRSA Journal* 20 (Fall): 6–7.

Kaplan, R. S., and D. P. Norton. 1996. *The balanced scorecard: Translating strategy into action.* Boston: The Harvard University School Press.

Lee, J. W., G. Bush, and E. W. Smith. 2005. Service learning: Practical learning experiences in sport and physical education. *Strategies* 18(3):11–13.

Matthews, D. O. 1984. *Managing intramurals and recreational sports.* Champaign, IL: Stipes Publishing.
Traces the roots of organized intramural sports programs and how they have become the recreational sports programs of today. Points out the many educational values of such programs.

NIRSA. 1997. *Changes, challanges and choices.* Corvallis, OR: NIRSA.
Presents a collection of papers ranging from effective management communication to fund-raising, marketing, and building successful programs.

———. 1993. *Instructional programming: A resource manual.* Corvallis, OR: NIRSA.
Describes the general standards and procedures for certification, contracts, safety, liability, scheduling, and fee assessment as they pertain to recreational sports instructional programs. Goals, expectations, and evaluations as well as potential intradepartmental and interdepartmental conflict are discussed.

———. 2004. *Planning principles for college and university recreation facilities.* Corvallis, OR: NIRSA.
Endorsed by Society for College and University Planning.

———. 2004. The value of recreational sports in higher education: Impact on student enrollment, success, and buying power. Corvallis, OR: NIRSA.

Roth, D., and S. Hudson. 1994. The Impact of the Americans with Disabilities Act on campus recreation. *NIRSA Journal* 18 (Spring): 22–25.

Special Olympics International. 2002. *Special Olympics University Curriculum.* Washington, DC: Special Olympics International.
Presents an overview of Special Olympics International's integrated sports offerings and strategies.

CHAPTER 5

Interscholastic, Intercollegiate, and Other Competitive Sport Programs

INSTRUCTIONAL OBJECTIVES AND COMPETENCIES TO BE ACHIEVED

After reading this chapter the student should be able to:

- Discuss the purpose of and the values derived from participating in competitive sport programs.
- Specify the duties performed by such key management personnel in competitive sport programs as the athletic director, coach, athletic trainer, and members of the sport council.
- Explain some of the management considerations involved in sport programs relating to scheduling, providing for the health, safety, and risk management of participants, contracts, officials, transportation, event and game management, crowd control, protests and forfeitures, awards, and records.
- Understand some of the central issues involved in such management problems concerned with competitive sport as recruitment, eligibility, scholarships and academic support, proselytizing, scouting, finances, and extra compensation for coaching.
- Describe the nature and scope of competitive sport programs in elementary, middle, junior high, and senior high schools; colleges and universities; and other organizations.
- Identify some of the key sports associations and the role they play in influencing organized sport competition in schools, colleges, and other organizations.
- Outline key provisions and issues of Title IX and gender equity concerning the conduct of interscholastic and intercollegiate sport.

Two primary components of the Physical Activity and Sport Continuum (PASC) have been presented: the basic instructional physical education program and the recreational sports program, which included intramural, fitness, open, and sport club offerings. This chapter focuses on competitive sport programs in schools, colleges, and other organizations.

Interscholastic, intercollegiate, and other organized sport programs represent an integral part of the total spectrum of human movement experience. In some cases involvement in competitive sport programs evolves from active participation in school physical education and recreational sports as well as the myriad sport programs that are housed elsewhere in the community.

Competitive sports, with their appeal to all age-groups, should play an integral role in the movement experience and help achieve the goals and educational objectives that have been discussed in previous chapters. They should also aid individual growth and development, and help all participants realize their full potential as citizens and contributing members of society.

The competitive sport program is usually designed for those individuals most talented in sport-specific endeavors. It is the domain of the most talented and highly skilled, and it receives more attention and publicity than most other phases of the PASC. The reason for this attention is not that the competitive sport program is more important or renders a greater contribution; instead, the attention is largely the result of popular appeal. Print and electronic media, alumni, the public, parents, and others discuss competitive sport in glowing terms, especially when it involves competition of one school, college, or community against another. This competition increases public awareness and creates enthusiasm and often a spirit of rivalry, which seems to be pervasive as sport plays out its role in society. The competitive spirit is not only a local phenomenon, but is national as well as international in scope and dimension. Unfortunately, this competitive enthusiasm occasionally erupts in dysfunctional, dangerous, and sometimes deadly behavior by participants, parents, spectators, and "associated" crowds.

The Hubert H. Humphrey Metrodome, home of the University of Minnesota football team.

Interscholastic and intercollegiate sport programs concomitantly have had more attendant difficulties than most other phases of the Physical Activity and Sport Continuum (PASC). The desire to win and to generate revenue has resulted in some unfortunate practices, such as unethical recruitment procedures, altering transcripts to make players eligible, admitting students to colleges and universities who may be academically unqualified, and the relaxing of academic and behavioral standards for student-athletes, not to mention substance abuse, violence, and player exploitation issues and concerns. Large stadiums and megasports complexes that require huge capital outlay and substantial revenue for their upkeep have been reengineered and constructed. Indeed, many collegiate and some school programs have been enticed off campus in hope for the big payday.

The challenge of providing sound educational programs in competitive or varsity interscholastic and intercollegiate sports is one that all physical education professionals recognize. The challenge can be met and resolved if physical educators and other professionals bring to the attention of administrators, the community, and the general public the true purposes of sports in their respective schools and institutions of higher education. A need exists for maintaining competitive sport programs within the school that meet the needs of everyone; that are professionally organized and managed with the welfare of the individual in mind; and that are conducted in a manner by which educational objectives are not compromised even when exposed to pressures from parents, alumni, community members, and the media.

THE ROLE OF SPORT IN SOCIETY

It is no secret that millions of Americans engage in competitive sport (more than six and one-half million young girls and boys participate in interscholastic sport) on a yearly basis. Serving as testimony to the status of sport in contemporary society are the facts that sport is a multibillion-dollar industry, that more than one-tenth of the *World Almanac* is devoted to sport, and that more people watched the World Cup than watched Neil Armstrong take the first step on the moon. Indeed, 217 million Americans report some type of participation in sport.

Sport's magnetism has been chronicled and debated by many who concentrate their effort on sport-specific exploration of our limits and inner selves; however, most researchers and organizations such as the National Federation of State High School Associations (NFHS) contend that sport possesses the following societal functions:

Emotional release. Sport serves to release emotions and relieve stress, acts as a safety valve, and provides a catharsis to relieve aggressive tendencies.

Affirmation of identity. Sport offers opportunities to be recognized and to express one's individual qualities.

Social control. Sport provides a means of control over and containment of people.

Socialization. Sport serves as a means of socializing those individuals who identify with it.

Change agent. Sport results in social change and new behavior patterns and is a factor that may contribute to changes in the course of history (e.g.,

interaction of classes, upward socioeconomic mobility based on ability, Ping-Pong diplomacy, gender equity, the demise of apartheid).

Collective conscience. Sport creates a communal spirit that brings people together in search of common goals, such as building community.

Success. Sport provides a feeling of success both for the participant and for the spectator when a player or team with whom one identifies achieves. To win in sport is also to win in life; it may serve as a predictor of later life success, and winning seems to be glorified by all.

BENEFITS OF COMPETITIVE SPORT

The values of participation in competitive sports are discussed under the headings of physical fitness, sport skill and knowledge, individual development, social development, and sport in the global village.

NCAA champion and now Assistant Coach Marty Morgan, University of Minnesota.

Physical Fitness

Competitive sports contribute to physical fitness by developing organic vigor, cardiovascular and cardiorespiratory endurance, neuromuscular skill, muscular strength and endurance, flexibility, and agility as well as desirable psychosocial attitudes toward play, fitness, and exercise. To develop and sustain a high degree of physical fitness, the individual must voluntarily submit to a vigorous program of physical training and exercise. Perhaps the most powerful force capable of motivating a person to engage in strenuous training regimens is the desire to excel in the arena of competitive sport.

Sport Skill and Knowledge

To achieve success in sport, individuals must develop neuromuscular skills that will enable them to respond instantly and effectively in a competitive sport situation. The resulting skill development will enable individuals to successfully respond to situations requiring strength, endurance, speed, and coordination, and to fit their skills within the framework of the sport-specific decision-making process.

Acquiring skill through sport also leads to a high level of proficiency and a further desire to engage in physical activity. Some research indicates that persons who participate in sports when they are young are more likely to lead physically active lives as they age. The development and mastery of physical skill holds many other benefits, such as feelings of accomplishment, recognition, and affiliation as well as contributing to a more positive self-image.

Individual Development

Self-realization, self-sufficiency, self-control, improved mood states, self-discipline, and perseverance are individual qualities frequently developed through competitive sport experience. Self-image and self-confidence are also enhanced through comparison and social evaluation of one's competitive interaction with others.

Participation in competitive sports facilitates the development of leadership, cooperation, teamwork, fair play, and loyalty. Furthermore, commit-

NCAA All-American Todd Yeagley, Indiana University.
Courtesy of Indiana University Instructional Support Services, Nick Judy, photographer.

ment, decision making, and self-worth seem to be enhanced through the rigors of the competitive sport process. Reduced drop-out rates, fewer discipline problems, and higher GPAs are also associated with interscholastic sport participation (ASEP/NFHS 2000).

Social Development

Competitive sport provides opportunities for competition, cooperation, and individualistic participation. Although competition is a part of life, at the same time life demands cooperation, self-sacrifice, and respect for other people (e.g., race, ethnicity, gender, age, disability). Competition, cooperation, and individualistic sport behaviors, therefore, must be interdependent. Sport provides a natural opportunity to achieve this multifaceted objective, because individuals must be both competitive and cooperative in some situations, whereas under other circumstances, the sport environment may require individualistic behaviors. Fairness, adherence to the rules of the game, the ability to accept defeat, gaining respect for others, and the love of the game continue to shape the player as the player shapes the game.

Student-athletes gain valuable social skills, self-image, and help build community.

There is little question that as greater numbers of individuals compete there will be more physical injury. Greater psychological and sociological stress, potential drug use (i.e., anabolic steroids, diuretics, ephedra, EPO) and the female athlete triad of eating disorders, amenorrhea, and osteoporosis are serious concerns and must be addressed, if indeed, competitive sport and physical activity as the President's Council on Physical Fitness and Sports suggests is a truly effective means of improving health, function, and quality of life (HHS/PCPFS 1997).

Sport in the Global Village

Since circa 776 B.C., sport has served to bring the world together, stop war, and open barriers often closed by geopolitics. Sport, if managed properly, can facilitate peace and understanding, create life-long friendships, and bring nations together. The 1996 Atlanta Olympic Games brought more nations (197) together on the field of competition than the United Nations roll call, and Sydney 2000 and Athens 2004 continued this inclusive trend. The Super Bowl was transmitted to 182 countries in 24 languages to over 800 million viewers, and who would have suspected that the NFL would be playing in European soccer stadiums, not to mention a number of talented U.S. soccer players? Educational institutions and other organizations such as Athletes in Action (AIA) and Partners of the Americas are taking advantage of the international competitive experience. The hosting via home stays of international teams at local tournaments such as the USA Cup Soccer Tournament in Blaine, Minnesota, where more than 18,000 youth representing 1,200 teams and 25 nations take part; an enlarged competitive format such as the PAC 10 men's and women's all-star basketball tour to Asia as well as the many intercollegiate teams that compete against university all-stars and clubs from Australia, Canada, Europe, and Asia; provide examples and serve as further evidence that sport can bring together the "global village."

There are, however, critics of the competitive sporting process, and table 5-1 offers some popular arguments for and against competitive sport.

MANAGEMENT PERSONNEL INVOLVED IN SPORTS PROGRAMS

Key management personnel involved in sports programs include the director of athletics, the coach, the certified athletic trainer, the athletic or sport council, and members of the academic support and compliance teams. In addition, the following personnel are also involved in sport programs, particularly at the college level: senior associate athletic director, assistant athletic directors, academic counselor, compliance officer, sports information director, athletic business manager, facility director, travel coordinator, administrative assistant, fund raiser, physician, sport psychologist or educator, equipment manager, event and game manager, ticket manager, marketing director, and coordinator of special events. For the purposes of this chapter, however, only the major sport management positions applicable to both high school and college competitive sport programs will be presented.

Table 5-1. Arguments For and Against Interscholastic Sport Programs	
Arguments For	**Arguments Against**
1. Involves students in school activities and increases interest in academic activities.	1. Distracts the attention of students away from academic activities.
2. Builds self-esteem, responsibility, achievement orientation, and teamwork skills required for adult participation in society.	2. Perpetuates dependence, conformity, and a power performance orientation and that is no longer appropriate in post-industrial society.
3. Stimulates interest in physical activities and fitness among students in the school.	3. Relegates most students to the role of spectator rather than active participant.
4. Generates the spirit and unity necessary to maintain the school as a viable organization.	4. Creates a superficial transitory spirit that has nothing to do with the educational goals of the school.
5. Promotes parental, alumni, and community support for all school programs.	5. Deprives educational programs of resources, facilities, staff, and community support.
6. Provides students opportunities to develop, display, and be recognized for their athletic prowess.	6. Applies excessive pressure on student-athletes.
	7. Causes too many serious injuries to participants.

Adapted from J. J. Coakley, *Sport in society: Issues and controversies*. Dubuque, IA: McGraw-Hill, 2004.

The Director of Athletics

The director of athletics implements the athletic policies as established by the state, school board, board of regents, or institution. Responsibilities and duties of the athletic director include preparing the budget; employing and evaluating coaches (see figures 5-1 and 5-2); purchasing equipment and supplies; media contact and contracts; marketing and promoting the program; fund-raising; scheduling; arranging for officials; supervising eligibility and compliance with league and governing body laws and regulations and health status requirements; arranging transportation; seeing that medical examinations, insurance coverage, and medical treatment are available and adequate; and generally supervising the total conduct of the program.

The athletic director should be professionally trained and possess a background in physical education and sport. Qualifications might include a major in physical education with additional preparation in sport management and business. Experiences as a player, coach, or manager should also remain experiential requisites. Although the scope and division of duties and responsibilities might vary from school to university level and from Division III to Division I, the basic human, conceptual, informational/technological, and leadership skills remain constant.

In a well-organized school, college, or other organization with a large sports program, the athletic director might work closely with a business manager, executive assistant, and associate or assistant athletic director whose responsibilities might include overseeing office staff; budget and financial record keeping; hiring, scheduling, and paying officials; risk management and security; and other contractual arrangements (e.g., insurance, clothing and media contracts, gate receipts, and guarantees).

The director of athletics in some complex Division I programs usually has an associate and assistants to help with such responsibilities as event and facilities management, scheduling, staff supervision, eligibility, fund-raising, corporate sponsorships, marketing, budgets, insurance and risk management, sports medicine, purchasing, travel, academic support, and compliance. There typically is a sports information or media relations director (SID) who prepares media releases, develops brochures, and manages such areas as photography, media, and public relations.

HIGH SCHOOL ATHLETES FORM TO EVALUATE COACHES

The primary purpose of this evaluation is to assist the coach and the Athletic Department in improving our program(s). Please return the evaluation to the coach by (Date) _____

The athletic program is _____ Coach _____
Specify if athlete is male or female: _____
I participated at the following level:

_____ Varsity   _____ Junior Varsity   _____ Sophomore

1. Please rate the coach/program in the following areas. Please explain any rating of 1 or 2 by making a comment where indicated.

	Poor	Weak	Average	Good	Excellent
Instruction in the basic fundamentals.	1	2	3	4	5
Provided a better understanding about my own ability as a result of participating on the team.	1	2	3	4	5
Established a sense of loyalty and responsibility to the school.	1	2	3	4	5
Encouraged a sense of fair play and sportsmanship.	1	2	3	4	5
Encouraged cooperative attitudes.	1	2	3	4	5
Developed my self-confidence.	1	2	3	4	5
Puts winning and losing in the proper perspective.	1	2	3	4	5
Encouraged responsible behavior.	1	2	3	4	5
Encouraged to continue participation in athletics.	1	2	3	4	5
Discipline was fair for all participants.	1	2	3	4	5
The program was well managed and organized.	1	2	3	4	5
Developed my sense of loyalty and responsibility to the team.	1	2	3	4	5
The importance of academics was stressed.	1	2	3	4	5
Chemical abuse issues were addressed.	1	2	3	4	5

Figure 5-1. An example of a form for student-athletes to use to evaluate their coach.

HIGH SCHOOL COACHING EVALUATION FORM
Rating Scale: 1-Excellent 2-Acceptable 3-Not acceptable

Coach's Name _____   Sport _____

I. PERSONAL AND PROFESSIONAL ATTRIBUTES (Circle One)

A. Personal Qualities
1. Is enthusiastic   1 2 3
2. Presents a positive role model
for the athletes   1 2 3
3. Has appropriate appearance   1 2 3
4. Uses appropriate language   1 2 3
5. Demonstrates appropriate
sportsmanship   1 2 3
6. Interacts appropriately with parents   1 2 3

B. Personal Conduct
1. Exhibits ethical/moral behavior   1 2 3
2. Maintains emotional control   1 2 3
3. Places the welfare of the athlete
above winning and would not
sacrifice values/principles to win   1 2 3

EVALUATOR'S COMMENTS:
_____
_____
_____

II. ADMINISTRATIVE PROCEDURAL ABILITIES

A. Practice Organization
1. Conducts well-planned sessions   1 2 3
2. Informs administrators and players
of practices and games as early
and as often as possible   1 2 3

B. Financial Resources
1. Adheres to budget policies and
procedures   1 2 3
2. Works within the constraints of
the budget   1 2 3

EVALUATOR'S COMMENTS:
_____
_____

III. KNOWLEDGE AND PRACTICE OF MEDICAL-LEGAL ASPECTS

1. Exhibits reasonable and prudent
conduct in preventing and handling
accidents and injuries   1 2 3
2. Follows the advise of the physician
regarding the participation of injured
athletes   1 2 3
3. Instructs players and supervises
implementation of the school's
Athletic Code   1 2 3
4. Reinforces the school policy concerning use and abuse of chemicals   1 2 3

EVALUATOR'S COMMENTS:
_____
_____

IV. THEORY AND TECHNIQUES OF COACHING

A. Coaching Methods
1. Demonstrates knowledge of the skills,
techniques, strategies and rules of
the sport   1 2 3
2. Demonstrates the ability to teach
fundamentals   1 2 3
3. Develops good team spirit and morale   1 2 3
4. Maintains discipline in a fair and
consistent manner   1 2 3
5. Makes students aware of behavior
expectations before and during season   1 2 3

B. Strategy
1. Is able to accurately assess players' skills   1 2 3
2. Consequences for behavior are
explained before participation and are
uniformly enforced   1 2 3

C. Rules and Regulations
1. Abides by the rules and regulations of the
sport and appropriate governing bodies   1 2 3
2. Demonstrates knowledge of the rules
and officiating techniques of the sport   1 2 3

EVALUATOR'S COMMENTS:
_____
_____

V. PERSONNEL MANAGEMENT

1. Monitors student's academic achievement   1 2 3
2. Develops and maintains a positive
attitude among the student-athletes   1 2 3

EVALUATOR'S COMMENTS:
_____
_____

VI. PUBLIC RELATIONS

1. Communicates effectively with assistant
coaches   1 2 3   1 2 3
2. Cooperates with the athletic coordinator   1 2 3
3. Cooperates with the administration   1 2 3
4. Communicates appropriately with the
media   1 2 3
5. Understands the concerns of parents of
the athletes and the general public   1 2 3
6. Communicates appropriately with parents   1 2 3
7. Communicates appropriately with the
administrator   1 2 3
8. Communicates appropriately with
school personnel   1 2 3

EVALUATOR'S COMMENTS:
_____
_____

NOTE: The coach's signature does not mean the coach agrees with the content of the evaluation.
However, the signature does acknowledge that the evaluation has been received and read.

Coach's Signature: _____   Date: _____
Athletic Coordinator's Signature _____   Date: _____
Principal's Signature _____   Date: _____

Figure 5-2. An example of an athletic and activities director's coaching evaluation form.

The NCAA also designates a Senior Woman Administrator (SWA) position in each collegiate athletic department. The SWA title goes to the highest-ranking female administrator involved with the conduct of the college's athletic program. The SWA usually, but not always, is a member of the athletic management team (associate or assistant AD) and participates in departmental, campus, conference, and national meetings, particularly those that may involve Title IX and gender equity.

The Coach

One of the most challenging management positions within the Physical Activity and Sport Continuum is that of coaching. Indeed, there are about 400,000 high school coaches, many of whom have no sport-related education. Many students who show exceptional skill in an interscholastic sport believe they would make good candidates for various coaching positions. They believe that because they have proved themselves outstanding athletes in high school, their skills will carry over into the coaching arena. This carryover, however, is not necessarily true. There is insufficient evidence to indicate that exceptional skill in sport will necessarily guarantee success in the teaching and coaching profession. Many qualities and properties—such as a thorough knowledge of the sport, educational degree, coaching license, professional attitude and commitment, and teaching prowess, combined with such personal characteristics as personality, intelligence, fairness, flexibility, integrity, honesty, leadership, and a sincere interest in working closely with youth and young men and women—must provide the foundation for coaching success.

Coaching should be recognized as a form of teaching. Because of the nature of the profession, a coach is in a more powerful position to affect participants than are most other members of a school faculty. Youths, in their inherent drive for activity and action and the quest for the excitement of sports competition, often look up to the coach and, in many cases, believe that the coach is a person to emulate. Coaches should recognize this role-modeling concept and strive to instill such values as character, honesty, self-discipline, personal responsibility,

and integrity. Although a coach must be a student and an expert of the game, these other characteristics including coaching ethics, are crucial to the job.

Coaching is regarded by many as a position of insecurity, political or parental jockeying, and a hot seat of psychosocial turmoil. On the other hand, coaching offers an interesting and satisfying career for many individuals who seem to become permanent fixtures on the sidelines. However, the coach should recognize the possibility of finding himself or herself in a situation in which the pressure to produce winning teams may be so great as to cause unhappiness, insecurity, job discomfort, and sometimes ill health. One need not look at schools like Notre Dame, Duke, Indiana, Minnesota, or Utah or into the professional ranks to examine these coaching concerns because they exist within every local community. Lopiano (1986) suggests that if the competent, ethical, and well-trained coach is the key to elimination of undesirable behavior for which sport is now being criticized, it seems obvious that the better organized we are in preparing and training this individual and the more reflective we are in employing and retaining a coach, the better our programs will be.

Of the qualifications needed to function as a credible coach, four are paramount. First, the coach must be a good teacher who is able to teach the fundamentals and strategies of the sport. Second, the coach needs to understand the player, that is, how the individual functions at a particular level of development, with a full appreciation of human growth and development, including psychosocial parameters. Third, the coach must understand the game; a thorough knowledge of techniques (e.g., biomechanics of running, heading a soccer ball), rules, strategies, and tactics is basic. Fourth, the coach must possess a desirable personality and character. Patience, understanding, kindness, honesty, ethical character, sense of right and wrong, courage, common sense, solid communication skills, cheerfulness, affection, humor, enthusiasm, and unending energy are imperative.

Many times the coach is working part-time at the school or club, and in many cases, men are coaching girls and young women. These situations present certain logistical problems and are further reasons why the contemporary coach must be a thorough professional in all regards.

Coaching Certification and Licensure

In some situations, the only qualification coaches possess is that they have played the game or sport in high school, college, or sometimes, as a professional. It is generally recognized, however, that the best preparation for a coach is training in physical education (Horine and Stotler 2004). In light of this, many states as well as state athletics and activity associations are requiring, or at least strongly recommending that coaches, particularly at the precollege level, have some training in physical education or exposure to various educational coaching programs offered through a variety of delivery systems.

Standards for coaching certification have been identified by the NASPE (National Association for Sport and Physical Education 2005), an association of AAHPERD, through their National Standards for Athletic Coaches. NASPE identified 37 standards that are grouped in the following domains:

- Injuries: prevention, care, and management
- Risk management
- Growth, development, and learning
- Training, conditioning, and nutrition
- Social/psychological dimensions
- Skills, tactics, and strategies
- Teaching, administration, and management
- Professional preparation and development

Coaches should be encouraged to seek training, even if certification or licensure standards have not yet been required by their particular state, school, or institution. Many coaching federations, such as the United States Soccer Federation, the United States Volleyball Association, USA Track and Field, and USA Triathlon, provide outstanding coaching licensure programs. Private concerns such as the American Sport Education Program (ASEP), the North American Youth Sport Institute (NAYSI), the National Youth Sport Coaches Association (NYSCA), the Program for Athletic

Brian Ivie, former captain of the U.S. Olympic volleyball team, conducts a coaching education and certification seminar.

Coaches Education (PACE), the National Federation of High School Coaches Education Program (NFHS/ASEP), and Special Olympics International also provide excellent coaching preparation and mentoring opportunities. Although the trend toward coaching certification and education is increasing, the thorough training of all coaches at all levels remains essential for the health, safety, and welfare of each participant.

A recent survey of the 50 states and District of Columbia provides the following information regarding coaching certification and education:

- 10 states require all coaches to hold a valid teaching certificate.
- 3 states require only the head coaches to hold a teaching certificate.
- 3 states require only selected sport head coaches to hold a teaching certificate.
- 24 states reported that coaches must be exposed to minimal education course content.
- 6 states leave the decision up to the individual local school district.
- 3 states require neither a teaching certificate, coaching licensure, or educational course work.

■ Some states, such as Nevada, New York, and Washington require personal background checks. More and more states are adopting such measures as part of risk management policy.

Table 5-2 illustrates some of the various states' teaching and coaching certification and licensure requirements, whereas table 5-3 offers a comprehensive coaching certification program.

Table 5-2. State Requirements Concerning Coaching Certification, Qualification, and Education (NFHS 2005).

Professional/Teacher Certification

All Coaches	All Head Coaches	Selected Head Coaches
Delaware	Arizona	Arkansas
Kansas	Georgia	Louisiana
Kentucky	Mississippi	Tennessee
Maryland		
Missouri		
Nebraska		
New Jersey		
New York		
Oklahoma		
Texas		

Coaching Education Only	State/District Decision	No Requirement
Alabama	California	Michigan
Alaska	Colorado	North Carolina
District of Columbia	Connecticut	North Dakota
Idaho	Florida	
Illinois	Hawaii	
Indiana	Ohio	
Iowa	Pennsylvania	
Maine	South Carolina	
Massachusetts		
Minnesota		
Montana		
Nevada		
New Hampshire		
New Mexico		
Oregon		
Rhode Island		
South Dakota		
Utah		
Vermont		
Virginia		
Washington		
West Virginia		
Wisconsin		
Wyoming		

Table 5-3. Course Requirements for the University of Minnesota Coaching Certificate Program

Course Number	Course Name
KIN 3113	First Responder for Athletic Coaches and Athletic Trainers (3) or current American Red Cross Standard First Aid and CPR/AED cards (1)
KIN 3114	Prevention and Care of Injuries (3) or *KIN 5620* Practicum: Prevention and Care of Athletic Injuries (3)
KIN SpSt Electives	*KIN 3126* Psychology and Sociology of Sport (3), *KIN 3385* Human Physiology (3), SpSt 3621 Applied Sport Psychology (2), *SpSt 3641* Training and Conditioning (2), *KIN 5126* Sport Psychology (3), *KIN 5136* Psychology of Coaching (3), *KIN 5375* Competitive Sport for Children and Youth (3), *KIN 5801* Legal Dimensions of Sport (4). Select one or more electives.
KIN 31xx Coaching courses	*3168* Soccer Coaching (1); *3169* Volleyball Coaching (1), *3171* Baseball Coaching (1), *3172* Basketball Coaching (1), *3173* Football Coaching (1), *3174* Golf Coaching (1), *3175* Gymnastics Coaching (1), *3176* Ice Hockey Coaching (1), *3177* Swimming and Diving Coaching (1), *3178* Tennis Coaching (1), *3179* Track and Field Coaching (1), *3181* Wrestling Coaching (1). Select one or more coaching courses or *KIN 5720* or *5740* Coaching Topics Courses.
KIN 3143	Organization and Management of Sport (3)
KIN 5697	Student Teaching: Coaching (3-4)

Box 5-1 Code of Ethics, Minnesota State High School Coaches' Association

As a Professional Educator, I Will

Strive to develop in each athlete the qualities of leadership, initiative, and good judgment.

Respect the integrity and personality of the individual athlete.

Encourage the highest standards of conduct and scholastic achievement among all athletes.

Seek to inculcate good health habits, including the establishment of sound training rules.

Fulfill responsibilities to provide health services and an environment free of safety hazards.

Exemplify the highest moral character, behavior, and leadership.

Promote ethical relationships among coaches.

Encourage a respect for all athletics and their values.

Abide by the rules of the game in letter and in spirit.

Respect the integrity and judgment of sports officials.

Display modesty in victory and graciousness in defeat.

Demonstrate a mastery of, and continuing interest in, coaching principles and techniques through professional improvement.

I Will Not

Approve commercialism, solicitation, subsidizing, or professionalism entering into high school athletics.

Most states and organizations provide a coach's code of ethics and many are now requiring the participants as well as their parents/guardians to sign a like document. Boxes 5-1 and 5-2 reflect excellent examples of a coach's code of conduct. It is important for all coaches to keep pace with the game, the profession, and their school, campus, or community sport organizations. This can be accomplished by joining and actively participating in their sport-specific coaching organization, reading,

Box 5-2   NFCA Coaches Code of Ethics

The function of a coach is to properly educate students through participation in interscholastic competition. The interscholastic program is designed to enhance academic achievement and should never interfere with opportunities for academic success. Each child should be treated as though they were the coach's own and their welfare shall be uppermost at all times. In recognition of this, the following guidelines for coaches have been adopted by the NFCA Board of Directors.

The coach must be aware that he or she has a tremendous influence, either good or bad, in the education of the student-athlete, and thus, shall never place the value of winning above the value of instilling the highest desirable ideals of character.

The coach must constantly uphold the honor and dignity of the profession. In all personal contact with the student-athlete, officials, athletic directors, school administrators, the state high school athletic association, the media, and the public, the coach shall strive to set an example of the highest ethical and moral conduct.

The coach shall take an active role in the prevention of drug, alcohol, and tobacco abuse and under no circumstances should authorize their use.

The coach shall promote the entire interscholastic program of the school and direct his or her program in harmony with the total school program.

The coach shall be thoroughly acquainted with the contest rules and is responsible for their interpretation to team members. The spirit and letter of rules should be regarded as mutual agreements. The coach shall not try to seek an advantage by circumvention of the spirit or letter of the rules.

Coaches shall actively use their influence to enhance sportsmanship by their spectators, working closely with cheerleaders, pep club sponsors, booster clubs, and administrators.

Contest officials shall have the respect and support of the coach. The coach shall not indulge in conduct that will incite players or spectators against the officials. Public criticism of officials or players is unethical.

Before and after contests, rival coaches should meet and exchange friendly greetings to set the correct tone for the event.

A coach shall not exert pressure on faculty members to give student-athletes special consideration.

It is unethical for coaches to scout opponents by any means other than those adopted by the league and/or state high school athletic association.

From the National Federation
Coaches Association

and studying, and attending workshops, clinics, institutes, camps, and conventions; however, there is no substitute for holding a degree in teaching and a creditable coaching license.

Certified Athletic Trainer/Sports Medicine Specialists

The profession of athletic training has taken on greater significance in recent years because of the guidance of the National Athletic Trainers Association (NATA) and the concomitant increase in sports programs and the recognition that the health and safety of the student-athlete is a top priority.

The role of the certified athletic trainer is the prevention, recognition, assessment, and management of injuries at all levels of competitive sport.

The contemporary certified athletic trainer needs special preparation to carry out athletic training duties, which include prevention of injuries, first aid, postinjury treatment, and rehabilitation, as well as educational counseling. Such preparation, if possible, should include a major in physical education, kinesiology, or sport science, NATA certification, or being a registered physical therapist. Also needed are such personal qualifications as emotional stability under stress, ability to act rationally when injuries occur, and a standard of ethics that places the welfare of the participant above the pressures for approval to play.

Many schools and colleges whose financial situation does not permit hiring a full-time certified athletic trainer are strongly encouraged to provide at the very minimum a part-time certified athletic trainer.

Qualifications for Certified Athletic Trainers

Certified athletic trainers should complete a four-year college curriculum that emphasizes the biological and physical sciences. The courses required in certified athletic trainers professional preparation programs also indicate some of the competencies needed. These courses include anatomy, physiology, exercise physiology, applied anatomy, biomechanics, sport psychology, sport sociology, organization and management of sport, first aid and safety, nutrition, remedial exercise, health, techniques of athletic training, counseling, and an internship/practicum in the techniques of athletic training.

The certified athletic trainer is a crucial part of the sports management team and must work closely with administrators, coaches, physicians, school medical personnel, athletes, and parents in a cooperative effort to provide the best possible safety and health care. In some community situations, the certified athletic trainer is also responsible for staff development, in-service training, and supervision of a student athletic training staff.

Prentice (2004) lists the following as the personal qualifications requisite for athletic trainers: good health, sense of fair play, maturity and emotional stability, good appearance, leadership, compassion, intellectual capacity, sense of humor, kindness and understanding, competence and responsibility, and a sound philosophy of life.

Additional information about the management of athletic training programs is provided in chapter 12.

The Athletic/Sport Council

Most schools and colleges have some type of athletic or sport council, advisory board, or committee that establishes and is responsible for the conduct of sport

Certified athletic trainer at work. University of Minnesota, Minneapolis.

policies and procedures for the institution or organization. Such councils, boards, or committees are responsible for providing proper direction and input to athletic directors and administrators as sport operates in the educational context of the organization.

The composition of such committees or councils varies widely from school to school and college to college. In a school, the superintendent or principal may serve as chairperson, or the director of physical education and/or athletics or other faculty member may hold this position. The committee may include coaches, members of the school board or board of education, faculty, students, parents, and members of the community at large.

Some of the functions of sport councils at the high school level mirror somewhat that of college faculty athletic committees (see chapter 2) and includes making, reviewing, and recommending policy; approving eligibility; advising the athletic director on issues or concerns; endorsing and approving schedules and budgets; evaluating the athletic and activities programs; investigating complaints; interviewing and recommending to athletic directors potential athletic personnel for hiring; approving codes of ethics; reviewing scholarship and award programs, approving pre- and postseason play and international educational competitions; and deciding if various sport programs should be added or discontinued.

Athletic councils at the collegiate level usually include several elected faculty members, an alumni representative, and several elected student-athletes. This group usually provides direct feedback to the athletic director concerning associated issues and concerns of student-athlete life. These may range from housing to equity and from community engagement (e.g., Learn-To-Read programs, Special Olympics, tsunami relief) efforts to training table nutrition and graduation rates. It is crucial no matter what level or type of program to have direct student-athlete or participant representation, involvement, and input into the sporting process.

Academic Support

In the last decade, many colleges and universities have made a concerted effort to improve their academic image and the graduation rates of student-athletes. The NCAA has also joined this athletic reform challenge and will now impose a series of graduated penalties (i.e. public warning, recruiting and scholarship restrictions, pre- and postseason bans, membership restriction) for those who do not graduate their student-athletes within acceptable peer institution guidelines. These actions, among others, have served to bring academic support programs to the forefront on the college campus. These program support services have as their mission to enable each student-athlete to become an educated, self-reliant, and self-confident member of the campus community. Once the student-

Academic support services are important for student-athletes.

athlete arrives on campus, many believe that academic support should play a significant role. Study halls, computer rooms, tutoring, time management and study skills classes all have found their way into the daily life of today's student-athletes and have drawn a certain amount of criticism from certain quarters. With the renewal of the effort to reform "big-time" intercollegiate athletics, academic support units will continue to grow and play an important role in the recruitment, retention, and academic prowess and progress of the student-athlete. Indeed, academic support and compliance is now becoming part of high school programs, especially in regard to NCAA eligibility. All high school athletics and activities personnel as well as counselors must be able to provide accurate and up-to-date direction for potential Division I and II college student athletes as they must adhere to the NCAA Initial-Eligibility Clearinghouse certification regulations concerning GPA and core units of specific academic coursework.

Compliance

Because of the complexities of Division I athletics and their intimate bond with the NCAA, most institutions have employed a full-time compliance officer to ensure that the rules of the day are obeyed. Most often, this individual reports directly to an academic administrator, but works closely with the athletic director. The role of the compliance officer is to develop an educational environment whereby everyone, directly or indirectly involved in the program (e.g., coaches, certified athletic trainers, alumni, family, significant others, boosters, agents, etc.), understands and complies with the rules of the sport-governing bodies and institutions involved. This is usually accomplished by an ongoing series of training and compliance seminars (e.g., rules, Title IX, academic progress, sexual harassment, employment, etc.), as well as a continuous stream of electronic reminders and case studies to insure attention to detail in this crucial domain.

SELECTED MANAGEMENT FUNCTIONS IN COMPETITIVE SPORT PROGRAMS

Many management functions are pertinent to the directing of a competitive sport program, including the following concerns: event, game, facility, and practice scheduling; contracts; health and safety of student-athletes; injuries, insurance, and risk management; officials; transportation; event and game management; crowd control; protests, forfeitures, and cancelled games; awards and honors; and record keeping.

Event, Game, Facility, and Practice Scheduling

Scheduling involves maintaining a proper balance between home and away contests, seeking contests with organizations and institutions of approximately the same size and caliber of play, and trying to restrict the scope of the geographical area in which contests are conducted to minimize transportation costs.

Where leagues and conferences are in place, schedules are usually made many months or years in advance, leaving the athletic director or coach few windows of opportunity for nonconference matches. In most instances, the high school league or association, NCAA, NAIA, NJCAA, or other appropriate governing body limits the number of scheduled matches as well as the length of the season. All contests, games, and competitive sport events should have the sanction and approval of school, state, college, or other organizational authorities. Season lengths should be arranged so

that they interfere as little as possible with institutional academic priorities. Practice schedules before the first contest should be adequate and appropriate so that the players are in match or game condition and thoroughly prepared to play.

Some factors that may affect scheduling include environmental conditions, maximizing gate receipts, number of participants and potential spectators, state playoffs and invitational tournaments, transportation and logistics, availability of facilities, different sports that appeal to the same students, limitations concerning number of games or contests permitted, rivalries, religious considerations, paid guarantees to travel and play, and potential educational impact on the student-athlete, ranging from tournament participation in Hawaii or international trips to Australia or Italy to number of class days missed.

Event, game, facility, and practice scheduling should be fairly and equitably managed (following Title IX guidelines) permitting equal time, opportunity, and accessibility for all sport participants. All coaches and other personnel involved in facilities utilization, travel, scheduling, and support services should be involved in management's decision-making process.

Contracts

Written contracts are essential in the management of interscholastic and intercollegiate sports programs (see figure 5-3). On the college level in particular, games are scheduled many months and sometimes years in advance. Memories, handshake agreements, and facts tend to fade and become obscure with time. To avoid misunderstanding and confusion, it is best to have a written contract between the schools, colleges or organizations, and all those concerned (e.g., athletic directors, coaches, business managers, officials, league commissioners, hotels, food service, transportation companies).

Contracts should be properly executed and signed by official representatives of all schools or colleges involved. Many sport associations, federations, and conferences provide specially prepared forms for use by member schools or colleges. Such forms usually contain the names of the schools,

ATHLETIC EVENTS AGREEMENT

THIS AGREEMENT, entered into this _____ day of _____ ,20 _____ , by and between
_____ , and the REGENTS OF THE UNIVERSITY
OF _____ , stipulates:

First: That the _____ teams representing the above institutions

    shall meet/play in _____ athletic contests as follows:

      At _____ Date _____ Time _____

      At _____ Date _____ Time _____

      At _____ Date _____ Time _____

      At _____ Date _____ Time _____

Second: That said contests and all arrangements incident thereto shall be conducted under the rules and

    regulations of _____

Third: That in consideration of playing said contests, the following financial arrangements

    are agreed _____

Fourth: That contest officials _____

Fifth: That radio rights _____

Sixth: That television rights _____

Seventh: That other provisions are

    A. _____

    B. _____

    C. _____

NOTE: Cancellation of this agreement may result in a financial penalty to the extent of actual costs incurred
by participating institution.

Recommended:

University of _____   Institution _____

By   By
_____   _____

Title   Title

Date   Date

REGENTS OF THE UNIVERSITY

By
_____   Return By _____

Title

WHITE—Central files   PINK—Institution   CANARY—Department

Figure 5-3. An example of an athletic events agreement.

dates, times, and circumstances and conditions under which the contests will be held. In addition, they usually provide for penalties if contracts are breached by either party.

Health, Safety, and Welfare of the Student-Athlete

Competitive sport should contribute to the health, function, and well-being of the student-athlete. Through wholesome physical activity, the participant should not only become more aware of the benefits of health-related fitness and exercise, but also become more physically, cognitively, affectively, emotionally, and psychosocially healthy.

One of the first requirements for every participant involved in a sport program should be a thorough, vigorous, preparticipation medical examination by an experienced physician to determine physical health status before engaging in strenuous activities. The nature of competitive sport and the sometimes stressful demands (both physical and psychological) placed on the participant make this yearly examination imperative.

Strength training and conditioning play important roles in contemporary sport. Kevin Yoxall, Strength Coach, Auburn University.

Everything possible should be done to protect the health and safety of the participant. A coach should always conduct the program with these objectives in mind. The coach should be licensed and possess current certification in first aid and CPR/AED and strictly adhere to progressive and prudent measures of training and conditioning.

Proper training and conditioning should take place before any player is subjected to competition. Such training and conditioning should always be progressive and gradual. The playing roster should contain ample players to allow for substitutions in the event a person is not physically fit or is otherwise unable to compete.

Proper and well-maintained facilities and equipment should be available to ensure the safety and health of the players. This means that facilities are constructed according to recommended standards concerning size, lighting, surfacing, and various safety features. Protective equipment meeting all current safety specifications (e.g., for football, lacrosse, and ice hockey) should be provided as required in the various sports. If appropriate facilities and equipment are not available, competition should be immediately suspended.

Games should be scheduled that result in equal and safe competition. The desire of small schools to compete against larger schools for a large guarantee, in which case the competition is not equal, often brings potentially disastrous results to the health, safety, and welfare of the players (primarily in the case of collision sports). Under such circumstances, one often hears the remark, "They really took a beating." Competition should be as equal and fair as possible.

Proper sanitary measures should be taken. Individual towels and drinking cups or bottles should be provided. The day of the team towel, shared water bottle or deodorant, and uncared for mat (bacteria, funguses, viruses, MRSA-methicellin-resistant staphylococcal-aureas) has passed. Equipment should be approved and well maintained, and uniforms should be laundered as often as necessary. Facilities (e.g., strength-training stations, exercise machines, and mats) should be cleaned daily and up to code. Locker, dressing, shower, toilet, and other facilities used by participants should also be kept clean and sanitary.

Playing areas should be well maintained, clean, and safe. Gymnasiums, pools, and other facilities should be maintained at the proper temperature, and every measure must be taken to ensure safe, healthful, and optimal learning and performance conditions.

Injuries, Insurance, and Risk Management

Prompt attention should be given to all injuries. Injured players should be examined and diagnosed by a physician and administered proper treatment. There should be complete medical supervision of the entire sports program. A physician should be present at all games and be on call for practice sessions, especially those involving contact and heavy exertion. The certified athletic trainer is not a substitute for a physician. The physician should determine the extent of injury. After being ill or hurt, a player should not be permitted to participate again until the coach receives an approved statement from the family, school, or college physician. The coach should make sure that, even though such permission is granted, the athlete is also psychosocially and physically prepared for practice, match, or game conditions.

In many states, the state high school association sponsors an athletic insurance plan. Some insurance companies have plans that allow a sports participation rider to be added to the student's basic student insurance policy. Such plans pay various medical, X-ray and MRI examinations, dental, hospitalization, and other expenses according to the terms of the plan. The amount of any payment for an injury is usually only the amount of the actual expenses incurred, but not in excess of the amounts listed in the schedule of allowance for such injury. To collect benefits, plan requirements must be met.

The insurance provided by various state and independent plans usually includes benefits for accidental death or dismemberment, hospital expenses, X-ray and MRI examination fees, physicians' fees, and surgical and dental expenses as well as emergency transportation. Dental benefits may or may not be included in the schedule of surgical benefits. In some plans, catastrophe benefits are also available for injuries requiring extensive medical care and long-term hospitalization. Coverage is normally provided on a deductible basis, with the insurance company paying 75 percent to 80 percent of the total cost over the deductible amount up to a maximum amount.

Every school, college, or organization involved in the delivery of competitive sport should have a written policy concerning health, safety, injury, insurance, and other forms of risk management relating to the competitive sport process. For example, an enterprise risk management plan enables management to effectively deal with uncertainty and associated risk and opportunity. Such a plan enhances risk response decisions (avoidance, reduction, sharing, acceptance) and reduces operational or programmatic surprises and losses. Furthermore, the administrator, coach, certified athletic trainer, team physician, parents, and players should be thoroughly familiar with the legal responsibilities, rights, and due process concerning all phases of the competitive sport program.

Officials

Officials play an integral role in any competitive sport program; therefore they should be well qualified, certified, and licensed, and hold membership in their respective officiating association. They should know the rules and be able to interpret them accurately, recognize their responsibility to the players, be good sportspersons, and be courteous, honest, friendly, cooperative, impartial, and able to control the game at all times.

To ensure that only high-quality officials are employed, procedures should be established to register and rate officials and determine which are best qualified. Officials should be medically and physically fit and required to pass examinations on rules and to demonstrate their competence. Rating scales have been developed to help make such assessments. Most sports associations have some

Umpires and officials play major roles in sports competition.

method of registering and certifying acceptable officials. These organizations, including state high school leagues and associations as well as collegiate conferences, also have committees that rate officials to insure that their performance is up to standards. In some states, the officials also rate the schools or colleges regarding facilities, environment, and circumstances surrounding the game. Officials' ratings can provide important feedback on coaching behavior and event and site management. In turn, coaches should rate every official.

Subject to contract differences, officials are frequently chosen by the home team with approval of opponents or the conference. The practice of the home team selecting officials without any consideration toward the wishes of other organizations has on occasion resulted in relations that have not been in the best interests of sport. The growing practice of having the conference, league, or association select officials has nullified many of these situations.

Officials should be duly notified of the date, time, and location of the contests to which they have been assigned and contracts awarded. Computer scheduling by commissioners or those charged with game assignments has greatly added to the efficiency of this process. Officials' fees vary from school to school and sport to sport, although some associations have assigned standard rates. It is usually considered best to pay a flat fee that includes both salary and expenses rather than to budget them separately.

Transportation

Transporting athletes to and from sporting contests presents many management problems: Who should be transported? In what kinds of vehicles should athletes be transported? Who should drive? Is sport part of a regular day-school program? Should private vehicles or school- and college-owned vehicles be used? What are the legal and risk management implications involved in transporting athletes to and from school- and college-sponsored events?

The present trend in high school is to view competitive sport as an integral part of the educational program so that public funds may be used for transportation. At the same time, however, statutes vary from state to state, and persons managing sport programs should carefully examine the statutes and policies concerning their own circumstance.

Many managers believe that athletes and representatives of the school or college, such as pep band members and cheerleaders, should travel only in transportation provided by the school. When private cars belonging to coaches, students, or other persons are used, the manager should be sure to determine whether the procedures are in conformity with the organization and state statutes regarding liability. Under no circumstances should students or other representatives be permitted to drive unless they are licensed drivers, and under most circumstances student-athletes should not be used as drivers.

The business manager is generally responsible for transportation. This responsibility usually involves a great deal of advance planning, and the coach, athletic director, and department representative assigned to handle transportation must work in consort to provide for the safest, most efficient, and cost-effective form and more on travel. The

---

Box 5-3   One Day in a Monthly Schedule of Sporting Events

April 8

Depart:	3:00 P.M.
From:	Senior High School Parking Lot, West Exit
Team:	Junior Varsity Baseball
To:	Jones High School Baseball Field, 3 Oak St., Cary, NC 27511
Phone:	919-555-0123
Students:	25
Pickup:	5:30 P.M. at Jones High School Baseball Field
Remarks:	Construction on Route 12 may require travel on Route 55. Please check before trip.
Contact:	Will Krotee 919-233-4655

---

director of athletics should submit a monthly calendar of athletic events, listing the date, time, and place of departure; event; destination; number of participants; time of pickup; mode of transport; and remarks (see box 5-3). These calendars should be posted and sent to all coaches, athletic staff, and athletes involved.

After the transportation has been scheduled with the appropriate school department or transportation company, a copy of the transportation contract is distributed to the athletic director, the coach, the principal, and the business manager. The procedure for submitting transportation requests varies in different schools and colleges, but written records should always be confirmed, scrutinized, and kept on file by the athletic director and coach.

Event and Game Management

Because so many details are associated with event or game management, it is possible to include only a brief statement concerning some of the more important items. To have an effectively and efficiently conducted event, good organization is important. Someone must be responsible. Indeed most large colleges hire event, game, and tournament managers on a full-time basis. Advance planning must be

done. Many details must be attended to, including (1) pregame responsibilities, (2) game responsibilities, (3) postgame responsibilities, (4) emergency plans, and (5) preparation for away games. Before an event or game, details such as contracts (e.g., officials, transportation, security, concessions, and facilities), eligibility records, equipment, facility availability, ticketing, public relations, medical supervision, and health status and insurance must be thoroughly checked. Responsibilities for home games might include checking such items as supplies and equipment, parking, pregame and halftime entertainment, tickets and credentials, security and volunteer ushers, score and message boards, game statistics, public-address system, emergency care procedures, availability of physician and certified athletic trainers, and locker room facilities for visiting teams and officials. The responsibilities after a home game consist of checking such items as payments to officials and visiting school, evaluation of officials, attendance and participation records, contact of local media outlets, and financial records and ticket sale reports and deposits. Preparations for an away game include such important details as parents' permissions, missed classes, transportation, funding, contracts, travel team, and records. In addition, after an away game, forms must be completed in order to accurately account for all travel-related expenses (see figure 5-4).

Crowd Control and Security

Crowd control and safety at sports contests have become increasingly important in light of post-9/11 concerns. Crowd control incidents involving unruly fans and players at high school and college (not to mention professional) sporting events have also served notice that more must be done to ensure the safety of all concerned. The elimination of evening sports events at the high school level has been on the increase, particularly in metropolitan areas. School districts and college authorities are taking increased precautions to avoid crowd problems at sporting contests. Good sports assemblies are being conducted, the community is being informed, and administrators are discussing the matter. Fair play assemblies are now presented at most

UNIVERSITY OF NEVADA, LAS VEGAS

Controller's Office
Accounts Payable Department
CLAIM FOR GROUP TRAVEL EXPENSES

Note: Do not use this form for submitting Travel Expenses for individual faculty/staff of UNLV.

Department to Travel: _____

Destination: _____

Dates of Travel: _____

Number of Students and Staff Members: _____

SUMMARY OF EXPENDITURES

Transportation:

    Method: _____

    Cost (Do not enter cost of any agency vehicle.) _____

Meals, lodging, and miscellaneous:

Dates						Total
Breakfasts						
Lunches						
Dinners						
Lodging						
Other						
Student Allowance						

Total Meals, Lodging, and Miscellaneous: ....

Total All Expenditures and/or Student Allowances......................
    (Must be substantiated by receipts)

Advance Received: ....

Balance due or to be reimbursed ....
    (If balance is to be reimbursed to the traveler submit a request
    for check in the amount of reimbursement.)

Account to be Charged: _____

        Signed by: _____

        Approved by: _____
                      Department Head

UNLV AP 270 4-06

(1) Controller's Office
(2) Controller's Office
(3) Department

Figure 5-4. Claim for group travel expenses.

state high school association competitions as well as at college level tournaments. Organizations—including the AAHPERD, the National Federation of State High School Associations (NFHS), and most conferences and high school leagues—have suggested numerous guidelines for crowd control, including parent and spectator codes of conduct and fair play. A summary of these recommendations may be found in appendix C. These approaches to crowd control should also be extended to include crowd emergencies such as lightning storms, earthquakes, tornadoes, bomb scares, and other environmental disasters in which crowd communication and safety are paramount. Security personnel, volunteer ushers, teachers, and parents who have received crowd control training and who are on duty before, during, and postevent are key elements to vigilant crowd control and safety.

Well-orchestrated crowd control and crisis management programs are crucial parts of risk management and essential if athletic and activity departments are going to provide an entertaining, exciting, and safe environment for all involved.

Protests, Forfeitures, and Called Games

Procedures for handling protests and forfeitures in connection with sports contests should be a matter of written policy. Of course, careful preventive action should be taken beforehand to avoid a situation in which such protests and forfeitures occur. Proper

Event management and control are crucial for the safe and successful conduct of any sporting venture.

interpretation of the rules, good officiating, elimination of undue pressures, and proper education of coaches, participants, parents, and officials about the philosophy and objectives of competitive sport will help prevent such action. However, the procedure for filing protests and forfeitures should be established. This procedure should be clearly stated in writing and should contain all the details, such as the person or responsible organization to whom the protest should be addressed. Time limits and time frame involved, person or group responsible for action, legal counsel, and any other necessary information should be readily available for the parties involved. One of the most frequent reasons for a protest is the use of ineligible players, which usually results in the forfeiture of any game in which ineligible players participated.

Calling games because of environmental (e.g., rain, ice, snow, cold, lightning, tornado, earthquake) or other unforeseen conditions (e.g., sickness or tragic circumstance) also requires following the policies and procedures set down by management. Oftentimes, short notice is the great concern, which is why communication via phone, fax, electronic mail, and walkie-talkie must be readily available.

Awards and Honors

Awards and honors in interscholastic and intercollegiate sport have long played an important role in the recognition of the student-athlete. The type and cost for these, for the most part, are dictated by the high school league, conference, and the NCAA. There are arguments for and against granting awards. Some individuals believe that the intrinsic values derived from playing a sport—fun, joy and satisfaction, physical and psychosocial benefits, among others—are sufficient and that no materialistic awards should be presented. Others argue that awards have been a symbolic recognition of achievement since the time of ancient Greece, and they should be an integral part of the competitive sport program.

The awards policy should be determined by the athletic or sport council, conference, league, or management team at each sporting level. The practice of granting awards in the form of letters, insignia, plaques, pins, medals, pennants, or some other symbol is almost universal. Along with traditional sporting honors, many organizations are beginning to recognize the academic achievement and sportsmanship of student-athletes (e.g., banquets and awards for academic excellence and sportsmanship). This practice is strongly encouraged.

When awards are given, they should be modest and meaningful. Some state athletic associations and other governing bodies have placed financial limits on awards to student-athletes. Furthermore, it seems wise not to distinguish between so-called major, or revenue-producing, sports and minor, or non-revenue-producing, sports when granting awards. Award criteria should call for equal treatment among potential recipients. Awards and honors (e.g., all-state, MVP, all-academic, captain) are personally meaningful for those student-athletes who receive them. College admissions officials or prospective employers often request such information, and sometimes admission and financial aid are directly related to such achievements.

Record Keeping

Management of any competitive sporting endeavor requires accurate records of all the details concerned with the sport-specific situation. The following records should be considered for inclusion in a secure computer or database file: health and medical status (HIPAA protected); parents' contact addresses, phone numbers, insurance information, and permission to participate; academic eligibility; budget, contract, and travel records; conference schedules; and transportation. Also online should be records on the conduct of various sports from year to year, season to season, and game to game, so that they can be compared over time or with

Extrinsic awards are commonplace in competitive sport programs. Edina High School, Edina, Minn.

other organizations or teams; statistical summaries of player participation and game performance tendencies that may assist the coach in determining weaknesses in game strategy or in quantifying players' or teams' performances vs. stated objectives; and other pertinent information essential to well-organized game preparation and management. Moreover, sound management practices, including risk management, demand accurate records of equipment, equipment repair and replacement, and supplies, officials, financial reports, injuries, and other crucial accountability items. All records should be safe, secure, and backed up.

SELECTED MANAGEMENT PROBLEMS ASSOCIATED WITH COMPETITIVE SPORT

Contemporary competitive sport at both the school and college levels has become a quagmire of seemingly ever-changing rules and regulations. Needless to say, the sport management team (athletic director, coaches, student-athletes, sport council, sports medicine staff, school and college personnel, etc.) is responsible for the conduct of a program of integrity. The management team is bound to encounter problems related to recruitment, eligibility, scholarships, proselytizing, scouting, finances, substance abuse, and compensation for coaching.

Recruitment

Recruiting student athletes is a controversial issue. Some educational institutions indicate that they do not condone recruiting for the primary purpose of developing winning teams. These institutions feel the admission process should be the same for all students, regardless of whether they are athletes, merit scholars, minority students, or others gifted in music, art, or architecture. No special consideration should be shown to any particular individual or group. The same standards, academic and otherwise, should prevail. This idealistic view, however, seems to be in constant conflict with most pragmatic practices at both the high school and college levels.

Some educational institutions, however, actively recruit athletes for their varsity teams. One has only to identify the country's leading high school football, basketball, or ice hockey teams to gain a realistic view of big-time high school recruiting. The main consideration here is to live up to rules of the state high school association or league, the conference, the NCAA, or other organizations in which the institution participates. To do otherwise should not be condoned.

In high school and college sports, teams should be made up of matriculated students attracted to the school or college because of its educational offerings, not its sports reputation. However, outstanding intercollegiate sports teams and outstanding recreational sports and physical education facilities have been identified as strong influences in the recruiting process, not only for athletes, but also for other prospective students and faculty as well. In some states, high school open enrollment continually causes problems that have not truly been addressed. At the college and university level, there is a population of student-athletes on whom millions of dollars are spent during the recruitment process. Management can do much to see that acceptable academic standards are observed in the recruitment process and that the cost of attracting qualified student-athletes is controlled. Recent NCAA reforms are beginning to address these problems. It should be made clear in writing that established rules will be observed and that any violation by the athletic department staff will be dealt with severely. Also, at many universities, athletic departments are hiring external consultants to assist compliance officers in conducting seminars for the management team, including coaching staffs, about effective and legal recruiting practices.

Eligibility

Standards regarding the eligibility of participants are essential. These standards should be in writing, disseminated widely, and clearly understood by all concerned so that players, coaches, parents, guardians, and other involved people will not become emotional when they "suddenly" realize that their star player is ineligible to compete.

Standards of eligibility in interscholastic circles usually include an age limit of not more than nineteen or twenty years; a requirement that an athlete be a bona fide student; rules concerning transfer students that frequently require them to be residents in the community served by the school; rules concerning international and exchange students; satisfactory class attendance, academic standing, and grades in school; permission to play on only one team during a season; playing on an outside all-star or select team during or after the season; and a requirement that the participant have a medical examination, amateur status, and parent's or guardian's consent. These eligibility regulations vary from school to school, conference to conference, and state to state.

The National Federation of State High School Associations (NFHS) considers a student ineligible for amateur standing if the student (1) has accepted money or compensation for playing in an athletic contest, (2) has played under an assumed name, (3) has competed with a team whose players were paid, or (4) has signed a contract to play with a professional team.

Eligibility requirements at the college and university level include rules concerning core courses, academic test scores (currently under study because of possible bias), residence, undergraduate status, academic grade point average and progress toward graduation, limits of game participation, transfer, substance abuse, and amateur status, including hiring of agents and professional tryouts. These rules have become quite complex, and athletic directors, coaches, counselors, academic support, and compliance staff must remain current.

Scholarships

Should athletes receive scholarships or special financial assistance from schools and colleges? Those in favor of scholarships and financial assistance claim that a student who excels in sport deserves to receive aid just as much as one who excels in various other academic pursuits. Those opposed point out that scholarships should be awarded on the basis of the need and academic qualifications, rather than physical prowess in a given sport.

Scholarships help student-athletes obtain a sound education while competing. University of California at Los Angeles.

The NCAA has continued to hold down the number of allowable scholarships, with the exception of women's soccer, which has caused a controversy concerning further limitations on students who without athletic scholarships would be unable to afford a Duke, Georgetown, Princeton, or Stanford education. The complex web of sport scholarships is not confined to the college campus. The situation even extends into the private high schools and preparatory schools, which seem to be in steady supply of high-powered athletes, whether in football, basketball, lacrosse, soccer, or ice hockey.

The controversy is a difficult one; however, with competitive sport being an integral part of the educational process, it seems that if sport can enable young people to further their education or can assist them in gaining admission to highly selective institutions, the student-athletes should take full advantage of those opportunities.

Proselytizing

Proselytizing is a term applied to a high school or college that has so strongly overemphasized sport that it has stooped to unethical behavior to secure outstanding talent or winning teams. High schools are not immune to this problem, and colleges seem to receive a lot of attention as well as visits from the staff of the NCAA office. Open enrollment, sports sponsorship, international exchange students, high-profile summer camps, and gracious financial incentives offered by private high schools lead to legitimate concerns about the management of competitive sport at the high school level. For the most part, state high school athletic associations and leagues have attempted to legislate and control these problems and have realized a fair amount of success. The NCAA, however, seems to be continuously investigating unscrupulous proselytizing practices and has reduced the length of the "recruiting season" for its member schools' coaches.

Scouting

Scouting has become an integral part of competitive sport at both the high school and college levels. Scouting might range from personally attending games to watching game film. By watching another team perform, one can learn the formations and plays used as well as discover certain team or individual player tendencies or weaknesses. These discoveries might range from watching players to determine mannerisms they possess that might give away a certain play to evaluating the personality of the opponent under stress.

Many schools and colleges are spending considerable money and time on scouting. Some schools scout a rival team every game during the season, using three or four persons on the same scouting assignment, and some study endless footage of exchanged or recorded videos.

Scouting is considered an important part of the game, and if scouting does occur, the head coach at the institution has direct responsibility for its con-

Intercollegiate volleyball provides opportunities for student-athletes to gain an education both on and off the court.

duct. Prior arrangements should be made about the game to be scouted or videos to be exchanged with the opposing team's athletic department. Although one hears stories of coaches falling out of trees while observing closed practices, scouting for the most part has been ethical and remains an important facet of game preparation.

Finances

Interscholastic and intercollegiate sport programs throughout the country are financed through many different sources. These sources include board of education and central university funds, gate receipts, donations and gifts, endowments, special projects, students' activity fees, pay-for-play assessment, physical education department funds, parking, game programs, sports apparel, and concessions. In major college and professional sport, preferred seating, luxury boxes, and corporate sponsor signage and partnerships, logo licensing, TV, cable, and cybercasts are also crucial strategies for producing new and enhanced revenue streams.

It has long been argued by leaders in physical education that competitive sport programs have great educational potential. They are curricular in nature rather than extracurricular. This means they contribute to the welfare of students like any other subject in the curriculum. On this basis, therefore, the finances necessary to support such a program should come from board of education or central administration funding sources. Sport programs should not have to be self-supporting or used as a means to support part or all of the other so-called extracurricular activities of a school or college. Sport programs represent an integral part of the educational program and as such deserve to be treated like other aspects of the educational program. This procedure is followed in some schools and colleges with benefits as well as limitations to all concerned.

Gate receipts are a primary source of funding for many competitive sport programs. Too often gate receipts become the point of emphasis rather than the vehicle that provides valuable educational opportunities and experiences to the participant. When this shift occurs, sport cannot justify its existence in the educational process.

Recent trends indicate that one out of every five U.S. schools has cut back sport programs, or may soon do so, as a result of fiscal difficulty. Gate receipts of revenue-producing sports alone can no longer support the number of men's and women's sport programs that are being offered at many institutions.

In some school districts, a student fee ranging from $50 to $500, which is collected from the interscholastic sport participant, as well as the formation of booster clubs has managed to keep competitive sport programs intact. And yes sports sponsorship is beginning to make its way into the high school sports' programs. Schools,

Interscholastic evening soccer match. Wayzata High School, Wayzata, Minn.

colleges, and universities will have to creatively address this fiscal issue because the sport "chopping" trend of the 1990s is unacceptable for the new millennium.

Coaching Compensation

A frequent topic of discussion at school meetings is whether teachers should receive extra pay for extra services. Parents, taxpayers, school boards, and administrators have been trying to decide whether sport coaches, adapted coaches, dance line and debate coaches, cheerleading advisors, band leaders, dramatics supervisors, yearbook advisors, and others who perform services in addition to their teaching load should receive additional compensation.

A sensible solution to this problem is essential to the morale of a school staff. Most school systems are demanding more and more services and have formulated pay scales to cover the extra duties. These scales often have compensation formulas including hours spent, length of season, number of participants, and experience, which may culminate in as much as $4,000 to $6,000 for a head coach of football or basketball and $1,500 to $3,500 for an assistant coach in a typical suburban senior high school.

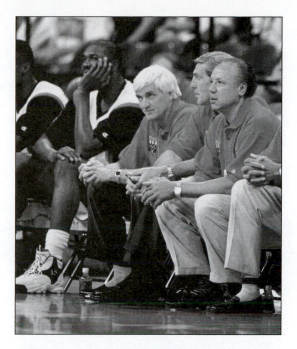

Coaching at the elite level can be a rewarding profession; U.S. Olympic basketball coaches. Courtesy of USA Basketball.

Coaching loads should be equalized as much as possible. If inequalities exist that cannot be corrected through extra pay, then extra staff and, sometimes, release time may be considered.

The compensation involved in competitive sport at the college or university level is not as clear-cut as in high school. At the NCAA Division III level, coaching might be part of the teaching or administrative responsibilities, whereas at the Division I level, coaching and its associated duties may be the only assignment. Within sport, differences range from seven-figure salaries, radio and television shows, cars, shoe and apparel contracts, and country club privileges to the "no perks club" of many non-revenue-producing sports. There seems to be a distinction between revenue-producing and non-revenue-producing sport coaches' compensation not to mention gender-based salary equity concerns.

For the majority of coaches, however, at both the high school and college level, compensation for coaching is similar to pay for teaching. It needs to improve and should be a top priority.

Substance Abuse

Substance abuse among junior high, middle, high school, and college students is a reality that must be recognized, treated, and combated with preventive measures. The student-athlete has no immunity to the use of drugs among students. Indeed, athletes and anabolic-androgenic steroid abuse are often mentioned in the same breath, which tarnishes the traditional belief that the young athlete was somehow above substance abuse.

The substance abuse problem in the world of professional and Olympic sports continues to gain the most media attention. The news media, public, parents, student-athletes, and, particularly, educators and coaches, should be equally concerned about the young athlete. Substance use and addiction are not limited to the adult world; they endanger the entire younger generation.

The Drug Education Committee of the NCAA has indicated that most athletes bring their substance use habits with them when they come to the college campus.

Therefore the committee concluded that "it may be more effective to deal with the problem at the secondary school level."

Alcohol is the most commonly abused drug, with 93 out of every 100 young athletes eleven to fourteen years of age coming in contact with this element. Marijuana is the next most popular drug on the list. The U.S. Department of Health and Human Services has pointed out that approximately one out of every three high school seniors has tried marijuana before entering high school.

Young athletes who hope to give themselves more energy use agents such as cocaine, including its derivatives crack and ice, and uppers such as amphetamines, caffeine, and ephedrine. Anabolic steroids, human growth hormone (HGH), as well as creatine, are also being used by these sport neophytes who hope to make themselves bigger, quicker, and stronger for sport competition.

These drugs are taking their toll on our young athletes as well as on the community as a whole.

Growth potential and maturity are being hampered, and side effects are causing poor health not to mention impairment of motor function, slower reaction times, improper coordination with poor execution of movement, altered perception of speed, and withdrawal and loss of friends. In sum, users are experiencing academic, psychosocial, and vocational failure.

Some school districts and high school leagues are coming to grips with drug abuse. Programs designed to identify those students who come to school under the influence of alcohol or other drugs are being implemented throughout the nation. Those students who exhibit overt behavior of drug abuse are usually referred to the school principal. Students who voluntarily admit use of drugs are then referred to the student assistance and counseling program. Voluntary self-referral to the student assistance program for drug abuse in some school districts is not a violation of the athletic code and student-athletes can remain active participants. In many high schools, however, substance abuse is forbidden, and immediate suspension from the team for various time lengths is prescribed.

Robert Kanaby, executive director of the National Federation of State High School Associations (NFHS) (which represents 17,346 schools and approximately 6.9 million student-athletes), believes that a drug program should stress education rather than enforcement. Such programs should reach and be actively supported by coaches, officials, parents, students, and educators in general.

The Minnesota State High School League (MSHSL) has been proactively involved in providing student-focused chemical health awareness programs since the early 1980s. The league's programs (see "TARGET Minnesota" in appendix D) have served as models for the National Federation of State High School Association programs which were designed to assist other states in addressing chemical abuse. In 1985, the MSHSL, the state of Minnesota, the Hazelden Foundation, and the KROC Foundation (founded by Joan Kroc, widow of McDonald's founder and San Diego Padre owner Ray Kroc) cooperatively founded Operation CORK and have constructed a $7 million training and treatment facility at Hazelden in Center City, Minnesota devoted to drug prevention and education. The MSHSL in cooperation with its region committees also select drug-free student athlete/activities leaders to serve on their 16 regional TARGET teams that provide chemical health awareness training and information to regional schools.

Many universities and high schools and, most recently, Olympic and professional sport have taken a proactive stance toward substance abuse; some of those relevant ideas and initiatives as well as the NCAA list of banned drug classes are offered in appendix D.

MANAGEMENT GUIDELINES FOR COMPETITIVE SPORT PROGRAMS

Competitive sport programs have existed in schools, colleges, and universities since 1852 when the Harvard and Yale crews dueled on the calm water of the Winnipesaukee River in New Hampshire.

Elementary, Junior High, and Middle Schools

Since competitive sport was first introduced to college campuses throughout the United States, high schools have embraced sport as part of their educational offerings. As a result, most high schools in America today have some form of interscholastic sport. It did not take long for our junior high, middle, and elementary schools to feel the impact of interscholastic sport programs. A survey by the National Association of Secondary School Principals (which included 2,296 junior high schools) revealed that 85.2 percent had some program of interscholastic sport.

For the most part, interscholastic sport has been phased out of the elementary school level, where educators agree that physical activities should focus on the development of basic motor skills and positive attitudes toward physical activity. An informal recreational sport program should be a part of all elementary programs, as should traditional May Days, Field Days, or

Low-organized sport focusing on confidence and skill development. The Woodlands, Texas.

observances of events such as National Running and Fitness Week (May 14–20), at which competitive intramural and extramural sport may be introduced.

The special nature of grades 6 through 9, representing a transition period between the elementary school and the senior high school and between childhood and adolescence, has raised a question in the minds of many educators about whether an interscholastic sport program is in the best interests of the students. Many junior high and middle schools do, however, have football, soccer, basketball, volleyball, cross-country, and track and field for young boys and girls.

Management Guidelines for Elementary School Sport

Many of the guidelines of the American Academy of Pediatrics may be applied at the elementary school level and to the type of sport competition that should be offered:

- All children should have opportunities to develop skill in a variety of activities.
- All such activities should take into account the age and developmental level of the child.
- Sport activities of elementary school children should be part of an overall school program.

- Competent medical supervision of each child should be ensured.
- Health observation by teachers and others should be encouraged and help given by the physician.
- Sport activities outside the school program should be entirely voluntary without undue emphasis on any special program or sport and without undue emphasis on winning. These programs should also include competent medical supervision.
- Competition is an inherent characteristic of growing, developing children; therefore, competitive programs organized at the school, neighborhood, and community levels that meet the needs of children should be provided.
- State, regional, and national tournaments, bowl games, and charity and exhibition games are not recommended for this age-group. Commercial exploitation in any form should be avoided.
- Body-contact and collision sports, particularly tackle football and boxing, are considered a physical risk and have no place in programs for children of this age.
- All competitive sport programs at this level should be organized with the cooperation of interested medical groups, who will ensure adequate medical care before and during such programs. This care should include thorough physical examinations at specified intervals and advising parents and coaches about such factors as injury, response to fatigue, individual emotional needs, and the risks of undue physical and emotional strains.

With a proper blend of common sense and sound management and leadership, competitive sport activities at the elementary school level can lay the foundation for a lifetime of wholesome physical activity. The primary consideration should be toward a diversity of wholesome childhood experiences that will aid in the proper physical, psychosocial, emotional, and moral development of the child rather than toward highly organized competition and performance outcome.

Management Guidelines for Junior High and Middle School Sport

The research regarding a highly organized sport program at the junior high or middle school level indicates the following points of substantial agreement:

- This age range is a period of transition from elementary school to senior high school and from childhood to adolescence. It is a time when students are trying to understand their bodies, gain independence, achieve adult social status, acquire self-confidence and body image, and establish a system of values. It is a time when a challenging and enjoyable program of education unique to this age-group is crucial to meet the needs, abilities, and broadening interests of students.

- The best educational program at the junior high and middle school level provides for enrichment that meets the needs of students. A well-designed and coordinated educational climate for these grades is needed to ensure that the program will be meaningful and provide quality experiences as students transition into senior high school.

- Coaches are needed whose full responsibilities lie in the junior high or middle school and whose training is appropriate to the needs of these students.

- The junior high and middle school should provide for exploratory experiences with sport-specific specialization delayed through the completion of senior high school.

- The junior high and middle school competitive sport environment should provide for the physical, cognitive, social, mental, and emotional development of students as well as for the development of a sound foundation of values and personal responsibility.

- The principal, athletic and activities director, physical education teacher, and other members of management have the responsibility for providing sound educational leadership in all school matters. The type of physical education, recreational, and competitive sport programs offered will reflect the type of leadership provided.

The interscholastic sport program, if offered at this level, should be provided only after fulfilling the prerequisites of physical education programs, adapted/developmental programs, and recreational sport or intramural programs and only if special controls regarding health and safety, risk management, facilities, game adaptation and supervision, classification of players, leadership, and qualified, certified coaches, sports medicine staff, and officials have been provided.

The competitive sport program should offer a favorable social and emotional climate for the student. The program should provide freedom from anxiety and fear, absence of tensions and stress, a feeling of belonging for each student, a social awareness that contributes to the development of such important traits as respect for the rights of others, and an atmosphere conducive to growing into social and emotional maturity.

All sport activities should be professionally supervised and a physician or certified athletic trainer should be intimately involved to ensure optimal health and safety conditions.

Competition itself is not the factor that makes sport dangerous to the student. Instead, the crucial factors are items such as the manner in which the program is conducted, type of activity, administrative and coaching leadership, facilities, and the health status and physical condition of the participant.

Competitive sport, if properly conducted, has the potential for satisfying such basic psychological needs as recognition, belonging, self-respect, and the feeling of achievement as well as providing a wholesome outlet for the physical activity drive. However, if conducted in light of adult interests, community pressure, and other questionable influences, it can prove psychosocially harmful.

Interscholastic sports, when conducted in accordance with desirable standards of leadership, educational philosophy, and other pertinent factors, have the potential for providing beneficial social effects for the student; but when not conducted in accordance with desirable standards, interscholastic sports at this level can be physically and psychosocially detrimental to all involved.

Management Guidelines for Interscholastic and Intercollegiate Sport Programs

Selected recommended standards for high school and college sport programs follow.

Organization

The wholesome conduct of the sport programs should be the ultimate responsibility of the school administration along with the school board or board of regents.

Sport policy should be developed, evaluated, modified when necessary, and supervised by an athletic or sport council, athletic association or faculty athletic committee. Sport policy should be implemented by the director of athletics and activities.

Sport should be organized as an integral part of the department of physical education at the high school level and should maintain strong positive relationships with associated departments (e.g., physical education, kinesiology, sport and leisure studies, business, public health, physical therapy) at the collegiate level.

Staff

Ideally, members of the coaching staff should be members of the faculty.

This is, of course, impossible for most large colleges; however, the focus when hiring coaches should remain on educational qualifications and not solely on their ability to produce winning teams.

Coaches should enjoy the same privileges of tenure, rank, and salary accorded other similarly qualified faculty members. This remains a major point of contention at many large universities.

High school coaches should be certified educators and hold a coaching minor or coaching certification including current first aid and CPR/AED training.

Good officiating is requisite for the protection and safety of the participant. Minnesota State High School League soccer play-off.

Finances

The financing of interscholastic and intercollegiate sport should be governed by the same policies that control the financing of all other educational activities within an institution.

Gate receipts and student fees should be considered a supplemental source of revenue, as should the myriad revenue streams ranging from TV to fund-raising and sponsorship ventures undertaken by both schools and colleges and their respective booster organizations.

Health, Safety, and Risk Management

Each school and participating partner should have an enterprise risk management plan that helps insure effective reporting and compliance with laws and regulations. This plan also helps avoid dangers to the school or institution's reputation and other risks (strategic, financial, operational, compliance) and associated consequences. An annual, thorough, preparticipation medical examination should be required of all participants; a physical examination on a seasonal basis would be preferable.

Each school should have a written policy outlining the responsibility for sport-related injuries and should provide or make available athletic accident insurance.

Each school should have a written policy for the implementation of an injury care and rehabilitation program.

A physician and certified athletic trainer should be present at all sport contests.

Only equipment that is fully certified as offering the best protection for the student-athlete should be purchased and utilized.

All protective equipment should fit players properly.

Competition should be scheduled between teams of comparable ability.

Games should not be played until players have had a minimum of two to three weeks of prudent and progressive physical training and conditioning.

Playing fields and surfaces should meet standards for size and safety for the participants.

Eligibility

All schools should join and fully participate, honor, and respect the eligibility rules and regulations of respective local, state, national, and international governing bodies and sport associations. Most schools and colleges have athletic councils, faculty athletic committees, and compliance officers who certify the integrity of this process.

Recruiting

The sport teams of each school should be composed of bona fide student-athletes who live in the school district or who were attracted to the institution by its educational programs. This is similar for most college student-athletes; however, contemporary sports recruiting and sport participation know no geographic or socioeconomic boundary and have provided an opportunity for many to gain a valuable and meaningful educational experience.

All candidates for admission to a school should be evaluated according to similar standards.

All financial aid should be administered with regard to need and according to the same standards for all students. The recipient of financial aid should be provided a statement of the amount, duration, and conditions of the award.

Sport scholarships, when possible, should be allocated on a full rather than partial basis to avoid inequitable distribution among team members. However, many coaches of nonrevenue sports choose to disperse their aid to a greater number of student-athletes to ensure team depth and interest.

Awards and Honors

The value of sport awards and honors is sometimes questioned. However, when the program is properly managed and kept in perspective, awards are a meaningful part of high school and college sport programs and are a positive recognition of hard work, dedication, skill, and school commitment. Many institutions have developed comprehensive award programs in which scholar-athlete honors and all-academic honors share the spotlight with traditional sport awards such as all-state, all-district, all-conference, and most valuable player.

Evaluation

Just as evaluation and assessment of physical education instructional programs, recreational sport programs, coaches, and officials should be practiced on an ongoing basis, so should evaluation and assessment of interscholastic and intercollegiate sports programs (see box 5-4). This scrutiny, sometimes from an external audit team, helps ensure, maintain, and enhance the quality and delivery of competitive sport programs.

Management Guidelines for Competitive Sport Programs in Other Organizations

Competitive sport programs also exist in forms other than the formal educational setting. Community organizations and businesses, recreation and park districts, Ys, and the traditional golf and

Box 5-4 Evaluation of a High School Sport Program

	Yes	No

1. Sport program as an integral part of total curriculum
    a. The sports are an outgrowth of the physical education program.
    b. A variety of sports is available for all students.
    c. The educational values of sport are foremost in the program's philosophy.
    d. All students have an opportunity to participate in a sport.
    e. Sports are used appropriately as a school's unifying force.
    f. Athletes are not excused from courses, including physical education, because of sport participation.
2. Coaches as faculty members
    a. Coaches have an adequate opportunity to exercise the same rights and privileges as other faculty members in determining school and curricular matters.
    b. Coaches attend, and they are scheduled so that they may attend, faculty meetings.
    c. Coaches are not expected to assume more duties of a general nature than are other faculty members.
    d. Tenure and other faculty privileges are available to coaches.
    e. Assignments for extra duties are made for coaches on the same basis as for other teachers.
3. Participants encouraged to perform adequately in academic areas
    a. Athletes are held accountable scholastically at the same level as other students.
    b. Practices are of such length and intensity that they do not deter students' academic pursuits.
    c. Game trips do not cause the students to miss an excessive number of classes.
    d. Counseling and support services emphasize the importance of academic performance on career education.
    e. Athletes are required to attend classes on days of contests.
4. Meeting philosophy of school board
    a. New coaches are made aware of the board policies and informed that they will be expected to follow them in spirit as well as to the letter.
    b. All coaches are regularly informed by the principal and athletic and activities director that they must conduct their programs within the framework of board policy.
    c. A procedure is available for the athletic and activities director and coaches to make recommendations regarding policy change.
    d. Noncoaching faculty members are made aware of board policy regarding sport so that they may discuss it from a base of fact.
    e. The philosophy of the board is written and made available to all personnel.
5. Awards
    a. Only those awards authorized by local conferences, state high school athletic associations, and NCAA or similar organizations are awarded.
    b. Diligence is exercised to ensure that outside groups or individuals do not cause violations of the award regulations.
    c. Care is taken to ensure that student-athletes are not granted privileges not available to the general student body.

Continued

Box 5-4   Evaluation of a High School Sport Program—cont'd

6. Projected program outcomes
   a. It is emphasized that participation in sport is a privilege.   _____ _____
   b. Development of critical thinking, decision making, and personal responsbility, as well   _____ _____
      as sport performance outcomes, are integral to the program.
   c. Development of self-direction and individual motivation are integral parts of the sport-   _____ _____
      ing experience.
   d. The athletes are allowed to develop at their own physical, cognitive, psychomotor, and   _____ _____
      affective readiness paces.
   e. Appropriate and accepted social values are used as standards of behavior both on and   _____ _____
      off the playing area.
7. Guarding against student exploitation
   a. The student is not used in sport performance to provide an activity that has as its main   _____ _____
      purpose entertainment of the community.
   b. The student's academic program is in no way altered to allow continued eligibility with_____ _____
      less than normal effort and academic progress.
   c. The students are not given a false impression of their ability through the device of sug-   _____ _____
      gesting the possibility of a college scholarship or professional career.
   d. The athletes are not given a false image of the value of athletic prowess to the sociocul-_____ _____
      tural success of a school and/or community.

Source: Adapted from the National Council of Secondary School Athletic Directors.

tennis clubs offer tremendous opportunities for all age-groups to compete. State games, senior games, local sports festivals, police athletic leagues, church leagues, aquatic clubs, Athletes in Action, Special Olympics, and the military are just some of the many sports delivery systems available to the competitive sport consumer.

These sport programs should be geared to the age, developmental level, and needs of the participants. Youth-serving agencies, for example, should observe the established standards for interscholastic programs, whereas adults and seniors might follow the standards applicable at the college and university level. Many advantages accrue from belonging to leagues and conferences rather than playing independently. Leagues and conferences often promote established procedures, rules, and regulations that are more likely to benefit the participant than if a team were organized independently.

Usually sports sponsored by educational institutions take special pains to provide for the health and safety of the participants. They fre-quently provide insurance options, physicians and certified athletic trainers, access to transportation, appropriate facilities and equipment, and other provisions that help guarantee safer participation.

Sometimes highly competitive sport programs in other organizations do not have the same concern for the safety and well-being of the players, especially as the participant gets older (e.g., senior rugby and soccer leagues); as a result, players sometimes participate more at their own risk than do players in institutionalized school sport.

It would be helpful if all sport organizations would examine and apply many of the procedures and standards set forth in this chapter designed for educational institutions.

Management Guidelines for Sport for People with Varying Disabilities

Persons with disabilities can receive the same benefits as well as harm from a program of competitive sport as does their nondisabled peer group.

The following reasons for including adapted or unified sport activities in the school sport programs are listed by Auxter, Pyfer, and Huettig (2005).

Many students assigned to an adapted physical education class are unable to correct an existing condition and also are unable to participate in regular physical education. A program of adapted sport would be ideal for such students because it would provide them additional opportunities to participate in various forms of physical activity, not to mention school life experiences.

Students in the adapted/developmental sport program need activities that have carryover value. They may continue exercise and fitness programs in the future, but they also need training in sports and games that will be useful in later life, such as learning to handle his or her body under a variety of circumstances that may assist in both the physical and mental (i.e., discipline, perseverance, personal responsibility) conduct of daily living.

A certain amount of emotional release also takes place in sport activities, and this release is just as important to the student-athlete with a disability as it is for the nondisabled student-athlete.

The Joseph P. Kennedy Jr. Foundation probably has focused more attention on sport for persons with disabilities than any other single organization. The most visible activity promoted by the Kennedy Foundation is the Special Olympics, which was organized in 1968. It was designed to provide mentally retarded youths, eight years of age and over, with opportunities to participate in a variety of sports and games on local, state, regional, national, and international levels.

The basic objectives of the Special Olympics follow:

- Encourage development of comprehensive physical education and recreation programs for the mentally impaired in schools, day-care centers, and residential facilities in every community.

Eunice Kennedy Shriver, founder of Special Olympics International.

- Prepare the impaired for sport competition—particularly where no opportunities and programs now exist.
- Supplement existing activities and programs in schools, communities, day-care centers, and residential facilities.
- Provide training for volunteer coaches to enable them to work with youth in physical fitness, recreation, and sports activities.

Since the enactment of the Amateur Sports Act of 1978, P.L. 95-606, the Committee on Sport for the Disabled (COSD) was established by the U.S. Olympic Committee, and other groups and associations have taken up the challenge to provide sport opportunities for athletes with disabilities (see appendix E). In 1995 the Minnesota State High School League became the first state league to offer high school tournaments for student-athletes with disabilities. Clearly we have a challenge within this crucial arena to provide safe and healthy sports experiences for all.

TITLE IX AND THE CHANGING ROLE OF GIRLS' AND WOMEN'S SPORT COMPETITION

Proponents of equality in girls' and women's sport and Title IX have continued to open the window of opportunity for participation in women's sport. Women have become accepted as athletes with full rights to join and experience the competitive sporting process so long restricted by our gender-dominated society.

Procedures and practices concerning inter-scholastic and intercollegiate sport competition for females vary from school to school, state to state, and university to university. Some schools and colleges have wide-ranging programs of interscholastic and intercollegiate sports, whereas others maintain limited opportunities to compete at the varsity level. Most states have not set up specific requirements for girls' sport, but believe that their established regulations apply to both girls and boys. A few universities still maintain independent men's and women's athletic departments (e.g., University of Tennessee, University of Arkansas, and Brigham Young University).

The National Association for Girls and Women in Sport (NAGWS) of AAHPERD (1977) helped launch the drive so that opportunities were provided for all girls and women who wanted to participate in competitive sport. Adequate and equitable funds, scholarship support, salaries, facilities, and support staff should be provided for these programs.

Title IX*

Although the 92nd Congress passed the Education Amendments Act on June 23, 1972, Section 901(a) (Title IX as it is commonly referred to) was not signed into law until 1975. Title IX of the Education Amendments Act of 1972 is a federal law that prohibits sex discrimination in any educational program or activity at any educational institution that is a recipient of federal funds. The "treatment" of students was considered inclusive of areas such as housing, course offerings such as physical education (presented in chapter 3), admissions, counseling, financial aid, insurance benefits, employment assistance, drama, band and other extracurricular activities, and sport participation. Although Title IX applied to all types of institutional programs, the most dramatically affected programs have been those associated with sport. This attention was not without reason. Research at that time indicated that budget dollars directed toward women's intercollegiate athletics were approximately 2 percent compared to men's revenue share, even though 15 percent of the participants at this level were female. Legal suits concerning basketball, baseball, golf, tennis, and track and field were levied in states ranging from New York to California (Clement 2004).

---

*Parts of this section have been taken directly from government documents relating to Title IX, particularly the following documents:

U.S. Department of Health, Education, and Welfare, Office of Civil Rights. 1995. *Final Title IX regulation implementing Education Amendments of 1972—prohibiting sex discrimination in education.* Washington, DC: U.S. Government Printing Office. July.

U.S. Department of Health, Education, and Welfare, Office for Civil Rights. 1975. *Memorandum to chief state school officers, superintendents of local educational agencies and college and university presidents; subject: elimination of sex discrimination in athletic programs.* Washington, DC: U.S. Government Printing Office. September.

Title IX of the Education Amendments of 1972, 1979. A policy interpretation: Title IX and intercollegiate athletics. *Federal Register* 44 (11 December): 227.

Title IX has provided increased opportunity for girls and women to participate in sport.

Since the passage of Title IX, girls' and women's sports programs have grown rapidly, and today, girls' and women's interscholastic and intercollegiate sport teams are in full evidence throughout the nation, providing athletes with challenges and championships on an equal basis with their male counterparts. Sport once again has contributed to breaking down discriminatory social barriers (e.g., gender, race, ethnicity, age), but although great strides have been taken, it is clear that we have a way to go to total equality in sport opportunity and delivery (Eitzen and Sage 2003).

Provisions of Title IX Affecting Sport Programs

Chapter 3 contained some background information about Title IX of the Education Amendments Act of 1972 and how its interpretation has influenced physical education programs. The following section offers some of the provisions of Title IX specifically affecting sport programs.

- Separate teams for boys and girls, or a coeducational team, must be provided in schools and colleges. For example, if there is only one team in a particular sport, such as swimming or nordic skiing, then students of both sexes must be permitted to try out for this team.

- Equal opportunities must be provided for both sexes in the educational institution in terms of competitive training facilities, equipment and supplies, facilities for practice and games, medical and athletic training services, coaching and academic support services such as tutoring, travel and per diem allowances, housing and dining facilities, compensation of coaches, and publicity. Equal aggregate expenditures are not required; however, equal opportunity for men and women is mandated. In situations in which men are given the opportunity for athletic scholarships, women must be given the same opportunity. Contact and collision sports such as football, basketball, boxing, wrestling, rugby, and ice hockey may be offered either separately or on a unitary basis.

- The emphasis of Title IX is to provide equal opportunity for both sexes. In determining whether equal opportunity is provided, it is important to know whether the interests and abilities of students of both sexes have been met and whether such items as adequate coaching, facilities, academic support, and equipment are equally available.

■ Title IX guidelines provide that expenditures on men's and women's sport be proportional to the number of men and women participating. This standard of substantially equal per capita expenditures must be met unless the institution can demonstrate that the differences are based on nondiscriminatory factors, such as the costs of a particular sport (e.g., the equipment required in football) or the scope of the competition (national rather than regional or local). This proportional standard applies to athletic scholarships, recruitment, and other readily measurable financial benefits such as equipment, supplies, travel, recruiting, and publicity.

■ According to the Department of Health and Human Services, the policy is designed to eliminate, over a reasonable period of time, the discriminatory effects, particularly at the college level, of the historic emphasis on men's sport and to facilitate the continued growth of women's sport. It requires colleges and universities to take specific steps to provide additional competitive sport opportunities for women—opportunities that will fully accommodate the increasing interest of women participating in sport.

Procedures for Assuring Compliance With Title IX

To make sure the provisions of Title IX have been complied with by an educational institution, certain procedures should be followed. Each educational institution usually has some member of the faculty or staff coordinate a self-evaluation and ensure compliance. Some universities have employed a full-time compliance officer.

The steps that have been followed in some sport programs involve first developing a statement of philosophy that provides a guide for equality of opportunity for both sexes. Then student

interest is determined about the activities in which students desire to participate. In addition, all written materials concerned with items such as mission statements, curriculum, employment, job descriptions, and organizational structures are reviewed to see that needed changes are made to ensure that equal and fair inclusion is described. Also, such factors as game and practice scheduling times for all teams, provision for supplies and equipment, travel expenses, number of coaches and support staff assigned to teams, and salaries of coaches are examined to see if any discrepancies exist between the sexes. The membership requirements for clubs and other student organizations associated with sport are also reviewed. The amount of publicity and information services provided for physical education and sport programs are checked. Eligibility requirements for scholarships and financial aid, medical and accident policies, award systems, and employment procedures are examined. Teaching loads, coaching assignments, coaches' gender, and facility (e.g., training, medical, housing, dining) assignments are also included in the appraisal.

According to Carpenter and Acosta (2005), many questions can be asked to determine if equality exists for men's and women's programs. For example, the question about *employment conditions* might be "Are men and women compensated the same for essentially the same work for both teaching and coaching?" For *physical education classes* the question might be "Are physical education requirements for graduation the same for boys and girls, men and women?" For *recreational sport opportunities,* "Are recreational sport programs provided for both sexes?" For *competitive sport,* "Does the total budget reflect comparable support to both the men's and women's programs?" Many other questions for determining if equality exists are listed in publications by AAHPERD and the Women's Sports Foundation.

One of the most effective methods for ensuring compliance has been the Department of Health and Human Services' three-prong test for institutional compliance and its continuous policy interpretations. To be in compliance, athletic programs must demonstrate one of the following:

Dedicated leaders including Julie Foudy, Holly Hunter, Geena Davis, and Dr. Donna Lopiano work hard to ensure Title IX will keep a level playing field.

1. That intercollegiate participation opportunities for its students of each sex are substantially proportionate to its male and female undergraduate enrollments, or

2. a history and continuing practice of program expansion responsive to developing interests and abilities of members of the underrepresented gender, or

3. that the interests and abilities of the "underrepresented sex" are "fully and effectively" accommodated by the existing program.

Compliance is established by satisfying any one of these three tests (Clement 2004).

The Office of Civil Rights is not only an enforcement agency, it can receive and initiate violation complaints. If found in violation, the institution has ninety days to voluntarily respond with a compliance agreement contract including a time frame for compliance attainment. Only when the institution fails to meet this agreement is it found in noncompliance; at that time, federal funds could be withheld or legal action seeking damages could be initiated.

A project of the Women's Equity Action League Educational and Legal Defense Fund has offered the following pros and cons of bringing a legal suit.

Some Pros of Filing a Complaint

It is possible to win! You may convince others to take legal action for other complaints. You may change discriminatory practices at your school or college. Many girls and women may benefit from your action. Your action may result in the Title IX compliance plan at your school becoming the subject of scrutiny. Schools that have been cited for complaints are more likely to come closer to compliance. You can seek and potentially win or settle for legal fees and damages.

Some Cons of Filing a Complaint

You can lose! You may lose your position or scholarship and be labeled a troublemaker. You may become frustrated in dealing with the many organizations' legal concerns involved. The procedure sometimes takes years to resolve.

Organizations that may be of help in case it is found that inequality exists are the Department of Health and Human Services; Office for Civil Rights; Equal Employment Opportunity Commission; Office of Federal Contract Compliance; and the U.S. Department of Labor–Wage and Hour Division of the Employment Standards Administration.

Title IX sport complaints have been filed against numerous institutions. The complaints are usually filed with the regional Office of Civil Rights and have been referred to the national headquarters in Washington, D.C.

Coeducational Sport and Title IX

Coeducational sport should be provided for students in schools and institutions of higher education because of the benefits that can accrue from such participation. In instances in which highly skilled females would not otherwise have the opportunity to participate in a particular sport, they must be allowed to participate on male teams. However, coeducational sport, in most cases, has been limited to the recreational sport level.

The primary reason for not advocating coeducational sport participation on interscholastic and intercollegiate levels in many sports is the physical difference between males and females. The ratio of strength to weight is greater in males than in females. Females thus would be at a decided disadvantage in those sports requiring speed, power, strength, and impact. As a consequence, teams would be male dominated.

The Impact of Title IX on Girls and Women in Sport

During the year before the birth of Title IX, 3,366,000 boys and 294,000 girls competed in interscholastic sport in the United States. After ten years, that figure increased to over 3,500,000 boys and 1,810,671 girls, and today, the National Federation of State High School Associations reports that 2,865,299 of the 6,903,522 participants in interscholastic sports are girls. Furthermore, the participation of girls increased from a pre– Title IX figure of 8 percent of the total number of students involved to 40 percent. Girls participate in more than twenty-nine high school sports. The five most popular sports, in terms of schools sponsoring teams and number of participants, are basketball, track and field, volleyball, softball, and soccer. College participation for women has more than quadrupled from 31,000 to 146,657 participants. Approximately 500 colleges offer sport scholarships to women athletes, and women receive almost 40 percent of the current scholarship pool of funds while making up 53 percent of the total undergraduate enrollment. Since the early 1980s when the NCAA took over the AIAW (despite its antitrust law suit—AIAW vs. NCAA, 1983, 506), the NCAA has provided increased opportunities for young women to participate in myriad championship events.

Although sport programs for men and women are still not equal in terms of funding, (i.e., budgets for boys' sport activities at the interscholastic level are on the average larger than those for girls' sport activities), sport programs for male and female student-athletes on all levels are far more equal, as well as more numerous, than ever before. It is unfortunate that financial constraints are now also equally affecting men's and women's programs, resulting in some significant loss of both men's (i.e., wrestling, gymnastics, and baseball) and women's sports, especially at the collegiate level.

Legislation such as Title IX has had, for the most part, a positive impact. One negative impact of Title IX, however, is that the number of female coaches in girls' and women's sport programs has decreased dramatically, from about 90 percent in the early 1970s to around 50 percent in the mid-1990s to about 44 percent today (Acosta and Carpenter 2004).

Title IX, the Courts, and Prospects for the Future

Since the passage of Title IX, the courts have played a crucial role in effecting change toward equality. The courts have caused some changes in Title IX. The 1984 U.S. Supreme Court decision in *Grove City College v. Bell* changed the interpretation of Title IX as formerly held. The court ruled that only the student aid office at Grove City College was covered by laws barring sex bias, because the only federal money that the institution received came through student aid Pell Grants. In the case of private institutions that received direct federal aid, the U.S. Commission on Civil Rights stated that only the program or activity that actually received the aid need abide by Title IX regulations. In other words, the federal law barring sex discrimination in education, according to the Grove City ruling, did not apply to schools and colleges as a whole, but only to those parts or subunits of an institution that directly received federal aid. The court ruling meant, for example, that if the sport programs do not receive federal aid directly, they are not covered by Title IX. This ruling raised a storm of protest from the Office of Civil Rights and other organizations supporting the original concept of Title IX—if an institution receives federal aid, then all programs within that organization should be covered by Title IX regulations. On March 2, 1988, the U.S. Senate voted 75 to 14 to approve Senate Bill 557, the Civil Rights Restoration Act, which served to counteract the 1984 Grove City College decision and return the enforcement of Title IX to an institutional rather than specific subunit basis.

Each institution and each educational program will face continued challenges in complying with Title IX. This challenge is true particularly in light of the budget crises that many schools and colleges face at present. For example, it will be difficult for many institutions to increase, or even maintain, budget items such as academic support services, scholarships, and facilities for an expanded sport program for girls and women without curtailing some other parts of the educational program at the same time. More realistically, it will become even more difficult to bear the increased costs of present sport programming that now provide females and males with comparable sport programs. If proportioned equally, however, reductions in programs would further serve to reduce the opportunities for girls and women to participate, causing compliance complications. Class action suits at Brown University, Indiana University of Pennsylvania, Colorado State University, and West Chester State University—because each institution attempted athletic department cost cutting by eliminating women's sports such as gymnastics, volleyball, field hockey, and softball—attest to the ongoing battle to keep or reinstate programs that were discontinued. Each suit led to reinstatement. Scholastic sports associations of Kentucky, Michigan, Montana, and Virginia have also been brought to court to equal the "playing field."

Many changes have taken place to comply with the spirit of Title IX. Sports such as soccer, rowing, ice hockey, lacrosse, rifle/pistol shooting, skiing, and water polo have been rapidly expanding at the college level, where women make up approximately 40 percent of all student-athletes (a 25 percent increase since 1992). These changes and others, although not completely leveling the playing field, are positive steps in breaking down the equity barrier in the arena of competitive sport. Title IX has cleared the way for behavioral change to take place concerning women's participation not only in the domain of competitive sport but also in all of society. While great strides have been made, clearly women's head coaching and administrative position appointments remain a work in progress.

SELECTED SPORTING ASSOCIATIONS

An individual school or college, by itself, finds it difficult to develop standards and control sport in a sound educational manner. However, uniting with similar schools and colleges makes such a formidable task possible. This coordinating has been done on local, state, regional, and national levels in the interest of enhanced sport for high schools and colleges. Establishing rules, policies, and procedures well in advance of playing seasons provides educators, sports managers, athletics and activities directors, and coaches the necessary guidelines and control for conducting sound competitive sport programs. It aids them in resisting pressures of alumni, students, parents, spectators, community, media, and others who do not always have the best interests of the student-athlete and the program in mind.

Various types of sport associations exist. The ones most prevalent in high schools and colleges are student athletic associations, local conferences or leagues, state high school associations or leagues, the National Federation of State High School Associations, the National Association of Intercollegiate Athletes, the National Collegiate Athletic Association, and their respective conferences that exist throughout the nation.

The student athletic association or board is an organization within a school designed to actively promote and participate in the conduct of the school sport program. It is usually open to all students who elect to pay fees, which further help support the competitive sport program. Such associations are found in many high schools and colleges throughout the country. These associations assist in the mobilization of ticket sales, program and event publicity and promotion, and overall school spirit and enthusiasm. Once mobilized, they add another educational component and dimension to the management structure of a well-managed sport program.

Various associations or boards, conferences, or leagues also bind together to facilitate sport competition and scheduling as well as to reduce travel expense. Usually several high schools within a particular geographical area will become members of a conference in order to construct schedules, assign officials, handle disputes, and maintain general guidance over the sport programs of the member schools.

The state high school athletic association or league that now exists in almost every state is yet another major influence in high school sport. The state association is usually open to all professionally accredited high schools within the state. It operates under a constitution, employs an administrative core of officers to conduct business, and usually possesses a board of directors. The number of members on the board varies widely but the board usually has a representative from each district or region. Fees or dues are usually assessed by the association on a per school basis or sometimes according to the size of the school or number of sports offered. Some states have no fees because the necessary revenue is derived from the gate receipts, sponsorships, and/or television revenue from tournament competition. State associations are interested in sound programs of sport competition within the confines of the state. They concern themselves with the usual problems that have to do with sport, such as eligibility of players, certification of coaches and officials, conduct of coaches, provision of assistance in the handling of protests and disputes, and the organization and conduct of state tournaments. These state associations are interested in promoting sound high school sport practices for all, equalizing athletic competition, protecting participants, and guarding the health, safety, and welfare of players. In some states, such as Minnesota, the association operates drug awareness and leadership programs throughout the state. State associations have been a positive influence and have won the respect of school administrators, coaches, and educators.

National Association for Girls and Women in Sport

Founded in 1899, as its own standing organization, the National Association for Girls and Women in Sport (NAGWS) is now one of the six associations of AAHPERD and is concerned with the conduct of sports for girls and women.

NAGWS strives to develop and deliver equitable and quality sport opportunities for "ALL" girls and women through relevant research, advocacy, leadership development, educational strategies, and programming in a manner that promotes social justice and change.

The specific goals of the NAGWS are to do the following:

- Increase programs and services for underserved populations.
- Maximize the utilization of members' professional expertise.
- Cultivate an active, involved, knowledgeable, and diverse membership.
- Develop and increase involvement at the grassroots level.
- Advocate for U.S. government laws and policies.
- Maintain and increase the number and quality of collaborative efforts.
- Capitalize on sport as a viable business.
- Capitalize on AAHPERD services in ways that enhance the work of NAGWS.
- Raise awareness of how legal, political, and social justice issues impact ALL girls and women in sport.

NAGWS offers gender-equity training to communities in their efforts to promote equity in the gymnasium, as well as on the field (Backyard and Beyond Program). They also sponsor National Girls and Women in Sports Day (in February), produce a host of professional development materials ranging from textbooks to community action tool kits, and twice a year publish the online *Women in Sport and Physical Activity Journal* (WSPAJ).

The National Council of Secondary School Athletic Directors

AAHPERD's National Association for Sport and Physical Education (NASPE) established the National Council of Secondary School Athletic Directors (NCSSAD) in the mid-1970s. The increased emphasis on sport and the important position of athletic and activities directors in the nation's secondary schools warranted a council by which increased services could be rendered to enhance the programs offered to the nation's youth. The membership in the National Council is open to members of AAHPERD who have primary responsibility in directing, administering, or coordinating interscholastic sport programs. The mission of NCSSAD is to extend professional services to secondary school athletic administrators and to enhance their professional status. The NCSSAD also looks to support and strengthen the role that secondary school athletic administrators play in helping to attain the educational objectives of secondary school education.

The purposes of the Council remain:

- to improve the educational aspects of interscholastic sport and their articulation in the total educational program
- to foster high standards of professional proficiency and ethics
- to improve understanding of sport throughout the nation
- to establish closer working relationships with related professional groups
- to promote greater unity, goodwill, and fellowship among all members
- to serve as a clearinghouse providing for an exchange of ideas
- to assist and cooperate with existing state and regional athletic directors' organizations
- to improve athletic administration by providing a national forum for the exchange of current practices and trends
- to make available to members special resource materials through publications, conferences, and consultant services

NCSSAD initiatives include accreditation of coaching education and national standards of coaching.

The National Federation of State High School Associations

High school competition for boys began in Michigan in the late 1890s and, subsequently, a Michigan state athletic association was developed. By the turn of the century, Illinois and Indiana had followed Michigan's lead. In New York, Luther Gulick established the New York City Public School Athletic League in 1903, which was followed in 1905 by the founding of a girls' branch under the direction of Elizabeth Burchenal. The Ohio High School Athletic Association was established in 1907.

The Midwest Federation of State High School Athletic Associations was established in 1920 with five states (Illinois, Indiana, Iowa, Michigan, and Wisconsin) participating. In 1923 the Federation became national in name and scope, and in the 1970s, Athletic was dropped from its title. Today all states and the District of Columbia, as well as eight Canadian associations, are included in the NFHS ranks. The National Federation is particularly concerned with the conduct of interstate sport competitions. Its constitution offers these objectives:

- To serve, protect, and enhance the interscholastic programs provided by the members for their schools and students
- To promote the educational values of interscholastic athletics and activities
- To regulate those activities which, in the determination of the members, can best be administered on a national level
- To sponsor meetings, publications, and activities for the benefit of members, related professional groups, and their constituents
- To promote efficiency in the administration of interscholastic athletics and activities
- To formulate, copyright, and publish competition rules for interscholastic athletics and activities
- To preserve interscholastic athletic records and the tradition and heritage of interscholastic sports
- To provide programs, services, materials, and assistance to members and individual professionals involved in the conduct and administration of interscholastic athletics and activities
- To serve as a national information resource for interscholastic athletics and activities
- To identify needs and problems related to interscholastic athletics and activities, and to work toward their solution

The NFHS's coaching arm, the National Federation Coaching Association (NFCA), offers the NFHS/ASEP Coaching Education Program, as well as liability and accident protection for its 155,000 members. The NFHS sponsors National High School Activities Week (in October), publishes the NFHS *Coaches and Officials Quarterly* magazines, and provides educational training programs to athletic and activities directors, officials, and its music, speech, and spirit divisions. The NFHS also offers playing rulebooks for seventeen sports, a video professional development series, and the *National High School Record Book*.

The National Federation has been responsible for many improvements in sport on a national scale, ranging from the delivery of leadership and officials training to its Citizenship Through Sport curriculum. The NFHS is housed in Indianapolis, Indiana.

The National Collegiate Athletic Association

The National Collegiate Athletic Association (NCAA) was formed in 1906. The alarming number of football injuries and the fact that there was no institutional control of the game led to a conference in New York City on December 12, 1905, attended by representatives from thirteen universities and colleges. Preliminary plans were made for a national agency to assist in the formulation of sound requirements for intercollegiate athletics, particularly football, and the name Intercollegiate Athletic Association (IAA) was suggested. At a meeting on March 31, 1906, a constitution and bylaws were adopted and issued. On December 29, 1910, the name of the IAA was changed to NCAA. Its first championship (track and field) was held in 1921. The purposes of the NCAA are as follows:

- To initiate, stimulate, and improve intercollegiate athletics programs for student-athletes, and to promote and develop educational leadership, physical fitness, athletics excellence, and athletics participation as a recreational pursuit
- To uphold the principle of institutional control of, and responsibility for, all intercollegiate

The NCAA conducts eighty-eight men's and women's championships in twenty-six sports.

sports in conformity with the constitution and bylaws of this association

- To encourage its members to adopt eligibility rules to comply with satisfactory standards of scholarship, sportsmanship, and amateurism
- To formulate, copyright, and publish rules of play governing intercollegiate athletics
- To preserve intercollegiate athletics records
- To supervise the conduct of, and to establish eligibility standards for, regional and national athletics events under the auspices of this association
- To cooperate with other amateur athletics organizations in promoting and conducting national and international athletics events
- To legislate, through bylaws or by resolutions of a convention, upon any subject of general

concern to the members related to the administration of intercollegiate athletics

- To study in general all phases of competitive intercollegiate athletics, and establish standards whereby the colleges and universities of the United States can maintain their athletics programs on a high level

Membership in the NCAA numbers more than 1,000 colleges and universities and over 130 conferences categorized in three divisions. The NCAA requires that an institution be accredited by a recognized academic accrediting body and compete in at least four sports for men and four for women each year, with at least one sport sponsored in each of the three traditional sport seasons.

The services provided by the NCAA are as extensive as its stated purposes for existence. These services include publication of official guides in various sports, provision of a film and video library, establishment of an eligibility code for athletes and provisions for the enforcement of this code, provisions for national meets and tournaments (such as the CBS's $6 billion basketball championship contract over 11 years) with appropriate eligibility rules for competition, provision of financial and other assistance to groups interested in the promotion and encouragement of intercollegiate and recreational sport, and provision of administrative services for U.S. universities and colleges concerning matters of international competition and student-athletes (insurance, postgraduate scholarships, community service). The NCAA headquarters is located in Indianapolis and offers eighty-eight women's and men's championships in twenty-six sports at the Division I, II, and III levels. From 2000 to 2001, 149,115 young women and 206,573 young men participated under the NCAA umbrella, with more than 44,600 student-athletes participating in championship events.

The National Association of Intercollegiate Athletics

Another sport association on the college and university level is the National Association of Intercollegiate Athletics (NAIA), which is located in Olathe,

Kansas. The NAIA has a membership of 290 institutions, mostly among the smaller colleges. This organization was instituted in 1937 as a basketball tournament association (National Association of Intercollegiate Basketball) and by 1952 emerged as a total sport association. Its primary function is to promote the education and development of students through intercollegiate athletic participation for those young men and women competing outside the "big-time" NCAA Division I level.

The NAIA hosts twenty-three national championships in thirteen sports for over 48,000 participants. One of its primary initiatives is its "Champions of Character" program, which focuses on respect, integrity, responsibility, servant leadership, and sportsmanship and serves as a model for youth sport character development. Its future goals include establishing an interactive sport museum and a Hall of Fame as it transitions into its new headquarters.

The National Junior College Athletic Association

The National Junior College Athletic Association (NJCAA) is an organization of junior colleges that has sponsored sport programs since its inception in 1937 in Fresno, California. It now has twenty-four regional offices with an elected regional director for each. Regional business matters are conducted within the framework of the constitution and bylaws of the parent organization. The regional directors, who are governed by an executive committee, hold an annual legislative assembly to determine the policies, programs, and procedures for the organization. The assembly's location rotates between NJCAA headquarters in Colorado Springs, Colorado (odd years), and regional sites (even years). The *Juco Review* is the official publication of the organization. Standing and special committees are appointed each year to cover special items and problems that develop. The role and membership guidelines of the NJCAA closely follow those outlined by the NCAA.

National championships, including nine Bowl games, are conducted in fifteen sports for men and thirteen for women of its more than 530 institutional members. The NJCAA is affiliated with the

National Federation of State High School Associations, the National Association of Intercollegiate Athletics, the United States Sports Academy, AAHPERD, the United States Olympic Committee, and the Women's Sports Foundation.

Some of the services offered by the NJCAA to its members include recognition of organizations and athletes, recognition in official records, a film and video library, and publications including guide books, a record book, and a professional handbook/casebook.

Amateur Athletic Union of the United States

Founded in 1888, the Amateur Athletic Union (AAU) of the United States is one of the oldest and largest single, nonprofit, volunteer organizations designed to regulate and promote the conduct of amateur sport. It serves over 500,000 participants, involves over 50,000 volunteers, and has "Sports for All, Forever" as its base. Certainly it is one of the most influential organizations governing amateur sport in the world.

The AAU is a federation of sport and athletic clubs, national and district associations, educational institutions, and amateur athletic organizations.

Many persons associate the AAU only with track and field. However, the organization is involved with many more sports and activities, including aerobics, cheerleading, basketball, baton twirling, boxing, diving, golf, gymnastics, in-line hockey, judo, karate, power lifting, softball, swimming, volleyball, trampoline and tumbling, weight lifting, and wrestling, among others. In addition to governing this multiplicity of sports and activities, the AAU is vitally concerned with ensuring that the amateur status of athletes is maintained at all times when participating in the amateur sport arena. To this end, the leaders of the AAU have developed explicit rules and promulgated a precise set of guidelines describing amateurism, which may be found on their web site.

Some of the other activities of the AAU include registering athletes (online) to identify and control the amateur status of participants in sport events, sponsoring local (over 10,000) and national (250)

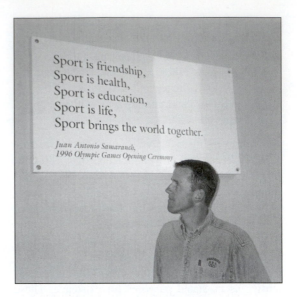

Sport, if managed properly, can serve to build a more inclusive global community.

championships, raising funds for the U.S. athletes for international competition, conducting tryouts for the selection of Junior Olympic competitors, and sponsoring the AAU Junior Olympic competition. The AAU Junior Olympics includes over 11,000 athletes competing in twenty-six different events and is conducted over a ten-day period in July and August. The AAU has established over thirty committees (e.g., golf, swimming, track and field, youth activities) to help with the monumental task of performing the myriad duties associated with governing such a large number of sports and activities. President and CEO Bobby Dodd and a staff of thirty are housed in Lake Buena Vista, Florida.

Other Organizations

Higher education also has many leagues, conferences, and associations formed by a limited number of schools for sport competition. Examples are the Ivy League, Big Ten, Big East, Big Twelve, Northern Sun, Pac 10, SEC, Southland, CIAA, and Atlantic Coast Conferences. These associations regulate sport competition among their members and settle problems that may arise in connection with such competition.

TAKE IT TO THE NET!

Amateur Athletic Union (AAU)
www.aausports.org

National Association for Girls and Women in Sport (NAGWS)
www.aahperd.org/nagws

National Association of Collegiate Directors of Athletics
www.nacda.com

National Association of Collegiate Women Athletic Administrators
www.nacwaa.org

National Association of Intercollegiate Athletics (NAIA)
www.naia.org

National Federation of State High School Associations (NFHS)
www.nfhs.org

National Junior College Athletic Association
www.nijcaa.org

National Standards for Athletes and Coaches
http://aahperd.org./naspe

Other groups related to sport and the sporting process include, but are not limited to, AAHPERD; the National Association of Collegiate Directors of Athletics (NACDA), National Association of Collegiate Women Athletic Administrators (NACWAA); the Society of State Directors of Health, Physical Education, and Recreation; the United States Olympic Committee (USOC); the United States Sports Academy (USSA); and the Women's Sports Foundation.

SUMMARY

The standards for competitive sport in schools, colleges, and other organizations have been clearly identified. There should be no doubt in any individual's mind about the types of interscholastic and intercollegiate programs that are educationally sound and operate in the best interests of student-athletes who participate in them. It is the responsibility of managers and others concerned with such programs to implement and monitor the various standards that have been established. The issue is not one of de-emphasis, but of reform and refocus along educational lines. Sound leadership can make the interscholastic and intercollegiate programs forces for quality education that have no equal.

Competitive sport is an integral part of the Physical Activity and Sport Continuum. The objectives stated earlier in this text for physical education also apply to interscholastic and intercollegiate sport. Managers should evaluate their programs in terms of the extent to which the listed objectives are being delivered and achieved.

Sport has tremendous value if it is conducted in a sound educational manner. The management in charge of competitive sport is largely responsible to see that it is conducted in accordance with the standards that have been set. In so doing, managers may be confronted with problems that periodically occur in these programs because of sport's high public visibility and the economics and politics involved. However, prudent managers know the goals to be achieved, the values to be transmitted, and the standards to be observed. They know right from wrong. Therefore, their responsibility is to see that the total competitive sport program is conducted accordingly.

SELF-ASSESSMENT ACTIVITIES

These activities will assist students in determining if material and competencies presented in this chapter have been mastered.

1. You are at a school district budget hearing when a taxpayer attacks the varsity sport program as costing too much money for the values derived. As a member of the athletic staff, you are asked to react to the taxpayer's statement. What values can you cite to support the need for a varsity sport program?

2. Write profiles of what you consider to be the ideal director of athletics and activities, and coach.

3. Divide the class into teams that discuss the pros and cons of competitive sports at each educational level.

4. As a director of athletics and activities at a high school, what administrative policy would you recommend regarding the following: Gate receipts, tournaments and championships, eligibility, scholarships, recruiting, proselytizing, and scouting?

5. Develop a set of standards that could be used to evaluate a sport program at the junior high or middle school level.

6. Identify the sporting association that governs your institution and the role it plays in the conduct of sport on your campus.

7. Prepare a report that provides pertinent facts about your school's competitive sport program and its compliance with Title IX.

REFERENCES

1. Acosta, R.V., and L. J. Carpenter. 2004. *Women in intercollegiate sport: A longitudinal study: Twenty-seven year update 1977–2004.* (Available from authors, P.O. Box 42, West Brookfield, MA 01585).

2. ASEP/NFHS. 2000. *Raising the standard.* Champaign, IL: Human Kinetics.

3. Auxter, D., J. Pyfer, and C. Huettig. 2005. *Principles and methods of adapted physical education and recreation.* New York: McGraw-Hill.

4. Carpenter, L., and R. Vivian Acosta. 2005. *Title IX.* Reston, VA: NAGWS.

5. Clement, A. 2004. *Law in sport and physical activity.* Dania, FL: Sport and Law Press.

6. Coakley, J. J. 2004. *Sport in society: Issues and controversies.* Dubuque, IA: McGraw-Hill.

7. Eitzen, D. S., and G. H. Sage. 2003. *Sociology of North American sport.* Dubuque, IA: McGraw-Hill.

8. HHS/PCPFS. 1997. *Physical activity and sport in the lives of girls.* Washington, DC: PCPFS.

9. Horine, L., and D. Stotlar. 2004. *Administration of physical education and sport programs.* Dubuque, IA: McGraw-Hill.

10. Lopiano, D. 1986. The certified coach: Central figure. *Journal of Physical Education, Recreation and Dance* 51(9):32–33.

11. NASPE. 2005. *Quality coaches, quality sports: National standards for athletic coaches.* Dubuque, IA: Kendall/Hunt.

12. Prentice, W. E. 2004. *Principles of athletic training.* WCB/McGraw-Hill.

SUGGESTED READINGS

Andre, J., and D. N. James. 1991. *Rethinking college athletics.* Philadelphia: Temple University Press.

Coakley, J. 2004. *Sport in society: Issues and controversies.* Dubuque, IA. McGraw-Hill.
   Provides a critical analysis of many of the salient sociological issues, concerns, and controversies in the sporting domain. Race, violence, social mobility, and politics as well as competitive sport are explored.

French, P.A. 2004. *Ethics and college sports.* Lanham, MD: Rowman Littlefield Publishers, Inc.

Frey, J., ed. 1982. *The governance of intercollegiate sports.* West Point, NY: Leisure Press.
   Examines the history of sport governance, sport cartels, alumni, law, and the "greening" of American athletes.

Houlihan, B. 1994. *Sport and international politics.* New York: Harvester Wheatsheaf.

Koehler, M. D. 1996. *Advising student athletes through the recruitment process.* Englewood Cliffs, NJ: Prentice Hall.

Lumpkin, A., S. K. Stoll, and J. M. Beller. 2003. *Sports ethics: Applications for fair play.* New York: McGraw-Hill.

Orlick, T. 2000. *In pursuit of excellence.* Champaign, IL: Human Kinetics.
   Explores the limits of human performance including commitment, self-control, goal setting, concentration, imagery. Also delves into coaching problems.

Stier, W. F. 1998. *Coaching concepts and strategies.* Boston, MA: American Press.
   Provides guidelines for coaches and athletes regarding various aspects of the psychology of sports, including psychological assessment, leadership, motivation, activation, aggression, and group dynamics. Also discusses characteristics such as coaching behavior, behavior modification, imagery, and team cohesion.

Thoma, J. E., and L. Chalip. 1996. *Sport governance in the global community.* Morgantown, WV: Fitness Information Technology.

Vargyas, E. J. 1994. *Breaking down barriers: A legal guide to Title IX.* Washington, DC: National Women's Law Center.

Wuest, D. A., and C. A. Bucher. 2003. *Foundations of physical education and sport.* New York: McGraw-Hill.
   Presents an overview of the various academic components of physical education; discusses sports-related careers, issues, and challenges facing the profession.

PART 3

Management of Physical Education and Sport Programs in the Public and Private Sector

CHAPTER 6

Physical Education and Sport Programs in the Public and Private Sector

Instructional Objectives and Competencies to Be Achieved

After reading this chapter the student should be able to:

- Identify physical education and sport careers and opportunities across the Physical Activity and Sport Continuum.
- Identify and describe the role of physical education and sport professionals in public and private sector settings.
- Understand some of the management and program responsibilities involved in various employment settings.

- Illustrate organizational structures and systems related to public and private sector physical education and sport programs.
- Identify current and future trends in public and private sector physical education and sport programs.
- Determine qualifications and professional preparation needed to successfully fulfill management responsibilities in the corporate and commercial health and fitness industry.

This text is devoted in great measure to the management processes, organizational structure, and functioning of physical education and sport programs housed within educational institutions at the kindergarten through twelve (K–12) and college levels. However, in recent years many potentially promising careers and employment opportunities have developed in set-

tings other than schools and colleges (see table 6-1). Just as participation in youth, high school, and college sport has grown, so also has interest in public and private sector physical education (fitness, health, wellness) and sport (foundations, leagues) (Meek 1997 and IHRSA 2003c). The Sporting Goods Manufacturing Association (SGMA), for example, reports that health club

Table 6-1. Physical Education, Recreation, and Sport Career Opportunities

Teaching Opportunities

School Setting	Nonschool Setting
Elementary school	Community recreation/sport programs (Ys/JCCs)
Junior high/middle school	Corporate recreation/fitness centers
High school	Commercial sport clubs
Junior/community college	Youth-serving agencies
College and university	Preschools
Basic instructional programs	Health clubs
Professional preparation programs	Military personnel programs (MRW)
Adapted physical education	Resort sport programs
International school programs	Senior care programs
Overseas school programs	Correctional institution programs
Military school programs	Sport tourism/theme parks
Department of Defense schools	State high school leagues

Coaching Opportunities

Interscholastic programs	Community sport programs
Intercollegiate programs	Military sport programs
Commercial sport camps	AAU and club sport programs
International sport camps	Strength and conditioning
Commercial sport clubs	

Fitness and Health-Related Opportunities

Cardiac rehabilitation	Corporate fitness programs
Sports medicine	Sports nutrition
Strength and conditioning specialist	Athletic training
Movement therapy	Weight control spas
Health clubs	Military personnel programs (MRW)
Community fitness programs	Country clubs
Personal fitness trainer	Nursing homes
Government fitness programs	
Dance studio	

Sport Management Opportunities

Athletic administration	Hotel/cruise ship recreation
Aquatic administration	Sport retailing
Sport facility management	Corporate recreation and wellness
Commercial sport club management	Resort and spa management
Community recreation/sport management	Bowl organizations
Recreational sport/campus recreation	Sport conference commissioner
U.S. Olympic Committee organizations	Professional sport associations
Sports governing bodies	Summer camps/guides
State high school leagues	Amateur sports agencies
Sport organization administration	Nonprofit youth agencies and charities
Health club management	Sport management groups (i.e., IMG, Octogon, Sfx, IEG)
Ticket manager	
Tournament management	

Sport Media Opportunities

Sports information	Sport broadcasting and production
Sport journalism	Sport art
Sport photography	Sport product advisor
Writing sport-oriented books	Sport museum/hall of fame
Sport publishing	

Sport-Related Opportunities

Sports agent	Sport officiating
Player personnel and community relations	Game/event entertainment
Sport law	Sport statistician
Professional athlete	Sport consulting
Entrepreneur	Compliance director
Research	Golf club and turf management
Academic support/counseling	Sport/educational psychologist
Sport agent	Sport technology expert
Corporate marketing	
Club pro	

Adapted from Wuest and Bucher 2003.

growth rates of participants aged thirty-five to fifty-four have climbed from 6.3 to 10.5 million and for age fifty-five and over from 1.9 to 5 million. They forecast these numbers to triple by 2020. Besides the tremendous growth in the health and fitness club and spa industry, corporations, businesses, athletic (golf, racquet, country) clubs, sports associations, therapeutic rehabilitation and wellness centers, planned housing and community complexes, hotels and resorts, senior citizen centers, Ys, recreation and park boards, and community centers among others have opened new windows of employment opportunity for physical educators. Indeed, there are over 64,000 fitness-type clubs in the United States (IHRSA 2003c).

This chapter is designed to provide the reader with information about representative public and private organizations at which physical educators may seek employment (even ownership) as instructors, personal trainers, consultants, program directors, and managers.

The chapter is divided into four sections. The first section presents corporate or workplace health and fitness career opportunities. Companies featured include International Business Machines (IBM), General Mills, Inc., Ford, the SAS Institute, Inc., and Rex Healthcare System. The second section provides a glimpse into the commercial fitness industry; Bally Total Fitness, Clark Hatch International, and the Radisson Hotel and Conference Center are presented. The third section explores various representative community-based programs, including a Y, a Jewish Community Center, a large recreation and parks department, and a local community recreation department. Examples of a state high school league program, a college conference, and a private not-for-profit sports foundation are also included. The final section explores the professional qualifications necessary to meet the roles and responsibilities in public and private sector physical education (fitness, health, wellness) and sport (associations, foundations, leagues) programs.

CORPORATE OR WORKPLACE HEALTH, FITNESS, AND WELLNESS PROGRAMS

In the last decade, many large and small corporations and businesses have begun to offer employee health, fitness, and wellness programs. These companies have found that improved fitness and wellness among their ranks lead to improved workplace health, decreased employee absenteeism, and higher levels of employee productivity and job satisfaction. Corporations and businesses have found that they can also attract, recruit, and retain top-notch employees by providing high-quality health-related fitness programs for both the employees and their families. Indeed, surveys and research by the U.S. Department of Health and Human Services (1987; 1999) report that more than half the U.S. companies with 750 or more employees, and almost 35 percent of the companies with 250 or more employees, offer some form of corporate or workplace health-related fitness and wellness program or benefit. The U.S. Department of Health and Human Services has set a goal for the decade of 2010 to have 75 percent of large companies provide health-related fitness and wellness programs for its employees (PHS/PCPFS 1999; USDHHS 2000).

These in-house health, fitness, and wellness (e.g., nutrition, smoking cessation, stress and weight management) programs save an estimated ten dollars for each one dollar invested, which is why over seven billion dollars is spent annually in health and fitness-related corporate environs (Eitzen and Sage 2003). In some instances corporate or workplace fitness programs are reaching out and partnering with the local community. Corporations have found that this concept not only boosts membership, but also improves and builds community relations, which leads to better business.

The following pages present representative corporate or workplace programs that go well beyond the scope of the traditional employee health, fitness, and wellness programs. The information about these creative programs has

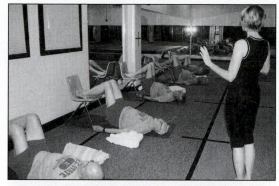

From the corporate to the university setting and from community centers to resorts and spas, healthy lifestyles are promoted in various fashion and design.

been gathered from the professional literature, from publications prepared by the corporations or companies, and directly from personnel of the respective organizations.

International Business Machines (IBM)

Source of Information

Stewart Sill, Wellness Program Manager
IBM Global Well-being Services & Health Benefits

General Information

IBM is the world's largest information technology company and for over 100 years has created a cutting edge corporate culture based on em-ployee talent, innovation, social responsibility, and high-quality management, products, and services. IBM is a fixture on *Fortune Magazine's* 100 Best Companies to Work For and has a tradition of concern and commitment for the health and well-being of its employees, retirees, and their families. In this regard, IBM's Global Well-being Services & Health Benefits has developed a comprehensive, integrated wellness strategy focusing on employee health risk reduction and maintenance of low health risk status for its over 133,000 employees based in the United States.

Management believes that healthy employees are more productive and enjoy a state of well-being that contributes to the quality of life at work, at home, and in the community. IBM, like other businesses across the country, recognizes that reducing health risks among its workforce pays off in a number of ways:

- Lower health-care costs
- Reduced absenteeism
- Improved productivity
- Decreased disability and workers compensation
- Increased morale
- Enhanced recruitment and retention

IBM's commitment to corporate citizenship and social responsibility is second to none and spans and impacts the globe. From programs and initiatives like Reinventing Education to On Demand Community and from arts and culture (State Hermitage Museum) projects to crises response, United Way, and Ameri-Corps VISTA support, IBM has clearly stepped to the forefront both at home and abroad.

Program Goals/Objectives

IBM's health promotion and wellness for employees took form in the 1960s and has evolved over time to a cutting edge three-step wellness intervention framework and delivery system (Assess-Plan-Act), which is accessible to all its employees. The ultimate goal of IBM's Wellness for Life Strategy is to foster long-term behavior change and commitment to healthy living and a healthy lifestyle. The corporate strategy is to reach as many employees as possible through innovative delivery and motivational packages including financial incentives (Physical Activity and Smoke-free Rebates) to encourage maximal employee reach and engagement. More than 9,000 employees and spouses or domestic partners recently engaged in IBM's smoking cessation (Smoke-free Rebate) program, while over 97,000 employees elected to participate in the Physical Activity Rebate program. Employees can choose to enter IBM's Wellness for Life programs at any step or stage based on their needs.

Program Description

The IBM Wellness for Life Strategy offers a comprehensive multidimensional program for all employees. It is wrapped in a three-step program of wellness intervention that usually begins with an ini-

tial voluntary Express Wellness Health Screening and Risk Appraisal. This step offered both on-site and online serves to provide the employee with baseline health status assessments. The next key step in the strategy is planning. Each participant receives assessment feedback from a trained professional, is informed of the types of action programs and "tools" available, and is assisted in setting healthy behavior targets or goals. The employee can also subscribe to "interactive wellness coaching" to help in selecting and designing the appropriate mix of "tools" to promote a positive change in health behavior.

The last step or action phase of the program consists of selecting from a menu of behavior change and maintenance tools. These include, but are not limited to, physical fitness and exercise programs delivered both on-site and "virtually" on-site; self-directed and online weight management programs; smoking cessation programs in self-directed kit form, through telephone counseling, or online; a variety of mental health programs; and clinical and condition management services ranging from immunization to disease management. Creative approaches to program delivery provide the greatest reach to IBM's large, diverse, and dispersed professional workforce. It is no surprise that many of the programs noted are electronically delivered, interactive, and offer flexible, cost-effective options to gain and maintain mass employee involvement to sustain a healthy workplace environment.

Program Specifics

As noted, IBM reaches its large population to a great extent through online interactive exchange not only with IBM specialists but with numerous well-credentialed and geographically diverse partners as well.

IBM also maintains a number of on-site fitness centers ranging from the IBM Club Fitness & Recreation Center at Research Triangle Park (RTP), North Carolina, to its state-of-the-art fitness centers in Armonk, New York. Other on-site locations include Austin, Poughkeepsie, and San Jose. The on-site facilities vary, but most include group exercise rooms and classrooms and basketball and tennis courts. At the RTP facility, IBMers pay a small yearly membership fee; complete a Health History Form and Rick Assessment Profile; and have the option to undergo a thorough fitness assessment conducted by center professionals. Each member then receives a personally designed fitness and exercise program that is monitored and updated throughout the year. Besides each member's individualized program, group exercise classes in core, cardio challenge, pilates, spin, step, yoga and Irresist-A-Ball among others are offered; classroom series in nutrition, weight management (Maintain But Don't Gain), osteoporosis, and stress reduction serve to compliment similar online behavior change and maintenance "tools." The center takes advantage of its surrounding forty acres and delivers a well-designed Recreation League Program ranging from softball and basketball to Ultimate Frisbee and from sand volleyball to soccer. Special events including golf outings, 5-K campus runs, fitness fairs, and "Fitness Makeover" provide over 2,500 busy IBMers well-balanced activities throughout the year. The center is open weekdays from 6 A.M. to 8 P.M., Saturday from 8 A.M. to 1 P.M., and Sunday from 10 A.M. to 3 P.M.

Personnel

Because of the decentralized nature of IBM's fitness centers, personnel requirements vary. IBM's RTP Fitness & Recreation Center has a highly qualified manager, two full-time assistants who coordinate group fitness and recreation respectively, a fitness/recreation specialist and fifty part-time employees. They are well trained, hold degrees in exercise science, and are committed to IBM's corporate Wellness for Life goals.

Contact Address

IBM-HR-USA
3039 Cornwallis Rd.
RTP, NC 27709

General Mills, Inc.
Source of Information

Andrew Wood, Manager of Health Promotion and Human Performance
TriHealthalon Program

General Information

General Mills is a Midwest-based firm that consists of a number of divisions: Big G Cereal, Betty Crocker, Pillsbury, Green Giant, and Yoplait/Columbo, and over 100 brands such as Cheerios and Haagen-Dazs.

Workplace health promotion began in earnest in the early 1980s under the title Framework—A Healthy Lifestyle Program. In 1984, the expanded TriHealthalon program began under the auspices of the Health and Human Services Department and now falls under the Health, Safety and Environment Department (see figure 6-1). The corporation and its Foundation are committed to social responsibility and are strong supporters of the Olympic Games, Special Olympics, Habitat for Humanity, and other worthy community-based programs, including children's school physical education through its Youth Fitness and Nutrition Champions Programs.

Program Goals/Objectives

The TriHealthalon is a program developed to improve the health of General Mills employees in the areas designated by the World Health Organization. These include the focal aspects of health—physical, mental, and social well-being.

- Physical well-being signifies exercising, eating well, controlling body weight, and being aware of the risk factors associated with cardiovascular heart disease, diabetes, and cancer.
- Mental well-being includes release of stress in one's life and involvement in activities that are recreational, relaxing, and healthy.
- Social well-being focuses on improving interpersonal relations, controlling chemical usage, and being aware of personal safety.

Program Description

Every employee who completes the online Personal Medical History and Lifestyle and Health Risk Appraisal forms is enrolled in the Total You and TriHealthalon programs. Each participant receives a computer-analyzed health recommendation plan and a Health Number Rating.

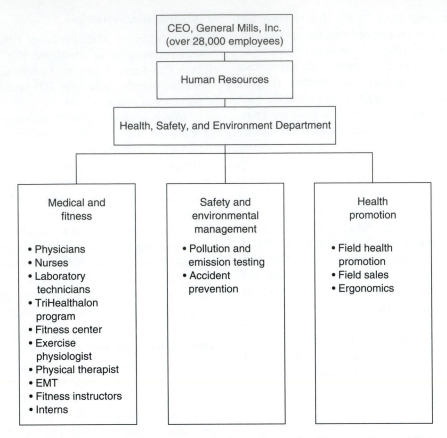

Figure 6-1. Organizational structure of a corporate health promotion and fitness program.

Health goals are determined, and three categories of participation are outlined in terms of physical, mental, and social well-being goals:

1. physical: fitness, nutrition and weight control, ergonomics, and cancer prevention

2. mental: stress management, recreation, relaxation, and entertainment

3. social: interpersonal relations, chemical usage, and safety

Program Specifics

A new Fitness Center at the main corporate offices consists of 8,000 square feet of space and provides services from 6 A.M. to 8 P.M. Monday through Friday and 8 A.M. to 12 noon on Saturday. The fitness center at the General Mills Research and Development facility is open and staffed twenty-four hours per day for its 3,000 employees. There are also fitness centers at the Lodi, California; Cedar Rapids, Iowa; and Kansas City, Missouri, plants. Completion of an orientation and a fitness/medical assessment and questionnaire is required before participation.

Health classes, seminars, and programs such as Weight Watchers are routinely scheduled to provide participants with information and guidance about physical, mental, and psychosocial well-being. Furthermore, individualized physical fitness programs are prescribed to address specific employee needs, and fitness assessments and follow-ups are ongoing.

The Fitness Center has weight-training stations, upright and recumbent bicycles, treadmills, cross-training, skiing, stair climbing, and rowing machines as well as other state-of-the-art exercise apparatus. Available fitness classes range from beginning to advanced level in activities such as stretching, aerobic exercise, conditioning, pilates, Tai Chi, yoga, exercise walking, and progressive relaxation.

Personnel

Director

Exercise physiologist/physical therapist/emergency medical technician

Physical fitness instructors (6)

Physician

Nurses

Laboratory technicians

University interns

Contact Address

General Mills TriHealthalon Program

Health, Safety, and Environment Department, 3C

Number One General Mills Blvd.

Minneapolis, MN 55426

UAW-Ford Wellness Center
Source of information

Vince Pozinski, Program Manager

Karin Fuzzey, Senior Fitness Specialist

Alexis Stockwell, Fitness Specialist

General Information

The UAW-Ford Wellness Center was first established in 1989 when the UAW leadership and Ford management at the Twin Cities Assembly Plant agreed to build an on-site fitness center for their employees. Due to the popularity of the center, a second center was added in 2002. The UAW-Ford Wellness Centers are funded locally and by the UAW-Ford National Programs Center.

It is managed by Park Nicollet *HealthSource,* which is a service provided by the Institute for Research and Education, HealthSystem Minnesota. It has been serving Minnesota and the Midwest with innovative worksite health promotion services since 1979.

Program Goals/Objectives

The UAW-Ford Wellness Centers are dedicated to serving the employees and retirees of the Twin Cities Assembly Plant by offering comprehensive and innovative health enhancement and improvement. In 1997, the Local 879 Twin Cities Assembly Plant UAW-Ford National Programs Center was awarded the annual R.I.S.E. (Recognition, Innovation, Service, and Excellence) award for local Employee Support Services Program based on their Wellness Program. This award is presented to companies for providing their employees with high-quality programming and service. The center is available for current employees and retirees; however, some health promotion programs are also open to spouses and family members. The UAW-Ford is an active participant in Ford's National Corporate Weight Loss Challenge Program.

Program Description/Specifics

The UAW-Ford Wellness Centers are open Monday through Thursday 7 A.M. to 4 A.M., and Fridays from 7 A.M. to midnight. The Wellness Center staff is available during all shifts to help employees with their health and fitness needs. The Wellness Center has two on-site fitness centers, which house over twenty-three resistance and twenty-one cardiovascular stations as well as a group fitness and exercise studio. The center maintains a library with health-related videos, books, and resource materials. A monthly newsletter is also published. Equipment available to employees includes the following:

- Quinton clubtrack treadmill with heart rate and a longer jogging deck
- Life Fitness 9500 HR treadmills with heart rate and Flex Tech technology

- Life Fitness 9500 HR recumbent and upright cycles
- Elliptical cross-trainers and cross-country ski machines
- Stair climbers and rowing machines
- Cybex selectorized resistance equipment
- Free-weight bench press, incline press, squat rack, and dumbbells
- Polar Heart Rate monitors for use in the Wellness Center
- Swiss/therapeutic and BOSU balls and resistance tubing
- Mats for exercise, stretching, and relaxation
- Exercise videos for check out or use in Wellness Center
- Body Trec, Body Mill, and upper body ergometers

Staff members design and lead employees through programs that are tailored to specific needs and desires. Besides personalized programs, classes in core and balance, abs, yoga, Tai Chi, pilates, circuit training, and "boot camp" are popular.

The Wellness Center has a variety of health assessment and health improvement programs offered throughout the year focusing on the following topics:

- Health risk appraisal on the interactive computer station
- Medical self-care and prevention
- Health-related fitness education
- Tobacco cessation
- Stress management/life balance
- Weight loss and maintenance
- Nutrition and healthy cooking
- Chronic disease management
- Massage therapy

Personnel

The UAW-Ford Wellness Center management structure consists of one program manager and seven fitness specialists.

Contact Address

Twin Cities Ford Assembly Plant
Wellness Center
966 South Mississippi River Blvd.
Saint Paul, MN 55116

The SAS Institute, Inc.
Source of Information

Jack D. Poll, Recreation and Employee Services Manager
Human Resources Division

General Information

The world's largest, privately owned software company, SAS, has been ranked as one of the best places to work by numerous institutions. Employee retention rates point to the success of the company's ideology that a positive work environment combined with a balanced personal life enable employees to work at peak performance. Situated under the Human Resources Division of the company, the Recreation and Fitness Center (RFC) at SAS was established in 1985 as an integral part of the SAS corporate culture. Combined with the related services offered by their Work-Life and Food Services Departments and the on-site Health Care Center, SAS's RFC provides a comprehensive, rich package of resources that supports the Institute's 5,000 employees and their families while simultaneously helping to control personnel and health-care costs. Over 90 percent of SAS employees participate in the programs.

Program Goals/Objectives

The RFC at SAS recognizes the health benefits that can be obtained through a balanced program of physical activities and educational programs including fitness, recreation, leisure, wellness, and personal convenience services. The RFC's daily activities offer outlets for stress reduction through exercise and recreation, helping employees face each workday feeling healthy and ready to meet the challenges of their jobs. Competitive and noncompetitive activities are offered for every skill level, while educational programs and

Employees at corporations such as Ford, IBM, and SAS participate in a wide range of physical activity and sport.

leisure/special events are regularly programmed to keep valued human resources of all ages motivated to stay active.

Program Description

The RFC at SAS recognizes that every person is an individual and provides services that appeal to a wide and varied audience. After completing the required medical and participation forms, employees gain the use of the facilties. An orientation for each employee and eligible family member is then conducted. A personal trainer also meets with each employee to design an exercise program geared toward each individual's fitness goals. Staff members are challenged to find innovative ways in which to motivate employees and provide incentives to keep them engaged. Employees can accumulate participation points as an individual or in "challenge teams," which transfer to RFC dollars that can be used to purchase entertainment tickets, clothing, or gift certificates. Classes and activities such as the Boot

Camp, the Walk to Run Program, Hydro-Challenge, 12 Days of Fitness, and Extreme Fitness Challenge are regularly scheduled, and RFC crews offer a variety of workout styles, modes, and intensities to help employees maintain interest.

The recreation and leisure program offers dozens of on-site and off-campus activities. Recreational and competitive sports include softball, soccer, ultimate frisbee, volleyball, racquetball, tennis, wallyball, and several aquatic-related games such as water-basketball and volleyball. Employees can also participate in marathon and triathlon training classes, and ski, kayaking, hiking, and whitewater rafting trips are regularly programmed. Dance, golf, painting, and decorating classes are also organized on a continual basis.

Wellness programs help the employees maintain a healthy balance between mind and body. Yoga, pilates, and Tai Chi classes are offered weekly to help participants reduce stress and maintain focus. Classes are also offered addressing specific issues such as self-defense, prenatal to cradle care, smoking cessation, and weight loss. The company also offers every employee a complete lifestyle and health assessment including personal consultations.

Program Specifics

The RFC at SAS is located at the two million-square-foot world headquarters in Cary, North Carolina. Spread over forty acres at the main campus with over 61,000 square feet of activity space in four buildings, the RFC facilities are staffed and open to employees from 6:30 A.M. to 8 P.M. Monday through Thursday, with a 7 P.M. closure on Friday. Closed on Saturday, the RFC is open on Sunday from 1–6 P.M. An adults-only complex during the week, the RFC reserves Sunday as family day, during which children of employees may participate in myriad play activities. The natatorium is also open to the children the first Sunday of every month. Ongoing swim lessons are provided to adults and children, and sport camps are conducted for children throughout the year.

The main gym houses staff and provides space for basketball, volleyball, wallyball, racquetball, table tennis, biliards, nautilus and free weights, cardio equipment, locker rooms, and meal "to-go" services. The gym annex houses additional locker rooms and aerobics and exercise space. The third building contains the natatorium, with its own locker rooms, while the fourth building houses SAS's wellness programs. Another fitness and wellness building has just been completed.

Designed not to be a typical corporate recreation and fitness center, SAS's RFC programs are limited only by the imagination of its highly trained staff.

Personnel

Recreation and Employee Services Manager
Assistant Manager
Aquatics Supervisor
Recreation and Fitness Program Specialists
Aquatic Specialist
Activity Instructor
Staff Assistant

Contact Address

Recreation and Employee Services Manager
SAS Institute Inc.
SAS Campus Drive
Cary, North Carolina 27513
(919) 677–8000
www.sas.com

Rex Wellness Centers
Source of Information

Judy Jackson, Operations Manager
Melanie Dean, Wellness Instructor

General Information

Housed within the Rex Healthcare System, Rex Wellness Centers (Raleigh, Cary, Garner) are one of the United States's first comprehensive medically supervised health and wellness center systems. Each center is within or proximate to a local Rex Healthcare complex. Rex Wellness Centers are not your typical corporate or commercial health, fitness, or wellness center as they serve not only their system employees but also referred outpatient clientele who need rehabilitation to return to their daily routine. The center also welcomes community members over eighteen years of age and maintains an active intern program for local universities.

Program Goals/Objectives

Since 1986 when the first center was opened, Rex Wellness has provided a model program that partners corporate, medical-related, and socially responsible community fitness and wellness. The goal of the center is to supply state-of-the-art facilities and comprehensive health and wellness programs that are delivered by highly qualified staff to provide members with the perfect opportunity, and lots of motivation, to get in shape and stay that way. Recognizing that there is not "one size fits all" exercise programs, all programs are expertly tailored, professionally supervised and designed for lifestyle change.

Program Description

To apply for membership to Rex Wellness, all potential members must undergo a medical and exercise screening. An introduction to cardiovascular exercise/stretching is offered in conjunction with the screening. This is followed by a thorough Fitness Assessment (aerobic submax test, blood pressure, heart rate, body composition, muscular strength and endurance, flexibility, functional movement). A third session targets weight training safety techniques and muscular strength and endurance baseline measures to shape the Individualized Personalized Exercise Program (IPEP) developed for each member. The IPEP is supervised and reviewed every three months. Besides the tailored IPEP, members can join in group exercise (aqua walking, body shaping, core, pilates), secure a personal trainer (jump start, prescription exercise, nutrition), take Healthy Way and Health Promotion classes (aquatics, CPR, Tai Chi, yoga basics, prenatal health yoga), or participate in various Well Quest educational and exercise classes.

Rex Wellness also conducts its PEAK Program (exercise and joint conditioning) designed for post-physical therapy patients recovering from injury or surgery. Rex prides itself in its continuous counseling, motivating, and high-quality service for all members.

Program Specifics

Rex Wellness Centers pride themselves as being "A Step Above"! Heated lap pool, a therapy pool, sauna, steam room, aquatic therapy and massage, child activity area, and full-service locker rooms are available to members. State-of-the-art equipment including treadmills, stair climbers, rowing and Nordic ski machines, computerized upright and recumbent bikes, upper body ergometers, as well as free and fixed weights are standard as are the staffs' commitment to members' well-being and lifestyle change. Centers are open Monday through Thursday 5:45 A.M. to 9:30 P.M., and Friday sessions end at 8 P.M. Saturday hours are from 8:30 A.M. to 6 P.M., and Sundays from 1 P.M. to 6 P.M. From aquatics to smoking cessation and from lipid and glucose screening and nutrition to prenatal HATHA yoga, there is a well-managed program for all.

Personnel

Each staff member is required to hold at least a bachelor's degree in physical education or exercise science as well as appropriate recognized certifications in his or her areas of instructional delivery (aerobic, aquatic, personal training, strength training). Staff members regularly meet with their area coordinators and are updated on the latest trends and research to apply to their respective center assignments. Each center has an operations manager, office and front desk staffs and coordinators of health promotion and aerobics; aquatics and nursery; and wellness and fitness. There are nine full-time floor instructors (including an exercise scientist and dietitian), a fully staffed physical therapy station, and seven to ten part-time instructors. The staff is highly qualified, well trained, and "A Step Above."

Contact Address

Rex Wellness Centers
1515 Southwest Cary Parkway
Cary, NC 27511

COMMERCIAL HEALTH, FITNESS, AND WELLNESS INDUSTRY

The commercial (for profit) health and fitness industry has grown significantly in the last decade (over 20,000 centers). Membership campaigns have attracted millions of men and women to health clubs and fitness centers (an estimated thirty-five million members), which seem to have become a permanent part of our society (IHRSA 2003c).

The commercial health and fitness industry focuses, for the most part, on adult fitness and sport pursuits, although most clubs are now catering to all age-groups to keep their competitive edge. The commercial health and fitness industry is profit motivated ($10 billion yearly), which differentiates it from many corporate and community-based physical education, health-related fitness, and sport programs. Their business structure is also arranged differently ranging from sole proprietorship to limited liability partnership (LLP) and from limited liability corporation (LLC) to general partnership and C and S corporate structures. Liability, tax treatment, access to capital and managerial control, operations, and programming, not to mention decision making, are all related to the business structure (Miller and Fielding 1996).

Facilities at a typical center might include exercise and aerobic exercise rooms, resistive-type exercise or strength-training equipment like Cybex, Ivanko, Keiser, Precor, Stairmaster, Magnum, Paramount, Universal, or Nautilus machines as well as free and selectorized weights, computerized treadmills, elliptical cross-training machines, rowing machines, recumbent bicycles, stair climbing equipment, and cross-country ski trainers. Cardio theaters, fitness cinemas, wireless fitness entertainment centers with Internet access, E-zone and netpulse educational linkages, and a bevy of health-related fitness software have also found their way to the gym. Swimming pools, day-care play areas, whirlpools, therapy pools, saunas, steam rooms, massage therapy rooms, cold plunges, oil baths, tanning rooms, and locker and shower areas, not to mention sport courts for volleyball, basketball, tennis, racquetball, and squash are commonplace.

Programs in commercial enterprises focus on such items as fitness assessment and profiling, exercise prescription, weight management and nutrition, strength training, yoga, pilates, various forms of kickboxing, aerobics of various types and intensity levels (e.g., core, step, spinning, exercise walking, chirunning), stress management, day care, and sport competitions, both in-house and against other clubs. Personnel often include instructors (physical educators), personal trainers, business managers, and sales, marketing, and promotions specialists. The following descriptions are representative examples of the commercial health and fitness industry.

Swimming remains a constant for both public and private sector fitness, exercise, and wellness programs.

Bally Total Fitness

Source of Information

Brent Roseth, Assistant Manager

General Information

Bally Total Fitness was a branch of Bally's Manufacturing and Entertainment, which also oversaw equipment manufacturing, casinos, and the Health and Tennis Corporation of America. Bally Total Fitness was spun off into its own corporate enterprise and, according to *Business Industry* magazine, with its 420 fitness centers and two million plus membership is one of the largest commercial fitness corporations in the world.

Program Goals/Objectives

Bally Total Fitness designs a personalized physical fitness program based on the member's needs (e.g., cardiovascular or muscular strength, nutrition, weight control, injury care). The company ranked first on *Club Industry's* (2000) revenue list at $861 million and has as its mission to maintain its position as the leading provider of fitness services by offering a first-rate product at a fair price, by at-

tracting and retaining committed members, and by employing quality staff who are focused on meeting customers' needs. Consonant with their mission, Bally's fitness centers adhere to a holistic approach to exercise in order to meet each individual's specific exercise needs.

Program Description

Each Bally Total Fitness center provides a wide array of programs, which include exercise and fitness, injury management, and a variety of counseling, assessment, and personal training services. Exercise and aerobic classes include low-impact, intermediate, and advanced levels as well as muscle conditioning (e.g., 30-Minute Workout, Boot Camp, Power Flex) and step, reaction cycling, and aqua-aerobics. These classes as well as Kwan Do are provided for members ranging from children to seniors. An online Meal Plan Program and Built to Fit weight loss nutrition and programs including phone counseling with a personal dietition are now also available nationwide to all Bally's members.

In the area of injury management, Extended Care is a holistic program available to members. The program is designed according to the individual's physical limitations and his or her physician's recommended prescription for exercise. Counseling is also an integral part of the program and is available for basic nutrition and in conjunction with body composition and metabolic assessment. Other assessment services that are tailored to meet individual needs are also offered (e.g., fitness level, posture, cholesterol, blood pressure).

Program Specifics

Each Bally Total Fitness center is well equipped with computerized resistance machines, eliptical trainers, exercise cycles, step ergometers, and rowing machines as well as an indoor jogging track and swimming pool. Some facilities also maintain racquetball, tennis, and squash courts.

Bally Total Fitness is open Monday through Thursday 5 A.M. to midnight, Friday 5 A.M. to 10 P.M., and Saturday and Sunday 8 A.M. to 8 P.M. Membership fees vary according to the local economy and state laws and regulations, with the average fee being twenty to forty-nine dollars per month. Each fitness center serves approximately 750 to 1,500 members (50–50 gender divide) daily and has on-site child care.

Personnel

Instructional staff are professionally trained, certified, and regularly updated with the most current principles and methods of fitness and exercise training. Standard black and red sport uniforms identify Bally Total Fitness staff. Each center has a manager in charge of operations, service, and scheduling; an assistant manager focusing on sales, marketing, and service; personal training director; five to fifteen personal trainers; twenty to thirty aerobics and fitness instructors; receptionists; and day-care and maintenance staff.

Contact Address

Bally Total Fitness
71 Minnesota Avenue
Little Canada, MN 55117

Clark Hatch International (CHI)
Source of Information

Clark G. Hatch, Founder
Randy Bozeman, President
Jeff Lum, Vice President
John L. Sheppard, Asia Regional Representative
William A. Monsen, President Clark Hatch, Hawaii

General Information

An international chain of fitness centers with more than 40,000 members worldwide in fourteen countries, the Clark Hatch organization began in Tokyo, Japan, in 1965. There are now more than sixty locations, which are either wholly owned, co-owned, in reciprocating status, leased or managed by CHI from their flagship center in Mont' Kaira Plaza, Kuala Lumpur, Malaysia. Clark Hatch has been the pioneer for physical fitness and health in the Pacific Rim, and his impact has set the pace and established the standard of quality, excellence, and professionalism for today's health and physical fitness manager and professional.

Program Goals/Objectives

Clark Hatch International offers a three-pronged approach to fitness management. First, by offering traditional fitness center operations; second, by offering in-house developmental and management fitness service to hotels, spas, resorts, and corporations throughout the world; and third, by offering the Clark Hatch Life Spa and Sport Lab initiative. Clark Hatch Life Spa focuses on health and wellness (e.g., massage, aromatherapy, reflexology). CHI also offers a worldwide consulting service to hotels, resorts, and spas. The Clark Hatch program has carved out a special niche in the fitness industry, with more than forty of the centers being located in prominent world-class hotels, which serve not only the hotel clientele, but also its immediate multicultural community users. CHI's goal is to expand to over 100 centers by 2115.

CHI's philosophy mirrors its founder's personal fitness, vigor, and enthusiasm for the industry, and this, in turn, is reflected in the managers and staff CHI recruits, employs, trains, and continually updates through yearly, if not more frequent, managerial and instructor seminars. CHI, although profit driven, is grounded in the underlying philosophy of promoting health and fitness throughout the world.

Program Description

Following an initial fitness assessment, which includes health history, injuries, nutrition, stress level, body measurements, and physical fitness appraisal, all members are scheduled for one-to-one exercise sessions. During these individualized sessions, a five-phase program of warm-up, aerobic exercise, flexibility, strength/conditioning, and cooldown is introduced. This individualized program provides a sound base from which all members progressively build more personalized challenging programs under the direction of a well-trained staff.

Clark Hatch International programs provide incentives such as educational seminars, newsletters, ongoing assessments, and individualized program readjustments to inspire adherence as well as attainment of fitness goals. Personalized, supportive service, high-quality and well-maintained facilities, and sound managerial skill are evident throughout the Clark Hatch International network.

Program Specifics

All centers are equipped with the most modern exercise equipment, an aerobics area, and one or more additional facilities (e.g., swimming pool, sauna, steam room, whirlpool, massage, and tennis, squash, or racquetball courts). Furthermore, the centers also sponsor outside events such as fun runs, hiking, kick boxing, outrigger canoeing, softball, futsal, and soccer. As an added amenity, members and hotel guests are provided with complimentary use of gym clothing, footwear, and towels.

Hours of operation vary from center to center (generally 6 A.M. to 10 P.M.). Members pay an initiation fee and monthly dues (forty-five to fifty-six dollars), which vary markedly from country to country and center to center. Special spousal, student, off-peak hours, and corporate memberships are also available. Memberships offer unlimited usage and are fully reciprocal at Clark Hatch International centers throughout the world.

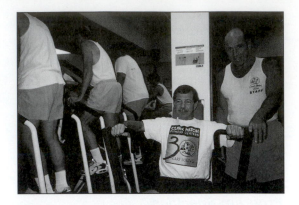

Clark Hatch International (CHI) fitness centers support a wide range of quality fitness activities and have set the standard in the international fitness marketplace.

Table 6-2.   Sample Budget of a Representative Commercial Fitness Center

Clark Hatch International Budget Sample

General and Administration Expenses	% of Gross Revenue
Payroll	34.0
Employee benefits	2.9
Rent	21.9
Repair/maintenance	4.2
Office expenses	1.7
Fitness center expenses	3.6
Advertisement/promotion/marketing	5.0
Entertainment/transportation/seminars	0.7
General excise tax	4.0
License fee	0.2
Insurance	1.0
Professional fees/outside services	1.3
Temporary instructors	0.2
Parking/miscellaneous	0.2
Depreciation	3.8
	84.7
PROFIT MARGIN (varies by country and site)	15.3

Table 6-2 presents an international representative breakdown of expenses for a Clark Hatch International center, which of course varies with country and location.

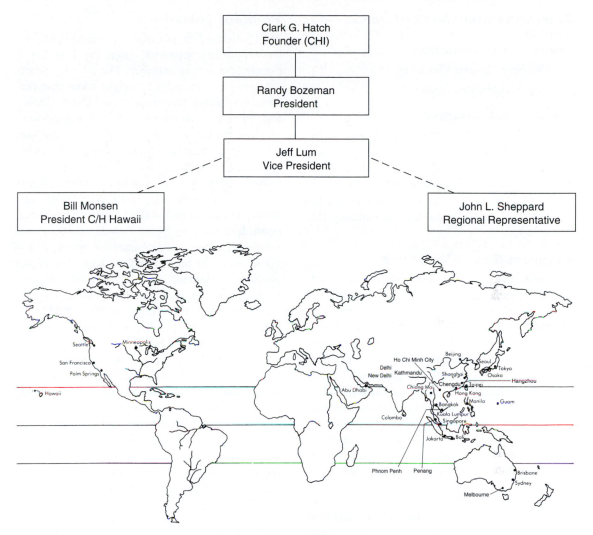

Figure 6-2. Representative organizational network of an international commercial fitness corporation (CHI).

Personnel

The worldwide Clark Hatch International network is illustrated in figure 6-2. Each location typically has a center manager, senior fitness instructor(s), aerobic exercise instructors, and support personnel ranging from on-site recreational staff to locker room attendants, and from sales and marketing to maintenance. The personnel, regardless of level or location, are people-oriented, pleasant, honest, and follow standardized corporation policies and procedures.

Contact Address

Clark Hatch Fitness of Hawaii
Hawaii Building
745 Fort Street
Honolulu, HI 96813
www.clarkhatch.com.my

Radisson Hotel and Conference Center

Source of Information

Mike Serr, General Manager

Barry McLaughlin, Manager

General Information

The Radisson Hotel and Conference Center and its Fitness Center opened August 1, 1991. The fitness center caters to guests of the 243-room hotel and to its conferees who attend intensive meetings and conferences as well as to a limited membership who work or reside in the local community (see figure 6-3).

Program Goals/Objectives

The objective of the Radisson Fitness Center is to provide exercise facilities and fitness programs for the guests of the Radisson Hotel and Conference Center and for club members from the surrounding corporate and residential community. The center seeks to promote health-related fitness and adherence to an exercise prescription program as well as to provide physical activities during stretch and fitness breaks for those attending corporate seminars at the conference center. The key is availability, accessibility, and personalized cooperative programming planned in coordination with the various corporate and conference seminar directors.

Program Description

The fitness center at the Radisson Hotel and Conference Center focuses on an exercise prescription program that is offered to all members. These services are tailored and designed to meet individual needs and to assist members in exercise adherence.

In order to meet the varied needs of the community clientele, the organization offers a wide range of membership options, including individual, joint, off-peak, family, short-term, and corporate memberships. The Fitness Center is not as membership driven as most commercial fitness centers are, because its services and facilities are intimately tied into corporate sales packages, including Silver Sneaker programs. Service and long-range planning are keys to its success.

Program Specifics

The Radisson Fitness Center is housed in a three-story building separated from the hotel by a twenty-foot atrium entrance. The 20,000-square-foot complex includes a weight room that features selectorial, free-weight, and Cybex/Trotter and Precor equipment; a 1,200 square-foot-aerobics room; and an exercise room equipped with steps, elliptical cross-training and rowing machines, treadmills, recumbent bicycles, and cross-country skiing machines. The facility maintains a swimming pool, whirlpool, and sauna, as well as racquetball courts, a basketball court, four outdoor lighted tennis courts, a sand volleyball court, and numerous jogging and biking trails in the immediate area. The center operates basketball, volleyball, wallyball, and racquetball leagues, a summer youth camp, and rents trail bikes to hotel guests. Additional amenities include a suntan bed, a massage therapy area, and a juice bar.

A schedule of aerobic exercise, pilates, Tai Chi, and yoga classes provides instruction over twenty-five different times each week (usually mornings, noons, and evenings). Center classes, functions, and special events are closely coordinated with the conference planning office.

Hours of operation are 6 A.M. to 11 P.M. Monday through Friday, 7 A.M. to 11 P.M. on Saturdays, and 8 A.M. to 9 P.M. on Sundays.

Personnel

The fitness center is staffed by five full-time employees, which include a manager, two personal trainers, a front desk supervisor, a fitness center attendant, and twenty part-time (twelve to twenty hours per week) employees. Responsibilities for all personnel involve front desk duties (e.g., communications/making reservations, accessibility, and some sales), directing fitness and wellness programs and sports leagues, safety audits, stocking the locker room and juice bar, and general maintenance and cleaning. Education, certification, experience, appearance, social skills, and communication are requisite to employment.

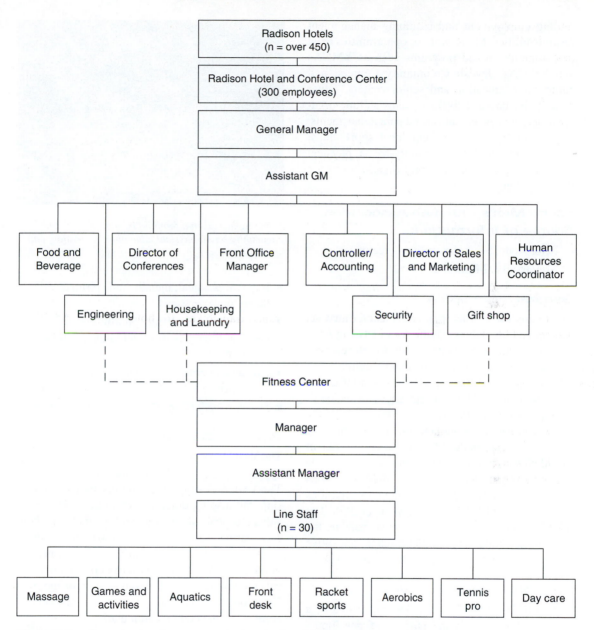

Figure 6-3. Organizational structure of a hotel-related fitness center.

Contact Address

Radisson Fitness Center

Radisson Hotel and Conference Center

3131 Campus Drive

Plymouth, MN 55441

COMMUNITY-BASED PHYSICAL EDUCATION, RECREATION, AND SPORT PROGRAMS

In addition to corporate fitness and commercial health, fitness, and wellness centers, there are other settings in which physical educators are finding employment and assuming management responsibilities. Many of these opportunities exist in community-based programs such as YMCAs and YWCAs, Jewish Community Centers, and community education and senior centers. Other community-based delivery systems include organizations such as recreation and park departments, Boys' and Girls' Clubs, and local sport clubs. Some representative community-based physical education, recreation, and sport organizations are described here.

Young Men's Christian Association
Source of Information

Peter Rodosovick, Executive Director

Minnetonka, Minnesota

General Information

The Young Men's Christian Association (YMCA) was founded by George Williams in 1844 in London, England. Initially the YMCA offered programs designed to teach adults and children (with an emphasis on young males) the values of health and Christianity. This concept was transnationalized to Montreal, Boston, and New York in the 1850s and spread throughout the urban centers of the United States in the 1870s when a commitment to add physical education to its educational agenda and curriculum was adopted. YMCA programs were the cradle from which sprang the inventions of basketball (1891) and volleyball (1895). The YMCA continues to play an active role in the building of strong communities through innovative programs of health, wellness, fitness, and sport.

Program Goals/Objectives

The YMCA is a worldwide fellowship united by a common loyalty with the purpose of developing strong kids, strong families, and strong communities and promoting values to building a better world. The goals for members include the following:

- Focus on character development and emphasize the Y's four core values; caring, honesty, respect, and responsibility
- Strengthen family life

Climbing has taken a foothold in many school and community-based physical education, recreation, and sport programs.

- Improve physical, mental, and spiritual well-being of all persons
- Provide life-enhancing opportunities for disadvantaged persons, including a scholarship program
- Advance international understanding, justice, and peace
- Develop leadership skills among the community

Program Description

The YMCA program promotes a spirit-mind-body approach to the health and fitness of its members. The YMCA is supported not only by its membership, but also by donations from individuals who value the ideals of the organization, including honesty, caring, respect, and responsibility. Today's YMCAs are open to all regardless of race, gender, or religion. They remain an active contributor to local communities from Raleigh to Nairobi and from Kingston to Hong Kong. Their U.S. membership approaches the eight million mark.

Program Specifics

Hours of operation at the Ridgedale YMCA are 5 A.M. to 10 P.M. Monday through Friday and 7 A.M. to 10 P.M. on Saturday and Sunday.

The facilities consist of a swimming pool, an indoor running track, four racquetball courts, and a gymnasium that can be partitioned to form two activity areas for basketball and/or volleyball. In addition, there is a free-weight room as well as areas for strength training equipment, dance, yoga, pilates, and aerobic exercise. Other facilities include a kids' gym and a conference and counseling area. State-of-the-art equipment in the exercise room includes a cardio theatre, ten recumbent exercise bicycles, ten stair climbing machines, two rowing machines, four cross-trainers, and a full complement of gymnastic apparatus. Added attractions of the Ridgedale YMCA are family locker rooms, a kids' play maze, sauna, and large whirlpool as well as a teen room, nursery, kitchen, and classroom facilities. The Y also has outdoor basketball courts and a well-equipped playground as well as day-camp facilities.

Programming includes exercise, fitness, and wellness instruction, classes in all forms of aerobic exercise, weight management, and basketball and volleyball leagues. The YMCA also offers a children's sport program, a Youth Exercise Initiative Program, teen nights, and a popular summer camp program. The contemporary community-based YMCA is truly committed to building strong families.

YMCAs have long been an integral part of many communities worldwide.

Personnel

The YMCA management structure consists of a director, associate director, and staff for the service and information desk. There are program directors and instructional staff for aquatics, adult fitness, gymnastics, children's and youth programs, camps, and special events as well as for family and community relations.

Contact Address

Ridgedale YMCA
12301 Ridgedale Dr.
Minnetonka, MN 55305
or
Your local YMCA/YWCA

Jewish Community Center
Source of Information

Mitch Silver, Assistant Executive Director
Schenectady, New York

General Information

The Robert and Dorothy Ludwig Schenectady Jewish Community Center (JCC) is a committed community-oriented organization that provides exercise, sport and recreational facilities, and associated programming for a wide range of local clientele.

Program Goals/Objectives

The objective of the JCC is to provide health and fitness, sport, and recreational opportunities for children and adults in an atmosphere of fair play, cooperation, and family. These physical education objectives are couched within the overall JCC goals of enhancing the mind, body, and spirit as well as the cultural dimension of the Jewish faith. The family and cultural preservation are important parts of the JCC. The JCC, however, is secular in nature, with 40 percent to 50 percent of its users being non-Jewish.

Program Description

The JCC offers a wide range of programming to meet the physical education and recreational needs of its 1,300 members, which include boys and girls, adults, senior citizens, and especially families. Programming includes instruction in aquatics, aerobics, aikido, kick boxing, and tennis and sport leagues for soccer, basketball, softball, and volleyball. Programs for seniors (e.g., water walking), preschool movement exploration offerings, and a popular after-school recreation program are also cornerstones of the JCC.

Program Specifics

The Schenectady JCC offers indoor facilities including a swimming pool, gymnasium, health club with steam room, whirlpool, and sauna; fitness, aerobics, and ceramics studios, a member lounge, and kitchen area. Outdoor facilities consist of a $1.5 million family park complex, which includes a 300,000-gallon swimming pool, a spray pool, tennis courts, sand volleyball courts, playing fields, amphitheater, and picnic area. This beautiful area is rented for a nominal fee to many school, community, and family groups who take advantage of the modern facilities. A $3 million, 3,000-square-foot fitness wing has been added to further meet the needs of the community.

The focus of the center is the after-school youth recreation program as well as the adult recreation program. A number of activities are available on an adults-only basis (Reebok Core, Sculpt, Guts and Butts). In addition, many aerobic activities are offered, including Lite Touch (low-impact aerobics), Bodyworks (intensive aerobics), and Aerobic Exercise (high-impact and step). The center's Well Fit and Cardio Combo remain mainstays of programming. Aquatics, ranging from Red Cross preschool programs and lifeguarding to YMCA certifications, are also very popular as are the myriad games and physical activities offered in the after-school program.

The operational hours are 5:30 A.M. to 10 P.M. Monday through Friday, 9 A.M. to 5 P.M. Sundays, and 12 P.M. to 6 P.M. on Saturday (Shabbat). Satur-

Movement exploration in the children's gym.

day is devoted to family and recreation day, and no competitive activities or games are practiced.

Personnel

The health and physical education department of the Schenectady JCC is comprised of a director, who manages all recreation and fitness programming as well as oversees the maintenance of the facilities; an aquatics program director, who directs water activities, including a staff of forty lifeguards; and a fitness director, who manages the center's certified aerobics instructors and fitness specialists. The staff is well-qualified and committed to the aims and objectives of the JCC.

Contact Address

Schenectady Jewish Community Center
2565 Balltown Road
Niskayuna, NY 12309

Recreation and Parks Department
Source of Information

Jay Lotthammer, Parks and Facilities Manager
Brooklyn Park, Minnesota

General Information

The Brooklyn Park Recreation and Parks Department was started in 1965. From its inception, the department has steadily grown to be one of the finest and most diverse departments in the nation and enjoys the distinction of being the first recreation program in the country to twice (1970 and 1981) receive the National Gold Medal Award for excellence in the field of park and recreation management.

Department Goals/Objectives

The basic objective of the Brooklyn Park Recreation and Parks Department is to provide quality facilities and programs to as many community residents as possible. Further goals of the organization are that the activities offered can assist both adults and children in gaining satisfaction, joy, and new friendships and that the activities provide an opportunity to improve skills while participating in meaningful leisure-time activities.

Program Description

The Brooklyn Park Recreation and Parks Department not only is well known for its comprehensive and quality sport programs across all ages, but also offers more than 500 diverse recreational programs for its users. Age-group activities include instruction and recreational activities in art, music, drama, dance, safety, health, fitness, sport, and wellness, which form the focus of their well-rounded program. The department is committed to enhancing the social, cultural, and aesthetic environment of its diverse community and serves as a focal point for many community activities.

Program Specifics

In addition to designing and conducting the aforementioned 500 programs, the city of Brooklyn Park oversees a park system that contains 2,400 acres of community park land, including sixty-three neighborhood parks. The system also includes three nature areas, a communitywide trail system, ten school/park sites, three major sports complexes, five separate community public meeting facilities, and the Community Activity Center/Armory, which is one of the finest centers of its kind in the nation. The park system also operates the restored Brooklyn Park Historical Farm, which showcases an 1890s farmstead, and two municipal golf courses (Brookland Executive Nine and Edinburgh U.S.A., which has been selected as one of the nation's top fifty public championship golf courses).

The Community Activity/Senior Center is home to the department's management staff and houses a gymnasium, ice arena, community room, and racquetball, volleyball, and wallyball courts as well as conference rooms and classrooms. These areas are shared with groups ranging from the Lions to the National Guard. The facility also provides a nursery and day-care facility and programs for persons with varying disabilities.

The center opens daily at 6 A.M. and ice time is typically programmed to 1 A.M. Summer park hours extend daily from 8 A.M. to 10 P.M. There are user fees for golf, tennis, racquetball, the ice arena, and the nursery, with other modest fees (ten to twenty-five dollars) associated with each specific program. The center in this regard is user friendly!

Personnel

The department employs a director, two assistants, four program supervisors, and six program specialists (youth, seniors, special populations, special events, aquatics, teens, and preschool), as well as 200 to 300 instructors and support staff necessary for providing first-class facilities and programming to all members of the community. The department also likes to provide summer jobs for qualified young men and women (high school/college). As implied by the depth, scope, and popularity of the programs, recreation and parks departments like

Children's aquatic programs are important to community health, wellness, and safety.

Brooklyn Park offer many employment opportunities for qualified physical educators and recreation specialists.

Contact Address

Brooklyn Park Recreation and Parks
Department
5600 85th Avenue North
Brooklyn Park, MN 55443

Hopkins-Minnetonka Recreation Services

Source of Information

Dave Johnson, Director
Ron Schwartz, Contractual Services Manager

General Information

Since 1967, the neighboring cities of Hopkins and Minnetonka as well as their respective school districts and Wayzata have joined forces to provide a high-quality community recreation department. Basically the two cities and school districts (see figure 6-4) provide the facilities and space to the department, which in turn provides the management and assures equal access to all residents. The services unit recently reorganized to provide more effective recreational programs, administrative services, facilities management, ice arena management, and contract services to the twenty-five communities and three school districts that it expertly serves.

Figure skating at Brooklyn Park Community Center.

Program Goals/Objectives

The mission statement of this innovative organization is "to develop, promote, and provide quality diversified recreational programs, activities and facilities that will enhance the leisure-time needs and interests of the Hopkins-Minnetonka community." To accomplish this shared mission, the Hopkins-Minnetonka Recreation Services have established the following goals:

- to provide quality customer services
- to hire and maintain a staff that is professional in their abilities and responsive to the needs of the public
- to be fiscally responsible
- to strengthen the organization's identity and presence in the community
- to provide and promote diversified recreational programs, activities, administrative services, and facilities to enhance the quality of life of the community

Program Description

The comprehensive recreation program includes league play activity ranging from T-ball to high school and senior league competition in basketball, volleyball, broomball, ice hockey, softball, football, soccer, and baseball. Year-round aquatic programs, low-impact aerobics, slimnastics, morning stretch, senior tennis league ladder, couples and family golf, indoor soccer, and figure and power skating as well as a nature environmental studies camp, sports clinics/camps, and sport schools are other features of this multidimensional community-based program. Recreation Services also offers special programs ranging from Tiny Tots (for three- and four-year-olds) to Over Forty and Fit and from New Horizons (integration of persons with disabilities) to monthly family recreational outings.

General activities include pool splash time, summer playground activities for preschool children, day camp, municipal swimming beaches, ice skating rinks with warming houses, open gymnasiums, and an adaptive recreational program. Other

Operating costs for the recreation program are apportioned to the two cities' general fund tax base on the basis of the average user attendance. Although the program's administrative offices are housed in the Minnetonka City Hall, its facilities are primarily those of the two cities as well as their respective school districts. The services unit, in joint cooperation with its two cities, just constructed another new full-service 92,000 sq. ft. fitness center, as well as a Cultural Arts Center, which houses its dance programs.

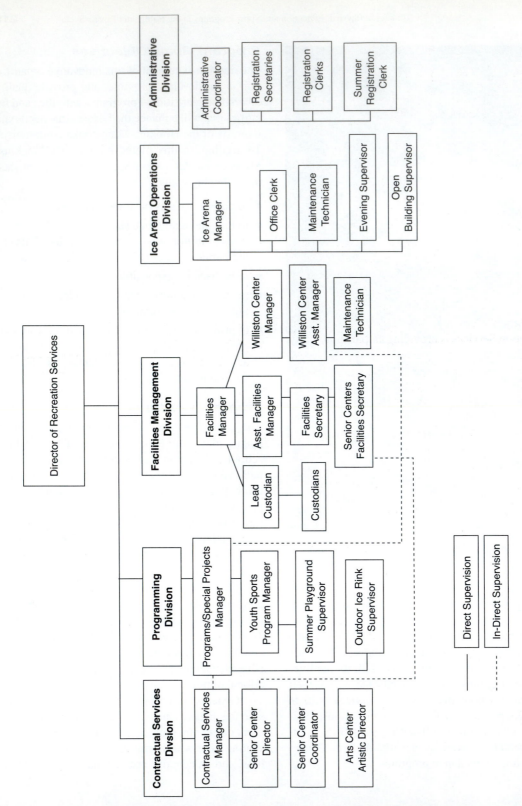

Figure 6-4. Organizational structure of a partnered community-based recreation program.

services provided by the department are day centers, clubs, outings and trips for teens, families, and senior citizens, group picnics, Kid's Fest, a USATF-certified 8-K, two-mile Fun Run and Tot Trot, and Breakfast With Santa.

Program Specifics

Recreation Department activities are available to all residents of Hopkins, Minnetonka, and the surrounding communities as well as any individuals who are employed full-time in either of these cities.

Programming for the department is developed and conducted by a joint recreation staff. Sport programs are low pressure and recreational in nature; they emphasize skill learning and development rather than highly competitive play.

An important focus for Hopkins-Minnetonka Recreation Services is providing ample opportunity for senior citizens to engage in meaningful and enjoyable leisure-time activities. The department offers an active seniors schedule that includes birding, gardening; hiking; line, square, and ballroom dancing; billiards; swimming; softball; tennis; and Tai Chi Chin as well as ceramics and parlor games. In addition, senior trips, outings, and tours are organized and promoted via the *Senior Script* newsletter.

The department's programs run year-round, and except during summer, they operate after school and on weekends. The fees involved typically sustain each of the programs and respective administrative overhead and provide a 10 to 30 percent profit margin.

Personnel

The Hopkins-Minnetonka Recreation Services is headed by the director, five division heads, five recreation supervisors, a clerical and support staff, and more than 500 contract instructors and supervisors who are responsible for the conduct of the various seasonal phases of the department's programs.

Contact Address

Hopkins-Minnetonka Recreation Services
Minnetonka City Hall
14600 Minnetonka Boulevard
Minnetonka, MN 55345

HIGH SCHOOL LEAGUES, COLLEGE CONFERENCES, AND FOUNDATIONS
The Minnesota State High School League
Source of Information

David V. Stead, Executive Director

Skip Peltier, Associate Director

Lisa Lissimore, Associate Director

Kevin Merkle, Associate Director

Jody Redman, Associate Director

General Information

The Minnesota State High School League (MSHSL) is a voluntary, nonprofit association of public and private schools with a history of service to Minnesota youth since 1916. The MSHSL has long been recognized as a national leader in student chemical health awareness and education (TARGET Minnesota), for its leadership in gender equity, and for developing activities and state championships for students with disabilities.

Community-building programs focus on peer mentoring, youth, and leadership skills.

Program Goals/Objectives

The MSHSL mission is to provide educational opportunities through interscholastic athletics and fine arts programs for students and leadership and support for its more than 480 member schools. To achieve the mission, the MSHSL adheres to the following governing values:

- equity, fairness, and justice
- activities that support the academic mission of schools
- fair play and honorable competition
- activities that support healthy lifestyles
- treating people with dignity and respect

Research indicates that students in league activities tend to have higher grade point averages, better attendance records, lower dropout rates, and fewer discipline problems than the general student population does.

Program Description

The MSHSL administers thirty-seven athletic and fine arts state tournaments for its member schools. They conduct fourteen tournaments for girls, thirteen for boys, and since 1995, four (bowling, floor hockey, softball, and soccer) for students with disabilities. State tournaments are also held for debate, fine arts, one act plays, music, and speech/debates. The MSHSL serves more than 200,000 students and involves more than 3,000 individuals in their committees and advisory boards.

Program Specifics

The MSHSL comprises more than 480 member high schools and is structured (see figure 6-5) in the form of an elected representative assembly and a twenty-member board of directors. The representative assembly is the rule- and policy-making body and develops bylaws that govern league activities. Member schools, activity associations, school board associations, and regional committees elect or appoint the members of the representative assembly. The league is financed primarily through state tournament gate receipts, broadcast rights fees, and corporate contributions. The league provides catastrophic insurance for league-sponsored programs and provides tournament liability insurance, rule books, a newsletter, training for contest officials and judges, and educational programs for coaches.

The MSHSL provides leadership in adapted athletics, gender equity (publishes an excellent manual), student chemical health programs (TARGET Minnesota, see appendix D), and student leadership development (ExCEL). It also promotes Spotlight on Scholarship and Academic, Arts and Athletics (Triple A) award programs and maintains a Hall of Fame. The league serves over 10,000 coaches and fine arts directors and 4,500 registered contest, and game officials and judges.

Personnel

The MSHSL consists of an executive director and four associate directors, as well as a fifteen-member office and support (accounting, publications, legal) staff.

Contact Address

Minnesota State High School League
2100 Freeway Blvd.
Brooklyn Center MN 55430

The Atlantic Coast Conference
Source of Information

Amy Yakola, Director of Public Relations
PO Drawer ACC
Greensboro, NC 27417-6274

General Information

The Atlantic Coast Conference was founded in May 1953 from seven schools that had been long-time members of the Southern Conference: Clemson University, Duke University, University of Maryland, North Carolina State University at Raleigh, University of North Carolina at Chapel Hill, University of South Carolina, and Wake Forest University. The University of Virginia joined late that same year. In 1954, the conference chose Wake Forest University Athletic

The ACC expands their reach and influence.

Director James H. Weaver as its first commissioner, and took up residence in Greensboro, North Carolina, where it remains today.

The University of South Carolina withdrew in 1971, and Georgia Institute of Technology joined in 1978. Florida State University was admitted in 1991 to become the ninth member. In 2003, the University of Miami and Virginia Polytechnic Institute and State University withdrew from the Big East Conference and joined the ACC. Effective July 1, 2005, Boston College became the twelfth member of the ACC.

The ACC is a National Collegiate Athletic Association Division IA conference. It is an "all sports" conference in that each member schools' sports teams must compete within the conference in each of the sports in which the conference sponsors a championship. The conference now sponsors twenty-five sports and twenty-four championships: baseball, women's field hockey, women's rowing, softball, women's volleyball, wrestling, and men's and women's basketball, cross-country, golf, indoor and outdoor track, lacrosse, soccer, swimming and diving, and tennis.

Program Goals/Objectives

The ACC mission is "to maximize the educational and athletic opportunities of its student-athletes while enriching their quality of life. It strives to do so by affording individuals equitable opportunity to pursue academic excellence and compete successfully at the highest level of intercollegiate athletics competition in a broad spectrum of sports and championships. The conference will provide leadership in attaining these goals by promoting diversity and mutual trust among its member institutions, in a spirit of fairness for all. It strongly adheres to the principles of integrity and sportsmanship, and supports the total development of the student-athlete and each member institution's athletics departmental staff, with the intent of producing enlightened leadership for tomorrow."

The purposes of the Atlantic Coast Conference can be summarized as follows:

- enhancing the academic and athletic achievement of student-athletes
- promoting competitive opportunities for student-athletes in the sports sponsored by the conference
- promoting amateurism, fostering rules compliance, and stimulating fair play and sportsmanship
- encouraging responsible fiscal management and fiscal stability at the conference and institutional levels
- providing leadership in developing positive public attitudes toward intercollegiate athletics
- promoting trust among member institutions and addressing their future athletic needs in a spirit of cooperation and mutual benefit.

Program Descriptions

The conference motto "A tradition of excellence . . . then, now, and always" expresses the ACC's attitude toward athletic competition and academic

MINNESOTA STATE HIGH SCHOOL LEAGUE
ORGANIZATION CHART

Membership

32 — AA Subregions
32 — A Subregions
 2 — Music A—AA
 2 — Speech A—AA
 2 — Athletic Directors Association
 2 — Coaches Association—Girls Sports
 2 — Coaches Association—Boys Sports
 8 — A School Board Representatives
 8 — AA School Board Representatives

LEGISLATION

Representative Assembly *
The 90-member legislative
body of the MSHSL

* Enacts and amends activity rules
as submitted by:
1. Any five (5) member schools
2. A region committee
3. A coaches association
4. The Board of Directors

ADMINISTRATION

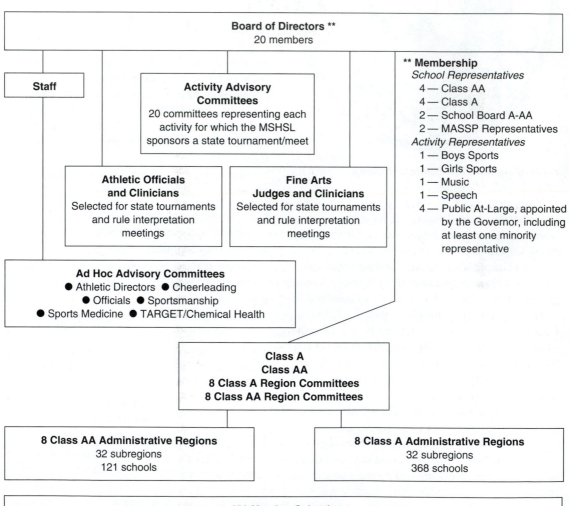

Board of Directors **
20 members

Staff

**Activity Advisory
Committees**
20 committees representing each
activity for which the MSHSL
sponsors a state tournament/meet

** **Membership**
School Representatives
 4 — Class AA
 4 — Class A
 2 — School Board A-AA
 2 — MASSP Representatives
Activity Representatives
 1 — Boys Sports
 1 — Girls Sports
 1 — Music
 1 — Speech
 4 — Public At-Large, appointed
      by the Governor, including
      at least one minority
      representative

**Athletic Officials
and Clinicians**
Selected for state tournaments
and rule interpretation
meetings

**Fine Arts
Judges and Clinicians**
Selected for state tournaments
and rule interpretation
meetings

Ad Hoc Advisory Committees
● Athletic Directors ● Cheerleading
● Officials ● Sportsmanship
● Sports Medicine ● TARGET/Chemical Health

**Class A
Class AA
8 Class A Region Committees
8 Class AA Region Committees**

8 Class AA Administrative Regions
32 subregions
121 schools

8 Class A Administrative Regions
32 subregions
368 schools

489 Member Schools
2 Official School Representatives from each member school to Region Meetings
Eligible: one school board member; one administrator or full-time faculty member

Figure 6-5. Minnesota State High School League organizational chart.

accomplishment. In its fifty-three years of competition, it has lived up to this tradition. Since 1953, ACC schools have won 91 national championships and 173 individual national titles. Among these accomplishments are ten national titles in football, eight in men's basketball, and one in women's basketball. The ACC also has the best bowl record of any conference. Throughout its history the ACC has also promoted and supported academic excellence. Among its important programs is one that offers yearly postgraduate scholarships to outstanding graduating senior student-athletes. In addition, the conference sponsors numerous outreach programs ranging from the Futures Internship Program to its Annual United Way Campaign in which its employees are actively engaged.

Program Specifics

Each member of the conference has one vote in all matters of conference business. The voting delegates of the respective institutions are appointed by their chief executive officers and "shall be a regular full-time member of the faculty at the time of appointment, with voting power, or an administrative officer in that institution . . . whose primary duty is not in athletics." In practice, each institution's NCAA Faculty Athletics Representative (FAR) is its voting delegate. A president, a vice-president, and a secretary-treasurer are elected for one year terms from among the voting (FAR) delegates on the basis of a rotation kept on file in the conference office.

The Chief Executive Officers of the member institutions, together with the Commissioner, constitute the Council of Presidents, which usually meets twice a year. The Council is responsible for voting on the admission and withdrawal of conference members and for the hiring of the Commissioner. Although the Council of Presidents can review any aspect of conference operation, most issues relating to conference management are dealt with by each CEO through the institution's voting delegate.

The officers of the conference, together with the past-president and the chair of the Council of Presidents, constitute the Executive Committee. The Executive Committee transacts the business of the conference between regular meetings and oversees the management and operation of the conference. Matters related to the operation of the conference are dealt with by the voting delegates. It is worth noting that the ACC vests the responsibility for voting on most matters related to conference management to faculty members (FARs) who are not members of their institution's athletic departments.

The Commissioner is the chief administrative officer of the conference and is responsible to the Executive Committee. In addition to administering the conference, the duties of the Commissioner include, but are not limited to, interpretation and enforcement of conference rules, calling regular and special meetings, assigning football and basketball officials for conference games, preparing publicity about the conference and its activities, preparation of an annual budget, and leading negotiation of television and other contracts on behalf of the conference. The Commissioner also engages the employees of the conference of which there are now twenty-seven. The major positions are Associate Commissioners for Men's Basketball, Women's Basketball, Finance and Administration, and Compliance and Governance; Assistant Commissioners for Football/External Relations, Media Relations, and Student-Athlete Welfare; Directors of Video Services and Information Systems, Championships, and Public Relations; and Four Assistant Directors including Compliance and Governance, Media Relations, Video Services, and Women's Basketball. There are also Coordinators of Football and Basketball Officials.

Much of the conference business is conducted by a number of committees appointed by the conference President and Commissioner and composed of voting delegates, athletics administrators, and conference employees. These committees deal with awards, constitution and bylaws, equity, finance, infractions and penalties, marketing and sponsorship, nominations, officiating, postgraduate scholarships, public relations, sportsmanship, student-athlete development, television, and one committee for each of the sports that the conference sponsors. In addition, the athletic directors and senior women administrators meet separately as committees and there is an active Student-Athlete Advisory Committee.

Formal conference business is conducted at four regularly scheduled meetings of the voting delegates, athletic directors, and senior women's administrators. The President presides at these meetings, and the agenda is prepared by the Commissioner in consultation with the membership.

Personnel

League Commissioner

Associate Commissioners (4)

Assistant Commissioners (3)

Directors (4)

Assistant Directors (4)

Coordinator of Football Officials

Business Manager

Contact Address

Mr. John D. Swofford, Commissioner

Atlantic Coast Conference

PO Drawer ACC

Greensboro, NC 27417-6274

Phone: 336-854-8787

Fax: 336-316-6097

www.theacc.com

Women's Sports Foundation
Source of Information

Donna A. Lopiano, Ph.D., Chief Executive Officer

General Information

Founded in 1974 by Billie Jean King, the Women's Sports Foundation is a national charitable educational organization seeking to advance the well-being and leadership skills of girls and women through sports and physical activity. The Foundation's Participation, Education, Advocacy, Research, and Leadership programs are made possible by gifts from individuals, foundations, and corporations. The nonprofit Foundation is located in Nassau County, New York.

Dr. Donna Lopiano, CEO of the Women's Sports Foundation, delivers a powerful and meaningful message for all girls and women involved in physical education and sport.

Program Goals/Objectives

The Foundation works for equal opportunity for our daughters to play sports so they too can derive the physiological, psychological, and sociological benefits of sports participation. Research has shown that high school girls who play sports are less likely to become pregnant, more likely to get better grades in school, and more likely to graduate than girls who do not play sports. Regular participation in physical activity can help reduce a girl's health risk for obesity, diabetes, heart disease, amenorrhea, osteoporosis, breast cancer, depression, stress, anxiety, disordered eating, and lack of self-esteem among others. Sport is where our children learn about teamwork, goal setting, ethics, and the pursuit of excellence. In an economic environment where two-income families are commonplace, our daughters must be well prepared for the highly competitive workplace, and participation in sport and physical activity is a proven training ground.

Program Description/Specifics

One of the top five public grant-giving women's funds in the United States, the Women's Sports Foundation distributes $10,000–20,000 per week to provide opportunities for socioeconomically underprivileged and inactive girls to participate in sports and physical activity. In the past thirty years, the Foundation has awarded $8 million in grants to advance participation, research, and leadership in sports and physical activity for girls and women.

The Foundation offers ten grant and scholarship programs that support female athletes, students, coaches, researchers, and organizations conducting sports programming. It produces over fifty publications, videos, and research projects and maintains an Information Referral Service; a Speaker Service of champion female athletes and experts; and various TV and publishing projects. The Foundation has continued to successfully defend the landmark civil rights statue Title IX and provide gender equity counseling and an attorney referral service and is a co-sponsor of National Girls and Women in Sports Day. The Women's Sports Foundation also conducts critical national research reports on various aspects of women's sports and has created seven local and national awards programs.

As the leading voice in girl's health through sport and physical activity for the last thirty years, on May 20, 2004, the Women's Sports Foundation launched GoGirlGo!—a national call-to-action to get one million girls aged eight to eighteen moving over the next three years and make physical activity part of their lives. The initiative will also aim to keep another one million girls from dropping out of sport participation. The Foundation wants the term "inactive girl" to disappear and wants regular physical activity to be an expected and enjoyable part of every girl's life. The Foundation wants every active girl and every adult to know how important it is to encourage girls to engage in movement, be an active role model, and understand how to get girls involved in physical activity.

The GoGirlGo! initiative includes $2.6 million in grants to provide activity opportunities to girls in underserved and economically disadvantaged communities, a national public education campaign, a mentoring program, a curriculum-based program for parents, coaches and girls and GoGirlGo! Days in local communities. The Foundation asks for everyone's help. Go to www.GoGirlGo.com, where adults can pledge to get a girl active and girls can learn about different activity choices. There are more than 100 activity choices for her—one just right for her skill level, body type, personality, and interests.

Personnel

The Foundation consists of twenty-eight full-time staff members and twelve to fifteen interns, led by a chief executive officers and a twenty-seven-member Board of Trustees.

Contact Address

Women's Sports Foundation
Eisenhower Park
East Meadow, NY 11554
(800) 227-3988
www.WomensSportsFoundation.org

PROFESSIONAL QUALIFICATIONS AND RESPONSIBILITIES OF PUBLIC AND PRIVATE SECTOR PHYSICAL EDUCATION AND SPORT PERSONNEL

The qualifications required to gain employment in the various public and private sector physical education and sport professions are similar in nature but expanded in scope, diversity, and intensity from that of the teacher, coach, or athletic director. Certainly a degree in physical education/kinesiology, sport management, recreation, exercise science (with basic business, marketing, or counseling background), or some allied or health-related degree is requisite. An internship in a public or private sector physical education or sport setting is also mandatory as is actual work experience in a similar setting.

In addition to a degree, solid communication and people skills are crucial, as well as professional credentials from the following:

- ACE (American Council on Exercise)
- ACSM (The American College of Sports Medicine)
- AFAA (Aerobics & Fitness Association of America)
- IFPA (International Fitness Professional Association)
- ISSA (International Sports Sciences Association)
- NASM (National Academy of Sports Medicine)
- NATA (National Athletic Trainers Association)
- NCSF (National Council for Strength & Fitness)
- NIHS (National Institute of Health Science)
- NSCA (National Strength & Conditioning Association)
- NSCA-CPT or CSCS (National Strength & Conditioning Association-Certified Personal Trainer or Certified Strength and Conditioning Specialist)
- NSPA (National Strength Professional Association)
- USPTA (U.S. Professional Tennis Association)

Education preparation and professional certification are crucial because they not only provide the employee with expertise to serve the user more effectively, but also provide experience, as well as rich management training (e.g., harassment, negligence) necessary in all physical activity environments. Certification has become an issue in the profession and fitness industry and will continue into the future. Some public and private sector members are turning to third-party accreditation of their certification procedures and protocols from independent, experienced, and nationally recognized accrediting bodies such as the National Commission for Certifying Agencies (NCCA),

which is the accrediting body for the National Organization for Competency Assurance.

Other qualifications that come in handy are the ability to repair and maintain equipment; construct online newsletters and Web sites; create and design a wide range of exercise, fitness, health, and wellness programs (including nutrition, stress, and weight management); sell, promote, and market memberships; and develop or adopt a personality and communication style conducive to the specific workplace setting. Technology skills are requisite for all personnel. The public and private sector job market is people-oriented, service and labor intensive, very competitive, comes with legal risks and challenges; and demands a great deal from the employee.

The responsibilities of personnel involved with corporate and workplace organizations; commercial fitness, health, and wellness industries; and community-based physical education and sport programs cover the total spectrum of work endeavor.

Other associated responsibilities of health and fitness industry professionals and specialists follow:

- Direct exercise, fitness, and health-related wellness programs, which may be oriented to prevention and/or rehabilitation
- Train, supervise, and counsel staff
- Develop and manage the program budget
- Design, manage, and maintain the facility
- Market and sell the program and facility
- Evaluate, in conjunction with a physician, each participant's medical and physical activity history, as well as perform graded exercise tests and various other fitness assessment procedures and protocols
- Develop individual exercise prescriptions and health-related training packages for participants
- Evaluate and/or counsel participants, upon request, about nutrition, smoking, substance abuse, weight control, and stress reduction
- Accumulate program data for statistical analysis, research, and reporting
- Maintain professional affiliations

Professional qualifications, education, experience, and communication skills are requisite for all workplace environs. Wright Wayne, North Carolina State University.

This list of responsibilities, however, must be supplemented with the following tasks, which often fall in the domain of the corporate, commercial, and community-based program manager:

- Instruct a wide variety of skills (e.g., aerobic exercise, racquetball, jogging, weight and circuit training)
- Participate with members in a wide variety of physical activity (e.g., jogging, squash, swimming)
- Counsel participants on fitness, health, wellness, and skill and technique development
- Serve as individual or personal trainer (IEP and computer analysis)
- Clean, maintain, and repair equipment (especially in an international setting where parts are sometimes difficult to acquire)
- Inventory, select, purchase, and care for equipment
- Be an accountant and money collector (maintain daily, weekly, and monthly statements)
- Supervise groundskeeping, maintenance, and cleaning crews
- Supervise and train lifeguards and staff (a critical legal responsibility)
- Write newsletters, construct media guides, and design corporate health, fitness, and wellness handbooks and guides

- Sell and sustain memberships (conduct tours of facilities)
- Seek new partnerships both internally and in the community
- Budget, schedule, promote, market, advertise, supervise, and assess programs and personnel
- Schedule members for interclub and intraclub activities and competitions (e.g., Boston Marathon, cycling tour of France, Green fun runs)
- Become a stress reducer and enabler for members and staff

These are just some of the responsibilities and duties required of personnel employed in a public or private sector physical education and sport environment (NASPE-NASSM, 2000). This profession offers a tremendous educational, physical, and psychosocial challenge, one that requires commitment, endless vigor, and personal excellence.

TAKE IT TO THE NET!

American College of Occupational and Environmental Medicine (ACOEM)
www.acoem.com

Club Industry's Fitness Business-Pro
www.fitnessbusiness-pro.com

Club Managers Association of America
www.cmaa.org

Fitness Management
www.fitnessmanagement.com

International Health, Racquet and Sportsclub Association (IHRSA)
www.ihrsa.org

National Strength & Conditioning Association (NSCA and NSCA-CPT)
www.nsca-cc.org

Online Sports Career Center (SGMA International)
www.sportlink.com

Potential Employment Options/Sports Careers
www.sportscareers.com

SUMMARY

Physical education and sport programs are not limited to schools, colleges, universities, and other educational institutions. Many other programs and settings exist in the larger community, including the international domain. Corporate enterprises, hospitals, foundations, health and fitness clubs, and other commercial fitness industry creations, as well as various community-based organizations ranging from Ys, community centers, and recreation and park-related services to local and state associations now play, and will continue to play, a vital role in the delivery of health, fitness, and wellness to the nation. These settings represent new, exciting, and challenging opportunities for well-trained and skilled physical educators and sport management students seeking employment as instructors, consultants, managers, and potential owners.

SELF-ASSESSMENT ACTIVITIES

These activities will assist students in determining if material and competencies presented in this chapter have been mastered.

1. Conduct a survey of your community, county, and state to determine various public and private sector physical education and sport programs providing employment opportunities.

2. Prepare a set of guidelines you would follow if asked to manage a commercial fitness club.

3. What physical education objectives might be accomplished in public and private sector physical education and sport programs?

4. Construct a job description for a manager of a corporate fitness and wellness center.

5. Conduct an interview with a public sector fitness, health, and wellness manager and construct a top ten list of key responsibilities.

6. Design a business plan to present to a hotel chain to convince them to include a fitness center component in their management scheme.

7. Describe how a community-based health and fitness center may partner with existing school district programs.

REFERENCES

1. Cohen, A. 2004. It's getting personal. *Athletic Business,* July, 52–60.
2. Eitzen, D. S., and G. H. Sage. 2003. *Sociology of North American sports.* Dubuque, IA: McGraw-Hill.
3. Ferreira, R. R. 1988. Effect of work shift and club size on employees. *Journal of Sport Management* 2:1–13.
4. IHRSA. 2003c. *The 2003 profiles of success report.* Boston: International Health, Racquet and Sportsclub Association.
5. Janda, J. 2000. The top 100. *Club Industry,* July, 33–56.
6. Meek, A. 1997. An estimate of the size and supported economic activity of the sports industry in the United States. *Sport Marketing Quarterly* 6(4): 15–21.
7. Miller, L. K., and L. W. Fielding. 1996. The appropriate business structure: A decision for sport managers. *Journal of Legal Aspects of Sports* 6(2): 101–116.
8. NASPE-NASSM. 2000. *NASPE-NASSM sport management program standards and review protocol.* Reston, VA: AAHPERD Publications.
9. U.S. Department of Health and Human Services. 1987. *National survey of worksite health promotion activities.* Washington, DC: Office of Disease Prevention and Health Promotion, Summer.
10. U.S. Department of Health and Human Services/Public Health Service/ PCPFS. 1999. *Healthy people 2010.* Conference edition. Washington, DC: United States Department of Health and Human Services.
11. U.S. Department of Health and Human Services. 2000. *Healthy people 2010: Understanding and improving health.* 2nd ed. Washington DC: U.S. Government Printing Office.
12. Wuest, D. S., and C. A. Bucher. 2003. *Foundations of physical education and sport.* New York: McGraw-Hill.

SUGGESTED READINGS

Anspaugh, D. J., M. B. Dignan, and S. L. Anspaugh. 2000. *Developing health promotions programs.* New York: McGraw-Hill.
Discusses health promotion, employment and career paths, legal issues, and corporate culture. Case studies are included.

Cordes, K. A., and H. M. Ibrahim. 2003. *Applications in recreation and leisure: For today and the future.* Dubuque, IA: McGraw-Hill.
Designed for students who are considering a career in recreation, physical education, and related professions.

The appendices list various organizations that may be of interest to physical educators.

Fitness Business Pro
Monthly publication for the health & fitness facility management industry. Published by Intertel Publishing, 9800 Metcalf Ave., Overland Park, KS 66212-2215.

Forouzesh, M. R., and L. E. Ratzker. 1984–1985. Health promotion and wellness programs: Insight into the Fortune 500. *Health Education* 15(6):18–22. Describes the nature and the extent of health promotion and wellness programs in Fortune 500 companies.

Kobak, E. T. 2000. *The 2000–2001 sports address bible & almanac.* Santa Monica, CA: Global Sports Productions.
A comprehensive list of public and private sector sports organizations.

Lumpkin, A. 2005. *Physical education and sport: A contemporary introduction.* 4th ed. New York: McGraw-Hill.
Provides lists of certifications and journals for newly entering professionals to the field of physical education and sport.

McLean, D. D., A. R. Hurd, and N. B. Rodgers. 2005. *Kraus' recreation and leisure in modern society.* Boston, MA: Jones and Bartlett.
Describes recreation, parks, and leisure service programs for various special-interest groups, with a focus on physical education and sport. Outlines commercial and private recreation enterprises.

McNeal, R. B. 1995. Extracurricular activities and high school dropouts. *Sociology of Education* 68 (January): 62–81.

Robbins, S. P., and M. Coulter. 2005. *Management.* Upper Saddle River, NJ: Prentice Hall.
Discusses social responsibility, value chain management, and building of organizational culture.

Thibault, L., T. Stack, and B. Hinings. 1994. Strategic planning for nonprofit sports organizations: Empirical verification of a framework. *Journal of Sport Management* 8:218–233.

PART 4

Management Functions

CHAPTER 7

Human Resource Management and Supervision

Instructional Objectives and Competencies to Be Achieved

After reading this chapter the student should be able to:

- Identify the laws of the land that affect human resource management.
- Understand the need for personnel policies.
- State the basic principles underlying effective personnel or human resource management.
- Summarize the qualifications needed by physical educators and coaches who work in schools, in institutions of higher education, or in the private sector.
- Trace the process for recruitment, selection, hiring, orientation, and preservice and in-service training

for professional development of new staff members.
- Discuss the subject of supervision, including the qualities needed by supervisory personnel, the role of group dynamics in the supervisory process, and the basic principles that should guide effective supervisory working relationships with staff members.
- State the various steps of procedural due process to which all personnel are entitled.
- Describe various methods of evaluating physical educators, coaches, and other personnel in physical education, sport, and recreation programs.

This text has been concerned thus far with a discussion of management theory, organization, and structure and of the management of various kinds of physical education and sport programs, including fitness, recreation, health, and wellness programs in the public and private sectors. Part IV contains a discussion of the main functions and du-

ties that managers must perform within these programs. The first of these is human resource management and supervision.

Originally, personnel management or industrial relations was mainly about selecting, placing, orienting, evaluating, and retaining people who were staff members of an organization. Contemporary personnel management that is now referred to as human resource management (HRM), however, has taken on a more mature connotation. Management no longer regards personnel as overhead or cost factors to be manipulated for greater gain and glory but instead views personnel, or human resources, as assets worthy of investment (e.g., compensation, professional development, recognition, reward) in order that the social capital of the organization can accumulate. Elements of social organization such as trust, norms, values, standards, and networks that improve the efficiency and effectiveness of an organization by facilitating coordinated and meaningful actions are its social capital. Human resources are more likely to cooperate for mutual benefit in this horizontally managed environment and to seek collective solutions to problems as well as to perform at a high level. Recruitment, selection, hiring, training, motivating, and other considerations become the responsibility not only of management, but of all staff or team members. As a result, human resource management depends on various individuals and groups understanding and accepting each other and working closely together to ultimately achieve the organization's goals. A contemporary definition of HRM is the process of accomplishing organizational objectives by finding, acquiring, developing, and keeping the right people to form a qualified workforce (Gibson, Ivancevich, and Donnelly 2003). Simply stated by John Chambers, CEO of Cisco, you get the best people in the industry to fit into your culture and you motivate them properly, then you are going to be an industry leader (Nakache 1997).

The nature of human resource management and supervision is changing because many institutions and businesses are adopting school-based and on-site management and responsibility-centered management concepts that provide for more decentralized decision making as well as responsibility sharing. Managers and supervisors are consulting more closely with faculty, staff members, and employees before making final decisions on hiring, staffing, curriculum, scheduling, evaluations, and workplace environment. Managers are also being required to negotiate with unions and nonunion workers in collective bargaining sessions. Manage-

ment and supervisory positions are no longer considered isolated levels at which all decision making takes place. School-based, site-based, and responsibility-centered management ensures that various faculty, staff, employees, user groups, students, and others who care about quality education and program delivery have a voice in departmental or institutional policy making.

For all these reasons, human resource management and the important articulating component of supervision (providing quality oversight, appropriate attention, and encouragement) are perhaps the most challenging responsibilities for managers as they attempt to establish an optimal working environment. Managers who do not have the confidence and cooperation of their human resource assets will have great difficulty implementing any decision, policy, or program (Williams 2005).

HUMAN RESOURCE POLICIES

With the help of staff members, management should see that a detailed handbook of personnel policies or human resource manual is developed. These policies, procedures, and rules should be sound, up-to-date, and consistent with contemporary human resource management theory and the laws of the land (see box 7-1). Selected areas that might be covered by a human resource policies manual include employee rights, terms of employment, assignments, promotions, due process, grievance procedure, harassment policy, separations, evaluations, hours of service and length of school year, compensation, schedules, fringe benefits, insurance, child care, absences, leaves, travel, in-service training, and conduct on the job (see box 7-2).

In some cases, human resource policies are not developed by the management, but rather by a bargaining contract or exclusive representative (e.g., union, association, or federation). In such cases, the bargaining contract as well as the organization's structure (i.e., LLC, LLP, sole proprietor) will probably affect the flexibility and guidelines within which the manager and management may operate. It is crucial that management understand

Federal Law/Order and Year	Main Provisions
Civil Rights Act of 1964	Title VII prohibits employment discrimination in hiring, compensation and terms, conditions or privileges of employment based on race, religion, color, sex, or national origin.
Executive Order (E.O.) 11246, 1965	Prohibits discrimination on the basis of race, religion, color, and national origin by federal agencies as well as those working under federal contracts.
Executive Order 11375, 1965	Adds sex-based discrimination to Executive Order 11246.
Age Discrimination in Employment Act of 1967 (amended in 1978 and 1986)	Protects employees forty to sixty-five years of age from discrimination. Later amended to age seventy, then amended to eliminate age limit altogether.
Executive Order 11478, 1969	Amended part of Executive Order 11246, states that practices in the federal government must be based on merit. Also prohibits discrimination based on political affiliation, marital status, or physical handicap.
Occupational Safety and Health Act (OSHA), 1970	Established mandatory safety and health standards in organizations.
Equal Employment Opportunity Act of 1972	Established the EEOC.
Vocational Rehabilitation Act of 1973	Prohibits employers who have federal contracts greater than $2,500 from discriminating against individuals with disabilities, racial minorities, and women.
Veterans Readjustment Act of 1974	Provides equal employment opportunities for Vietnam War veterans.
Age Discrimination Act of 1978	Increased mandatory retirement age from sixty-five to seventy. Later amended to eliminate upper age limit.
Pregnancy Discrimination Act of 1978	Affords EEOC protection to pregnant workers and requires pregnancy to be treated like any other disability.
Immigration Reform and Control Act of 1986, 1990, 1996	Established penalties for employers who knowingly hire illegal aliens; prohibits employment discrimination on the basis of national origin or citizenship.
Older Workers Benefit Protection Act of 1990	Prohibits age-based discrimination in early retirement and other benefit plans.
Americans with Disabilities Act of 1990	Prohibits discrimination against an essentially qualified individual and requires enterprises to reasonably accommodate individuals.
Civil Rights Act of 1991	Nullifies selected Supreme Court decisions. Reinstates burden of proof by employer. Allows for punitive and compensatory damages through jury trials.
Family and Medical Leave Act of 1993	Permits employees in organizations of fifty or more workers to take up to twelve weeks of unpaid leave for family or medical reasons each year.

Adapted from Gibson, Ivancevich, and Donnelly 2003.

Box 7-2	Human Resources Manual Content

Vision and Mission Statement

Organizational Structure and Infrastructure

Employee Status Designation (professional, staff, hourly, seasonal)

Rules, Roles, and Assignments (work duties and obligations)

Rights and Responsibilities (personnel files, representatives)

Contract, Salary, and Terms of Agreement (temporary, probationary, salary, hiring, and termination)

Benefits Packages (hospitalization, retirement, life and health insurance)

Leaves of Absence (sick, personal, professional)

Grievance Definitions and Procedures (abuse, harassment)

Staff and In-Service Development Opportunities (legal, compliance, training, work life issues)

Assessment, Evaluation, Performance, and Approval Procedures and Timeframe

Promotion, Advancement, and Bonus Schedules

Physical and Health Status (physical ability, appearance)

Injury, Insurance, and Risk Management (disability, substance abuse)

such exclusive representatives and that the guidelines prescribed are contained in full in the human resource policies handbook or manual (Miller 1997; Mathis and Jackson 2005).

PRINCIPLES OF HUMAN RESOURCE AND SUPERVISORY MANAGEMENT

Productive human resource management and supervision do not just happen. They occur as a result of adhering to a prescribed set of basic principles.

The Individual as a Member of an Organization

Management and supervision should seek to imbue the organization with the idea that every individual is an asset and has a personal investment in the enterprise. The organization's undertakings can be successful (i.e., quality, productivity, service) only

if all persons contribute by working to their fullest potential; then success brings satisfaction to all. Submergence of self to this end is necessary for achievement of the organization's goals. In this regard, Ouchi's Theory Z and Total Quality Management concepts discussed in chapter 1 are typically employed by high-quality managers. Organizational development through the involvement of employees (ODIE) has also proved to be an effective model in introducing and integrating the employee into the workplace. Managers that pay attention, are responsive, and involve employees in the decision-making process usually secure positive results.

Building a Culture of Cooperation, Character, and Trust

To achieve cooperation, build character and trust, and ensure that their service will be most productive and effective, the talents and unique abilities of individuals must be utilized, continuously developed, encouraged, reinforced, and rewarded. Maintaining cooperation, character, and trust among the staff will largely depend on staff satisfaction in the work environment and fulfillment of the organization's obligations, mission, and goals. The function of management and supervision is to see that these essentials as well as a wholesome and safe work environment are provided and sustained.

Ethics and HRM: Social Responsibility

Educators, sports managers, and leaders, regardless of their work-site employment, are faced with ethical decision making every day. Philosophy, values, beliefs, behavior, and the laws of the land are constantly being tested by, and are crucial to, not only the organization, but also each of its members, as well as the many publics the organization may serve. Theorists often cite bureaucratization, rationalization, and routinization as "unethical props," as well as the specialized, technocratic, elite-controlled, and seemingly impersonal nature of sport and those who manage its structures, systems, and processes.

Therefore, it is critical that teachers, coaches, sport managers, and leaders bring to the table personal and moral commitment, honesty, a positive attitude (cognitive, affective, behavioral), and integrity. Not only do contemporary managers and leaders have to possess vision and value and respect human resources/human capital, but they must be aware of their ethical, legal (i.e., discrimination, harassment), and social responsibilities (serve to benefit community/society). Some general ethical principles that are often adhered to by high-quality managers and leaders include the following:

- Religious injunction: Never take any action that does not build a sense of community.
- Government requirements: Never violate the law because the law represents the minimum moral standard.
- Utilitarian benefits: Never take action that does not create greater good for the society.
- Individual rights: Never infringe on other's agreed-on rights.
- Distributive justice: Never take actions that harm the least among us.
- Long-term self-interest: Never take action not in the long-term interests of the organization.
- Personal virtue: Never do anything that is not ethical, honest, open, and truthful.

HRM Authority and Power

The existing authority of management belongs to the position and not to the person. Power and authority do not reside in one human being, but in the best thinking, judgment, and imagination that the organization can summon. Therefore, authority and power come from the organization. This is the value of the school-based or workplace management approach. Individuals possess only the authority that goes with their position. In turn, this authority is respected, valued, and appreciated by other members whose work is closely allied to achieving the objectives for which the organization exists. Final authority and power rest in those who, because of their positions, are responsible for ultimate decisions.

Department heads, sport and fitness staffs, various committees, task forces, and staff consultants issue reports interpreting the facts. Their judgments, conclusions, and recommendations contribute to the formulation of final decisions, which are the responsibility of the manager (e.g., teacher, coach, athletic and activities director, principal, fitness center manager). If these interpretations, judgments, conclusions, and recommendations are not accepted, the organization is not only weakened but may fail. Furthermore, individuals cannot be induced to contribute their full efforts to an organization that has little respect for their thinking. Authority and power permeate any organization and should be a shared concept, and skilled managers use their legitimate authority to empower their human resource base.

Building Human Resource Morale

Management should continually strive to create conditions that facilitate good staff morale. The degree to which high staff morale positively permeates the organization will be in direct proportion to the degree to which such conditions are satisfied (Hunter 1989).

Leadership

The quality of management will, to a great degree, determine staff morale. From the top down, all leaders/managers should be carefully selected. Other things being equal, staff and employees who contribute and produce more will possess better morale. These individuals usually have more respect for managers who are leaders in the true sense of the word. Leaders are managers who are a stride ahead in leading the way. Leaders ask what we should be doing and influence others in the group or team to do it. Leaders who possess a lucid, long-term vision for the future, including constructive change, will inspire, motivate, and empower employees, embrace diversity, and create and build trust and confidence. Leaders build social capital through sound human resource management.

Physical and Social Environment

A contributing, enabling, and supportive physical and social environment is essential to good staff morale. The organization must provide for the physical health, wellness, and safety of its human resources. All occupational safety and health (OSHA) guidelines and standards including ergonomics should be followed, and workplace security (theft, violence, harassment) practices set in place. The organization must also make provisions for mental and emotional health, including proper supervision, mentoring, and counseling; opportunity for advancement through professional and staff or student development; and avenues for intellectual enhancement (e.g., paid tuition, sabbatical leaves, paid staff development, and health promotion assistance).

The social environment is also an important consideration. Individuals with whom a person interacts and the activities in which those individuals engage both in and outside the workplace can strengthen or diminish a person's drive for excellence. Therefore it is important for a person to associate with those individuals who can serve as facilitators, mentors, and motivators, not only to accomplish the goals of the organization, but also to build positive social relationships that are conducive to individual development and continued satisfaction.

Mentoring

Many organizations are using mentoring not only to improve productivity, but also to develop managerial talents and potential successors. Mentoring is not a new concept, nor is it new to physical education, sport, or the sporting process. Greek literature notes that Mentor was hired by Odysseus to tutor/mentor his son before departing on his odyssey. In Japan, sumos have for centuries served as mentors (senpai) to develop future successors. Today, student teachers, and student coaches serve under cooperating teachers, and coaches, graduate assistants under head coaches, teaching assistants and research assistants serve under advisors, and even the U.S. Olympic Committee has an educational mentoring program. Mentoring usually takes place when a senior member advises and supports a junior member in order for that person to succeed and/or climb the professional ladder (Hunt 2001). All managers are encouraged to employ the various forms of mentoring—informal life, infor-

mal career, program, project, organizational, and external (community)—in the appropriate situation so that personnel may develop to their fullest potential.

Advancement

Each individual likes to believe that he or she is progressing on the job and in the world. Each member of an organization must be aware of what is essential for retention, progress, reward, and promotion. Opportunities should be provided (human resource development) for learning new skills and knowledge and for gaining new experiences. Encouragement, incentive (e.g., financial, flex time), and top-line resources and support (workshops, staff development, and training) should be provided to those individuals who wish to improve and are willing to devote extra time and effort to this end.

Recognition of Meritorious Service

Everyone possesses the need to be recognized. People who make outstanding contributions to the organization should be so honored. Investing in this positive reinforcement or celebration of "culture" dimension is important to the future of the organization as well as to individual self-enhancement, self-esteem, and self-worth. Recognition functions and award programs should be implemented.

Individual Differences and Diversity

Important principles of human resource management are recognizing individual differences, promoting diversity, and identifying different types of work. Building and managing diversity is a delicate balancing act and usually makes it more challenging to build a unified team. However, diverse teams bring multiple perspectives to the table, and heterogeneous teams increase the likelihood that unique and creative solutions will be identified and team effectiveness and empowerment will occur. Individuals differ in many ways—abilities, skills, and training as well as physical, mental, and social qualities. Various types of work require different skills, abilities, personalities, preparation, and training. These differences should be recognized

Recognition of accomplishment is valued at all levels. Mike Hebert and All-American Katrein DeDecker, University of Minnesota.

by the manager, who must make sure that the right person is in the right position at the right time. An individual who is a square peg in a round hole does not contribute to his or her own or the organization's welfare.

The status granted any one person should be in line with the talents, training, and capacities of that individual and with the importance of the function he or she performs. To be placed in a position that should be held by a person with lesser qualifications or vice versa is unjust and sometimes destabilizing or even emotionally devastating. Many disruptive features can develop if individual abilities are not recognized or if proper incentives and rewards are not provided in accordance with training, qualification, fairness, equity, and affirmative action.

Differentiated Staffing

Management must recognize staff members' interests, talents, training, and general suitability for each position or task that is assigned or delegated.

Whether in a school (i.e., teacher, coach) or in a fitness club setting (i.e., sales, personal training), staff should be assigned activities that are allied to their particular training skill sets, and abilities. Organizations are also employing persons such as paraprofessionals, activity specialists, interns, teacher's aides, technology consultants, maintenance staff, and equipment and facility managers to perform specialized tasks. All staff members must be carefully and selectively integrated into the whole so that each may develop to his or her fullest potential and add to the organization's efficiency and effectiveness.

HUMAN RESOURCE RECRUITMENT AND SELECTION

Personnel recruitment and selection are important functions of management. These functions include consideration of the special qualifications for teaching and coaching, and the unique qualifications of people working in other private and public sector physical education and sport settings. A thorough job analysis (the purposeful, systematic process for gathering information on all job-related aspects) begins this critical human resources related process that leads to a job description and specific job specifications. Orientation, pretraining, in-service training, and professional development are also responsibilities that go with staff recruitment, selection, and retention on what is hoped to be a long-term basis.

Special Qualifications for Physical Educators and Coaches

One of the most important considerations in human resource management is recruiting, selecting, and hiring the most qualified personnel. The members of an organization determine whether it will succeed or fail. Therefore, management must recognize the following qualifications needed to meaningfully deliver physical education and sport.

The teacher/coach should be a graduate of an accredited institution that prepares professionals for a career in physical education and sport. Knowledge and reputation of the college or uni-

Good coaches should have expertise in and be able to enthusiastically present the fundamentals of complex skills.

Nadia Comenici conducts a coaches' clinic at the University of Minnesota to help present instructional strategies for stimulating and motivating students.

versity that the potential employee has attended may play a part in the selection process.

Because physical education and sport is grounded in the sciences of anatomy, exercise physiology, biomechanics, sport sociology and psychology, and sport management, physical educators and coaches should be conversant in these disciplines as well as in research methods that will permit the teacher or coach to survey and apply appropriate research findings to the classroom and/or sport-specific situation.

The general education of physical educators and coaches is under continuous scrutiny and, at times, criticism. Knowledge of world affairs and other cultures, mastery of the arts, and possession of other cognitive and educational attributes are imperative. Because the position also requires frequent appearances in public, appearance and communication skills are deemed essential.

Teaching physical education and coaching are intense and strenuous activities and therefore demand that members of the profession be in good physical and mental condition in order to carry out their duties efficiently and effectively. Physical educators and coaches are supposed to help build healthy bodies and minds and are often expected by students, community, and management to be role models. Therefore, physical educators and coaches should be in good physical condition and conduct themselves in a professional manner at all times.

Values, ethics, and morals are often developed through participation in games, sports, and other physical education activities. It is essential that professional physical educators and coaches stress ethics, discipline, fair play, responsibility, and sound values. Their leadership should develop a recognition of the importance of high moral and ethical behavior and should significantly contribute to the development and enhancement of sound human relation and interpersonal skills.

Physical educators and coaches should have a sincere interest in and enjoy teaching, participating in activities, and helping others realize the enjoyment of participation and of becoming physically fit and physically educated. Unless the individual has a firm belief in the value of physical activity and a desire to help extend the benefits of such an endeavor to others, he or she will not be an asset to the profession.

The physical educator and coach should also possess an acceptable standard of motor ability and skill level. To teach and coach various games and activities to others and to fully appreciate the discipline, stress, and anxiety as well as the intricate finesse, technique, and strategies that accompany such activities, it is most helpful to possess the expertise, skills, and ability to demonstrate.

The qualifications and the qualities of a good teacher and coach are synonymous. Many experts consider the following qualities to be desirable ones.

- Thorough knowledge of the subject matter
- Expertise in making an enthusiastic presentation of the fundamentals involved
- Ability to take a personal interest in each student
- Sound preparation and organization skills
- Respect from and for the students
- Ability to inspire and motivate the students to think and act
- Ability to make the subject matter/sport come to life
- Willingness to work with change
- Originality, innovation, and creativity in teaching style and methods
- Good communication skills
- Neat, well-groomed appearance
- Good sense of humor
- Consistent, firm, fair, and honest approach in dealing with students
- Understanding, respect, and kindness
- Exemplary conduct and adherence to school policy and procedure

- Knowledge of clear boundaries between teacher/coach and student
- Emotional stability, self-control, and sensitivity in all situations

Beginning teachers, instructors, and coaches need considerable encouragement and support to hone their skills and gain confidence and experience. Management should be aware of these needs and should work to ensure that those needs are met. A survey of instructors indicated the problems associated with new practitioners in the profession:

- Conflicting messages between what was learned during academic training and what is encountered in the workplace where traditional systems with established patterns and expectations of experienced teachers, coaches, and administrators seem dominant
- Discipline problems with students
- Instructional and other assignments in addition to the primary responsibility of teaching physical education and coaching
- Large classes, making it difficult to instruct effectively
- Difficulty keeping records, reports, lesson plans, and other paperwork up to date
- Difficulties arising from a lack of facilities
- Difficulties with the administration or supervisory personnel directly above
- Problems encountered in obtaining books, equipment, materials, and supplies
- Problems encountered in obtaining cooperative attitude from other teachers, instructors, and coaches
- Lack of departmental meetings and forums to discuss common problems
- Inability to find time for personal recreation

Unique Qualifications for Physical Education Professionals in Other Settings

The professional who seeks employment in settings other than schools and institutions of higher education needs to possess those qualifications

Education, unique experiences, expertise, ethics, integrity, and leadership provide opportunity at the highest level of physical education and sport. Mike Mularky and March Krotee discuss the future.

listed for physical educators and coaches and, in addition, the special training and qualifications needed to work in the activity-specific institution, agency, or area in which he or she seeks employment. For example, a physical educator who seeks employment in the corporate fitness and wellness setting should have as much experience as possible in exercise science, nutrition, and fitness assessment, because many of the duties will involve fitness testing and the development of individualized exercise prescriptions for employees. It would also be helpful to be familiar with the various types of exercise equipment that are used in these programs. If the physical educator plans to seek a position in a community-based recreation program, he or she should have a wide variety of skills in activities that will interest youth, adults, and seniors. Furthermore, he or she will need to be familiar with program planning and structuring, scheduling, facility maintenance, public relations, marketing, and promotion.

To be successful in such settings as health and fitness clubs, ski areas, golf and tennis centers, senior centers, and youth-serving agencies, the physical educator should know the characteristics and needs of the population or user groups being served. For example, the professional working with the elderly must understand senior citizens—their lifestyles, interests, needs, fears, concerns, and physical fitness status—and the activities, programs, and personal attention that will contribute to their total well-being.

In a health and fitness club setting, the educator must be able to sell, promote, and market the program, to keep books, to design individualized fitness and health-related wellness programs, and to supervise the implementation of those programs. The bottom line is that in order to gain meaningful employment, today's professional must be well-educated, physically educated, highly skilled, multitalented, and be able to effectively fit into the organization.

Guidelines for Human Resource Recruitment

Here are several guidelines for the recruitment of qualified personnel.

A job description should be prepared that includes the various duties or job specifications and qualifications that the position requires. This description is often preceded by a thorough and systematic job analysis. The job description should provide such details as the position title, a list of specific duties and tasks involved, educational and experience requirements (qualifications, certifications), type and length of appointment, as well as starting and closing dates and salary and benefits package. In addition, it is standard practice to declare that the employing organization or agency is an equal opportunity employer (in accordance with the Equal Opportunity Employment Act of 1972), to invite the application of qualified women, minorities, and people with disabilities, and to state that the organization complies with federal and state laws prohibiting discrimination in employment.

Notices of the position vacancy should be distributed within the organization, to professional departments and placement offices in colleges and universities, and to respected leaders and colleagues in the field; the vacancy should also be advertised in professional publications such as

JOPERD, the *Chronicle of Higher Education*, and the *NCAA News;* in local and regional newspapers; and on appropriate Web sites and job boards such as Career Mosaic or the Monster Board.

Candidates for the position should be asked to submit their resumes, college transcripts, and confidential references (or persons who can be contacted by the employing organization). A file should be prepared on each candidate that includes records of references and other pertinent information. Candidates should be duly notified when their files are complete or if more information might be needed to fulfill completion requirements. Completed files should be forwarded to members of the search committee or human resource department who are assigned the task of selecting the most promising candidates to bring in to interview. This committee should consist of at least three members, be representative and diverse, and possess knowledge concerning the tasks and challenges of the position.

Guidelines for Human Resource Selection

Many organizations have a search or Human Resource (HR) committee as well as an affirmative action officer that recruits and interviews candidates for vacancies and makes recommendations to management. Guidelines for the selection of human resources follow.

The search, HR, personnel, or other committee or individual should review the files of all candidates, select three to five viable candidates for the position, and invite each of them for a personal interview. Persons within the organization who apply for the position should be evaluated by the same criteria as the outside candidates.

The personal interview offers an opportunity to meet the candidate firsthand and to discuss the position with him or her. During a personal interview, it is important to assess the candidate's personality, character, education, experience, demeanor under stress, and other job specific qualifications. Questions asked might revolve around his or her interest in the position, qualifications, understanding of the employing organization, in-

volvement in various professional activities, and background experience and education. The candidate's philosophy, leadership, value judgments, and potential to be a team player are also assessed. Some organizations require that the candidate make a presentation before faculty, staff, and students. Many organizations find it useful to develop applicant qualification forms and interview assessment forms, not only to assist in quantifying applicants' qualifications and strengths but also to serve as a guide to the human resource or search committee on what the organization believes is crucial to the interview and selection process. In this respect, there is also some information that may be discriminatory to inquire about. The applicant's ethnicity or date of birth, the nationality of the applicant's parents or spouse, and the applicant's religion or political affiliation are some questions that fall into this category.

On the basis of a personal interview and a further examination of credentials and references, a recommendation should be made to management that includes either one or several applicants, giving management the prerogative to select the most qualified and capable person for the position.

Another consideration that should be discussed is contracts. Contractual items such as salary and benefits, educational step level, length of employment, duties, tenure considerations, vacation time and sick days, and other job details should be made very clear to the prospective employee. These additional considerations could be the deciding factor that prompts an outstanding person to accept a position. Such benefits as health insurance, retirement, sick leave, annual leave, professional development, family benefit and recreational opportunities, and travel support are an important consideration in the minds of many prospective employees. Managers should make sure applicants clearly understand all aspects of the position for which a candidate is being hired. Offers and acceptance of employment can be made orally at first, but should be followed up immediately with a written contract. Those candidates who were not hired should promptly receive a letter thanking them for their interest in the organization.

ORIENTATION OF NEW STAFF

The new staff member needs considerable orientation and help in adjusting to a new position. On hiring a new staff member, management should provide guidance and assistance concerning housing, transportation, educational system, hospitals, shopping, recreational areas, places to worship, and other items necessary to getting settled into the community. A preorientation that familiarizes the person with the organization and its management and human resources personnel should also be conducted before the opening of school or first week of work. A specific departmental orientation in order to discuss, reinforce, and clarify the new staff member's duties and responsibilities should also be presented. The new member should know the person to whom he or she is responsible and should know the lines of communication within the organization and any protocol including due process and grievance procedures that must be observed. The new person will have many questions; these should be expected and answered quickly and frankly. Quality preservice and orientation programs should result in a happier, more settled, and more productive member of the organization. A peer mentoring program is also strongly recommended.

IN-SERVICE TRAINING AND STAFF DEVELOPMENT

Because of the rapid changes occurring within the profession, staff members should attend regular in-service and staff development training programs. New methods of management, programming, teaching, assessment, and evaluation have implications for all professionals.

Some suggestions for in-service training and staff development include the following:

- Conducting workshops for staff members in which new trends and developments are examined
- Holding retreats or arranging workshops that will enhance faculty and staff development by inviting consultants and professional colleagues who are specialists in facilities, curriculum development, methods delivery such as cooperative learning, activity and sport

Staff orientation and in-service training are important for efficient functioning of any program.

skills, and technology to meet with staff members and share new concepts, developments, and techniques

- Developing a professional library or resource room with the latest computer linkages and computer-based learning packages, books, journals and periodicals, films, videos, CDs, DVDs and other multimedia-based training materials, and making them readily accessible to staff members

- Devoting some staff meetings to discussions of new developments or issues like burnout, workplace security and health, sexual harassment, or substance abuse

- Encouraging, supporting, and subsidizing staff members' attendance at professional meetings, seminars, certification programs, and conferences

- Using staff members with special talents to upgrade the knowledge and competence levels of other staff members (e.g., stress management, relaxation, creative thinking, cooperative learning, diversity training, and team building)

- Providing presemester or summer orientation sessions for staff members

- Conducting research and experimentation within the organization's own program and linking in-house information and research systems with local university or public sector information systems

- Arranging for the local college or university to come to the school and conduct cohort group graduate classes and workshops or setting up an interactive TV link for distance education opportunities

- Providing training seminars in such activities as problem solving, computer applications, teacher assistant teaming, social and emotional health issues, and mainstream collaborative modeling to enhance teacher performance

- Encouraging sabbaticals, staff educational leave, and travel for professional enhancement

In-service training and staff development are vital to building a cooperative team of teachers, coaches, and personnel. Such activities build esprit de corps and promote communication, enthusiasm, creativity, and sharing. Often these investments in personnel (human capital), or in the organization's assets, pay huge dividends in the form of successful and high-quality programs. Professional enhancement and training opportunities play a significant role in motivating staff to perform to their fullest potential and should be an integral part in all management structures (Kraut and Korman 1999).

SUPERVISION

Supervision is the managerial function concerned with overseeing, assisting, and assessing the empowerment potential of the situation within each human resource function. Supervisors serve as links to management and transmit policy, procedures, and decisions to personnel and ensure that feedback is relayed in the other direction. Supervisors serve as coaches (impart knowledge, motivate), as counselors (encourage, resolve conflict), and as quality control guarantors (assessment and evaluation). The supervisor should act to improve the ability of teachers, coaches, or other personnel to complete their assigned duties. Supervisors must recognize each individual staff member and the contribution he or she makes to the organization, see that staff members are assigned to tasks in line with their abilities, be willing to delegate responsibility, establish high (yet attainable) standards, provide a complete analysis of each position in the organization, establish accountability for staff members, and help each member realize a sense of accomplishment and affiliation.

Supervision will be effective if sound leadership is provided with the supervisor's focus of attention not on his or her own interests or power, but on the needs, interests, and development of the employee.

Qualities of the Supervisor Who Is a Leader

People years ago believed that leaders were born and not made, and that some people by virtue of beliefs or qualities lead and others follow. These statements are not valid. Research indicates that personality, personal characteristics such as self-confidence, emotional stability and attitude, drive, experience, and behavior help shape and determine leadership qualities.

Group leaders are found to outperform other staff members in such areas as acceptance of responsibility, participation, scholarship, and socioeconomic status. Leaders influence others to work hard, stay on task, achieve goals, and challenge the status quo. Leaders encourage creativity and, when problems arise, motivate the individual or group to find a reasonable solution. They are considerate and provide the map for a satisfied and productive workforce.

Studies further reveal that the closer an individual conforms to the accepted norms of the group, the better liked he or she will be; the style of the leader is determined more by the expectations of the membership or group and the requirements of the situation than by the personal traits of the leader. The leader will be followed more faithfully the more he or she makes it possible for the members to achieve their personal goals along with the group goals. In a small group, authoritarian leadership is less effective than democratic leadership in holding the group together and getting its work done.

Hershey, Blanchard, and Johnson's (2001) Situational Leadership Theory suggests that to be an outstanding leader, the individual will change behavior with each situation. The theory is based on factors such as the interaction between the one who aspires to be a leader and the followers, the group's socioemotional support, two-way communication with the group, maturity level of followers, and education and experience of individuals or groups who are being led.

The physical educator or coach who desires to obtain and excel in a leadership and supervisory position in an organization should study the literature on management, supervision, and situational leadership. This research will expose potential supervisors to a variety of situations that may contribute to a greater understanding of the issues and concerns pertaining to leadership.

The physical educator and coach should also recognize that various personal qualities are essential for providing supervisory leadership. These personal qualities include a sense of humor; empathy; sensitivity; feeling of adequacy; ability to instill confidence, trust, and respect; enthusiasm; originality; sincerity; and resourcefulness. Supervision requires the ability to coach staff members in envisaging their own strengths and weaknesses, provide assistance in helping them solve problems, resolve personnel conflicts, improve morale, objectively judge and assess personal performance, and make recommendations for promotions, retention, and other rewards. To accomplish these tasks, the supervisor must be able to promote staff development; create effective channels of communication; establish staff accountability and assessment standards; set goals; provide effective motivation, nurturing, and adequate rewards; and supply a proper dosage of positive reinforcement.

GROUP DYNAMICS/TEAMWORK

Group dynamics are important in supervision. Group dynamics are about understanding the nature and role of groups in modern living. In this text, group dynamics and teamwork are considered in light of the supervisory role in physical education and sport programs. Research has revolved around the structure of groups, how groups operate, the relationships of members within a group and between groups, the factors that affect group attitudes and productivity, and what types of leadership are most effective in varying stages of group relationships and team building.

Physical educators and coaches can benefit from the study of group dynamics because they work with various groups of people in their programs and because they are interested in getting groups to enter into, participate, and support their activities and programs. Teamwork and cooperative effort are essential when working with organizations, agencies, and other groups. Managers and supervisors must be able to work comfortably both inside and outside the organizational framework and should be familiar with the various methodologies employed to examine group behavior.

Research in group dynamics and team building has yielded the following approaches to the study of groups:

■ *Formal models research:* theoretical models of the structure and behavior of groups are developed.

■ *Field theory:* the behavior of groups and individuals within a group results from many interrelated and interdependent phenomena.

■ *Sociometric research:* the choices of the group on an interpersonal basis among members play a major role.

■ *Systems approach:* the group is viewed as a structure of interlocking elements, and group inputs and outputs are analyzed.

■ *Psychoanalytic approach:* the factors that groups and individuals use for motivation and defensive actions form the basis for investigation.

■ *Empirical approach:* groups are observed, observational behaviors are recorded, and statistical procedures are employed to develop basic concepts and guidelines regarding group decisions.

Research has shown that supervisors must understand certain factors about groups in order to work effectively with them. These factors include an understanding of the group's mission in working with other groups, the power the group has over its own members, whether the group's activities are informal or highly structured, and the satisfaction derived by members of the group as a result of such group association. Other factors include the similarities of members of the group, the relationship of members with each other, the degree to which members actively participate in group activities, the case of access to group membership, significance of the group to its members, overall stability of the group, and the structure of the group as it affects the status of each of its members.

Strategies for group dynamics are taught in winter survival course training.

Research also suggests the following reasons why teamwork, and cooperative efforts are effective:

■ Team performance provides increased motivation over individual performance.

■ Teams usually produce better solutions to problems than do people working alone.

■ Teams are able to learn faster than individuals can by themselves.

■ More new and innovative ideas and solutions are generated by both individuals and groups when there is an absence of critical evaluation.

An understanding of group dynamics and team building can enhance the physical educator's and/or coach's role in the supervisory process. The study of group dynamics and coaching is an evolving area that has great potential for increasing the productivity and interpersonal relationships of any organization.

Further recommendations concerning the responsibilities and guidelines of effective supervision may be found in box 7-3.

THE WORKING RELATIONSHIP BETWEEN SUPERVISORS AND STAFF

Effective working relationships between supervisors and staff members will be discussed in two sections: (1) responsibilities of supervisors and (2) responsibilities of staff members. These sections will be supported by informational boxes relating to common points of conflict, effective supervision, and a checklist for effective working relationships.

Responsibilities of Supervisors

Supervisors Should Possess a Sound Understanding of Human Nature to Work Effectively with People

Physical educators and coaches should not look on supervising as impersonal but should always keep in mind human dimensions and potentialities and give human needs, concerns, and problems high priority (see box 7-3).

Supervisors Should Understand Their Own Behavior

Supervisors should see conflicts where they exist and not fabricate them where they do not exist. Supervisors should present an accurate account of group expectations although they may not be in agreement with those expectations. They should recognize the differences and rationale between their own views and egos and those of others.

Supervisors Should Exercise Wisely the Authority Vested in Their Positions

Authority goes with the position, not with the person. Supervisors should recognize that the position exists to further the goals of the organization and that it should never be used for personal gain.

Supervisors Should Establish Effective Means of Communication among Members of the Organization

Opportunities should be readily available to meet and discuss professional and personal (if appropri-

ate) problems, new ideas, and ways to improve the effective functioning of the organization.

Supervisors Should Provide Maximal Opportunity for Personal Self-fulfillment

Each person has a basic psychological need to be recognized, to have self-respect, to be considered, to be fairly rewarded, and to belong. Within the organizational structure, supervisors should strive to make this possible for every group member.

Box 7-3   A Guide to Effective Supervision

1. Establish high, yet attainable, standards and goals.
2. Create a positive working environment of trust and teamwork.
3. Place staff in jobs that match their interests, talents, and passion.
4. Encourage, enable, and acknowledge staff contributions to the total enterprise.
5. Provide staff with tools, resources, support, and motivation to perform a quality job.
6. Avoid threats, punishments, and fear by use of appropriate counseling to improve performance and behavior.
7. Encourage staff to be full partners in policy and decision making, and program development and implementation.
8. Be firm and fair in enforcing organizational policy and goals.
9. Serve as a communicative link between management and employee.
10. Appraise staff on objective, measurable performance criteria taking into account the situation (individual differences and task difficulty).
11. Avoid playing favorites and seek to reward all. Make each feel like an integral part of the team.
12. Be approachable, friendly, sympathetic, and reliable, yet maintain a sense of dignity that comes with a supervisory position.

Supervisors Should Provide Leadership and Promote Staff Growth

Supervising requires leadership qualities that bring out maximal individual effort in the context of the total coordinated effort of the group. Supervisors should encourage and reinforce staff to be self-sufficient and to take initiative with projects.

Supervisors Should Provide Clear-cut Procedures

Sound procedures are essential to the effective and efficient functioning of an organization. Procedures should be carefully developed; thoroughly discussed with those concerned; written and articulated in clear, concise language; implemented; nurtured; and assessed.

Supervisors Should Plan Meaningful Meetings

Staff meetings should be carefully planned and effectively conducted. Meetings should not be called on impulse or dominated by the supervisor. Agendas should be set and followed, and procedures agreed on at such meetings should be carried out.

Supervisors Should Recommend Promotions on the Basis of Merit, without Politics or Favoritism

Recommendations for pay increases, promotions, retention, contract length, tenure, and change of status or grade, when requested, should be attained through careful and systematic evaluation of each person's qualifications in relation to objective criteria. Each member of the staff (teaching or coaching) should be observed two to three times per year, with follow-up meetings and written evaluations submitted to management.

Supervisors Should Protect and Enhance the Mental and Physical Health of Staff Members

The supervisor should attempt to eliminate barriers and petty annoyances and worries that can weigh heavily on staff members. This concern in turn will increase the satisfaction each person derives from

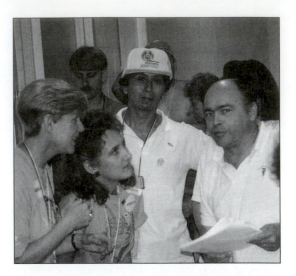

Supervisors provide clear-cut procedures that are essential to effective and efficient functioning.

the organization, promote friendly relationships, develop esprit de corps, improve respect for the status of staff members, and establish a climate of understanding that promotes goodwill as well as personal and organizational development. See box 7-4 for points of conflict between supervisors and staff members.

Supervisors Should Identify Talented Staff Members

The supervisor serves as a link to management and, thus, as part of the staff appraisal process can identify qualified potential staff for future leadership positions within the organization. This is a form of human resource succession planning that should take place in all organizations.

Responsibilities of Staff Members
Physical Educators and Coaches Should Support the Total Program

Each staff member must fulfill his or her responsibility to the program. This responsibility means serving on committees, attending meetings, contributing ideas, and participation in and lending support to worthy projects, initiatives, and developments regardless of the phase of the program to

Box 7-4 Common Points of Conflict between Supervisors and Staff Members

Areas in which poor working relationships may occur include the following:

- the failure of supervisors to recognize physical education and sport as a vital part of the program
- the existence of authoritarian and undemocratic supervision
- the failure to clarify goals, tasks, and responsibilities for the organization and for each member of the organization
- the failure of supervisors to provide dynamic leadership
- the failure of supervisors to provide clearly defined procedures
- the failure of supervisors to build trust and respect with staff
- the practice of supervisors encroaching on classes and schedules without good reason or adequate previous announcement
- the assignment of unreasonable and inequitable workloads
- the failure of staff members to read and respond to correspondence (bulletins, notices, e-mail) that contain important announcements
- the failure of supervisors to assume conscientiously the duties and responsibilities associated with supervision
- the failure of supervisors to keep up to date on staff evaluations
- the existence of unsatisfactory working conditions
- the failure of supervisors to listen to concerns posed by staff
- the lack of adequate space, materials, supplies, and equipment

which he or she belongs. Staff members should view their own fields of specialization in proper perspective within the conceptual or total organizational endeavor. This form of organizational commitment is requisite for success and positive outcomes.

Physical Educators and Coaches Should Take an Interest in Supervision

By actively participating in policy formation and decision making, by forecasting and role playing the problems and pressures faced by the supervisor, and by contributing ideas that will help cut down on red tape and thus streamline the process, physical educators and coaches can have significant impact on the entire organization.

Physical Educators and Coaches Should Carry Out Their Individual Responsibilities Efficiently

If each individual job is performed effectively, if proper procedure, attention to detail, and follow-up is maintained, the organization as a whole will function more efficiently. Performance outcome and organizational commitment go hand in hand.

Physical Educators and Coaches Should Be Prompt in Completing Administrative Responsibilities

Purchase requisitions, attendance, excuse and accident reports, lesson plans, curriculum, grade reports and many other administrative tasks have to be completed on schedule.

Physical Educators and Coaches Should Be Loyal

Each staff member must be loyal to the organization. Disagreement about supervision and differences of opinion can exist, but loyalty to the management and the organization is essential and must be maintained.

Physical Educators and Coaches Should Observe Proper Protocol

Staff members should discuss problems with immediate supervisors before going to higher authority. Lines of authority and chains of command should be recognized and followed. This means starting with the immediate supervisor.

Physical Educators and Coaches Should Be Professional

Professional and ethical behavior is essential in relationships with colleagues, supervisors, managers, administrators, parents, students, and the general public. Confidences should not be betrayed, and professional and personal problems and issues should be settled within the appropriate management infrastructure. Policies and procedures concerning grievance and due process should be articulated and understood.

EVALUATION/ASSESSMENT

Performance evaluation should determine the extent to which the employee is contributing to the overall mission of the organization. These evaluations are crucial in providing information into the organization's reward and sometimes punishment system.

Managers and supervisors need to establish methods to accurately assess human resource effectiveness; to make sound decisions for retention, compensation adjustments, promotion, and tenure; and to help staff members improve and grow. Assessment may also serve to identify weaknesses in the organization's infrastructure (i.e., training, equipment, facilities, support, supervisory, and mentoring programs) and lead to improvements in these domains. Management should encourage a program of assessment. To evaluate is to determine the value or worth of someone (e.g., human resource, user group) or something (e.g., program, equipment, facility). Assessment should be viewed as a positive and ongoing cooperative venture based on the organization's objectives. It is usually accomplished by observations, reports of peers and students, and self-evaluations. Staff members need assistance and support to improve their effectiveness, and assessment is one means to systematically assist in the achievement of this goal. Records should be maintained to determine and chart progress. Box 7-5 will help you formulate some questions to keep in mind when evaluating members of your program.

Here are some guidelines for evaluating staff members.

Appraisal should involve staff members themselves. Assessment is a cooperative venture, and staff members should be included in developing the criteria for evaluation because they need to understand the process. There also is a place for self-evaluation.

Evaluation should be relevant. The appraisal should be centered on specified, agreed-upon job performance criteria, with extraneous factors considered as secondary.

Assessment should be about helping staff members grow on the job. The purpose of evaluation is to help individuals evaluate themselves and develop or maintain strengths and reduce weaknesses.

Assessment should look to the future. Evaluation should be concerned with developing an improved physical education, sport, and recreation program and a better organization. Assessment can also be used to identify programmatic shortcomings and to develop training programs and other interventions to correct and improve these.

Assessment of staff members should be well organized, systematic, and reliable. A step-by-step approach with clearly outlined evaluation criteria should be provided for both teacher and coach. The appraisals should be reliable, meaning that other evaluators using the same evaluation criteria input, will arrive at similar conclusions.

Management evaluative and assessment techniques and strategies can be very helpful in assessing programs. Problems such as depressed economic conditions, changing enrollments, human resource shortages, cost effectiveness, and increased travel and competition can be analyzed more objectively by using management techniques to improve productivity, increase efficiency, and reduce costs. When such techniques are employed and departmental and programmatic assessment has taken place and has been examined, then informed decision making can take place.

Methods of Evaluation/Assessment

Some methods of evaluating human resources follow:

Observation of Teachers, Instructors, and Coaches

Teachers, instructors, and coaches should be notified in advance that the observation will take place, and a conference should follow the observation,

Box 7-5   Checklist for Effective Working Relationships among Managers, Supervisors, Physical Educators, and Athletic and Activities Directors

	Yes	No
1. Job descriptions of all positions are formulated, written, and disseminated to each individual involved.	____	____
2. Policies are cooperatively formulated.	____	____
3. Staff members are encouraged to participate in the determination of policies. Management uses inclusive committees to develop policies.	____	____
4. Policies cover priorities in the use of physical education and sport facilities.	____	____
5. Policies have been developed and are in writing for the major areas of the enterprise as well as specifically for physical education and sport.	____	____
6. Departmental policies and procedures are up to date and complete.	____	____
7. The board or management establishes and approves policies and programs.	____	____
8. Physical educators and coaches know the policies of their organization and work within this framework.	____	____
9. Open channels of communication are maintained between manager, supervisor, and staff.	____	____
10. Preservice, in-service, and staff development is provided.	____	____
11. Staff members are encouraged to participate in professional service and engagement activities of the organizations.	____	____
12. Supervisors act in an advisory, and not a managerial, capacity.	____	____
13. The teaching load of all instructors is equitable in that such factors as the following are considered: work hours per week and number of clientele per week.	____	____
14. Physical education and sport programs are open to all and conducted according to sound educational principles and the laws of the land.	____	____
15. Policies that cover the organization and management of sport are in writing and disseminated.	____	____
16. Coaches are certified in physical education, teacher education, or coaching.	____	____
17. The group process is effectively used in staff and committee meetings.	____	____
18. There is a strong belief in and a willingness to have democratic management.	____	____
19. Staff meetings are well organized.	____	____
20. New staff members are oriented with respect to responsibilities, policies, and other items essential to their effective functioning.	____	____
21. Departmental budgets and other reports are submitted on time and in proper form.	____	____
22. Staff members attend meetings regularly.	____	____
23. Staff members participate in curriculum development.	____	____
24. Class interruptions are kept to an absolute minimum.	____	____
25. Proper management channels are followed.	____	____
26. Relationships with colleagues are based on mutual integrity, understanding, and respect.	____	____
27. Management is interested in the human problems within the organization.	____	____
28. Maximal opportunity is provided for personal self-fulfillment consistent with organization requirements.	____	____
29. Department heads are selected on the basis of qualifications rather than seniority.	____	____
30. Staff members are enthusiastic about their work.	____	____
31. All personnel are provided opportunities to contribute to the improved functioning of the organization.	____	____

Box 7-5   Checklist for Effective Working Relationships among Managers, Supervisors, Physical Educators, and Athletic and Activities Directors—cont'd

	Yes	No
32. The board's executive officer executes policy.	____	____
33. Faculty and staff assignments are educationally sound.	____	____
34. Management works continually to improve the workplace environment.	____	____
35. Responsibilities and tasks are equitably distributed.	____	____
36. Management provides recreational and social outlets for the staff.	____	____
37. Management recognizes and rewards quality work.	____	____
38. Physical educators and coaches seek to improve themselves professionally.	____	____
39. Physical educators and coaches view with proper perspective their special roles and that of the profession in the total educational enterprise.	____	____
40. Physical educators and coaches organize and plan their programs to best meet the needs and interests of the participants.	____	____
41. Physical educators and coaches continually evaluate themselves and the professional job they are doing in the organization.	____	____
42. Budgetary allocations are equitably made among departments, units, and programs.	____	____
43. Management is sensitive to the specific abilities and interests of staff.	____	____
44. Physical educators and coaches take an active role in planning and decision making.	____	____
45. Physical education and sport objectives are consistent with general education objectives.	____	____
46. Management recognizes and gives respect and prestige to each area of specialization in the organization.	____	____
47. Physical educators and coaches are consulted when new facilities are planned in their areas of specialization.	____	____
48. Funds are available for professional library materials, professional travel, and quality in-service and staff development programs.	____	____
49. Physical educators and coaches carefully consider constructive criticism when provided by the management.	____	____
50. Management is skilled, informed, and up to date in organization and administration.	____	____

with the performance outcomes being discussed and evaluated. A written report should follow and be kept on file.

Student Progress

With the student progress method, standardized tests including physical performance appraisals are used to determine what progress the student has made as a result of exposure to the program, teacher, instructor, or coach.

Ratings

Ratings vary and may consist of an overall estimate of a teacher's, instructor's, or coach's effectiveness or consist of separate evaluations of specific teacher/coach behaviors and traits. Self-ratings may also be used. Ratings may be conducted by peers, by students, players, or by management and may include judgments based on observation of student or team progress, comparative or paired comparisons, or behavior-anchored rating scales (BARS). To be effective, rating scales must be based on criteria that maintain objectivity, reliability, sensitivity, validity, and utility.

At colleges and universities, the evaluation of teacher performance is sometimes more difficult than at other schools, agencies, or institutions because of the unwillingness of the faculty to permit managers or others to observe them. Various

Supervision, evaluation, certification, quality instruction, and safety go hand in hand.

methods have been devised to rate faculty members, including statements from department heads and ratings by peers, students, supervisors, personnel committees, and other administrative personnel. The athletic and activities director, parents, other teachers and coaches, and student-athletes usually rate the coaches' performance.

What constitutes effective evaluation as it relates to a teacher, instructor, or coach in a particular school or college? Research reveals, for example, only a slight correlation between intelligence and the rated success of an instructor. Therefore, within reasonable limits, the degree of intelligence a teacher possesses seems to have little value as a criterion. The relationship of knowledge of subject matter to effectiveness appears to depend on the particular teaching situation. A teacher's demonstration of good scholarship (e.g., publication and presentation record) appears to have little relationship to good teaching. Some evidence indi-

cates that teachers who have demonstrated high levels of professional knowledge on national teachers' examinations and gained board certification are more effective teachers. The relationship of experience to teacher/coaching effectiveness also needs to be further explored. Experience during the first five years of teaching seems to enhance teacher effectiveness but after five years, effectiveness seems to level off. Little or no relationship has been found between teaching effectiveness and cultural background, socioeconomic status, gender, or marital status. More systematic research, however, must be accomplished in this domain, including public and private sector settings, to establish what constitutes sound teaching and coaching effectiveness.

Accountability

Accountability may be defined as a means of holding the teacher or coach (and other staff members) responsible for what the students or other individuals learn or achieve.

How can accountability be assessed? The first obstacle that must be overcome to have valid accountability is the acceptance by teachers and coaches of certain objectives that must be met. This acceptance can usually be accomplished by developing performance objectives and learning outcomes. Once objectives and learning outcomes have been developed, the student, instructor, and coach, know what is expected of them. Accountability can be based on how well the staff or students satisfy the stated performance objectives. Some people have suggested that student performance should be a basis for merit pay increases for teachers and coaches. This method of outcome-based education has its pros and cons.

Student Evaluations

The student is the one most exposed to the teacher, instructor, or coach and his or her method. Therefore the student should have some input concerning the evaluation process. Some factors that students believe are related to teacher or coach effectiveness include knowledge of subject, fairness, interest in students, patience, leadership that is amicable but firm, enthusiasm, and skill in activities.

Many teachers, instructors, and coaches are using student opinion questionnaires for evaluation. The student is asked to respond to multiple choice or Likert scale questions that indicate items such as (1) interest level in activity, (2) skills learned, (3) time spent outside of class on activity, (4) knowledge gained, and (5) rating of instructor concerning course objectives, clarity of instructions, organization of presentation, enthusiasm, knowledge, skill, and accessibility to students. Space is often left for students to express in paragraph form any recommended changes in curriculum, teaching style, or method.

Self-Evaluation

An area of evaluation that is sometimes overlooked is self-evaluation, which is often the key to self-improvement. Physical educators and coaches should ask themselves some of the following questions: Have I been innovative? Do I alter my teaching to meet the different student needs and ability levels? Are my classes planned well in advance to ensure adequate teaching space, equipment, and facility use? Do I equally involve all my students and/or athletes? Do I stress cognitive, psychosocial, and affective behavioral objectives? Do I change my activities and practices from year to year and try new concepts such as contract grading, performance objectives and learning outcomes, and self-directed and cooperative learning? Do I continually assess my programs? Do I integrate technology in an effective manner? Do I try to improve myself by continuing my education?

Questions such as these can help the teacher, instructor, and coach begin the process of self-evaluation. Self-evaluation is not easy, but it can be a valuable assessment tool and may help improve personal performance and program delivery.

Independent or External Evaluators

In recent years, the trend has been moving toward using independent evaluators or examiners because they may be more objective in assessing a teacher's or coach's abilities or a program's effectiveness. Independent evaluators should be thoroughly trained and familiar with the subject they are evaluating and should have a teaching, coaching, and administrative background. Often evaluators are drawn from consultant groups, professional organizations, or colleges and universities. The evaluators should have little or no previous links with present organizational personnel or the institution being evaluated.

Evaluating the Prospective Teacher and Coach

The competence of the prospective teacher and coach is an important facet of the total educational evaluation system. Traditionally the undergraduate education major was evaluated in terms of grade point average, completion of required coursework including student teaching and student coaching experience, and a minimum grade level in major subjects. Such evaluation techniques alone obviously are not sufficient to produce quality teachers. New assessment criteria must be established to include such factors as (1) comprehensive testing to ascertain mastery of both general and specific knowledge as well as teacher education objectives; (2) performance testing based on teaching task analysis; (3) the development of a professional portfolio that includes a résumé and examples of job-related skills and experiences; and (4) an internship to develop teaching and coaching skills as well as to learn to perform in an organization's professional culture.

The prospective teacher and coach should be field-oriented, with much of his or her undergraduate training spent in school-related or community-based tasks. During undergraduate years, the individual should have experience in construction and design of lesson plans, IEPs, and learning packages, as well as in grading papers, keeping records, going on field trips, tutoring, and teaching and coaching. The teacher or coach who has graduated from such an experiential-based program and has satisfied the assessment criteria where theory and practice have been effectively linked will be a better teacher or coach and will also have an easier and more enjoyable adjustment to the first few years of teaching. Some teacher preparation departments are extending their programs an additional year in the form of postbaccalaureate programs to provide such extensive in-school training and preparation.

Performance-Based Education

One trend today, as has been pointed out earlier in this text, is toward performance- or outcome-based education. Under this plan, the prospective teacher, instructor, or coach is evaluated not in terms of courses taken and GPA, but in terms of certain competencies (skills, knowledge, abilities) that have been determined essential to satisfactory job performance. The prospective employee is evaluated by scientific assessment techniques that are performance based. A major consideration is whether the individual possesses or can develop the skills requisite to changing consumer (i.e., student, athlete, club member) behavior as well as performance through his or her teaching and coaching.

Evaluation of Physical Educators in Other Settings

Much of what has been said about the evaluation of teachers of physical education and coaches is also true about the evaluation of physical education professionals who work in capacities other than in school environs. They are also held accountable for the effective performance of assigned duties. This accountability is determined, for the most part, by on-the-job observation, by opinions elicited from persons who have been served by the instructors, and by their productivity. Productivity in a commercial establishment such as a health and fitness club, unfortunately, is sometimes judged by how many customers are attracted and maintained and what the bottom-line profit and loss statement says. This judgment is similar to looking at the win-loss ratio for the coach, which, although it may seem unfair, still appears to be the nature of the business.

The main concern of all physical educators and coaches, wherever and however they are employed, is to do the best job possible and let the evaluation take care of itself. In other words, one should be enthusiastic, develop as much expertise as possible about the position and responsibilities

one has, and provide the best experience possible to all persons being served. One should also strive to develop good human relations and rapport with everyone. If these suggestions are followed, the physical educator, instructor, and coach should not have to worry about the evaluation process. The satisfaction of doing the best job possible will lead to productivity, and advancement will result.

HUMAN RESOURCE PROBLEMS REQUIRING SPECIAL ATTENTION

Selected personnel problems that need special attention are teacher burnout, stress management, unionism, affirmative action, use of certified and noncertified personnel, and grievance and due process.

Teacher Burnout

Teacher burnout has been described as a physical, emotional, and attitudinal exhaustion. Depression, fatigue, lack of concentration, anger, loss of sleep, and decreased productiveness are just some of the symptoms that seem to be prevalent in today's professions. Large classes, lack of administrative support, repetitiveness, lack of facilities and resources, workplace violence, shrinking employment opportunities, austere budgets, ill-conceived curricular movements, undue public criticism, lack of community support, heavier teaching loads or workloads, overemphasis on accountability and teacher "testing," discipline problems, and inadequate salaries are a few of the conditions contributing to teacher burnout, as well as heavy turnover.

Some teachers and coaches are tired of their work and the many problems and pressures they face. As a result, the students are being short-changed by teachers and coaches who are complacent, dissatisfied, restless, and suffering physically and sometimes emotionally.

What can be done to cope with burnout? How can teachers and coaches who are suffering from it be helped? What procedures will result in self-renewal and revival for overburdened teachers and stressed-out coaches? More important, how can teacher and coach burnout be prevented?

Many suggestions have been made for eliminating and avoiding burnout. They are listed here so that beginning teachers, coaches, and other professionals currently on the job will be familiar with ways to avoid it or, if already afflicted, can find a remedy for it.

A review of the literature suggests the following activities as antidotes to teacher and coach burnout: participate in visitations and exchange programs, participate in structured learning experiences, become involved in professional organizations, reassess instructional strategies, reevaluate curricular offerings, reassess reading habits, contribute to professional publications, develop a quest for new knowledge, join a fitness and wellness program, get involved in community service functions, and explore additional personal and family development opportunities.

Other potential solutions include the following: use holidays and vacations for personal and professional revitalization, transfer to another school, transfer to another position within the educational system, find a job outside education, or participate in professional development education. Burnout must be attacked on several fronts because no single cause or solution exists. Therefore a teacher or coach experiencing burnout must recognize the problem and then develop a meaningful plan of correction and coping. These plans can range from exercise to prayer and from sabbatical leaves to hobbies. Many educational and corporate environments now provide wellness counseling, a health-related fitness program benefit, and self-help groups to alleviate this serious and growing problem. Support of family, friends, and significant others is also of great help in coping with stress and burnout symptoms.

Stress Management

Stress can be harmful or beneficial, depending on the nature of the stimulus or stressor, as the causal agent is called. Harmful stress affects the ability of the body to maintain stable conditions within itself. Beneficial stress can result in euphoria and greater personal achievements. Negative stress should be reduced to avoid developing physical or emotional health problems. In many cases, physical activity provides an excellent means of intervention (passive coping) and of stress reduction.

Some symptoms of stress that may represent danger signs are irritability, boredom, eating disorders, headaches, muscular tension, back pain, loss of appetite, nightmares, depression, emotional tension, and heart palpitations. The late Hans Selye, endocrinologist, philosopher, scientist, and pioneer in modern stress theory, defined stress as the "nonspecific response of the body to any demand placed upon it" (Selye 1976). He indicated that the body's response to stress follows a three-stage pattern:

Alarm state—the body mobilizes its resources to fight the hostile stressor.

Resistance state—the body adjusts to stress by using its maximal ability to withstand the stressor.

Exhaustion state—the body becomes devitalized and loses its ability to resist stress, leading to serious illness and even death. Many mental and physical reasons have been set forth proclaiming the benefits of physical activity and sport in stress reduction. Through physical activity, individuals can improve mind-body harmony and thus reduce harmful stress, thereby contributing to their own health, wellness, and fitness.

Exactly how physical activity reduces stress is not completely understood. It has been generally established that the mind can influence the body and the body can influence the mind. Research suggests that physical activity can result in a positive psychological response. One theory is that exercise burns up stress hormones (catecholamines). The human body reacts to stress by a response known as fight or flight. As a result, a number of hormonal and physiological changes take place as stress by-products are created.

If one responds to the stressor by engaging in physical activity, the stress by-products are depleted. Selye suggested that the person who exercises regularly is able to resist stressors better and

Teachers attend in-service training on stress management.

that stressful situations do not represent as much harm to the physically active person as to the sedentary individual.

A second explanation is that activity helps remove distress by releasing the tension that can accumulate when one is under stress. Activities such as jogging, bicycling, and brisk walking produce an increased target heart rate and respiration rate and result in significant stress reduction for tense persons. Physical activity also appears to provide a mental diversion or "time out" from problems and concerns that cause stress (Krotee and Hatfield 1979). A stress-regulated and controlled lifestyle should provide a balance between work, exercise, rest, and structured relaxation training.

Many experts report that endurance exercise promotes the secretion of hormones called endorphins that produce the jogger's high. Endorphins are reported to be far more powerful than morphine and serve as nature's way of rendering negative psychological feelings inert and of producing a natural feeling of well-being. Other experts point out that regular and vigorous exercise helps reduce stress by contributing to a lower heart rate, lower blood pressure, improved condition of blood vessels, fewer circulatory disorders, increased core body temperature, and improved body composition (Corbin et al. 2005).

The negative image that some people have about their own body, whether the image is caused by being overweight, weak muscular development, poor posture, or low fitness level, can also be a stressor. Exercise can not only improve body and fitness level development, but it can also assist in enhancement of a person's self-image, self-concept, or body image.

Stress can also be managed by utilizing various kinds of coping strategies and interventions such as progressive relaxation techniques, biofeedback, music, cognitive restructuring, self-talk, imagery, Tai Chi, yoga, and meditation. Box 7-6, Selye's General Guidelines for Stress Reduction, is provided so that teachers and coaches can take full advantage of the suggested interventions to develop successful personalized stress management and active and passive coping programs. Remember stress management requires learning skills that must be practiced.

Exclusive Representation, Unionism

Exclusive representation (e.g., federation of teachers, labor unions, professional organizations) is widespread, and management, teachers, coaches, and other staff members should understand the nature of such an association and be able to work effectively within their exclusive representative framework, including personnel and contractual agreements.

The emphasis in physical education and sport over the years has been for teachers and coaches to become involved in their professional organizations. But since the Public Employment Labor Relations Act of 1971 (PELRA), very little has been introduced to orient the manager, teacher, or coach to exclusive representation.

Managers, especially, need to understand teacher bargaining units, binding arbitration, and civil agreements to be able to work effectively with all personnel. If involved with exclusive representation negotiations, managers should look on negotiations as an opportunity to improve relationships rather than to harm such relationships. It is a time to adjust to negotiations and make the best of the working relationship, advance the organization, and improve its democratic atmosphere. The manager should insist on being a part of the negotiation process, protect the right to be the professional leader of the organization, and strive to promote mutual trust, understanding, respect, and cooperation. Other strategies contained in the Harvard Negotiation Project (Fisher and Brown 1988) and related literature should also be a part of the shared decision making in the negotiation process.

Box 7-6 Selye's General Guidelines for Stress Reduction

Try not to be a perfectionist—instead, perform and work within your capabilities.

Spend your time in ways other than trying to befriend those persons who don't want to experience your love and friendship.

Enjoy the simple things in life.

Strive and fight only for those things that are really worthwhile.

Accent the positive and the pleasant side of life.

On experiencing a defeat or setback, maintain your self-confidence by remembering past accomplishments and successes.

Don't delay tackling the unpleasant tasks that must be done; instead, get after them immediately.

Evaluate people's progress on the basis of their performance.

Recognize that leaders, to be leaders, must have the respect of their followers.

Adopt the motto that you will live in a way that will earn your neighbor's love.

Try to live your life in such a way that your existence may be useful to someone.

Clarify your values.

Take constructive action to eliminate a source of stress.

Other Suggestions

Maintain good physical and mental health.

Accept what you cannot change.

Serve other people and some worthy cause.

Share worries with someone you can trust.

Pay attention to your body.

Balance work, recreation, and relaxation.

Improve your qualifications for the realistic goals you aspire to.

Avoid reliance on things such as drugs and alcohol.

Don't be narcissistic.

Manage your time effectively.

Laugh at yourself.

Get enough rest and sleep.

Don't be too hard on yourself.

Improve your self-esteem.

Managers should know and be conversant as to their responsibilities in professional negotiations, and these responsibilities should be included within their job descriptions. If managers perform within the responsibilities as stated, they should receive solid backing from those whom they represent.

Teachers and coaches should understand that pursuant to PELRA, nothing contained in any exclusive representation agreement should be construed to limit, impair, or affect their right to express a view or opinion, to grieve, or to complain, as long as their duties are conducted faithfully.

Affirmative Action

Managers need to understand and conform to affirmative action guidelines. Among other things, these guidelines, first outlined in Title VII, Civil Rights Act of 1964, and again in The Equal Employment Opportunity Act of 1972, indicate that no discrimination can exist on the basis of gender, race, age, religion, color, ethnic background, national origin, handicap, or creed. All individuals must be afforded equal opportunities to achieve their destinies. In hiring, attention must be given to adequate and appropriate posting and publicity of vacancies (e.g., time; appropriate journals; local, regional, and national electronic and print media), to equal consideration of all applications, and to objective selection based on each individual's qualifications. No discrimination can exist against members of minority groups in employment, retention, discharging salary, or promotion. Recent reverse discrimination litigation and banning of race and gender-based discrimination in college admissions (Proposition 209, California), government hiring, and contracting awards have placed a more controversial light on affirmative action. Also, organizations should strive to achieve representative diversity as well as to promote equal opportunity for professional growth and economic security. The general purpose of diversity programs is to create a positive work environment where no one is advantaged or disadvantaged.

Many organizations employ individuals whose responsibilities include promoting and overseeing the process of equal opportunity and affirmative action within their department, school, or division. Managers should continually consult with these individuals and keep up-to-date with the current interpretation of the law to make the workplace a level playing field. If no such individual exists in an organization, the manager should be thoroughly familiar with and committed to affirmative action and diversity guidelines and goals.

Use of Noncertified and Temporary Personnel

A recent trend has been to use noncertified and temporary personnel in physical education and sport to teach and coach activities when permanent certified personnel are not available or when workloads have become too heavy for the full-time faculty. The shortage of teachers, especially in urban environs that are surrounded by higher-paying suburban areas (i.e., The United Federation of Teachers report that 14 percent of New York City's teachers are not certified) remain a challenging problem. The profession has suggested the following guidelines:

- Activities and sports including athletic training in which students and other consumers are interested in participating need to be conducted by regular full-time, licensed faculty and staff.
- In hiring new faculty, attention should be given to applicants who have the qualifications to teach and coach. If no certified faculty member is available to teach or coach an activity, certified part-time personnel should be hired. If no certified person is available, then noncertified temporary personnel may be considered.
- Noncertified personnel should have expertise in the activity to be taught or coached, and proper supervision should be provided for the noncertified person.
- The noncertified and/or temporary person should be replaced with regular full-time certified and licensed faculty and staff when they become available.

There is considerable discussion in sport programs as to whether coaches and athletic trainers should be certified. Most experts who have explored

Employment and retention of well-qualified, certified and licensed human resources, including teachers, coaches, athletic trainers, and sports administrators, is vital to attain positive outcomes.

this question believe that each needs to be qualified and certified because tasks such as progressive training and conditioning programs as well as issues such as risk, safety, and legal liability can lead to serious problems if coaches are not well trained and well qualified. The same holds true with the profession of athletic training. There is evidence that most states agree with these positions concerning qualification and certification.

Grievance and Due Process

In most educational organizations, a prescribed procedure is set forth to be followed by a staff member or other person who has a grievance. Grievance implies that the person believes he or she has not been treated fairly or wronged or that a hardship, harm, or harassment has been realized and that he or she has a just cause for protest and complaint.

The established procedure usually includes discussing the grievance with persons in the chain of command and trying to solve and correct the problem at the grassroots level. If the problem cannot be solved at the lowest level, it moves on to a higher level or is submitted to a grievance committee. This committee discusses the facts in the case

and attempts to arrive at a solution that is right and, if possible, satisfactory to all concerned.

Management should always be alert to situations in which grievances may occur and should try to solve personal and other problems before they reach the grievance stage. At the same time, some problems are impossible to solve, and therefore an established grievance procedure is essential.

Due process refers to an established procedure requiring certain prescribed steps that are designed to safeguard the legal rights of the individual under the Fourteenth Amendment. For example, when a person is accused of some wrongdoing and could be fired or suspended from the job or denied the right to participate in sport, that person is protected legally by having the right to pursue a judicial procedure that enables both sides to present their facts before a final decision is made. In general, procedural due process includes the individual's right (1) to be informed of all charges and complaints, (2) to a hearing, (3) to secure counsel, (4) to have adequate time to prepare and respond to the charge or complaint, (5) to present his or her side of the issue, (6) to call witnesses and to cross-examine opposing witnesses and parties, and (7) to a fair trial.

SUMMARY

One of the most important functions that management has to perform is that of human resource management. Management is responsible for such actions as establishing policies under which the staff will operate, attracting and recruiting qualified members for the organization according to federal and state equal opportunity guidelines, seeing that staff morale is high, providing adequate supervision and quality control, employing group dynamics and cooperative approaches in the achievement of organizational goals, and providing creative ways to prevent such problems as undue stress and teacher and coach burnout (Barney and Wright 1998). Furthermore, managers must be able to work harmoniously with exclusive representatives and the various publics in general. Last, staff members need to be evaluated periodically in an objective,

TAKE IT TO THE NET!

American Institute for Stress
www.stress.org

Career Mosaic
www.careermosaic.com

Department of Labor
www.dol.gov

Monstertrak
www.jobtrak.com

Occupational Safety and Health Administration
(OSHA)
www.osha.gov

Society for Human Resource Management (SHRM)
www.shrm.org

Sports Careers
www.sportscareers.com

The Monster Board
www.monster.com

U.S. Equal Employment Opportunity Commission
www.eeoc.gov

reliable, and fair manner so that performance can be improved and deserving staff members are appropriately rewarded.

SELF-ASSESSMENT ACTIVITIES

These activities will assist students in determining if material and competencies presented in this chapter have been mastered.

1. Define what is meant by human resource management and supervision and describe the guiding principles for a physical education supervisor.

2. If you were hiring an instructor for a health and fitness club or corporate setting, what qualifications would you look for?

3. Prepare a step-by-step procedure for the recruitment, selection, orientation, in-service, and pro-

fessional development training of a new member of a physical education staff.

4. You are scheduled to be interviewed by a superintendent of schools who is looking for a person to supervise the work of coaches employed within the school system. Discuss the evaluation technique that you would employ to evaluate those coaches within your program. Present to your class what you told the superintendent. Then have the class decide whether you would be hired for the position.

5. Develop a performance-based outcome rating scale you would use to evaluate the work of a physical educator at a senior high school.

6. Prepare a job description for a junior high or middle school girls' volleyball coach.

7. A teacher named in a misconduct complaint by a student should be entitled to what due process steps?

REFERENCES

1. Barney, J. B., and P. M. Wright. 1998. On becoming a strategic partner: The role of human resources in gaining competitive advantage. *Human Resource Management* 37(1):31–46.

2. Corbin, C.B., G. J. Welk, W.R. Corbin, and K.A. Welk. 2005. *Concepts of physical fitness: Active lifestyles for wellness.* New York: McGraw-Hill.

3. Fisher, R., and S. Brown. 1988. *Getting together: Building relationships as we negotiate.* Boston: Houghton Mifflin.

4. Gibson, J. L., J. M. Ivancevich, and J. H. Donnelly. 2003. *Organizations: Behavior, structure and processes.* New York: McGraw-Hill.

5. Hershey, P., K. H. Blanchard, and D. E. Johnson. 2001. *Management of organizational behavior.* Old Tappan, NJ: Prentice Hall.

6. Hunt, D. M. 2001. *Mentoring: The right tool for the right job.* Cincinnati, OH: Thompson International Custom Publications.

7. Hunter, M. 1989. *Mastering coaching and supervision.* El Segundo, CA: Tip Publications.

8. Kraut, A. I., and A. K. Korman. 1999. *Evolving practices in human resource management: Response to a changing world.* San Francisco: Jossey-Bass.

9. Krotee, M. L., and F. C. Hatfield. 1979. *The theory and practice of physical activity.* Dubuque, IA: Kendall/Hunt.

10. Mathis, R. L., and J. H. Jackson. 2005. *Human resources management*. Mason: OH, South-Western.

11. Miller, L. K. 1997. *Sport business management*. Gaithersburg, MD: Aspen Publishers.

12. Nakache, P. 1997. Cisco's recruiting edge. *Fortune,* September 29, 275–276.

13. Selye, H. 1976. *The stress of life*. New York: McGraw-Hill.

14. Williams, C. 2005. *Management*. Mason, OH: South-Western.

SUGGESTED READINGS

Avolio, B. J. 1999. *Full leadership development*. Thousand Oaks, CA: Sage.

Presents a framework concerning leadership, performance, and motivation. Leadership is viewed as a system that can optimize the vital force of each individual.

Fournies, F. F. 2000. *Coaching for improved work performance*. Dubuque, IA: McGraw-Hill.

Greengard, S. 1998. Putting online recruiting to work. *Workforce* 77, 73–77.

Discusses various means to attract, recruit, and enter the workforce/marketplace.

Harvey, C., and M. J. Allard. 2005. *Understanding diversity*. Old Tappan, NJ: Prentice Hall.

Hitt, M., J. S. Black, and L. W. Porter. 2005. *Management* Old Tappan, NJ: Prentice Hall.

Presents crucial information on establishing culture, team building, motivation, and monitoring and evaluation.

Iacocca, L. 1984. *Iacocca—An autobiography*. New York: Bantam.

Tells the story of one of today's most successful managers in industry. As chief executive officer of the Chrysler Corporation, he transformed a dying company into a great success. Relates how he worked with his staff to achieve results.

Kelly, B. C., and D. L. Gill. 1993. An examination of personal/situational variables, stress appraisal, and burnout in collegiate teacher-coaches. *Research Quarterly for Exercise and Sport,* March, 94–101.

Kraus, R. G., and J. E. Curtis. 2000. *Creative management in recreation, parks, and leisure services*. New York: McGraw-Hill.

Outlines the scope and process of personnel management, including information about such items as job descriptions, competency-based approaches to hiring personnel, professional preparation, employment standards, supervisory practices, training approaches, and working with unions.

Nahavand, A. 2003. *The art and science of leadership*. Old Tappan, NJ: Prentice Hall.

Discusses current issues and trends in leadership and provides a salient biography concerning the art and science of leadership.

Ouchi, W. G. 1981. *Theory Z: How American business can meet the Japanese challenge*. Reading, MA: Addison-Wesley.

Discusses the Theory Z management style in which employees are key to increased productivity and organizations foster close interchange between work and social life in order to build trust.

Peters, T. 1987. *Thriving on chaos*. New York: Alfred Knopf.

Introduces the revolution of personnel recruiting and covers topics such as reducing structure and the reorganization of the manager's role. Presents a model for empowering personnel and measuring what is important to the organization.

CHAPTER 8

Program Development

INSTRUCTIONAL OBJECTIVES AND COMPETENCIES TO BE ACHIEVED

After reading this chapter the student should be able to;

- Explain why program development is an important part of the management process and what programs of physical education and sport should accomplish.
- Identify the factors that influence program development.
- Outline a step-by-step process for program development, including the

personnel or groups that will be involved.

- Describe a systems- and competency-based approach to program development.
- Discuss significant elements of program development as illustrated by the Krotee Program Development System (KPDS).
- Develop a procedure for assessing a program.

Chapter 7 focused on human resource management, and supervision, some of the most important functions that directors, chairs, teachers, coaches, instructors, and other professionals involved with managerial aspects in physical education and sport have to assume. Chapter 8 presents another important function of management—to provide the leadership and support needed to plan, design, develop, integrate, and deliver a program that will achieve the objectives of physical education, recreation, and sport. A program can refer to a single event, such as an elementary school track and field day, a 5K fun run or a weekend coaching workshop, or it could be a planned sequence of curricular activities in team-building games. The key point is that the program depends on the "pro-

grammer," or manager of the program who provides expert leadership, intervention, and services to facilitate the total development of the participant or consumer.

The term *program development* as used in this text refers to the total learning experiences provided to consumers to achieve the objectives of physical education, recreation, and sport. Program development is about managing the component parts of physical education, recreation, and sport programs, and integrating the needs of the consumer with the objectives of the organization. It is about managing resources (e.g., human, physical, financial, informational/technological, and technical) involved in planning, implementing, and assessing these learning experiences, so the program can be continually improved. Physical education, recreation, and sport management is involved with programs in schools and colleges as well as various public and private sector organizations as described in chapter 6. Contemporary program development and management demands a team approach with management, school or institution, agency, professional organization (i.e., AAHPERD, The Society of State Directors of Health, Physical Education, and Recreation), and community as well as all people who share a need and concern about the delivery of quality physical education, recreation, and sport programs. Today the trend is to provide carefully planned, fully integrated, value-based programs rooted in the following considerations: (1) the needs and abilities of the participant, consumer or user, (2) the needs of community and society, (3) the practical meaningfulness and usefulness of various knowledge and skills, and (4) the social psychology of learning.

WHAT PROGRAM GOALS SHOULD PHYSICAL EDUCATION AND SPORT MANAGEMENT SUPPORT?

The main goals that physical education, recreation, and sport programs should strive to accomplish pertain to four areas. The physical education and sport program should (1) develop health-related and motor performance-related fitness, (2) develop skill in a wide range of physical activities, (3) develop an understanding and appreciation of physical activity and sport, and their role in the lifelong process, and (4) provide a meaningful psychosocial experience (Mohnsen 2003). This last goal may be accomplished by designing new and challenging physical activity opportunities (e.g., physical education, recreational sport, varsity sport) and having people (e.g., teachers, coaches, instructors, fitness leaders) intervene in the social interaction. Such intervention should create and manipulate learning environments in a fashion that provides quality experiences and outcomes for everyone participating in the physical education and sporting process (SSDHPER 1998).

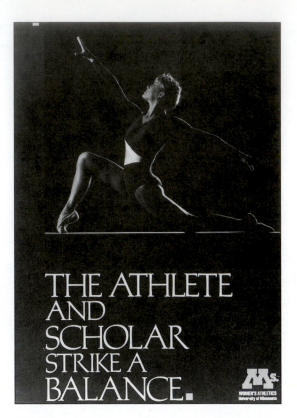

Programs must balance student-athlete activities with academic pursuits.

Develop Health-Related and Motor Performance–Related Fitness

The physical education and sport program should develop such physical characteristics as adequate cardiovascular and respiratory endurance and function, proper body composition, strength, flexibility, body awareness, muscular power and endurance, coordination, speed, reaction time, balance, agility, and proper posture. It is crucial that programs emphasize not only the development of motor performance-related fitness but also its intimate relationship to health and physical activity, which are of national concern.

Develop Skill in Activities

The physical education and sport program should also develop skill in activities such as basic movement patterns and fundamentals (e.g., running, jumping, throwing, kicking, skipping) as well as in individual, team, and lifetime sports. Gymnastics, aquatics, low organizational and cooperative games, and rhythmic activities (such as dance) that incorporate such factors as space, time, and flow should be integral components of the program. Management should also provide support for activities that will assist in any way the development of the various components of health-related and motor performance–related physical fitness (e.g., aerobic exercise, biking, jogging, skating, martial arts, strength and circuit training, orienteering, outdoor pursuit). Mastery of the basic motor skills in physical education, recreation, and sport programs, should be a primary target.

Develop an Understanding of Physical Activity

The program should also foster an understanding and appreciation of, among other things, the contribution of physical activity to physical health (reduction of risk factors, weight control, nutrition), biomechanical principles (role of gravity, levers, acceleration, force), human factors (the ability to integrate human movement with machines) and the contribution of physical health to mental health (relief of nervous tension and stress, building of self-esteem). Also, physical education and sport managers should help students and other individuals gain self-management skills, so they can assess their own fitness level and personal developmental needs and set goals that lead to building and maintaining a healthy lifestyle (Petifor 1999). Box 8-1 contains examples of common physical fitness test components employed by AAHPERD (Physical Best) and PCPFS (The President's Challenge).

Provide a Meaningful Psychosocial Experience

Physical education and sport programs should provide for such psychosocial goals as the human desire for affiliation, mastery, and success in play activities. Cooperative effort experiences, followership, recognition of ability, self-reliance, personal responsibility, respect for leadership, self-discipline, positive attitude formation, con-

cern for others, and increased cultural understanding may also be gained. Managers (e.g., teachers, coaches, instructors) not only should build the program to provide meaningful psychosocial experiences through physical activity, but also must be proactive and enabling role models in the formation of their participants' psychosocial capital (e.g., trust, norms, network, etc.).

IMPORTANCE OF PROGRAM DEVELOPMENT AND THE ROLE OF MANAGEMENT

Researchers indicate that management should pay attention to three basic program development concerns. The first is what ought to be taught (the ideal program), the second is what is being taught (the real program), and the third is what can be taught (the practical program).

Program development should determine what must be learned and achieved (i.e., graduation standards, fitness level, target heart rate) and then should provide the means for seeing that these goals are accomplished. Because no two people are exactly alike, a wide range of physical activity, recreational, and sport experiences that meet the needs of all participants is requisite.

Management plays an important part in program design and planning. The goal of management is to provide quality teaching, instruction, and coaching, an optimal learning environment, and healthful and safe activities and experiences to achieve the established program objectives. Because problems constantly arise and unmet needs continue to exist or remain unrecognized, continuous and adaptable planning, monitoring, and assessment is always a management priority. The manager, who may be the programmer, provides the leadership required to accomplish this ongoing, dynamic task.

Program construction requires the selection, guidance, and evaluation of needs, experiences, and activities to achieve both long-term and more immediate short-term goals. Program construction provides for a periodic assessment of the entire program to make changes whenever necessary. Consideration is given to factors such

Box 8-1   Health-Related Physical Fitness Components

Item A: Distance Run (One-Mile Run/Walk)

Fitness component: Cardiorespiratory fitness/aerobic capacity

Purpose: To measure the maximal function and endurance of the cardiorespiratory system

Item description:

Walking may be interspersed with running; however, students are encouraged to give their best effort to cover the one-mile distance in as short of time as possible after the "Go" signal usually on a one-quarter mile track. Procedures and norms are provided for the one-mile run/walk for time by both the AAHPERD and PCPFS. They are based on the principle that the profession should send children and youth ages six to eighteen into adulthood with a physical status to buffer the myriad degenerative or hypokinetic diseases associated with lifestyle and aging (Corbin, Welk, Corbin, and Welk 2006).

Item B: Sum of Skin Folds (Triceps and Calf)

Fitness component: Body composition/percent body fat

Purpose: To assess the level of body fatness

Item description:

In a number of regions of the body, the subcutaneous adipose tissue may be lifted with the thumb and forefinger to form a skin fold. The skin fold consists of a double layer of subcutaneous fat and skin whose thickness may be measured with a skin-fold caliper. The skin-fold sites (triceps and calf) have been chosen for this test because they are easily measured and are highly correlated with total body fat. The skin folds should be lifted from a relaxed limb at the midposterior or back of the right arm and on the medial or inside at the largest part of the calf girth.

Equipment: Harpenden or Lange skin-fold calipers or lower-cost plastic calipers.

Item C: Sit-ups (Curl-ups)

Fitness component: Muscular strength/endurance

Purpose: To evaluate muscular strength and endurance of the abdominal muscles

Item description:

Students lie on their backs with knees flexed, feet on the floor with heels between twelve and eighteen inches from the buttocks. The arms are crossed on the chest with hands on the opposite shoulder. Feet are held by a partner to keep them in touch with the testing surface. Upon the signal "go," students, by tightening their abdominal muscles, curl to the sitting position. Arm contact with the chest must be maintained. The sit-up or curl is completed when elbows touch the thighs. Students return to down position until the midback makes contact with the testing surface. Repetitions are counted for a sixty-second time period.

Item D: Back Saver Sit-and-Reach/V-Sit-and-Reach

Fitness component: Flexibility

Purpose: To measure the flexibility of the lower back and hamstrings

Item description:

The students remove their shoes and assume the sitting position with knees fully extended and feet against the sit and reach apparatus or a line drawn on the floor shoulder width apart. The arms are straight and extended forward with the hands placed one on top of the other. The students reach directly forward, palms down, along the measuring scale. In this position, each student slowly stretches forward four times and holds the position of maximum reach on the fourth count for one second. The base of the apparatus, or the line where the soles of the feet are placed, is at the twenty-three-centimeter or zero-inch level, respectively. The Back Saver Sit-and-Reach modification employed in the FITNESSGRAM uses the same method; however, only one leg is extended while the other remains bent. Both sides are then alternately measured in a similar manner as the V-Sit-and-Reach.

*Notes: Medical clearance and warm-ups should precede all tests and the cognitive (i.e., concepts of physical fitness) and affective (i.e., attitudes, feelings, commitment) domains should also be assessed. The FITNESSGRAM Physical Activity Questionnaire 6.0 software may be employed. Other often-used health-related fitness tests include the shuttle run (speed, agility), the PACER (aerobic capacity), pull-ups or flexed arm hang (muscular strength, endurance), trunk lift (strength and flexibility), push-ups (strength), and the nine and twelve minute run or walk. Modifications for students with physical disabilities are often provided. For specific information concerning the conduct of the FITNESSGRAM see their Web site (AAHPERD 1999; Baumgartner, Jackson, Mahar, and Rowe 2003; The Cooper Institute for Aerobics Research 2005).

Students learn the importance of stretching.

as participants, the community, the organization, existing facilities and space, human resources, the environment, time allotments, national trends, and state and federal laws and regulations. Program construction provides a conceptual framework for a progressive plan that serves as a guide to physical education recreational and sport personnel so that they are better able to achieve educational and organizational goals.

Although program development is in many cases a staff and faculty responsibility, management plays a very important role in bringing about program development process and reform. Management assesses and forecasts the organization's needs, recruits and hires human resources, assigns tasks, and sees that the mechanism is set in motion to develop and effectively deliver a quality program that meets not only the organization's objectives but those of the consumer (e.g., beginners, lifelong learners, student-athletes) and the immediate community.

PROGRAM DEVELOPMENT PLAYERS

Program planning is a role and responsibility that involves the entire organization as well as vital external sources and resources. The considerations of managers, staff members, professional agencies, organizations and groups, participants, parents and community leaders, and other significant individuals are crucial to sound and effective program development.

Managers

Managers are key personnel in program planning. They serve as the catalytic force that sets curriculum and program initiatives into motion; as the leadership that encourages and stimulates interest in providing optimal learning experiences; as the barrier clearers who provide the time, place, space, and resources to accomplish the task; and as the implementers who help carry out appropriate recommendations of such plans.

For example, the roles of principals and athletic and activities directors of schools in program development are to serve as management links between the central administration, parents, and staff when it comes to program development. Principals of schools influence program development by discussing curriculum and programs with boards of education and superintendents, by seeing that state and federal government mandates are implemented, and by providing for preservice and inservice training and professional staff development of teachers and coaches.

Athletic and activities directors are charged to place together a team of program developers who can work cooperatively and effectively, provide this team with direction (e.g., organizational philosophy and goals), and supply the team with the necessary motivation as well as human, financial, physical, technical, and informational/technological resources to accomplish the task of designing a quality program.

Staff

Staff members lie at the grassroots level of program development. The staff member can contribute his or her experiences and knowledge and can provide data to support recommendations of desired programmatic construction, change, or reform. Teachers' and coaches' comments, based on their immediate understanding of students' needs and interests, can make a valuable contribution. Committees and task forces are an effective way to use staff members. They can be established to study specific instructional or programmatic areas; identify deficiencies, weaknesses, and inequities as well as strengths; and recommend solutions as

Children and their student-teacher plan the next activity.

well as implement changes and reforms. Staff input and perceived ownership are necessary before a program is designed and implemented as well as during its evaluative stage.

Professional Groups, Agencies, and Organizations

Most states have many groups, agencies, and organizations who can assist in physical education, recreation, and sport planning. These include the state departments of public instruction, education, and/or health; colleges and universities; corporate groups; private voluntary organizations (PVOs), such as the Partners of the Americas or the Rotary; state high school associations or leagues; the NCAA; and state AAHPERD affiliates. All these organizations as well as various community-based service groups can provide meaningful input. These groups may provide program assistance, courses of study, volunteer teaching aids, mentors, materials, consulting services, advice, and even physical resources (e.g., space, facilities) that will prove to be invaluable in the planning and conduct of any program.

The Participant

The participants (ranging from student-athletes to older citizens) should play a part in program development. Their thinking in regard to what constitutes desirable or satisfying activities or instructional strategies concerning program content, intensity, duration, frequency, time, and delivery modality, for example, is vital. Participants today are more actively involved in expressing their program desires as well as their concerns and hesitations. They want to be heard, identified, included, and play a meaningful role in planning the various activities and experiences that a quality program should provide.

Parents, Guardians, and Significant Others

Dialogue with parents, guardians, and significant others sometimes helps communicate to the public, as well as the participant, what physical education and sport programs within the school or institution are trying to achieve. Parents and significant others can make significant contributions by supplying input and support in terms of desired outcomes and other programmatic recommendations. Parents, guardians, and significant others also actively express their desires, expectations, and views concerning program content, conduct and outcomes. Parents are a crucial lifeline for all programs and ensuring their full participation and satisfaction is vital to managing any program in an effective and efficient manner. The establishment of a parent and community liaison to serve alongside the program developer and the programmer is a useful strategy to meet this end.

Community Leaders and Other Significant Individuals

Program development should include the services of all interested individuals especially in the immediate community. Professionals such as physicians, nurses, lawyers, architects, bankers, barbers, construction workers, engineers, recreation leaders, and business leaders (e.g., finance and marketing executives) and virtually all citizens who reside in the community can make worthwhile contributions by examining offerings and providing input for various programmatic initiatives and support services. In many instances, citizens support these programs with extra funding (e.g., equipment, uniforms) as well as other resources that significantly add to

Parents, teachers, and coaches play an active role in program development.

Sport managers must envision the needs of the community. Hall of Famer Peggy Kirk Bell delivers a community golf clinic in Pine Needles, North Carolina.

program conduct and quality. It is management's charge to ensure the full participation of all valuable human capital that may significantly contribute to building and sustaining a quality program.

FACTORS THAT INFLUENCE PROGRAM DEVELOPMENT

Factors that directly and indirectly influence program development in physical education, recreation, and sport include (1) the community; (2) federal and state legislation; (3) professional organizations; (4) attitude, leadership, and vision of managers, faculty, students, and consumers; (5) facilities and equipment; (6) class schedules; (7) class and team size; (8) physical education and coaching staff; (9) research; (10) climate and geographical considerations; and (11) social forces ranging from culture to religion.

The Community

The community has considerable influence on physical education and sport program development. In public schools and other institutions in particular, the community provides the funds, facilities, and space for the program; therefore there are vital implications for program development. The community wants to be, and should be, involved.

In the Darien, Connecticut, public schools, a task force on physical education curriculum was appointed by the board of education. The task force

consisted of thirteen members who were active in the community. This group established the programmatic objectives they wished to accomplish and the strategy they would use to achieve their goals. The strategy provided for a survey of all students in the school system, the district's coaches and staff members, 1,000 Darien residents selected from tax rolls, and 40 organizations with a direct or indirect interest in sport and recreation. Furthermore, the task force established evaluation criteria for program assessment.

This community involvement project resulted in rewriting K–12 curriculum guides, setting up student advisory boards and student recreational sport councils, creating a physical education inventory system, creating faculty manager positions in the secondary school, instituting staff development opportunities for physical education teachers and coaches, holding regular meetings with community agencies, and developing a coaches' handbook.

Communities are becoming more aware of their role and responsibility in the planning and program development process, and good management practice allows for full and active participation. Managers in turn must be aware of the physical characteristics of their community (boundaries, constituents, housing, parks) as well as its economic base, political systems, and culture.

Federal Legislation

Although the governmental authority primarily responsible for education is the local authority and the state, the federal government is active in shaping educational programs. The Department of Health and Human Services is responsible for recommending many legislative changes in various fields, including education.

Title IX had a profound effect on physical education and sport programs by prohibiting sex discrimination in educational programs. As a result, many school districts revised their curriculum and redesigned the mode and access of delivery to meet the mandate. Many more sports teams have also been brought into the educational fold, providing for marked increases in female participation at all levels. Unfortunately, at the university level, the National Coalition for Athletes Equity reports that decreases in men's minor sports programs (i.e., baseball, gymnastics, swimming, wrestling) have also occurred.

P.L. 94-142, now IDEA and the Americans with Disabilities Act, and its continual reauthorization and upgrading has also had an effect on school programs in physical education and sport by requiring schools to provide educational services, opportunity, and classes for persons with disabilities from birth through age twenty-one. The upgrading of facilities and personnel has been a direct result of these mandates. Equal opportunity laws and affirmative action continue to play a role in the conduct and staffing of any program.

Sensitivity to issues of diversity has also brought about initiatives such as the Multicultural Education Project of the National Association for Sport and Physical Education (NASPE). Multicultural physical education shall

- include examination of prejudice based on race, ethnicity, language, religion, gender, and exceptionality
- be directed toward elimination of stereotypes and biases and toward achievement of full commitment to cultural pluralism

- be designed for students of both minority and dominant cultures
- promote equity and the maintenance of diverse cultural identities

To further clarify the definition, the following components were established:

- appreciation of (and pride in) a person's own unique cultural heritage, as reflected in history, philosophy and values, customs and traditions, and contemporary concerns
- appreciation of (and respect for) persons of different ethnic groups and their varying cultural perspectives
- appreciation of (and respect for) persons of both sexes and their differing cultural perspectives
- appreciation of (and respect for) persons of all racial groups and their varying cultural perspectives
- appreciation of (and respect for) persons of other religious affiliations and their varying cultural perspectives
- recognition of differences in goals of individuals within a culturally diverse population
- recognition of common goals and concerns of all persons within a culturally diverse population as a basis for positive personal interaction within and across cultural groups

All programs, including those of physical education, recreation, and sport, must lead the way to provide for inclusion, appreciation, respect, and fair and equitable opportunity for all.

State Legislation

The state is the governmental authority primarily responsible for education. Local boards of education are responsible to the state for operating schools as well as recreation and park boards in their respective local school districts. They must adhere to the rules and regulations established by state departments of education. Most schools are also members of their

A peer teacher promotes participation and motivation in a game of tug-of-war.

state high school leagues or associations, which in turn set regulations for participation in many extracurricular activities including sport.

State departments of education set policies about credits to be earned for graduation and courses (e.g., physical education, health) to be included in the curriculum and set requirements about physical education, including the number of hours and days per week as well as the opportunity for participation by persons with disabilities.

In most cases, the regulations adopted by state departments of education set minimum standards. In an ideal situation, local school management sets the standards. Management must continue to play a proactive role in advocating and lobbying for daily physical education initiatives as well as recreation sport programs at both the state and local governmental levels.

Professional Organizations

National, state, and local professional organizations are constantly engaged in activities that influence physical education and sport programs. Through such activities as workshops, health fairs,

play days, conferences, clinics, research, and publications and videos, these organizations provide needed informational resources crucial to program advocacy and development. Resources such as AAHPERD's *Physical Best* (1999), Jump Rope for Heart and Hoop Kits, and NASPE's *Basic Stuff Series I and II* (AAHPERD 1987) as well as its guidelines for elementary, middle, and secondary school physical education; and National Standards for Physical Education (2004) and Sport Coaches (2005); the President's Council on Physical Fitness and Sports; President's Challenge Physical Fitness Program (2004); the surgeon general's *Healthy People 2010: National Health Promotion and Disease Prevention Objectives;* the U.S. Olympic Committee's K–9 enrichment units and its *Olympic Spirit: Building Resiliency in Youth* project materials, for example, can serve to guide, shape, and supplement program development.

AAHPERD also sponsors many national, regional, and state conferences of vital importance to physical education, recreation, and sport professionals. Research studies; workshops; demonstrations of new activities, equipment, methods, and materials; and a general exchange of ideas are presented at these conferences. Also, on request, AAHPERD will suggest knowledgeable consultants to work with school and college personnel in program development, evaluation, and revision. The National Education Association, American College of Sport Medicine, and various sporting and coaching organizations ranging from sports federations such as the U.S. Soccer Federation and USA Triathlon to Special Olympics International also provide meaningful program and human resource support services.

State and local professional organizations such as Be Active North Carolina also provide valuable program development resources, materials, and information. Physical educators, recreation leaders, and coaches should join and support these associations to keep abreast of the latest trends, issues, concerns, and activities. Programs ranging from the American Association of Adapted Sports Program's (AAASP) Project A.S.P.I.R.E.: Getting America's Sidelined Kids into the Game to local programs for

Arnold Schwarzenegger, Governor of California and former chair of the President's Council on Physical Fitness and Sports, addresses AAHPERD members.

the frail and elderly serve notice that we have a long way to go in program diversity, service learning, and professional outreach. This participation is not only good public relations but also a way to keep programs in step with societal trends and demands.

Attitude, Leadership, and Vision of Managers, Faculty, Students, and Participants

In education, the scope and content of physical education, recreation, and sport programs are influenced by attitudes, leadership, and vision of school managers, teachers, and coaches. If physical education and sport programs are viewed as an integral part of the school program, attempts will be made to provide the necessary support, financial and otherwise, for quality program development and delivery. If, on the other hand, they are viewed as extraneous or interfering with "academic" programs, attempts may be made to diminish and downsize sound programs. The attitudes of teachers, students, and the community toward physical education and sport can also affect the kind of program offered.

Management has the responsibility for leading and interpreting and setting the tone for the program to students, faculty, school boards, and the community. A written statement of philosophy, mission, and policies should be provided and included in the curriculum guide as well as in other school materials (e.g., community services and school handbook, policy manual).

Students' and participants' attitudes should not be overlooked by program planners. The way students and student-athletes feel about their programs and experiences will influence their participation in, and support for, the program. A well-designed needs-and-opinions questionnaire is one way of determining attitudes toward physical education, recreation, and sport programs. This questionnaire will enable the programmer to identify specific program development and population needs and outline a strategic blueprint for operation, improvement, and ongoing assessment.

Physical Education and Coaching Staff

The number of and qualifications of physical education and coaching staff members influence the program. Are teachers and coaches qualified, licensed, and certified? Is there a supervisor of physical education and/or athletic and activities director to coordinate physical education and sport in the school district? These important questions need to be considered because sound physical education and sport programs depend on the quality of the teaching and coaching staffs. The faculty of every school should include human resources who have expertise and interest in physical education and sport.

Physical education specialists responsible for delivering the subject matter should have completed a sequence of courses relating to their specialty. Too often physical education is taught by individuals with limited physical education experiences. Coaches often are assigned because of willingness rather than qualification. Management should require that only qualified, licensed, and certified personnel be employed in carrying out programmatic plans.

Facilities and Equipment

The provision of adequate physical resources (e.g., facilities, equipment, maintenance, and upkeep) can help in influencing attitudes and facilitating programmatic success. Attractive and well-maintained indoor and outdoor facilities entice participation and adherence and thus help in shaping a quality program. They also foster a sense of pride to all concerned. The extent, nature, and condition of the facilities depend on such factors as the number of students, other user groups, financial support, and the geographical location (e.g., urban, rural) of the program. Chapter 9 provides in-depth treatment of facility management.

Class Schedules and Sports Offered

The number of classes of physical education provided each week, the length of these classes, and who delivers them affect the program. The minimum time for all subjects is set by state departments of education. However, local school managers can increase the amount of time spent on physical education just as they can for other subjects. Scheduling strategy such as block scheduling or alternate week can also provide the programmer with creative opportunity.

The sports opportunities offered to males, females, and special populations also depend on attitudes, leadership, vision, financial resources, and

the interests of the community, school, and user groups. It is the manager's role to marshal and coordinate these human resources, to implement to full advantage the laws of the land (e.g., Title IX, IDEA, ADA), and to provide quality, equitable opportunities and programs for all.

Class and Team Size

The type of activity being taught, the environment, and the number of teachers will determine the class size and frequency of offering. Under normal circumstances, the number of children in a physical education class should not exceed thirty-five. Size of classes in adapted/developmental physical education should be determined by the specific needs of the students. In school districts in which physical education is accepted as an integral part of the school curriculum, class size is kept at a level that promotes optimal learning and safety. The school management, and sometimes the local exclusive representative, can do much to see that class size is reasonable for achieving learning goals and maximizing safety.

Team size should allow for inclusion of all participants who want the sporting experience within the limitations of quality staff, supervision, and facility specifications. Title IX stresses equal opportunity for both physical education and sport programs.

Research

Although some school districts, institutions, and corporations rely on research to assist them in developing and revising their physical education and sport programs, too many fail to recognize the value of the latest research about health, physical education, and sport.

Important research studies that affect curriculum offerings in physical education are being conducted by researchers in a variety of disciplines. An example of the results of research that have influenced physical education programs are studies relating to the fitness of United States children and youths. Results have indicated that a majority of our children and youths are lacking in many fitness components, and curricula have been revised accordingly to focus on the upgrading of physical fitness levels and transmission of health-related fitness knowledge.

Relevant research in the social, psychological, and movement sciences as they relate to human movement and learning should guide physical education program planning. Researchers are investigating topics ranging from cooperative learning and team building to effective movement patterns, from mainstreaming to exercise and fitness program adherence; their research has implications for program development at all levels of education. Researchers have an opportunity and challenge to meaningfully contribute to the classroom, field, pool, and gymnasium and chart a course for the new millennium. This research dimension for the most part must be enhanced and advanced through cooperative program ventures, and the gap between research and practical application must be bridged. Needs analysis and market forecasts as well as evaluative assessment and instructional strategy research should play a significant role in the design, delivery, and enhancement of all physical education, recreation, and sport programs.

Climate and Geographical Considerations

The content of the program in physical education, recreation, and sport is also influenced by environmental conditions including weather and geographical location. Program designers should take advantage of the environmental aspects of school locations. For example, many outdoor activities (e.g., rock climbing, sailing) can be scheduled in areas where the weather and terrain are favorable. Schools in areas with an abundance of water might offer various aquatic activities (kayaking, rafting), whereas those located in northern environs might include skating, alpine and nordic skiing instruction, and winter and survival camping. Extreme temperature conditions may also dictate yearly scheduling and curricular programming. Management's role is to turn climatic and environmental barriers into challenges and to transform creative ideas into satisfying program offerings. The opportunity to bring or expose learners to varied geographic or even global regions should be a part of all programming.

Social Forces and Pressure Groups

Social forces such as the civil and equal rights movements, culture, religion, booster clubs, mass communication, student activism, and sports promotion have implications for program development. Times, customs, and habits change; laws and their interpretations vary; rules vary; and the role of schools, institutions, corporations and their responsibilities to society are also altered over time.

Influential and special interest groups ranging from the National Sports Federations and Foundations to labor unions, ROTC to PTOs, and alumni boards to booster clubs should be monitored in order to gain their positive support and potential intellectual and financial contributions in program development and implementation. It takes an inclusive village to build and sustain a successful program.

SELECTED APPROACHES TO MANAGING PROGRAM EXPERIENCES

Many approaches and models have been designed for the development and organization of program and curriculum experiences. For example, Jewett, Bain, and Ennis (1994) and Kelly and Melograno (2004) describe what they believe are sound models for contemporary program development, models that are designed to provide a basis for decisions about the selection, structuring, and sequencing of educational experiences. These models are listed under titles such as developmental education, humanistic physical education, fitness and movement education, kinesiological studies, sport and play education, and personal meaning.

Four widely employed approaches that have been used to organize program and curricular experiences are the systems, conceptual, competency-based and activity-based approaches.

Systems Approach

In recent years, physical educators have tried to develop a more systematic means of determining what activities to include in a program. In some cases, formulas have been created; in other instances, step-by-step procedures have been developed to match activities to goals and learning outcomes. Such methods of program development are encouraging because they represent an attempt to make program development a more scientific process.

A systems approach for developing a physical education program may be helpful to the physical educator because it provides a scientific, logical, and systematic method for program preparation that meets the needs of the participants. This systems approach to program development is composed of seven basic steps:

1. Identify the developmental objectives to be achieved in physical education (e.g., physical fitness development, motor skill development, cognitive development, and social-emotional-affective development) or sport.

2. Divide each of the developmental objectives listed in the first step into subobjectives. Identifying the subobjectives brings into sharper focus what must be accomplished and makes the achievement of the developmental objective more manageable. The following are examples of some subobjectives of each of the development objectives:

Senior groups' participation in physical activity and sport are important to all programs and communities.

Physical Fitness Development Objective

Subobjectives: health-related fitness components

Cardiovascular and cardiorespiratory endurance (e.g., one-mile run/walk)

Muscular strength and endurance (e.g., pull-ups and curls or sit-ups)

Flexibility (sit-and-reach)

Body composition (leaness/fatness)

Subobjectives: motor performance-related components

Agility

Balance

Coordination

Posture

Reaction time

Speed and power

Motor Skill Development Objective

Subobjectives

Locomotor (e.g., running, walking, jumping, hopping, skipping, leaping) and nonlocomotor or stability (e.g., bending, stretching, pulling, pushing) skills

Movement or manipulation fundamentals (e.g., balancing, throwing, kicking, striking, or catching and trapping)

General motor ability and efficiency

Specific motor ability in game and sport skills (e.g., Hyde archery test, Yeagley soccer test)

Cognitive Development Objective

Subobjectives

Understanding the principles of movement (e.g., gravity, force, time, acceleration, flow)

Knowledge of rules and strategies of games and sports (e.g., Scott badminton knowledge test, River Crossing cooperation game)

Knowledge of contribution of physical activity to health-related fitness

Awareness of contribution of physical activity to academic achievement

Problem-solving and decision-making ability

Affective Development Objective

Subobjectives

Fair play

Values clarification

Affiliation

Perceived competence or self-efficacy

Cooperation in group work

Positive attitude toward physical education and sport

Development of self-concept

Respect for self, other students, and teammates (worthiness)

3. Identify participant characteristics or norms in terms of each subobjective identified in step 2. A cardiorespiratory endurance characteristic, for example, of junior high or middle school students under the physical fitness development objective is that they may tire easily during a one-mile run/walk activity because of their rapid, uneven growth, whereas in grades 10 to 12, students possess a more mature physiological capacity and therefore are better equipped to engage in and complete this type of vigorous activity.

   The characteristics or norms of participants at each educational level must be determined in terms of each of the subobjectives identified in step 2. It is then possible to determine the relationship between the goals and specific participant growth and development characteristics.

4. Determine participant needs in relation to the characteristics outlined in step 3. For each subobjective, the needs of the participant must be identified. For example, a cardiorespiratory endurance characteristic of students in grades 7 to 9 indicates that they tire easily. Therefore a need exists for physical education and sport programming experiences that overcome fatiguing factors associated with time, distance, frequency, duration, intensity, persistence, and game pressures. Students also need guidance concerning nutrition habits, rest, and sleep.

5. Identify developmentally appropriate activities. For example, the activities scheduled for students in grades 7 to 9 that meet their needs should include large-muscle activities such as soccer, field hockey, volleyball, or floor hockey. Use of modified rules, including shortened periods of play, smaller playing areas, frequent timeouts, and unlimited substitutions are recommended. Health-related fitness activities such as jogging, cycling, circuit training, strength training, and fitness walking should also be prudently utilized.

6. List specific performance objectives for the participants in relation to their objectives, characteristics, norms, and needs and the activities appropriate to their age, fitness level, and ability. For each of the subobjectives, specific performance objectives should be listed. For example, a performance objective for the cardiorespiratory endurance subobjective for 7th- to 9th-grade students could be an exercise that measures cardiorespiratory endurance (e.g., the 600-yard run/walk) that the student is able to perform without undue fatigue and to promptly achieve heart rate recovery. A performance objective for 10th- to 12th-grade students might be having the student engage in a one-mile run/walk and be able to perform without undue fatigue and with a quick recovery time as measured by pulse rate. Of course, all performance objectives should consider the characteristics and needs of the specific students involved. Performance objectives provide specific levels or standards of accomplishment that indicate whether progression toward the desired goals occurs.

7. Identify the teaching methods (e.g. play-teach-play, direct, etc.), instructional strategies, and procedures that will most

effectively achieve the desired goals and learning outcomes. These instructional strategies provide for variety and should incorporate sound learning theories (e.g., activity theory, cooperative learning). They reinforce concepts related to accomplishing the objectives (e.g., follow-through contributes to accuracy, a concept in motor skill development).

Methods that can be employed to develop the subobjective of cardiorespiratory endurance for 7th to 9th graders include viewing a laboratory experiment comparing conditioned and nonconditioned adults. Participants may also be educated and motivated by studying an explanation of the role and value of cardiorespiratory endurance in health-related physical fitness development and a presentation of research that outlines the comparative physical fitness level of their U.S. age-group, (such as the fitness levels found in the FITNESS-GRAM) in figure 8-1, or with others throughout the world. Participation in activities that develop this type of endurance, together with an explanation of performance objectives and guidance in

Children use an objectives chart for a balance beam activity.

practice and self-evaluation, will assist the learner and facilitate efforts toward successful achievement of the objectives.

The seven-step systems approach to program development provides a logical, systematic, step-by-step method for determining the activities that will achieve the objectives, meet the characteristics and needs of participants, and provide the performance or outcome-based objectives to assess whether students are progressing or have met each objective. A systems approach may enhance a meaningful physical education program aimed at helping participants become truly physically educated and making physical education a viable, well-planned offering that achieves specific educational and developmental goals.

Conceptual Approach

During the past two decades, many disciplines have instituted major program reforms that emphasize the conceptual approach to program and curriculum development. Curriculum models based on the conceptual approach have been designed for mathematics, science, biology, social studies, and health education.

In addition to studying national curriculum models, physical education program planners and other educators interested in the conceptual approach should also become acquainted with the theoretical aspects of concept development.

A definition of *concept* is needed to better understand the conceptual approach to program development. Woodruff (1964) defines a concept as "some amount of meaning more or less organized in an individual's mind as a result of sensory perception of external objects or events and the cognitive interpretation of the perceived data." It is the "why" and "how" questions that seem to always come up in class!

According to Woodruff, several kinds of concepts can be identified, including concepts that might be a mental construct, an abstraction, a symbolic response, or some other connotation. Although a concept might be a high-level abstraction, many concepts can be presented as concrete,

Joe Jogger
Fitnessgram Jr. High School
FITNESSGRAM Test District

Instructor: Mr. James
Grade: 06   **Period:** 09   **Age:** 12

Test Date	Height	Weight
MO - YR	FT - IN	LBS
03-06	5.00	101
03-06	5.03	112

AEROBIC CAPACITY

HEALTHY FITNESS ZONE

One Mile Walk/Run

Needs Improvement	Good	Better
* * * * * * * * * * * * *	* * * * * * * * * * * * * * *	
* * * * * * * * * * * * *	* * * * * * * * * * * * * * *	

10 : 30   08 : 00

	Current	Past
	min : sec	
	8:56	9:12
	ml/kg/min	
	47	47

VO₂ₘₐₓ Indicates ability to use oxygen. Expressed as ml of oxygen per kg body weight per minute. Healthy Fitness Zone = 35 + for girls & 42 + for boys.

MUSCLE STRENGTH, ENDURANCE & FLEXIBILITY

HEALTHY FITNESS ZONE

Curl–up (Abdominal)

Needs Improvement	Good	Better
* * * * * * * *		
* * * * * * * *		

18   36

# performed	
12	10

Push–up (Upper body)

Needs Improvement	Good	Better
* * * * * * * * * * *	* * * * * * * * * * * * * * * * * * * *	* * *
* * * * * * * * * * *	* * * * * * * * * * * * * * * * * * * *	* * *

10   20

# performed	
27	20

Trunk Lift (Trunk Extension)

Needs Improvement	Good	Better
* * * * * * * * * * * *	* * * * * * * * *	
* * * * * * * * * * * *	* * * * * * * * *	

9   12

Inches	
10	10

The test of flexibility is optional. If given, it is scored pass or fail and is performed on the right and left.
Test given: Back Saver Sit–and–Reach

Right	P
Left	P

BODY COMPOSITION

HEALTHY FITNESS ZONE

Percent Body Fat

Needs Improvement	Good	Better
* * * * *		
* * * * *		

25.0   10.0

% Fat	
39.9	48.7

You can improve your abdominal strength with curl-ups 2 to 4 times a week. Remember your knees are bent and no one holds your feet.

Your upper-body strength was very good. Try to maintain your fitness by doing strengthening activities at least 2 or 3 times each week.

To improve your body composition, Joe, extend the length of vigorous activity each day and follow a balanced nutritional program, eating more fruits and vegetables and fewer fats and sugars. Improving body composition may also help improve your other fitness scores.

Your aerobic capacity is in the Healthy Fitness Zone. Maintain your fitness by doing 20–30 minutes of vigorous activity at least 3 or 4 times each week.

Figure 8-1.   The FITNESSGRAM provides profiles for an individual's level of fitness to help assess if program objectives are being met.

easy-to-understand ideas. For example, a concept in health-related physical fitness could be related to the cardiac response to exercise: the heart rate increases during exercise. This concept can be illustrated by having students take their resting pulse rate, engage in one of AAHPERD's *Physical Best* (1999) or health-related physical fitness components (see box 8-1), and then measure their pulse rate again to note the increase as a result of exercise. Concept learning has been tested and found useful for students at the upper elementary school level.

The following is an example of the conceptual approach based on movement activities. It is broken down into the key concept, the concept, and subconcepts. Some conceptual statements are then provided:

- *Key concept:* Individual development can be enhanced through movement activities.
- *Concept:* The development of locomotor skills is necessary for effective and efficient movement. These skills are also necessary for later development of competency in specialized games, sports, and other recreational and leisure activities.
- *Subconcept:* Sprints and distance running are two specialized forms of one locomotor movement—running.

Examples of Conceptual Statements in Physical Education and Sport

Proper techniques and skill in starting are necessary for mastery of sprint running. The ability to understand and carry out the concept of pacing (the idea of running at a gradually increased speed to have enough energy left to sprint the last part of the race) is necessary for distance running. Leg strength is important in sprint running. Proper leg strength, endurance, and cardiovascular-respiratory endurance are important concepts in distance running. A knowledge of the cognitive aspects related to both sprint and distance running and a positive attitude about running are necessary to the development of these running skills.

Basic Stuff Series I and II

The National Association of Sport and Physical Education (NASPE) of AAHPERD has created *Basic Stuff Series I and II* (1987). The purpose behind this project has been to identify the basic knowledge that applies to physical education programs and organize it in a manner that can be utilized by physical education and other professionals. It is applicable to elementary, middle, and secondary school children and youth at a time when the foundations are being laid down for adult years. It presents—in clear, concise language—basic concepts in the areas of exercise science, kinesiology, motor learning, psychosocial aspects of physical education, humanities (art, history, and philosophy), and motor development. A booklet has been prepared covering the basic concepts in each of the six areas; it is designed for preservice and in-service teachers. *Series I* represents the body of knowledge that supports the worth and interconnectedness of physical education.

The chapters in each pamphlet in the series share a similar organizational format relating to questions asked by students, such as (1) What do you have (e.g., self-concept, health, weight control) to help me? (2) How do I get it? (3) Why does it happen this way? Concepts are presented and then the student is shown how they can best be grasped, understood, and realized or controlled. It also explains why the concepts are valid and work.

Series II, which has been designed for teachers in the field, provides learning experience booklets with examples of instructional activities for early childhood (ages three to eight), childhood (ages nine to twelve), and adolescence (ages thirteen to eighteen). The scientific knowledge in the six areas in *Series I* is related directly to physical education and sport and enables physical educators and coaches to have at their disposal the basic information and learning activities that will make it possible to educate the students. General concepts such as how to learn a new skill, how to better one's performance, and the beneficial effects of exercise are identified. The booklets also include ways to present the concepts in activity programs so that students may realize the importance of these concepts. This realization is accomplished by relating the concepts to the motives most children and young people possess. These motives are health (they want to feel good), appearance (they want to look good), achievement (they want to achieve), social (they want to develop aesthetic and affective qualities and to belong), and coping with the environment (they want to survive and be empowered). Furthermore, the *Basic Stuff Series* makes it possible for teachers and coaches to tell and show students what concepts are important in physical education and sport as well as how and why they are important.

Starting skills are crucial to sprint running.

Concept-based programs and curriculum such as *Basic Stuff Series I and II* have been cooperatively developed by teachers and researchers who are experts in their particular disciplines, and seek to develop the participant's ability to understand, synthesize, analyze, and evaluate, not only each learning experience, but also the importance of physical education and sport in building a healthy and socially productive lifestyle.

Competency-Based Approach

Competency-based learning has evolved because of a public and professional concern for accountability. Students are taught by means of defined student-centered program or content standards and performance objectives based on cognitive, psychomotor, and affective tasks. Students are not in competition with each other, but with themselves and various norms. The teacher becomes a facilitator to learning rather than a taskmaster, and each student proceeds at his or her own rate. In addition, resource materials are made available to students to help further challenge their behavioral and cognitive skills.

How competency-based instruction or learning actually takes place can be better understood by reviewing the competency-based instruction at the high school level in Montclair, New Jersey. The performance objectives are developed and written by a team of physical educators and based on general physical fitness, motor skill, cognitive, and affective goals. A competency-based learning unit for the health-related activity of gymnastics, for example, is divided into a three-week unit centered around seven performance standards including skill, routines, risk management, peer improvement, social behavior, and self-expression. A lecture and demonstration of the thirty-four selected gymnastic stunts are presented to the students followed by a unit in instruction, safety, and practice. The grading system for the skills unit is based on performance mastery of the number of stunts as determined by the teacher:

16 to 28 stunts = A
10 to 15 stunts = B
6 to 9 stunts = C
3 to 5 stunts = D
0 to 2 stunts = F

Activity-Based Approach

This approach is common, not only in educational systems (especially at the high school level), but also in those programs offered in the public and private sectors. It is grounded in major activity areas such as aquatics, dance, fitness, gymnastics, outdoor pursuit, and sports (team, individual, lifelong, etc.). Activities such as badminton, tennis, and golf in the lifelong sports unit provide students with active learning experiences to achieve program objectives. Lecture, demonstration, practice, teacher, peer, and video feedback are the mainstays of instructional delivery.

The activity-based approach stresses the development of fine and gross skill fundamentals essential for proficiency at the sport. The activity approach is very popular and physical educators and program managers must ensure programmatic balance and scope, as well as systematic evaluation and promotion of the cognitive and affective objectives associated with program delivery.

Regardless of which model or approach that is employed by the program manager, there remains a common link to benefits-based management. That is, clear programmatic goals and objectives are identified by a team of experts; the program is structured and tailored around these goals; effective, efficient, objective, and systematic monitoring and assessment systems are in place to document and track goal-related outcomes and achievement; and a comprehensive public relations and informational communication system is used to inform the various publics (school, parents, community, etc.) of the outcomes and successes of the program. We certainly need to meet these challenges, especially in regard to reporting and promoting the successful outcomes and values concerning our physical education programs.

Guidelines

Regardless of which program approach is used to organize students into learners, programmers must take into consideration the following factors when constructing the framework, steps, and stages of program development.

1. *Motivation:* What choices do students have about what is being taught and how it is being presented?

2. *Activity:* How do students get involved? Are programs accessible? Are there equal and fair opportunities provided for all students?

3. *Interaction:* How will students discuss concepts? Can students try their ideas and receive feedback about their thinking or inquiry?

4. *Integration:* How do students connect what they are learning with their previous experience, and how do these concepts fit with other core courses?

Only when careful and thorough program development steps are outlined; only when students, learners, and team members are given a chance to become actively involved with the creation, design, implementation, operation, assessment, and revision of their program; and only when students' demonstrated performance is evaluated using clearly defined, concept- and context-specific criteria; only then will we truly optimize learning and personal growth and development. These crucial steps, as well as key management principles in program and curriculum development and the Krotee Program Development System (see figure 8-2) follow.

STEPS IN PROGRAM DEVELOPMENT

Many dimensions should be studied when constructing a quality program. The four example approaches presented previously illustrate some of the crucial ingredients and considerations of program development. Although ideally, perfect physical education, recreation, and sport programs are implemented right from the start, the reality is that quality programs are developed over time by trial and enhancement within a systematic program development plan. The major steps involved in program development include (1) determining the organizational objectives, (2) analyzing the objectives in terms of the program, (3) analyzing the objectives in terms of activities, (4) providing program guides and teaching aids, and (5) evaluating the program.

Determining the Organizational Objectives

Determining the organizational objectives involves studying such factors as the philosophy, vision, climate, and nature of the organization and society to be served; developmental program trends; the learning process; and the needs and makeup of the participant or target population so that objectives may be clearly formulated.

Figure 8-2. Krotee Program Development System (KPDS).

If the main objective of physical education and sport is to produce a physically educated person, this should be the focus of the program objectives. For example, a physically educated person is one who engages in a program of physical education or sport and is able to demonstrate competency in motor skills and movement patterns; understand concepts, principles, and strategies; participates regularly in physical activity and is fit; and values physical activity and its contribution to a healthful lifestyle (see chapter 2; NASPE 2004).

Analyzing the Objectives in Terms of the Program

Having determined the organizational objectives and philosophy and knowing the characteristics of the participant as well as the various constraints, barriers, and challanges associated with the task, those developing a program can now target, outline, and define broad categories of experiences and activities and assign relative emphases to the various phases of the design and program developmental process. The specialized fields of physical education and sport should be viewed as part of the total educational program and process. As a consequence, their specific objectives should relate to the overall objectives of the organization.

Analyzing the Objectives in Terms of Activities

The next step is to focus attention on the activities needed to achieve the set objectives and program goals. For example, the cognitive, affective, and psychomotor needs of the participants necessitate providing a wide range of physical activities as well as emphasizing the growth and development characteristics of participants throughout the life span. In addition, enabling participants to become self-educative throughout their lives provides a tremendous challenge to program developers.

Providing Program Guides and Teaching Resources

Curriculum and program guides and teaching resources, such as books, equipment, technology (hand held devices, heart rate monitors), and visual

Box 8-2   Management Principles to Consider in Program Development

Although program development varies from organization to organization, the following general principles are applicable to all situations:

Learning experiences and activities should be selected and developed to achieve desired outcomes.

The value of program development is determined by enhanced instruction and results.

Program development is a continuous and dynamic effort rather than one accomplished at periodic intervals.

The leadership in program development rests primarily with managers, supervisors, and programmers.

Management should consult (wherever possible and practical) teachers, coaches, community, students, participants, state consultants, and other persons who can contribute to the development of the best program possible. The work should not, however, place an unreasonable demand on any one person's time and effort.

Program development depends on a thorough knowledge of the needs and characteristics, developmental levels, capacities, and maturity levels of participants as well as an understanding of their environments and lifestyles.

Program development should permit staff members to explore sound principles of learning when selecting and developing experiences.

Physical education should be viewed in its broadest scope and include all activity-based programs provided by the school, including recreational and varsity sports.

Physical education and sport should be integrated with other areas in the organization.

Physical education and sport activities should be selected using valid criteria including needs assessment.

Physical education programs should be student-centered, and be organized around content standards and learning outcomes.

Working relationships should be sought with recreational sport and athletic departments as well as with community-based public and private sector programs.

aids, offer opportunities to use educationally sound and challenging materials to achieve objectives during this program implementation phase. Computer software programs, videos, and behavior modification counseling are other means to support program operation. Well-qualified staff are vital to operationalize the program plan.

Assessing the Program

Assessment represents the culmination of the program development process—what actually takes place in the classroom, gymnasium, arena, fitness center, or natatorium. The learning that takes place, the skills and movement patterns acquired, physical fitness level achieved, the understanding and respect for others, materials and human resources employed, and the outcomes accomplished determine the success or failure or worth of the program to both the organization and the community.

Assessment is a dynamic process that helps determine the progress being made in meeting program objectives. It can identify strengths, weaknesses, and omissions and show where needed resources, balance, or emphases might be shifted in order to enhance the program. It also helps the participants determine their own progress (e.g., competence, individuality, socialization, integration) within the program and is useful to the manager for interpreting and reporting program outcomes to both the organization and the public (see boxes 8-2 and 8-3).

The relationship between program planning and assessment should be recognized and understood by all individuals involved in the program. All programmatic learning experiences should be evaluated. Evaluation is primarily concerned with: (1) meeting participant needs, (2) meeting the objectives of the program, and (3) considering the requirements of parents, community, staff members, the profession, and organization members.

Goodlad (1964) indicates that program evaluation usually employs the following four means to determine the worth of a new program: (1) observing

> **Box 8-3   Management Steps in Program and Curriculum Development**
>
> - Establish a philosophy.
> - Construct a conceptual framework to guide program formation.
> - Analyze the situation, system, and culture of the community.
> - Analyze the characteristics and needs of the participants.
> - Determine program objectives, integrating the participants and the institution's needs, values, and beliefs.
> - Identify barriers and challenges (i.e., budget, laws, space).
> - Select appropriate activities arranging them in instructional delivery packages or units (progressive, sequenced, cross-curricular learning opportunities, and developmentally appropriate).
> - Construct a year-long delivery plan.
> - Assess, adapt, and modify each unit (i.e., content, scope, interdisciplinary focus, level, time, sequence, location, and enjoyment).

Master teachers employ technology to evaluate and provide feedback to students.

individuals who have been exposed to the new program and the progress they have made, (2) systematic questioning of people involved in the program, (3) testing participants periodically to determine their progress, and (4) comparative testing of participants under both the new and old programs to determine the progress of each.

Evaluation may be a yearly procedure, handled by members of a department, or it may be a review or audit of the entire organization by a visiting team of external specialists. The process of evaluation itself involves rating or judging the program according to selected criteria and standards. Some standardized forms have been developed to evaluate various phases of physical education programs (e.g., by NASPE/NCATE).

In situations in which standardized tests or norms are not available to judge programs or parts of programs, criteria based on authoritative models, research and textbook sources, or the judgment of experts in the field must be established.

The following are sample questions, which may be answered *poor, fair, good,* or *excellent;* or may be scored on a scale of 1 to 10; or may be scored on a Likert scale wherein the respondent reacts to a five-point scale indicating *strongly agree, agree, uncertain, disagree,* or *strongly disagree.* Select program areas are listed with sample questions about various factors that managers must take into full consideration. Box 8-4, the Suggested Outline of a School Physical Education Program Assessment Checklist, also provides a criteria checklist to help assess program curricula.

Basic Instructional Physical Education Program

- Does the program devote equitable time and programmatic balance to team, individual, and lifetime sports as well as to rhythms, aquatics, dance, cooperative games, and gymnastic activities?
- Are the available equipment, facilities, and space adequate to allow for maximal as well as safe participation?
- Are reasonable budgetary allotments made for the program?
- Are accurate evaluation procedures conducted and records kept?
- Are minimal participation requirements met by all students?

Box 8-4 Suggested Outline of a School Physical Education Program Assessment Checklist

The following evaluation checklist for physical education programs suggests criteria for assessing curriculum development in this area.

	Yes	No
1. Does the physical education curriculum meet the established objectives?	___	___
2. Does the physical education curriculum provide for the keeping of records to chart student progress?	___	___
3. Is evaluation used to help each student find out where he or she is in relation to the program objectives?	___	___
4. Are objective, as well as subjective, measures used to determine the progress of students in attaining program objectives?	___	___
5. Are the students required to have medical examinations in order to participate?	___	___
6. Does the physical education curriculum provide for the administration of physical fitness tests to determine the fitness level of each student?	___	___
7. Does the physical education program provide for the testing of motor skills using specific ability tests?	___	___
8. Does the physical education curriculum provide for cognitive testing of students?	___	___
9. Does the physical education curriculum provide for the assessment of the social and affective dimension of each student?	___	___
10. Are the attitudes and interests of the students evaluated?	___	___
11. If scientific methods of testing are not feasible, does the physical education curriculum provide for teacher-made tests?	___	___
12. Does the physical education program use test results in planning and revising activity or program units?	___	___
13. Does the physical education curriculum provide for mobility of students on the basis of evaluation results?	___	___
14. Does the physical education curriculum provide for teacher evaluation as well as student evaluation?	___	___
15. Does the physical education program provide for the recognition of curriculum problems and appropriate reform?	___	___
16. Once change is needed in the curriculum, is it easy to bring about that change?	___	___
17. Is the physical education staff receptive to change?	___	___
18. Is there a provision for ongoing evaluation of programs in reference to satisfying objectives according to an established schedule?	___	___
19. Does the physical education curriculum provide for the needs of students with varying disabilities?	___	___

- Are participants meeting proper physical education requirements in regard to participation?
- Are proper safety and risk management measures implemented in all activities?
- Are opportunities for developing student leadership being provided in the program?
- Are cognitive and affective evaluation systematically employed?

Adapted/Developmental Program

- Do adequate screening and assessment procedures exist for its participants?
- Are proper supervision and instruction afforded each individual participant?
- Are adequate facilities, equipment, time, and space made available to the program?

- Is school and parental approval obtained for each individual's regimen of activity?
- Do participants engage in their least restrictive environment as well as any recommended developmental classes?
- Are careful records and progress charts (e.g., IEP objectives) kept for each student?
- Is the financial allotment to the program reasonable?
- Does student achievement reflect the value of the program?

Recreational Sport Programs

- Are intramural, extramural, fitness, open, outdoor, and club sports offered to all students, including the disabled?
- Are enough activities (e.g., level, coed, individual, outdoor pursuit, special student) offered to the student population?
- Has the percentage of participation in these programs increased during the past three years?
- Is prudent supervision and quality instruction available to all participants?
- Is adequate financial assistance given to this phase of the program?
- Are accurate records maintained about the participants and their awards, protests, satisfaction, and conduct violations?
- Does the reward or point system emphasize the joys of participation rather than focus on the value of the reward?
- Is the equipment utilized for the program safe and adequate for the number of participants?
- Is equipment properly maintained and stored to gain the most use from it?
- Are competitive experiences safe, wholesome, and worthwhile for all participants?
- Is the level of organization appropriate to the activity?
- Are risk management plans in place in all areas and programs involved?

Interscholastic and Intercollegiate Sport Programs

- Is adequate financial support provided by the school for this program?
- Is there equitable financial support and opportunity for all sports in the program?
- Are equal numbers of interscholastic sports available to boys and girls?
- Does the program meet established Title IX mandates?
- Are adequate health and safety standards being met in respect to number of practices and games, health and fitness level of participants, level of competition, and certified equipment?
- Is competition provided by schools of a similar size?
- Is the program justifiable as an important facet of the educational process?
- Are academic standards for participants maintained?
- What sports have been added/deleted in the last three years?
- Are good public relations with the community furthered through this program?
- Are sport offerings healthful and safe for all participants?
- Are qualified and certified medical staff available at practices and games?

Management should provide opportunities for gifted students to reach the highest level of skill development.

Staff and Faculty

- Is the teaching and coaching staff well qualified, certified, licensed, and capable of carrying out the program?

- Is the program run efficiently, with little loss of teaching time or space, and is maximal use made of facilities?

- Are professional or exclusive representative standards maintained regarding class size and teacher/coach assignment?

- Does the departmental organization function on a democratic basis, with members sharing in the decision-making process?

- Do members of the staff function in a professional fashion?

- Do staff members attend professional meetings and keep up with the latest developments in the profession?

- Do staff members apply current research findings to various programmatic activities?

- Are staff development opportunities supported?

These are just a few sample questions that may be used in assessing program management and conduct. A sample evaluation criteria checklist for a school physical education program is also offered (see box 8-4). The key to successful assessment of this type lies in the follow-up steps for program improvement and enrichment.

Regardless of which evaluation method, style, or technique is used for physical education, recreation, and sport programs, assessment is an important and vital part of program development. Assessment helps the programmer improve and service programs; analyzes the value of various component parts of programs (e.g., jump rope or strength-training unit, booster club); should boost staff, student, or participant morale; and may even result in discovering new needs that should be addressed. Assessment should be realistic, functional, systematic and continuous in order to fulfill its major purpose of providing meaningful quality assurance for programs that benefit all involved.

MANAGEMENT AND PROGRAM CHANGE

Because assessment is a continuous process, it effects future program development, establishes accountability to determine if program development goals are being met, and serves to change (e.g., reform, revise, reengineer, cut, and enhance) existing programs. Many factors have an impact on programs, and the physical educator, coach, athletic and activities director, and program manager must make informed and prudent decisions about program change. Here are five questions that managers might ask themselves in evaluating changes:

1. *What are the functions of the organization?* How does the suggested change conform to the philosophy, culture, climate, and purpose of the organization?

2. *Am I sufficiently well informed to make an intelligent decision?* Managers need to be knowledgeable about the learning process; health-related fitness patterns; human growth and development; current program and participant needs, issues, and mandates; and the needs and interests of the local community.

3. *How does the change relate to staff, facility, budget, future program development, and other important managerial considerations?* The change must be practical to implement and make the best use of human and physical resources.

4. *What do the experts say?* What is the thinking, opinion, and position of professionals and organizations who have conducted research, thoroughly studied the problem, and piloted like programs? Expert testimony may be helpful in making sound program decisions.

5. *Who is the assessment for, and who will take action based on the results?* Change is not accomplished in a vacuum and both personal and political motives for change must be studied.

Considerations in Program Change

Program revision cannot occur without considering the following:

1. *Participants.* The number of participants, their needs and interests, and other characteristics such as sociocultural background or gender need to be considered before initiating any program change.

2. *Staff members.* Staff members play a key role in program revision. Important considerations include, for example, the attitude of the staff toward change, present workloads, comprehension of goals of the school, attitudes toward after-school sport programs, competencies in curriculum revision, and past training and experience. Change in curriculum might mean new staff members being added, reassignment, or a different type of competency being represented on the staff.

3. *Physical facility.* The adequacy of the physical plant and facility for present and future programs must be considered. Information should be available on capabilities and limitations of the present physical plant (e.g., pool, arena, and field space). New demands may be placed on facilities through program revision that brings about changes in class size, scheduling, alternative site planning, and partnering.

4. *Budget.* The budget is another important consideration. What will the new program cost? What are the sources of support? Before staff members expend time and effort to study program change, they need reasonable assurance that proposed changes are economically feasible. In systems using a planning-programming-budgeting-evaluation-system, or PPBES, budgets are formulated on the basis of the objectives of the program; PPBES also provides for evaluation techniques that may require further program change or modification if goals are not being met.

5. *Program.* Because any new program proposal is likely to reflect current practices to some degree, it seems logical that the present program needs careful scrutiny to determine what has happened over the years, the degree to which staff members have brought about change, and the general direction in which the institution is moving.

6. *Legality.* New program additions or subtractions must conform to the laws of the land (e.g., Title IX, ADA). Programs and their resources must be accessible and equally and fairly apportioned.

7. *Management.* Staff members must take a hard look at the managerial leadership. The philosophy of management and its views toward change should be carefully weighed. Managers will need to approve budgetary and resource allocations as well as required expenditures in order to affect the proposed program initiative or change.

Research in Program Changes in Physical Education and Sport

Advancing the frontiers of knowledge in physical education and sport is urgently needed. Too many unsupported claims about the value of physical education and sport have been set forth. Its worth needs to be determined through valid research findings: basic research that will advance knowledge and perhaps more critically applied research that will determine the best ways to design and effectively implement and deliver this knowledge so individuals can come closer to realizing their full potential.

Many questions are still unanswered, such as: What is the most effective way to develop physical fitness? What activities are most effective for developing muscular strength and power? How many times per week is physical education needed to enhance self-concept? What activities can the employee on the job perform to enhance or maintain his or her physical fitness level? What are the fundamental patterns of human movement? What activities are best conducted cooperatively? What is the relationship of personality development to motor performance? What is the relationship of academic achievement to physical fitness level? What is the therapeutic value of physical activity? What

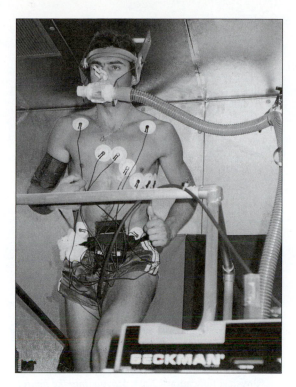

Research is vital to physical education and sports programs. Courtesy of the Division of Kinesiology, Laboratory of Physiological Hygiene and Exercise Science, University of Minnesota.

TAKE IT TO THE NET!

American Sport Education Program (ASEP)
www.asep.com

Diversity Training University International
www.diversityuintl.com

FITNESSGRAM/ACTIVITYGRAM
www.cooperinst.org

International Council for Sport Science and
Physical Education (ICSSPE)
www.icsspe.org

National Coalition for Promoting Physical Activity
www.ncppr.org

National Education Association (NEA)
www.nea.org

PE Central
www.pe.central.org

President's Challenge (PCPFS)
www.presidentschallenge.org

The Society for College and University Planning
www.scup.org

The Society of State Directors of Health, Physical
Education, and Recreation
www.thesociety.com

U.S. Department of Education
www.ed.gov

types of feedback are most effective to promote exercise and sport adherence? How does family structure contribute to participation pattern and performance? What instructional strategies are most effective in mainstreaming? What about physical education and sport in other societies and cultures?

Research opportunity abounds in the classroom, arena, and gymnasium. There is no question that more systematic research is crucial to the development of the profession and that many program development improvements will result from such concerted research effort.

SUMMARY

Management has the responsibility to see that quality physical education, recreation, and sport programs are developed, systematically reviewed, assessed, and changed or modified when necessary to better meet the needs of the participant as well as the organization. This responsibility includes deciding what goals and objectives should be created and supported; enlisting the help of key individuals and groups in the construction of the program and its standards; taking into account the factors and groups that influence and are influenced by the program; following the proper procedures, policies, and steps, and selecting the best approach in program development; and being aware of the current trends and issues in the field for which the program is being targeted. In other words, management is responsible for providing effective vision and leadership as well as the structural and support resources and motivation to fully, effectively, and efficiently carry out the program development process.

SELF-ASSESSMENT ACTIVITIES

These activities will assist students in determining if material and competencies presented in this chapter have been mastered:

1. Explain to the class what is meant by program development, the role of management in this process, and the ways in which program change occurs.

2. If you were an athletic and activities director of a junior high or middle school, what factors would influence the various activities included in your program?

3. You have been assigned to chair a committee to develop a physical education program for your school. Whom would you select to serve on a curriculum committee?

4. List and discuss several principles you would observe in developing a middle school curriculum.

5. Using the systems approach, trace the program development process for a high school.

6. You have been hired as a consultant to evaluate a physical education program in a developing nation. Describe the process you will follow in conducting this task.

7. Discuss various components in the KPDS that may influence the shape and conduct of the physical education program at your school or institution.

REFERENCES

1. AAHPERD (American Alliance for Health, Physical Education, Recreation and Dance). 1987. *Basic stuff series, I and II.* Reston, VA: AAHPERD.

2. AAHPERD (American Alliance for Health, Physical Education, Recreation and Dance). 1999. *Physical best: Activity Guides for the elementary level, the secondary level, and the teacher.* Champaign, IL: Human Kinetics.

3. Baumgartner, T. A., A. S. Jackson, M. T. Mahar, and D. A. Rowe. 2003. *Measurement for evaluation in physical education and exercise science.* New York: McGraw-Hill.

4. The Cooper Institute for Aerobics Research. 2005: FITNESSGRAM/ACTIVITYGRAM: Test manual. 2005. *Test administration manual.* Champaign, IL: Human Kinetics.

5. Corbin, C. B., G. J. Welk, W. R. Corbin, and K. A. Welk. 2005. *Concepts of physical fitness: Active lifestyles for wellness.* New York: McGraw-Hill.

6. Goodlad, J. L.1964. *School curriculum reform in the United States.* New York: The Fund for Advancement of Education.

7. Human Kinetics with B. Petifor. 1999. *Physical education methods for classroom teachers.* Champaign, IL: Human Kinetics.

8. Jewett, A. E., L. L. Bain, and C. Ennis. 1994. *The curriculum process in physical education.* Dubuque, IA: Wm. C. Brown.

9. Kelly, L. E., and V. J. Melograno. 2004. *Developing the physical education curriculum.* Champaign, Ill.: Human Kinetics.

10. Mohnsen, B. 2003. *Concepts and principles of physical education: What every student needs to know.* Reston, VA: NASPE.

11. NASPE (National Association for Sport and Physical Education). 2004. *Moving into the future: National standards for physical education.* Dubuque, IA: McGraw-Hill.

12. ———. 2005. *Quality coaches, quality sports: National standards for sport coaches.* 2005. Reston, VA: NASPE.

13. President's Council on Physical Fitness and Sports. 2004. President's Challenge Physical Fitness Program. *GET FIT.* Washington, DC: PCPFS.

14. SSDHPER. 1998. *School programs of health education and physical education: A statement of beliefs.* Reston, VA: SSDHPER.

15. U.S. Department of Health and Human Services/Public Health Service/PCPFS. 1999. *Healthy people 2010: Conference edition.* Washington, DC: United States Department of Health and Human Services.

16. Woodruff, A. D. 1964. The use of concepts in teaching and learning. *Journal of Teacher Education* 20(March):84.

SUGGESTED READINGS

Chepko, S., and R. K. Arnold. 2000. *Guidelines for physical education programs.* Needham Heights, MA: Allyn and Bacon.
Presents guidelines concerning standards, objectives, and assessments for K–12 physical education

programs. Compiled in a joint effort by the NASPE Outcomes Committee Task force and AAHPERD's Eastern District.

Csikszentmihalyi, M. 1991. *Flow: The psychology of optimal experience.* New York: Harper Perennial.

Edginton, C. R., S. D. Hudson, R. B. Dieser, and S. R. Edginton. 2004. *Leisure programming: A service-centered and benefits approach.* Dubuque, IA: McGraw-Hill.
Discusses perspectives of the philosophies and principles of leisure programming. Presents information about how the knowledge base of leisure and sport relates to career potentials.

Glover, D. R., and L. A. Anderson. 2003. *Character education.* Champaign, IL: Human Kinetics.
Presents community and team-building concepts and strategies while helping teachers and team leaders meet National Association for Sport and Physical Education curriculum content standards.

Kelly, L. E., and V. J. Melograno. 2004. *Developing the physical education curriculum.* Champaign, IL: Human Kinetics.
Provides help in the development of a curriculum in physical education for the secondary school level. Includes such topics as objectives, curriculum planning, research, program organization, the curriculum guide, evaluation, and management guidelines for programs.

NASPE (National Association for Sport and Physical Education). 2004. *Moving into the future: National standards for physical education.* Dubuque, IA: McGraw-Hill.

Newell, S., and J. Swan. 1995. The diffusion of innovations in sport organizations: An evaluative framework. *Journal of Sport Management* 9:317–37.

Rink, J. E. 2002. *Teaching physical education for learning.* Dubuque, IA: McGraw-Hill.
Has implications for the implementation of the curriculum in physical education through the improvement of the efficiency of instruction, quality of teaching, and other factors that should be considered in seeing that students reap the greatest benefits from planned programs. Presents comprehensive coverage of sequential learning experiences.

Rossman, J. R., and B. Schlatter. 2002. *Recreation programming: Designing leisure experiences.* Champaign, IL: Sagamore Publishing.

Stark, J. S., and L. R. Lattuca. 1997. *Shaping the college curriculum.* Boston, MA: Allyn and Bacon.

CHAPTER 9

Facility Management

INSTRUCTIONAL OBJECTIVES AND COMPETENCIES TO BE ACHIEVED

After reading this chapter the student should be able to:

- Describe the duties and responsibilities that contemporary facilities managers should be able to effectively practice at their respective workplaces.
- Prepare a list of principles that could be used in planning, constructing, and managing facilities for physical education, recreation, and sport programs.
- List the procedures involved in working with an architect.
- Describe the indoor facilities (type, size, location) needed for physical education, recreation, and sport programs, and prepare guidelines for managers to follow in planning such facilities.

- Describe the outdoor facilities (type, size, location) needed for physical education, recreation, and sport programs, and prepare guidelines for managers to follow when planning such facilities.
- Determine the number of teaching stations/areas needed, given the total number of participants, size of classes, and classes per week.
- Discuss contemporary features and developments in the design and construction of physical education, recreation, and sport facilities.
- Show how to provide facilities that will be conducive to a healthful, safe, and risk-free environment for conducting physical education, recreation, and sport programs.

Traditionally, at the K–12, college, and public sector levels (e.g., YMCA/YWCA, local health and fitness clubs, community centers, etc.), the responsibility of facility management falls to those persons who are in charge of physical education, recreation, and sport programs. The facilities for which they are responsible include outdoor facilities—such as playgrounds, beaches, pools, skate parks, courts, and fields—and indoor facilities—such as locker and shower rooms, natatoriums, racket sport courts, weight and exercise rooms, arenas, climbing walls, multipurpose rooms, gymnasiums, and sometimes a golf course. Facility management includes not only the effective operation, scheduling, and maintenance of such facilities but also, at times,

Box 9-1   Total Facility Management Package (TFMP)

Planning and Design
    Feasibility and needs assessment
    Economic impact studies
    Market analysis
    Financial planning
    Site selection
    Team building/inclusion
Administration
    Facilities programming/scheduling
    Systems analysis
    Evaluation
    Personnel negotiating
    Networking
Operations
    Personnel hiring and training (HR)
    Concessions/novelties
    Security
    Event management
    Information systems
    Ticketing and rentals
    Maintenance
    Medical, emergency, and disaster services
    Parking/tailgating
    Scheduling
    Technology
    Transportation

Marketing
    Promotion/pricing
    Event procurements/bookings
    Public and media relations
    Licensing
    Televison, Web, and cable rights
    Sponsorship/signage
    Naming rights
Finance
    Accounting
    Budget analyses/forecasting
    Capital planning
    Costing systems
    Inventory and purchasing
    Travel
Legal
    Contract negotiations
    Sponsorship procurement
    Insurance
    Labor
    Employee relations
    Risk management
    Laws, codes, and regulations (ADA)

planning new and reengineered structures to keep pace with the growing demand for participation in physical education, recreation, and sport programs. Contemporary sport facilities management at the university and community level, in some instances, has taken on a whole new meaning. (Pate, Moffit, and Fugett 1997). Facility management at many large universities, for example, has become a full-time profession. Facility management groups ranging from Spectacor and Signature Sports to Ogden and International Management Group (IMG) have created profitable multimillion-dollar businesses that professionally manage large sports complexes like the Hubert H. Humphrey Metrodome, the Xcel Energy Center, the RBC Center, or the RCA Dome. In addition to their operation's traditional responsibilities, facilities managers are now involved in the Total Facility Management Package (see box 9-1), which includes conceiving, planning and design, administering, operating, marketing, financing, and attending to the legal ramifications of facility management. Contemporary facility managers need to be well schooled in all dimensions of their profession. (Appenzeller 2004; Kraus and Curtis 2000).

Additional developments have critical implications for facility management. The cost of materials and labor is rising as a result of inflation, making it very difficult for new capital building projects to go forward. High interest rates make it difficult to get bond issues passed for facility construction. Facilities must be accessible for persons with disabilities (per ADA) and must be brought up to code concerning myriad safety and environmental standards. Energy, environmental, and land conservation and sustained maintenance and repair costs must also be taken into consideration, not to mention security.

Because little or no money is available in some situations or because capital expenditure for building is so high, alternative methods are being used to see that physical education, recreation, and sport programs have the facilities necessary to conduct quality programs. Methods such as renovating, retrofitting, and converting existing structures and instituting multiple use of present facilities are emerging. When funds are limited, fiscal responsibility involves following design and construction plans that are most economical not only in cost but in construction time, maintenance and the use of energy.

Joint ventures and partnering between school, community and public and private sector interest groups (e.g., Ys, health and fitness clubs) are be-

The Hubert H. Humphrey Metrodome is shared by the community, Minnesota State High School League, and the University of Minnesota as well as the area's other intercollegiate and professional sport teams.

coming commonplace. Even though the partnering groups may not share the same goals, each entity desires quality facilities for its consumer or user groups. So from Geneva, Illinois, to Springfield, Massachusetts, and from Wayzata, Minnesota, to Cary, North Carolina, Ys and medical centers are partnering and sharing with communities and private health and fitness clubs are sharing with school districts to form common ground facilities projects. On a larger scale, enterprises such as Disney and corporations such as Toro and Cybex have also combined resources, for example, at Disney's 200-acre Wide World of Sports complex.

Physical plants whether in schools, municipalities, or private settings require careful planning and consultation with specialists in architectural planning and design. Managers, physical educators, coaches, fitness and recreation specialists, consultants, and other personnel should participate in the planning and design phase of new facilities (Tharrett and Peterson 1997). Other participants, depending on the type of facility, should include representatives from the school board, institutional policy board, municipal sports facilities commissions, building and grounds, maintenance, public safety, and numerous building task force groups including disabilities, risk management, and security. The facility manager must be knowledgeable not only about the facility's specific structure but also its function and maintenance in the context of the organizations mission and vision. Trends and innovative structural design concepts should be thoroughly examined to provide a healthful, safe, environmentally friendly, and efficient physical plant.

The physical plant is a major consideration in most physical education, recreation, and sport programs. New architectural design ideas are constantly being introduced and new concepts developed that have a more economical, accessible, and functional management scheme. Some building concepts include *convertibility,* in which interiors are rearranged by employing movable walls, curtains, and partitions. Such a concept facilitates using the gymnasium, cafeteria, and amphitheater as multipurpose activity stations that can accommodate small or large activity-specific groups. This concept provides instruction and independent study and fly spaces for a number of varied activities and is becoming a trend as plant space and fiscal restraint become crucial to the survival of programs.

Some suggested resources that are aimed exclusively at planning facilities for physical education and sport are listed at the end of the chapter and should be consulted by those who desire a more thorough treatment of this subject. Once a facility comes online, however, there are certain facility management fundamentals embedded in the Total Facility Management Package (TFMP) that must be placed into practice to ensure a high level of service for all user groups.

MANAGING THE FACILITY

As mentioned, facilities management has evolved into a full-time profession within many large institutions and private and public venues. Facilities management has its own professional organizations (International Facility Management Association— IFMA) and International Association of Assembly Managers (IAAM), a bimonthly *Facility Management Journal* and *Facility Management Magazine*, and its own stream of professional research, development, certifications, standards, and even its own "language." For the purpose of this text, facility management is the profession, function, duty, or responsibility of those in charge to ensure the functionality of the built environment by effectively and efficiently integrating people, place, process, and technology. For most contemporary facility caretakers or operations managers (department heads, athletic and activities directors, teachers, coaches, recreation and fitness program managers), managing facilities means providing leadership and making decisions concerning the supply of services that enables or enhances the ability of the organization or program to create, improve, and raise the standards of all dimensions of the delivery of physical education, recreation, and sport.

It means the return to the fundamental elements of the Total Facility Management Package (TFMP) through excellent operations management by highly qualified, well-trained, and committed professionals. The facility, large or small, indoor or outdoor, multipurpose or activity-specific (aquatics, golf, group exercise, ice arena), partnered or private, must be expertly and effectively served. These fundamental, yet key, facility management services include, but are not limited to, the effective integration of the following:

- Safety and security
- Accessibility, inclusion, and control
- Cleanliness (crucial)
- Capacity and inventory
- Functionality and technology

Additional service quality measures include courtesy, cleanliness, speed of service, effectiveness and meaningfulness of communication, and providing a healthful and friendly learning environment. The implementation of these basic facility management practices seems simplistic; however, the implementation remains a continuous challenge to the profession. Decision making about these basics must be conducted (assigned, ordered, scheduled, monitored, serviced, and assessed) many times in a cross-functional (housekeeping, maintenance, contracted services, purchasing) fashion both within the infrastructure of the organization's TFMP and sometimes outside. It is crucial that effective communications, teamwork, and networking be maintained.

So whether it is to provide an electronic lock and key or check-in system; a clean climate-controlled bathroom, locker room, or racquetball court; a wireless environment for handheld heart rate assessment or security signal system; ordering and controlling the flow of first-rate equipment (including safety equipment); scheduling more well-trained employees during peak usage; or promoting the facility and its programs including providing appropriate incentives to reach out to students, employees or the community: facility management and those professionals engaged in its process are crucial to providing high-quality programs as well as to meeting organizational goals and objectives.

PLANNING THE FACILITY

At the outset, two principles relating to facility management should be uppermost in the minds of professionals: (1) facilities are built as a result of community and program needs, and (2) cooperative planning is essential to design and construct quality facilities. After determining the needs via a needs assessment study, a feasibility study is usually conducted. The purpose of the feasibility study is to identify the costs, both short and long term, associated with the project (e.g., operations and maintenance, equipment, financing, etc.); the potential site; primary target and user group population; environment, economic, and community impact; the legal feasibility (e.g., deed, ownership, easements, restrictive zoning, etc.); as well as the design and management feasibility and capability. This information is then fed into the design of a master plan or building scheme that identifies the organization's needs and priorities. Program objectives; user group needs; priority activities; instructional strategies, delivery, and materials; management philosophy; policies; equipment; technology; and supplies and maintenance all represent considerations regarding facilities. The educational and recreational needs of both the school and community; the vision and thinking of the managers, physical educators, and coaches; the advice of architects, city planners, and engineers; and input from other groups mentioned earlier are other inputs requisite if facilities are to be planned wisely.

Management guidelines and principles for facility planning that apply to all educational levels and organizations include the following:

- Facilities should be planned primarily for the participants and user groups.

- Facilities should be planned for multiple and shared usage as well as potential growth patterns and trends.

- All planning should be based on goals that recognize that the total physical and nonphysical environments must be safe, secure, attractive, comfortable, clean, healthful, practical, accessible, and adaptable to the needs of the individual.

- Facilities must be economical and easy to operate, control, and maintain.

- The planning should include a consideration of the total physical education, recreation, and sport facilities community. The programs and facilities of these common areas are closely allied, and planning should be coordinated and cooperative, based on the needs and character of the total community.

- Facility planning must take into consideration protection for the community (e.g., traffic, sound, lighting, civil services—fire, police, transport, medical emergency). The facility must be accessible to user groups, yet isolated enough so that the activity is not a distraction to other programs.

- Facilities should be geared to health, safety, and legal codes and standards, which are important in protecting the health, welfare, and safety of user groups, as well as the environment.

- Facilities should be planned so that they are easily accessible (ADA) and secure for all individuals, including those with disabilities.

- Facility planning must be long-term in nature to include adaptability, convertibility, and expandability to meet the needs of a changing society. This includes adequate acreage for expansion.

- Facilities play a part in a healthful environment. The extent to which organizations provide ample and safe play area space, sanitary considerations (e.g., drainage, lighting), and proper ventilation, heating, and cleanliness will to some extent determine how effectively health and wellness are promoted.

Managers must make plans for facilities long before an architect is consulted. Technical information can be obtained in the form of standards, codes, and guides from various sources, such as state departments of health and education, sports organizations and federations, professional journals and literature (e.g., *Athletic Business, Facility Manager, Facility Management Journal, Fitness Business*

From construction to operation—University of Minnesota Sports Complex.

Pro, The Academy of Management Review, Special Events, Aquatics), as well as from appropriate groups such as the American Association of School Administrators, AAHPERD, NASPE, NASSM, CFE (Council on Facilities and Equipment), NCAA, and the American Institute of Architects.

Standards may be used as guides and as a starting point; however, it is important to keep in mind that standards cannot always be implemented entirely as envisaged. They usually have to be modified in light of community needs, environmental conditions, and scarce inputs, including fiscal and space constraints.

Building safety and environmental and sanitation codes managed by the local and state departments of public health and the technical advice and consultation services available through these sources should be identified and implemented by managers during the planning phase as well as the construction phase of the facilities. Information about quality building materials, safety specifications, minimal standards of sanitation, power, sound and light, and other details may be secured from these sources.

Physical education, recreation, and sport human resources should play important roles in planning, providing needs and feasibility studies, administering, operating, marketing, and promoting new and renovated facilities. The specialized knowledge and experience that such individuals have is important. Provisions should be made so that their expert opinion will be used to promote healthful, safe, optimal learning environments.

Facilities should be planned only after thorough needs and demand assessments and market and economic impact studies and forecasts are performed. Too often, facilities are constructed, outdated, and outgrown within a very short time. Building units should be large enough to accommodate peak-load participation for various activities at all user group levels. The peak-load estimates should be made with future growth of the target user group, community, and activity in mind.

Planning should provide adequate allotment of space to each activity and program area. Space allotment should fit into an overall plan of program priorities (e.g., cardio and strength training, dance, open fitness, group exercise, lifetime sports, spectator sports). Office space and service and storage units, although important, should not be planned and developed in a spacious and luxurious manner that goes beyond efficiency and necessity.

Geographical, ecological, and climatic conditions should be considered when planning facilities. By doing this, the full potential for conducting activities outdoors as well as indoors can be realized.

Architects are not always fully aware of the special educational and health features when planning physical education, recreation, and sport buildings and facilities. Therefore it is important that they be briefed on certain requirements and specifications that physical educators and other professionals believe are essential so that the health, safety, and welfare of children, youth, and adults may be better served. Such a procedure is usually welcomed by the architect and facility planning committee and will aid them in rendering a greater service to the community.

Facilities should include all the safety, security, and risk management features essential in physical education, recreation, and sport programs. Health and sports medicine services and office locations near the gymnasium, pool, arena, and other activity and play areas, proper surfacing of activity areas, adequate space, temperature and humidity control, communication, and proper lighting are a few of these considerations (see box 9-2).

The construction of school physical education, recreation, and sport facilities often tends to set a pattern and elicit a positive reaction that will influence community, civic leaders, parents, and others. This in turn promotes a healthful and safe environment for the entire community to take pride in.

HEALTH CONSIDERATIONS IN FACILITY PLANNING

The participant must be provided a safe, healthful, pleasant, and emotionally secure environment in which to participate. This environment also includes the outdoors, where everything possible

> ### Box 9-2   Role of Management in Facility Planning and Development
>
> - Management should familiarize itself with background information (needs, feasibility and impact studies) pertinent to the facility plan and should be actively involved in all planning sessions.
> - Management should visit sites of other like facilities and talk to appropriate personnel.
> - Management should meet and discuss the facility project with all people (e.g., user groups, community) who have a stake in the project. Management should be familiar with the views of such people and consider their input carefully.
> - Management should insist on being involved in selecting the architect or engineer who is going to do the master plan. Management should press strongly for selecting competent and qualified people to do the job rather than the lowest bidder or the firm with political connections. This is also the case with materials and equipment.
> - Management should attend planning conferences to present the department's point of view on facility design, construction, and detailing.
> - Management should conduct regular site audits after construction begins. All problems should be noted, recorded, and reported to the appropriate facility planning team or "change" committee.
> - Management should insist that all details and standards incorporated in the project be carried out exactly as specified. Management should not approve any facility or authorize payment unless this has been done.
> - Management should initiate a "time frame" for each phase of the plan, so appropriate "construction tracking" can be continuously monitored and updated.
> - Management should see that appropriate standards and codes recommended by such organizations as the American National Standard Institute (ANSI), ASTM International, Occupational Safety and Health Administration (OSHA), the Environmental Protection Agency (EPA), the American College of Sports Medicine (ACSM), and National Spa and Pool Institute (NSPI) are closely followed.

should be done to protect and enhance land, water, air, and other delicate ecosystems. The total learning, playing, and working environment should be integrated, healthful, and pleasant for all, whether staff member, employee, or participant.

Another set of principles basic to facility planning concerns the optimal promotion of a healthful environment for not only the participants but also the community. Included in this set of principles is the provision for facilities that consider the physiological needs of the participant (i.e., intergenerational activities), including proper climate control, lighting, water supply, and acoustic (noise) level. A second principle is to provide safe and secure facilities. The facilities should be planned so that the possibility of mechanical accidents, the danger of fire, and the hazards involved in traffic, and crowd safety and control would be eliminated or kept to a minimum. Risk management, emergency, and disaster plans are vital. A third principle is to protect

A safe, pleasant learning environment is necessary for positive academic performance.

against disease. This means attention to items such as proper sewage disposal, sanitation procedures and policies, and quality water, air, and materials supply. A fourth principle is the need to provide a healthful psychosocial environment.

This has implications for space, capacity control, location of activities, color schemes, and elimination of distractions through such means as soundproof and light sensitive construction materials and design.

The general health features of the physical environment include site, building, lighting, environmental impact, climate control, plant sanitation, and acoustics.

Site

There are many aspects to consider in selecting a suitable facility location. These considerations will differ, depending on the community. Whether it is a rural or an urban community will have a bearing on the site selection. In an urban community, it is desirable to have a school situated near transportation facilities but at the same time located away from industrial concerns, railroads, noise, heavy traffic, toxic fumes, and smoke. A rural facility site might bring more attention to readily accessible initiatives including cable and fiber optics, transportation, and parking as well as access to medical, emergency, and fire services. Real estate, surrounding neighbors, zoning, toxification, sewage, environment, security, topography, and legal constraints also are crucial site variables. Consideration should also be given to demographic trends, population forecasts, and future development of the area in which the buildings and space for activity are planned. Adequate space for play, recreation, and community involvement should be provided. The play area should consist of a minimum of 100 square feet for each young child and 125 square feet for each high school student. Some school standards recommend five acres of land for elementary schools, ten to twelve acres for junior high or middle schools, and twenty acres for senior high schools.

Attention also should be given to the aesthetic features of a site because of their effect on the physical and psychosocial well-being of participants and staff members as well as the community. The surroundings (e.g., site walkways, walking and bike paths, green space, etc.) should be well landscaped, attractive, and free from disturbing noises, odors, or other external interferences.

Building

The trend in schools and community-based building projects is toward one-story construction, with stress on planning from a functional rather than an ornamental point of view. The building should be constructed for optimal *use* and, when possible, be multipurpose in design. The materials selected should be high quality, up to code, and make the building attractive and safe. Every precaution should be taken to protect against accidents, fire, slippery floors, and other dangers and risks. The walls should be painted with light colors, a matte or new glossy finish, and treated with acoustic materials. Doors should open outward. Space for clothing/storage should be provided. Provisions for persons with disabilities and for older citizen community user groups, including nonslip ramps, walkways, split entrance accessibility, toilet facilities with grab bars, and others discussed in chapter 3, should be major considerations when building, renovating, or retrofitting an existing facility.

Lighting

Proper lighting is important to protect and conserve vision, prevent fatigue, provide a safe environment, and improve morale. It is recommended when possible to have a combination of natural (windows, skylights) and artificial (direct and indirect) lighting. Artificial light (e.g., mercury-vapor, fluorescent, metal halide, high-pressure sodium, quartz, incandescent), moreover, should come from many sources rather than a few to prevent too much concentration of light in one place (glare). Lighting intensity (especially high-intensity outdoor lighting) should be uniform in accordance with recommended standards and color rendering indices. Switches and other power sources for artificial light should be located in secure parts of the facility and of course should be recessed and enclosed for protection.

In gymnasiums, arenas, field houses, and swimming pools, light intensity should range from 50 to 100 foot-candles, depending on the type of activity being conducted. Outdoor recreational areas and high school stadiums also

Natural, direct, and indirect lighting are features at Reily Recreation Center at Tulane University in New Orleans.

should have at least 50 foot-candles of light while professional stadiums and parks range from 150 to 300 (pro baseball infield) foot-candles. Group exercise, dance, cardio and strength training areas, and most sport courts should range from 50 to 70 foot-candles, whereas classroom and laboratory settings require 100 to 150 foot-candles of illumination. Glare, reflection, and shadows are undesirable hazards that should be eliminated, especially in aquatic facilities to ensure the safety of the participant and protect sight lines for lifeguards. Overhead or other multistage lights should be properly installed (twenty-four feet above the playing surface), recessed, protected (transparent polycarbonate), and adjusted for best results. Some new facilities are employing occupancy or motion sensors or preprogrammed computers to control their lighting systems. Strong contrasts of color such as light walls and dark floors should also be avoided if possible.

Environmental Climate Control

Efficiency in the classroom, gymnasium, fitness center, arena, special activities rooms, and other places is determined to some extent by thermal comfort, which is mainly determined by heating, ventilation, and air conditioning (HVAC).

The purposes of heating, ventilation, and air conditioning are to remove excess heat and humidity, unpleasant odors, and in some cases, gases, vapors, fumes, and dust from the room; to promote balanced radient temperature and uniformity; to diffuse the heat within a room; and to supply heat to counteract loss from the human body through radiation and otherwise.

Heating and air conditioning standards vary according to the activities engaged in, number of participants, the participant's clothing, and the geographical location of the facility. Usually the air temperature is maintained between 64 and 72 degrees, whereas the humidity ranges between 40 and 60 percent.

For ventilation, the range of recommendations is from eight to twenty-one cubic feet of fresh air per minute per occupant. Adequate ventilating and condensing systems are especially needed in dressing, shower, and locker rooms; steam and storage rooms; toilets; gymnasiums; and swimming pools; in fact, all rooms require adequate ventilation. The type and amount of ventilation including air conditioning will vary with the specific needs and location of the particular activity or special area. Computer-controlled HVAC "smart systems" that control not only the environment, but also fire alarms and security and communications systems are coming online. Preventative HVAC maintenance and corrective services and repair are requisite for health and risk management purposes. The American Society of Heating and Ventilation Engineers is a good resource for specifications.

Plant Sanitation

Plant sanitation should not be overlooked. Sanitation facilities should be well planned and maintained. The water supply should be safe and adequate. If any question exists, the health department should be

A rowing tank facility at Trinity College, Hartford, Conn.

consulted. One authority suggests that at least twenty gallons of water per individual per day is needed for all purposes.

Drinking fountains of various heights should be recessed in corridor walls and should consist of material that is easily cleaned. A stream of water should flow from the fountain so that it is not necessary for the mouth of the drinker to get too near the water outlet or drain bowl.

Water closets, urinals, lavatories, shower rooms, and washroom equipment such as soap dispensers, toilet paper holders, waste containers, safety mirrors, bookshelves, and grooming facilities should be provided keeping in mind reasonable accomodations for persons with disabilities.

Waste disposal should be regularly collected and monitored. There should be provision for cleanup, removal, and recycling of paper and other materials that make the grounds and buildings a health and safety hazard as well as unsightly. Proper sewage disposal and prompt garbage, trash, and recycling services should also be provided. Frequent plant and facility sanitation audits are strongly encouraged.

Acoustics

Noise disturbs, causes nervous strain, and detracts from the many benefits of participating in physical activity. Therefore the sonic environment or noise (e.g., background, echoing, etc.) should be eliminated, absorbed, and reflected as effectively as possible. Walls, including double wall construction, dividers, fences, bermes, trees, and water all provide a means of sound control. Sound control can also be achieved by acoustical treatment of such important places as corridors, gymnasiums, arenas, and swimming pools.

Acoustical materials include glazes, plasters, fibers, boards, acoustic tiles, matting, turf, and various fabrics. Floor covering that reduces noise should be used in corridors, and acoustical material should be used in walls and ceilings. Gymnasiums, arenas, swimming and diving pools, and racket courts need special treatment to control the various noises associated with enthusiastic play and participation. Of course, sound and sound systems (i.e., group exercise and dance rooms, public address systems), when appropriate, must also be taken into full consideration.

DETERMINING NUMBER OF TEACHING STATIONS NEEDED

The teaching station concept should be considered when planning and designing physical education, recreation, and sport facilities. A teaching station is the space or setting in which one teacher or staff member can conduct physical activities for one group of participants. The number and size of teaching stations available together with the number of teachers or instructors on the staff, the size of the group, the number of times the group meets, the number of periods in the school or college day, and the program of activities are important items to consider when planning.

The following formulas may be used to determine the number of teaching stations necessary for effective teaching and learning (Sawyer 2005).

Elementary Schools

The formula for computing the number of teaching stations needed for physical education in the elementary schools is as follows:

Minimum number of teaching stations =

$$\frac{\text{Number of classes or units of students} \times \text{Number of physical education periods per week per class}}{\text{Total physical education periods in school week}}$$

For example, for an elementary school of six grades, with three classes at each grade level (approximately 450 to 540 students), ten 30-minute physical education periods per day (fifty per week), and physical education conducted on a daily basis, the teaching station needs are calculated as follows:

Minimum number of teaching stations =

$$\frac{18 \text{ units} \times 5 \text{ periods/week} \ (3 \text{ classrooms} \times 6 \text{ grades})}{50 \text{ total periods in school week} \ (10 \text{ periods/days} \times 5 \text{ days})} = \frac{90}{50} = 1.8$$

Secondary Schools and Colleges

The formula for computing the number of teaching stations needed for physical education in secondary schools and colleges is as follows:

Minimum number of teaching stations =

$$\frac{\text{Number of students} \times \text{Number of periods class meets each week}}{\text{Average number of student/instructor} \times \text{Total number of class periods in school week}}$$

For example, if a school system projects its enrollment as 700 students and plans six physical education class periods a day with an average class size of thirty students and physical education class meets three times per week, the formula is as follows:

Minimum number of teaching stations =

$$\frac{700 \text{ students}}{30 \text{ per class}} \times \frac{3 \text{ classes/week}}{30 \text{ periods/week}} = \frac{2100}{900} = 2.4$$

Athletic Training Facilities

An average athletic training facility ranges from 1,000 to 2,500 square feet. A formula for consideration is as follows:

$$\frac{\text{Number of athletes at peak hour}}{20 \text{ athletes per table per day}} \times 100 = \text{Total square footage}$$

For example, if 250 athletes arrive at peak practice time, it would be requisite to have at least 1,250 square feet of operational space.

$$\frac{250 \text{ athletes}}{20 \text{ athletic training stations}} = 12.5 \times 100 = \frac{1,250}{\text{square feet}}$$

Other Teaching (Gymnasiums) Space

Further teaching space recommendations include at least 100 square feet per K–6 grade participant and 125 square feet per grade 6 through postsecondary school. A minimum gymnasium teaching space with safety buffer should be at least 54×90 or 4,860 square feet with twenty-two- to twenty-four-feet-high ceilings. Auxiliary indoor teaching stations should provide for at least sixty to eighty square feet per participant and, at a minimum, 1,800 square feet with eighteen-foot ceilings. Storage, electrical outlets, and accessibility to toilet facilities are also considerations.

Storage and Equipment Issue Area

Storage of inventory and adequate issue and control areas are often problematic for some institutions and fitness clubs. Location proximate to primary facility and locker room, security, double doors, climate control and computerized inventory control, and checkout are mandatory. A first aid, AED, and communication center should also be found in this important hub location. While there are no specific space requirements for this type of ancillary or support space, 20 percent of the activity area has been suggested.

THE TEAM APPROACH TO FACILITY PLANNING

Facility planning requires a team approach that includes many crucial players (Ammon, Southall, and Blair 2004). The planning team may include the architect (design, landscape), engineer (civil, electrical, etc.), business manager, physical plant and maintenance staff, physical education, recreation, and sport managers, coaches, and consultants in facility safety and risk management, technology, the environment, and health. In order to ensure optimal results in obtaining a quality facility, certain facility planning procedural processes should be followed.

First, form a planning team (needs and feasibility assessment team) that will identify needs, perform a feasibility study, and prepare a project proposal. Included on this team may be the project coordinator for the organization for whom the facility is being planned, the architect, a representative from the physical education and sport area, a community government representative, and a budget director or business manager. Team members should understand the role each plays in the facility planning process.

Second, secure consultants (i.e., AAPAR's Facilities and Equipment Council) during the early stages of the project because team members may not have expertise in all aspects of facility design, multipurpose programming, or sustained maintenance and finance. Consultants can help close the gap between architectural theory and physical education and sport practice, not to mention fiscal shortcomings and legal responsibility.

Third, stress faculty, staff, student, participant, and community involvement. Each of these representative team members can provide important input about their specific area of facility interest and involvement. These key players can also be used to form a public relations team to articulate or "sell" the facility to the community. For example, an adapted/developmental physical education teacher, specialist in biomechanics, eronomics, and exercise science, an aquatics director, park board member, group exercise instructor, or tennis, rowing, gymnastics, or swimming coach could provide meaningful information about the projected facility, laboratory space and special needs.

Fourth, visit and gather information and materials from other like facilities. Planning team members can obtain valuable ideas and advice that may contribute to improving the facility plan. Appendix F provides a checklist for potential facility planners.

Finally, the plan, after approval by higher administration and management, evolves into a request for proposals (RFP). The RFP issuance is a call for bids that outlines the overall facility picture and its fiscal outlook and requirements. Bids are received, presentations made, RFPs and performance bonds received, contracts negotiated, and, with luck, ground is broken. Lost time in this process often translates into higher costs. The total process from planning and design to moving in usually takes from twenty-four to thirty months.

The planning team should also be aware when making facility recommendations about long-term maintenance and operational costs. When construction is under way, not only the architect and consultants but also the physical education, recreation, and sport specialists as well as other key members of the planning team should systematically monitor and audit the work. By doing this, many potential errors and flaws may be avoided and if a mistake does occur, it can be documented and submitted to the change team.

WORKING WITH THE ARCHITECT

The architect is the specialist in facility planning and leads the design team in the planning and construction of new physical education and sport facilities. The architect, through his or her training and experience, is a specialist who is competent to give advisory service in most aspects of facility management.

Donald E. Krotee, the chief operations officer for a group of architects in Santa Ana, California, points out that a strong, positive relationship between the architect, the school, and the community is crucial for effective planning. Lines of communication within the school, between the school and the architect, and within the architect's office must be based on mutual understanding, accurate information, and

The architect and physical educators cooperatively planned for facilities at the Bob Carpenter Sports/Convocation Center at the University of Delaware, Newark.

teamwork. Communication about program and space needs and requirements must be continuous. These are the hallmarks of the satisfied and successful facility planner.

Physical educators and coaches should carefully think through their own ideas and plans for any special facilities needs (security, technology, storage) and submit them in writing to the planning team during the early stages of planning. The architect and physical education, recreation, and sports specialists should have regular team meetings in which they exchange views and consider architectural potentials, possibilities, and acceptable alternatives.

Some architects may be limited in their knowledge about physical education, recreation, and sport programs and therefore welcome the advice of specialists. The architect might be furnished with such information as the names of institutions or communities where excellent facilities exist; kinds of activities that will constitute the program; space and rules requirements for various age-appropriate activities; storage and equipment areas needed; lighting and climate control requirements; relation of dressing, showering, and toilet facilities to the program; teaching stations needed; athletic training, therapy, and first-aid rooms; specific construction materials for activity areas; and lighting, acoustical, security, and accessibility requirements. The physical educator, athletic and activities director, and coach may not have all this information readily available, including some of the latest trends and standards recommended for his or her specific field or sport. However, such information can be obtained through the literature and Web sites of professional organizations and federations as well as from other schools and organizations where outstanding facilities have been developed, financed, constructed, and marketed.

The Donald Krotee Partnership, a professional planning and architectural firm, together with Comprehensive Planning Services, a Newport Beach, California, planning firm, has developed a procedural facility planning outline that lists some essential considerations for physical educators and sports administrators and managers when planning with architects and facility planning firms. Some of the main points follow.

Educational Specifications

Adequate educational specifications provide the basis for sound planning by the architect:

1. General description of the program, such as the number of teaching stations necessary to service the physical education program for a total student body of approximately (n = ?) boys and (n = ?) girls. The general description should also include school or institutional philosophy, primary user group (e.g., age and developmental level), size of team, number of spectators to accommodate, accessibility and security issues, and other user group specifications, including the projected popularity of physical activities to be delivered.

2. Basic criteria that pertain to the gymnasium or facility being planned, including the number of teaching periods per day; capacities, number,

size, and types of courts and lockers; and total multipurpose prioritized uses and delivery times projected for the facility:

a. Availability and accessibility to the community (e.g., foot, bicycle, skating, wheelchair).

b. Proximity to parks and community centers.

c. Parking, transportation, traffic patterns, and accessibility (e.g., persons with disabilities, medical emergency units, police, fire department).

d. Popularity and type of activities for primary and other appropriate user groups (construct a prioritized list including latest trends).

e. Size and nature of groups and activities that will be accommodated after school hours.

f. Whether locker rooms and facilities will be made available for public use.

3. Specific description of various aspects of the physical education and sport program that affect the architects:

a. Class size, scheduling, office space, and number of instructors—present and future projection.

b. Preferred method of handling students or spectators—for example, flow of traffic in corridors, classrooms, gyms, pools, office areas, locker rooms, and shower rooms—and distance to outside play areas.

c. Storage requirements (e.g., size and space by square footage) and preferred method of handling permanent equipment and supplies.

d. Primary user groups and other extracurricular and after-school use of facilities (It helps the architect if the educational specifications detail a typical week's use flow chart of the proposed facility, which would include a typical daily program, after-school use, and potential community integration).

e. Sport- or activity-specific requests such as synthetic tracks or fields, metal halide/incandescent underwater lights,

spectator glass walls, acoustics, energy conservation power water pump system, skylights, wood surface floors, modular basaltic granite climbing wall system, and so on.

f. Rules, regulations, standards, laws (IDEA, Title IX, ADA, NCAA, etc.), and safety codes concerning various user groups and physical activities should be reaffirmed. All user groups must be involved in the facility planning process.

g. Any sport or competition-specific rules or regulations ranging from water temperature to ceiling height and from pool depth and length (to accommodate electric timing or moveable bulkheads) to field length and width, including special markings must be accounted for.

4. Risk management features should be built into the design process:

a. Nonslip surfaces, safety buffer zones around playing areas, unprotected glass such as mirrors, light fixtures, doors, trophy cases, fire extinguisher covers, and acoustic tile all must be reinforced.

b. Closed circuit supervisory and control systems, identification entry points and systems, storage, isolated areas or dead spaces must all be accounted for.

c. From lighting to sight lines and from equipment placement to placement of lifeguard stations and from ADA to OSHA compliance, specific and prudent research and facility planning must occur.

Meeting with the Architect

At this point, it is advisable for the team to meet with the architect to discuss specifications to ensure complete understanding and to allow the architect to point out certain restrictions or limitations that may be anticipated even before the first preliminary plan and design are made. There is no use creating elaborate plans if the only space available is one that is directly over an earthquake fault line or there is no money in the bank!

Facilities must be planned with specific user groups in mind. Removable synthetic flooring, portable bleachers, electronic scoreboard messaging systems, club rooms, and a historic hall of fame walkway have enhanced what was once an old ice hockey arena. Sports Pavilion, University of Minnesota, Minneapolis.

Design

The following factors might be considered in the design of the facility and discussed with the architect.

1. *Budget.* An adequate budget should be allocated for the participants and the community to be proud of the completed project. It is important to secure the best (most affordable) facility possible because, in most cases, it will be a long time before another opportunity to build presents itself.

2. *Function.* Physical education, recreation, and sport facilities should be long lasting (at least twenty-five to thirty years), durable, multipurpose, accessible, easily maintained, functional, safe, secure, and user friendly.

3. *Acoustics.* Use the service of acoustical consultants. Take their sound advice!

4. *Public address system.* How is it to be used—for instruction, sporting events, general communication?

5. *Aesthetics.* The design and color scheme should be compatible with surrounding environs, including existing structures, school colors, and the immediate community.

6. *Fenestration (window treatment).* Consider light control, potential window and skylight breakage, vision panel, natural light; windows in gymnasium areas and all high-traffic areas should have safety glass and be well protected and marked.

7. *Heating, ventilation, and air conditioning (HVAC).* The various areas should be zoned for flexibility of use and control. This means greater ventilation when a larger number of

users or spectators are present or a reduction for single class and smaller groups or in isolated areas such as locker and storage rooms. Special attention must be given to proper ventilation of washing and drying rooms, gymnasium storage areas, and locker, sauna, steam room, and shower areas. Ventilation, air exchange, heating, and air conditioning equipment should have a low noise level and maximal efficiency rating.

8. *Supplementary equipment in the gymnasium.* Such equipment should be held to a minimum. Supplementary equipment, such as fire boxes, AEDs, drinking fountains, phone and electrical power sources should be recessed, well marked, yet accessible for all user groups. Storage should be built into your design.

9. *Compactness and integration.* Keep volume compact—large, barnlike spaces are unpleasant and are costly to heat and maintain. Divide and integrate the facility as far as budget permits.

10. *Mechanical or electrical features.* Special attention should be given to location of electrical panel boards, light controls, scoreboards, timing systems, video and closed-circuit television monitors, fire alarms, folding doors, and drop nets. All must be easy to use, secure, and safe to operate.

Further Critique with the Architect

The architect begins to develop plans from an understanding of the initial requirements he or she has considered in relation to the design factors listed. Aesthetics (how it looks), project budget, function, codes, laws, technology, and master plan integration will significantly determine the shape of your facility plans.

When the basic plan is set (e.g., square footage, cost estimate in lump sum and unit pricing), the architect will usually call in consulting engineers to discuss the structural and mechanical systems before approval of the plan. These systems will have been outlined by the architect, but usually are not discussed with planning teams other than in generalities before the plan is in approximate final form.

More meetings are then conducted regarding approval of preliminary plans and proposed structural and mechanical systems, including the use of materials, technology, and sometimes equipment after the incorporation in the preliminary plans.

If supplementary financing by government or private sector agencies is involved, the plans or set of drawings will have been submitted to those agencies with a project outline or specifications as soon as the plan has been sufficiently developed. If the agency approves the application as submitted by the architect, the final preliminary working drawings are started.

Final Processing

It is advisable to settle all matters that can be settled during preliminary planning to save time and expense. If this method is employed, greater clarity is ensured and less changing or misunderstanding results (see box 9-3). On completion of the preliminary facility plan and agreement of the planning committee, the plans are then submitted to higher administration (e.g., school board, board of regents or directors) for approval, and competitive bids are sent out as described previously in the section titled The Team Approach to Facility Planning. A cooperative and coordinated effort including systematic walk-throughs, audits, and meetings between the planning team (representing the user), architect, and contractor remains in place until the facility is online. Even after opening, many consultations will be needed to ensure facility integrity.

INDOOR FACILITIES

Indoor facilities are unique, special, and crucial to quality physical education, recreation, and sport programs. These typically include such areas as management and staff offices; locker, shower and drying rooms; gymnasiums; special activity areas; and indoor swimming pools.

Box 9-3 Common Errors Made by Managers in Facility Planning and Development

Some common errors made by managers and athletic and activity directors in facility planning and development include the following:

- Failure to adequately project or forecast enrollment, demand, and program needs into the future (facilities are difficult to expand or change, so this is a significant error).
- Failure to build an expert and representative planning and design team inclusive of participants, community, and individuals with various disabilities.
- Failure to provide for multiple use of facilities.
- Failure to provide for adequate accessibility for students in physical education and recreational sport and also for myriad community user groups.
- Failure to observe basic health codes and factors regarding lighting, safety, and ventilation.
- Failure to provide adequate space, including safety buffer zones, for the conduct of a comprehensive program of physical education and sport activities.
- Failure to provide removable accommodations for spectators and participants with disabilities.
- Failure to soundproof areas of the facility in which noise will interfere with educational functions.
- Failure to meet with the architect to present views on program needs early in the planning process.
- Failure to provide adequate staff offices.
- Failure to provide adequate storage space.
- Failure to provide adequate space for privacy for medical and counseling services.
- Failure to provide entrances large enough to transport equipment.
- Failure to observe desirable current professional standards, codes, and regulations.
- Failure to provide for adequate study of cost in terms of durability, time, money, and effective instruction and efficiency.

- Failure to properly locate teaching stations with service facilities.
- Failure to provide adequate and accessible locker, dressing, toilet, and grooming space.
- Failure to plan dressing, grooming, and shower area so as to reduce foot traffic to a minimum and establish clean, dry aisles for bare feet.
- Failure to provide a nonskid surface on dressing, shower, and drying room floors.
- Inadequate provision for drinking fountains.
- Failure to provide acoustical treatment where needed.
- Failure to provide and properly locate toilet facilities to serve *all* participants and users.
- Failure to provide doorways, hallways, or ramps so that equipment may be transported easily.
- Failure to design equipment rooms for convenient and quick check-in and check-out, including technology.
- Failure to provide safety mirrors, electrical outlets, and shelving for dressing facilities.
- Failure to plan locker and dressing rooms with safe traffic pattern and control to swimming pools.
- Failure to construct shower, toilet, dressing, and grooming rooms with sufficient floor slope and properly located drains.
- Failure to place showerheads low enough and in such a position that the spray is kept within the shower room.
- Failure to provide shelves in the toilet and drying rooms.
- Failure to comply with ADA regulations.
- Failure to provide proper safety signage.
- Failure to provide a safe, secure, and supervisable area and environment (e.g., simple entry, monitored ID system, etc.).

It is important, as far as practical and possible, for physical educators, coaches, recreation and fitness managers, and athletic and activities directors to have a section of a building set aside for management and staff offices. At minimum, the area should be a large central office with an outer office that can serve as a waiting room and reception area. The central office provides a place where secretarial and clerical work is performed; computer systems are housed; and records, files, and office supplies are secured.

Separate offices for the staff members should be provided, if possible. Separate offices provide a place where conferences can be conducted in private and without interruption. This is an important consideration for counseling, meeting with students, participants, and parents, and discussing other work-related business. If separate offices are not practical, a desk, computer, bookshelf, storage cabinet, and office divider should be provided for each staff member. There should, however, be a private room available for conferences.

Other facilities that make the administrative and staff setup more efficient and enjoyable are staff locker and dressing rooms, a staff lounge, departmental library, conference room, and private toilet, lavatory, and grooming facilities.

Locker, Shower, and Drying Rooms

Physical education and sport activities require facilities for storage of clothes and workout gear as well as for showering and drying. These facilities are essential to good personal hygiene and health and to a well-organized program.

Locker and shower rooms should be readily accessible to all users, close to activity areas, and, when possible, of the same floor level of aquatic facilities. Locker rooms should not be congested places that people want to get out of as soon as possible. Instead, they should provide ample room for storage and dressing lockers, stationary benches, safety mirrors, recessed lighting fixtures, scales, sauna, toilets, grooming area, and drinking fountains. Athletic training, therapy, and first-aid stations may also be part of a well-designed locker room area. Amenities such as saunas, steam and massage/therapy room, team rooms, jacuzzis (each requiring twelve to fifteen square feet per participant), towel service, and swimsuit dryers are becoming commonplace because of the multiple use and partnering arrangements that many facilities are now being constructed under. Most locker rooms are designed with "soft" surrounding space (storage, meeting rooms) for potential future expansion.

A minimum of fifteen to twenty square feet per individual at peak load, exclusive of the locker space, is generally required to provide proper locker room space. Generally the number of lockers in a facility range from 60 to 70 percent of the total peak-load demand.

Storage lockers should also be provided for each participant. An additional number of lockers equal to 10 percent of those needed should be installed for expanded enrollments or membership. Lockers are typically permanently assigned and can be used to hold essential clothing and other necessary supplies. They can be smaller than the dressing lockers; some recommended sizes are 7½ by 12 by 24 inches, 6 by 12 by 36 inches, and 7½ by 12 by 18 inches. Basket lockers are not favored by many experts because of hygiene problems, because an attendant is required, and because of the logistics involved in carting the baskets from place to place.

Dressing lockers are used by participants only when actually engaging in activity. They are large, usually 12 by 12 by 54 inches or 12 by 12 by 48 inches in elementary schools, and 12 by 12 by 72 inches or 12 by 15 by 60 for junior high, middle, and secondary schools and colleges as well as for community physical activity programs.

Locker rooms should provide seated dressing areas and storage lockers for all participants. Adequate space should be provided so that dressing

Locker rooms should present a healthful and inviting environment.

zones relieve cramped quarters. At least one multiple-use private changing or family changing and shower area should be provided for participants' special needs. Some end lockers may also be reserved for special populations usage. Lockers should also have proper ventilation, be periodically inspected, and be kept clean at all times.

Shower rooms that have both group and cubicle showers should be provided. Some facility planners recommend that the number of showerheads be equal to 30 to 40 percent of the enrollment at peak load, whereas others rely on a 1:20 shower to locker ratio. Another recommendation suggests a 1:4 shower to person ratio at peak load; University National Standards insist on 10 showerheads for the first 30 users with an additional 1:40 ratio thereafter. Showers should be four feet apart or dispersed in a circular group pattern, and a graded change of water temperature and controlled water flow are recommended. Shower height may be varied for multiple user groups. Shower rooms should also be equipped with liquid soap dispensers, good ventilation and heating, nonslip floors, and recessed plumbing. The ceiling should be constructed to prevent condensation. The shower area should be washed daily to prevent athlete's foot and other contaminations. A towel and laundry service should be initiated if it does not already exist.

A drying area adjacent to the shower room is essential. This should be equipped with proper drainage, good ventilation, towel and grab bars, drinking fountain, mirrors, swimsuit dryers, and appropriate grooming area accessible to all user groups.

Gymnasiums

The type and number of gymnasiums and teaching facilities that should be part of a school, community, recreation, or fitness center physical plant depends on the number of individuals who will be participating and the variety of activities that will be conducted.

School gymnasiums are best located in a separate wing of the building to isolate and control the potential noise and traffic and to provide a conven-

ient location for community-based groups that will be anxious to use such facilities. Parking should be close by.

Many gymnasiums have folding doors or curtains that divide them into halves, thirds, or fourths and allow activities to be conducted simultaneously. This has proved satisfactory where separate gymnasiums or teaching stations could not be provided.

General construction features for gymnasiums include smooth, matte-finished, acoustically treated walls, hardwood floors (maple—laid lengthwise—is preferred), recessed lights, recessed and protected HVAC systems, safety windows, and storage space for the apparatus and other portable equipment. Many gymnasiums are now being floored with various types of resilient synthetic materials.

In elementary schools that need only one teaching station, a minimum floor space of 36 by 52 feet is suggested. Where two teaching stations are desired, floor space of fifty-four by ninety feet, which may be divided by a folding partition, is recommended. The general rule of 110 to 150 square feet per student and 4,680 square feet per gymnasium should be strived for in the facility planning process. The ceiling should be at least twenty-two feet high.

In junior, middle, and senior high schools where only one teaching station is desired, a minimum floor space of 66 by 96 feet exclusive of

A typical elementary school teaching station divided by electronic folding doors. Birchview Elementary School, Wayzata, Minn.

bleachers will provide adequate space. Typically, 125 square feet of activity space for each individual participant per class at peak usage time should be honored. The ceiling should be at least 24 feet high. If seating capacity is desired, additional space will be needed. If more than two teaching stations are desired, the gymnasium area may be extended to provide an additional station, or activity rooms (e.g., strength training, combatives, group exercise, etc.) may be added. Of course, the addition of a swimming pool also provides another functional teaching station.

Other considerations for gymnasiums might include provisions for basketball backboards, mountings for floor plates for various apparatus and standards that will be used, places for hanging and storing mats, outlets for various instructional technology (e.g., video, computer analysis, interactive videodisk), proper line markings for activities, bulletin boards, a false wall for rock climbing, and other essentials necessary for a well-rounded program.

Safe and properly constructed and maintained equipment should be a part of all physical education facilities. Adequate space should be provided for all the activity phases of the program, whether they are in the gymnasium, swimming pool, adapted room, dance area, or auxiliary areas. Mats should be used as a protective measure on walls, floors, and other areas in which participants may be at risk. Drinking fountains and cuspidors should be recessed, and doors should open away from the playing floor. Proper flooring should be used; tile-cement and some types of vinyl floors are sometimes undesirable where activity takes place. Appropriate and architecturally barrier-free space should be provided for people with disabilities so that all facilities (indoor, outdoor, locker room, etc.) are fully accessible. Equipment storage space is a commodity often overlooked during facility planning. Approved HVAC systems, storage racks, shelves, and bins, and an office and workplace area for observation and making minor equipment repair are also desirable.

Clothing and equipment used in physical education activities should meet health and safety standards. Appropriate, clean, and safe clothing, including nonscuff sport footwear, should be required.

Guidelines for Gymnasium Planning

The following guidelines are valid for management, architects, board members, consultants, and other persons involved in gymnasium planning. Many of these guidelines are overlooked by those responsible for gymnasium construction.

The Roof and Ceilings If the roof is not properly designed before construction, costly changes in equipment installation may occur later. Ceiling support beams that may be part of the construction could also be employed by the physical educator to make maximal use of the facility. The design of the roof should allow for support beams strong enough to absorb the stress placed on them in various activities. Support beams should be placed to allow maximal flexibility for the placement of equipment such as scoreboards and gymnastic apparatus. Ceilings should be insulated, reflect light, and be acoustically treated. The distance from the floor to the exposed beams should be at least 22 to 24 feet for the main gymnasium and minimally twelve to fifteen feet for specialty areas such as dance, combatives, wrestling, and strength training.

The Floor The floor is a vital part of the gymnasium and should be constructed from hardwood, not tile. Although more expensive, hardwood is safer, more resilient, lasts longer, does not become slick, and is better for sports performance. Plates for floor apparatus such as the high bar or tennis and volleyball standards should be designed with safety and flexibility in mind. Floor markings should be placed after the prime coat of seal has been applied and before the application of the finishing coat. Synthetic surfaces (polyvinyl chloride and polyurethane) may also be a consideration; however, for heavy use and longevity, wood is recommended.

The Walls It is a good idea to provide a smooth, acoustically glazed, nonabrasive, nonmarkable wall for participants to practice their throwing, catching, and striking skills. A line could be taped along the wall to indicate the height of the tennis or badminton net. The wall can also be used for climbing (cargo nets) or other assorted targets and goals. Walls behind baskets should be recessed and padded. Electrical outlets should be provided (at fifty-foot intervals) throughout the gymnasium so that instructional technology can be used at each teaching station. Computers, timing devices, scoreboards, embedded cork and white boards, public address systems, and outlets for the media should be kept in mind.

Lighting Proper illumination that meets approved standards, with selective controls to vary intensity depending on activity, is a necessity. Fifty foot-candles or higher is recommended for teaching stations and spectator consideration. Many gymnasiums are employing metal halide, fluorescent, high-pressure sodium, or reo-stat quartz lighting used in combination with natural lighting. Durable lighting with recessed and protected fixtures is essential. This helps prevent bulb or tube breakage from ball activities.

Acoustics Noise and sound control should be primary considerations in any gymnasium construction. Acoustic treatment of ceilings, floors, and walls can help reduce or eliminate noise and provide for an optimal learning environment. Sound systems should also be part of the facility design for instruction, communication, and security.

Special Activity Areas

Although gymnasiums take up considerable space, there should still be additional areas for activities essential to high-quality physical education, recreation, and sport programs.

Wherever possible, additional activity areas and teaching stations should be provided for remedial or adapted activities, strength training, tennis (one court/400 school population), racquetball/wallyball, handball, squash, strength training, combatives, dance, rhythms, fencing, and exhibitions and shows. The activities to be provided will depend on the interests of the user groups and type of activities involved in the program. The recom-

Special activity teaching stations should be well designed and constructed.

mended size for such teaching stations is 30 by 60 by 24 feet, or 40 by 60 by 24 feet. A 54 by 90 foot auxiliary gymnasium with a twenty-four foot ceiling is ideal. Many special activity facilities are utilizing lower ceilings, ranging from twelve to eighteen feet depending on their multipurpose usage requirements. The adapted/developmental activities room, if the school is fortunate enough to have one, should be equipped with items such as balance beams and stablizers, horizontal ladders, safety mirrors, mats, climbing ropes, stall bars and benches, fixed and free weights, dumbbells, exercise balls, and other equipment and assessment materials, including technological feedback systems, suited to individual or small group instruction.

Regulation classrooms and other multipurpose space can be converted into additional teaching stations. This alternative may be feasible in situations in which the actual construction of such costly facilities may not be practical.

Auxiliary Rooms

The main auxiliary rooms that must be considered in facility planning are equipment, storage, supply, checkout, custodial, and laundry rooms.

Equipment, storage, and supply rooms should be easily accessible from the gymnasium and other activity areas. Balls, exercise mats, nets, goals, standards, port-a-pits, and other equipment and supplies needed for the program are stored, inventoried, and maintained in these rooms. Towels and uniforms can also be distributed from this area, as can first aid materials and AEDs when necessary. The size of these rooms varies according to the number of participants, the number of activities offered, and the size and scope of the program as well as the size of the physical plant.

Checkout rooms should be provided seasonally. They house the equipment and supplies used in various seasonal activities. They may be less centrally located and more proximate to fields, courts, arenas, or rinks.

Custodial rooms and janitorial closets provide places for storing some equipment and supplies used to maintain these specialized facilities. They should be centrally located, proximate to bathroom and locker rooms, appropriately maintained and appointed (e.g., sinks, work table, shelving, etc.), and provide a comfortable environmental setting.

Laundry rooms should be large enough to accommodate the washing, drying, and storage of such essential items as towels and uniforms. They should be well ventilated, properly wired and floored, and possess adjustable shelving necessary for a well-organized and neat appearance.

Indoor Swimming Pools

Major design decisions must be made if an organization decides to construct a pool. These decisions include items such as the nature of the program to be conducted, philosophy of management as well as user groups, type of overflow system, dimensions, shape and depth of pool, type of finish, type of drains, filters, and water treatment system, construction material, amount of deck area, dry and wet teaching stations, types of air handling and environmental climate control systems, illumination and sound systems, and number of spectators to be accommodated.

Some mistakes that should be avoided in the construction of a pool include the following: locker rooms that open onto the deep rather than the shallow end of the pool; pool base that is finished with slippery material such as glazed tile; insufficient depth of water for diving and racing

The University of Minnesota Aquatics Center in operation.

starts; improper placement of ladders and guard rails; placement of starting blocks in the shallow end of the pool; water recirculation at an insufficient rate to accommodate peak participation loads; inadequate storage space; failure to use acoustic material on ceiling and walls; insufficient illumination; no ADA pool entry; slippery tile on decks; and an inadequate overflow system at the ends of the pool.

Some trends and innovations in pool design and operation include the Rim-Flow Overflow System, inflatable roof structure, the skydome design, pool tent cover, floating swimming pool complex including movable bulkheads, prefabrication of pool tanks, automation of pool recirculating and filter systems, drain covers to prevent entanglement and entrapment, regenerative cycle filter system, heat recovery and chiller preheating systems, adjustable height diving platform, variable bottom depths, pool lifts, fluorescent and incandescent underwater lights, portable underwater sound systems, automatic cleaning systems, computerized and interactive chemical control, in-deck wiring systems for automatic timing, and wave-making machines. Play areas, water slides, and indoor/outdoor sundecks are also growing in popularity.

Swimming pools have two main objectives: to provide instructional and competitive programs and to provide recreation.

The swimming pool should be located on or above the ground level, have a southern exposure, be isolated from other units in the building, and be easily accessible from the central dressing and locker rooms. Materials that have been found most adaptive to swimming pools are smooth, glazed, acoustically treated, light-colored tile or brick.

The standard indoor pool is 75 feet 1 inch long. The width should be a multiple of 7 or 9 feet, with a minimum of 35 feet. Depths vary from 2 feet 6 inches at the shallow end to 4 feet 6 inches at the outer limits of the shallow area. The shallow or instructional area should make up about two-thirds of the pool and be separated by pool lane dividers from the deeper areas, which taper to 9 to 12 feet in depth. An added important factor is a movable bulkhead that can be used to divide a large pool into various instructional or practice areas. Most colleges and many communities are moving toward 50-meter pools.

Water depth under the 1- or 3-meter board should be 12 feet or more and under any platform, 18 feet or more. Racing starts require 4 feet to be measured 15 feet from the end wall.

The deck space around the pool should be constructed of a nonslip, nonglazed material and must provide ample space for land drills, demonstrations, and potential spectators. The area above the water should be unobstructed. The ceiling should be at least 25 feet above the water and 20 feet above the diving board height if this is part of the complex. The walls and the ceiling of the pool area should be acoustically treated.

The swimming pool should be constructed to receive as much natural light as possible, with the windows located on the sides rather than on the ends. Artificial lighting should be recessed in the ceiling. Good lighting (70 foot-candles) is essential, especially near the diving board, where glare should be eliminated. Underwater lighting (50 foot-candles) is a risk management feature and is attractive as well.

There should be an efficient system for adequately heating and circulating the water. When possible, solar and self-heating systems should be adopted to save energy and reduce pool overhead costs. The temperature of the water should range from 78° to 82° F and the in-house humidity should be between 50 to 60 percent. Temperatures for multipurpose pools may range from 83° to 86° F while therapy pools (86°–94° F) and spas (104° F max) may provide for higher temperatures. Chemical balance (pH 7.2–8.0) is specified by code and must be regularly monitored.

Other pool-support spaces that should be considered in pool design include the following: staff and lifeguard offices and changing rooms, dry and wet classrooms, meet management and seminar rooms, first-aid station, research/drug testing laboratory, athletic training and therapy room, strength-training area, technology support room (viewing underwater feedback) and, of course, appropriate storage and janitorial rooms.

An office adjacent to the pool, with open vision to the pool, in which communication and first aid supplies can be stored is advisable. Such an office should be equipped with windows that overlook the entire length of the pool. Also, toilet facilities should be available and, of course, the pool must be fully accessible.

The swimming pool is a costly operation. Therefore it is essential that it be planned with the assistance of aquatic experts. Specialists who are well acquainted with such facilities, including maintenance, cost control, technology, and marketing, and who conduct aquatic activities should be brought into planning meetings with the architect, a representative from the public health department (water-borne illness), and experts in essentials such as lighting (fenestration), environmental climate control, filtration including drain systems, acoustics, construction, and risk management. Figure 9-1 illustrates the planning and design of a large university aquatics facility.

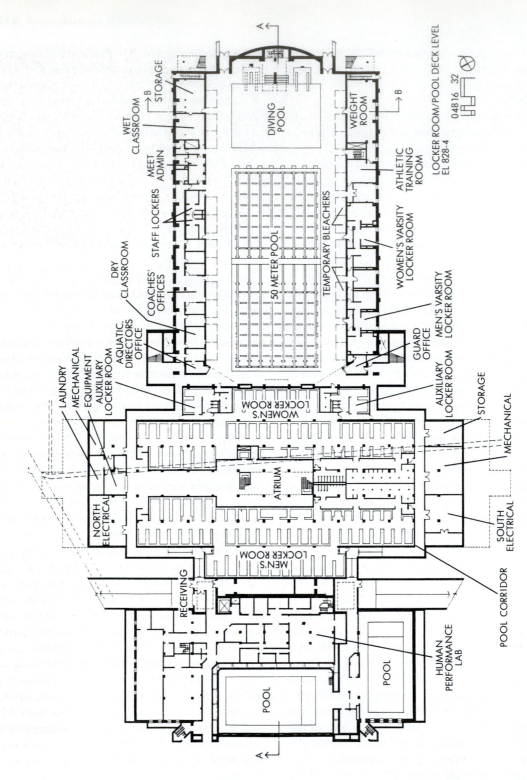

Figure 9-1. The planning and design of the University of Minnesota Aquatics Center.

Health Considerations for Swimming Pools

Swimming pools need special attention whether indoors or outdoors. First, the pool should be properly constructed to provide for adequate filtration, circulation, and chemical treatment. The computer can assist in uniform regulation and conduct of these tasks. Next to water treatment, air handling is crucial to maintain a proper educational and competitive environment. A daily log should be kept on information such as water temperature, water saturation index, facility humidity, hydrogen ion concentration, residual chlorine, and other important factors. Regulations and rules for pool use as well as safety and emergency procedures should be established and appropriately posted; all employees (lifeguards) and user groups should be well-acquainted with them.

Athletic Training and Sports Medicine Facilities

Athletic training, sports medicine, health, and therapy services are an important part of some programs and require adequate facilities. These facets of physical education and sport are addressed in chapter 12.

OUTDOOR FACILITIES

The outdoor facilities discussed in this section are play areas, game areas, outdoor swimming pools, outdoor pursuit, facilities for persons with disabilities, and other special activity areas.

Play Areas

Many factors must be considered when planning outdoor facilities for schools and colleges. Before a site is selected, it is important to appraise the location, topography, soil drainage, irrigation, water supply and table, acreage, shape, and natural features. The outdoor facilities should be as near the gymnasium and locker rooms as possible, yet far enough from the classrooms so that noise and activity will not be a distraction. Other factors that apply also to indoor facility planning, such as accessibility, integration with physical

Outdoor facilities are necessary for quality physical education programs.

plant (e.g., gymnasium, school classrooms), adaptability, convertibility, and expandability, should play a salient role in the facility planning process.

Play areas should serve the needs and interests of the students for the entire school year and at the same time provide a setting for activities during after school hours and vacation periods. The needs and interests of the community must also be considered, especially in communities in which physical plants and facilities such as schools and recreation centers are shared. Because the community uses the areas after the school day a joint planning, program, and management team with community input is strongly recommended.

The size of the area should be determined on the basis of the number and type of activities offered in the program and the number of individuals who will be using the facilities at peak load. Possibilities for expansion and partnered usage should also be kept in mind. Playing fields and playgrounds should have good turf and be clear of rocks, holes, and uneven surfaces. A dirty, dusty surface, for example, can aggravate conditions such as emphysema, chronic bronchitis, and allergies. Safety precautions should also be provided through regular inspection and risk management audits of facilities, play areas, and equipment. Playfields and playgrounds should be fenced in, particularly where there is heavy traffic adjoining these facilities. Rubber, asphalt, synthetic materials, and other substances that require little maintenance and help to free an area from cinders, gravel, stones, dirt, and dust are being used on many outdoor surfaces. In some sections of the country, limited shelters are also being utilized to provide protection from the cold, rain, wind, and sun. All outdoor areas should be fully accessible and possess sanitary drinking fountains and toilet facilities.

Elementary School

The activities program in the K–6 learning environment suggests what facilities should be available. Children in the primary grades engage in large muscle activity involving adaptations of climbing, jumping, skipping, kicking, throwing, leaping, and catching. Children in the intermediate and upper elementary grades perform these fundamental skill activities and others in low organization games and various cooperative and team activities.

The playground area for an elementary school should be located near the building and should be easily accessible from the classrooms. Children in kindergarten should have a section of the playground for their exclusive use. This section should be at least 5,000 square feet and separated from the rest of the playground. It should consist of a surfaced area, a grass area, a play area, and a place for sand and digging. The sand area should be enclosed to prevent it from being scattered or shared by local pets. It is also wise to have a shaded area where storytelling, educational demonstrations, and similar quiet activities may be conducted.

The surfaced area may serve as a year-round multipurpose activities center for both school and community. It can house basketball, shuffleboard, tennis, and sport courts and provide space for games of minimal organization and other creative activities. This area should be paved with material that provides resilience, safety, and durability. Rapid and efficient drainage is also essential. Lines may be painted on the area for various games.

The grass area provides space for varied and modified field and team games such as speedball, soccer, field hockey, softball, and fieldball. The play area should provide for essential health-related fitness equipment such as climbing and horizontal bars, swings, slides, seesaws, climbing and sliding structures, and built-in seats and tables also might be placed in this area. The area should have ample space for maximum safety and supervision of the participants. The shaded area may provide space for activities such as marbles, hopscotch, ring toss, and storytelling. Schools should allow additional space adjacent to this area for possible future expansion.

Other community-based recreation areas that have important implications for K–6 students include any landscaped, parklike areas. These provide a place for quiet activities such as dramatics and informal gatherings, fitness trails, biking, hiking, jogging, skating, walking, and a place for children to have "team" and confidence building activities as well as gardening and picnic opportunities.

Junior High and Middle School

The junior high or middle school play and recreation area, planned and developed for the children who attend the school and also for the citizens of the community, should be located on a site that consists of 10 to 25 acres. Local conditions will determine the amount of land available.

Many of the facilities addressed in the elementary school section may be incorporated in the junior high or middle school. In many cases, however, the various play areas should be increased in size. The necessary facilities should provide for those activities that will be part of the basic physical education, recreational sport, and school sport programs. Football, soccer, baseball, volleyball, softball, and track and field seem to be prevalent at most junior high and middle schools.

Oftentimes the community shares or may even possess co-ownership of this space, so ample field, court, arena, and gymnasium space with lighting is recommended.

A landscaped, parklike area should also be provided for various recreational activities for the students and the community. Activities such as walking, picnicking, in-line skating, bicycling, beach volleyball, broomball, bocce, nordic skiing, sailing, and fly casting might be considered appropriate.

Senior High School

The senior high school physical education program is characterized by individual and lifetime sports as well as by team game activities. This emphasis, together with the popularity of recreational and interscholastic sport and the fact that facilities are typically needed for shared recreational use by the community, requires an even larger area than those for the two previous educational levels. Estimates range from 10 to 40 acres for high school physical plants.

Most of the environmental design concepts and activity areas that have been listed in discussing elementary and middle schools should be included at the senior high level. Considerably more space, however, is needed for the delivery of high school physical education, recreational sports, and interscholastic sport programs because of the need for regulation-size field and game areas. These facilities often include baseball, field hockey, football, lacrosse, soccer, and softball fields, as well as tennis, basketball, volleyball, badminton, handball, and shuffleboard courts, and a track among others.

Game Areas

Football, soccer, and track can be provided for in an area of approximately four acres, with the football/soccer field placed within an enlarged 400-meter track oval that includes at least one 120-meter straight-away six to eight meters wide and appropriate jumping and throwing areas. Baseball and softball need an area of about two acres to allow

Multisport facilities are popular in both schools and communities; evening winter broomball (summer beach volleyball) in Minneapolis, Minn.

safe participation whereas one acre will accommodate four tennis courts, four sport courts, three badminton courts, and two volleyball courts. With so many user teams playing and practicing, including community and youth groups, game space should be protected from daily wear and tear, so additional field space with lighting capacity is strongly recommended.

Winter activities should not be forgotten. With such activities gaining in popularity, provisions should be made for ice skating, nordic or cross-country skiing, broomball, ice hockey, and other winter activities. The more field space and safe, creative, multiuse game area configurations (ice hockey/broomball to sand soccer/volleyball) that can be adapted, the better.

Some recommended dimensions for game areas for physical education, recreation, and sport programs as outlined by the profession are illustrated in table 9-1. Please note that most dimensions can be modified for varying age user groups, special populations, or space restriction.

Table 9-1. Recommended Dimensions for Game Areas

	Elementary	Upper Grades	High School (Adults)	Side and End Safety Space
Basketball	40' × 60'	42' × 74'	50' × 84' (94' univ.)	6'; 8'
Volleyball	25' × 50'	30' × 50'	30' × 60'	6'; 6'
Badminton			20' × 44' × 24'	6'; 8'
Paddle tennis			20' × 50' × 12'	10'; 5'
Platform tennis			30' × 60' × 12'	
Deck tennis			18' × 40'	4'; 5'
Tennis		36' × 78'	36' × 78'	12'; 24'
Ice hockey			85' × 200'	
Field hockey			180' × 300'	8'; 8'
Horseshoes		10' × 40'	10' × 50'	
Shuffleboard			6' × 39'	2'; 6'6"
Lacrosse			180' × 330'	3'; 9'
Lawn bowling			14' × 110'	
Tetherball	10' circle	12' circle	12' circle	
Croquet	40' × 50'	50' × 63'	84' × 105'	
Bocce			18' × 62'	
Handball/Racquetball	18' × 26'	18' × 26'	20' × 40' × 20'/14'	
Baseball			350' × 350'	
Archery		50' × 150'	50' × 300'	15'; 50'
Softball (12" ball)	150' × 150'	200' × 200'	250' × 250'	
Football—with 400-yard track— 220-yard straightaway			300' × 600'	
Touch/flag football			120' × 300'	
6-person football			120' × 240'	
Soccer	40' × 60'	165' × 360'	225' × 360'	8'; 8'
Squash			21' × 32'	
Water polo			75' × 100'	
Wrestling/combatives			24' × 24'	5'; 5'
Fencing		4' × 30'	6' × 46'	9'; 6'
Table tennis			5' × 9' × 2'6"	5';15'
Ultimate			120' × 240'	
Team Handball (indoor)			60' × 126'	

OTHER SPECIAL ACTIVITY AREAS

Other special activity areas also requiring special attention include those involving dance, golf gymnastics, strength training, combatives and martial arts, racquetball/handball, squash, and ice hockey (i.e., in-line hockey and skating, floor hockey, and indoor soccer). Research laboratories, technology-enhanced teaching stations, and assessment facili-

ties, especially at colleges and universities, should also be provided not only for direct use by the students, staff, and faculty, but also to enable researchers to contribute to the body of knowledge of the profession.

Because dance has always been, and continues to be, a very popular activity, special facilities should be provided. It is recommended that a minimum of 100 square feet of space per student and sixteen- to twenty-four-foot ceilings be provided. Full-length mirrors, a sound and video system, and practice barres eight inches from the mirror on one wall at heights of thirty-six and forty-two inches are requisite for program enhancement. The floor (nonslip, floating, resilient) is an important consideration, and it should consist of sealed and buffed hard northern maple. Proper acoustics, wiring, and other appropriate and wide-ranging dance-specific equipment and supplies should also be available, as should adequate storage.

With over 2.5 million golfers playing on over 15,000 golf courses, golf instruction should not be overlooked. A multipurpose room with a dozen striking bays, a video area, and golf simulator space adds value to any program. Synthetic putting surfaces are also becoming popular.

Gymnastics is another special activity area, and recommended space allotment is 90×120 feet of floor space, with a minimum ceiling height of twenty-four feet. Appropriate floor plates and performance pits are also important for skill acquisition, fun, and safety.

Strength training and open fitness lifting are very popular activities for both girls and boys. A minimum of 2,500 square feet should be provided with selectorized, fixed and free weights available. An updated strength-training facility design is presented in figure 9-2 (adapted from Hatfield and Krotee 1984).

A wrestling and martial arts area of a minimum fifty by 100 feet will provide enough space for two forty-two by forty-two foot mats. Judo, Karate, Tai Chi, Tai Kwan Do, and self-defense, among other combatives, have become popular activities for all age levels and should be housed in an appropriate space that is well cushioned, climate controlled, and cleaned daily to prevent the spread of various communicable germs (e.g., impetigo, herpes simplex).

Racquetball, handball, and squash courts are common, particularly in colleges, universities, and club settings. Each four-wall court is forty feet long and twenty feet wide, with a ceiling height of twenty feet. Modified squash courts ($18.5 \times 32 \times 16$ feet) can also be housed within this area.

Another multipurpose facility to be considered is that of an ice arena (85×200 feet) that can also be converted for in-line skating, roller and floor hockey, and indoor soccer, not to mention other court sports. About 25,000 square feet are needed to add such a valuable school and community commodity.

Such activities as indoor tennis, fencing, archery, golf, skating, Nordic skiing, ropes courses, and rock climbing also deserve full consideration when designing facilities. Technology ranging from synthetic floors and portable sport courts to computerized golf simulators has enabled many of these activities to be delivered indoors at any time of year.

An integral part of many facility designs, especially at the college and university level, are research, assessment, and teaching laboratories. Space for exercise assessment and research (e.g., biomechanics, exercise physiology), psychosocial training (e.g., psychological performance, biofeedback, and skill enhancement), and human factors, as well as sport medicine (athletic training, therapy, and first-aid rooms) should be provided for all students, staff, and faculty. These integrated facilities must also be accessible, well-maintained, functional, and in budgetary alignment with the mission of the school, department, college, or community in which they are housed.

Outdoor Swimming Pools

The outdoor swimming pool is a popular and important facility in almost all communities. Waterparks are also becoming quite popular in many areas of the country. To a great degree, climatic conditions determine the advisability of such a facility.

Outdoor pools including activity pools are built in various shapes, including oval, circular, T- and L-shaped, and rectangular. Rectangular pools are most popular because of easier construction, practicality of conducting competitive aquatic events, and accommodation of standard

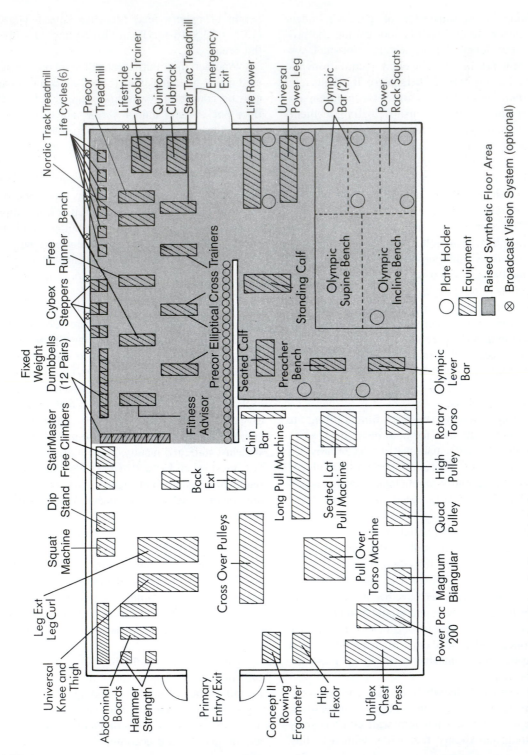

Figure 9-2. Strength training facility and design.

Outdoor aquatic facilities must be secure at all times; Texas A&M University.

Mezzanine retrofitting, direct and indirect lighting, and proper spacing of equipment lead to a healthy and productive environment.

equipment as well as various creative slide configurations and water spray units including wave-generation machines.

The size of pools varies, depending on the number of persons they are to serve. One recommendation has been made that twelve square feet of water space per swimmer be allotted for swimming purposes or, if the deck is taken into consideration, twenty square feet of space for swimming and walking area per swimmer.

The decks for outdoor pools should be larger than those for indoor pools. This larger space will accommodate more people and also provide space for relaxing, lounging, socializing, and sunbathing.

Shower facilities should be provided to ensure that every swimmer is clean before entering the water. A basket system for storing clothes has been found useful, but when the pool is located adjacent to a school, it is sometimes practical to use the school's locker and shower facilities. However, it is strongly advised that wherever possible, separate shower, locker, changing, grooming, and toilet facilities be provided, and that safety and accessibility for all participants is ensured.

Because swimming is popular at night as well as in the daytime, lights should be provided so that the community may participate in this healthful and enjoyable activity.

Diving boards generally are constructed of fiberglass or plastic, and the standard heights of one and three meters are typically found in most outdoor aquatic facilities. The board or any diving takeoff area should have a nonskid surface, be securely fastened to the ground or foundation, and conform to state safety standards and recommendations for water depth as previously discussed in the section on indoor swimming pools.

The rules and regulations concerning the facility, including diving and sliding, should be clearly posted near the appropriate areas. Clear markings, firm dividers of shallow and deep water, proper drains (entrapment), and a certified and well-trained guard staff are also a must for all aquatic facilities. Management should provide clear emergency guidelines (see figure 9-3) concerning active and passive drowning victims as well as facility emergency. These sample emergency guidelines should serve as models to develop emergency policies and procedures (for all facilities and programs) that are crucial to sound facility management.

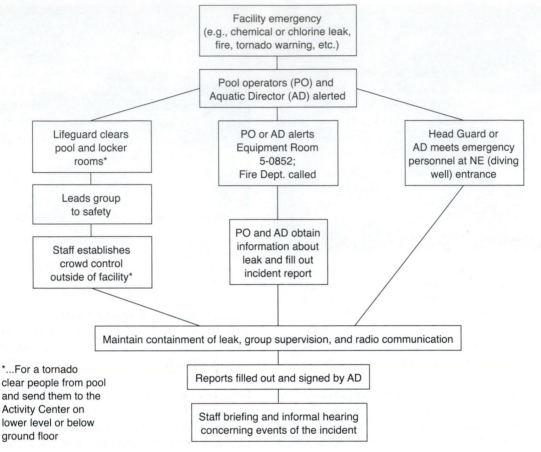

Figure 9-3. Facility emergency guidelines.

Outdoor Pursuits

Because outdoor pursuits (biking, canoeing, golf, hiking, backpacking, rock climbing, skiing, kayaking, sailing, camping, etc.) are becoming increasingly popular, they should receive full consideration for inclusion in a quality physical education or any activity program. Outdoor areas, including fitness trails, par course, and camping areas, should be located within easy reach of the school and community. They should be in locations desirable from the standpoints of scenic beauty, safety, accessibility, clear and unobstructed water, and natural resources pertinent to the program offered. Activities usually offered include hiking, rock climbing, orienteering, swimming, camp-craft, boating and small craft, ecostudy, fishing, and appropriate winter activities (e.g., alpine and cross-country skiing, snowshoeing). The natural terrain and other resources can contribute much toward such a program.

There should be housing, shelter, eating, sanitation, waterfront, and other facilities essential to outdoor activity. These facilities do not have to be elaborate, but they should provide adequate protection against the elements or in case of emergency. Facilities should also meet acceptable standards of health and sanitation. In general, camp structures should be adapted to the climatic and environmental conditions of the particular area in which the facility is located. It is wise to consult public health authorities, departments of natural resources, state and local park boards, or other appropriate professionals when selecting outdoor facility sites. Sometimes existing facilities can be shared (e.g., Ys, Scouts) or converted to camp use. Outdoor pursuit acreage could also be purchased outright by the school system or community, or acquired under a long-term lease agreement by coordinating with other local user groups or school districts. Again, strict policies and procedures for usage are crucial.

FACILITIES FOR PEOPLE WITH DISABILITIES

Since the passage of the Architecture Barriers Act of 1968 (P.L. 90-480), Section 504 of the Rehabilitation Act of 1973, P.L. 94-142 in 1975, and more recently ADA in 1990 and IDEA in 1997, more consideration has been given to the facility needs of people with disabilities. Physical education and sport facilities in particular are concerned with the students' and participants' programs of specialized developmental exercises, perceptual-motor ability activities, health-related and fitness activities, modified sports, stress management, rest, therapy, and relaxation. Facilities for individuals with disabilities usually vary from school to school and according to the disabling conditions of those served.

Contemporary physical education and sport has the person with disabilities participating in the least restrictive environment (LRE) and, whenever appropriate and possible, integrated, included, or mainstreamed into regular physical activities. Special multidisciplinary case teams design appropriate user IEPs, and some special equipment may be necessary; however, mainstreaming or inclusion into the gymnasium as well as the classroom is the trend. This trend requires accessibility, sound planning, support, supervision and a committed team effort by administration, faculty, and support staff.

For those schools and communities that provide people with disabilities separate developmental space, a minimum area of 40×60 feet is recommended. Creative and committed teachers, however, can construct challenging curriculum utilizing much of the standard equipment and physical resources (e.g., aquatic facilities, balance beams, exercise balls, mats) already available.

Some schools also make use of nearby community or private facilities, and this partnering trend will grow as more specialized resources concerning physical activity are needed, not only by the estimated five million individuals with varying disabilities, but also by our older generation who will demand increased physical activity opportunities. With scarce financial inputs it is envisaged that the school and community will have to work even more closely together in order to meet the facility and experiential needs of these special user groups.

Management of any facility should establish an ADA/IDEA audit team made up of teachers, staff, health-care professionals, parents, and individuals with varying disabilities among others to carefully "walk through" the facility and its programs and make recommendations for enhancement.

CONSTRUCTION TRENDS IN PHYSICAL EDUCATION AND SPORT FACILITIES

There are many new trends in facilities, supplies, and materials for physical education, recreation, and sport programs, including new paving, surface, and subfloor materials, mobile floor coverage and storage systems, and new types of equipment ranging from therapy balls and rolls to wave eating racing lanes. Personal moisture-resistant storage units (lockers), exhibit halls, air-supported, cover-all structures, improved landscape design, new ceiling and lighting systems, new shapes for swimming and activity pools, partial shelters and minigyms, and synthetic grass and field turf, just to name a few. Combination indoor-outdoor pools, including water slides, physical fitness equipment for outdoor use, all-weather tennis, sport courts, and games areas, and various kinds of climbing wall technology are other new developments that have had an impact on physical education, recreation, and sport facility management as well as on program development.

In gymnasium renovation and construction, some of the new features include using modern engineering techniques and materials, which has resulted in welded steel and laminated wood modular frames; arched, vaulted, and gabled roofs; domes that provide areas completely free from internal supports; exterior surfaces of aluminum, steel, fiberglass, and plastics; hydraulic floors; translucent window patterns and styles; myriad floor surfaces including nonslip material; prefabricated and protected wall surfaces; and uniform lighting systems with reduced glare and spillage control. Facilities are moving from using regular glass to using treated thermal pane, plastic, or fiberglass panel or an overhead skydome.

Lightweight fiberglass, sandwich panels, or fabricated sheets of translucent fiberglass laminated over an aluminum framework are proving popular in minigyms or sport halls. These require no painting; little maintenance, and material cost is lower. Modern HVAC and air-handling systems and solar radiation make these minigyms and sport courts functional and cost effective.

Locker rooms with built-in locks with combination changers, quiet tone control, and even computerized "Smarte Lockes" have also made their way into sport facilities where ID cards are being scanned for admittance and "tracking." Ceramic nonslip tile and terrazo are used extensively because of its durability and low-cost maintenance. Wall-hung toilet compartments permitting easier maintenance and sanitation with no chance for rust are being installed. Odor control is being effectively handled by new HVAC dispensers and dehumidification systems. New thin-profile HVAC fan coil units are now being used to provide improved air quality, ventilation, heating, and humidity control. More walls and floors are being constructed of easily cleansed materials, which aids in improving sanitation.

New developments in indoor swimming pools include computers that have direct control over all filters, chlorinators, chemical pumps, and lever

The University of Idaho has a portable football field. The tartan turf is 200 feet by 370 feet and can be rolled up and stored on a 210-foot-long steel drum.

controllers; much larger deck space areas constructed of nonslip ceramic tile; greater use of diatomaceous earth rather than sand filters to filter out small particles of matter including some bacteria; underwater lighting and sound; water level deck pools (the overflow gutters are placed in the deck surrounding the pool instead of in the pool's side walls, and provision is made for grating designed so that the water that overflows is drained to a trench under the deck without the possibility of debris returning to the pool); air-supported roofs that can serve as removable tops in a combination indoor-outdoor pool; fiberglass and PVC pool membranes; and movable bulkheads.

New developments for outdoor swimming centers involve new shapes, including oval, wedge, kidney, figure-8, cloverleaf, and bean; water play and sprayparks; as well as modern accessories, including wave-making machines, pool and water slides and tubes, gas heaters, pool blankets, automatic water levelers, and retractable roofs and sides. More supplemental recreational facilities (such as shuffleboard and beach volleyball courts) and more deck equipment (including guard rails, slides, pool lifts, and pool covers) are being included around larger pools.

Air-Supported Structures

An air-supported structure consists of a large fabric or plastic bubble that is inflated and supported by continuous air pressure. It is the least expensive building that can be erected, costing from one-fifth to one-half of what a solid structure may cost. These bubblelike facilities have housed tennis courts, swimming pools, indoor tracks, golf ranges, classrooms, and gymnasiums.

The outside construction is usually made of vinyl-coated Teflon or Dacron polyester-type material, which is lightweight, strong, and flexible. The fabric is flame-retardant, waterproof, tear-resistant, mildew-resistant, and unaffected by ultraviolet rays. Installation is simple and may be completed in a few hours by a minimal crew. The installation process includes placement of the fabric-type (vinyl- or PVDF-coated) envelope and inflation. The bubble is supported by a blower that

provides a constant flow of air pressure. The bubble may be easily dismantled by stopping the blower, opening the door, disconnecting the attachments, and folding the bubble compactly.

Of course there are other types of more complex, and larger fabric-covered facilities (tension, cable sports domes) than the single air bubble that might be employed to add facilities ranging from indoor tennis courts to pools to your school or community physical plant. These range from the Metrodome of Minneapolis and the Silverdome in Pontiac, Michigan, to the "tent" at LaVerne College in California and the DakotaDome at the University of South Dakota in Vermillion. Other fabric bubbles are insulated like the Lindsay Park Sports Centre in Calgary, Canada.

Minigyms and Fitness Corners

Minigyms and fitness corners can be operated in the classrooms, halls, and alcoves of any school building or facility. Creative corners and minigyms can be used between classes, at time-out sessions, during lunch, or other appropriate break times. They can also be used as regularly scheduled activity areas for small or specialized groups (e.g., seniors or special needs populations, etc.). Recommended equipment includes mats, plastic stepping devices, a computerized stationary bike and rowing machine, a portable treadmill, lightweight dumbbells, climbing simulation, exercise balls, and even a small innovative fitness and strength system (i.e., Keiser, Magnum, Paramount, etc.). Chairs, benches, desks, and classroom computers already present can be arranged to provide a structured and fully functional activity area for delivery of physical education and fitness activity.

Other New Developments

New and improved developments in physical education, recreation, and sport facilities are numerous. Sculptured play apparatus including climbing walls have been produced by a number of firms. They have been designed to be more conducive to imaginative movements and creativity than conventional equipment. Hard-surfaced, rubberized, synthetic turf; all-weather running and court surfaces; radiant

Facilities such as the Super Tent at LaVerne College, Calif., and the Metrodome in Minneapolis, Minn., provide year-round multisport playing opportunity.

heating of decks on swimming and therapy pools and outdoor elevated courts; heated wet rooms for aquatics instruction; floating roofs that eliminate non-load-bearing walls; improved interior climate control and indoor and outdoor lighting; new refrigeration systems for ice rinks; padding for use under apparatus and on fences and walls; translucent plastic materials for swimming pool canopies, blankets, and other uses; underwater treadmills and therapy aquacisers; and electrically operated machinery to move equipment and partitions and "tutor" students in volleyball and soccer. Portable bleachers, electronic messaging scoreboards, and cardio theatres are just a few of the many facility enhancements that have been, and continue to be, upgraded.

Other contemporary facility developments for physical education and sport include synthetic ice and snow centers, snowless ski hills, BMX biking, in-line skating, and waterparks, mezzanine additions, convertible roofs, mobile locker rooms, with phenolic lockers, illuminated game lines, folding racquet and sport courts, movable pool floors and lifts, computerized pool treatment, AED stations, and myriad other factors that may influence the management and planning of a physical education, recreation, and sport program. Security control systems and software, computerized energy conservation systems, and total facility communication, and surveillance systems, not to mention the new lines of fitness and exercise equipment, make facility management a challenge.

With the contemporary trend toward scarce inputs (e.g., lack of money, space, and land), facility planning, sharing, and creative and cooperative management of new and existing facilities are more crucial than ever.

FACILITY MAINTENANCE

Planning for the construction or remodeling of facilities is an important management function. An equally important responsibility of facility management is maintenance. With proper maintenance, a facility will last longer, provide a healthier and safer environment, be less costly, and provide a more satisfying experience for user groups. Planning and constructing facilities in physical education, recreation, and sport are team efforts. If proper plans, construction, and materials are selected, then maintenance including energy conservation should be made easier. Nothing is more embarrassing than a new facility that is a maintenance nightmare because of poor management decisions in the design and planning phases of the construction process, not to mention the purchase of equipment, scheduling, and hiring of staff. Given an adequate facility, it is up to the physical education, recreational sports, and athletic departments' management and all user groups as well as the maintenance staffs to work together in taking pride in their facility and putting forth a special effort to see that it is maintained in as near perfect condition as possible.

SHARED FACILITIES

Schools and colleges continually receive requests to open their facilities to various community and other user groups. Facilities are also being planned, developed, constructed, and brought on-

The tennis complex at Northwest Athletic Club promotes the shared facilities concept. Bloomington, Minn.

line through creative partnering between Boys and Girls Clubs and YMCAs and communities, as well as universities and school districts and private sector enterprises ranging from fitness clubs to hospital systems and building developers. It is therefore imperative that management establish guidelines and policies ensuring that appropriate precautions are taken (e.g., legal and fiscal) and that such facilities are used properly when approval is granted. Shared facilities means shared responsibilities, including maintenance, equipment, and insurance.

First, management should see that a written policy is established and approved by proper authorities regarding shared, community, and outside group use of facilities (who can use facilities, at what times, under what conditions). Second, procedures regarding outside use should be established. This usually includes such procedures as making a proper application, obtaining the liability insurance coverage necessary, signing appropriate waiver forms, setting the fee structure and type of payment, and making stipulations regarding maintenance, supervision, and security. Third, management controls should be established to see that policies and procedures are carried out as specified in the user contract.

Schools Using Community Resources

Such facilities as parks, campgrounds, bowling alleys, golf courses, swimming pools, waterparks, ski areas, Ys, fitness centers, and skating parks and leisure ice arenas can extend and enhance the school physical education and recreational sport programs as well as related sport activities. Most community facilities can be used during off-hours or nonpeak hours, and the charge is frequently nominal. Sometimes barter and partnering agreements can be arranged. Those procedures described in community use of school facilities apply in reverse.

With bond issues and fiscal inputs becoming difficult to obtain, it is imperative that management and the community (public and private sector) work together to build model programs that might be impossible to accomplish alone. This mode of cooperation is a challenge to management and all those intimately involved in long-range strategic facility planning.

(a)

(b)

From (a) Camden Yards Ball Park, Baltimore, Md., to (b) the Hong Kong National Stadium, Hong Kong, PRC, high-quality stadiums make an international statement about sport management's impact on community development.

TAKE IT TO THE NET!

American National Standards Institute
www.ansi.org

ASTM International (formerly the American Society for Testing and Materials)
www.astm.org

American Society of Heating, Refrigerating, and Air Conditioning Engineers (ASHRAE)
www.ashrae.org

Facilities Net
www.facilitiesnet.com

International Association of Administrative Professionals (IAAP)
www.iaap-hq.org

International Association of Assembly Managers (IAAM)
www.iaam.org

International Facility Management Association (IFMA)
www.ifma.org

Occupational Safety and Health Administration (OSHA)
www.osha.org

SUMMARY

Facility management is an important managerial responsibility. It requires prudent planning based on physical education, recreation, and sport program philosophy and participant, school, and community needs, taking health, safety, security, and environmental conditions into consideration. Predicted demand, cost of facilities, timing, trends, and business strategy also play a key role. Working with an architect and planning team and being aware of the latest developments, issues, concerns, standards, codes, and laws in facility construction are also crucial parts of facility management. A basic knowledge of the requirements of both indoor and outdoor facilities is also important so that the needs of all participants, including those with disabilities, may be met. Facility management also includes establishing sound emergency and disaster procedures and policies. Management should be concerned with the renovation, multiple use, maintenance, repair, and cleanliness of the facilities because these factors are crucial to effective and efficient programming and delivery. Furthermore, most physical education, recreation, and sport facilities are used by people other than just the students and members of one institution or organization. It is common practice for community residents and other community-based organizations (e.g., youth groups, seniors, special populations) to use such facilities. Therefore consideration should be given to the development of policies, procedures, and priorities for such usage. Creative and cooperative facility management is requisite in this time of scarce financial inputs.

SELF-ASSESSMENT ACTIVITIES

These activities will assist students in determining if material and competencies presented in this chapter have been mastered.

1. List the basic considerations that should be followed by management in planning physical education and sport facilities.

2. As director of a physical education program, what steps would you follow in working with an architect in the construction of a gymnasium?

3. Prepare a sketch of what you consider to be an ideal high school indoor cardio and strength training facility.

4. Develop a list of standards for outdoor areas in physical education and sport, including a play area and swimming pool, for a junior high or middle school.

5. Construct an emergency procedure plan for your local high school or community center.

6. Divide the class into teams and visit neighboring schools, interviewing students and staff about a facility needs assessment. Present your findings to the class.

7. Prepare a checklist for a physical education and sport facility that will ensure that it is safe, healthful, and accessible for all participants.

REFERENCES

1. Ammon, R., R. M. Southall, and D.A. Blair. 2004. *Sport facility management: Organizing events and mitigating risk.* Morgantown, WV: Fit Information Technology.
2. Appenzeller, H. 2004. *Risk management in sport: Issues and strategies.* Durham, NC: Carolina Academic Press.
3. Hatfield, F. C., and M. L. Krotee. 1984. *Personalized weight training for fitness and athletics.* Dubuque, IA: Kendall/Hunt.
4. Kraus, R. G., and J. E. Curtis. 2000. *Creative management of recreation, parks, and leisure services.* 6th ed. New York: McGraw-Hill.
5. Pate, D. W., E. Moffit, and D. Fugett. 1997. Current trends in use, design/construction, and finishing of sports facilities. *Sports Marketing Quarterly* 2(4): 9–14.
6. Sawyer, T. H. (Editor-in-Chief). 2005. *Facilities design and management for health, fitness, physical activity, recreation and sports facility development: Concepts and applications.* Champaign, IL: Sagamore Publishing.
7. Tharrett, S. J., and J. A. Peterson. 1997. *ACSM's health/fitness facility standards and guidelines.* Champaign, IL: Human Kinetics.

SUGGESTED READINGS

Clayton, R., and D. B. Thomas. 1989. *Professional aquatic management.* Champaign, Ill.: Human Kinetics. Discusses a wide range of aquatic trends in facility management. Also includes a thorough overview of rules, procedures, and policies necessary for effective management.

Cohen, A. 1996. Togetherness. *Athletic Business,* October, 31–38.

Crompton, J. L. 1995. Economic impact analysis of sports facilities and events: Eleven sources of misapplication. *Journal of Sport Management* 9:14–35.

Dunn, J. M. 1997. *Special physical education.* Dubuque, IA: Brown & Benchmark.
Discusses, suggests, and provides guidelines for adapted physical education facilities. Outlines how facilities can be modified and planned to meet the needs of persons with disabilities.

Farmer, P. J., A. L. Mulrooney, and R. Ammon, Jr. 1996. *Sport facility planning and management.* Morgantown, WV: Fitness Information Technology.

Flynn, R. B. 1993. *Planning facilities for athletics, physical education and recreation.* Reston, VA: AAHPERD.

Flynn, R. B. 1983. Planning facilities. *Journal of Physical Education and Recreation* 54 (June):19–38.

Mood, D. P., F. F. Musker, and J. E. Rink. 2003. *Sports and recreational activities.* Dubuque, IA: McGraw-Hill.

Olson, J. R. 1997. *Facility and equipment management for sports directors.* Champaign, IL: Human Kinetics.

Sawyer, T. H. (Editor-in-Chief). 2002. *Facilities planning for physical activity and sport.* Dubuque, IA: Kendall/Hunt.

Sawyer, T. H., and O. S. Smith. 1999. *The management of clubs, recreation, and sport: Concepts and applications.* Champaign, IL: Sagamore Publishing.
Discusses steps in the process of facility development and planning, including the role of the manager, the planning process, and event and risk management.

Walker, M. L., and D. K. Stotlar. 1997. *Sport facility management.* Sudbury, MA: Jones and Bartlett Publications.

CHAPTER 10

Fiscal Management

INSTRUCTIONAL OBJECTIVES AND COMPETENCIES TO BE ACHIEVED

After reading this chapter the student should be able to:

- Support the need for sound fiscal management in physical education, recreation, and sport programs.
- Explain the budgeting process and formulate a physical education, recreation, and sport budget.
- Apply a planning-programming-budgeting-evaluation system (PPBES) in the management of a physical education, recreation, and sport program.

- Understand the role of school and college business managers or administrators in fiscal management.
- Outline principles necessary for managers to follow to ensure financial accountability in a physical education, recreation, and sport program.
- Discuss zero-base budgeting as applied to a physical education, recreation, and sport program.

One of the most crucial functions of management involves securing the funds necessary to provide sound physical education, recreation, and sport programs. Adequate funding must be procured, programs and budgets planned and implemented, and accountability for funds established. Finances are the engine that drives the total management process of any organization. This chapter deals with this managerial crucial function.

Fiscal management and control have become increasingly important responsibilities for management in light of current financial problems, issues, and constraints. In recent years, financial problems caused by inadequate financial forecasting and monitoring, insufficient levy referendum coverage, and rising, building, operational, and maintenance costs have made it much more difficult to fund physical education, recreation, and sport programs even though sport is a 200-billion-dollar enterprise ($25 billion dollars just for footwear). Other compounding reasons for fiscal difficulty include the high price of supplies, equipment, security, technology, and travel and transportation; the need to finance an increasing number of girls and boys who are participating in physical activity and sport; crowd control costs at sporting events as a result of violence; expensive liability insurance packages; and an inflationary spiral that is resulting in rising costs for human resources, including labor, teachers, coaches, certified athletic trainers, officials, and other associated human resources. The recent pause of the National Hockey League (NHL), the demise of the Women's Professional Soccer League (WPSL), the continuous deletion of various NCAA sports teams and the demise of the Olympic sports of baseball and softball serve as reminders that sound fiscal planning and management are requisites for survival.

As a result many schools' physical education, athletics and activities program managers, and directors have had to institute cost-control measures including, but not limited to, the following:

- Reduce the number of paid teachers and assistant coaches and increase the number of volunteers.
- Reduce equipment, supplies, and maintenance budgets.
- Reduce numbers of participants and levels of sports offered.
- Reduce travel distance and combine transportation where possible.
- Reduce the number of games, matches, and contests.
- Seek sponsorship and external funding.
- Increase fund-raising and booster club presence.
- Raise ticket prices.
- Charge for parking.

Pay-to-play costs ranging from $25 to $350 have also been applied to many programs and operating with increased private funding has become commonplace, bringing management's fiscal responsibility to a new level. President Clinton while visiting the ARCO U.S. Olympic Training Center in Chula Vista, California, called for greater coordination of public and private sector partnerships to ensure and better prepare the nation's young people for lifelong physical fitness (see appendix A for Healthy People 2010 Objectives). The 106th Congress's passage of the $400 million Carol M. White Physical Education for Progress Act (PEP) in an effort to initiate, expand, or improve K–12 physical education over a five-year period sets the standard for such public partnerships. In 2004, over $70 million was awarded to over 230 school districts. Contemporary managers, more than ever

Girls' and women's physical education and sport programs are expanding, as evidenced by the initiation of women's soccer into the Big Ten Conference.

before, must be well schooled in the practice of effective and efficient fiscal management.

Efficient fiscal management is an essential management function that ensures proper budgeting financial accountability, and fiscal responsibility. Therefore managers must thoroughly understand the philosophy and strategic vision of the organization as well as the fiscal needs. Management must be able to set objectives, performance benchmarks, and priorities of all the departments or subdivisions under their supervision. They must be able to craft a budgetary strategy to accomplish organizational goals. Budgeting deals with departmental requests as well as fiscal procurement and control. The fiscal management of an institution, department, league, or program deals with goal setting, design of a budget that is targeted to achieve these goals, the process of budget review and approval, the certification that funds have been appropriately expended and that sound accounting procedures are in place, and the actual management of the program. Fiscal management, including assessment and budget review and initiating corrective adjustments, is a critical and challenging responsibility (American Management Association 1986).

IMPORTANCE AND FUNCTION OF FISCAL MANAGEMENT

The services and benefits that a program provides, whether human resources, facilities, event management, or purchase of supplies and equipment, usually involve the gathering and disbursement of funds. This money must be secured from appropriate sources, be expended for approved and proper purposes, and be accounted for item by item. The budget (from the French *bougette,* meaning bag or wallet), the master financial plan to procure and allocate funds for the organization, is constructed with these guidepoints in mind.

Policies for raising and spending money must be set within organizational limits. Persons responsible should know the procedures for procurement and handling such funds with integrity, responsibility, security, and accountability, the basic purposes for which the program exists, as well as the laws, codes, and current regulations concerning fiscal management. Only when funds are implemented wisely and in the best interests of all concerned can the outlay of monies be justified (Robbins and Coulter 2005).

Place of Fiscal Management in Physical Education, Recreation, and Sport Programs

In schools, colleges, or other agencies and organizations, physical education, recreation, and sport require a major outlay of funds. As much as 25 percent of many school and college physical resources (assets) are devoted to these programs. Human resources, health services, insurance, facilities, maintenance, supplies and equipment, security, and transportation are only a few of the line items that quickly amount to significant sums of money. Probably as many as 700,000 physical educators and coaches are collectively paid millions of dollars in annual salaries and benefits, and more than sixty million students participate in school physical education and sport programs with another forty million frequenting local health and fitness clubs and youth sport playing fields. Gymnasiums, campus recreation centers, stadiums, arenas, aquatic complexes, athletic training, research and weight and exercise areas, playgrounds, and other school and college facilities are being constructed and stocked with state-of-the-art equipment at huge costs to the taxpayers as well as to fee paying students at institutions of higher learning.

The cost of facilities, programs, and human resources is increasing.

What is true of fiscal management in schools and colleges is also true in community-based, corporate, and other public and private sector settings in which physical education, recreation, and sport programs have become an intimate part of their organizational structure and culture. Sound fiscal management is requisite to quality organizations.

Responsibility

The responsibility for fiscal management, although falling largely on the shoulders of management (e.g., department chairs, athletic and activities directors, coaches, recreation directors), involves every member of the staff. In schools and colleges, students should also play an active part in fiscal management as should the member/consumer in the public and private sector physical activity setting. In this regard fiscal management is similar to strategic planning; it is a team effort (see box 10-1).

Formulating and preparing the budget are cooperative enterprises. They are based on information, reports, and forecasts that have been forwarded by staff members from various departments, subdivisions, and budget teams of the organization. These reports must contain accurate information on enrollments, inventories, programs, projects, obligations that exist, funds that have been spent, and monies that have been received from various sources (e.g., grants, interest-bearing investments, endorsements, carryovers, signage, sponsorships, user fees). Sometimes management brings in a group of experts to consult (Nominal group technique) or seeks autonomous input (Delphi technique) to insure budget integrity. Managers must have a conceptual or

Some of the principal purposes of financial management in physical education and sport programs are the following:

To prevent misuse and waste of funds that have been allocated to these special areas.

To help coordinate and relate the objectives of physical education and sport programs with the money appropriated for achieving such outcomes.

To ensure that monies allocated to physical education and sport will be based on research, study and a careful analysis of the pertinent conditions that influence such a process.

To involve the entire staff in formulating policies and procedures and in preparing budgetary items that will help ensure that the appropriate program directions are taken.

To use funds to develop high-quality physical education, recreation, and sport programs.

To exercise control over the process of fiscal management to guarantee that the entire financial process has integrity and purpose.

To make the greatest use of human and physical resources, supplies, equipment, and other forms of assets and capital involved in accomplishing organizational objectives.

overall picture of the enterprise at their fingertips. They must be cognizant of the work being done throughout the organization, functions that should be carried out, needs and resources of every facet of the organization, and other items (e.g., capital improvements, operations, maintenance, equipment, external funding) that must be considered in preparing the budget. The advent of the computer and its myriad software packages provide for more sophisticated accounting procedures (identifying, entering, recording, measuring, forecasting, and communicating statistical, demographic, and financial information) that make budgeting a far less labor-intensive task as well as a far more accurate management venture.

BUDGETING

Budgeting is the formulation of a financial plan in terms of work to be accomplished and services to be performed. The budget reflects what is expected to happen. It is based on the estimated expenditures to be made and the expected income to be generated within each organization's unique environment and culture and on sound accounting procedures (what has fiscally happened within and without the organization and its subordinates). All expenditures should be closely related to the philosophy, mission, and objectives the organization is trying to achieve. In this control aspect, management plays an important part.

Budgets should be planned and prepared with thought and vision to the future. They are an important part of management's three-year, five-year, or seven-year plan as well as the program of accomplishment outlined for a fiscal period. Projects of any size should be integrated progressively over many years. Thus the outlay of monies to realize such aims requires long-term, strategic planning. Downsizing or budget reduction or revision as well as adding assets (e.g., a new women's sport, such as rowing or ice hockey, to comply with gender equity) should also follow a similar planning path.

According to the strict interpretation of the word, a budget is merely an orderly record of receipts or income and expenditures. As used here, however, it reflects the long-term planning of the organization, pointing up user needs and projected costs and then ensuring that a realistic program is planned and effectively implemented that will fit into the proposed financial plan. Budgets, forecasts, revenues, and expenses for a period of one year (usually July 1 to June 30), known as the fiscal year, are the most common in school, community, and college physical education, recreation, and sport programs.

Types of Budgets

There are short-term and long-term budgets. The short-term budget is usually the annual budget. The long-term budget represents long-term fiscal planning, possibly for a five- or ten-year period. Most physical education, recreation, and sport managers will be concerned with short-term or annual budgets, whereby they plan their financial needs for a period covering the school or fiscal year. Budgets can be financial (i.e., cash flow, capital expenditure, balance sheet), operational (i.e., sales/income, expenses, profits), and nonmonetary (i.e., labor/time; motion, space, production) in nature.

Budgets may also be categorized into (1) object classification (e.g., numbering system applied to personnel, supplies and equipment, travel, salaries), (2) line-item functions (e.g., aquatics director, fitness coordinator), (3) organizational unit (e.g., football, swimming, lifetime sports), and (4) classification by fund (e.g., 0100-state, municipal bond, trust fund, user fee).

Budgets are also classified into (1) operational, (2) equipment and supply, (3) human resource, and (4) capital outlay. Usually the first two types are directly managed by the chair or director of the respective physical education, recreation, or sport program. Capital outlay management and human resource management sometimes reside at a higher level (e.g., principal, executive director of finance, vice president) with top-down input usually applied. Each budget classification may also be accompanied by a reserve fund.

Budgets may also be variable in nature, so if the actual output deviates from the planned output then adjustments to supporting budgets (i.e., marketing, equipment) may be automatically instituted. A variable budget, also known as a flexible budget, outlines the levels of resources to be allocated for each organizational activity according to the level of participation or productivity within the organization. It follows, then, that a variable budget automatically indicates an increase in the amount of resources allocated for various organizational activities when revenue streams increase or, in some instances, incur a decrease such as a fund-raising shortfall. Variable budgets provide for continual year-long monthly projections based on, for example, last month's income, participation rates, or fund-raising inititives. In this way the most recent budget inputs are included in the budgeting process.

Regardless of the type of budget, the budgeting process (see figure 10-1) is a critical part of

Figure 10-1. The budgeting process consists of prudent actions and decisions that affect the entire organization.

They express the plan and program for physical education and sport. They determine things such as (a) size of classes, (b) supplies, equipment, and facilities, (c) methods used, (d) results and educational values sought, and (e) human and technological resources available.

They reflect the philosophy, mission, vision, and policies of the professions of physical education and sport. They provide an overview of the work to be accomplished, benchmarks to be met, and services to be performed.

They determine what phases of the program are to be emphasized and help analyze all aspects of physical education, recreation, and sport programs.

They interpret the need, space, and funds necessary for effective conduct physical education and sport.

In a school program, they help determine, together with the budgets of other subdivisions, the tax levy for the school district.

They make it possible to manage the physical education and sport programs economically by improving accounting procedures.

They make it possible, on approval by the proper authority, to authorize expenditures for physical education and sport programs.

the management function (planning and control) and demands continuous attention to detail (see box 10-2).

Responsibility for Budgets

The responsibility for the preparation of the budget may vary from one locality or institution to another. In most school systems, the superintendent of schools is responsible. In colleges, budgeting may be the responsibility of the president, provost, vice president, dean, or department chair. In other organizations, the athletic director or head coach plays a key role. It is often possible for school managers, department heads, teachers, professors, coaches, technology specialists, and

members of the organization to participate in preparing the budget by submitting various specific requests for item expenditures. In other situations, a comprehensive budget may first be prepared and then submitted to the appropriate subdivisions, departments, or resource teams for consideration and input.

In some large school systems, the superintendent of schools frequently delegates much of the budget responsibility to an executive director of finance, business manager, or assistant or associate superintendent. The final official school authority concerned with school budgets is the board of education and, in colleges, the board of governors, regents, or trustees. In some organizations other than schools, it is the chief financial officer or controller who possesses authority to approve, reject, or amend budgets. Beyond the board of education rests the authority of the people, or stakeholders who in most communities, also have the right to approve, reject, or significantly influence budget proposals. The state in most instances also maintains an oversight auditing responsibility for taxpayer dollars.

In colleges, the budget may be handled in the dean's office, the director or chairperson of the physical education department, or a budget and fees committee may have the responsibility. In most cases, the director of athletics is responsible for the intercollegiate or interscholastic sport budget. Within school departments of physical education and sport, the chairperson, department head, or director is the person responsible for the budget. However, he or she will usually consult with members of the department (aquatics director, intramural director, technology support) to consider their input, opinions, and projections. This type of bottom-up management is most effective in schools and community-based physical education, recreation, and sport programs. Top-down management, where the budget is designed by management and passed down to the employee, can be found, for example, in most private sector organizations within the club industry where managers have found this type of budgeting system more effective.

Criteria for a Sound Budget

A budget for physical education and sport should meet the following criteria:

- The budget clearly presents the financial needs of the entire program in relation to the objectives sought. Goals and objectives drive the budget.
- Key and representative persons in the organization have been consulted.
- External experts have been consulted.
- The budget provides a realistic estimate of income to balance the expenditures anticipated.
- The budget reflects equitable allocations to boys' and girls' physical education, recreation, and sport programs.
- The possibility of emergencies is recognized through flexibility in the financial plan.
- Human relations factors have been taken into consideration.
- The budget was prepared well in advance of the fiscal year to leave ample time for analysis, thought, criticism, review, and potential modification.
- Budget requests are realistic, not padded.
- The budget meets the essential requirements of students, user group, faculty, community, staff, and management.

Budget Preparation

Budget preparation is a continuous and ongoing process. There are seven basic steps to this process:

Planning. Management uses the input power of staff, community stakeholders, and external experts in creative and cooperative planning as well as in identifying user needs. Past budgets and plans also play a significant role and serve as a solid reference point.

Coordinating. Management coordinates and integrates staff and community suggestions and recommendations into a unified whole that realizes the goals, vision, and mission of the organization.

Technology developments add to new budget items.

Interpreting. To have support for the budget, proper interpretation of plans and actions must be effectively communicated both within and outside the organization. Communication and consensus building are a continual part of budgetary preparation and strategic planning.

Presenting. Management presents the budget in a simplified version so that it can be readily understood. Pictures, diagrams, graphics including GANTT and load charts and PERT network analysis, and other visual materials make such a presentation more attractive, interesting, and informative.

Approving. Adoption of the budget is but the formal approval of many projects that have been studied and considered throughout the year. In fact, this year's budget is usually based on last year's budget decisions with special attention to targeted areas or new organizational goals. Management is continually planning, researching, and studying various budgetary items.

Administering. The budget, when approved, serves as management's guide throughout the year as to how monies will be allocated and spent and what activities will be conducted and supported. Budget flexibility, however, is critical for efficient management.

Appraising. Appraisal is a continuous process indicating how the budget is functioning. Methods used include daily, monthly, and quarterly observation, cost accounting records and reports, surveys, audits, checklists, and staff studies. Benchmarking, ratio analysis, and break-even analysis are control tools to be considered.

There are four general procedures, or stages, in budget planning that physical education, recreation, and sport personnel might consider. First is actual preparation of the budget by the chairperson of the department or unit with his or her staff (a team approach), listing the various estimated revenue, expenditures, and any other information that needs to be included, ranging from additional revenue streams such as grants to loss of state or local funding. Second, the budget is presented to the principal, superintendent, dean, board of education, or other person or group that represents the proper authority and has the responsibility and legal authorization for reviewing it. Third, after formal approval of the budget, it is used as a guide for the execution of the financial management plan of the department or organization. Fourth, periodic critical evaluation of the budget takes place to determine its effectiveness in meeting organizational goals, targets, and needs, with notations being made for the next year's budget.

The preparation of the budget, representing the first step, is a long-term endeavor that cannot be accomplished in one or two days. The budget can be prepared only after a careful review of last year's (or the last three years') program effectiveness and extensive appraisal. Oftentimes, economic forecasts, projections, adjustments, and fiscal targets will be passed down from the administration. However, the actual completion of the budget usually is accomplished in the early spring after a detailed inventory of program needs and outcomes has been taken. The director of physical education or athletics and activities, after close consultation with staff members, coaches, athletic trainers, the principal, dean, superintendent of schools, or other responsible management, should formulate the budget.

Involvement of Staff Members

Involving staff members (teachers, coaches, volunteers, athletic trainers, technology support) in the budget-making process is crucial to responsibility-

centered fiscal management (Miller 1997). Some suggestions that permit effective and dynamic involvement follow:

- Teachers, coaches, and equipment managers should maintain inventory records that indicate supplies and equipment on hand.

- Teachers, coaches, and athletic and activity directors should keep accurate records of all income and expenditures for each activity, sport, or piece of equipment.

- Teaching staff and coaches should determine the items that were not a part of this year's budget, but that should be included in the budget for the coming year (e.g., new equipment, repairs, PEP grant, subscriptions to professional journals).

- Accurate records and receipts should be kept by staff members regarding funds allocated and spent each year. Then it should be determined whether funds were expended for purposes that were initially listed.

- When all pertinent information has been collected and analyzed, management should meet with all staff members and go over budget requests.

- Management should prepare total physical education or sport budgets, including all valid requests. The budget should not be padded, but provision should be made for emergencies.

Management and staff members must do their homework by having the latest price lists for supplies and equipment; the number of students or other user groups projected for the program; the cost of such items as officials, travel, print material, phone, recruiting, meals, lodging, insurance, security, and medical supervision; the amount of money needed for instructional aids, video, equipment repair, and other teaching, coaching, and technological support and staff development needs, such as attending professional meetings, certification clinics, and seminars.

Many records and reports are essential to budget preparation and should be part of a central database. The inventory of supplies and equipment on hand will be useful, and copies of inventories, contracts, and budgets from previous years will provide good references and projection points. Comparison of budgetary items with peer organizations of similar size may also be of help. Accounting records are also a valuable source through which to review income and expenditure flow.

All records, reports, inventories, past budgets, and budget requests should be part of management's database. Lexington, Massachusetts,' and Wayzata, Minnesota, public schools provide such a fiscal system that enables each teacher and coach to project and assess their budgetary status and requirements.

The budget is based on forecasts that can be overtaken by reality; therefore, some flexibility for readjustment is necessary. It is difficult to accurately and specifically list each detail in the way it will be needed and executed; however, budgets should also be reasonably rigid (see boxes 10-3 and 10-4).

The budget should represent a schedule that can be justified. This means that each budgetary item must satisfy the needs and interests of everyone concerned. Furthermore, each item that constitutes an expenditure should be reflected in budget specifications. A typical high school varsity sport budget and a sample intercollegiate recreational sport budget, accompanied by the monthly budget balance and year-to-date ledger balance with transactions for supplies, equipment, and other expenses, may be found in appendix G. Sample budgets for community-based youth and club sport organizations and a YMCA are also included in this appendix.

Box 10-3   A School Budget

Proposed Budget Classification by Major Function

	Salaries, Fees, and Benefits	Equipment and Supplies	Services and Other Expenses	Totals
Board of Education and District Administration				
Board/district administration	$ 183,400	$ 11,400	$ 45,900	$ 240,700
District insurance			74,600	74,600
Claims, property tax, administrative costs			78,300	78,300
Category total				$ 393,600
Instruction				
Building administration	302,600	19,700	8,600	330,900
Salaries and materials	3,178,300	169,000	439,700	3,787,000
Student services and health	264,200	2,900	14,600	281,700
Student activities	57,300	22,900	6,700	86,900
Category total				$4,486,500
Support Services				
Transportation	287,600	106,500	36,300	430,400
Operation and maintenance	362,000	42,900	378,400	783,300
School lunch program			5,000	5,000
Category total				$1,218,700
Employee Benefits	1,293,400			$1,293,400
Total operating expenses	$5,928,800	$375,300	$1,088,100	$7,392,200
Debt Service			765,600	765,600
TOTAL BUDGET				$8,157,800

Box 10-4 Budgetary Allocations for Regular Instructional Programs

The programs listed below describe the funding for regular classroom instruction. The costs of general classroom teachers in grades 1 through 5 are divided among the language arts, mathematics, and environment programs, according to the estimated percentage of instructional time each subject receives in the classroom curriculum.

Program costs in grades 6 through 12 are based on the division of staff members by academic specialization.

The unclassified group contains those general supply and equipment items that support the entire program and cannot be allocated by the program.

	Salaries	Benefits	Equipment	Supplies	Services	Total
Art	$ 136,761	$ 38,434	$ 522	$ 10,401	$ 677	$ 186,795
Business education	66,465	18,681	2,150	1,638	1,350	90,284
Driver education	4,410	1,239	550	10,850	—	17,049
Environment	151,747	42,650	—	1,999	300	196,696
Health education	2,290	627	—	400	420	3,737
Life skills	39,609	11,313	—	3,341	447	54,528
Industrial arts	70,837	19,910	471	5,335	675	97,228
Kindergarten	47,203	13,267	—	1,255	—	61,725
Language arts	613,255	172,365	—	14,375	2,900	802,895
Foreign languages	158,078	44,430	—	5,361	1,715	209,584
Mathematics	452,918	127,291	710	7,489	560	588,968
Music	141,035	39,635	516	2,439	850	184,485
Physical education	233,176	65,552	2,147	6,069	2,590	309,534
Reading (special)	83,162	23,372	—	915	400	107,849
Science	333,804	87,083	3,124	11,140	1,850	437,001
Speech	10,751	3,018	—	261	—	14,030
Social studies	283,827	79,774	—	4,509	3,500	371,610
Unclassified	146,898	41,286	1,737	22,009	9,080	221,010
TOTAL	$2,976,226	$829,745	$11,927	$109,786	$27,314	$3,954,998

Budget Organization

Budgets can be organized in many ways. One pattern that can prove useful for the physical education, recreation, and sport manager is a four-phased program. First, a brief introductory message enables management to present the financial proposals in terms a person outside the educational or professional domain might readily understand. This might include the philosophy, mission, objectives, and goals of the total organization.

The second phase presents an overall graphic view of the budget, with expenditures and anticipated revenues arranged clearly and systematically so that any person can compare the two.

Phase three includes a more detailed estimate of receipts and expenditures, enabling a principal, superintendent of schools, board of education, or other interested individual or group to understand the specific budget item expenditure and projected income, not only for the total budget, but also for each appropriate cost area or center.

A fourth phase includes supporting documentation to provide additional evidence for the requests outlined in the budget. A budget often has a

The capital outlay for a weightroom is significant for many sport programs.

better chance of approval if it is accompanied by sufficient documentation to support some items. For example, extra compensation for coaches may be supported by presenting salary schedules for coaches in cohort school systems.

Another form of budget organization consists of the following three parts: (1) an introductory statement of the objectives, policies, and programs of the physical education or sport department; (2) a résumé of the objectives, policies, and programs interpreted in terms of proposed expenditures; and (3) a financial plan for meeting the needs during the fiscal period.

Not all budgets are broken down into these three or four representative phases. For example, some larger programs may organize their total budget into minibudgets, cost centers, or units that can usually be found on their organizational chart. This is a form of responsibility-based management. The same sound budget preparation and planning are still followed; however, each specific area (e.g., aquatics, women's basketball, open fitness, group exercise, youth camps, distance education) is broken out for scrutiny. Whatever their form, however, all budgets do present an itemized account of revenue streams, receipts, and expenditures.

In a physical education or sport budget, common inclusions are items concerning instruction, such as extra compensation for coaches; matters of capital outlay, such as a new swimming pool or strength training mezzanine; operations such as running the pool; replacement of expendable equipment, such as basketballs and softball helmets; and provision for maintenance and repair, such as refurbishing football uniforms or resurfacing the playground. Many of these items cannot be estimated without making a careful inventory and analysis of the condition of the facilities and equipment on hand. This analysis can be accomplished yearly (e.g., facility and inventory audit) and maintained in the computer database. This status can then be updated each year with adjustable or modified future projections and needs assessment.

FUND-RAISING FOR PHYSICAL EDUCATION AND SPORT PROGRAMS

The sources of income for most school and college physical education and sport programs include the general school fund (e.g., local taxes, millage, state appropriations, bonds) or college fund, gate receipts, broadcast rights, concessions, and general organization and activity fees. However, these sources sometimes do not provide sufficient monies to provide quality programs. It has been estimated that less than 40 percent of large and 16 percent of smaller colleges' sports programs pay their own way (Masteralexis, Barr, and Hums 2005).

The budget crunch in many school districts and institutions of higher education has caused physical education and sport directors to find additional ways of raising revenues for their programs (Stier 1997). In Massachusetts, for example, school districts as well as physical education and athletic departments are getting business organizations to provide matching funds for specific programs by conducting fundraising campaigns among alumni, by soliciting local citizens to make tax-free donations and gift provisions in their wills, and by selling two-for-one passbooks to the public for sport and activity contests.

Other sources of additional revenue streams are special foundation, governmental, or individual grants or gifts; sale of television, cable, and radio rights; signage, sponsorship, and naming rights; concessions at sport contests and physical education events; and special fund-raising events such as games involving faculty vs. the media, alumni, or a local professional team.

Many physical educators at the college level also look to replenish and supplement their funds with grants and external funding. Local and federal sources (e.g., U.S. Department of Education, State Department, National Institutes on Aging or Health) are approached with well-written proposals, as are various private foundations, corporations, and PVOs (e.g., Bush Foundation, Kellogg Foundation, Inter-America Foundation, Partners of the Americas, Pacific Cultural Foundation). Such proposals outline the proposed project, goals, projected budget, and outcomes of the project itself including its significance to the local or global community. These competitive funding channels are difficult to tap; however, all avenues to support worthwhile programs should be explored.

The principles of fund-raising are simple and easy to apply. A successful campaign is the combination of a good cause, careful planning, fact finding and "homework", and skillful communication. Good public relations are essential. Secondary schools and community-based programs have a product with which many people like to be associated: sport. Physical education is not quite as attractive to many potential sponsors; however, if presented in the right fashion with students as a point of focus, it also can be a recipient of fund-raising and grant rewards. Indeed, many parent and community groups recognize the value of quality physical education and often provide additional funds to purchase equipment and support other programmatical and instructional needs.

To be effective, a program of fund-raising should have excellent organization, clearly articulated objectives, effective management, and a sound organizational philosophy. It is recommended that a policy manual containing guidelines for the conduct of fund-raisers be developed. Insurance, risk management, sales permits and permissions, and gambling are just some of the issues that should be addressed.

Fund-raising to increase revenue is crucial to many physical education, recreation, and sport programs; a charity golf event in New Bern, North Carolina, draws Michael Jordan, four-time NC State All-American, Kelly Mitchem, Peter Jacobson, and Curtis Strange.

Some illustrations of successful fund-raising are associated with booster clubs. The question of using booster clubs may be controversial because sometimes such clubs want to influence the operation of the physical education and sport programs. With proper guidelines and procedures, however, opportunity for this to occur is minimal.

Christian Brothers High School in Sacramento, California, has the La Salle Club, which raises money for the physical education and sport programs by means such as the Old Timer Baseball Night, a golf tournament, and a fireworks booth for the 4th of July. Davis Senior High School in Davis, California, has an annual Lift-A-Thon for its football program to raise money. Notre Dame High School in Sherman Oaks, California, uses its booster club membership as a major contributor to their sport fund. The Dell Rapids, South Dakota, school system sells advertising on its scoreboards to help finance its programs. Wayzata High School in Wayzata, Minnesota, has booster clubs for almost all its girls' and boys' sports. Pig roasts, potlucks, and the selling of T-shirts, sweatshirts, and other items raise ample sums of money that are used to employ assistant coaches and provide needed supplies, equipment, or transport.

Box 10-5 Popular Fund-Raising Activities	
A-thons:	Jog-a-thon, swim-a-thon, bike-a-thon
Specialty sales:	Pizza, candy, cookie, holiday items, wrapping paper
Concessions:	Programs, food items, bake sales
Raffles:	Donated items from local merchants, preferred seating
Clothing sales:	Sweatshirts, T-shirts, pins
Car washes:	Sponsored by various teams and clubs
Specialty meals:	"Roasts," barbecues, dinners, breakfasts
Novelty sports competitions:	Basketball, volleyball, tug-of-war, faculty vs. _____ !
Summer sports camps and clinics:	Camps usually run by coaches
Booster club:	Donations, sponsored activities
Memorial gifting:	Managed by school board
Souvenirs:	School items, key chains, towels, seat backs
Celebrity tournaments:	Local media vs. _____ !
Equipment sales and exchanges:	Used equipment "exchanges"
Signage naming rights:	Arenas, scoreboards
Sponsorship:	Local businesses supply uniforms, food
Discount tickets:	Tickets for special populations, groups

Some high schools across the country use professional organizations to assist with their fund-raising. These novelty or fund-raising vendors and suppliers usually work through the school and/or organization to help sell and market everything from "creative school promotions" to candy and fruit, and from buttons, pins, and clothing to paperweights, cushions, and chairs among many other specialty items.

Most programs, however, usually rely on talented parents and a supportive community who are willing to get the job done in this ever-crucial process of budget supplementation. It seems that each year fund-raising, ranging from golf tournaments to turkey sales and from candy sales to scoreboard signage, plays a greater role in the conduct of physical education and sport programs. See box 10-5 for ideas about raising additional revenues to help support physical education, recreation, and sport programs.

PAY-TO-PLAY POLICY

Many high school sport and activity programs are requiring students who wish to participate to pay fees. This popular policy is being initiated because school sport programs have outgrown their projected budgets. The National Council of Secondary School Athletic Directors indicates that the average high school athletic budget has been reduced by at least 25 percent and some even by 75 percent. This reduction seems to be the trend as the year 2010 approaches. Cuts in funding combined with increased costs are prompting schools to defray expenses through student participation fees ranging typically from $25 to $300 depending on the sport or activity. Some schools have been forced to drop various sport programs as well as to reduce paid teaching, coaching, and supervisory staff.

Although some states, such as Iowa and Michigan, have ruled against the pay-to-play practice, California courts have upheld user fees. A citizens' group called "The Coalition Opposing Student Fees" lost a suit against the Santa Barbara School Board. The ruling stated that fees were permissible because sport takes place outside the regular school day, students volunteer for the activity, fees are used only to pay the cost of administering such a program, and fees do not violate the equal opportunity clauses of federal and state constitutions; that is, financially disadvantaged students are exempt from fees.

Many sport programs have instituted a pay-to-play policy.

A school instituting a pay-to-play policy should make sure that the fee charged is reasonable, that disadvantaged students (those who are financially unable to pay) are exempt, and that fees are used solely to cover program operation costs on an equal and fair basis (e.g., both boys and girls and their teams have equal opportunities).

TRADITIONAL SOURCES OF INCOME

General School or College Fund

In elementary and secondary schools, the physical education and sport program usually is financed through the general fund (e.g., local taxes and state appropriation). At most colleges and universities, the general fund of the institution also represents a major source of income, especially for physical education and recreational sport programs. Today, most universities at the Division I and II levels (athletic scholarship providers) are being asked to be self-supporting. Division III and most community and junior colleges, however, still rely on general funds to conduct their programs. The theme and issues of self-support and budgeting contribution and taxation for all physical education, recreation, and sport programs both within the school setting (high school and college) and in the surrounding community or corporate structure will continue to dominate the beginning of the twenty-first century.

Gate Receipts

In some schools, gate receipts play an important part in financing at least part of the physical education and sport program. Although gate receipts are usually less important at lower educational levels, some colleges and universities finance a large share of their sports programs, including recreational sports and physical education programs, through gate receipts. One example is at the University of Nebraska at Lincoln, where an assessment charge for each home football ticket will raise a projected $9.9 million toward the debt service of their new campus recreation center used primarily for physical education and recreational sports. At some high schools throughout the country, gate receipts have been abolished because of the belief that if sports represent an important part of the education program, they should be paid for in the same way that science and mathematics programs are financed. Table 10-1 shows a partial general organization financial statement of expenses and receipts for a typical interscholastic sports program. Appendix G offers further sample budgets of school district sports programs, intercollegiate recreational sports programs, and community-based youth sport and YMCA programs.

General Organization and Activity Fees

Some high schools either require or make available to students separate general organization or activity fees and tickets or some other inducement that enables them to attend sporting, dramatic, and musical events as well as receive various school publications and yearbooks. In colleges and universities, a similar plan is sometimes

Table 10-1.   A Partial General Organization Athletic Account—Financial Report* (Sept.–Dec.)

Program	Expenses	
Football		
Officials (four home games)	$480.00	
Equipment and supplies	2364.02	
Transportation	275.00	
Supervision (police, security, ticketing)	952.00	
Reconditioning and cleaning equipment	1,313.20	
Medical supplies	125.40	
Scouting	60.00	
Film/video	131.36	
Guarantees	520.00	
Football banquet	331.00	
Miscellaneous (printing tickets, meeting)	172.00	
TOTAL		$6,723.98
Cheerleaders		
Transportation	$152.20	
Sixteen new uniforms	520.00	
Cleaning uniforms	196.00	
TOTAL		$868.20
Total expenses		$7,592.18
	Receipts	
Football games		
Newburgh	$1,311.70	
Norwalk	1,819.60	
Yonkers	1,129.50	
Bridgeport	1,100.00	
Guarantee (New Haven)	120.00	
Total receipts		$5,480.80

*Does not include girl's and boy's cross-country and soccer.

Stands such as those at the Metrodome in Minneapolis must be filled to meet budget projections.

olina State University, Texas A&M University, University of Maryland). Just as professional sports' owners have used creative public and private finance and partnering (i.e., city and sales taxes, bonds, naming rights, luxury seating, etc.) to construct and renovate new facilities ranging from the Alamodome in San Antonio, Texas, to the World Cup "Big Stadium" in Paris, France; schools, colleges and communities are also now being asked to follow a similar pattern of creative financing (Walker and Stotlar 1997).

ESTIMATING RECEIPTS/CREDITS

Some steps for projecting receipts in the general school budget that also have application to physical education and sport budgeting include gathering and analyzing all pertinent data, estimating all income based on a comprehensive view of income sources and revenue streams, organizing and classifying receipts in appropriate categories (e.g., ticket sales and gate receipts, membership fees, priority seating, parking, programs, concessions), estimating revenue from all gathered data, comparing estimates with previous years, and computing a final draft of credits as well as debits.

employed as a part of a student activity fee, thus providing students with reduced rates to the various extracurricular activities offered by the institution. Student referendums are another means to raise capital to construct new physical education and sport (both intercollegiate and recreational) facilities (e.g., University of Southern Mississippi, University of Texas at Austin, North Car-

EXPENDITURES

In physical education and sport budgets, typical examples of expenditures are items of capital outlay, such as constructing or remodeling a swimming pool or strength training room; expendable equipment, such as badminton shuttlecocks and soccer balls; and a maintenance and repair provision, such as towel and laundry service and the refurbishing of equipment and uniforms. See appendix G for a sample list of potential budget-coded line-item expenditures to support various interscholastic and community sport programs.

Some expenditures are easy to estimate (i.e., coaching and staff salaries and benefits), but others are more difficult, requiring accurate inventories, past records, and careful analysis of the condition of inventoried equipment. Some items and services, such as equipment cleaning and repair, will need to be figured by averaging costs over a period of years. Awards, new equipment needs, transportation, guarantees to visiting teams, insurance, security, and medical services for emergencies are other expenditures that must be forecast.

Here are some sound procedures to follow in estimating expenditures: determine objectives and goals of the program; analyze expenditures in terms of program objectives; prepare a budgetary calendar that states what accomplishments or outcomes are expected and by what date; estimate expenditures by also considering past, present, and future needs; compare estimates with expenditures from the previous three years as well as consult with peer programs; and thoroughly evaluate (using a budget team) estimates before preparing a final budget draft. Don't forget a cost-of-living adjustment.

Cost-Cutting Procedures

In light of current economic challenges and problems, some managers are cutting costs. Some of the strategies employed, for example, are doing away with low participation or low revenue producing sports, reducing squad sizes and grade-level sport offerings, reducing referees' pay, eliminating or purchasing group insurance, permitting fewer contests, reducing the number of coaches, using volunteer coaches, discontinuing the purchase of personally used equipment (e.g., bats, hockey sticks, tennis rackets), lowering coaches' salaries, eliminating sports where rental facilities are used, and scheduling teams (e.g., girls' and boys' soccer) on the same day and combining transportation, coaches, and officials for these contests. Contemporary managers must be more creative not only to keep programs intact, but also to provide more opportunities for all.

BUDGET PRESENTATION AND ADOPTION

After being prepared, school physical education and sport budgets are usually submitted to the superintendent through the principal's office. The principal is the person in charge of his or her particular building; therefore subdivision budgets should be presented to him or her for approval. Good management means, furthermore, that the budgetary items have been reviewed and shared with the principal during their preparation so that approval is usually routine.

In colleges and universities, the proper budgeting channels should be followed. This might mean clearance through a dean or other management officer or budget committee. Each person who is responsible for budget preparation and presentation should be familiar with the proper working channels, procedures, and protocols.

For successful presentation and adoption, the budget should be prepared in final form only after careful consideration and consultation with appropriate budget committees so that little change will be needed. Requests for funds should be justifiable, and ample preliminary discussion of the budget with persons and groups most directly concerned (the fee payers) should be held so that needless fiscal conflict will be avoided and a strong and unified proposal can be presented.

BUDGET MANAGEMENT

After the presentation and approval of the budget, the next step is to see that it is managed properly. The budget should be followed closely with periodic checks (audits) on various line-item expenditures to see that they are properly recorded and fall within the budget appropriations and guidelines provided. The budget should be a guide to economical and efficient management.

Budget time frames such as Program Evaluation Review Techniques (PERT) and Critical Path Method (CPM) are often applied in budget management to assist in time expectation management. To employ these management techniques, the project must (1) have a clear objective and end point, (2) be divided into a series of stages or phases, (3) have projected due dates accompanying each phase or assigned task, and (4) have a kick-off or starting date.

Numerous systems are employed in the management of budgets. Line-item or object classification budgets (see appendix G) are the most common methods of categorizing incomes and expenses. Each system provides a class, type, or number code (i.e., equipment and supplies) and a corresponding special line item of expense or income. These in turn may be further itemized or broken down (e.g., photocopying paper, stamps, technology, etc.) if necessary for auditing purposes. Incremental budgeting is another common budgeting system that takes each line item and increases, decreases, or maintains its current status with each new or projected budget plan. Other systematic forms of budgeting, such as zero-base budgeting and planning-programming-budgeting-evaluation system (PPBES), are explained next.

ZERO-BASE BUDGETING

Zero-base budgeting (Dirsmith and Jablonsky 1979) is a procedure and system based on a justification for all expenditures of an organization at the time the budget is formulated. It allows management to, in effect, start over and not be influenced by previous budgets. Zero-base budgeting (ZBB) was developed and introduced by the Texas Instruments Company in 1969.

The traditional method (incremental budgeting) of developing a budget is to use the previous year's budget as a base and then require a justification for any increase that is requested for the ensuing year. For example, if $500 had been allocated for recreational sports the previous year and the recreational sports director asked for $900 this year, then only the $400 incremental line-item increase would have to be justified. In some instances a flat 3 percent incremental increase is applied across the board to all aspects of the budget.

Zero-base budgeting, on the other hand, requires a justification of all expenditures that are requested. In the example just given, the entire $900 would have to be justified. In other words, each element, subdivision, unit, or cost center of an organization that is allocated funds starts from zero, and all funds requested must be justified in light of their contribution to the achievement of the objectives of the organization. It requires planning for how these subdivisions can contribute to the achievement of the organization's goals and brings decision making into the procedure. Zero-base budgeting could mean that some elements, units, programs, or sports of an organization have outgrown their usefulness and will no longer receive any funds whatsoever. It could also mean that new programs would be more likely to receive funds if they can be shown to be in line with, and capable of contributing to, organizational goals.

The steps to follow in zero-base budgeting include identifying the goals of the organization, gathering data about the program to be supported, planning a program to meet goals, identifying alternative ways to achieve goals in light of budgetary constraints, including formula and partial funding, performing a cost analysis of the alternatives, and then arriving at a decision about what programs, functions, or alternatives should receive funding and how much.

Zero-base budgeting could be especially valuable to organizations so steeped in tradition that they are not capitalizing on current trends and developments; they may need to implement new and creative ideas including formula funding, programs, and projects. This system of budgeting can also make it possible to see that funds are used in the most effective way to achieve organizational goals and insure program integrity.

PPBES: PLANNING-PROGRAMMING-BUDGETING-EVALUATION SYSTEM

PPBES came about as a solution to problems of fiscal accountability and optimal use of scarce inputs or limited resources. PPBS, as it was originally known, started in 1949 when the Hoover Commission Report on the organization of the executive branch recommended that the government adopt a budget based on three critical factors—function, activities, and objectives. In 1954, the Rand Corporation developed a performance budget for use in military spending. PPBS (Planning-Programming-Budgeting System) was the title given to this system. The DuPont Corporation and the Ford Motor Company were among the first to implement PPBS. In the early 1960s, Robert McNamara introduced the system to the Defense Department. The results of the system were so impressive that President Johnson ordered all federal departments and agencies to adopt PPBS by August 1965. PPBS became PPBES when the function of evaluation was added. At present, many schools, colleges, and other organizations are using this system, and many more are researching the feasibility of employing it.

Definition of PPBES

PPBES (see figure 10-2) may be defined as a long-range plan to accomplish an organization's objectives by using continual feedback and updating of information to allow for greater efficiency in the decision-making process (Apostolou and Crumbley 1988). The four elements of PPBES are as follows:

1. *Planning*—establishing clear goals and objectives
2. *Programming*—developing activities, programs, and events to produce distinguishable and measurable results toward meeting organizational objectives
3. *Budgeting*—allocating resources; the financial plan for meeting program needs and objectives
4. *Evaluating*—determining how adequately the budget fits the program and the program

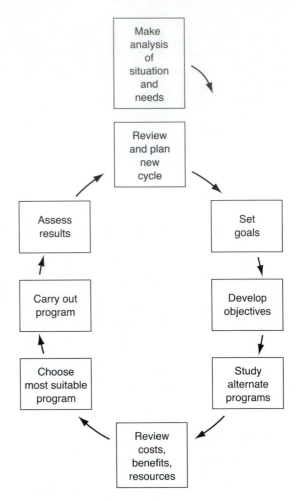

Figure 10-2. The PPBES cycle.

meets the objectives; and evaluating the relationship of accomplishments, outcomes, and risk to cost.

To implement PPBES, the objectives of the organization must be clearly defined. All activities that contribute to the same objective, regardless of placement in the organization, are clustered or grouped together. A financial plan designed to reach these objectives is formulated for a particular time period (PERT or CPM techniques may be utilized). An analysis document assesses long-range needs and evaluates the adequacy, effectiveness, costs, benefits, barriers, and difficulties inherent in the proposed program. Under PPBES, funds must be used with definitive goals in mind. Accountability for expenditures is stressed. In using PPBES, each activity and educational program is considered, not only by itself, but also with respect to other educational programs that make up the whole system. In this way, the needs of the entire school system or organization are considered.

The following steps are necessary to effectively apply PPBES:

1. *Goals and objectives.* Goals and objectives should be stated in terms of "authentic" behavior and performance outcome (Avery 1999). The results of the program should also be determined in relation to knowledge, understanding, skills, and attitudes.

2. *Statement of needs and problems.* Needs and problems of the particular organization and user group must be adequately defined.

3. *Determination of expected satisfaction of needs.* Numbers of persons and skills needed must also be determined.

4. *Constraints, barriers, problems, and feasibility.* These items must be evaluated to determine whether the system can overcome certain limitations (human resources, cost, lost time, materials, facilities). The system may need modification in terms of needs or objectives to overcome existing limitations and barriers.

5. *Alternative programs.* These programs outline the different ways the organization can reach its goals. Alternative programs should be evaluated in terms of needs, goals, cost effectiveness, and constraints of the system.

6. *Resource requirements.* The resource needs of each alternative must be computed. One way to accomplish this might be to derive the cost per student per activity or credit hour and then add department overhead costs such as advising, coaching, counseling, management, equipment, and technical support.

7. *Estimate of benefits.* The benefits of the program must be determined in relationship to student, participant, user group, school, or organizational accomplishment at present and in the future.

8. *Development of an operating plan.* From the data collected, all alternatives should be weighed against criteria such as cost of implementation, risk, and safety involved, estimated benefits, and future budget allocations.

9. *Pilot implementation of best alternative.* A pilot program should be conducted at a level at which it could be modified or changed without involved or costly effort.

10. *Evaluation.* The data from the pilot program should be used to determine whether it is meeting the objectives of the organization. The program should be modified accordingly.

11. *Feedback and further modification.* Once PPBES is in process, it should be continually reevaluated and modified to ensure that the goals and objectives agreed on are being met.

12. *Situational analysis.* This is both a beginning and end process determined by the present state of the situation. This is a crucial and meaningful assessment of needs and value of the program.

Advantages and Disadvantages of PPBES

Before implementing PPBES in an institution, management must be thoroughly familiar with the advantages and disadvantages of such a system. Each situation differs, and careful situational analysis before and after implementation is essential. Here are some of the advantages of PPBES:

1. The system assists in formulating goals, objectives, and identifying skills requisite to program conduct.

2. Curriculum and programs can be designed to meet the objectives formulated.

3. Staff members can be provided with prior planning and professional development experiences and resource materials.

4. Alternative plans can be more systematically analyzed.

5. Costs, accomplishments, and risks may be systematically compared.

6. Staff members are more involved in decision making; and morale, motivation, and productivity may be increased.

7. Instructional and operational costs may be easily identified.

8. Innovation, integration, and coordination can be promoted in programs as well as within the entire organization.

9. New, creative ideas and programs that have been scrutinized and tested are continually applied to the system.

10. Public awareness, understanding, and communication are increased.

Some disadvantages of PPBES include the following:

1. Staff time is limited, and staff members with sufficient technical skills in these areas may also be limited.

2. Implementation may lead to conflict and resistance from community members and sometimes from within the organization.

3. Cost-benefit analysis is difficult to quantify; some benefits from education are not easily measurable.

4. Communication among staff members may be limited as a result of centralization of system planning.

5. PPBES is a method of indicating the best use of funds; however, in doing so, funds are also expended, and limited budgets may not be able to justify implementation of such a system.

6. The vocabulary is vague to those who are not directly involved in using such a system.

7. PPBES may be mistakenly seen as a substitute for management rather than as a tool of management.

8. Alternatives with great potential are passed up because of their high risk or chance of failure according to PPBES criteria.

9. Some persons may believe that they are answerable to the "system" for their program; however, the system should be an aid, not a deterrent.

Many schools and public and private sector organizations in the United States employ PPBES with their budgets because it helps them use available funds wisely, identify problem areas, and improve program weaknesses. Another important attribute of PPBES is the way it relates program costs and risks to expected accomplishments and outcomes. In addition, the public not only is given input into the process, but also is offered clear, transparent, and understandable data and information to assist in adopting and supporting sound fiscal budgeting.

COST ANALYSIS

Cost analysis of resources used in a program is a derivative of cost accounting. Cost analysis is needed to assist the manager in the evaluation of present operations and projection of future planning and budget development. Cost analysis is limited to the types of accounting systems being used as well as to designating the unit to be compared. It is particularly applicable to schools and colleges. For example, some schools operate on K–12, others, on K–6 or K–8 or some other educational pattern. Naturally, a great difference in expenditures per student would occur depending on the various patterns of organization.

Various units are employed in cost analysis in a school's general education fund. The number of students in attendance, the census, average daily attendance, and average daily membership or students enrolled in the school are some of those numbers used. Each of the various units has advantages and disadvantages.

As a raw measure of educational costs, the average daily membership is better than the average daily attendance. Teachers' salaries must be paid whether students are in 90 percent or 100 percent attendance, and desks, books, supplies, and equipment must be available whether students are in attendance or not. With respect to raw per capita

Maintenance, equipment, and human resources must be considered when designing any budget.

units, the average daily membership is also a better unit to measure the educational costs than is the average daily attendance unit. Tradition, however, has favored the average daily attendance unit over average daily membership.

Cost analysis as it relates to supplies and equipment for physical education and sport may be simply handled by allowing a certain number of dollars per student or per participant, depending on whether one is concerned with a school, corporate, or other public or private sector program.

Some experts in fiscal management believe a per capita expenditure allocation for physical education, recreation, and sport represents a solid foundation to provide high-quality service (see appendix G for sample net cost per participant data). However, they recommend in addition (1) an extra percentage allocation for program enrichment, (2) an extra percentage allocation for variation in enrollment, and (3) a reference to a commodity index (current prices of supplies and equipment) that may indicate need for changes in the per capita expenditure because of current increase or decrease in the value of the items being considered for purchase.

The following example can be used as a guideline to determine the amount of money needed for physical education and sport programs. The director of physical education or athletic and activities director submits and substantiates the needs for the

coming school year: increased expenditures—a sound estimate of projected increases of student participation based on increased enrollments, student interest, program changes, and the anticipated cost of equipment and supplies; inventory—equipment and supplies on hand and the condition of these items; and the previous year's budget—amounts allocated in the previous year or years. These items represent the basis on which most allocations of funds to physical education and sport programs are determined.

Most managers of physical education, recreation, and sport programs believe that any increases in per capita allocations that they were granted were the result of such factors as a documented increase in the number of participants, a careful evaluation of the number of participants and of the time those participants spent using the equipment, space, and supplies, the cost per hour, and an excellent working rapport with the board of education and community.

THE EXECUTIVE DIRECTOR OF FINANCE OR BUSINESS MANAGER: FISCAL MANAGEMENT IN SCHOOLS AND COLLEGES

Schools and colleges today are in the business of education. The size of the physical plant and the large expenditures necessary to deliver high-quality programs require the talents of a qualified executive director of finance, business manager, or budget officer. The school or college business manager is an integral part of the entire management team and ideally should possess experience in both business administration and education. Most business managers have earned a master's degree, usually in business administration/finance. Some are certified public accountants, and others have taken courses from management institutes. Many school, college, and university business managers are recruited from outside the domain of education. The manager is primarily responsible for the efficient and economic management of business matters concerning the educational institution or agency and often its physical education, recreation, and sport programs.

Physical education and athletic and activity directors must understand and appreciate the vital role of the business manager. Many management functions of physical educators or public and private physical activity and fitness directors, including fiscal management, fall within the responsibility of the business manager. The business manager is a specialist in this area, and educators, coaches, instructors, and staff should work closely with this individual in reference to business-related matters. It is up to teachers, coaches, and representatives of other cost centers to supply the business manager with an accurate and up-to-date database (debits, receipts, equipment costs, membership trends, etc.).

The school, college, or private sector business manager is responsible for budget preparation and fiscal accounting, investment of endowment and other gift monies, bids for planning and construction of buildings, data processing, management of research and other contracts, business aspects of loans, debt service, travel, purchase cards, and other authorized activities.

Regardless of who performs the role of business manager or what title he or she assumes, the functions outlined and the working relationship with physical education, recreation, and sport personnel are similar to or have implications for physical educators in colleges as well as other public and private sector organizations.

Function

The business manager's function is strictly limited by the size of the educational triangle—programs, receipts/credits, expenditures/debits (see figure 10-3). The greater the perimeter of the triangle, the larger the sphere of operations. This applies to all departments within the system. Likewise, in times of inflation, the expenditures and receipts may increase, but the program side may remain stable. Hence it is obvious that the business manager must accurately project and forecast both costs and expenditures and revenue and receipts if a physical education or sport program is going to be maintained, sustained, or expanded.

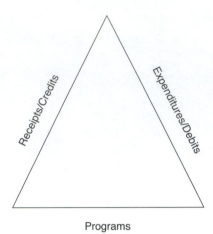

Figure 10-3. The business manager's isosceles triangle.

The business office represents a means to an end, and it can be evaluated in terms of how well it contributes to the realization of the objectives of the organization (educational or other).

Objectives

In serving schools and colleges, the business manager constantly has the goal of helping them obtain the greatest educational service possible from each tax, general fund, student fee, or other dollar spent. He or she should take a democratic approach to decisions affecting others, be they user groups, parents, alumni, coaches, or management. The decisions reached will then be for the best and will include assurances that the educational benefits are worth the cost and any associated risks.

The business manager or finance director is part of the management team—along with principals, superintendents, board members, presidents, directors, chairs, athletic and activities directors, and coaches—who may be expected to look into the years ahead and present long-term ideas regarding the future plans of the school or college as well as its programs.

Responsibilities

The business manager's responsibilities are varied. He or she must be familiar with employee and participant health and accident insurance and benefit programs as well as with state and federal allocations for education. In the smaller school districts, the business responsibilities may be incorporated into the duties of the chief school administrator. As districts grow, they usually hire a person to oversee all the noninstructional areas of the district so that the chief school administrator is free to devote more time to the educational programs of the district. No two districts are alike in handling business responsibilities.

Frederick W. Hill, past president of the Association of School Business Officials, offers a list of some duties of the contemporary business manager:

Budget and financial planning. This is an area in which the business manager has to be sensitive to the needs of staff members to carry out a program. Knowledge of revenue streams, credit, and financial planning are crucial in this role. A business manager also must have a sixth sense to understand how much the community or user group can expend on the program. This experience can be related to the isosceles triangle in figure 10-3. A direct relationship must exist among all the components that make up the three sides of the triangle.

Purchasing and supply management. The business manager must use the best and most effective purchasing techniques to obtain maximal value for every dollar spent. Equipment offered at the lowest bid price is not always the most economical to purchase. After purchases are made and goods received, he or she is responsible for warehousing, storage, computerized inventory control, distribution, and collection records.

Planning. The business manager works with administrators, teachers, coaches, architects, attorneys, and citizens of the community in developing plans for expansion, renovation, and construction of facilities. This must be a team approach.

Human resources. The business manager's duties vary in relation to the size of the district. In a large district, he or she may be in charge of the nonteaching personnel, and in a small district, he or she may be in charge of all human resources. In this capacity, the manager has to maintain records and pay and benefit schedules, initiate strategic compensation plans, generate payroll and retirement reports, and keep other human resource management records. The business manager must also be a master of personal, professional, and sick leave as well as retirement packages.

Staff development. The business manager is always interested in upgrading the people under his or her jurisdiction by providing workshops, professional development, and in-service courses covering the latest developments in the field of fiscal management systems and services.

Community relations. Without community support the school would not operate. Some managers tend to forget this truism and become too far removed from the community. There is always a need to interpret and effectively communicate the financial responsibility and accountability of the institution and program to the public. Newsletter contributions and personal engagement are recommended.

Transportation. It has often been said that boards of education find themselves spending too much time on the three Bs—buses, buildings, and bonds. When this occurs, it is time to look into hiring a business manager. Transportation is vital—and together with the raising cost of fuel, repairs, and maintenance— is one of the most complex and costly line items to control.

Food services. The business manager is responsible for the efficient and effective management of food services. All federal programs must be explored and brought into fiscal play.

Accounting and reporting. The business manager establishes and supervises the financial accounting procedures, including recording, data entry, measuring, reconciling and communicating financial information to appropriate sources.

Debt service. The business manager is involved with various capital developments and financial planning through short-term and long-term financial programs. The financial rating of a school district is judged in part on the way its debt service is managed.

Insurance. Insurance is an important component of risk management. The business manager must be familiar with a large schedule of insurance provisions ranging from fire and liability to health, injury, and disability. He or she must maintain records for proof in case of loss, harm, or injury.

Legal matters. The business manager has to be familiar with education and school law and be aware of the legal constraints on pay systems such as the Fair Labor Standards Act, must know when to consult with attorneys, who are typically retained by most school districts, colleges, corporations, and other public and private sector organizations.

Money raising. The business manager is frequently called on to lead or organize fund-raising campaigns or drives for schools, colleges, and universities. The business manager may also work with public relations consultants and community and advocacy groups to help pass school tax referendums.

Grants and financial aid. The business manager must be aware of money available for programs through private, state, and federal agencies. Grants, assistance programs, financial aid, and other monies available for scholarships from private and public sources should also fall into his or her domain.

Systems analysis. The business manager must constantly question and challenge existing systems to see if they can be improved so that

Transportation costs add significant expenses to budgets at all levels.

managerial tasks, such as budget forecasting, can be performed more efficiently and effectively. SWOT (strengths, weaknesses, opportunities, threats) analysis is often employed to research new systems or evaluate existing ones.

In many public schools, the collectibles and accountables are transferred via computer to the business manager's centralized database. Thus the role of the teacher and coach is to feed specialized information (e.g., equipment types and prices) to the central office. The business manager, via computer, can then check out the item, comparison shop, project and audit the existing equipment budget, evaluate alternative purchase offers, and produce vendor requisitions and purchase orders as well as update the existing equipment inventory and provide documentation back to the physical education chair or athletic and activities director.

Similar procedures for budgeting exist that ensure increased accuracy and "real-time" feedback. Standardized budget request, requisition, and payment forms help provide appropriate copies and feedback to affected management, and provide crucial inputs to help continually track and audit the existing budget area or cost center.

From budgeting to data storage, and from scheduling to breakdown of plays, technology helps all dimensions of physical education and sport programs maintain accountability and integrity.

FINANCIAL ACCOUNTABILITY

The large amount of money involved in physical education, recreation, and sport programs makes strict accountability mandatory. This accountability includes the maintenance of accurate records and receipts, proper distribution of materials, and adequate appraisal and evaluation of procedures. Financial accounting should provide a record of budget, income, and expenditures for all departmental transactions. With help from the computer, the process should also provide permanent records of all financial transactions, which can help form a pattern of expenditures as related to the approved budget. Documenting compliance with mandates and requests imposed either by law or by administrative action, evaluating and accounting to ensure that funds are dealt with honestly, and managing properly with respect to control, cost and risk analysis, reporting, and communication all fall within the domain of the business manager (see box 10-6).

Box 10-6   Reasons for Financial Accounting

To provide a method of authorizing expenditures for items and services that have been included and approved in the budget. This means proper accounting procedures and record keeping are being used.

To provide authorized procedures for making purchases of equipment, supplies, and other materials and to let contracts for various services.

To provide authorized procedures for paying the proper amounts (a) for purchases of equipment, supplies, and other materials, which have been checked upon receipt; (b) for actual labor; and (c) for other services rendered.

To provide a record of each payment made, including the date, to whom, for what purpose, and other pertinent information and material.

To provide authorized procedures for handling various receipts and sources of income.

To provide detailed information essential for properly auditing accounts, such as confirmation that money has been spent for specified items.

To provide informational resources for the preparation of future budgets.

To provide a tangible base for developing future policies relating to financial planning.

To serve as control for various cost centers.

Management Policies for Financial Accounting

Management has the final responsibility for accountability for all monies, equipment, and supplies (see box 10-7). Departments should establish and enforce policies covering loss, damage, theft, misappropriation, or destruction of appropriate departmental resources. A system of accurate and secure record keeping should be established and uniformly applied throughout the organization. The person to whom equipment and supplies are issued should be held accountable for these materials, and accurate inventories must be maintained.

Box 10-7   The Role of the Manager in Budgeting

A. Preliminary considerations in preparing the budget
   1. Program additions or deletions
   2. Staff changes
   3. Inventory of supplies and equipment on hand
   4. Program participant numbers
B. Budget preparation: additional considerations
   1. Gate receipts and expenditures—athletic booster fund, other revenue streams, such as concessions, signage or sponsorships
   2. Board of education budget—allocations for physical education, including athletics and activities and recreational sport
   3. Coaches' requests and requests of teachers and department heads
   4. Comparison of requests with inventories
   5. Itemizing and coding requests
   6. Budget conferences with administration
   7. Justification of requests
C. Athletic and activities association funds: considerations
   1. Estimated income
      a. Gate receipts
      b. Student activities tickets
      c. Tournament receipts
      d. Concessions
      e. Programs, parking, and signage
   2. Estimated expenditures
      a. Awards
      b. Tournament fees
      c. Videos and photos
      d. Miscellaneous
      e. Surplus
D. General budget: considerations
   1. Breakdown
      a. By sport or activity (cost center)
      b. By gender and per student
      c. Transportation/fuel
      d. Salaries
      e. Insurance and benefits
      f. Reconditioning and repair of equipment
      g. Supervision
      h. Equipment/uniforms
      i. Officials
      j. Security
      k. General and miscellaneous

2. Codes (selected)
   a. Advertising
   b. Travel
   c. Conference and membership fees
   d. Printing
   e. Office supplies
   f. Equipment/uniforms
   g. Facility rental
   h. Postage, copying, faxing
E. Postbudget procedures
   1. Selection of equipment and supplies
   2. Preparation of list of deals to bid
   3. Request for price quotations
   4. Requisitions
   5. Care, maintenance, and repair of equipment
   6. Notification to teachers and coaches of amounts approved
F. Ordering procedures
   1. Study the quality of various products
   2. Accept no substitutes for items ordered
   3. Submit request for price quotations
   4. Select low quotes or justify higher quotes
   5. Submit purchase orders
   6. Check, count, and document all shipments
   7. Record items received on inventory cards or computer
   8. Provide for equipment and supply accountability and audits
G. Relationships with management
   1. Consultation—program plans with building principal and/or superintendent
   2. Make budget recommendations to administration
   3. Advise business manager of procedures followed
   4. Discuss items approved and deleted with business manager
   5. Advise teachers and coaches of amounts available and adjust requests
H. Suggestions for prospective directors of physical education and sport and activity programs
   1. Develop a philosophy and transparent approach to budgeting
   2. Consult with staff for their suggestions
   3. Select quality merchandise

> **Box 10-7   The Role of the Manager in Budgeting—cont'd**
>
> 4. Provide proper care and maintenance of equipment and supplies
> 5. Provide for all programs on an equitable basis
> 6. Budget adequately but not elaborately
> 7. Provide a sound, well-rounded program of physical education and sport
> 8. Emphasize equality for all segments of the program.
> 9. Provide for balanced physical education (including adapted), recreational, and sports programs
> 10. Conduct a year-round public relations campaign
> 11. Try to overcome these possible shortcomings:
>   a. Board of education not oriented to needs of physical education and sport
>   b. Program not achieving established goals
>   c. Budget not in line with school and program objectives
>   d. Staff not adequately informed and involved in management process
>   e. Try to move toward compliance for Title IX, ADA, and Healthy People 2010 Objectives for the Nation

Once again the computer is user friendly for these types of budgetary and control systems (Howard and Compton 2004).

Accounting for Receipts and Expenditures

A centralized accounting system, with all funds being deposited with the business manager, treasurer, or other designated responsible person, is advantageous. Purchase orders and other forms are usually then countersigned or certified by the proper official, thus better guaranteeing integrity in the use of funds. A system of bookkeeping wherein books and databases are housed in the central office by the business manager helps ensure better control of finances and allows all subdivisions, units, departments, or cost centers in a system to be uniformly controlled. The central accounting system fund accounts, in which the physical education and sport funds are located, should be audited annually by qualified persons. An annual financial report should be developed and publicized to indicate revenue, expenditures, and other pertinent data associated with the enterprise.

All receipts and expenditures should be properly recorded in the ledger or computer, providing important information like the fund or object code into which the transaction has been deposited or from which it was debited. The money received from sources such as sport participation fees, rental agreements, concessions, and organization dues should be recorded with sufficient credit cross-references and detailed information. Supporting vouchers should also be maintained, copied to appropriate people, and readily accessible for inspection. Tickets to sports and other events should be numbered consecutively and checked to get an accurate record of ticket sales. Students should not be permitted to handle funds except under the supervision of management, staff, or authorized personnel.

Purchase orders on standardized and authorized forms issued by the organization should be used so that accurate records may be kept. To place an order or receive permission to "go ahead" orally without a written follow-up is a questionable policy. Preparing written purchase orders on standardized forms and according to sound accounting practice and procedure better ensures the legality of the contract together with prompt delivery and payment (see box 10-8).

	Yes	No

1. Has a complete inventory been taken, itemized, and recorded on proper forms as a guide in estimating equipment and supply needs?

2. Does the equipment inventory include a detailed account of the number of items on hand, size and quantity, type, condition, date of certification and manufacturing, and repair, etc.?

3. Is the inventory complete, current, and up to date?

4. Are budgetary estimates as accurate and realistic as possible without padding?

5. Are provisions made in the budget for increases expected in enrollments, increased student participation, and changes in the cost of equipment, supplies, transportation, and insurance?

6. Has the business manager been consulted on the cost of new equipment?

7. Has the director of physical education or athletics and activities consulted with the staff on various budget items?

8. Has the director of physical education or athletics consulted with the school business manager in respect to the total budget for the department?

9. Are new equipment and supply needs for physical education and sport determined and budgeted at least 1 year in advance?

10. Was the budget prepared according to the standards recommended by the school administrator or business manager?

11. Are databases and information for previous year's budgets available as a means of comparison?

12. Is there a summary of revenue and expenditures listed so that the total budget can be quickly seen?

13. If receipts from sport or other special funds are to be added to the budget, is this shown?

14. Are there alternate program plans with budgetary changes in the event the budget is not approved?

15. Has a statement of objectives of the program been included that reflects the overall educational philosophy of the total school and community?

16. Has the budget been prepared so that the major aspects may be viewed readily by those persons desiring a quick review and also in more detail for those persons desiring a further delineation of the budgetary items?

17. Is the period of time for which the budget has been prepared clearly indicated? developed to attain the goals and purposes agreed on by management and staff within the framework of the total school's philosophy and mission?

18. Is the physical education and sport budget based on an educational plan developed to attain the goals and purposes agreed on by management and staff within the framework of the total school's philosophy and mission?

19. Is the physical education and sport plan a comprehensive one reflecting an environment to ensure healthy and productive lifestyles?

20. Does the plan include a statement of the objectives of the physical education and sport programs, and are these reflected in the budget?

21. Are both long-range and short-range plans for achieving and assessing the purposes of the program and it's outcomes provided?

Box 10-8   Checklist for Budgeting and Financial Accounting—cont'd

	Yes	No
22. Have provisions been made in the budget for emergencies?	___	___
23. Are accurate records kept on such activities involving expenditures of money as transportation, insurance, officials, fuel, laundry, awards, guarantees, repairs, new equipment, medical expenses, and publicity?	___	___
24. Are accurate records kept on the receipt of monies from such sources as gate receipts, concessions, sponsorships, student fees, and advertising revenue?	___	___
25. Once the budget has been approved, is there a specific plan or system provided for authorizing expenditures?	___	___
26. Are specific standardized forms used for recording purchase transactions?	___	___
27. Are purchases on all major items based on competitive bidding?	___	___
28. Are requisitions used in obtaining supplies and equipment?	___	___
29. Are requisitions numbered and do they include such information as the name of the person originating the requisition, when the item to be purchased will be needed, where to ship the item, the sescription and/or code number, quantity, unit price, and amount?	___	___
30. With the exception of petty cash accounts, is a central purchasing system in effect?	___	___
31. Is the policy of quantity and cooperative purchasing power followed whenever possible?	___	___
32. If quantity purchasing is used, are advanced thought and planning given to storage and maintenance facilities and procedures?	___	___
33. Are performance tests and inspections made on items purchased? Are state, regional, or national testing bureaus or laboratories utilized where feasible?	___	___
34. Are receipts of equipment and supplies checked carefully?	___	___
35. Is an audit made of all expenditures?	___	___
36. Are specific procedures in effect to safeguard money, property, and employees?	___	___
37. Is there an audit or check to determine that established standards, policies, and procedures have been followed?	___	___
38. Are procedures in operation to check condition and use of equipment, supplies and facilities?	___	___
39. Is a financial report made periodically?	___	___
40. Are there proper procedures for the care and maintenance and inventory of all equipment and supplies?	___	___
41. Are accurate records kept on all equipment and supplies, including condition, site, age, repair, and replacement?	___	___
42. Have established procedures been developed and are they followed in regard to the issuance, use, and return of equipment?	___	___
43. Have provisions been made for making regular notations of future needs?	___	___

SUMMARY

The management of physical education, recreation, and sport programs must be concerned with proper fiscal management. The lack of money from traditional sources such as the general fund of a school district or institution of higher education is prompting many organizations to look to government, foundations, the corporate sector, and other external sources for help in meeting their fiscal needs and budgetary requirements. Other organizations are engaging in special fund-raising projects ranging from raffles to T-shirt sales and from "a-thons" to lotteries in order to secure the financial help they need to conduct quality programs. Management of funds also requires a knowledge of how to prepare and implement budgets; how to determine proper costs of supplies and equipment; how to apply systems such as incremental, variable, and zero-base budgeting, PPBES, and PERT; and how to provide for fiscal accountability within the organization. Computerization should also come into play to ensure greater accuracy and control of new revenue streams as well as to streamline fiscal operations.

SELF-ASSESSMENT ACTIVITIES

These activities will assist students in determining if material and competencies presented in this chapter have been mastered.

1. What are the reasons for fiscal management in physical education, recreation, and sport programs?
2. Outline the procedure you would follow in preparing a zero-base budget if you were the chair of a department of recreational sports for a citywide program.
3. Develop a detailed PPBES plan for a department of athletics at the junior high school level (see appendix G for budget guide).
4. As a business manager in a school system, what aspects of fiscal management would involve you and the management of a physical education and sport program?
5. Prepare a budget for a new varsity sport that will be presented to the community at next month's school board meeting.
6. Design and defend a pay-to-play policy for an interscholastic varsity sport program.

REFERENCES

1. American Management Association. 1986. *Financial management.* New York: American Management Association.
2. Apostolou, N. G., and D. L. Crumbley. 1988. *Handbook of government accounting and finance.* New York: John Wiley & Sons.
3. Avery, P. G.1999. Authentic instruction and assessment. *Social Education* 65(6):368–373.
4. Dirsmith, M. W., and S. F. Jablonsky. 1979. Zero-base budgeting as a management technique and political strategy. *Academy of Management Review* 4(4):555–565.
5. Howard, D. R., and J. L. Crompton. 2004. *Financing sport.* Morgantown, WV: Fitness Information Technology, Inc.

6. Masteralexis, L. P., C. A. Barr, and M. A. Hums. 2005. *Principles and practice of sport management.* Gaithersburg, MD: Aspen Publishers.

7. Miller, L. K.1997. *Sport business management.* Gaithersburg, MD: Aspen Publishers, Inc.

8. Robbins, S.P., and M. Coulter. 2005. *Management.* Upper Saddle River, NJ: Pearson Prentice Hall.

9. Stier, W. F., Jr. 1997. *More fantastic fundraisers for sport and recreation.* Champaign, IL: Human Kinetics.

10. Walker, M. L., and D. K. Stotlar. 1997. *Sport facility management.* Sudbury, MA: Jones and Bartlett.

SUGGESTED READINGS

Ambrosio, J. 1993. Funding the athletic department's capital improvements: A growing dilemma. *Athletic Administration* 28(October):56–57.
Discusses how sources of funds that affect physical education and sport programs have been reduced. Lists strategies for funding and sustaining physical education and sport programs.

Baim, D. 1994. *The sports stadium as a municipal investment.* Westport, CT: Greenwood Press.

DeSchriver, T. D., and D. K. Stotlar. 1996. An economic analysis of cartel behavior within the NCAA. *Journal of Sport Management* 10:388–400.

DuBrin, A. J., R. D. Ireland, and J. C. Williams. 2005. *Management and organization.* Mason, OH: South-Western Publishing.
Presents control methods and techniques relative to budgeting and finance. Discusses various network analysis techniques such as PERT and cost-profit schemes.

Fried, G., S. J. Shapiro, and T.D. Deschriver. 2003. *Sport finance.* Champaign, IL: Human Kinetics.

Howard, D. R., and J. L. Crompton. 2004. *Financial sport.* Morgantown, WV: Fitness Information Technology.
Discusses various financial resource avenues for public and private sector funding.

Kanter, S. L., Z. F. Gamson, and H. B. London. 1997. *Revitalizing general education in time of scarcity.* Needham Heights, MA: Allyn and Bacon.

Mahony, D.F., and D.R. Howard. 2001. Sport business in the next decade: A general overview of expected trends. *Journal of Sport Management.* 15: 275–296.

Miller, L. K. 1997. *Sport business management.* Gaithersburg, MD: Aspen Publishers, Inc.
Discusses financial management, including such aspects as operating versus capital budgets, types of budgets, preparing and presenting the budget, and sources of funding. Explores marketing tools and sponsorship.

Miller, L. K. 1997. *Sport business: Operational management.* Gaithersburg, MD.
Discusses financial management, including such aspects as operating versus capital budgets, types of budgets, preparing and presenting the budget, and sources of funding. Explores marketing tools and sponsorship.

Phyrr, P. A. 1970. Zero-base budgeting. *Harvard Business Review,* November–December, 111–121.

Stier, W. F. 1994. *Successful sport fund-raising.* Dubuque, IA: Brown & Benchmark.
Accentuates the need to raise funds for physical education and sport programs in schools and colleges. Suggests that such outside sources need to be tapped if these programs are to survive. Provides suggestions for procuring external funds.

VanderZwaag, H. J. 1998. *Policy development in sport management.* Westport, CT: Praeger.

Williams, J. C. 2005. *Management.* Mason, OH: South-Western.
Presents control methods and techniques relative to budgeting and finance. Discusses various network analysis techniques such as PERT and cost-profit schemes.

CHAPTER 11

Purchase and Care of Supplies and Equipment

INSTRUCTIONAL OBJECTIVES AND COMPETENCIES TO BE ACHIEVED

After reading this chapter the student should be able to:

- Explain why sound supply and equipment management is important and explain the basis on which supplies and equipment should be selected for physical education, recreation, and sport programs.
- Discuss the various procedures and principles that should be followed in purchasing supplies and equipment.
- List guidelines for the selection of an equipment manager and for the management of the equipment room.
- Establish a system for checking, issuing, and maintaining supplies and equipment.
- Justify the need for various types of technology-related supplies and equipment for physical education, recreation, and sport programs.
- Identify professional organizations involved with certification of prophylactic or protective equipment.

Chapter 10, Fiscal Management, showed that a significant portion of the physical education and sport budget is allocated for the purchase of supplies and equipment. Management is responsible for seeing that the supplies and equipment that are purchased will meet program needs, be of good quality, be safe, measure up to code, and be acquired via a procedural pattern that reflects efficient, effective, and ethical practices. Management (equipment managers at large institutions and

recreation centers) is also concerned with fit of equipment (especially prophylactic or protective equipment), maintenance, accountability, and development of policies and procedures for effective and efficient conduct of this important segment of any program.

Physical education, recreation, and sport programs use supplies and equipment that cost thousands of dollars. It is estimated that the sports equipment industry generates over 70 billion per year. *Supplies* are those materials that are expendable and have to be replaced at frequent intervals, such as shuttlecocks, tennis balls, and adhesive tape. *Equipment* refers to those items that are not considered expendable, but are used for a period of years, such as balance beams, volleyball standards, strength training equipment, soccer goals, canoes, mats, and videotape recorders.

Because so much money is spent on supplies and equipment and because such materials are vital to the health and safety of participants, to good playing conditions and environment, and to values derived from the programs, it is important that the management aspects related to supplies and equipment are well planned, carefully developed, effectively and and ethically implemented, and appropriately controlled and monitored. In addition, the purchase of supplies and equipment should be related to achieving program objectives designated by PPBES and inventory control represented by Economic Order Quality (EOQ) and Order-Point Systems. These models assume a constant demand for supplies and equipment, constant lead-time for ordering and purchase, lot ordering, stable equipment demand and supply, and predictable pricing. This permits independent replenishment of equipment on the basis of programmatic philosophy, needs, and demands (Schroeder 2004). Physical educators, coaches, fitness directors, and equipment managers and personnel should express their needs for supplies and equipment in terms of these models and programmatic goals, keeping in mind at all times quality and safety.

Many different sources for purchasing equipment exist, many grades and qualities of materials are available, and many methods of storing, repairing, and maintaining such merchandise may be utilized. Some of these sources, grades, methods, and procedures are good whereas others are extremely questionable. To obtain the best value for the investment of scarce financial inputs, basic principles of selecting, purchasing, controlling, and maintaining equipment need to be understood and applied. The checklist at the end of this chap-

Proper care of supplies and equipment is crucial to all physical activity, recreation, and sport programs.

ter provides some guidelines that should be followed in the purchase and care of supplies and equipment.

DETERMINING SUPPLY AND EQUIPMENT NEEDS

Supply and equipment needs vary according to a wide range of factors, including the level of the program or participants, demographics (age, experience) of the user group, type and frequency of activities being offered, number of participants, and, of course, finance. Other factors are the facilities and physical plant, athletic training rooms (see chapter 12), playing space available, inventory on hand, demand for specific equipment because of rules or accommodation requirements, and number of activities or sports being offered. Some organizations have only limited physical education, recreation, and sport programs and facilities. Under such conditions, the supplies and equipment needed differ from those required in settings in which more spacious and sophisticated accommodations exist. Other factors to consider are the nature of the clientele (age, gender, skill level, and number), the length of playing seasons, the environment, and health, safety, and security provisions. Those responsible

Specialized equipment being assembled for basketball.

for purchasing supplies and equipment should carefully study their own particular situations and estimate and forecast their needs objectively and realistically.

In the physical education instructional domain, all types of balls, apparatus, nets, mats, standards, implements (e.g., gloves, bats, racquets), and accompanying storage will be needed for the conduct of individual and team sports as well as for aquatics, dance, group exercise, and other physical activities. These same types of supplies and equipment may also be used in the recreational sport program and sometimes by community education. Many times, in fact, the same human, physical, informational, and technical (facility, supplies, equipment, risk management protocols, set-up and directions) resources are utilized in joint or shared arrangement.

Physical education, recreation, and sport supply and equipment needs, and the manner by which they are determined, vary from organization to organization. For example, an elementary school may be given an equipment budget based on the

Rolling equipment carts make it easy to transport, store, and account for costly equipment. University of California at Irvine.

number of students enrolled. Then, within the parameters of the budget, teachers request at the end of each year the equipment and supplies they will need the following year. Another procedure that might be followed in a high school, in which various units of different activities constitute the program, would be to conduct an inventory of supplies at the conclusion of each teaching unit. A third procedure followed in some school districts and communities is, in the interest of economy, ordering all supplies and equipment through a central management center system for all schools and organizations within the city or district. In such cases, items may be stored and controlled from a centrally located warehouse, from where they can be obtained or distributed as needed.

In sport programs, inventories are usually taken and purchase requests instituted at the end of each respective sport season. In this process, the sport-specific coach, equipment manager, and athletic and activities director usually cooperate to develop a five-year revolving plan and budget to ensure that the necessary supplies and equipment are available for the beginning of the next playing season.

GUIDELINES FOR SELECTING SUPPLIES AND EQUIPMENT

Selection should be based on local needs and demands. Supplies and equipment should be specified and selected because they are needed in a particular situation and by a particular user group. Items should be selected that represent materials and equipment needed to effectively, efficiently, and safely carry out both programmatic and organizational goals and objectives.

Selection should be based on quality. This remains a top priority and, in the long run, the item of good quality will be the least expensive and the safest. Bargain goods too often consist of inferior materials that wear out much earlier and perhaps do not supply the protection needed for safe participation. Only the best grade of football equipment, for

Strength training equipment is costly, yet if maintained properly, it can last for many years.

example, should be purchased. Serious football-related injuries and deaths that occur at an approximate rate of 1.44 per 100,000 participants reveal that many of these resulted from the use of inferior or poorly fitting helmets and other substandard, out-of-date, or modified equipment. What is true of football is also true of other activities.

Selection should consider whether the product is both budget and maintenance friendly. When planning for everything from uniforms to artificial surfaces, management must consider not only the initial capital outlay for an item (e.g., shoulder pads, ice hockey breezers, pool lane dividers, fitness equipment, golf mats), but also the maintenance, shelf life, and upkeep. Managers many times will purchase the "label" of, for example, strength training equipment (Cybex, Nautilus, Stair Master, Magnum, OEI Life Fitness, York, Keiser, etc.), but should first shop around because alternate equipment may be found at significant savings without compromising quality or service.

Equipment that has readily replaceable parts that are "recommended by the manufacturer" for liability purposes should be the only type of equipment purchased and maintained. (Athletic Business 2005; Fitness Business Pro 2004; Recreation Management 2004).

Selection should be made by professional personnel. The persons selecting the supplies and equipment needed in physical education and sport programs should be knowledgeable and competent. Performing this responsibility efficiently means examining many types and brands of products; researching and conducting comparative experiments to determine economy, durability, and safety; listing and weighing the advantages and disadvantages of different items; and knowing how each item is going to be used and how long it will last. The person selecting supplies and equipment should be interested in this responsibility, have the time to do a thorough job, be a certified member of the Athletic Equipment Managers Association (AEMA), be a team player and able communicator and be able to perform the function efficiently. Some organizations have purchasing agents who are specially trained in these matters whereas oth-

Safety equipment such as helmets must be certified and regularly inspected to meet acceptable standards.

ers use athletic equipment managers or an equipment committee. In small organizations, the department chair, director, coach, physical education teacher or team leader, frequently performs this responsibility. Regardless of who is responsible for ordering supplies and equipment the participant/consumer, teacher, fitness leader, and coach should have direct input concerning the specific items being considered for selection.

Selecting should be continuous. A product that ranks as the best available this year may not necessarily be the best in the next ordering cycle. Manufacturers are constantly conducting research to develop and produce a safer and improved product. There is keen competition in the marketplace; management, therefore, cannot be complacent, thinking that because a certain product has served well in the past, it remains the best buy for the future. The search for the best product available must be a continuous process. With the help of professional organizations such as AAHPERD, AEMA, and the National Sporting Goods Association, and resources such as Runner's World and Athletic Business, an expert equipment manager, with the use of a computer, can track the latest sources and trends.

Selection should consider service and replacement needs. Supplies and equipment may be difficult to obtain in volume. On receipt of merchandise, sizes of uniforms may be wrong, and colors may be mixed up. Additional materials may be needed on short notice (JIT, or just-in-time ordering). Therefore, one should select items that will be available in volume, if needed, and deal with reliable business firms that will service and replace materials with manufacturer's approved parts and take care of emergencies without delay or controversy. Local merchants should be strongly considered in the purchasing process.

Selection should consider whether old equipment can be reconditioned successfully or whether new equipment should be purchased. Management should make this decision based on factors such as safety, cost, and suitability for effective use in activities in which the item is required. In some cases, repairing old equipment may be costly; therefore, buying new equipment may be more beneficial. If the safety of participants is in question, the decision definitely should be in favor of new safety or protective equipment versus new jerseys or uniforms.

Selection should consider those persons with disabilities. Members of various special population user groups may need special types of supplies, equipment, or materials to participate in some of the activities that are a part of the physical education and sport program. Equipment may be needed for such aspects of the program as perceptual-motor activities or correction of postural deviations. For the most part, however, regular equipment can be adopted and adapted for those with disabilities, because the trend is to have students with disabilities integrated or "included" (inclusion) into as many regular classes as possible. This notion holds true with recreational sports and sport participation as well.

Dunn (1997) and Sherrill (2004) discuss equipment and supplies for special populations. Information about topics such as ordering and maintenance of equipment, safety, supervision required, and storage space is provided as well as a list of equipment suppliers.

Selection should consider acceptable standards and rules for athletic equipment. The stamp of approval of the National Operating Committee on Standards for Athletic Equipment (NOCSAE) should be on football, lacrosse, baseball, and softball helmets whereas the Hockey Equipment Certification Council's (HECC) seal should be on ice hockey protective equipment. These seals will ensure that the helmets have been properly constructed and certified. NOCSAE researches sports equipment and encourages acceptable standards in manufacturing. It also distributes information about sport standards and safety to various organizations and individuals in the interests of safety, utility, and legal considerations. Furthermore, it provides an opportunity for individuals and organizations to study the problems regarding various aspects of sports equipment and how those problems can be solved. The National Federation of High School Associations (NFHS) and the NCAA have rules concerning the fitting and wearing of some protective equipment. From polycarbonate eye protection to sport bras (Cooper's ligament), protective equipment is continually improving and essential to all programs (Arnheim and Prentice 2000).

Equipment and uniform selection should be up-to-date. University of Colorado, Boulder.

Selection should consider trends in sports equipment and uniforms (Olson 1997). The emerging trends in sports equipment and uniforms also should be taken into consideration. Some significant changes include ventilated mesh cloth, waterproof and breathable Gore-Tex and similar materials, screen-printed lettering, and one-piece wrestling uniforms, not to mention the numerous fabrics (e.g., nylon filament, "shark skin," stretch nylon, spandex, cotton, acrylic, lycra, polypropylene, and polyester). Additional accessories to basketball uniforms (e.g., T-shirts and sports bras might be worn under the uniform shirt and spandex tights under the pants) are also popular.

Developments in equipment are improving both safety and sport performance. Modifications in equipment ranging from ice hockey skate blades and pads to composite tennis racquets and from eye protection to high-tech ski bindings have made continuous updating requisite to providing the most current, safe, and effective equipment for the physical activity and sport consumer.

GUIDELINES FOR PURCHASING SUPPLIES AND EQUIPMENT

Purchases should meet the organization's requirements and have management approval. Each organization has its own policy providing for the purchase of supplies and equipment. It is essential that the prescribed pattern be followed and that proper management approval be obtained. Requisition forms that contain specific descriptions of items, amounts, and costs (see figure 11-1), purchase orders that place the buying procedure on a written or contract basis (see figure 11-2), and voucher forms that show date of receipt, date manufactured, and the condition of materials received should be used as prescribed by regulations. The physical education instructor and sport or equipment manager and staff should all be familiar with and adhere to the purchasing policies and procedures of the organization and should be sure that their policies include standards such as those of NOCSAE and the U.S. Consumer Product Safety Commission.

Purchasing, when possible and practical, should be done in advance of need. The majority of supplies and equipment for physical education and sport programs should be ordered in bulk and well in advance of the time the materials will be used (see box 11-1 presenting EOQ Plan). Late orders, rushed through at the last moment, may mean mistakes or substitutions on the part of the manufacturer. When purchase orders are placed early, manufacturers have more time to carry out their responsibilities efficiently and often "early bird" and prepay discount prices are available. Also, goods that do not meet specifications can be returned and replaced. Items needed in the fall should be ordered not later than the preceding spring, and items desired for spring use should be ordered not later than the preceding fall (see box 11-2). Just after the postseason inventory is a recommended time to order new equipment. This early bird ordering as well as preday or early day plans may serve not only to save money but also establish a positive vendor relationship, which usually results in better service.

Supplies and equipment should be standardized. Ease of ordering is accomplished and larger quantities of materials can be purchased at a savings when standardized supplies and equipment are used. This also assists in last-minute or JIT (just-in-time) ordering when it is not possible or practical to buy ahead of time. Standardization means that certain colors, styles, sizes, and types of material or equipment remain constant over time and therefore may be ordered on a revolving basis. This procedure can be followed after careful research to determine which are the best, most reliable, and most serviceable products for the money. However, standardization of supplies and equipment should never mean termination of further study and research to find the best products to meet program objectives.

Specifications should be clearly set forth. The trademark or brand name, item serial number, catalog number, type of material, and other important specifications should be clearly stated when purchasing supplies, equipment, and other materials to avoid any misunderstanding of what is being ordered (see figure 11-1). This procedure ensures

REQUISITION FORM
BLOOMINGTON SCHOOL DISTRICT 271

REQUISITION NO. 158236

ALL REQUISITIONS MUST BE TYPEWRITTEN

Name & Address of Vendor

Required Delivery Date

SHIP TO:

Today's Date

Source of Price:
Estimate ☐   Catalog ☐   Contract ☐
Verbal Quote ☐   Written Quote ☐   (Attach copies of all quotes received)
Requisitions in excess of $1,000.00 require competitive written quotes.

(Vendor Information Below This Line)

Quantity	Unit of measure	Catalog/Serial Number	Give complete information as to color, size, brand name, dimensions, copyright date, edition, etc. — state if book, film, magazine, etc.	Unit Price	Total Price Each
1.					
2.					
3.					
4.					
5.					
6.					
7.					
8.					
9.					
10.					

PURCHASE REQUISITION

Purchase requisitions are generally initiated by a school or department to cover requirements, which are needed during the school year that are to be purchased from a supplier. Requisitions should be made in duplicate:

1. Original sent to business office for processing
2. Duplicate retained by initiating school or department

TOTAL

ADDITIONAL INFORMATION — (INFORMATION SHOWN BELOW THIS LINE WILL NOT GO TO VENDOR)

COMMENTS:

DIST.	SCHOOL & DEPT.	REQUESTED BY	DATE	PURCHASE ORDER	T	VEVDOR
271			39 44	45 50	51	52

G/E	ACCOUNT NUMBER						C R	PURCHASE ORDER	P O C	B L T	C R	AMOUNT	T P 1	T P 2	INVOICE NUMBER	P T L
	FD	ORG	PRG	FIN	OBJ	CRS		AMOUNT								
9 10	11 13	14 16	17 19	20 22	23 25	26	27		37	36	26	27	37	38	58	68
						000										
						000										
						000										
						000										
						000										
						000										

Principal _____

District Administrator _____

PURCHASE ORDER

45   50

DATE OF ORDER

39   44

Figure 11-1. Requisition form.

Figure 11-2. Purchase order.

that quality merchandise will be received when it is ordered. It also makes it possible to objectively compare bids of competing business firms. For example, if a particular brand of baseball, basketball, or sweat suit is desired, the trademark, item serial number, and catalog number should be clearly stated on the bid form, along with a written notice that no substitutes will be accepted.

Cost should be kept as low as possible without loss of quality. Quality of materials is a major consideration. However, among various manufacturers and business concerns, prices vary for products of equal quality. Because supplies and equipment are usually purchased in considerable volume, a few cents per unit could represent a savings of many hundreds of dollars to departments, participants, and taxpayers. Therefore, if quality can be maintained, materials should be purchased at the lowest cost figure.

Purchases should be made from reputable business firms. In some cases, higher management authorities such as the state or district decide the firm from which supplies and equipment are to be purchased. In the event of such a procedure, this principle is academic. However, when physical education, recreation, and sport personnel are

Box 11-1   Athletic Equipment Buyers' Economic Order Quality (EOQ) Plan

MONTH	TYPE OF SPORTS EQUIPMENT			
	FOOTBALL	BASEBALL	BASKETBALL	TRACK
JANUARY	ORDER NEW EQUIPMENT	ORDER NEW EQUIPMENT	PRACTICE FREE THROWS	ORDER NEW EQUIPMENT
FEBRUARY	ORDER NEW EQUIPMENT	TIME IS RUNNING OUT		TIME IS RUNNING OUT
MARCH	ORDER NEW EQUIPMENT	DELIVERY	TAKE INVENTORY	
APRIL	TIME IS RUNNING OUT	MARK AND SAFETY CHECK EQUIPMENT	ORDER NEW EQUIPMENT	
MAY	PRINCIPAL'S RETREAT		ORDER NEW EQUIPMENT	ATTEND TAC MEETING
JUNE	ATTEND SCHOOL BOARD PICNIC	TAKE INVENTORY	ORDER NEW EQUIPMENT	TAKE INVENTORY
JULY	DELIVERY		ORDER NEW EQUIPMENT	
AUGUST	MARK AND SAFETY CHECK EQUIPMENT	ATTEND STATE FAIR	TIME IS RUNNING OUT	
SEPTEMBER		SECURE METRODOME	DELIVERY	DELIVERY
OCTOBER		ORDER NEW EQUIPMENT	MARK AND SAFETY CHECK EQUIPMENT	MARK AND SAFETY CHECK EQUIPMENT
NOVEMBER	TAKE INVENTORY	ORDER NEW EQUIPMENT	FINAL FOUR MEETING	ORDER NEW EQUIPMENT
DECEMBER	ORDER NEW EQUIPMENT	ORDER NEW EQUIPMENT		ORDER NEW EQUIPMENT

ORDER NEW EQUIPMENT   TIME IS RUNNING OUT   YOU MAY BE TOO LATE determining the business firm from which purchases will be made, they are wise to deal with established, reputable businesses that are known to have reasonable prices, reliable materials, ample manufacturer-approved inventory for replacement, and good service. In the long run, purchasing from reputable companies is the best way to conduct business.

Direct purchasing is an expedient way to conduct business. Direct purchasing takes place when the school board, institution, or club enables the buyer (e.g., physical education teacher, coach, fitness leader) to purchase from whoever the buyer believes is the best supplier. Most schools or organizations have a direct purchasing policy limiting the buy to $100 to $500, and with the present capability of online purchasing and the use of procurement cards (P-Cards), direct purchasing is increasingly common. However, purchasers must be aware that they must be able to establish the authenticity of the vendor and comply with the stipulations and guidelines attached to the card (purchase item restrictions and limitations, delivery time frames). The advantages of direct purchasing are that it is usually fast, local, and promotes good vendor relationships. The downside is that money may be directly handled and that favoritism and a higher price may result.

Central purchasing can result in greater economy. Some school districts and other organizations or consortiums purchase supplies and equipment for several schools, school districts, clubs, or other groups. In this way, the purchasers can buy larger amounts at a reduced price per unit. In some cases, large school districts even go so far as to standardize their uniform types and colors, thus enabling them to purchase uniforms at lower prices. These systems also usually computerize their purchase orders, bids, contracts, and other records, not to mention their entire budgetary, purchasing, distribution, and auditing processes. Databases for maintaining and tracking inventory and equipment lists are also made immediately available. The physical educator, coach, and instructor should be called on for their valuable input, as the typical downside to central purchasing is that a less expensive or not acceptable substitute sometimes appears rather than the desired product.

Local firms should be considered. Management's main concern must be to obtain quality value for money expended. If local firms can offer equal values, render equal or better service for the same money, and are reliable, then preference should be given to local dealers. In some cases, it is advantageous to use local dealers because they

NOTICE TO BIDDERS

(For use in advertising)

The board of education of ___(legal name)___ School District

No. ____ of the Town(s) of _____ popularly known

as _____ , (in accordance with Section 103 of

Article 5-A of the General Municipal Law) hereby invites the sub-

mission of sealed bids on _____ for use in the

schools of the district. Bids will be received until _____ on the

(hour)

_____ day of _____ , 20 ____ , at _____

(date)   (month)   (place of bid

opening) , at which time and place all bids will be publicly opened.

Specifications and bid form may be obtained at the same office. The

board of education reserves the right to reject all bids. Any bid

submitted will be binding for _____ days subsequent to the date of

bid opening.

Board of Education

_____ School District No. ____

of the Town(s) of _____

County(ies) of _____

_____

(Address)

By _____

(Purchasing Agent)

_____

(Date)

Note: The hour should indicate whether it is Eastern Standard or
Eastern Daylight Saving Time.

Figure 11-3. Sample notice to bidders form.

are more readily accessible and can provide quicker and better service than firms located farther away. Buying locally also makes for good public relations.

Bids should be obtained. A sound management procedure that helps eliminate any accusation of favoritism and helps obtain the best price available is competitive bidding. This procedure requires that special forms be distributed to the many dealers and vendors who handle the supplies and equipment desired (see figure 11-3). These forms should clearly state the specifics re-

garding the description (e.g., kind, make, model, serial number), amount, and quality of articles desired. After bids have been obtained, usually over a six-week time period, the choice of vendor can be made. Low bids sometimes do not have to be accepted; however, a decision not to honor one must be justified. Such justification could be that a company's reputation is in question, the service rendered is poor, delivery cannot be made on time, or that the company is situated at such a great distance that communication and service are hampered.

Horine and Stotlar (2004) discuss the question of whether the competitive bidding process is desirable. They point out that this process sometimes increases costs, slows down the purchasing process, discourages bids from local dealers, and encourages dealers to cut corners in order to submit lower bids. Oftentimes the result leads to an inferior product being delivered.

Advantages of the bidding system are that it may stimulate honest competition, resulting in lower prices; it may promote on-time delivery; it can provide for better and more reliable service; it spreads the purchasing among more vendors; it eliminates favoritism; and it may reduce the risk of poor-quality merchandise.

Gifts or favors should not be accepted from dealers. Some dealers and their representatives (reps) are happy to present management or staff members with a set of golf clubs, a nice training outfit, tennis racquet, or other gifts if, by so doing, they believe it is possible to acquire an account. In most cases, accepting such gifts or favors is poor policy. Accepting such a gift may place a person under obligation to an individual or firm and can result only in difficulties and harm to the program. Managers or staff members should never profit personally from any materials purchased for use in their programs. Therefore, such gifts or favors should be scrutinized carefully in light of professional ethics (see box 11-3). Many vendors, of course, do leave sample items with the department to be field-tested and researched for further consideration.

At the high school level, sponsorships are now coming into play. This casts a gray area about the acceptance of free or discounted equipment and supplies. At the university level, however, large companies often have contracts with the administration or the coach to provide free or discounted rates on supplies and equipment. In this case, with approval of higher authority, gratis and reduced cost equipment may be received.

A complete and accurate inventory analysis is essential before purchasing. Before purchases are made, the amount of supplies and equipment on hand and the condition, including when these items

---

Box 11-3   Management's Code of Ethics for Human Resources Involved in Purchasing

1. To consider first the interests of the organization and the enhancement of the program.
2. To be receptive to advice and suggestions of others, both in the department and in management, including the participant, insofar as the advice is compatible with legal and moral requirements.
3. To endeavor to obtain the most value for every dollar spent.
4. To strive to develop expertise and knowledge of supplies and equipment that ensure recommendations for purchases of best value and user safety and impact.
5. To insist on honesty in the sales representation of every product submitted for consideration for purchase.
6. To give all responsible bidders equal consideration in determining whether their product meets specifications and the educational needs of the program.
7. To discourage and to decline gifts that in any way might influence a purchase.
8. To provide a courteous reception for all persons who conduct business regarding supplies and equipment.
9. To counsel and help others involved in purchasing.
10. To cooperate with all professional organizations or persons helping in the development of sound management procedures and policies in the procurement of supplies and equipment.

---

were purchased, should be known and entered in a data bank. This knowledge prevents overbuying and having large stockpiles of materials that may become outdated or unsafe when they are needed. Inventories should be taken at specified times, such as at the end of a sport season or before ordering for the next season, or semester or on an annual basis. In most organizations, the inventory is computerized and kept up-to-date on a continuing basis. (See box 11-4.)

Computers connected to centralized databases help determine equipment needs as well as inventory.

GUIDELINES FOR THE EQUIPMENT ROOM AND THE EQUIPMENT MANAGER

The equipment manager's position is very important. The money spent on uniforms, supplies, and equipment amounts to a large part of an organization's budget. Therefore, the person in charge of the equipment and supply room, whether a paid employee, intern, or student volunteer, should be selected with care. A qualified person will be able to help make equipment and supplies last longer through proper maintenance, storage, cleaning, and care. Accountability for equipment will be better ensured because a system of sound policies (see figure 11-4) and good record keeping

Box 11-4	Steps in Purchasing Supplies and Equipment
Need	Staff identifies need or demand for equipment in program and checks inventory.
Consultation	Staff consults with management and grassroots personnel supporting need for equipment and discusses whether to lease or purchase.
Initiation	A request is made for equipment to fulfill, augment, supplement, or improve the program.
Review of request	Proper management approve or disapprove request after careful consideration of need. Sometimes the request is modified!
Review of budget allocation	A budget code number is assigned after availability of funds in that category has been determined.
Preparation of specifications	Specifications are prepared in detail, giving exact quality requirements, and made available to prospective contractors or vendors.
Receipt of bids	Contractors or vendors submit price quotations.
Comparisons	Careful evaluation is made to determine exact fulfillment of quality requirements.
Recommendations	The business manager prepares specific recommendations for approval.
Purchase order to supplier	After approval, a purchase order that fulfills the requirements at a competitive price is made.
Follow-up	Purchasing agent makes a follow-up inquiry if equipment is not received when due.
Receipt of goods	Central receiving receives goods, checks them against specifications, and returns purchase order with approval.
Payment	Purchasing agent and appropriate authority (department head, board of education) approve purchase for payment and accounting office pays.
Accountability	Goods are sent to the department that is held accountable for equipment.
User receives	Staff picks up equipment at designated place and inspects via safety audit before payment.
Inventory	Equipment staff inventories, via computer, labels, and properly stores equipment.

Athletic Equipment Room Policies

The Athletic Department at the University of _____ provides each student-athlete with the best available equipment that can be purchased within its athletic equipment budget. It is the intention of the Athletic Equipment Room to provide each student-athlete with the most up-to-date and protective equipment possible. This is in line with our avowed intention of creating a safe and professional atmosphere at all times. This is an expensive proposition, so certain policies have been adopted to ensure that each student-athlete will make every attempt to protect his or her equipment.

1. Each student-athlete is directly responsible for each and every piece of equipment issued to him or her. Once an item of equipment has been issued to a student-athlete and it leaves the confines of the equipment room, that student-athlete becomes responsible for the safe-keeping and return of that piece of equipment.

2. All equipment issued to the student-athlete must be returned promptly and in person to the equipment room at the end of the season, upon termination of his or her participation on his or her team, or at the equipment manager's request. All equipment must be returned unless directed otherwise by the equipment manager.

3. Failure to return any equipment for any reason in a timely manner will result in a bill being sent to the student-athlete for the missing equipment through the Bursar's office. Prices for equipment are based on single unit replacement. Bills are nonrefundable and nonnegotiable.

4. Athletic equipment is to be worn only by the person who has been issued that equipment and used solely for sanctioned university events or participation. Equipment room personnel does not issue "loaner" equipment, and will not issue additional equipment without billing the student-athlete.

5. Any issued athletic equipment that breaks omit or wears out due to sanctioned athletic participation or use will be repaired or replaced free of charge upon its return to the equipment room. Replacement costs for any athletic equipment damaged outside of sanctioned athletic participation or not exchanged will be passed on to the student-athlete.

6. All issued athletic equipment will be cleaned, laundered, and inspected for safety on a regular basis by the equipment staff if that equipment is returned to the equipment room in a timely manner as requested by the equipment room staff.

7. Any athletic clothes or equipment that becomes damaged or ruined because the student-athlete has not returned his or her game or practice equipment to the equipment room in a timely manner as directed by the equipment manager will be billed to the student-athlete.

These policies are not intended to harass the student-athlete but rather to ensure that each student-athlete has quality equipment at all times and to ensure that the university adheres to NCAA guidelines.

I have read, understand, and agree to comply with the official policy of the University of _____ Equipment Room.

_____   _____

Date   Signature

_____   _____

Student I.D. #   Print Full Name

You will be held to these policies whether you have taken the time to read the above or not.

Figure 11-4. Sample athletic equipment room policies.

will be established and less equipment will be lost (see figures 11-5 and 11-6). Also, a qualified manager will be able to make sound recommendations regarding the purchasing of athletic supplies and equipment. In light of such important responsibilities, the equipment manager selected should have qualifications that include technical equipment skills, organizational ability, computer skills, an interest in keeping equipment in excellent condition, an understanding of the purchase, care, and maintenance of sports equipment and supplies, a willingness to learn, the ability to get along with people, trustworthiness, patience, and the ability to effectively supervise and communicate with other people. Equipment managers should be familiar with inventory systems and ordering procedures, as well as the latest rule changes that might affect equipment, fitting, or other AEMA role criteria. The equipment manager should also possess thorough understanding of the philosophy, goals, and objectives of the program and how this position fits in the total process.

The equipment and supply room is an important facility in physical education, recreation, and sport programs. It is important to have sufficient space with proper climate control to take care of the various purposes for which such a room exists (e.g., laundry, drying, storage). Space should be sufficient to store, label, inspect, inventory, and identify the equipment and supplies needed in the program. Adequate bins, shelves, and racks for equipment are needed. Space should be sufficient to permit movement for handling the routine functions of issuing equipment and supplies. People working in the equipment room should be able to move with ease throughout the facility. Space should be provided for drying equipment, such as football or soccer uniforms that have become wet when practices or games are held in the rain. The equipment and supply room should be well organized, secure, computerized, and a model of efficiency, cleanliness, and sound organization. The equipment room manager and personnel team are important and valued members of the organization and deserve to be treated as such by all concerned (staff, students, faculty, user groups).

EQUIPMENT/CLOTHING ISSUE

Date ....

I .... have

accepted school property ....

....(write in article, description and its code number)

and agree to return it clean and in good condition or pay for said equipment.

Signed ....

Student I.D. #..................   Locker # ....

Home Phone #............................. Home Address ....

E-mail...

Figure 11-5. Form for checking out physical education, recreation, and sports inventory.

EQUIPMENT CHECKOUT RECORD

Player_____ Home Room_____

Address_____ Phone_____

E-mail_____

Class_____ Height_____ Weight_____ Age_____

Parents Waiver_____ Medical Examination_____ Insurance_____

Notes:_ _.

Football   Cross Country   Basketball   Swimming   Wrestling   Hockey

Baseball   Track   Tennis   Golf   Softball   Soccer

_ _

	Out	In	Game Equipment	Out	In
Blocking pads			White jersey		
Shoulder pads			Maroon jersey		
Hip pads			White pants		
Thigh pads			Maroon pants		
Knee pads			Warm-up pants		
Helmet			Warm-up jacket		
Shoes			Stockings		
Practice pants					
Practice jersey					

I hereby certify that I have received the above-listed athletic equipment and will return same not later than the day following the last game of the season for the sport checked.

Signature_____

Figure 11-6. Equipment checkout record.

GUIDELINES FOR CHECKING, STORING, ISSUING, AND MAINTAINING SUPPLIES AND EQUIPMENT

All supplies and equipment should be carefully inspected upon receipt. Supplies and equipment that have been ordered should not be paid for until they have been thoroughly inspected and deemed whole, safe, within code guidelines and specifications, and complete (including directions). The equipment should then be inventoried as to amount, type, quality, size, and other specifications listed on the purchase order. Any discrepancies that are noted should be reported and corrected before payment is made. This inspection is an important responsibility and should be followed carefully. It represents sound and prudent management practice and indeed is an important part of risk management.

Supplies and equipment requiring organization identification should be labeled. Equipment and supplies are often moved from location to location and sometimes are part of an integrated or multiuser (e.g., physical education, recreational sports, community education, fitness clubs) locker room system. It is a good practice to ID, stencil, or stamp inventory with the organization's logo in order to identify it. This identification system also helps to trace and locate missing articles, discourage misappropriation of such items, and determine what is and what is not departmental property.

Procedures should be established for issuing and checking in supplies and equipment. Considerable loss of material can result if poor accounting procedures are followed. Procedures should be established so that items are issued and collected as prescribed, proper forms are completed, records are maintained, and all materials can be traced and located (see figures 11-5 and 11-6). Articles should be listed on the records according to various specifications of amount, size, or color, together with the name of the person or user group to whom the item is issued. The individual's record should be classified according to name, street address, telephone, locker number, student ID, or other information important for identification.

There are numerous supply and equipment issue and retrieval systems employed in most equipment rooms, especially those with in-house laundry facilities. Towel replacement and uniform services, roll and bag/pin systems, all have their pros and cons, but these services facilitate participation, promote a healthy lifestyle, and should be provided. Laundry drops and pick-up points including various locker systems should, like equipment and supply points, be clean, secure, and well organized. In all cases, the person or persons to whom the supplies and equipment are issued should be held accountable.

In instances of multiple user groups, sound issuing procedures will enable management to track the amount of user time for each piece of equipment, which will not only justify the need for future purchasing considerations but also identify the user group budget code that might be held accountable.

Equipment should be in constant repair. Equipment should always be maintained in a safe and serviceable condition. This is sound preventive maintenance. Maintenance procedures for equipment should be routinized so that repairs are provided as needed. All used equipment should be checked and then repaired, replaced, or serviced as needed. A record of date and type of repair should be maintained and placed on file. Repair can be justified, however, only when the cost for such is within reason and when manufacturer's approved parts can be obtained. Supplies should also be replaced before they have been depleted.

Equipment and supplies should be stored properly. Equipment and supplies should be handled efficiently so that space can be properly organized for storing. A procedure should be established for identification and location, and proper safeguards should be taken to protect against fire and theft. Convenient bins, racks, shelves, hangers, and other accessories should be available. Temperature, humidity, lighting, and ventilation are also important considerations. Items going into the storeroom should be properly checked for quality and quantity before acceptance is confirmed. Cleanliness should also

Maintaining an organized inventory is crucial to sound purchasing and distribution practices.

be requisite; many schools place the participant in charge of not only uniform cleaning but minor repairs as well. An inventory should be readily available for all items on hand in the storeroom. Computerization is strongly recommended for this function. Every precaution should be taken to provide for the quality care of all materials so that investments are properly maintained and protected.

Garments should be cleaned and cared for properly. According to the Rawlings Sporting Goods Company, garment care has four categories: (1) New garments should be kept in original packing boxes and stored in a cool, dry area with low humidity. (2) During the season, garments should be cared for immediately after a game. Before being sent to the cleaner, they should be inspected for tears or other defects and repaired immediately. (3) For away contests, garments should be packed for the trip and then hung up as soon as possible on arrival as well as on return. If an extended trip is being made, or if the trip home will not take place until the following day, the garments should be hung up for drying and inspection after each game. (4) Upon completion of the season, final cleaning, repair, and storage of the garments are crucial. If followed, proper cleaning and storing procedures will extend the life of the garments, help maintain attractiveness,

Box 11-5 Suggestions for Cleaning Sports Equipment

- The person responsible for cleaning should be informed about the need for special handling of various garments. Read the labels!
- Dry cleaning usually will remove dirt and stains but normally will not remove perspiration. Therefore, garments that can be cleaned by soap and water rather than by dry cleaning should be purchased.
- Garments of different colors should not be laundered together. Careful sorting is requisite.
- Strong chemicals or alkalies should not be used because they will fade colors and may damage the material.
- Soaking and treating soiled laundry is a sound practice.
- Chlorine bleach should not be used, except for towels and whites.
- Water levels in washing equipment should be kept high if lower mechanical action is desired, but kept low if uniforms are badly soiled, to increase chemical mechanical action. Do not overload washing equipment.
- When using a commercial steam press, it is recommended that garments should be stretched back to original size.
- Uniforms and other garments should be dry before being stored.
- Water temperatures above 120° F may fade colors and cause shrinkage.
- Specialized all-automatic sport laundry facilities that are owned by the organization are recommended as a means of protecting garments against shrinkage, color fading, snags, and bleeding. Human resources must be thoroughly trained to make this system effective.

and save time and money (see box 11-5). This is crucial for many programs as the number of sports and participants are increasing and budgets are not keeping pace, so uniforms usually have to last longer than in the past.

Instructional technology systems, including computers and audiovisual equipment, must be maintained and kept secure.

GUIDELINES FOR EQUIPMENT AND RISK MANAGEMENT

Physical education, recreation, and sport managers, equipment managers, and those dealing with equipment in various physical activity programs must be aware of the issues regarding equipment product liability and other legal concerns (see chapter 13, Legal Liability, Risk, and Insurance Management). Most equipment-related legal action generally falls into four categories:

- Modification or misuse of products (e.g., removing an ear flap from a softball helmet)
- Failure to follow manufacturer's guidelines related to selection, fitting, maintenance, or product replacement (e.g., using a youth helmet on an adult because it fits better)
- Inadequate instruction to participants related to the use of the products or equipment
- Failure to warn participants, parents, or guardians of the ability of the products to reduce the risk of participation

It is therefore crucial that equipment personnel be thoroughly trained and certified (AEMA) in order to not only protect the participant, but the organization. Equipment policies covering duties of equipment managers, teachers, fitness instructors, and coaches concerning such things as the assigning and proper fitting of equipment, providing guidelines on proper use, documenting the participant warning process, and equipment safety inspection, among others, must be thoroughly implemented (Appenzeller 2004).

AUDIOVISUAL SUPPLIES AND TECHNOLOGY-RELATED EQUIPMENT

Audiovisual aids and materials are an important and essential part of physical education, recreation, and sport programs for delivering instruction, providing feedback, conducting in-depth analysis of movement patterns, and scouting sport opponents.

As modern society embraces the rapid development of audiovisual equipment and other technological advances, it is crucial that managers in physical education, recreation, and sport programming remain cognizant of available equipment and technical possibilities, as well as the development of future trends. Audiovisual equipment has long been useful for providing valuable instruction in the acquisition of motor skills and for encouraging and motivating people to be physically fit. While current audiovisual media supplement traditional materials such as wall charts and posters, the advent of new instructional materials and tools such as computer simulations (e.g., golf and bowling), various CD-ROMs, PowerPoint presentations, digital video recorders (TiVo), and interactive videodiscs, which facilitate self-paced programs, have significantly impacted physical education, recreation, and sport program delivery. Additionally, the availability of tools such as Blackboard and WebCT have created a host of new approaches for using Web-based and Web-assisted instruction and assessment. However, along with these new capabilities and opportunities come myriad management considerations for the selection and purchasing process. Continuous computer development and matching software position what was today's state-of-the-art technology into the race to keep pace. It is crucial to have in place an insightful revolving technology plan to continue to provide high-quality physical education, recreation, and sport programs as we move forward in the first decade of the new millennium.

Reasons for Increased Use of Audiovisual Materials in Physical Education, Recreation, and Sport Programs

They enable the viewer to better understand concepts concerning the performance of a skill, event, game, and other experiences. Use of instructional technologies including DVDs, laser discs, graphics, or other materials provides a clearer idea of the subject being taught, whether it is how a heart functions, selecting a well-balanced diet, or how to groove a golf swing.

They help provide variety to teaching. When audiovisual aids are used in addition to other teaching techniques, structures, and strategies, motivation is enhanced and the attention span is prolonged. The subject matter comes alive and is more exciting, meaningful, and sometimes personalized.

They increase motivation on the part of the viewer. To see a game played, a skill performed, or an experiment conducted in clear, understandable virtual reality or graphic representation helps motivate a person to engage in a game, perform a skill more effectively, or want to know more about the relationship of physical activity to health-related fitness. This motivation is particularly true in digital video replay or computer simulation, whereby a person sees how he or she performs a skill and then can compare the performance to a model program or movement pattern.

The recent innovation of the interactive videodisk carries the video concept one step further. Students not only view the video, but also are asked to respond to questions about strategies or skill execution. Correct responses allow the program to proceed whereas incorrect answers key the disk to repeat the learning sequence. This instructional strategy provides immediate feedback of results, is student-paced, and offers out-of-class learning options for students who need additional practice time.

They provide an extension of what can normally be taught or delivered in a classroom, gymnasium, pool, or playground. Instructional technology enables the viewer to experience other countries and cultures as well as to view sporting events in other parts of the United States. Digital videos enable the viewer to assess the Internet and view appropriate educational materials at any time in any place. All these experiences are important to the objectives of physical education, recreation, and sport programs.

They provide a historical reference for physical education, recreation, and sport. Outstanding and sometimes traumatic events and personal drama (e.g., the 1972 Munich Olympics, Magic Johnson, Arthur Ashe, Lance Armstrong, the 1980 Miracle On Ice in Lake Placid, Glory Road, Kathie Freeman) in sports, physical education, and health that have occurred in past years can be brought to life before the viewer's eyes. In this way, the student obtains a better understanding of these events and the important role they might play in our society as well as within the global village.

Guidelines for Selecting and Using Audiovisual Aids

Audiovisual materials should be carefully selected and screened before purchasing and use. Appropriateness for age and maturity level of students and others, accuracy of subject matter, technical qualities, inclusion of current information, cost, and other related factors are important to ascertain before selecting audiovisual materials. This process should be undertaken by a representative "curriculum team" or resource committee. (See box 11-6.)

Management should see that the presentation of materials is carefully planned and sequenced to provide continuity in the subject matter being presented. Instructors should select and use materials that amplify and illustrate some important part of the material being covered. Furthermore, audiovisual aids should be employed at a time that logically fits into the presentation of certain material and concepts.

Management should realize that slow-motion and stop-action projections are best when a pattern of coordination of movements in a skill or strategy is to be taught. When teaching a skill or strategy the physical educator or coach usually likes to analyze the various parts of the whole and also to stop and discuss aspects of the skill with the participants.

Box 11-6 Checklist of Selective Items to Consider in the Purchase and Care of Supplies and Equipment

	Yes	No
1. Selection of supplies and equipment is related to the achievement of the goals and objectives of physical education and sport programs.	___	___
2. Supplies and equipment are selected in accordance with the needs and capacities of the participants, including consideration for age, gender, skill, disability, and interest.	___	___
3. A manual or written policies have been prepared regarding the procedure for purchasing, care, use, and control of all supplies and equipment.	___	___
4. Mechanics of purchasing such as the following are used: requisitions, specifications, bids and quotations, contracts and purchase orders, delivery data, receipt of merchandise, audit and inspection of goods, vendor invoices, and payment.	___	___
5. The relationship of functions such as the following to purchasing is considered: organizational goals, programming, budgeting and financing, auditing and accounting, maintenance, legal rules and regulations, ethics, and organizational philosophy.	___	___
6. Principles of purchasing such as the following are adhered to: need, quality, safety, quantity, storage, inventory, control, and trade in or carry over value.	___	___
7. A close working relationship exists between the department head and school or college business manager or athletic and activities director and the equipment manager and equipment room personnel.	___	___
8. Participants provide and maintain their own equipment and supplies when appropriate.	___	___
9. Merchandise is purchased only from reputable manufacturers and distributors, and consideration is also given to replacement and the services provided.	___	___
10. The greatest value is achieved for each dollar expended.	___	___
11. Management possesses current knowledge and understanding of equipment and supplies.	___	___
12. Management is receptive to advice and suggestions from colleagues who know, use, and purchase supplies and equipment.	___	___
13. The teacher or coach of the sport is contacted when ordering merchandise for his or her activity, and specifications and other matters are checked.	___	___
14. The director of physical education and athletics and activities consults with the business manager when supplies and equipment are needed and ordered.	___	___
15. Regulations for competitive purchasing are followed.	___	___
16. Supply and equipment purchases are standardized whenever possible to make replacement easier.	___	___
17. Management is alert to improvements and advantages and disadvantages of various types of supplies and equipment.	___	___
18. Brand, trademark, and catalog specifications are clearly defined in the purchase requisitions.	___	___
19. Purchase orders are made on standardized school or institutional forms.	___	___
20. Functional quality of merchandise and the safety it affords are major considerations.	___	___
21. The inventory is computerized and is used to plan for replacements and additions.	___	___

Continued

Box 11-6 Checklist of Selective Items to Consider in the Purchase and Care of Supplies and Equipment—cont'd	Yes	No
22. Complete and accurate records are kept on all products purchased.		
23. New equipment and supply needs are determined well in advance.		
24. New materials and equipment are tested and evaluated before being purchased in quantity.		
25. New equipment complies with minimal safety requirements.		
26. Honesty is expected in all sales representations.		
27. State contracts are used when they are available.		
28. Management is prompt and courteous in receiving legitimate sales and business people.		
29. All competitors and vendors who sell merchandise are given fair and equal consideration.		
30. Gifts or favors offered by salespeople or manufacturers are refused.		
31. Materials received are checked with respect to quality, quantity, and safety and whether they meet purchasing specifications that have been indicated on standardized requisition forms.		
32. Prompt payment is ensured on contracts that have been accepted.		
33. All orders are checked carefully for damaged and outdated merchandise, shortages, and errors prior to officially signing for the shipment.		
34. Policies have been established for designating procedures to be followed when there is theft, loss, or destruction of equipment.		
35. Inventories and audits are taken periodically to account for all materials.		
36. A uniform plan is established for marking, labeling, and inventorying supplies and equipment.		
37. A written procedure has been established for borrowing and returning or issuing and dropping off supplies and equipment.		
38. A procedure has been established for holding participants or users accountable for supplies and equipment that are not returned or are returned damaged.		
39. Proper storage facilities have been provided for all purchases.		
40. Equipment is cleaned and repaired when necessary before replacements are ordered.		

Management should ensure that dependable, functional, and quality audiovisual equipment is purchased. Large capital outlays are required for audiovisual equipment, computers, and accompanying software, whether purchased or used by equipment personnel or by staff and other user groups. The new equipment should be compatible with that already used by the organization and should be secured and protected from the elements when not in use. Cool, dust-free storage is best and uninterrupted power sources (UPS) with backup are requisite.

Management should carefully evaluate the audiovisual materials after they have been screened and used. Whether materials are used a second time or purchased for the physical education, recreation, and sport organization or library should be determined on the basis of their value the first time they were implemented or field-tested. Evaluation records should be maintained by the teacher, coach, media resource center, or other school or institutional personnel.

Management should see that equipment is properly maintained and repaired. Videotape players, computers, projectors, record and disc players, television and VCR equipment, and other materials need to be maintained in good

TAKE IT TO THE NET!

Athletic Business
www.athleticbusiness.com

Athletic Equipment Managers Association (AEMA)
www.aema/AEMA.com

Fitness Business Pro
www.fitnessbusiness-pro.com

National Operating Committee on Standards for
Athletic Equipment (NOCSAE)
www.nocsae.org

National School Supply and Equipment Association
www.nssea.com

National Sporting Goods Association
www.nsga.org

Runner's World
www.runnersworld.com

U.S. Consumer Product Safety Commision
www.cpsc.gov

operating condition and serviced on a regular basis. Proper care by qualified technical support ensures the longevity of equipment. An efficient and cost-effective audiovisual and technology program and its accompanying staff development sessions are vital to every physical education, recreation, and sport setting.

SUMMARY

Physical education and sport programs spend thousands of dollars on supplies and equipment in order to provide a meaningful and varied program of activities for their user groups. Because a large expenditure of funds is made for supplies and equipment, it is important that this management responsibility be carried out in a businesslike manner. Supply and equipment needs must be accurately determined, selection accomplished according to sound guidelines (e.g., user or organization needs, demands, goals, and objectives), and purchasing conducted within organizational policy

and requirements. Storage, security, maintenance, inventory, and repair of these items are also crucial to the effective and efficient operation of a well-managed physical education and sport program. The computer should be utilized in this vital management function.

SELF-ASSESSMENT ACTIVITIES

The following questions and activities will assist students in determining if material and competencies presented in this chapter have been mastered.

1. Why is supply and equipment management important, and what factors need to be considered regarding this management responsibility?

2. List and discuss five guidelines for equipment selection that should be followed before buying or tendering competitive bids.

3. Discuss the steps that should be considered in purchasing supplies and equipment.

4. Establish a job description for the position of equipment manager.

5. Prepare a management plan that you as chair of a physical education department would recommend for checking, issuing, and maintaining physical education supplies and equipment.

6. Prepare a volleyball lesson plan that includes the use of audiovisual aids and explain how and when audiovisuals could be used most effectively.

7. Design a model equipment room facility.

8. Construct a complete set of forms to assist a high school to purchase, maintain, and keep track of its athletic supplies and equipment.

REFERENCES

1. Appenzeller, H. 2004. *Risk management in sport.* Durham, NC: Carolina Academic Press.
2. Arnheim, D. D., and W. E. Prentice. 2000. *Principles of athletic training.* New York: McGraw-Hill.
3. Athletic business. February 2005. *Buyers guide.* Madison, WI: Athletic Business Publications.
4. Dunn, J.1997. *Special physical education.* Dubuque, IA: Brown & Benchmark.
5. Fitness Business Pro. 2004. *Buyers guide.* Fort Washington, PA: Intertec Publishing.

6. Horine, L., and D. Stotlar. 2004. *Administration of physical education and sport programs.* 4th ed. New York: McGraw-Hill.

7. Olson, J. R. 1997. *Facility and equipment management for sport directors.* Champaign, IL: Human Kinetics.

8. Prentice, W. E. 1999. *Fitness and wellness for life.* New York: McGraw-Hill.

9. Recreation Management. December 2004. *Buyers guide.* Palatine, IL: CAB Communications, Inc.

10. Schroeder, R. G. 2004. *Operations management.* New York: McGraw-Hill.

11. Sherrill, C. 2004. *Adapted physical activity, recreation, and sport.* Dubuque IA: McGraw-Hill.

SUGGESTED READINGS

Athletic Equipment Managers Association. 2000. Certification Manual. Oxford, OH: Health Care Forum, Inc.

Athletic Business. February 2005. *Buyers guide.* Madison, WI: Athletic Business Publications.
Provides a purchasing resource and reference base for physical education, sport, recreation, and fitness. Includes a facility specification guide, a manufacturers and suppliers directory, and a directory of associations to explore equipment purchase opportunities.

Clement, A. 2004. *Law in sport and physical activity.* Dania, FL: Sport and Law Press.
Presents various concepts and legal implications concerning care, safety, and maintenance of equipment.

Fitness Business Pro. 2004. *Buyers guide.* Fort Washington, PA: Intertec Publishing.

Miller, L. K., L. W. Fielding, M. Gupta, and B. G. Pitts. 1995. Case study: Hillerich and Bradsby Co., Inc. *Journal of Sport Management* 9:249–62.
Presents views on just-in-time manufacturing, ordering, and purchasing concepts.

Raia, E. 1995. JIT in the 90s: Zeroing in on leadtimes. *Purchasing* 12(September):54–57.
Discusses the just-in-time concept revolution as well as the *kanban* inventory management system.

Stephenson, H., and D. Otterson. 1995. *Marketing mastery: Your seven step guide to success.* Grants Pass, OR: The Oasis Press/PSI Research.
Presents concepts on sales, purchasing, product images, distribution, and pricing.

Street, S. A., and D. Runkle. 2000. *Athletic protective equipment: Care, selection and fitting.* New York: McGraw-Hill.
Provides a thorough guide on the issues and concerns of care, selection, and fitting of sporting equipment.

Walker, M. L., and T. L. Seidler. 1993. *Sports equipment management.* Boston: Jones and Bartlett.

CHAPTER 12

Management and the Athletic Training Program

INSTRUCTIONAL OBJECTIVES AND COMPETENCIES TO BE ACHIEVED

After reading this chapter the student should be able to:

- Understand and discuss the importance of a quality athletic training program and how it affects both the physical educator and the coach.
- Summarize the incidence of injuries among athletes.
- Understand the role of prevention and care of injuries in physical activity and sport programs.
- Discuss the qualifications, duties, and responsibilities of team physicians and certified athletic trainers.

- Discuss some risk management procedures that should be undertaken to emphasize safety in a school or other organized physical activity or sport program.
- Understand the functions and role of the certified athletic trainer.
- Identify some injury data collection systems and their role in the management of athletic training programs.
- Identify the appropriate supplies that should be included in an athletic trainer's kit.

Throughout history, the profession of physical education and sport has had an intimate and complementary relationship with sports medicine and athletic training. Indeed, Michael Murphy, the famed University of Pennsylvania track coach and athletic trainer, authored the classic book *Athletic Training* in 1914 followed by Bilik's *The Trainer's Bible* in 1917. The National Athletic Trainers' Association (NATA) was founded in Kansas City in 1950, whereas the American College of Sports Medicine (ACSM) was inaugurated in New York in 1954 at the annual AAHPERD professional conference. The original competencies for NATA were authored by Gary Delforge in 1983. Today, all athletic training education programs must be accredited by the Commission on Accreditation of Allied Health Education Programs (CAAHEP). The NATA publishes both the *NATA News* and the *Journal of Athletic*

Training to advance the profession and enhance health care worldwide. There are currently almost 300 accredited universities offering undergraduate athletic training education programs as well as 14 offering accredited graduate programs. These important relationships have evolved and grown over time because the health and safety of students, student-athletes, and other user groups must be provided for by physical educators, coaches, directors of athletics and activities, and other members of management involved in the delivery of high-quality physical activity and sport programs. The increasing number of participants in physical activity and sports programs makes it particularly important to provide sound education and proper training and conditioning protocols, as well as appropriate preventative and protective techniques and practices to reduce the number of injuries that may occur in both physical education and sport programs. These services, in many instances, can be best provided by a certified athletic trainer (ATC). This chapter addresses the need, nature, scope, complementary relationship, and responsibilities of management in providing a quality athletic training program.

THE NEED FOR CERTIFIED ATHLETIC TRAINERS (ATCs)

The number of high school athletes injured increases each year. Over two million sport injuries requiring hospital treatment with a cost approaching a million dollars will occur each year: 50 percent of the six million girls and boys participating in interscholastic sport in 24,000 high schools will incur injury. About one-sixth of these injuries will be time-loss classified (one to two lost days per year), whereas another 4 to 8 percent will force students to miss three weeks of school or more; however, most injured athletes return to school within a few days of the injury (Powell and Barber-Foss 1999).

Each year, more than one million boys participate in high school football, another 75,000 play at college, and still another estimated 300,000 participate in other community-based organizations (e.g., Pop Warner). An estimated 300,000 football injuries occur every year (35 percent of all varsity high school players). Sixty percent of these injuries

occur at practice and 80 percent are minor in nature and scope. Injuries are caused by factors such as general trauma, illness, hazardous playing surfaces, and players returning to action before fully recovered from injuries (Prentice 2003).

Basketball has the second highest injury rate of all competitive sports. The National Athletic Trainers' Association (NATA) projects that two players on every high school team, regardless of gender, are likely to be injured. In 2001, over 200,000 children ages five to fourteen were treated in hospital emergency rooms for basketball-related injuries. Injuries to the ankles and knees, stress fractures, and other serious contusions (hip, thigh, leg) are most prominent. In baseball and softball, most injuries occur to the hands, wrist, arm (hit by the ball), and shoulder (throwing), and some injuries are caused by improper sliding techniques and spikes. For ages five to fourteen, baseball reported the highest fatality rate of any sport. With the tremendous growth of youth soccer, injuries in this sport have also increased. Lower extremity injuries (ankle and knee ligaments, fractures) are seen most often, while occasional heat exhaustion and dehydration also cause problems. The NATA also reports that wrestling, gymnastics, and cross-country running rate high in injury incidences.

Although research seems to support that injury tends to be sport specific and that for the most part well-trained and conditioned female athletes are no more likely to sustain injury than are male athletes

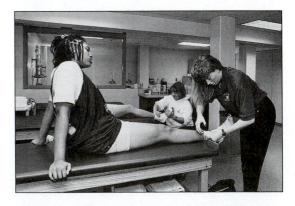

A student-athlete receives attention from a certified athletic trainer.

(Rochman 1996), the total number of injuries and the incidence of serious injury over time seems to fall on the female participant (Chandy and Grana 1985; Whieldon and Cerny 1990; Powell and Barber-Foss 1999). For example, anterior cruciate ligament (ACL) injury requiring surgery in basketball and soccer are significantly more prevalent in females than in their male counterpart (Schenck 1997; Arendt, Agel, and Dick 1999). Some suspect a hormonal connection; most experts recommend a sound nutritional as well as strength training and conditioning program concerning the muscle groups involved in order to attempt to reduce the number of these types of serious injuries.

With the tremendous increase of individuals involved in physical education and sport programs (e.g., more than six million participants in interscholastic activities, more than thirty million children between ages six and sixteen in out-of-school sports activities, and twenty million adults involved with various sports activities) and with subsequent reported and projected injury rates, the crucial need to provide quality sports medicine services at all levels of participation is evident. In June 1990, the American Medical Association (AMA) officially recognized athletic training as an allied health profession that is charged to enhance the quality of health care for the physically active through education, research in prevention, evaluation, rehabilitation, and management of injuries. In 1998, the AMA recommended that certified athletic trainers be part of the health-care team at every high school.

Despite the well-documented need and crucial link between the professions of physical education and sport and athletic training, the NATA reports that less than 50 percent of the nation's 24,000 high schools provide certified athletic trainers for their programs (approximately 1:417 ATC [Athletic Trainer Certified]: student-athlete ratio). Although this is an improvement compared to 1988 when only 10 percent of the nation's high schools provided such crucial services for its sports programs, clearly more strides must be made in this crucial area.

Although Division I and professional level sports are keeping pace with the needs of athletes (approximately 1:20–40 ATC: athlete), the picture in corporate and private sector physical education, sport, and fitness needs improvement. The NATA, however, projects that many certified athletic trainers will be filling this void as the need and challenge are evident, and sound and prudent management practice mandates providing quality sports medicine services to all participants in physical activity and sport programs.

THE SPORTS MEDICINE MANAGEMENT TEAM

Although this chapter has strong implications for all persons who participate in physical education and recreational sport at all levels and ages, athletic health-care services are especially important for student-athletes. It is therefore vital that the physical educator, coach, and athletic and activities director understand not only their role and responsibilities but also those of the athletic trainer in the overall scheme of their sport and physical activity settings. Not only does the growth of sport programs support this notion, but the medical and legal community does as well. School systems and their coaches would be less likely to be held liable for injuries if a certified athletic trainer was on

A sports medicine team on call at the U.S. Intercollegiate Handball Championships.

staff. Even more crucial is the fact that contemporary management philosophy makes the individual student-athlete a high priority that mandates accessibility to quality sports medicine services. The complexities of student athletics (e.g., physical, psychological, psychosocial) and the rigor of training regimens, ranging from preseason to off-season, make it requisite that a team approach to total quality management of sports and sports medicine services be applied. This team approach includes all professionals who are concerned with enhancing the performance and health care of all participants engaged in physical activity and sport.

The Team Physician

The physician is the leader of the sports medicine team (see box 12-1) and oversees all aspects of the athletic health-care program, including preparticipation medical examinations, monitoring the participant's medical needs (e.g., prescriptions for exercise-induced asthma), training and conditioning to prevent injury, emergency care, protocol for injury and illness, as well as evaluation, treatment, and rehabilitation of injuries.

A team physician must be selected with care. He or she must not neglect team responsibilities because of a growing practice or other commitments. The physician should remain objective and avoid being influenced by student-athletes, parents, and coaches. If a physician is needed and none is available, the local medical society, medical school, or HMO should be consulted for a recommendation of one or perhaps several physicians who will jointly care for the team. A team dentist and physical therapist may also be identified in the same fashion. Some of the duties of the team physician are listed in box 12-2.

Although it might be impossible to have a physician present for all sport contests, including practices where most (about 60 percent) of the injuries occur, some suggestions for sport management in such cases might include the following:

- At contests or matches at which a physician cannot be present, have a cell phone, beeper, or pager number where he or she can be contacted on short notice.

Box 12-1   Sport Medicine Team Members

Physician team (general practitioner, orthopaedic surgeon, physician assistant)
Athletic and activities director
Coach and physical education or fitness instructor
Certified athletic trainer (ATC)
Chiropractor
Sport psychologist/educator
School counselor/psychologist/social worker
Exercise scientist (physiology, biomechanics)
Dentist
Emergency medical technician (EMT)
Nurse
Nutritionist
Physical/massage therapist
Podiatrist/orthoist/prosthitist
School health services
Strength and conditioning coach
The athlete, participant, family and significant others

- Provide a certified athletic trainer (ATC).
- Refer the injured student-athlete to the family physician at parents' request. Have emergency contact number on file.
- Provide for emergency (EMT) and ambulance service to the closest medical center emergency room.
- Prepare and keep on hand a complete athletic trainer's kit, including a defibrillator (AED) for ATC use and a first aid kit if no ATC is on-site.
- Prepare and keep on file an accident report containing all essential injury-related information, including nature and extent of injury, date, time, place, and witnesses.
- Have the participant's medical prescriptions available for emergency treatment. The participant, however, must administer these with ATC assistance if needed.

Athletic Trainers

The importance of certified athletic trainers (ATC) in sports injury prevention, recognition and care,

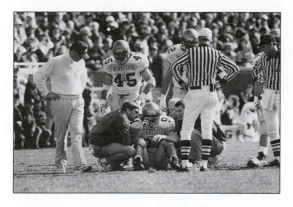

The physician plays an important part in the sports medicine team.

risk management, education, counseling, treatment, and rehabilitation cannot be overlooked by management. The ATC serves as the extension of the team physician and a crucial link between the sports medicine team (see box 12-1), the participant, and the administration. The athletic trainer is most directly responsible for all phases of health care in the athletic milieu, including preventing injury, providing initial first aid and injury management, evaluating injuries (only physicians can diagnose injuries), and designing and supervising a timely and effective program of rehabilitation. It is unfortunate that in the secondary schools where certified athletic trainers are most needed, they are underrepresented. Compounding this situation is the inadequate medical and injury prevention training of most coaches (i.e., many are not licensed and have not taken a first-aid or CPR course). Even if the coach has been well schooled in first aid and injury management, he or she simply does not have sufficient time or qualification to carry out both coaching duties and the responsibilities of an athletic trainer.

In 1980, 10 percent of public secondary schools had athletic trainers, but only 5 percent were certified by the NATA. Of the private secondary schools, 15 percent had athletic trainers, but only 5 percent were NATA approved. On the college level, 16 percent of the two-year colleges had athletic trainers, but only 7 percent were NATA approved; whereas 40 percent of the four-year colleges had

Box 12-2 The Team Physician's Duties

- Preparing and compiling medical histories of students, noting injuries and other health conditions.
- Examining athletes, reporting to parents, administrators, ATCs, and coaches the results of such health status examinations, and making recommendations about whether the player can participate or under what conditions he or she can play.
- Supervising, directing, and advising athletic trainers and working with coaches, student-athletes, and parents in determining the best course of action to follow.
- Attending all games and also practices, if possible.
- Working cooperatively with the athletic trainer, coach, and the athletic and activities director in preparing emergency procedures.
- Examining, diagnosing, and treating all injuries and illnesses and making recommendations about the future play of the athlete. The player must receive the physician's approval to participate.
- Providing time for students' queries regarding such matters as nutrition, conditioning, substance abuse, and injuries.
- Engaging in in-service self-education to keep abreast of the latest developments in prevention and care, and sports medicine.
- Making recommendations to the athletic trainer and coaches regarding injury prevention, rehabilitation, and care.
- Verifying injuries when required for insurance, high school league, the NATA, or NCAA purposes.
- Making recommendations about and helping to select and fit proper protective equipment.
- Working cooperatively with coaches, ATCs, and athletic and activities directors to promote and maintain a high level of health care for the student athlete.

athletic trainers, with 28 percent being NATA certified. Those figures have improved because today the NATA boasts more than 24,000 ATCs; however, many more are needed to keep the nation's middle, junior and senior high school programs on pace for the twenty-first century when it comes to providing quality athletic health care for their student-athletes. The NATA reports that approximately 18 percent and 20 percent, respectively, of their certified members are situated in the high school and college setting, while hospitals/clinics (24 percent), professional sports (3 percent), and corporate and industrial settings (about 2 percent) provide other professional opportunities. Clearly we have a long way to go in our obligations to provide quality health care for all who participate in sport and physical activity. Only at major Division I colleges and universities and at the professional level do we seem to find acceptable athlete-to-ATC ratios (Booher and Thibodeau 2000).

In the past the athletic trainer simply wrapped ankles and administered first aid to athletes. He or she usually had no special preparation for this role, but had learned through on-the-job training. Often such an individual had little scientific knowledge about the prevention and care of sports injuries.

Today, however, sports medicine and athletic training in particular has become a science as well as an art. The functions of the athletic trainer have become varied and complex, and the on-the-job-training philosophy, although crucial, is no longer all that is required. An explosion of scientific information about exercise physiology, nutrition, biomechanics, sport psychology, and sociology as well as sophisticated rehabilitation and treatment equipment make it a requirement for the athletic trainer to have an undergraduate major from an accredited athletic training program. This is requisite to be eligible to sit for the Board of Certification Examination. (See box 12-3).

The qualifications for an athletic trainer (Prentice and Arnheim 2005) are both personal and professional. Personal qualifications include poise, good health, intelligence, maturity, emotional stability, compassion, cleanliness, ethics, fairness, and stamina. Professional qualifications include a knowledge of anatomy and applied physiology, psychology and sociology of sport, sport and risk management, pathology and prevention of injury and illness, pharmacology, training and conditioning, nutrition, NATA and OSHA bloodborne pathogen protocols, rehabilitation techniques, taping, methods for preventing injury, substance abuse, counseling, and protective equipment. Furthermore, the athletic trainer should possess qualities and communication skills that provide a harmonious and productive rapport with the team physician, coaches, sports managers, student-

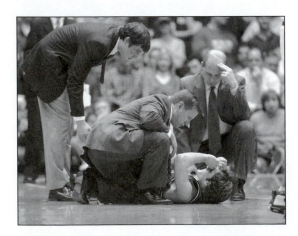

A certified athletic trainer looks after an injured student-athlete.

Box 12-3   The Role of the Certified Athletic Trainer

- Prevention of athletic injury and illness
- Prevention, evaluation, and assessment of athletic injury and illness, including medical referral
- First-aid and emergency care
- Treatment, rehabilitation, and reconditioning under direction of a physician
- Organizational and administrative tasks (e.g., accident reports, injury records, and reporting, etc.)
- Counseling and guidance (i.e., nutrition)
- Educational development initiatives for coaches and student-athletes
- Help prepare training and conditioning programs
- Assist in selection and fitting of equipment
- Work cooperatively with coaching staff and medical team.

athletes, parents, and the public in general. The athletic trainer must be able to practice good human relations as well as protect the student-athletes' well-being and confidence. It is also strongly recommended that the NATA Code of Ethics be adopted (see appendix D).

The NATA's basic minimum requirements for the professional preparation of certified athletic trainers are recommended by the Board of Certification (BOC). These standards include graduating from an approved (The Commission on Accreditation of Allied Health Education Programs) undergraduate or graduate program that meets specific criteria set forth by CAAHEP. Persons preparing for positions in athletic training must also be certified by the BOC. To achieve this certification, they must have proper training and pass the BOC examination. Other formal training in preparing to be an athletic trainer (in addition to those previously mentioned) include kinesiology/biomechanics, first aid and safety, CPR, therapeutic exercise and modalities, psychology of sport injury, exercise physiology, health-care administration, techniques of athletic training, psychosocial behavioral disorders (e.g., bulimia, anorexia nervosa), illness and injury recognition and intervention, ethics, legal aspects, communication, and sport management.

Just as the traditional functions of the athletic trainer have changed, so has the opportunity for

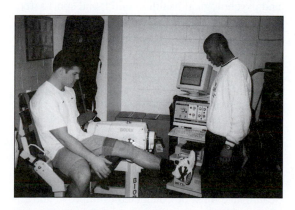

A certified athletic trainer(ATC) assists in the rehabilitation process using isokinetic equipment.

women to enter the profession. At present, 50 percent of the students involved in the athletic training educational process are women; the NATA's female membership numbers 47 percent of its more than 30,000 members.

The athletic trainer's function is crucial and rewarding, but it is also very demanding and entails long hours, working closely with administration, coaching staffs, and other sports medicine team members, and of course, total commitment.

THE ATHLETIC TRAINING ROOM

Elaborate athletic training rooms and equipment are not always essential in sports programs. Indeed, most high schools do not have much in the way of an athletic training room. A well-lighted and properly climate controlled private room with several treatment tables, a desk, file cabinet with lock, shelf space, phone, and a few chairs is the minimal requirement. However, a quality athletic training room should be provided if possible, for it will serve both physical education and sport programs as a multi-purpose place for first aid, physical examinations, bandaging and taping, exercise rehabilitation, treatment, keeping records, and other functions concerned with the health and care of students, athletes, and staff members. The athletic training room should be accessible, near the locker room, shower, and playing areas. A telephone, proper lumination, ice machine or refrigerator, whirlpool and, if possible, equipment for thermal massage, and mechanical therapy, electrotherapy, and hydrotherapy should be provided. A separate office that can be secured for keeping medical records should be maintained as per Health Insurance Portability and Accountability Act (HIPAA) guidelines.

If the sport program involves a great number of participants, special service sections or areas should be separated by low walls or partitions. For those institutions that desire more sophisticated facilities, separate sections would include those for taping, bandaging, and orthotics; thermal, and massage therapy; electrotherapy; hydrotherapy; functional therapy (Swiss exercise balls and standard exercises). An assessment, reconditioning, and functional rehabilitation area with equipment such as Biodex, Cybex, treadmill and stair-climbing machines, and stationary bicycles is also recommended. Of course, there should be an area for storage so that adequate training supplies and well-stocked athletic training kits would always be readily available. The Checklist for Athletic Trainer's Kit, box 12-4, provides a list of recommended supplies for the athletic trainer's kit.

The athletic training room is crucial to any sport program. It is a meeting place, a safe haven for the student-athlete, and a place to share problems and gain counsel. It may also serve as a classroom or teaching station. The athletic training room should be accessible, open, well supervised, and staffed year-round and should be fully supported by management with the appropriate financial, physical, informational, technical, and human resources.

MANAGEMENT'S RESPONSIBILITY IN ATHLETIC TRAINING

What is the management's responsibility in providing quality sports medicine services and preventing sports injuries? The first responsibility is to hire or subcontract, when possible, fully qualified and licensed physicians and certified athletic trainers who understand sports injuries and know how to prevent, treat, and rehabilitate them. These persons should be aware of the latest preventive measures and techniques necessary for sports safety and injury prevention. The American Medical Association's Committee on Medical Aspects of Sport, The American Academy of Orthopaedic Surgeons, the NATA, NCAA Committee on Competitive Safeguards and Medical Aspects of Sports, and the National Federation of State High School Associations (NFHS) provide further elaboration on this topic, which may be found in box 12-5.

Other key elements of injury prevention are complete and thorough preparticipation medical examinations, including cardiac, blood, and urine tests, for every participant. Athletes who are immature physically, who have sustained previous injuries, or who are inadequately conditioned are

Water, rest, and sound training and conditioning procedures help prevent injury.

prone to sports injuries. Crash diets and dehydration (sometimes practiced in wrestling and gymnastics) are injurious to an athlete's health and should be abolished. Training practices based on sound physiological, psychological, and biomechanical principles are some of the best ways to avoid sports injuries. Of course, proper protective equipment must be used in appropriate sports. Facilities and equipment as well as educational curriculum (e.g., nutrition, substance abuse, behavior) must be developed with safety and both physical and psychological health in mind, and sport safety and legal regulations must be reviewed. Management, coaches, and ATCs must keep abreast concerning the latest position statements, research, and educational materials (i.e., The National Institute on Drug Abuse's ATLAS and ATHENA nutritional and steroid programs, the National Center for Drug Free Sport, the NCAA Health Sciences Program) by professional organizations and qualified sports scientists, ranging from heading a soccer ball to various questionable supplements (i.e., creatine, androstindion, ephedra, steroids). Research also must be conducted to improve and enhance all dimensions of the athletic training and health-care process.

Box 12-4 Checklist for Athletic Trainer's Kit*

Item	Amount	Item	Amount
Accident/injury report forms	1 Pad	Knee immobilizer	
Adhesive bandages (1" × 3")	3 dozen	Insurance information	
Adhesive tape		Instant cold/heat packs	4
½-inch (1.25 cm)	1 roll	Liniment	2 ounces
1-inch (2.5 cm)	2 rolls	Lighter/matches	1
1 ½-inch (3.75 cm)	6 rolls	Medicated ointment	2 ounces
2-inch (5 cm)	1 roll	Mirror (hand)	13
Alcohol or iodine	4 ounces	Moleskin (bandaids, butterflys)	6" × 6" sheet
Analgesic balm	½ pound	Money pieces (quarters)	
Ace-elastic wraps		Mouth/nose guards	2
3-inch (7.5 cm)	2 rolls	Nail clippers	1
4-inch (10 cm)	2 rolls	Nonadhering sterile pad (3" × 3")	12
6-inch (15 cm)	2 rolls	Oral screw	1
Antacid tablets or liquid	100	Oral thermometer	1
Antibacterial ointment/betadine	6 ounces	Paper, pen, and pencil	
Antidiarrheal meds	6	Peroxide	2 ounces
Antiglare salve	4 ounces	Plastic cups	1 dozen
Antiseptic/baby powder	4 ounces	Polysporin	
Antiseptic soap (liquid)	4 ounces	Prewrap	2 rolls
Aspirin, ibuprofen, Advil, tablets	50	Saline/Visine solution	6 ounces
(with physician permission)		Save-A-Tooth	
Biohazard waste bags	3	Scissors (tape, shark, iris, cuticle)	1 each
Burn ointment	4 oz.	Shoehorn	1
Butterfly bandages/band aids		Skin lubricant/Vaseline	12 ounces
(sterile strips)		Sling	1
Medium	3 dozen	Splints (air, leg, vacu)	2 (L/R)
Small	3 dozen	Sphygmomanometer	1
Cell phone	1	Sterile gauze pads (3" × 3")	6
Cervicle collar	1	Stethoscope	1
Contact case/solution		Stockinet	3 inch
Cotton balls (sterile)	1 ounce	Sunscreen	12 ounces
Cotton-tipped applicators	2 dozen	Tampon	1 box
Cough drops	box	Tape adherent/Tuf-skin	6-ounce
CPR face shield	1		spray can
Cramergesic	1 tub	Tape remover	2 ounces
Elastic tape roll (3-inch)	2 rolls	Tongue depressors	5
Eyewash	2 ounces	Triangular bandages	2
Felt		Tweezers	1
¼-inch (0.6 cm);		Underwrap or prewrap	2 rolls
½-inch (1.25 cm)	6" × 6" sheets	Vinyl foam	
Flashlight or penlight		⅛-inch (0.3 cm)	6" × 6" sheet
Flexible collodion	2 ounces	¼-inch (0.6 cm)	6" × 6" sheet
Foot antifungus powder	2 ounces	½-inch (1.25 cm)	6" × 6" sheet
Gloves (nonlatex)	2 pair	Water bottles	2
Glucose tablets	100	Waterproof tape (1-inch)	1 roll
Goggles (safety)	1 pair	Wrist immobilizer	R/L
Heel cups/lace pads	2	Zinc oxide	6 ounces
Hydrogen peroxide	6 ounces		

*Extra amounts of items such as tape and protective padding are carried in other bags.
*Many ATCs/EMTs are also carrying portable defibrillator units.

Box 12-5   Safeguarding the Health of the Student-Athlete

A joint statement of the Committee on the Medical Aspects of the American Medical Association and the National Federation of State High School Associations.

A checklist to help evaluate five major factors in health-related supervision of sport.

Participation in sport is a privilege involving both responsibilities and rights. The athletes' responsibilities are to play fair, to train and to conduct themselves with credit to their sport and their school. In turn they have the right to optimal protection against injury as this may be ensured through sound conditioning and technical instruction, proper regulations and conditions of play, and adequate health-care supervision.

Periodic evaluation of each of the factors will help ensure a safe and healthful experience for players. The checklist below contains the kinds of questions to be answered in such an appraisal.

PROPER CONDITIONING helps prevent injuries by strengthening the body and increasing resistance to fatigue.

1. Are prospective players given directions and activities for preseason conditioning?
2. Is there a minimum of 3 weeks of practice before the first game or contest?
3. Are precautions taken to prevent heat exhaustion and heat stroke?
4. Is each player required to warm up thoroughly before participation?
5. Are substitutions made without hesitation when players evidence disability?

CAREFUL COACHING leads to skillful performance, which lowers the incidence of injuries.

1. Is emphasis given to safety in teaching techniques and elements of play?
2. Are injuries analyzed to determine causes and to suggest preventive measures and programs?
3. Are tactics discouraged that may increase the hazards and thus the incidence of injuries?
4. Are practice periods carefully planned and of reasonable duration?

GOOD OFFICIATING promotes enjoyment of the game and protection of players.

1. Are players, as well as coaches, thoroughly schooled in the rules and spirit of the game?
2. Are rules and regulations strictly enforced in practice periods as well as in games?
3. Are officials qualified both technically and emotionally for their responsibilities?
4. Do players and coaches respect the decisions of officials?

PROPER EQUIPMENT AND FACILITIES serve a unique purpose in protection of players.

1. Is the best protective equipment provided for use in collision/contact sports?
2. Is careful attention given to proper fit and adjustment of equipment?
3. Is equipment properly maintained and worn, with outmoded items discarded?
4. Are appropriate and safe areas for play provided and carefully maintained?

ADEQUATE MEDICAL CARE is a necessity in the prevention and control of injuries.

1. Is there a participatory health history and thorough medical examination?
2. Is a physician present at contests and readily available during practice sessions?
3. Does the physician make the decision as to whether an athlete should return to play following injury during games?
4. Is authority from a physician required before an athlete can return to practice after being out of play because of disabling injury?
5. Is the care given athletes by coach or athletic trainer limited to first aid and medically prescribed services?

Certified athletic trainers assist in the design of sound training and conditioning programs.

Protective equipment that fits well is crucial to all collision sports, including ice hockey.

Proper Conditioning of Athletes

Conditioning of athletes helps prevent sport injuries. This means preseason training as well as proper conditioning maintenance during the season. Certified/licensed athletic trainers, licensed educators, and coaches who know how to coach fundamentals and how to convey proper sport training procedures are crucial to this process. Careful selection and fitting of equipment and protective strapping as well as counseling athletes about risk and safety, use of equipment, nutrition and rest also play an important part in the total training and conditioning package.

Conditioning exercises for sport should be compatible with the athlete's capacity, developmental and fitness level and should include a warm-up, a progressive exercise routine including preseason, in-season and out-of-season, and special exercises to increase muscular strength and endurance, flexibility, and relaxation. Special attention should be paid to overuse and overreaching during training by monitoring feedback from the participant.

Protective Sports Equipment

Sports equipment that protects vulnerable parts of the athlete's body from injury is important, particularly in such collision/contact sports as football, ice and field hockey, soccer, and lacrosse. For example, football helmets should be purchased in accordance with standards established by the National Operating Committee on Standards for Athletic Equipment (NOCSAE). The NOCSAE seal on a football, baseball, or softball helmet indicates that the manufacturer has complied with prescribed standards for protection of the head. Mouth guards and head or eye protection should be worn, when appropriate, in a number of sports (e.g., baseball, basketball, football, field hockey, ice hockey, lacrosse, squash, racquetball). Shoes and all other equipment should always be carefully selected to ensure proper fit, comfort, and maximal support and protection. Furthermore, proper equipment to protect the chest, ribs, elbows, knees, and shins is critical in certain sports (e.g., football, field and ice hockey, lacrosse, volleyball, soccer).

Protective equipment must be tested for adequacy, must be maintained in good repair, and in essence be as good as new to prevent injury and avoid legal problems. The equipment, which, if possible, will be certified (e.g., Consumer Product Safety Commission, NOCSAE, HECC), should be selected with respect to the injury or potential trauma site (e.g., elbow pads, helmets, and face shields in ice hockey), should fit properly, and should be continuously monitored and evaluated; educational information about its use should be effectively transmitted.

Taping, Bandaging, and Padding

Protective taping, bandaging, and padding can help prevent as well as provide care for injuries. Bandaging is needed at times to protect wounds from infection, to immobilize or limit range of motion of an injured area, to protect an injury, to support an injured part, to hold protective equipment in place, and to make arm slings and eye bandages. Padding and orthotic devices (e.g., usually made from malleable plastics such as polyethylene) are needed to cushion against injury, to restrict the athlete's range of joint motion, and to be used as foot pads. Orthotic devices can help in knee and shoulder bracing, as well as to improve the biomechanics of the foot. Measuring, shaping, and fitting orthotic devices require special skill and knowledge including the team orthopaedic surgeon, orthoist, and podiatrist.

Nutrition

Proper nutrition is important to the health of the athlete for physical fitness and stamina, recuperation from fatigue, energy, and for the repair and regeneration of damaged cells and tissues. Nutrition is a fundamental component of all athletic training programs. Many questions will be asked of the gatekeeper (ATC) regarding nutrition. High pro-

Athletic trainers assist in measuring and fitting approved and certified athletic equipment.

tein and carbohydrate diets, pre-event, during, and postcontest fluid and caloric intake, rest patterning, menstrual cycle, electrolyte balance, and "supplement" questions ranging from creatine edge to bioengineered beverages are some examples. Athletes should include proper amounts of carbohydrates, fats (lipids), proteins, minerals, vitamins, and water in their diets. Typically, a well-balanced diet of 55–60 percent carbohydrates, 25–30 percent fats, and 15–20 percent protein and following the latest USDA food guide pyramid with ample water intake (2.5 liters) provides a solid foundation. Substance, including supplement abuse, eating disorders, osteoporosis, stress, anger, violence, and HIV are further examples of topics that should be presented in quality athletic training and health-care programs.

Ergogenic Aids

Ergogenic aids are supplements or agents that supposedly enhance sport performance. In other words, they are work-producing aids and are supposed to improve physical effort and performance outcome. They include drugs, food, herbs, physical stimulants such as caffeine and amphetamines, and even hypnosis. Some of these agents are questionable and unethical. The athletic trainer should be familiar with the ramifications of ergogenic aids as well as substance use and abuse.

Coaches, athletic trainers, physical educators, and fitness professionals should endorse only ethically and morally sound training practices. Under no circumstances should chemical substances, including over-the-counter (OTC) drugs (e.g., Doan's pills, acetaminophen, aspirin, diet pills), be administered to minor student-athletes for ingestion. Usually OTC first-aid preparations for skin wounds such as topical antibiotics are permitted, but the athletic trainer should refer to school and other professional sports organization's policies for direction.

Some sport and athletic associations (e.g., NCAA, NFHS, USOC, IOC) and sports medicine organizations (AMA, the NATA) have taken a strong position against the use of agents or drugs that enhance performance through artificial means. Substances ranging from amphetamines (to reduce fatigue) to anabolic steroids and growth hormones (to gain weight, build muscle and strength) and from dimethyl sulfoxide to crack cocaine and all illegal drugs have been placed on the banned substance list. The procedures and policies described in chapter 5 and appendix D fall well within the domain of those involved in athletic training and the athletic health-care profession.

SAFETY IN PHYSICAL EDUCATION AND SPORT

In light of the increased participation in physical education and sport, management must give attention to providing for the health and safety of persons engaging in these activities. Besides those maladies that might restrict active participation, injury to the participant is the paramount concern. Injuries are related not only to actual participation in these activities, but also to factors such as the equipment provided, conditions of playing fields, lighting, and myriad other factors associated with safe play (see chapter 13).

Participatory growth in selected sports results in an increase in accidents and injuries. For example, during the 1980s there were an estimated 7.5 million

The sports medicine team of the Pittsburgh Steelers consults daily on team injury status.

racquetball players and more than 850 registered racquetball clubs. The increase in injuries to the eyes and the facial area was dramatic. Approximately 3,000 swimmers drown each year, and fatal or paralyzing football injuries, although not numerous, have increased. Injuries in basketball (640,755), bicycling (632,000), baseball/softball (433,799), skateboarding (82,428), and now snow-boarding, in-line skating, mountain biking and racing, and women's ice hockey will all contribute to the estimated two million plus amateur athletes visiting U.S. emergency rooms each year. Given the large number of participants, including the tremendous increase in girl's and women's sports and physical activities as well as accidents, the first risk management step should be to create an accident, injury, and emergency policy and action plan that is prepared by each subunit involved in specific activities. Written policy, a sound and practiced action plan, including thorough documentation has been a valuable tool not only in enforcing safety regulations but in lowering incidence of injury as well as legal action.

Another management recommendation is the appointment of an individual who will be responsible for the safety compliance and risk management program of the organization. In large organizations, such a position would pay for itself by reducing the accident rate and therefore the loss of production and other human resource costs related to accidents and injuries. If a full-time professional cannot be employed, this responsibility should be assigned to a staff member (e.g., certified athletic trainer). This professional would have responsibilities such as developing policies and procedures, regularly inspecting facilities and equipment, conducting safety and risk management research, developing educational materials, and reporting incidents and accidents to appropriate networks.

One such network organization that collects data on athletic injuries as related to consumer products is the National Electronic Injury Surveillance System (NEISS). Participating schools receive periodic reports about the number and types of injuries in various sports. The NCAA Injury Surveillance System (ISS), started in 1982, also provides its

Helmets for bicycling, roller-skating, in-line skating, skateboarding, and snowboarding among other activities are commonplace and help prevent injury.

position, injury type, severity, and location) injury rate breakdown both in practice and in game-related situations (Prentice 2003).

The development of a proper accident/injury reporting system is another important management recommendation. Athletic trainers must accurately and systematically record injury information. The SOAP (Subjective, Objective, Assessment, Plan for treatment) format is a concise method for recording injury data. This includes what the injured athlete tells the ATC about the injury including past history, what the ATC learns while evaluating the injury (pain, range of motion), what the ATC's professional opinion is about the injury, and what the plan for injury management (treatment and rehabilitation) may entail. According to the National Safety Council, a well-organized reporting system is essential to a safety program. The council points out that use of accident/injury reports (see figure 12-1: Sports Medicine Accident/Injury Report Form) along with other systematic reporting helps prevent further accidents and injuries by getting at the causes of unsafe acts (i.e., strength training about the lower back or knee) and conditions and by developing a program or training protocol that results in the removal of such acts and conditions. Software packages such as the Integrated Injury Tracking System (Micro Integration Systems), Athletic Injury Management (Cramer, Inc.), Med Sports Systems' Sports Injury Monitoring System, and the Sports Ware Injury Tracking System (Computer Sports Medicine, Inc.) are available and facilitate making accident/injury reporting a crucial part of all athletic training programs.

In schools, mandatory preparation of a school risk management and safety handbook is recommended. The handbook should contain specific guidelines for maintaining a safe and risk-free physical activity and sporting environment, should identify individual responsibilities (e.g., student-athlete, parent, coach, athletic and activities director, certified athletic trainer, director of sports medicine), and should initiate and facilitate safety awareness and other creative risk management strategies.

member institutions with injury data. For the most part, athletic trainers are primarily involved in the collection and transmission of injury data. Since 1977, The National Center for Catastrophic Sports Injury Research housed at the University of North Carolina, Chapel Hill, has gathered data on catastrophic injuries at all levels of men's and women's sports. Another organization that is very much concerned with equipment standards and injury reduction in sports is the American Society for Testing and Materials (ASTM), an organization composed of manufacturers, consumers, and technical experts. One of the technical committees of this organization is the National Operating Committee on Standards for Athletic Equipment or NOCSAE. NOCSAE has a subcommittee concerned with helmets and face guards for sports such as football, baseball, softball, lacrosse, and ice hockey. ASTM also researches the number and types of injuries suffered by both male and female athletes. The NATA sponsors a National High School Injury Registry (NHSIR). Developed in 1986, NHSIR provides current and reliable data on injury trends in interscholastic sport. It provides a sport (by gender,

**SPORTS MEDICINE
ACCIDENT/INJURY REPORT FORM**

Name: _____ Sport: _____

During/Sport yes no _____ Practice _____ Conditioning _____ Game _____

Date/Time occurred _____ Date/Time reported _____

How and where occurred:

Anatomical Site:

Subjective:
   History:

Objective:
   Observation:

   Palpation:

   Functional Testing:

Assessment:
   Initial:

   Referral? yes no Physician's name: _____ Date: _____

   Physician's assessment: _____ Date: _____

Plan for treatment*: (include initial action and any meds or equipment provided as well as type and duration of
        treatment program)

Results (include date of discontinuation and summary):

Database and reporting: (NCAA, SIMS, NEISS, NHSSIR, NCCSIR, Risk management committee):

Certified Athletic Trainer: _____

*ATCs render service under the direction of a physician.

Figure 12-1. Sample sports medicine accident/injury report form.

Technology plays an increasing role in the athletic training room.

American Academy of Orthopaedic Surgeons (AAOS)
www.aaos.org

The American Orthopaedic Society for Sports Medicine (AOSSM)
www.sportsmed.org

American Physical Therapy Association (APTA)
www.apta.org

Athletic Trainer.com
www.athletictrainer.com

Board of Certification for the Athletic Trainer (BOC)
www.bocatc.org

Center for Drug Free Sport, Inc.
www.drugfreesport.com

International Sports Sciences Association (ISSA)
www.fitnesseducation.com

Joint Review Committee on Educational Programs in Athletic Training (JRC-AT)
www.jrt-at.org

NATA Educational Council
www.nataec.org

National Athletic Trainers Association (NATA)
www.nata.org

National Council of Strength & Fitness (NCSF)
www.ncsf.org

NIAMS/National Institutes of Health
www.niams.nih.gov

A concluding management recommendation is the establishment of a safety and risk management committee. Safety committees have proved helpful in gaining organizational support for sound safety and risk management practices and awareness. The functions of such a committee are to develop procedures for implementing safety and risk management recommendations, to hold regular meetings for discussion of safety promotion, to conduct periodic inspections and safety audits, to investigate accidents/injuries, to recommend changes in equipment, training protocols, and the physical plant in order to eliminate hazards and reduce injury incidence, and to promote health and safety in all phases of the physical education and sport program.

SUMMARY

An important responsibility in physical education and sport management is to provide for the health and safety of participants. This responsibility requires establishing policies, plans, and procedures that will provide for proper sports medicine and athletic training health-care services, seeing that coaches have an understanding, appreciation, and skill in sound sport and athletic training procedures, providing a full-time certi-

fied athletic trainer when possible, and ensuring that proper equipment and safe and risk-free sport environs are provided.

The number of injuries that occur in sports programs today requires management to oversee the programs to make sure that sound sports medicine and athletic training policies, procedures, and practices exist so that such injuries are kept to a minimum and are evaluated, treated, and rehabili-

Certified athletic trainers (ATCs) do more than just treat injuries.

tated effectively and efficiently. Risk management awareness and education are crucial to quality athletic training services and sound physical education, recreation, and sport programs.

SELF-ASSESSMENT ACTIVITIES

These activities will assist students in determining if material and competencies presented in this chapter have been mastered.

1. Prepare an accident/injury report that includes the nature and scope of the injuries that have just occurred at your middle school volleyball match. Outline the procedures that were followed.

2. As a coach of a soccer team, what steps should you take if a player breaks a leg in practice?

3. Discuss the role and relationship between one of the coaches at your university and the assigned certified athletic trainer.

4. Prepare a list of arguments to present to the board of education to justify the addition of a certified athletic trainer to the school staff.

5. List the desirable qualifications and functions of a certified athletic trainer.

6. You are an athletic trainer at the high school level; design your ideal training room, including space and equipment needs.

REFERENCES

1. Arendt, E. A., J. Agel, and R. Dick. 1999. Anterior cruciate ligament injury patterns among collegiate men and women. *Journal of Athletic Training* 34 (2):86–92.

2. Booher, J. M., and G. A. Thibodeau. 2000. *Athletic injury assessment.* New York: McGraw-Hill.

3. Chandy, T. A., and W. A. Grana. 1985. Secondary school athletic injury in boys and girls: A three-year comparison. *The Physician and Sports Medicine* 13(March):106.

4. Powell, J. W., and K. D. Barber-Foss. 1999. Injury patterns in selected high school sports: A review of the 1995–1997 seasons. *Journal of Athletic Training* 34(3):277–87.

5. Prentice, W. E. 2003. *Arnheim's principles of athletic training.* Dubuque, IA: McGraw-Hill.

6. Prentice, W. E., and D. D. Arnheim. 2005. *Essentials of athletic injury management.* Dubuque, IA: McGraw-Hill.

7. Rochman, S.1996. Gender inequity. *Training and conditioning* 6(5):13–20.

8. Schenck, R. C.1997. *Athletic training and sports medicine.* Rosemont, IL: American Academy of Orthopaedic Surgeons.

9. Whieldon, T. J., and F. Cerny. 1990. Incidence and severity of high school athletic injuries. *Athletic Training Journal of the NATA* 25(4):344–50.

SUGGESTED READINGS

Clain, M. R., and E. B. Hershman. 1989. Overuse injuries in children and adolescents. *The Physician and Sports Medicine* 17(9):111–23.
Discusses the implications of overuse injury in young athletes in regard to growth plate damage, which can result in such problems as traction apophysitis and Little League elbow. Provides information about appropriate interventions that can prevent potential long-term complications.

Curtis, N. 1996. Job outlook for athletic trainers. *Athletic Therapy Today* 1(2):7–11.

Prentice, W. E. 2006. *Athletic training: An introduction to professional practice.* Dubuque, IA: McGraw-Hill.

Prentice, W. E. 2003. *Therapeutic modalities in sports medicine.* Dubuque, IA: McGraw-Hill.
Concerns the prevention, evaluation, management, and rehabilitation of athletic injuries.

Rankin, J. M., and C. D. Ingersoll. 2006. *Athletic training management: Concepts and applications.* Dubuque, IA: McGraw-Hill.
Provides a thorough overview of management concepts as they relate to the profession of athletic training.

Ray, R. 2005. *Management strategies in athletic training.* Champaign, IL: Human Kinetics.
Addresses the NATA domains of professional development, risk management, and athletic health-care management.

Street, S., and D. Runkle. 2002. *Athletic protective equipment: Care, selection and fitting.* Dubuque, IA: McGraw-Hill.

Stuart, M. J. 1998. On-field examination and care: An emergency checklist. *The Physician and Sports Medicine* 26 (November):51–55.
Presents a step-by-step guide for the sports medicine professional for on-field emergency care.

White, J. 1998. Alternative medicine. *The Physician and Sports Medicine* 26(June):92–105.
Presents information that provides prospective athletic trainers with a background in alternative medicine as opposed to the more traditional therapeutic approaches to treatment.

Wilmore, J. H., and D. L. Costill. 2004. *Physiology of sport and exercise.* Champaign, IL: Human Kinetics.
Provides the sport practitioner, coach, athlete, certified athletic trainer, and team physician with a basic understanding of physiological principles underlying physical conditioning and performance in physical education, recreation, and sport.

CHAPTER 13

Legal Liability, Risk, and Insurance Management

INSTRUCTIONAL OBJECTIVES AND COMPETENCIES TO BE ACHIEVED

After reading this chapter the student should be able to:

- Define each of the following terms: legal liability, tort, negligence, intentional tort, product liability, immunity, risk management, and insurance management.
- Indicate the legal basis for physical education programs throughout the United States and the implications that this legal basis has for making physical education a requirement for all students.
- Discuss recent court interpretations regarding sport product liability, violence, and civil rights in physical education and sport.
- Describe what constitutes negligent behavior on the part of physical

educators and coaches and what constitutes defense against negligence.
- Identify common areas of negligence in the conduct of physical education and sport programs, and explain what can be done to reduce or eliminate such negligence.
- Appreciate the relationship of Title IX to legal liability in the conduct of physical education and sport programs.
- Discuss precautions that physical educators can take to prevent accidents and provide for the safety of students and other individuals who participate in their programs.
- Recommend sound risk and insurance management plans for physical education and sport programs.

Among the most important management responsibilities of the physical educator and coach is conducting programs and events within the standard of care appropriate to the profession. This standard of care, although not written out in detail as it is in some professions, is based on the best thinking contained in physical education and sport curriculum and planning materials, and in sport skill information premised on the valid principles of exercise science, biomechanics, ergonomics, psychology, sociology, and pedagogy. Unlike other programs that relate to academic pursuits, physical education and sport programs take place in a variety of high-risk settings where some participants may be at risk and injuries may occur. Accidents are happening in the schools and other physical activity and sport settings; students' and participants' civil rights are being ignored and we, as professionals, must be prepared to face the fact that we could be sued. Therefore, every effort must be taken to provide preventive safety measures (i.e., risk assessment and safety audits, professional development programs) that will keep such injuries and cases to a minimum. These measures include hiring competent, qualified, and certified personnel to plan, conduct, supervise, and oversee programs and activities; purchasing approved and quality equipment; providing facilities and play areas that are safe and well maintained; and acquiring and recommending appropriate liability insurance. Establishing procedures for health status and preparticipatory medical examinations, assessment of baseline fitness levels, prephysical activity and sport orientation, skill progression, and use of protective gear; educating and reminding the participants of the risk of the activity; selecting opponents to avoid dangerous mismatches and eliminating horseplay and harassment and honoring the rights of all are also factors to be fully considered. Teachers, coaches, recreation leaders, and those involved with exercise, fitness, and physical activity programs will be wise to learn tort and civil rights laws (including the First, Fourth, and Fourteenth Amendments), be aware of how the courts are making decisions in the context of these laws, and be vigilant in creating a safe and civil environment so that injuries and unfortunate prejudicial incidents are reduced and, when they do occur, steps are taken immediately to care for the physically or psychologically injured person. This chapter explores those aspects of legal liability and responsibility and risk and insurance management that are pertinent to the prudent management of physical education and sport programs.

According to *Black's Law Dictionary*, liability is the responsibility, the state of one who is bound in law and justice to do something which may be en-

Physical activity, recreation, and sport injuries can lead to questions of legal liability.

forced by action (Black 1990). Other definitions describe liability as the condition of affairs that gives rise to a legal responsibility, duty, or obligation to do a particular thing to be enforced by court action (Appenzeller 2005; Clement 2004; Kaiser 1986).

The tremendous increase in participation in all physical education and sport endeavors across the Physical Activity and Sport Continuum (e.g., youth sport, increased women's participation, lifetime sport, health and fitness clubs and resorts, Sport for All) concomitant with our contemporary legal climate makes it requisite that all physical education and sport professionals be knowledgeable of not only injury incidence reduction but also the legal ramifications (i.e., civil rights laws) that are intimately interwoven with the profession (e.g., program, facilities, equipment, supervision, and safety policies).

When an accident resulting in personal injury (physical or psychological) occurs, the question often arises about whether damages can be recovered.

Not only is the cost of damages at issue, but also the cost of hiring an attorney and mounting a defense, which can at times exceed any damages that may be awarded. All employees run the risk of being sued by injured persons on the basis of alleged tort or wrongdoing that caused the injury. Such injuries occur in playgrounds, sports fields (including the stands), parks, ski areas, golf courses, gymnasiums, arenas, natitoriums, classrooms, locker rooms, fitness laboratories, and the myriad places where physical education, recreation, and sport activities take place.

The legal rights of the individuals involved in such cases are worthy of study. Although the law varies from state to state and case to case, it is possible to discuss liability and legal responsibility in a way that has implications for most settings in which physical educators and coaches work.* First, it is important to understand the legal basis for physical education and sport and for those domains that fall under the Physical Activity and Sport Continuum that was presented in chapter 1.

LEGAL LIABILITY IN PHYSICAL EDUCATION AND SPORT

Litigation in physical education and sport has increased in recent years and was, until sexual harassment complaints, clearly the number one area for litigation in the school setting. Some experts have pointed to increased availability of legal services (e.g., more lawyers, contingency fees), a public more sophisticated about their legal rights, the modification of the doctrine of governmental immunity (e.g., state and local governments and educational institutions can now be sued), a public attitude that groups such as insurance companies and schools have endless sources of revenue, and the movement toward the doctrine of comparative rather than contributory negligence, wherein prorated settlements evolve between litigious parties,

as the main reasons for increased legal action. Other contributory litigious trends that directly affect physical education and sport management include litigation involving discrimination in respect to persons with disabilities, Title IX related cases, and increased legal negligence or foreseeability cases wherein participants were not properly warned that injury could result from their participation (Appenzeller 2004 and 2005; Fried 1999; Baley and Matthews 1989). A decrease in the amount of time dedicated to physical play and activity, decreased fitness level, increase in obesity and focused competitive youth sports programs with little provided for the average child, and the desire for youth to take risks are other factors that find physical education and coaching professionals involved in more than their share of legal action (Clement 2004).

Some years ago the courts recognized the hazards involved in the play activities that are a part of the educational program. A boy sustained an injury while playing tag. The court recognized the possibility and risk of some injury in physical education programs and would not award damages. However, it pointed out that care must be taken by both the participant and the authorities in charge. It further implied that the benefits derived from participating in physical education activities such as tag offset the risk that occasional injury might occur.

The decision regarding the benefits derived from participating in physical education programs was handed down at a time when the attitude of the law was that no governmental agency (e.g., federal, state, local, public school, or college) could be held liable for the acts of its employees unless it so consented. Since that time, a changing attitude in the courts has been evident. The immunity derived from the old common-law rule that "the King or Sovereign could do no wrong" (*Russell v. Men of Devon*, 100 Eng. Rep 359 [1788]) and that a government agency cannot be sued without its consent has changed so that federal, state, and local governments may be sued (Kaiser 1986; Dougherty et al., 1994).

In 1959, the Illinois Supreme Court (*Molitor v. Kaneland Community Unit*, District No. 302, 163 NE 2d 89) overruled the immunity doctrine. The

---

*If a legal issue does arise, seeking advice from the school, institutional, or association legal counsel or hiring a private attorney is recommended.

Signs with rules that are clearly articulated and appropriately placed are important for activity areas.

supreme courts of Wisconsin and Arizona and the Minnesota legislature followed suit; however, in 1963, the Minnesota legislature restored the rule but provided that school districts that had liability insurance were responsible for damages up to the amount of coverage. The principle of governmental immunity has also been tested in courts in Colorado, Iowa, Kansas, Montana, Oregon, Pennsylvania, and Utah. However, the courts in some of these states have been hesitant to depart from the precedent and insist that the legislature of the state rather than the courts should waive the rule.

In some incidences, immunity has been upheld. In the case of *Cerrone v. Milton School District*, 479 A. 2d 675 (Pa. 1984), Cerrone received an injury while wrestling in high school. As a result of a suit against the Milton School District in Pennsylvania, the court ruled that the school district was immune from suit as provided by the Tort Claims Act. In another case, *Kain v. Rockridge Community Unit School District #300*, 453 NE 2d 118 (Ill. 1983), a football coach was granted immunity when Kraig Kain sued the Rockridge Community Unit School District for alleged negligent conduct by the coach, who let him play in a game without observing the required number of practices before participation.

In most cases, however, governmental immunity has been modified, abrogated, or subjected to exceptions by either legislation or judicial decision. Schools and school districts may legally purchase liability insurance (many states expressly authorize school districts to carry liability insurance) to protect themselves when they become involved in lawsuits, although this insurance does not necessarily mean governmental immunity has been or will be waived (NEA 1950). Of course, in the absence of insurance and save harmless laws (laws requiring that school districts assume the liability of the teacher whether negligence is proved or not), any judgment rendered against a school district must be met out of personal funds. School districts in Connecticut, Massachusetts, New Jersey, and New York have save harmless laws. Wyoming also permits school districts to indemnify or financially protect employees.

A strong belief exists among educators and many people in the legal profession that the doctrine of sovereign immunity should be abandoned. In some states, students injured as a result of negligence are ensured recompense for damages directly or indirectly, either because governmental immunity has been abrogated or because school districts are legally required to indemnify school employees against financial loss. In other states, if liability insurance has been secured, a possibility exists that the injured may recover damages incurred. When searching for liability insurance, it is important to secure coverage that covers damages as well as the cost of defense.

Although school districts have been granted governmental immunity in many states, teachers, coaches, and administrators do not have such immunity. A 1938 decision of an Iowa court provides some of the thinking regarding teachers' responsibilities for their own actions (*Montanick v. McMillin*, 225 Iowa 442, 452–453, 458, 280 NW 608 [1938]):

> [The employee's liability] is not predicated upon any relationship growing out of his [her] employment, but is based upon the fundamental and underlying laws of torts, that he [she] who does injury to the person or property of another is civilly

liable in damages for the injuries inflicted ... The doctrine of *respondeat superior*, literally, "let the principle answer," is an extension of the fundamental principle of torts, and an added remedy to the injured party, under which a party injured by some act of misfeasance may hold both the servant and the master liable. The exemption of governmental bodies and their officers from liability under the doctrine of *respondeat superior* is a limitation of exception to the rule of *respondeat superior* and in no way affects the fundamental principle of torts that one who wrongfully inflicts injury upon another is liable to the injured person for damages. . . . An act of misfeasance is a positive wrong, and every employee, whether employed by a private person or a municipal corporation, owes a duty not to injure another by a negligent act of commission.

In *Short v. Griffiths, Lee, & Redman*, 255 S.E. 2d 479 (1979), the baseball coach and athletic director were not entitled to assert a governmental immunity defense for their acts of negligence even though the school and school board received immunity. Therefore sports managers, teachers, instructors, and coaches have the responsibility and the duty to be aware of salient factors and situations that can lead to litigation. Some potential litigious factors include ignorance of the law,

Only qualified and certified personnel should deal with injury.

ignoring the law, failure to act, and failure to warn (Appenzeller 2005, Clement 2004). Failing to provide accessibility for persons with disabilities to classes or programs, ignoring Title IX and equal protection mandates concerning equal opportunity, failure to inspect facilities and equipment on a regular basis, and failure to properly repair or replace equipment, omitting warning and hazard signs or failing to issue warning statements during strenuous and potentially hazardous activities are domains of litigation that have produced individual awards in excess of $1–2 million (Appenzeller and Baron 1995; Uberstien 1996).

Most often, the physical educator, coach, or athletic and activities director is responsible for many of the ministerial or operational acts cited. This notion was upheld in the Michigan Court of Appeals in *Ross v. Consumer Power Company* (1984), in which it was contended that individual government employees are immune from liability only when they are

1. Acting during the course of their employment, and are acting, or reasonably believe that they are acting, within the scope of their authority
2. Acting in good faith
3. Performing discretionary-decisional, as opposed to ministerial-operational, acts

Hence, when a student in a beginning swimming class, as in *Webber v. Yio*, 383 NW 2d 230 (1985), dove into a pool and failed to surface, and efforts to revive him failed, the court held that the system of rescue was a discretionary act for which the instructor was immune from liability; however, the instructor's failure to warn participants about the danger and risks of the activity and the negligent supervision and resuscitation procedures were ministerial acts for which the instructor may be held liable (Clement 2004; Fried 1999).

The courts have also heard legal liability cases involving such areas as negligence, intentional torts, supervision, product liability, and civil rights including gender equity, American's with disabilities, and procedural due process.

LEGAL CONCEPTS IMPACTING PHYSICAL EDUCATION AND SPORT

Tort, contract, and constitutional law are to lawyers what lesson plans, bats, balance boards, and soccer balls are to physical education teachers, coaches, and recreation specialists. This section will explore some of the legal concepts that serve as the basis for adjudication in most regular and civil courts in the United States, as well as in many other countries in the global community. Some of the legal concepts that will be addressed are torts, including negligence, supervisory negligence, intentional torts, and product liability.

Tort

A *tort*, derived from the Latin *torquere* meaning to twist, is a legal wrong resulting in direct or indirect injury to another individual or to property or to one's reputation. A tortious act is a wrongful act for which the court will provide a remedy often in the form of damages. The broad categories of tort most often found in physical education, recreation, and sport include negligence, including supervisory negligence, intentional tort, and product liability.

Negligence

Negligence is often described as carelessness. It is doing something a reasonable person would not be expected to do or failing to do something a reasonable person would be expected to do. Negligence occurs when a professional does or fails to do an act that another person would be expected to do. It is conduct that falls below the standard expected for the activity (Restatement of the Law of Torts, Second, 1965). For a person to be found negligent by the courts all five elements of negligence must be present: duty, breach of duty owed, breach of the duty causing the injury (causation), proximate cause (foreseeable consequences), and damage or harm that is measurable in terms of monetary compensation. Physical educators, recreation specialists, and sport managers have a high professional duty as a result of their positions. This duty is much higher than the duty of an ordinary person. Two factors contribute significantly to this duty. One is the image he or she projects to the public. The other

involves the skills and qualifications recognized as essential to the position. For example, it is recognized that a physical educator or coach has a professional duty to the students with whom he or she works. In addition, the job description suggests that the physical educator will have special skills in exercise science, sport psychology, and sport management, among others. Further, the physical educator or coach will know skill progressions and systems for assessing readiness of students for those activities to be employed. Also, the public assumes that first-aid and emergency care provisions will be readily available should they be needed.

Duty and legal standard of care are principally the same and used interchangeably in this chapter. The court determines duty by using experts, texts, curriculum resources, professional standards, and the expertise of persons holding similar positions. Within the medical profession written documents spell out the professional's duty and standard of care. No such documents exist in physical education and sport. This forces the court making decisions concerning physical education and sport to turn to experts for information and advice.

Once the duty has been established, parties to the lawsuit will bring forward information from the plaintiff to document that the duty was breached and from the defendant to document that the duty was honored. At times all parties agree that the duty existed and was breached. If it is found that the duty has been breached, then a direct cause between the injury and breached duty must be established. Yes, the person was injured. Yes, there was a duty of care and the duty was breached. But did the breach cause the injury? Again, evidence will be presented to the court by both parties in an effort to establish the fact of causation. Proximate cause of the injury is determined by whether or not the harm to the injured person was foreseeable. Could the professional have anticipated that harm would result from the activity and/or the specific actions? And last, are there substantial injuries?

To be found negligent the court must prove that the teacher or coach had a duty to the injured victim, that the duty was breached, that the breached

Box 13-1   An Employee May Be Negligent Because of the Following Reasons:

- Appropriate and reasonable care was not taken (carelessness).
- Provided faulty instruction or supervision.
- Although due care was exercised, he or she acted in circumstances that created risks.
- His or her acts created an unreasonable risk of direct and immediate injury to others, such as in unreasonable matching of participants.
- He or she set in motion a force that was unreasonably hazardous to others.
- He or she created a situation in which third persons such as students or inanimate forces, such as gymnastic equipment, or soccer goals may reasonably have been expected to injure others.
- He or she allowed students to use dangerous equipment or devices although they were untrained to use them.
- He or she failed to provide emergency plan, protocol, and care.
- He or she permitted students to participate in a risk activity beyond their capacity.
- He or she violated a law, statute, or regulation.
- He or she did not control a third person such as a special child, whom he or she knew to be likely to inflict intended injury on others.
- He or she did not give adequate warning, concerning hidden dangers.
- He or she did not look out for persons, such as students, who were in danger or at risk.
- He or she acted without sufficient skill and care.
- He or she did not make sufficient preparation, such as inspecting the facility, to avoid an injury to students before beginning an activity in which such preparation is reasonably necessary.
- He or she failed to inspect and/or repair equipment or devices to be used by students.
- He or she prevented someone, such as another teacher, from assisting a student who was endangered or injured, although the student's peril was not caused by his or her negligence.

The ability to foresee potential danger is crucial to physical educators, recreation specialists, and coaches.

duty was the cause or reason for the injury, and that the harm was foreseeable. If any one of those elements is missing the teacher or coach usually will not be found negligent (see box 13-1).

So far our discussion has been of general negligence. Gross negligence and willful, wanton, and reckless misconduct are more severe types of

Expert teaching, careful supervision, and quality equipment make for fun as well as safe participation.

Box 13-2   Cardinal Principles of Supervision

- Always be there!
- Be qualified and certified (first aid, CPR/AED)
- Be active and hands-on
- Know participants' health status
- Know participants' fitness and developmental level
- Monitor and enforce rules and regulations
- Monitor and scrutinize the environment
- Inform participants of potential hazards and dangers
- Inform students of safety and emergency plan procedures
- Be vigilant and in control
- Be prudent, careful, prepared, and trained

negligence. It should be noted that only general negligence is covered under immunity statutes. Yasser et al. (2003), in contrasting the forms of negligence refer to general negligence as a failure to exercise great care concerning conduct that is unreasonably risky; gross negligence as failure to exercise even that care that a careless person would use; and willful, wanton, and reckless misconduct as an intentional act of unreasonable character in total disregard of human safety (see box 13-2).

Negligence will be litigated under its individual state law. To be found negligent in Illinois, for example, the teacher or coach will have to have violated the gross negligence standard, whereas most states will find the teacher or coach negligent under the general standard. There is no research that indicates that there is less chance of a professional being found negligent in a state where the standard is higher or requires gross negligence than in a state where one need only meet the general negligence standard.

Defenses to Negligence

Defenses to negligence are contributory negligence, comparative negligence, and assumption of risk. When the injured party has done something that contributed to the cause of his or her injury it is called contributory negligence. A student who refuses to follow instructions, a person who will not wear prescribed protective equipment, and one who ignores safety instructions may be found guilty of contributory negligence. A contributory negligence claim against a minor is more difficult to prove than the same claim would be against an adult; however, contributory negligence has served as a defense helpful to teachers, recreation leaders, and coaches (see box 13-3).

Comparative negligence (an approach to fault) that has been accepted in most states is a mathematical formula to allocate fault to both plaintiff and defendant on a percentage basis. Traditionally, if a person was over 50 percent at fault, he or she was considered to be 100 percent at fault. Under comparative negligence or comparative fault, the parties are liable for financial resources according to their percentage of fault. This change in the law has been of concern to conscientious professionals who believe that they may be given a small percentage of 5 or 10 percent fault when their work has been exemplary. Persons attempting to make professionals more safety conscious often use this as a reason to improve safety.

Box 13-3 Coaches' Guide to Avoid Charges of Negligence

- Be familiar with the health status of students.
- Be familiar with the student's fitness, skill, and maturation level so appropriate matching is enabled.
- Require medical clearance of students who have been seriously injured or ill.
- Render services only in those areas in which one is fully qualified and certified.
- Follow proper procedures in the case of injury, illness, or emergency.
- See that medical personnel are available at all games and are on call for practice sessions.
- See that all activities are conducted in safe areas.
- Be careful not to diagnose or treat a student's injuries.
- See that approved protective equipment is properly fitted and worn regularly by players who need such equipment.
- See that teaching and coaching techniques and methods are current and provide for the safety of the participants.
- See that only qualified personnel are assigned specific responsibilities.
- See that proper instruction and warning are given before students are permitted to engage in class or contests.
- See that a careful and accurate record is kept of injuries and illness and HIPAA procedures followed.
- Act as a prudent, careful, and discerning teacher or coach whose students are the first consideration.

Assumption of risk is another defense. The courts tend to assume that persons engaging in sport know that they are taking risks, sometimes taking big risks. Sport and physical activity is one of the few areas in which society can learn to take risks in a controlled environment. Risk taking is an inherent aspect of physical activity and sport. Therefore, risks will be present in our programs. The important component for the physical educa-tion and sport professional to keep in mind is that the participants must be fully aware of the risks so that they can make an informed decision about tak-ing the risks, that no student is forced to perform beyond his or her capacity, that instructors have ad-equate documentation to prove that students are ready for risk-taking activities, that all persons are informed in writing and verbally of the risks in-volved, and that each has signed a statement ac-knowledging his or her understanding of the risks. There are two kinds of assumption of risk, express (signing a document) and implied (merely taking part in the activity). A defense of assumption of risk is valuable only when the parties know of the risks, understand the nature of the risks, and freely choose to incur the risk (Clement 2004).

Damages for Negligence

Damages for negligence are compensatory, or money to pay for medical, rehabilitation, and other expenses directly related to the incident. Comparative fault must be considered in the compensatory damage award. If the comparative fault for a $1,000,000 damage award is 40 per-cent to the plaintiff or injured victim and 60 per-cent to the school district, the victim will receive $600,000.

Cases Involving Negligence

The majority of the cases involving physical edu-cation and sport seem to be negligence cases. They tend to be found in improper supervision, or faulty instruction, faulty facilities, and inappro-priate or damaged equipment (Clement 2004). Supervision is an important consideration in all professional activities and programs and profes-sionals need to assess the adequacy of supervision at all times. It is impossible to be focused on all students at all times. Professionals should design their lesson plans with supervision in mind. Can you justify, explain, or if need be, defend your lo-cation in the gymnasium, field, or pool at all times. What is your scanning technique? And what do you look for? Another topic often men-tioned in litigation is unmatched participants.

Unmatched means a significant difference in either size or skill. Many professionals are conscious of difference in size or maturation; however, differences in skill may be a greater factor in injuries. Such simple things as using a tag game among a wide range of games may subject some children not only to constant failure and humiliation but also to risk and ultimately injury.

Faulty instruction may be teaching the skill incorrectly, failing to assess the student's readiness for an advanced skill or stunt, requiring students to perform beyond their ability, or failing to challenge highly skilled students causing them to create their own challenges. An in-depth analysis of the faulty teaching standard argues for using an individualized approach in the classroom and gymnasium.

Individuals assume risk when participating in collision sports such as soccer.

Fourteen-year-old Michael Iverson suffered a double fracture of his right forearm while playing soccer in a physical education class. He sued the physical education teacher and the school district for negligent instruction and supervision; he attributed his injuries to the school's failure in these areas. The district maintained that soccer was a hazardous recreational activity that fell within the description of a body contact sport as defined in the immunity standards for hazardous activities. "Government Code section 831.7 provides a public entity immunity against liability for negligence when brought by anyone who participates in a hazardous recreational activity that created a substantial risk of injury" (*Iverson v. Muroc Unified School District* et al., 221 [1995]). The Superior Court of California found for the school district on the basis of immunity. Iverson appealed. The Court of Appeals of California, Fifth Appellate District, reversed and ruled for Iverson stating, a body contact sport incorporated into a school time physical education class is not a "recreational" activity within the meaning of section 831.7.

In *Rieger v. Altona Area School District*, 768 A. 2d 912 (2001), thirteen-year-old Erika Rieger, a member of the junior high cheerleading squad, sustained dental and facial lacerations from a fall following a failed stunt. She fell from the shoulders of her new partner as they were executing a "liberty," a stunt involving a shoulder sit. Erika fell hitting the hardwood floor. Her parents filed a negligence claim against the school. Within the complaint was a claim that mats should have been used to protect their daughter from the fall. The school district responded that it was entitled to immunity. The trial court found for the school. The Riegers appealed, stressing the need for mats in this type of practice and documenting cases that had required the use of mats in executing stunts. The defendants moved to the defense of real property extension, in this case the 42 Pa. C.S. section 8543(b)(3). This is a new type of immunity becoming popular in physical injury cases. The court stated, "Even assuming that failure to provide mats in the cheerleading practice areas amounted to a negligent act causing Erika's injury, such negligent conduct would not fall within the real property exception to the act." Thus, the trial and appeals courts found for the school.

Thirteen-year-old David Lupash tripped and fell in the ocean during the final event of a Junior Lifeguard competition in Long Beach, California. David ran down the beach and into the surf, he stepped into something like a hole, lost his balance, and fell face down. He is now a quadriplegic. Lupash was an accomplished swimmer and distance freestyler. Weeks before the incident he took part in a Junior Lifeguard program on beach safety. He was repeatedly admonished not to dive into shallow water because you could hit your head on the bottom and break your neck, which would cause spinal cord injury or other types of serious injuries. Instead he was told to use a dolphin dive to protect his head (*Lupash v. City of Seal Beach* et al., 922–923 [1999]). Witnesses said he did a racing dive into very shallow water. Among his complaints to the court was that the city was negligent in using the beach for the lifeguard competition and in telling him to run into the water as fast as he could without doing a bottom check. The trial and court of appeals found for the city. They noted that hidden sandbars occur as a natural condition of beaches and that California courts had consistently held that, "public entities do not owe a general duty of care to the public to provide safe beaches or to warn against concealed dangers caused by natural conditions of the ocean." Further, they noted that if Lupash as a junior guard were encouraged to walk slowly down the beach and carefully check every component of the bottom before entering the water to execute a rescue, he would jeopardize the safety and lives of others.

Max Draughon died of heat stroke one day after collapsing following the first morning of contact football practice. He was doing wind sprints at the time he collapsed. The temperature was 78 degrees, and humidity exceeded 70 percent on the day of the incident. Although water was available, it was unclear whether Max had received any (*Draughon v. Harnett County Board of Education*, No. COA02-646, 2003 N.C. App. LEXIS 1047).

Plaintiff filed a wrongful death action against the school and individuals involved. The trial court granted summary judgment to the school; it appealed. The Court of Appeals of North Carolina affirmed the trial court's decision: "No genuine issue of material fact exists regarding the liability to the plaintiff."

Saul Cruz, a member of the Tottenville High School varsity football team, was practicing under supervision when he ran into a push sled that had been stored within three or four feet of the sidelines. The court agreed that the push sled was in a dangerous position; however, sufficient confusion existed over who was responsible for placing the equipment on the sidelines that the court chose to dismiss the case.

Negligence and Supervision

Children are entrusted by parents to physical education, physical activity, and sport programs, and parents expect that adequate supervision will be provided to minimize the possibility of accidents. Reasonable supervision includes the duty to establish minimum and maximum levels of supervision for each supervisor and/or activity and the duty to implement and monitor these crucial standards. Questions of liability regarding supervision usually pertain to two points: (1) the extent of the supervision (number and type [i.e., age, fitness level] of children and location) and (2) the quality of the supervision (certification, experience qualification,).

The first point, the extent of supervision, raises the question of whether adequate supervision was provided. This question is difficult to answer because it varies from situation to situation. However, the answers to these questions help determine adequate supervision: "Would additional supervision have eliminated the accident?" and "Is it reasonable to expect that additional supervision should have been provided?"

The second point, the quality of the supervision, addresses expectations that competent personnel should handle specialized programs in physical education, recreation, and sport. If the supervisors of such activities do not possess proper training in such work, the question of negligence can be raised.

Proper supervision is required for safe participation in physical activity and sport.

Playground activities need to be supervised to minimize the risk of injury.

It is crucial to have preservice, in-service, and continual professional development for all employees to ensure that proper training, including supervision, is an ongoing feature of the management scheme. Policy manuals containing supervision ratios and qualifications are also recommended.

Even with these safeguards legal experts estimate that over 50 percent of all court cases concerning physical education, recreation, and sports injuries deal with some dimension of supervision. Whether checking on the health status of the participant or managing a weight room or teaching a physical education class, qualified supervisors must be in charge. In Michigan, a high school principal and athletic director were sued for allegedly breaching their duty to a fifteen-year-old boy who

was severely injured when weights fell on him (*Vargo v. Svitchan*, 301 NW 2d 1 [Mich. 1981]). The boy accused the administration of negligence for failing to supervise his coach, to provide for proper ventilation in the weight room, and to observe rule violations for illegal summer football practice. The boy further charged the school's athletic director with negligence for failing to supervise the sports program. The Michigan court noted that the athletic director had the responsibility of enforcing the rules and supervising activities because of his specialized training in sports. It also reasoned that the athletic director had the authority to eliminate unsafe practices engaged in by the coaches under his direction.

In *Niles v. San Rafael*, 116 Cal. Rptr. 733 (Ca. 1974), a city park was held responsible for failure to properly supervise a physical activity when a student was hit over the head with a bat during a softball game. The nature, location, training, and number of supervisors should always be of concern to prudent management.

In another case, *Chudasama v. Metropolitan Government of Nashville*, 914 SW2d 922 (Tenn. App. 1995), a seventh-grade female requested permission to use the locker-room bathroom, where she was assaulted by several female class-

Careful selection and fitting of quality equipment keeps potential product liability suits to a minimum.

mates. Even though the teacher could not be in the boys' and girls' locker rooms at the same time, the case was dismissed because of unforeseeable circumstances.

In *Gifford v. Grime*, et al., No. 233667, 202 Mich. App. LEXIS. 1047 (2002), twelve-year-old Gifford, attending her first volleyball practice, was asked to move the volleyball standards from the gymnasium to the cafeteria. As she and a friend were dragging the poles to the new location, one of the poles became detached from the base and landed on her foot, crushing her toe and bones of the foot. The volunteer coach overseeing the practice did not inspect the poles before they were moved nor did she give instructions about moving the poles. Gifford sued the superintendent, athletic director, principal, three physical education teachers, and the volunteer coach. She alleged breach of their duty of supervision, staff training, inspection of equipment, and provision of adequate emer-

gency care. Defendants claimed immunity. The trial and court of appeals held for the school on immunity.

Jeremy Arteman, in *Arteman v. Clinton Community Unit School District*, No. 15. 198 Ill. 2d 475 N.E. 756 (2000), broke two bones in his right leg while roller blading in a physical education class. The students had an option of running laps or renting roller blades and roller blading laps. The rented roller blades had a toe brake. The school district did not provide skin guards, elbow guards, knee guards, helmets, gloves, or any other safety equipment. Arteman, represented by his father, sued. He alleged negligence and willful or wanton misconduct in the school's failure to provide safety equipment and suitable roller blades and failure to supervise the equipment and the activity.

The school district claimed immunity. The trial court found for the school under immunity, which provided "immunity from claims alleging a failure to supervise and that the plaintiff's failure to allege sufficient facts to establish willful and wanton misconduct, an exception to . . . immunity." The county circuit court granted the school district's motion to dismiss. The appellate court reversed. This case bridges on the gap between the first main category of tort (negligence) and the second main category, that of intentional torts.

Intentional Torts

Intentional torts are injuries caused by an intended or deliberate act or failure to act. The act is intentional; it is not necessary to intend to harm someone. Battery, assault, and offensive touching are examples of intentional torts to persons. Battery is hitting someone; assault is threatening someone so that they believe their life is in danger. Assault does not involve physical contact. Offensive touching is making contact with another in a way that is offensive to the second party; it ranges from continuous poking among children to sexual misconduct. Offensive touching is often part of the civil rights theory of sexual harassment and may even be part of the criminal act of rape.

Defenses to Intentional Torts

Defenses to intentional torts are consent, self-defense, or defense of others, and necessity or discipline. Consent is actively working to obtain the behavior and/or accepting the behavior; self-defense is fighting to save oneself or another. Necessity or discipline is using intentional force because the situation warrants it for the safety and well-being of others or the individuals involved. The latter should never be used unless it is the last resort. Professionals no longer have the power to use physical force to discipline children; they may attempt to break up a fight and separate the fighters if the fight could bring harm to one of the participants or to others in the vicinity.

Horseplay and/or hazing is an intentional tort of grave concern in physical education and sport. Traditionally, considerable horseplay and hazing existed during initiations and in the rituals of winning. Not long ago swimming meets ended with the swimmers, coaches, officials, and often tables and chairs, being tossed into the water. Today, throwing someone into the water is an intentional tort and should the person thrown into the water die as a result of making contact with the edge of the pool or some other permanent fixture, the person who threw him or her into the water could be brought to criminal court and could serve time in prison.

Damages for Intentional Torts

Damages for intentional torts are compensatory damages including medical expenses, rehabilitation costs, and other expenses to make the victim whole. Punitive damages, a money damage award based on the assets of the person, institution, or agency that caused the injury, may also be awarded. This punitive damage award is a sum assessed to the injury-causing party to stop him or her from repeating a similar behavior. High-profile punitive damage awards are often mistaken by the public as compensatory damage awards. Unless a state has a specific lid on punitive damage awards the awards are established through an analysis of the dollar sum that will make the offending party

hurt. A thousand dollar damage award against a first-year teacher might equal a million dollar award against a large corporation.

Cases Involving Intentional Torts

Sport initiations (hazing) and horseplay are often the areas that involve intentional torts. In an initiation of students to the football team Brian Seamons was tied unclothed to a horizontal towel bar with athletic tape by his Sky View High School football teammates in the boys' locker room (*Seamons v. Snow*, 1229 [1996]). A girl he had dated was brought into the shower room to see him. Brian reported the incident to school administrators and other authorities, including the football coach and the principal. The coach brought Brian before the football team, accused Brian of betraying the team by bringing the incident to the attention of the administration and others, and told Brian to apologize to the team. Brian refused to apologize, was dismissed from the team, and brought a cause of action against the school. The trial court found for the school; the court of appeals affirmed the trial court's intentional tort claim but remanded Brian's First Amendment right to tell authorities about the incident for further proceedings.

Reckless misconduct and intentional tort cases such as *Nabozny v. Barnhill*, 31 Ill. App. 3d 212 (1975), in which a goalie was kicked in the head during a high school soccer match and *Oswald v. Township High School District*, 84 Ill. App. 3d 723 (1980), in which a student sued another student for kicking him while participating in a physical education basketball class often seem to go unnoticed until very serious injury such as in some most recent ice hockey cases or where high-profile professional players are involved. Teachers and coaches, however, face a continuous and serious challenge in this arena.

SPORT PRODUCT LIABILITY

The sale of sporting goods is a multibillion-dollar industry. The term *sport product liability* refers to the liability of the manufacturer, processor, wholesaler, retailer, seller, lessor, or anyone furnishing a defective product to the market (i.e., participant, consumer). Owners and agencies leasing sports and physical activity equipment may also be sued under product liability. Product liability is one of the "strict" or automatic liability areas. A product is considered defective when the defect existed at the time the product left the manufacturer. The defect may be a manufacturer's defect, a design defect, or a failure to warn. A product may be defective when it (1) contains a manufacturing defect and departs from its intended design even though all possible care was exercised in the preparation and marketing of the product; (2) is defective in design and the foreseeable risks of harm posed by the product could have been reduced or avoided by the adoption of a reasonable alternative design; (3) is defective because of inadequate instructions or warnings when the foreseeable risks of harm posed by the product could have been reduced; or (4) fails to comply with safety standards, misrepresentation or recall. (Restatement of the Law, of Torts, Third, Product Liability 1997). Professionals, sport personnel, owners, teachers, coaches, camp leaders, and others responsible for selection and purchase of sport and fitness equipment need to be aware of product liability. Professionals in physical education and sport may become primary parties to a product liability case only when they fail to follow the manufacturer's, retailer's, and seller's instructions for using and/or maintaining a product or for failing to pass on warnings to those who will ultimately use the product.

To sue for product liability, the injured party has only to prove the product caused the injury. The injured party does not have to prove specific elements as found in negligence. Courts are placing more and more responsibility on the manufacturer to provide a reasonable standard of product to the market and to discover weaknesses and defects in the product. It is reasoned that the manufacturer or seller is in a better position than the consumer to become aware of, and to correct or eliminate, the defect. The manufacturer is re-

quired to exercise due care in designing, manufacturing, providing directions for specific use, as well as packaging and labeling (e.g., warning labels if appropriate) of the product, including making available new replacement parts, and if needed to recall the product. Many manufacturers and retailers often send additional copies of the directions and warning labels to the purchaser and management in case they have been thrown away by those who assemble the equipment (e.g., diving boards, flooring). The manufacturer guarantees the product to be safe for consumer use if the product is used in the specific way it was intended. Failure to do so is negligence in product liability.

Defenses to Sport Product Liability

Defenses to product liability are contributory negligence, assumption of risk, misuse, and disclaimers. Contributory negligence means the injured party was negligent in the use of the equipment. Assumption of risk is the same as explained earlier; sport is a controlled risk environment and there is risk in using various types of equipment in sport. Misuse is the use of equipment for something other than its intended use. Purchase of equipment for sport that is clearly beyond the participants' level of skill is a form of misuse. Disclaimers provide the industry the opportunity to point out the proper and intended use for the equipment and to clearly state in writing where its liability toward the purchaser and potential user stops.

Damages

Damages are compensatory, comparative where appropriate, and punitive. Injunctions, the court stopping the use of a product, are also common to this area.

Sport Product Liability Court Cases

When a high school student-athlete was injured by a pitching machine whose manufacturer failed to include operating instructions, as in *Schmidt v. Dudley*

Sports Co., 279 NE 2d Indiana Court of Appeals, 2d Dist., 266 (1972), the jury found the company negligent.

Under the strict liability doctrine, the plaintiff must establish proof that the product contained a defect causing the injury or damage. In addition to this doctrine, a breach of the manufacturer's warranty in which the product or object fails to function according to its written specifications can also be just cause for awarding damages. A breached warranty does not require the injured party to prove negligence or recklessness.

The number of suits involving product liability has increased dramatically in the last few years, with football helmets and equipment being most often mentioned. Defective design, fitting, and failure to warn were the basis for many of the complaints. In *Rawlings Sporting Goods Company, Inc. v. Daniels*, 619 SW 2d 435 (1981) the manufacturer's failure to warn that the helmet could not protect against injuries was key in Daniels being awarded $1.5 million from the district court.

Kelly Fiske sustained severe injuries resulting in quadriplegia when he tackled an opposing player. He sued not only the helmet manufacturer but also his coach for negligent coaching and supervision. He was awarded over $12 million from the manufacturer, but the court found for the coach in *Fiske v. MacGregor Division of Brunswick*, et al., 464 A.2d 719 (1983). Similar product liability cases in 1991, 2001, and 2004 have awarded over $10 million (Clement 2004).

Other frequent targets of product liability litigation besides the manufacturers of football equipment, include those producing diving boards, flooring, gymnastics, exercise, and ski equipment.

Sporting goods manufacturers are now calling for a national product liability standard that would stabilize the rules under which they operate. However, legislators are having difficulty finding a solution acceptable to both consumers and business. At present the clarity about how product liability cases will be treated contributes to the high cost and the availability of product liability insurance (see boxes 13-4 and 13-5).

Box 13-4 Reducing the Risks Associated with Sport Product Liability

- Establish and enforce written policies and procedures related to equipment usage. These must be distributed to and adhered to by all.
- Become involved in collecting pertinent facts and information associated with injury and illness. This procedure can result in discouraging unwarranted claims.
- Purchase the best quality equipment available. Equipment should be carefully inspected, evaluated, and tested. When equipment is purchased, records should be kept regarding such items as date of purchase, parts list, assembly directions, and operating instructions.
- Purchase only from reputable dealers. Reputable dealers stand behind their products and provide certified or appropriate replacements when called for.
- Use only reputable reconditioning equipment companies that have high standards. For example, the NOCSAE stamp of approval should apply to reconditioned football and lacrosse helmets.
- Keep a maintenance, repair, reconditioning, and replacement log.
- Follow manufacturer's instructions for fitting, adjusting, and repairing equipment, particularly protective equipment. Also, urge participants to wear protective equipment regularly.
- Be careful not to blame someone or something for the injury without just cause. Furthermore, it is best to confine such remarks to the accident report.
- Good teaching and prudent supervising are important. Do not use any drills or techniques not approved by professional associations and respected leaders in the field.
- An emergency care plan should be prepared and ready to be implemented when needed.
- Insurance coverage for accident and general liability should be purchased or be available to all parties concerned, including students, athletes, staff members, and schools.
- When and if serious injuries occur, preserve items of evidence associated with the injury, such as pieces of equipment.

Box 13-5	Recommendations Regarding Helmets

- Only the best as well as certified and approved equipment should be purchased.
- All players should have proper and certified equipment.
- The coach with guidance from professionals should see that the helmet fits properly. Only professionals should alter or change equipment.
- The helmet should be inspected weekly.
- Both players and parents should be informed about risk involved in using the helmet as well as the risk of engaging in the activity.
- Teach proper techniques in the use of the helmet.
- In event of injury, no one should remove the helmet during transportation to the hospital.
- The helmet should be removed safely by appropriate personnel.

CIVIL RIGHTS, SPORTS, AND THE COURTS

In recent years civil rights laws have played a significant role in the physical education and sporting scene. These laws have evolved from the application of the Constitution including the First Amendment (prayer in practice and at games in the public school); the Fourth Amendment (search and seizure), including drug testing; and the Fourteenth Amendment that plays a principal role in all forms of equity and due process complaints. Title IX and ADA may be classified as adjunct constitutional issues. Professionals at all levels of involvement in the physical education and sporting process must be aware and sensitive to not only local and state litigation, but also district and national court opinions and actions when civil rights are challenged.

First Amendment

The First Amendment states, "Congress shall make no law respecting an establishment of religion, or prohibiting the free exercise thereof; or abridging the freedom of speech or of the press; or the right of the people peaceably to assemble, and to petition the government for a redress of grievances." First Amendment rights are the freedom of religion, speech, and press.

Freedom of religion as it relates to prayer in graduation ceremonies, sports competitions, and in the locker room has become highly controversial. Results of litigation over the past ten years permitted student-initiated prayer in the public school (*Board of Education of Westside Community Schools v. Mergens*, 1990; and *Doe v. Duncanville Independent School District*, 1993, 1995). Prayer initiated by school authorities was denied (*Lee v. Weisman*, 1992). All of this changed in June 2000, in *Santa Fe v. Doe* et al., 530 U.S. 290; 120 S.Ct. 2266 (2000), when the United States Supreme Court in Santa Fe Independent School District found that student-led, student-initiated school prayer at football games violated the First Amendment Establishment Clause.

Fourth Amendment

The Fourth Amendment to the United States Constitution grants "The right of the people to be secure in their persons, houses, papers, and effects, against unreasonable searches and seizures." Drug testing and searches of an athlete or student's personal effects is the Fourth Amendment violation most often litigated in physical education and sport. *Vernonia School District v. Acton*, 515 U.S. 646; 115 S.Ct. 2386 (1995) is the United States Supreme Court decision that upheld the right of public school systems to randomly test athletes for drugs. The Oregon town of Vernonia created a policy for drug testing of athletes. When a seventh-grade student asked his parents to sign the consent form for drug testing so he could play football they said "no" and filed suit against the school for declaratory and injunctive relief. The parents' petition to the court said that the school's request violated Acton's Fourth, Fourteenth, and Oregon constitutional rights. The district court found for the school, the U.S. Court of Appeals, Ninth Circuit, reversed the finding for Acton. The Supreme Court affirmed the trial court's decision and reversed the court of appeals, and found that Vernonia School District's student-athlete drug policy was constitutional.

In *Gruenke v. Seip*, 225F. 3d 290 (2000), a swimming coach suspected one of his high school swimmers, also a minor, of being pregnant and required her to take a pregnancy test. She and her mother, Joan Gruenke, sued under both the Fourth Amendment rights as well as her First Amendment free speech and association rights. The coach was found not be entitled to immunity as Seip's conduct violated clearly established rights, including maintaining order in an environment in which one can safely participate.

Fourteenth Amendment

The Fourteenth Amendment to the United States Constitution has two clauses of extreme importance to professionals in physical education and sport. The equal protection clause is the basis for the Americans With Disabilities Act and for Title IX of the Education Amendments of 1972, often referred to as gender equity. The due process clause of the Fourteenth Amendment provides a system for challenging and or appealing the removal of a person's right to life, liberty, and freedom.

Equal Protection Clause

The equal protection clause of the Fourteenth Amendment to the United States Constitution states, "No state shall make or enforce any law which shall . . . deny to any person within its jurisdiction the equal protection of the law." To be effective in the courts an equal protection challenge must show that groups of people are being treated differently without justification. In sport an equal protection challenge, for example, would show that a group of people (women) were being treated differently from others (men) and that no legitimate reason existed to justify the difference in treatment. Title IX of the Education Amendment of 1972, statutory law in its broad context, addresses the concerns similar to those found in the equal protection clause and states that, "No person in the United States shall, on the basis of sex, be excluded

from participation in, be denied the benefit of, or be subject to discrimination under any education program or activity receiving federal financial assistance" (20 USC Section 1681[a], 1990).

An understanding of the difference between the United States Constitution and statutory law is helpful to understanding court decisions in gender equity, challenged legislation, and other civil rights. The Constitution represents traditional law upon which numerous court decisions on a wide range of topics have been made. It requires that the person filing a complaint obtain legal counsel, be willing to place his or her name on the complaint telling the world of his or her views, and be willing to take part in a trial. The decision, usually a federal court decision, becomes controlling law for the federal jurisdiction in which it was made. If made in the United States Supreme Court it will be controlling legislation for the entire United States.

Statutory law, in contrast, usually has a government administrative agency that oversees the law. This means that a person who believes that his or her rights have been violated files a complaint with the designated administrative agency. The complaint is anonymous, the process is free; the agency investigates the complaint and attempts to correct the situation. The decision is good for the person filing the complaint; no precedent beyond that person is guaranteed.

The results of the use of Constitutional law differ considerably from the results of the use of statutory law. The party successfully using the Constitution possesses the power to change the system; the party using statutory law merely corrects the immediate targeted behavior.

Gender Equity Litigation

Gender equity litigation is enormous, so only a brief example will be presented. Parents of young children used the equal protection clause of the United States Constitution in the courts to fight their battles for equity before Title IX. They included *Brenden v. Independent School District* (1972, 1973) where women were granted an opportunity to try out and participate on men's teams of cross-country skiing, running, and tennis when no team existed for women. Susan Hollander challenged and was denied an opportunity to participate in cross-country skiing (*Hollander v. Connecticut Interscholastic Athletic Conference, Inc.*, 1971, 1972), whereas Reed was granted her request to play golf (*Reed v. Nebraska*, 1972). Although golfer Haas was denied her injunction to play on the men's team by the trial court, the Supreme Court of Indiana reversed the trial court's decision stating, "that the regulation, while fair on its face, was discrimination in effect because a women's program did not exist and, thus, there was no opportunity for interscholastic competition. Note should be made that requests were granted in Nebraska, Minnesota, and Indiana, and denied in Connecticut" (Clement 2004). Each of these decisions had significant effects on the areas in which the litigation had been filed and probably served as building blocks for the impact that Title IX eventually has played on physical education and sport.

Title IX of the Education Amendments of 1972 was legislation dedicated to encouraging women to take an active role in science, mathematics, and medicine, and to make the educational environment one in which talented women would seek higher education. Little, if any, attention in the legislation was focused on sport. Whether it was the NCAA's very public efforts to fight Title IX or society's notion that sport was far more important than education that caused attention to turn to athletics is unclear. The punishment for a violation of Title IX is the removal of federal funding to an elementary, middle, secondary school, or institution of higher education. No school has ever lost its funding because of a violation of Title IX. The reader will note in the following cases that it is the Equal Protection Clause of the United States Constitution, not Title IX, that has changed the face of women's athletics. The results of litigation under the equal protection clause has often used disparate impact theory or equity by enrollment. Recent litigation under Ti-

Title IX ensures that physical education and sport opportunities are open to everyone. Coeducational flag football is popular at many schools.

tle IX uses the Office of Civil Rights' three-prong recommendations that examine (1) sport participation in the context of enrollment, (2) a continuous practice of expanding opportunities for women and, (3) accommodating the interests and abilities of women. Although the three areas are investigated in these cases, compliance with number one, sport participation in the context of enrollment, the old equal protection theory, is the easiest and most satisfactory means of reaching compliance. Also, note should be made that gender equity is one of the few areas in litigation in sport where nearly all the cases have been won by the plaintiffs; this is not true of litigation in tort. Among the classic collegiate cases in gender equity are *Haffer v. Temple* (1987), *Roberts v. Colorado State Board of Agriculture* (1993), *Cohen v. Brown University* 117 S.Ct. 1469 (1997), and *Pederson v. Louisiana State University*, et al., 213 F. 3d 858 (2000).

Haffer was a ten-year court process in which current participating and projected future athletes organized a class action suit to obtain equity in competitive opportunities, resources, and financial aid for women at Temple University. The complaint alleged discrimination in opportunities to compete, expenditure, recruiting, coaching, travel and per diem allowance, uniforms, equipment, supplies, training facilities and services, housing and dining facilities, academic tutoring, and publicity; all in violation of the Equal Protection Clause of the Fourteenth Amendment to the Constitution and the Pennsylvania Equal Rights Amendment. With the exception of meals, tutoring, facilities, and scheduling, the court ruled for the plaintiff in all areas.

Roberts was a suit against Colorado State University by women's fast-pitch softball players challenging the elimination of the sport during budget cuts. Colorado State failed all three components of the Office of Civil Rights recommendation. There was a difference of over 10 percent in the enrollment equation (5 percent or less is now required); no new teams for women had been added in the past twelve years, and persuasive evidence was provided to support the university's failure to accommodate the interests and abilities of women. The athletes succeeded in every request. Colorado State's petition to the United States Supreme Court was denied.

Cohen v. Brown University (1997) involved the demotion of women's gymnastics and volleyball teams from varsity to club status; men's water polo and golf were also demoted. An injunction was granted to the women athletes so that their teams could continue practicing and competing pending litigation. After a lengthy trial, the district court found Brown University in violation of Title IX (*Brown*, 1995). Among items in the remedial order Brown was required to "elevate and maintain as university-funded varsity status women's gymnastics, fencing, skiing, and water polo" (*Brown*, 1995). On November 21, 1996, the United States Court of Appeals affirmed the District Court's ruling; Brown had violated Title IX in demoting women's volleyball and gymnastics.

Pederson (2000), a recent case in collegiate gender equity, not only confirms the successes of plaintiffs, but leaves the door open for punitive

damages. Punitive damages are those damages awarded to punish an agency that has, in this case, intentionally discriminated against a person or persons and in the tort situation, one who has behaved in an outrageous manner. Pederson and others filed a class action suit, claiming violation of Title IX and the Equal Protection Clause of the United States Constitution against Louisiana State University in the United States District Court for the Middle District of Louisiana. They were denied an "equal opportunity to participate in intercollegiate athletics, equal opportunity to compete for and to receive athletic scholarships, and equal access to the benefits and services that LSU provides to its varsity intercollegiate athletes, and by discriminating against women in the provision of athletic scholarships and in the compensation paid coaches" (*Pederson, et al. v. Louisiana State University*, 858 [2000]). The suit was against the athletic director and chancellor in their individual and official capacity, and LSU board of supervisors, in its official capacity. They sought declaratory, injunctive, and monetary relief. The district court found that the enrollment ratio was 51 percent male and 49 percent female and the athletic participation ratio was 71 percent male and 29 percent female; that no opportunities for women had been added since 1993, thus failing the history of increasing sport participation; and that the women athletes were denied their request to add soccer and fast-pitch softball. Thus, the district court found Louisiana State University in violation of Title IX (*Pederson*, 917 [1996]). In the 1996 decision, Pederson had failed to create a class action or find that LSU had intentionally discriminated against women. So Pederson appealed to the United States Court of Appeals for the Fifth Circuit to review these issues. The Fifth Circuit affirmed the district court's judgment that Louisiana violated Title IX, reversed the district court's ruling on class, and sent the case back to court for further proceedings on these issues and damages.

The *Pederson* case has opened the door for awarding of potential punitive damages for discrimination and certainly has set a precedent for recent actions such as in *Barrett*, et al. *v. West Chester University of Pennsylvania of the State System of Higher Education*, et al., Civil Action No. 03-CV-4978, U.S. Dist. LEXIS 21095 (2003) where eight members of the gymnastics team brought suit when their team was eliminated. The university fell short in proving that it had treated the team equally and the court granted an injunction to restore the team. In a recent Supreme Court decision, *Jackson v. Birmingham Board of Education*, No. 02-1672 (2005), the Court has further broadened Title IX's interpretation to include whistle-blowers—male or female who report unequal treatment. Roderick Jackson, a physical education teacher and high school girls' basketball coach, was fired after he complained of discrimination against his players. Justice Sandra Day O'Conner in the Court's majority decision stated that without protection from discrimination, individuals who witness discrimination would likely not report it. Those who whistle blow will now receive roughly the same rights to sue for retaliation as those who raise charges for racial discrimination in employment. In such cases, now without fear that their institution will retaliate against them, teachers and coaches can be the ultimate enforcers of Title IX, which, it is reasoned, will perhaps hasten the leveling of our playing fields in a time when the politics of Title IX remain heated.

Title IX and gender equity litigation have not been limited to the arena of intercollegiate athletics. In 1978 a federal judge in Dayton, Ohio, ruled that girls may not be barred from playing on boys' school sport teams, even in such collision sports as football and wrestling. In the decision, the judge pointed out there might be many reasons why girls would not want to play on boys' teams, such as "reasons of stature or weight, or reasons of temperament, motivation, or interest. This is a matter of choice. But a prohibition without exception based on sex is not." The judge also indicated that the ruling would have national implications.

A ruling by the State Division on Civil Rights of New Jersey requires Little League baseball teams to permit girls to play. New Jersey was the first state to have such a ruling. The order also requires that both boys and girls be notified of team tryouts and that children of both sexes be treated equally. New York State also provides that no one may be disqualified from school sports teams because of gender.

In *Yellow Springs Exempted Village School District v. Ohio High School Athletic Association*, 647 F. 2d 651 (1981), it was found that the OHSAA rule preventing girls from playing on boys' teams was unconstitutional. The Indiana Supreme Court has also ruled that it is discriminatory for a high school to sponsor a boys' team and not a girls' team.

Although these decisions seem to be straightforward, they also have opened the doors for boys to participate on some girls' teams (i.e., softball) if appropriate opportunity is not afforded. Recently at a world Little League softball tournament several international teams forfeited their championship games rather than permit their all-girls teams to play a mixed gender U.S.–based team. As professionals, we must fight discriminating actions that continue to take place in our schools, clubs, playing fields, and stadiums. Hopefully the positive power of the sporting experience will serve to "level the playing fields" in the international arena as well.

Americans With Disabilities Act

The Americans With Disabilities Act (ADA) became law in 1990 and became effective in 1992. It relies on the Civil Rights Act of 1964 and the Rehabilitation Act of 1973. To qualify under the act the victim must prove that the violation occurred in a program receiving federal financial support, he or she is handicapped, qualified for the activity, and has been discriminated against because of the handicap. The Act has five titles that include (1) employment discrimination, (2) state and local government (schools), (3) public accommodations, (4) communication, and (5) retaliation. (20 USC, Section 1400, 1996).

Section two is a major concern of physical education teachers and section three (public accommodations) affects anyone managing physical activity, fitness, recreation, or entertainment enterprises. Title II works in conjunction with the Individuals With Disabilities Education Act (IDEA) and provides the basis for individualized education programs (20 USC, Section 1401, 1996, 20). Title III, Public Accommodations, provides for all persons with disabilities to have enjoyment of goods, services, facilities, privileges, and advantages of a facility operated by private enterprise. Penalties for violations can be as high as $50,000 for the first offense and $100,000 for each offense after that. The Civil Rights Act of 1991 added attorney fees and compensatory and punitive damage awards into the mix.

The Americans With Disabilities Act has created a great deal of litigation among special student-athletes who have lost interscholastic sport eligibility as a result of being too old. Accommodations for age discrimination have been unsuccessfully challenged in Michigan and Missouri where age was found not to be discriminatory because their peers of the same age were also denied eligibility (Appenzeller and Baron 1995). Few challenges concerning the integration of special needs students into the physical education setting have been litigated (Appenzeller 2005; Clement 2004).

Procedural Due Process

Procedural due process is a system created to enable a person whose right to life, liberty, or property has been challenged to receive fair treatment including an opportunity to state his or her side of the issue. Due process systems must exist whenever there is a possibility that either a liberty or property right will be removed. The removal of a swimming pool or health club membership, for example, may be deemed as the removal of a property right or not permitting an entire team to play be-

cause of a single player's behavior may not be a fair action as in *Diaz v. Board of Education of the City of New York and PSAL*, 618 NYS 2d 948 (N.Y. 1994). In *Hone v. Cortland City School District*, 985 F.Supp. 262 (N.D.N.Y. 1997), Hone, a sports reporter, sued the district because his access to school premises was denied. He sued stating his right to freedom of the press, freedom of association, and due process were violated. Hone lost his due process case because access to school premises is not a constitutionally protected right especially in this case where Hone was making unfavorable advances to the school's physical education teacher.

Due process usually, but not always, includes a hearing. It will include a written statement of charges and reasons for the charges and provide an opportunity for the defending party to present evidence, and if necessary, prepare for a hearing. The decision should be made by an impartial decision maker with the ruling based on the evidence provided. Again a policy manual governing the conduct of your organization in regard to due process is crucial.

LAWSUITS

Lawsuits need only a complaint to exist. The NCAA Committee on Competitive Safeguards and Medical Aspects of Sports assumes that those who sponsor and govern sport programs and events have accepted the responsibility of attempting to keep the risk of injury to a minimum. Because lawsuits are apt to arise in cases of injury that occurred despite the efforts of teachers, coaches, athletic directors, fitness instructors, and event managers, attempts should be made to ensure legal protection. The committee contends that the principal defense against an unwarranted complaint is documentation that adequate measures have been taken and programs, procedures, and policies have been established to minimize the risk inherent in physical activity and sport. No checklist is ever complete, but the Lawsuit Avoidance Checklist that follows should serve as a review of safety considerations for those people responsible for the management of interscholastic and intercollegiate sport programs. The list can also certainly be extrapolated for use in all physical activity environments and settings.

Lawsuit Avoidance Checklist
Preparticipation Medical Examination

Before a student or athlete is permitted to participate in physical education, organized sport, or physical activity, he or she should have a health status evaluation including a thorough medical examination by a well-trained physician. An annual update of a participant's health history, with the use of referral exams when warranted, should be sufficient. The NCAA Committee on Competitive Safeguards and Medical Aspects of Sports and the National Interscholastic Athletic Administrators Association (NIAAA) have developed health questionnaires and guidelines to assist in conducting preparticipation medical examinations as well as other sports medicine procedures.

Health and Liability Insurance

Each student-athlete should have, by parental or guardian coverage or institutional plan, access to customary hospitalization and medical benefits for defraying the cost of a significant injury or illness. Each participant and his or her parents should be informed in both writing and in the preseason meeting of what is and what is not covered, as well as various limitations of health and liability insurance coverage.

Preseason Preparation

Particular practices and controls should protect participants from premature exposure to the full rigors of the activity or sport. Preseason conditioning recommendations from the coaching staff and sports medicine team will help but not ensure, that the candidates arrive at the first practice in good condition. Attention to heat stress, dehydration, preseason fitness evaluation, and cautious competitive matching of candidates during the first weeks of practice are additional considerations.

Acceptance of Risk (Waivers and Consent)

Informed consent or waiver of responsibility by student-athletes, and/or their parents if the athlete is a minor, should be based on an informed awareness and acceptance of the risk of injury as a result of the student-athlete's participation in the sport. Not only does the individual share responsibility in preventive measures, but he or she also should fully appreciate the nature and significance of the risk involved. The forms (i.e., waiver, consent, permission) should be discussed with the student and parent during a preactivity or team meeting, and both students and parents should sign the forms.

A parent cannot waive the rights of a minor. Parents who sign waiver slips are merely waiving their right to sue for damages. Kaiser (1986) and Clement (2004) point out that although the courts have a penchant not to enforce liability waivers (*Wagenblast v. Odessa School District*, 758 P. 2d 968 [Wash. 1988]) such waivers are still helpful in risk management programs because they may discourage lawsuits and enhance legal defense of assumption of risk by increasing the participant's awareness of programmatic risk, rigors, and hazards. Consent forms that are clear, unambiguous, explicit and concise offer protection from the

Proper equipment, careful oversight, and certified personnel reduce risk as well as liability.

standpoint of showing that the child's parents/ participants were informed of the risks, understood the risks, agreed to encounter them, and have signed the form documenting permission to participate or engage in the activity.

Planning and Supervision

Proper supervision of a sizable group of energetic and highly motivated student-athletes can be attained only by appropriate planning. Such planning should ensure both general supervision and organized and professionally sequenced instruction. Instruction should provide individualized attention to the progressive refinement of skills and conditioning. Planning for specific health and safety concerns, including first-aid, emergency, and disaster plans should also take into consideration conditions encountered during team travel.

Equipment

As a result of the increase in product liability litigation, purchasers of equipment should be aware of impending, as well as current, safety standards recommended by authoritative groups and should purchase materials only from reputable dealers. In addition, attention should be directed to the proper repair and fitting of equipment.

In accordance with the preceding paragraph, one should know, for instance, that NOCSAE has established a football helmet standard that has been adopted by the NCAA, the National Association for Intercollegiate Athletics, the National Junior College Athletic Association, and the National Federation of State High School Associations. All new helmets purchased by high schools and colleges must bear the NOCSAE seal. According to NCAA football rules, if a helmet is in need of repair, it must be reconditioned according to the NOCSAE Football Helmet Standard recertification procedures. Equipment should be inspected on a regular basis.

Facilities

The adequacy and condition of the facilities, including fields used for all physical activities sports, should not be overlooked. The facilities, like equip-

Emergency medical technicians (EMTs) and immediate medical transportation should be available at all sporting events.

ment, should be examined and inspected regularly. Inspection should include warm-up areas, locker and shower rooms, and adjacent spectator areas as well as the actual competitive playing area.

Emergency Care

Most experts contend that attention to all possible preventive measures will help to eliminate sports injuries. At each practice session or game, the following should be available:

- The presence or immediate availability of a person qualified and delegated to render emergency care to an injured participant.
- Planned access to a physician by cell phone or nearby presence for prompt medical evaluation of the situation when warranted.
- Planned access to a medical facility—including a plan for communication and transportation between the sport or event site and medical facility—for prompt medical services when needed.
- A thorough understanding by all persons involved in the contest, class, activity, event, or practice, including the management of visiting teams, of the emergency personnel, as well as the policies and procedures involved.

Records

Documentation is fundamental to management. Authoritative sports safety regulations, standards, and guidelines should be kept current and on file. Permission slips, waiver and risk management audit forms, as well as equipment repair records may not prevent lawsuits, but they help reflect organizational control and attention to risk management. These forms need to be kept up-to-date as does the student-athletes' health status, insurance, and eligibility (see box 13-6).

Daily and weekly lessons and practice plans (including handouts) documenting the method and effort to inform students of safety and risk issues (including emergency procedures) as well as planned progressions of activity should be maintained by both teachers and coaches. Injury, accident, and incident reports must also be thorough and retained on record (see figure 13-1).

Required Physical Education

One legal implication for schools is that of requiring students to enroll in physical education classes. The schools should be flexible enough to provide alternatives for those cases in which activities such as dancing or swimming may be against a participant's sociocultural principles or religion.

Travel and Off-Campus Activities

Off-campus physical education, recreation, and sport course offerings and competitions have become popular in many communities, schools, and colleges. Of primary concern is whether due care is provided. It is the responsibility of the organization and its management to exercise care and prudence in selecting appropriate sites to be used, providing qualified personnel to see that quality instruction is being delivered, and ensuring that proper supervision is provided.

Many institutions enter independent contractor relationships for their off-campus activities (skiing, outdoor pursuit, horseback riding). The employer has no control over the selection, train-

ing, and sometimes the methods of instruction. The employer is not liable for the torts of independent contractors or their employees except when the work/instructional environment is hazardous. It is important for the institution (employer) to enter into agreements with reputable parties with a history of high-quality and safe service.

Box 13-6 Precautions to Be Taken by the Physical Educator to Avoid Possible Legal Liability

- Be familiar with the health status of each person in the program.
- Inform students of the potential risk involved in the activity.
- Consider each individual's skill, fitness, and developmental levels when teaching new activities.
- Group participants together on equal competitive skill, fitness, and developmental levels.
- Perform proper warm-up and progression leading up to all activities.
- Be sure equipment, uniforms, facilities, and environs are safe.
- Organize, plan, and carefully supervise the activity. Never leave the class unattended—even in emergencies. If an emergency occurs, secure a replacement before leaving the room.
- Administer only first aid, CPR, and AED if trained—never prescribe or diagnose.
- Use only qualified personnel to aid in classrooms.
- Keep accurate accident, incident, repair, replacement, and insurance records.
- Provide proper instruction, especially in potentially high risk activities.
- Make sure any injured person receives immediate medical attention and follow-up.
- Inform all and practice your emergency action plans and procedures.

INCIDENT REPORT FORM

A. NAME _____ GENDER _____ AGE _____ GRADE _____ SCHOOL _____

PARENT/GUARDIAN _____ HOME ADDRESS _____ HOME PHONE _____

DATE/TIME INCIDENT OCCURRED _____ PARENTS WORK PHONE _____

ADULT/SUPERVISOR IN CHARGE _____ ADULT PRESENT? YES _____ NO _____

WITNESS: NAME _____ POSITION _____ PHONE _____

B. NATURE OF INJURY/INCIDENT
1. Abrasion_____   10. Fracture_____
2. Amputa._____   11. Head Inj._____
3. Bite_____   12. Lacera/Cuts_____
4. Breath_____   13. Poisoning_____
5. Bruise_____   14. Puncture_____
6. Burn_____   15. Scratches_____
7. Dislocate_____   16. Sprain/Strain_____
8. Elect. Shock_____   17. Other (Specify)____
9. Foreign Body_____   _____

C. PART OF THE BODY INVOLVED
1. Abdomen_____   12. Hand_____
2. Ankle_____   13. Head _____
3. Arm _____   14. Hip_____
4. Back/Neck_____   15. Knee_____
5. Chest/Rib_____   16. Leg _____
6. Ear _____   17. Mouth _____
7. Elbow_____   18. Nose_____
8. Eye_____   19. Shoulder_____
9. Face _____   20. Tooth_____
10. Finger/Thumb_____ 21. Wrist _____
11. Foot/Toes_____ 22. Other (Spec) _____

D. LOCATION
1. Sport Field_____   11. Pool_____
2. Auditorium_____   12. Restroom_____
3. Cafeteria_____   13. Sch. Grds._____
4. Classroom_____   14. Stairs_____
5. Corridor_____   15. To/From Sch._____
6. Gymnasium_____   16. Field Trip_____
7. Home Econ._____   17. Ice Arena_____
8. Laboratories_____   18. Weight Room_____
9. Locker Rm._____   19. Wrestling Rm._____
10. Media Center_____   20. Other (specify)____

E. ACTIVITY
1. Physical Ed._____ What?_____
2. Rec. Sports_____ What?_____
3. Athletics_____ What?_____
4. Recess/Playground_____ What?_____
5. Equip. a. athletics/PE/recess/IM_____
   b. classroom_____ c. other_____
   What?_____
6. Medication-related_____
7. Name of Class_____

Figure 13-1.   Incident report form.

434

DESCRIPTION OF INCIDENT

F.

1. Description of the incident:

2. Description of the injury:

3. First aid treatment:

4. First aid provider:

ACTION TAKEN AND FOLLOW-UP

G.

1. Returned to class_____ 2. Sent home_____ Referred to nurse_____

3. Sent to physician (name) _____ Phone # _____

4. Sent to hospital (name) _____ Phone # _____

5. Parent/other notified?_____ Time_____ By whom?_____

6. School insurance: Yes_____ No_____ Claim Form to Parent_____

7. Report to: Principal_____ School Nurse_____ Adm. Records_____
                Date   Date   Date

8. Follow-up report_____

9. Person completing report:_____ Date/Time of report:_____
             (Name)   (Position)

Figure 13-1. Incident report form—continued.

GOVERNMENTAL VERSUS PROPRIETARY FUNCTIONS

The government in a legal sense is engaged in two types of activity: governmental and proprietary.

The *governmental function* refers to particular activities of a sovereign nature. This theory dates back to the time when kings ruled under the divine right theory, were absolute in their power, and could do no wrong. As such, sovereigns were granted immunity and could not be sued without their consent for failing to exercise governmental powers or for negligence. Furthermore, a subordinate agency of the sovereign could not be sued. The state college or university, public high school, or municipality, according to this interpretation, acts as an agent of the state in a governmental capacity. The logic behind this reasoning is that the municipality is helping the state govern the people who live within its geographical limits.

Many activities are classified under the governmental function, such as education, police protection, and public health. The courts hold that public education is a governmental function and therefore is entitled to state's immunity from liability for its own negligence. As has previously been pointed out, however, the attitude of the courts has changed and for the most part the doctrine of immunity has been neutralized.

Proprietary function pertains to government functions similar to those of a business enterprise. Such functions are for the benefit of the constituents within the corporate limits of the governmental agency. An example of this would be the renting of a school's gymnasium or ice skating rink to the private sector. In proprietary functions, a governmental agency can be held liable in the same manner that an individual or a private corporation would be held liable.

In *Watson v. School District of Bay City* (324 Mich. 1, 36 NW 2d 195), a decision was handed down by the supreme court of Michigan in February 1949. In this case, a fifteen-year-old girl attended a high school night football game. In going to her car, she was required to walk around a concrete wall. As she attempted to do this, she fell over the wall and onto a ramp. She suffered paralysis and died eight months later. The parking area was very poorly lighted. The supreme court held that staging a high school football game was a governmental function and refused to impose liability on the district.

From this discussion, it can be seen that education, recreation, and health programs are governmental functions. The distinction between governmental and proprietary functions precludes a recovery from the governmental agency if the function was governmental. However, if the high school had rented its stadium to another entity and the same action occurred, the outcome might have been different because a proprietary function would have been involved.

FEES AND FUNCTION

Many public recreation activities, facilities, and the like are offered free to the public. However, certain activities, because of the expenses involved, necessitate a fee to cover operational costs. For example, golf courses and ice arenas are expensive, and charges are usually levied so that they may be maintained. This charge is sometimes also found at facilities such as camps, tennis courts, and swimming pools.

The fees charged have a bearing on whether the activity is a governmental or a proprietary function. The courts in most states have upheld recreation as a governmental function because of its contribution to public health and welfare and also because its programs are free to the public at large. When fees are charged, however, the whole or conceptual picture takes on a different aspect.

The attitude of the courts has been that the amount of the fee and whether the activity was profitable are considerations in determining whether recreation and sport is a governmental or a proprietary function. Incidental fees used in the conduct of the enterprise do not usually change the nature of the enterprise. If the enterprise is run for profit or to create a revenue stream, however, such as a health and fitness club, or school youth sport camp, the function changes from governmental to proprietary.

LIABILITY OF THE MUNICIPALITY

It has been previously noted that a municipality as a governmental agency performs both governmental and proprietary functions.

When the municipality is performing a governmental function, it is acting in the interests of the state, it receives no profit or advantage, and it is not liable for negligence on the part of its employees or for failure to perform these functions. However, these factors would not hold if a specific tort claim statute imposed liability for negligence. When the municipality is performing a proprietary function—some function for profit or advantage of the agency or people it comprises—rather than the public in general, it is liable for negligence of the people carrying out the function. As previously pointed out, many states and municipalities have instituted specific statutes and permitted purchase of insurance recognizing the trend to permit injured citizens to recover damages from the managing agency for the torts of its employees.

LIABILITY OF THE SCHOOL DISTRICT

As a general rule, the school district is not held liable for acts of negligence on the part of its management or employees, provided a state statute does not exist to the contrary. The reasoning behind this is that the school district or school board in maintaining public schools acts as an agent of the state. It performs a purely public or governmental duty imposed on it by law for the benefit of the public and, in so doing, it receives no profit or advantage.

Some state laws, however, provide that school districts may be sued in cases of negligence, intentional torts, or reckless misconduct in the performance of certain duties, such as providing for a safe environment and competent and qualified leadership. Furthermore, the school district's immunity in many cases does not cover acts that bring damage or injury through trespass of another's premises or where a nuisance exists on a school district's property, resulting in damage to other property. Just as protection of the state and municipality is on the wane, so too is that of the school district.

LIABILITY OF SCHOOL BOARD MEMBERS

In general, school board members are not personally liable for any duties in their corporate capacities as board members that they perform negligently. Furthermore, they usually cannot be held personally liable for acts of employees of the district or organization over which they have jurisdiction on the theory of *respondeat superior* (let the master pay for the servant). However, they may be held for vicarious liability or being indirectly responsible for someone else's action arising out of legal responsibility (Clement 2004). Board members act in a corporate capacity and do not act for themselves. For example, in the state of Oregon, the general rule about the personal liability of members of district school boards is stated in 56C.J., page 348, section 223, as follows:

> School officers, or members of the board of education, or directors, trustees, or the like, of a school or other local school organization are not

personally liable for the negligence of persons rightfully employed by them in behalf of the district, and not under the direct personal supervision or control of such officer or member in doing the negligent act, since such employee is a servant of the district and not of the officer or board members, and the doctrine of *respondeat superior* accordingly has no application; and members of a district board are not personally liable for the negligence or other wrong of the board as such. A school officer or member of a district board is, however, personally liable for his own negligence or other tort, or that of an agent or employee of the district when acting directly under his supervision or by his direction.

However, a board member can be held liable for a ministerial act (an act or duty prescribed by law for a particular administrative office) even though he or she cannot be held for the exercise of discretion as a member of the board. If the board acts in bad faith and with unworthy motives, and if this can be shown, the board can also be held liable. Furthermore, acts of individual board members beyond their legal scope of duties are *ultra vires* (beyond their authority) acts, for which they may be held liable.

LIABILITY OF TEACHERS, COACHES, AND LEADERS

The individual is responsible for negligence of his or her own acts. With the exception of specific types of immunity, the teacher, coach, or leader in programs of physical education and sport is responsible for what he or she does. The Supreme Court has reaffirmed this principle, and everyone should recognize its important implications. Immunity of a government agency such as a state, school district, or board does not release the teacher, coach, or leader from liability for his or her own acts.

In New York (*Keesee v. Board of Education of City of New York,* 5 NYS. 2d 300 [1962]), a junior high school girl was injured while playing line soccer. She was kicked by another player. The board of education syllabus listed line soccer as a game and stated that "after sufficient skill has

Off-campus activities such as rock climbing add increased risk to physical education, recreation, and sports programs.

been acquired two or more forwards may be selected from each team." The syllabus called for ten to twenty players on each team and required a space of thirty to forty feet. The physical education teacher divided into two teams some forty to forty-five students who did not possess any experience in soccer. An expert witness in such matters testified that to avoid accidents, no more than two people should be on the ball at any time and criticized the board syllabus for permitting the use of more than two forwards. The expert also testified that students should have experience in kicking, dribbling, and passing before being permitted to play line soccer. The evidence showed that the teacher permitted six to eight inexperi-

enced students to be on the ball at one time. The court held that possible injury was at least reasonably foreseeable under such conditions, and the teacher's negligence was the cause of the student being injured.

Teachers and leaders are expected to conduct their various activities carefully and prudently. If such conduct is not observed, they are exposing themselves to lawsuits for their own negligence.

Many schools and agencies in states that have passed indemnification statutes allow the school district or agency to pay tort damage judgments against their employees. This payment is not mandatory, however, and includes only those actions that are within the scope of the job responsibility. There can also be no willful or intentional act by the employee. Actions outside the scope of their job that result in negligent behavior may find even the volunteer (who is classified as an employee) personally liable. All teachers, coaches, and leaders (even if volunteers) should check with their employers to determine the type and extent of liability coverage and plan accordingly for complete professional coverage. Private enterprises do not fall under the doctrine of governmental immunity.

RISK MANAGEMENT

Risk management is the systematic process by which management protects not only the participants from personal injury but also the organization from financial loss through claims for damages. Risk management is an ongoing process of risk identification, evaluation, analysis, and control as it relates to instruction, programming, supervision, and operations.

A risk management program requires a systematic examination of the environment, with identification of potential for exposure to loss and legal liability (Clement 2004). In recent years, a public relations component has been added to the system because it appears that a business may be forced to go bankrupt after a disaster even though no one was sued. When people no longer come to a facility or take part in an activity a business may fail as readily as when the courts award them a large damage award. Further, only a few insurance policies protect people against public relations disaster.

The first component of the risk management system is to identify all potential risks that exist in the activity program, facility, and so forth. The following are to be considered: local, state, and federal regulations, professional organization and industry standards, policies and procedures, facilities, equipment, human resources, supervision, instruction, participant education, and fiscal and contract information. Each identified risk domain should be analyzed and evaluated according to the following: probability that it could occur, severity of damage to people and property if it did occur, and the magnitude or number of people that would be affected if it did occur. Once all of this information is available the following choices exist: accept the risk and assume responsibility; retain the activity and transfer the risk through contract or insurance; alter the activity or event to reduce the risk; or eliminate the activity, event, or program.

Risk management is a team effort; however, each organization should appoint a risk manager whose duties are to conduct audits, develop policy and procedure, and to ensure their implementation (via audits) to avoid, limit, control, and reduce risk.

It is important to take every precaution possible to prevent accidents by providing for the safety of students and other individuals who participate in physical education and sport programs (see box 13-7). If such sound risk management precautions are taken, the likelihood of injury is lessened, of a lawsuit is diminished, and of negligence is minimized. The following are recommended precautions to which the teacher, coach, or sport manager should adhere:

- Be properly trained, licensed, certified, and qualified to perform specialized work.
- Require medical examinations of all participants. Know current health status of the participant.
- Be present at all organized activities (e.g., meetings, workshops, staff development, etc.) in the program.

Box 13-7 Safety Code for the Physical Education Teacher or Coach

The following safety codes should be followed by the physical education teacher or coach:

Have a proper and current teaching certificate and coaching license, including first aid and CPR.

Operate and teach at all times within the scope of employment as defined by the rules and regulations of the employing board of education or employer imposed by the state.

Provide the safeguards and warnings designed to minimize the dangers inherent in a particular activity.

Provide the required amount of supervision for each activity to ensure the maximal safety of all participants.

Inspect equipment and facilities regularly to determine whether they are safe for use.

Notify, in writing if necessary, the proper authorities forthwith concerning the existence of any dangerous condition, especially if it continues to exist.

Provide proper instruction in skill acquisition of any activity before exposing students to its hazards.

Be certain the activity is approved by the employer and is age and developmentally appropriate for the students involved.

Do not force a student to perform a physical feat the student obviously feels incapable of performing.

Act promptly, prudently, and use discretion in giving first aid, CPR, and AED to an injured student.

Exercise due care in practicing his or her profession.

Act as a reasonably prudent person would under the given circumstances.

Anticipate the dangers that should be apparent to a trained, intelligent professional (foreseeability).

Be a member of your professional organization and carry proper amounts and types of insurance.

Training and certification in first aid, CPR, and AED is crucial for all involved in physical education, recreation, and sport programs.

- Organize classes/activities properly according to class size, activity, environmental conditions, and other factors that have a bearing on safety and health of the participant.

- Have a planned, written, and approved program for proper disposition of participants who are injured or become sick or in case of other emergencies.

- Make regular inspections of items such as equipment, apparatus, ropes, or chains, testing them and taking other precautions to make sure they are safe. These items should also be checked for deterioration, looseness, fraying, and splinters.

- Avoid overcrowding at sport and other events, adhere to building specifications and codes and fire regulations, and provide adequate lighting and proper safety warning signs for all facilities.

- Use approved protective equipment, such as mats, helmets, and eye guards, wherever needed. Any hazards such as projections or obstacles in an area in which physical activity is taking place should be eliminated. Floors should not be slippery. Shower rooms should have surfaces conducive to secure footing.

- Require the wearing of gym shoes on gymnasium floors and safe and appropriate clothing for each activity.

- Adapt activities to the age and developmental maturity level, and fitness level of the participants; provide proper and competent supervision; and use trained spotters in gymnastics and other similar high-risk activities.

- Utilize teaching methods, procedures, and progressions that are consistent with professional and institutional guidelines and standards.

- Instruct students and other participants in the correct use of apparatus, equipment, and performance of physical activities, and duly warn them of the risk involved. Any misuse of equipment or horseplay should be prohibited.

- Inspect the environs, buildings, grounds, and other facilities regularly for safety hazards such as loose tiles, broken fences, cracked glass, uneven pavement, and wet surfaces. Defects should be recorded and reported immediately to responsible persons, and necessary precautions taken.

- Utilize thorough and approved releases, consent forms, and waivers when appropriate.

In planning play and other instructional activities, the following precautions should be taken:

Space should be sufficient for all activities and games. Games using balls and other equipment that can cause damage should be conducted in areas containing minimal danger of injuring someone. Quiet games and activities requiring working at benches, such as arts and crafts, should be undertaken in places that are well protected.

Emergency action plans should be put in writing and prepared with input by the entire school, institution, or agency. The professional should be part of the planning of the emergency action system, and become aware of it before the first day on the job. In the event of an accident, the following or similar procedure should be followed:

1. The nearest teacher, coach, supervisor, or sport or recreation manager should immediately proceed to the scene, notifying the person in charge and medical personnel, if available, by phone or messenger.

Special care should be provided for high-risk activities such as diving, jumping, water slides, and scuba diving.

2. A preliminary first-aid survey of the injured person will provide some idea of the nature and extent of the injury and the emergency of the situation. If necessary, the person in charge should call 911 for emergency medical services (EMS).

3. If the teacher, instructor, or coach at the scene is well versed in first aid, assistance should be given, paying particular attention to the ABCs of first aid (airway, breathing, and circulation). Current first-aid, CPR, and AED certification and the undertaking of proper procedures will usually absolve the teacher of negligence.

   Every teacher, instructor, coach, and sport manager should hold first aid, CPR, and AED certification. In any event, everything should be done to make the injured person comfortable until EMT or care by a medical team can be secured.

4. After the injured person has been provided for, the person in charge should fill out the appropriate accident report forms, take the statements of appropriate witnesses, and file the report for future reference. Reports of accidents should be prepared promptly and sent through appropriate managerial channels.

5. There should be a complete follow-up of the accident, an analysis of the situation, and an eradication or correction of any existing hazards or flaws in the organization's safety system or program.

   The Standard Student Accident Report Committee of the National Safety Council listed the following reasons why detailed injury reports are important for school authorities:

1. They aid in protecting school districts and school personnel from associated publicity and from liability suits growing out of student injury cases.

2. They aid in evaluating the relative importance of the various safety areas and the emphasis that each area merits in the total school safety plan.

3. They suggest modification in the structure, use, maintenance, and repair of buildings, facilities, grounds, and equipment.

The rapid growth of collision sports such as soccer has led to an increase in risk management issues.

Appropriate warning signs should be posted at all events.

4. They suggest curriculum adjustments to meet immediate concerns and safety requirements.

5. They provide significant data for risk management planning.

6. They give substance to the school managers' appeal for community support of the school safety program.

7. They aid school management in guiding the school's safety activities for parents, personnel, students, and all user groups.

INSURANCE MANAGEMENT

Insurance management is an element of risk management that seeks to divert or shift risk onto another party (the other elements include assignment and agreement indemnification).

Schools and other organizations employ three major types of insurance management to protect themselves against loss. The first is insurance for property. The second is insurance for liability protection when financial loss might arise from personal injury or property damage for which the school district or organization is liable. The third is insurance for crime protection against a financial loss that might be incurred as a result of theft or other illegal act. This section on insurance management addresses liability protection.

A definite trend can be seen in school districts toward having some form of school accident insurance not only to protect students against injury but to shield teachers, coaches, and staff against injury and liability as well. The same is true wherever physical education and sport programs are conducted. Along with this trend can be seen the impact on casualty and life insurance companies that offer insurance policies. The premium costs of accident policies vary from community to community and also in accordance with the age of the insured, type of plan offered, sport or activity to be covered, and number of like or pool groups involved in the contract. Interscholastic sport has been responsible for the development of many state athletic protection plans usually available through state high school leagues or NFHS as well as the issuance of special policies (riders) by commercial insurance companies, ranging from basic athletic injury or event insurance to lifetime catastrophic injury. Because accidents are the primary cause of death among students between the ages of five and eighteen, adequate and ample protection is requisite to a well-managed program of physical education and sport (see box 13-8). Although insurance companies traditionally defend and pay damages in negligence and employment cases they

Box 13-8 Some Common Features of Insurance Management Plans

A safety committee is formed (including an insurance agent) to develop the insurance plan.

Some plans include cooperative or pooled ventures (league, districts, federations) to help reduce the costs of premiums.

Premiums are paid for by the school, by the parent, or jointly by the school and parent.

Schools obtain their money for payment of premiums from the board of education, general organization fund, or a pooling of funds from gate receipts of games or events.

Schools place the responsibility on the parents to pay for any injuries incurred.

Schools place the responsibility on their employees to obtain appropriate insurance coverage.

Employees or schools might contractually deflect some of their liability (i.e., to the facility user, event sponsor, independent contractor).

Blanket coverage is a very common policy for insurance companies to offer.

Insurance companies frequently offer insurance coverage for athletic injuries as part of a package plan that also includes an accident plan for all students.

Most schools have insurance plans for the protection of athletes or belong to organizations such as the NEA, NFHS, or the NCAA that can offer various coverage plans including catastrophic injury.

Hospitalization, X-ray and MRI examinations, emergency transportation, medical fees, and dental fees are increasingly becoming part of the insurance coverage in schools. Be sure to know your coverage!

Specialty insurance riders might also be considered in addition to standard coverage.

Common Features of School Insurance Management Plans

Some school boards have found it a good policy to pay the premium on insurance policies because full coverage of students provides peace of mind for both parents and teachers. Furthermore, many liability suits have been avoided in this manner.

Other school officials investigate the various insurance plans available and then recommend a particular plan, and the student-athlete's parents or guardians deal directly with the company or through the school to guarantee coverage. Such parent-paid plans are frequently divided into two options: (1) they provide coverage for the student on a door-to-door basis (to and from school, while at school, and in school-sponsored activities) or (2) they provide twenty-four-hour accident coverage. The school-only policy rates are based on age, with rates for children in the elementary grades lower than for high school students. These policies usually run only for the school year.

Student accident insurance provides coverage for all accidents regardless of whether the insured is hospitalized or treated in a doctor's office. Some medical plans, such as Blue Cross and Blue Shield as well as various HMOs, may be limited in the payments they make. Student accident insurance policies, as a general rule, offer reasonable rates and are a good investment for all concerned. Parents should be encouraged, however, to examine their existing family policies before taking out such policies to avoid overlapping coverage.

Schools and other agencies should consider the following practices and procedures when selecting an insurance policy for their user groups:

- Some responsible individual or group of persons, preferably a committee of experts, should be delegated to review insurance policies and, after developing a set of criteria, should purchase the best one possible.

- Where feasible, cooperative plans with other schools or agencies on a county, district, association, state high school league, or other basis should be encouraged to secure less expensive group rates.

rarely pay expenses or damages for intentional acts that violate a plaintiff's civil rights. Civil rights cases often involve intentional acts to deprive someone of his or her liberty. Civil rights cases include Americans With Disability Act cases, Title IX cases, students' property rights issues, and discrimination cases.

- Criteria for selecting an insurance policy should, in addition to cost, relate to such important benefits as maximum medical coverage, excluded benefits, maximum hospital coverage, dental benefits, dismemberment, surgery, X-ray and MRI examinations, and physical and rehabilitation therapy.
- The greatest possible coverage for cost involved should be an important basis for selecting a policy.
- For contact and collision sports especially, a catastrophic clause should be investigated as possible additional coverage.
- Deductible clause policies should not be purchased, if possible.
- Dental injury benefits are an important consideration.
- Determine what claims the insurance company will and will not pay.
- The school should insist on 100 percent enrollment in the athletic insurance program.
- Schools and agencies should have a central location for keeping insurance records, and an annual audit should be conducted to ascertain all the pertinent facts about the cost effectiveness and quality of coverage.

Procedure for Insurance Management

Every school should be covered by insurance. Five types of accident insurance may be obtained: (1) commercial insurance policies written on an individual basis, (2) student medical benefit plans written on a group basis by commercial insurers, (3) state high school athletic association benefit plans, (4) medical benefit plans operated by specific city or district school systems, and (5) self-insurance. Before adoption by any school or athletic association, each type of insurance should be carefully explored and weighed so that the best coverage is obtained for the type and scope of program or event sponsored.

The most inexpensive insurance policy is the employment of master teachers and coaches.

Sport and Insurance Coverage

Some schools and colleges do not provide a sport insurance program. If a student is injured in a sporting event, the family is then responsible for all medical expenditures. No provision is made for the school or college to reimburse the family for its expense. Of course, the school or college is always open to a lawsuit by the parents as well as by the participant in an effort to reclaim expenses. A lawsuit is expensive for the school or college, because if the claim is settled in favor of the participant and parents, the school's or college's insurance premiums for the next few years are increased and because of the intangible effect to the school's or college's reputation and public image. In these cases, the high school is usually, through its membership in a state high school association, supplied with insurance options, including catastrophic insurance, to supplement the individual's personal coverage.

An alternative is to provide an opportunity for students to purchase athletic insurance (many high schools provide this option) or, better yet, for the school or college to purchase a policy for student-athletes (most collegiate athletic departments provide insurance). Of course, the latter is the best method because all students are then covered, regardless of their economic status, and the students' liability policy is not subject to suit. Most parents are interested only in recovering monies actually spent, and they are satisfied accordingly. Usually a blanket policy purchased by the school or college can be obtained at a lower unit cost than a policy purchased by individuals. The athletic insurance program should be managed through the business office of the school district or of the athletic department or by a local or regional broker, relieving the school, college, or association of going into the insurance business.

It is the responsibility of the director of physical education or athletics and activities to maintain and supply accurate lists of participating students to the business office before the beginning of the various sport seasons. It is also imperative that the coaches and athletic medical team personnel be made aware of the types of insurance coverage plans so that when accidents happen, they can inform the athletes and parents of the proper procedure to follow in seeking appropriate care as well as in filing reports and claims. Usually the business or athletic and activities office will supply policies for every participant in a covered sport team or program.

Not only should the coach be knowledgeable about insurance coverage, but he or she should also show concern for accident victims as well as injured players. This concern is not only a form of good human and public relations, but it may also make the difference in the parents' minds about potential litigation. The coaches must also be instructed by management in the proper attitude to take when such mishaps occur. Legal counsel, if required, should be made available through the school, institution, or agency. If not, a private attorney should be retained (see box 13-9).

School Sport Insurance

Sport protection funds usually have these characteristics: they are a nonprofit venture, they are not compulsory, a specific fee is charged for each person registered with the plan, and provision is made for recovery for specific injuries. Generally the money is not paid out of tax funds, but instead is paid either by participant fee or by the school or other agency.

In connection with such plans, an individual, after receiving benefits, could in most states still bring action against the coach or other leader whose negligence contributed to the injury.

States vary in whether they pay for liability and accident insurance out of public tax funds. Some states do not permit tax money to be used for liability or accident insurance to cover students in physical education and sport activities. On the other hand, the state legislature of Oregon permits school districts to carry liability insurance. This section is stated as follows in the revised code, O.R.S.:

> 332.180 Liability insurance; medical and hospital benefits insurance. Any district school board may enter into contracts of insurance for liability coverage of all activities engaged in by the district, for medical and hospital benefits for students engaging in athletic contests and for public liability and property damage covering motor vehicles operated by the district, and may pay the necessary premiums thereon. Failure to procure such insurance shall in no case be construed as negligence or lack of diligence on the part of the district school board or the members thereof.

Some athletic insurance plans in use in the schools today are entirely inadequate. These plans indicate a certain amount of money as the maximum that can be collected. For example, a boy may lose the sight in one eye. According to the athletic protection fund, the loss of an eye will draw $5,000. This amount does not come close to paying for such a serious injury. In this case, as a hypothetical example, the parents sue the athletic protection fund and the teacher for $50,000. In some states, if the case is lost, the athletic fund will pay the $5,000 and the teacher will pay the other $45,000. It is evident that some of these insurance plans do not give complete and adequate coverage and protection to all concerned. It is crucial, therefore, that teachers, coaches, and all involved in physical education and sport know the details and specifics concerning their insurance coverage (see box 13-10).

In many states, physical educators and coaches need additional protection against being sued for accidental injury to students and student-athletes.

Box 13-9   The Prudent Manager

The following exercise should provide personal guidance for management as to the establishment of an appropriate degree of prudence commensurate with the professional as well as legal responsibility of the contemporary manager in physical education and sport.

	Degree of compliance			
	Always	**Frequently**	**Rarely**	**Never**

The prudent manager:

1. Seeks to prohibit the situation that may lead to litigation through constant foresight and care inherent in the professional role he or she holds. _____ _____ _____ _____

2. Assigns instructional and supervisory duties for an activity to only those people who are qualified and certified for that particular activity. _____ _____ _____ _____

3. Conducts regular inspections/audits of all equipment used and insists on full repair of faulty items before use. _____ _____ _____ _____

4. Establishes policies and procedures and enforces rules for safe use of equipment and proper fitting of all uniforms and protective gear. _____ _____ _____ _____

5. Has written plans with adequate review procedures to ensure that participants do not move too rapidly into areas of skill performance beyond their present skill level. _____

6. Selects opponents for each participant/team with care to avoid potentially dangerous mismatching. _____ _____ _____ _____

7. Establishes and scrupulously enforces rules regarding reporting of illness or injury, to include compilation of written records and names and address of witnesses. _____ _____ _____ _____

8. Does not treat injuries unless professionally prepared and certified to do so. _____ _____ _____ _____

9. Regularly updates first-aid, CPR, AED, and emergency medical care credentials. _____ _____ _____ _____

10. Does not permit participation in any activity without medical approval following serious illness or injury. _____ _____ _____ _____

11. Regularly inspects facilities and readily recognizes the presence of any attractive nuisance, and initiates firm control measures. _____ _____ _____ _____

12. Posts safety rules for use of facilities, and orients and warns students and colleagues to danger areas in activities, facilities, equipment, and personal conduct. _____ _____ _____ _____

13. Does not place the activity area in the control of unqualified personnel for _any_ reason. _____ _____ _____ _____

14. Relies on waiver forms, not as a negation of responsibility for injury, but only as a means of ensuring that parents/guardians recognize students' intent to participate. _____ _____ _____ _____

15. Does not permit zeal for accomplishment or emotion of the moment to suppress rational behavior. _____ _____ _____ _____

Box 13-9   The Prudent Manager—cont'd

| | Degree of compliance | | | |
	Always	Frequently	Rarely	Never
16. Provides in letter and spirit nondiscriminatory programs and fair and equitable treatment for all participants.	_____	_____	_____	_____
17. Cancels transportation plans if unable to be thoroughly convinced of the personal and prudent reliability of drivers, means of transportation, weather, and adequacy of insurance coverage.	_____	_____	_____	_____
18. Does not conduct an activity, practice, or contest without an emergency plan for medical assistance in the event of injury or illness, regardless of the setting.	_____	_____	_____	_____
19. Holds liability insurance of significant dollar dimensions and pertinent applicability to professional pursuits involving physical activity and sport.	_____	_____	_____	_____
20. Does not permit excessive concern about legal liability to prohibit the development of a challenging and accountable physical education/sport experience for each participant.	_____	_____	_____	_____

Box 13-10   Common Inquiries Concerning Insurance

- Who or what is covered?
- How much coverage is received?
- What actions and harms are covered?
- Is there subrogation (the insurance company takes your financial position)?
- How long and under what circumstances will the coverage apply?
- Is there a deductible?
- How much are the premiums?
- Who covers the costs of defense?
- What is excluded by the coverage (so further liability deflection can be managed)?

Legislation is needed permitting school funds to be used as protection against student injuries. In this way, a school would be legally permitted, and could be required, to purchase liability insurance to cover all students, teachers, staff members, and coaches.

THE EXPANDED SCOPE OF LAW AND SPORT

The tremendous growth and development of physical activity and sport has been accompanied by the expanded role that law has played in ensuring a safe, smooth, and level playing field. This growth includes: labor and antitrust regulations; collective bargaining; contracts; eligibility; lease negotiations including concessions, parking, advertising, and stadium boxes; players and sports team representation; media negotiations; sponsorship; taxes; worker compensation and salary arbitration; and trademark and team licensing including ambush marketing, just to mention a few. Although these topics seem out of the range of this text, today's professional involved in physical education and sport will nonetheless be called on to explore, extract, and extrapolate relevant knowledge from such areas. It is strongly recommended that further study (see Suggested Readings) into sport and law be undertaken by all professionals involved in physical education and sport.

American Bar Association
www.aba.org

CaseCites
www.lexisone.com

Education Law Association (formerly NOLPE)
www.educationlaw.org

FindLaw
www.findlaw.com

From the Gym to the Jury
www.gym2jury.com

Law Library of Congress
www.loc.gov/law

Minnesota State Bar Association (MSBA)
www.mnbar.org

National Sports Law Institute
www.mu.edu.law/sports

Policy.com
www.policy.com

SUMMARY

Legal liability, risk, and insurance management are important functions of management of physical education and sport programs. In managing such programs, the persons in charge should be familiar with the laws and legal basis for physical education and sport programs and the responsibilities associated with factors such as torts, negligence, supervisory negligence, intentional torts, product liability, and civil rights, including gender equity. Sound policies and procedures concerning risk and insurance management should also be in place and serve as guideposts for all programs. Furthermore, management should be aware that citizens (e.g., parents and student-athletes) are becoming increasingly aware of the meaning of laws that concern their programs and

of their individual rights, including due process and equal protection in such matters. As a result, the prospect of litigation has significantly increased. Management, therefore, should be prepared to do all it can to prevent not only injury but also possible litigation.

SELF-ASSESSMENT ACTIVITIES

These activities will assist students in determining if material and competencies presented in this chapter have been mastered.

1. Without consulting your text, construct a definition for each of the following terms: *legal liability, tort, negligence, respondeat superior, assumption of risk,* and *risk and insurance management.*

2. Prepare a set of guidelines that teachers of physical activity in grades K–12 should follow to prevent student injury and violation of an individual's civil rights.

3. Discuss sport product liability and the methods you would take to ensure adequate protection for your ice hockey team.

4. Arrange a mock trial in your class. Have a jury, prosecutor, plaintiff, defendant, witnesses, and other features characteristic of a regular court trial. The case before the court is that the coach of a high school football team, in the final minutes of a game, used a player who had incurred a head injury in the first quarter. The player later suffered brain damage.

5. Conduct a risk management survey of the physical education and sport facilities at your school and identify any areas of concern that might exist. If any problem or risk areas are found, recommend how they can be corrected.

6. Prepare a step-by-step list of emergency safety procedures that should be followed by every physical education teacher at a middle school to provide for the welfare of all students.

7. Take a field trip to a local community playground and chart the various safety concerns observed.

REFERENCES

1. Appenzeller, H. 2004. *Managing sports and risk management strategies.* Durham, NC: Carolina Academic Press.
2. ———2005. *Risk management in sport: Issues and strategies.* Durham, NC: Carolina Academic Press.
3. Appenzeller, H., and R. Baron. 1995. *From the gym to the jury.* Vol. 7, 2:9. Durham, NC: Carolina Academic Press.
4. Appenzeller, T. 2000. *Youth sport and the law.* Durham, NC: Carolina Academic Press.
5. Baley, J. A., and D. L. Matthews. 1989. *Law and liability in athletics, physical education, and recreation.* Dubuque, IA: Brown & Benchmark.
6. Black, H. C. 1990. *Black's law dictionary.* 8th ed. St. Paul, MN: West Publishing.
7. Clement, A. 2004. *Law in sport and physical activity.* Dania, FL: Sport and Law Press.
8. Dougherty, N. J., D. Auxter, A. S. Goldberg, E. R. Goldberger and G. S. Heinzman. 1994. *Sport, physical activity, and the law.* Champaign, IL: Human Kinetics.
9. Fried, G. B. 1999. *Safe at first.* Durham, NC: Carolina Academic Press.
10. Kaiser, R. A. 1986. *Liability and law in recreation, parks, and sport.* Englewood Cliffs, NJ: Prentice Hall.
11. National Education Association, Research Division for the National Commission on Safety Education. 1950. *Who is liable for pupil injuries?* Washington, DC: National Education Association.
12. Restatement of the Law of Torts, Second, 1965. St. Paul, MN: American Law Institute.
13. Restatement of the Law of Torts, Third. Product Liability. 1997. St. Paul, MN: American Law Institute.
14. Uberstien, G. A., ed. 1996. *The law and professional and amateur sports.* Deerfield, IL: Clark Boardman Callaghen.
15. Yasser, R., J. R. McCurdy, C. P. Goplerud, and M. A. Weston. 2003. *Sports law: Cases and materials.* Cincinnati, OH: Anderson.

SUGGESTED READINGS

Carpenter, L. J. 1995. *Legal concepts in sport: A primer.* Reston, VA: AAHPERD.
    Addresses topics such as sexual harassment, corporal punishment, and product liability.

Colker, R., and A. A. Milani. 2005. *The law of disability discrimination.* Albany, NY: Matthew Berder & Company.

Cotten, D. J., and J. T. Wolohan. 2003. *Law for recreation and sport managers.* Dubuque, IA: Kendall/Hunt.

From the Gym to the Jury. Summerfield, NC 27358.
    A physical education, recreation, and sports law newsletter providing information about various legal issues, concerns, and cases.

Gallup, E. M. 1995. *The law and the team physician.* Champaign, IL: Human Kinetics.
    Discusses such topics as accountability, duty, negligence, and relationships with the sport management team.

Krotee, M. L., and E. S. Lincoln. 1981. Sport and law. *Choice* 18:1055–65.
    Delves into sport and law in regard to sports injuries, sex discrimination, education, contracts, and taxation. Describes the role of law in society and its effect on prudent management.

Miller, W. 2002. *Political risk management in sports.* Durham, NC: Carolina Academic Press.

Uberstien, G. A., ed. 1996. *The law and professional and amateur sports.* Deerfield, IL: Clark Boardman Callaghen.
    Gives a thorough overview of the multibillion-dollar industry that is associated with sport, entertainment, and recreation. It covers topics from antitrust law to violence and from collective bargaining to spectator rights.

van der Smissen, B. 1990–1995. *Legal liability and risk management for public and private entities.* 3 vols. and supp. Cincinnati, OH: Anderson.
    A three-volume exploration of physical education and sport and the law. Thoroughly treats legal liability and risk management for public and private sports-related organizations.

Wong, G. M. 2002. *Essentials of sports law.* Westport, CT: Praeger.
    Presents an overview of the court systems in the United States along with those entities that govern amateur sport. Contract law, tort law, drug testing, and sex discrimination cases are explored.

Wong, G. W., and M. Burke. 1993. Informed consent. *Athletic Business* 17(December):10.
    Discusses the pros and cons of liability waivers and shows how they can discourage lawsuits and enhance legal defenses by increasing participant awareness.

CHAPTER 14

Public Relations and Marketing

INSTRUCTIONAL OBJECTIVES AND COMPETENCIES TO BE ACHIEVED

After reading this chapter the student should be able to:

- Define the term *public relations* and its purpose and importance to physical education, recreation, and sport programs.
- Understand the relationship of marketing to a public relations program.
- Recognize the constituents and needs of various publics in physical education, recreation, and sport.
- Describe key guidelines of a sound public relations program.
- Be familiar with various public relations media and how they can best be used to promote physical education, recreation, and sport programs.
- Describe the six Ps as they relate to marketing strategy.
- Be familiar with the construction of a press release.
- Identify some professional organizations that can serve as resources for the conduct of public relations programs.
- Understand the importance of interpersonal and mass communications to the public relations and marketing agenda.

Abraham Lincoln once said, "Public sentiment is everything. With public sentiment, nothing can fail; without it, nothing can succeed." The management teams of physical education, recreation, and sport programs need positive public recognition that the programs under their jurisdiction are meeting the needs and wants of their "publics" (i.e., customer, user, community). To accomplish this, the consumer, user, and the public in general (community) should be familiar with, understand, accept, and support the services these programs render.

Therefore, to have sound public relations, quality programs must exist, effective and continuous communication with the various publics must take place, and the media (print, radio, TV, outdoor, Internet) must be utilized in a manner that effectively presents the vision, philosophy, purpose, values, objectives, successes, and image of the organization to the public at large. It is the management function of public relations that guides, protects, develops, cultivates, projects, and promotes this image or message to the various publics.

Once a positive balance between the organization or program, customer/user, the media, and the community is established, marketing comes into play. The ultimate goal of most marketing activity is to plan, develop, and execute strategies in order to facilitate mutually satisfying exchanges of goods and services between parties (Kotler 2003). Both public relations and marketing should play integral roles in all physical education, recreation, and sport programs. Although each share many common characteristics, concepts, and processes (some experts place public relations as a vital part of the marketing process), for the purposes of this text each will, for the most part, be presented as separate yet crucial management functions.

PUBLIC RELATIONS, PHYSICAL EDUCATION, AND SPORT

Public relations is an all-encompassing term. It is commonly defined as the planned effort to influence opinion through good character and socially responsible performance, based on mutually satisfactory two-way communications (Cutlip, Center, and Broom 2000). Whatever an organization does that affects the opinions of its various publics toward it is public relations (Appley 1956). Public relations indicates the positive relationship of the institution, program, or organization and its total complement of human resources as well as its public constituencies (Williams 2000; Milne and McDonald 1999). *Public Relations News* further adds that it is the management function that analyzes and evaluates public attitudes, identifies the policies and procedures of an individual or organization with the public interest, and plans and executes a program of action to earn or create public understanding, linkage, and acceptance. Two key ingredients of public relations are careful planning and proper conduct, which in turn will result in gaining public understanding, trust, and confidence. Public relations includes attempts to modify and shape the attitudes and actions of the public through advocacy, lobbying, persuasion, and education and to integrate the attitudes and actions of the public with those of the organization or people

Public relations starts at the top as President Clinton and Chief Program and Planning Officer for the Women's Sports Foundation, Dr. Marjorie Snyder, meet at the White House.

who are conducting the public relations as well as its marketing program. Public relations is the entire body of relationships that makes up our impressions of an individual, institution, organization, program, product, or idea. Used properly it can be a powerful tool to help drive the unique $200 billion physical education and sports industry (Pitts and Stotlar 2002; Meek 1998).

These concepts of public relations help clarify its importance for any organization, institution, or group of individuals trying to develop an enterprise, program, product, profession, or business. Public relations considers important factors such as consumer or user interest, human relationships, public understanding, and goodwill. In business, public relations attempts to show the important place that specialized enterprises have in society and how they exist and operate in the public interest. In education, public relations is concerned with improving public opinion, proclaiming and transmitting the needs of the school or college, and acquainting constituents with the value of programs and what is being done in the "public's" interest. Public relations also should inform the participant, media, and community about the problems and challenges that must be addressed, confronted, and overcome for education to render a greater service.

Purposes of public relations in schools include (1) serving as a positive public information source about school activities, programs, participants, and accomplishments; (2) promoting confidence in the schools or school-related organizations and programs; (3) gathering support for school, programmatic, or organizational funding and programs; (4) stressing the value of education for all individuals; (5) improving communication, understanding, and acceptance among students, teachers, coaches, parents, and community members; (6) establishing communications with electronic, Internet, and print media; (7) evaluating school and organization programs; (8) evaluating the public's attitudes and issues of concern; (9) correcting misunderstandings and misinformation including crisis management about the mission and objectives of the school, its programs, and other organizations; and (10) building a wholesome environment (image) for physical education and sport. This environment or image will enable public relations personnel (i.e., teacher, coach, sports information director) to maintain and sustain their programs. It also permits the marketers to adjust their strategy and marketing mix (product/program, publics, place, price, production, promotion) and help clarify and identify new marketing opportunities.

Physical education, recreation, and sport desperately need public relations because the public does not always recognize or understand the positive contributions that these programs make to all the people of a community. Many individuals believe that these programs, especially high-profile sport, are appendages to schools' academic programs and are sources of entertainment rather than education. Sound public relations programs both internally (e.g., faculty, staff, students, parents, alumni) and externally (e.g., community, media, business) are needed to correct and reshape these misunderstandings and ensure that an effective communication network is established based on research analysis, needs, and how these needs can be satisfied through the delivery of quality physical education and sport programs.

The goals of physical education and sport as presented in chapter 2 are educational and individual in nature and can be achieved through well-planned and effectively and efficiently managed programs as well as through the hiring of expert teachers, coaches, and support personnel. These aims and objectives together with the program's needs and challenges should be communicated to the public, both internal and external, through various media as well as through the sustained pursuit of excellence in the programs.

The practice of public relations has been related to education since a publicity bureau was established at Harvard in 1900. Since that time, public relations has invaded all areas of human endeavor, including education, business, politics, religion, media, military, government (U.S. Commission on Public Information 1917), and labor as well as physical education, recreation, and sport (e.g., AAHPERD's Physical Education Public Information Commission, and now its Department of Media and Public Affairs). A sound public relations program is not hit-or-miss. It is intelligently and consciously planned, employing the steps outlined previously in the planning process. Great amounts of time, effort, and human capital are necessary to produce meaningful results. Furthermore, it is not something in which only top management, executives, or administrative officers should be interested. For any organization to have a good program, all members must be conscious of public relations.

The extent to which interest in public relations has grown is indicated by the number of individuals specializing in it. A growing number of these people are involved in physical education, recreation, and sport programs. Indeed, almost every NCAA Division I institution designates a school official to manage its public relations efforts (e.g., sports information, public, community, or external affairs or relations).

Public relations is steadily being recognized for the impact it has not only in the business or corporate world, but also in the arena of physical education, recreation, and sport. All programs need public acceptance, support and understanding to survive. A sound program of public relations

Public relations, sponsorship, and marketing are coordinated, integrated, and cooperative efforts.

Public relations and advocacy must be well planned, coordinated, and managed. The NCAAHPERD Leadership Team meets to chart its course.

including educating and "reaching" out helps not only sustain programs but also make them grow and flourish. There is no substitute for a great program to drive public relations. A lot of work, however, has yet to be accomplished in public relations at both the grassroots and the national level, especially in regard to our physical education programs. Clearly, advocacy and lobbying must play a more prominent role in the profession's public relations plan or promotional mix.

THE MANY PUBLICS

For public relations and marketing programs to be successful, accurate facts must be systematically gathered and clearly articulated to the public in a meaningful fashion. To establish what facts or messages are to be packaged and presented to the public, management needs to identify the consumers, user groups, or target population of the product, program, or service. Marketing people call this market segmentation. Such factors as psychographic and socioeconomic status, education, proximity, transportation, parking, brand loyalty, and other product-service needs are used to identify the target population. These factors play a significant role in helping management select which popula-

tion it wishes to target, segment, and direct its efforts toward (Lamb, Hair, and McDaniel 2006).

A public is a group of individuals drawn together by common interests who are in a specific geographical location, community, or area or are characterized by some other common feature (e.g., age, interest, lifestyle, marital status, motivation, opinion). The United States, because of its diversity, is made up of hundreds of different publics—farmers, senior citizens, organized workers, students, professional and blue-collar workers, veterans, teens, and so on. The various publics may be national, regional, and local. They can be classified according to race, gender, ethnicity, age, religion, occupation, politics, disability, income, profession, benefit, usage, or background (business, fraternal, or educational). Each organization or group with a special interest represents a public. All publics possess common elements to which public relations and marketing efforts must be sensitive. Each public (e.g., internal, external, immediate, associated) usually needs to belong, wants to have input, and desires to be included (psychosocial ownership) in order to maintain its interest and enhance its reputation. Public relations-minded and dependent organizations (e.g., education, physical education, recreation, and sport) should always think in terms of the publics with which they wish to interact and serve in order to promote understanding as well as to determine how those publics can best be reached and satisfied. The AIDA concept or **a**ttention, interest, desire, and action is a classic model often employed to promote consumer involvement and ultimately "action."

To have a meaningful and purposeful public relations and marketing program, it is essential to visit, interact, and gain the attention of the community; obtain accurate facts about these publics; and gain an understanding of their needs, interests, desires, lifestyle practices, and likes and dislikes as well as other essential information. It is also important to consider what is good for most of the people in the community.

Public opinion, along with other factors, helps determine whether a profession or program (e.g., physical education, recreation, and sport) is important, whether it meets an essential need, and whether it is making a meaningful contribution to society. Public opinion can influence the success or failure of a department, program, course, class, school, institution, business, bond issue, event, or, indeed, an entire profession. Public opinion is dynamic and results from the interaction of people, the media, and all those involved with the physical education and/or

The Rolling Timberwolves display their skills while serving as PR ambassadors for individuals with disabilities.

sporting process. Public opinion has great impact, and any group, program, institution, or organization that wants to survive, sustain, and succeed should learn as much about its process as possible.

To gather information on what the public thinks, why it thinks as it does, and how it reaches its conclusions, various techniques may be explored. Surveys, questionnaires, opinion polls, interviews, focus groups, expert opinions, discussions, town meetings, observations, sampling, and other methods of probing needs have proved valuable. Anyone interested in public relations and marketing should be acquainted with these various techniques.

Some forms of public opinion are shaped as a result of influences in early life, such as the effect of parents, peers, coaches, and school and community environment. Individuals' everyday lifestyles, attitudes, and culture and what they see, hear, and experience in other ways also contribute to the establishment of public opinions. Furthermore, the media, including newspapers, magazines, billboards, radio, television, and the Internet, play a significant role in influencing the formation and strength of people's opinions. One must not only be aware of these facts but also remember that one is dealing with many different publics (e.g., unaware nonconsumer, aware nonconsumer, competitor, sanctioner, support, media consumer, light user, dropout, etc.). Each public requires a special source of probing needs, research, data gathering, and study in order to plan the most meaningful way to develop, organize, and manage an effective, efficient, and beneficial public relations and marketing campaign. The more that can be known about a particular public, the easier it is to plan such effective campaigns (i.e., Target Market Tour for teen antismoking).

PLANNING THE PUBLIC RELATIONS PROGRAM

Public relations programs are more effective when they are planned by a team of interested and informed individuals and groups. Individuals and groups such as school boards, management personnel, teachers, students, alumni, administrators, coaches, and citizens' task forces and committees can provide valuable input and assistance in certain areas of the public relations program. These people, serving directly with and in an advisory capacity to physical education, recreation, and sport professionals, can help immeasurably in planning an effective community public relations program by following these specific steps:

- Establish a sound public relations policy based on organizational mission and what your strengths are at the time.
- Identify the target market (community youth ages six to twelve).
- Conduct an audit to determine what users and nonusers want, need, believe, know, and do not know concerning your program (i.e., values, benefits).
- Identify the services, programs, and products that are needed and will yield the greatest dividends.
- Decide what facts and ideas will best enable the targeted consumers and nonconsumers to better understand the benefits obtained from quality programs.
- Decide what service or human, physical, and technological resources improvements will be needed to conduct or enhance programs.
- Make full use of effective planning techniques to generate mission statements, objectives, policies, goal setting, understanding, and appreciation.
- Relate cost to opportunity for participants to learn, experience, maintain, and improve health and achieve fitness.
- Decide who is going to perform specific public relations tasks or assignments at particular times.

After the public relations plan is put into operation, it is important to assess and evaluate its results to see if its goals are being met and to improve the quality and effectiveness of the program.

GUIDELINES TO SOUND PUBLIC RELATIONS

The role of management to provide sound public relations is vital to any institution or organization. Whether it is to create a more favorable image for your organization or program; increase participation in programs or activities; gain legislative, financial, community/volunteer support; or correct and reshape public misunderstandings, common guidelines to observe in developing a good public relations program should be followed:

- Public relations should be considered internally before being developed externally. The support of all substructures and representatives within the organization, from top management to operational staff, should be obtained. A team effort is crucial! Furthermore, such items as mission and purpose of program, person or persons responsible, funding sources, media involvement, and controlled communication and persuasion tools (e.g., brochures, flyers, in-house publications available) to carry on the program should be primary considerations before implementation.
- Managers involved in the public relations process must determine the organization's image from the public's point of view, relate this finding to the organization's public relations authority, and make suggestions on how this image can be positively enhanced before the public relations plan is set.
- A public relations program should be outlined and put in writing, and members of the organization should have meaningful input as well as the responsibility to become familiar with the program. The better its mission, goals, and objectives are known and understood, the better chance the program has of succeeding.
- The persons directly in charge of the public relations program must have thorough knowledge of the services being rendered and the expertise of members of the organization who will deliver the program, and the needs and attitude of the targeted public.

- The persons in charge should know the nature and potential reactions of the customer or user group, as well as, all the publics directly or indirectly related to the task at hand.

- After all relevant information has been gathered, a program that meets the needs of the organization and the public or community should be developed. The program should be based on through and reliable market or opinion research and not on the whims of management.

- Adequate funds and resources should be made available to do the job. Furthermore, all support services necessary to allow the public relations program to succeed should be mobilized to ensure the campaign a fair chance to meet its stated objectives.

- The formation of a public relations staff will be determined by the needs of the organization, the amount of money available, the attitude of the management, and the size, philosophy, and resources of the organization. If additional staff members are needed, specific job descriptions should be developed so that talented individuals can be sought and trained for the public relations team.

- Individuals who are assigned public relations work should, if deemed appropriate by the nature of the program, stay in the background instead of seeking the limelight.

- Public relations workers should keep abreast of the factors and influences that affect the program and develop and maintain a wide sphere of public contacts.

- As a public relations program is developed, the following items should be checked. Does the organization have a handbook, policy or guideline manual, or newsletter to keep members informed as to both their role and place in the overall picture? Does the organization have a system for disseminating information to local electronic (i.e., radio, television, Internet site) and newsprint outlets? Has the organization created a booklet, flyer, or other controlled printed matter that tells its story? Do members of the organization participate in community activities? Has the organization made provisions for a speakers' bureau so that civic and service clubs, schools, and other organizations may obtain someone to speak on various topics? Does the organization hold open houses, clinics, service learning projects, or educational seminars for interested persons? Does the organization have a video, DVD, or other visual or printed material that explains and interprets the work of the organization that can be shown and distributed to interested groups or publics? Are interinstitutional or intrainstitutional Internet being utilized to its fullest capacity?

- A good public relations program will employ all available human, technical, and informational resources to disseminate crucial information to the public to ensure meaningful dialogue among the consumer, potential consumer, community, media, and the organization.

These guidelines together with an honest, ethical, sincere, and fair approach; well-trained and courteous personnel who make customers, users, and community feel welcome and involved; and a thoughtful, considerate, and service-oriented cul-

Public relations promotes everyone involved in physical education, recreation, and sport.

tural climate will go a long way in building quality and sustainable physical education, recreation, and sport programs.

PROGRAM, STAFF, AND PUBLIC RELATIONS

The program and the staff represent perhaps the best opportunities for establishing an effective public relations program. Any school, college, department, or program can build much goodwill by providing leadership, activities, experiences, and meaningful interactions (e.g., sample programs, clinics, lecture series, workshops, health fairs).

Some of the most effective community relations occurs on a person-to-person basis. This contact might be teacher to student, student to parent, teacher to citizen, or physical educator or coach to participant. Research about communication, persuasion, and customer relationship management

PROCLAMATION

WHEREAS, the City of Wayzata, Minnesota is actively concerned and involved in nurturing and supporting the educational and physical development and achievements of its natives and residents; and

WHEREAS, the achievements academically and athletically of our native citizen, **Libby Nelson**, are a source of great community pride and interest as she represents our hometown in the nation and at the University of Minnesota as an accomplished athlete and scholar; and

WHEREAS, she will be especially honored during ceremonies at the University of Minnesota; and "Hometown Days" celebration of her achievements is representative of the recognition our City supports:

NOW, THEREFORE, BE IT RESOLVED, as Mayor of the City of Wayzata, Minnesota, I hereby do declare the date of

APRIL 5, 2006 AS OFFICIAL LIBBY NELSON WAYZATA HOMETOWN DAY IN THE CITY

Proclaimed by the City Council of the City of Wayzata this 2nd day of April, 2006.

Robert D. Gisvold, Mayor

Many communities are recognizing the contributions of their homegrown student-athletes.

indicates that one-to-one communication is a very effective tool. Data from the fitness industry about the popularity of personal training also seems to support this notion. Physical educators, coaches, and sport managers must enter and experience the community if their programs are to be meaningful and sustained.

PUBLIC RELATIONS, PUBLICITY, AND THE MEDIA

Many media (e.g., electronic, Internet, and newsprint) can and should be employed in public relations initiatives. Some media have more significance than others in certain localities (e.g., your local sports writer), and some are more readily accessible than others (e.g., local cable television, school newspapers, Internet). Physical educators, athletic and activity directors, and coaches should survey their communities to determine which media networks they have access to and which can be used most effectively and meaningfully to promote their programs, institutions, and the communities they represent to their targeted publics.

Discussion groups, focus groups, forums, coffee klatches, civic groups, town hall, and other similar meetings are frequently held in educational institutions and communities. At such gatherings, representatives from the community, including educators, parents, business people, physicians, lawyers, clergy, labor leaders, politicians, and others, discuss topics of general interest. These gatherings provide an excellent setting for physical education, recreation, and sport representatives to enlighten civic and community leaders about the value and benefits of their programs, clarify issues, clear up misunderstandings, and discuss the pros and cons of their programs and projects. Attending these types of meetings are a good way to get to know the "public" (Frigstad 1995). Physical educators, coaches, and public and private sector sport managers should play a larger role in such meetings than in the past. Much good could be done for all through proactive representation in this medium of public relations.

Someone once said, "There is no such thing as an original idea." Time allows ideas, methodologies, and concepts to be refined over and over again. Physical education, recreation, and sport managers must not be afraid to listen to people who are in the community. One of the most effective ways to keep current on the pulse of community sentiment is to form an advisory group. The purpose of the group is simple—to stay in touch with community needs, attitudes, opinions, wants, and desires. Members of an advisory group will invariably be from all walks of life. The group may be started with friends in the business community or parents of children in the organization who have an interest in certain opportunities that the program can offer.

The group should meet as often as is reasonable to discuss and brainstorm about the possibilities that exist in the immediate community to promote your programs and attract participants and advocates. Weekly e-mail or conference calls can also be conducted. Surprising results can be achieved by information relayed through school or company newsletters, updated Web sites, word of mouth, payroll envelope, e-mail, or mail box stuffers, and other ideas that have been generated at these informal meetings. In addition, allowing ownership, partnership, and inclusion in the program by including outside parties and making them feel that they are an important part of the program can only serve to expand the organization's programmatic and informational resource base for the future.

Print Media/Press and News Releases

The newsprint medium is one of the most common and useful means for disseminating information. It reaches a large audience and can be helpful in presenting and interpreting physical education, recreation, and sport to the public at large. Although news and press releases are uncontrolled once they leave the writer's hands, they provide a crucial link between the school and its programs and the public (see box 14-1).

Box 14-1   Press Release Format Example

School or Institution Name
and Address Here
Contact: (Your Name)
Day Phone:
Night Phone:
E-mail:

Release Date and Time

THE TITLE GOES HERE, ALL UPPER
CASE AND UNDERLINED LIKE THIS

The Point of Origin Dateline Goes Here—The body of the release should begin one-third of the way down the page to leave enough room for the editor or copy person to write remarks. The release proper should be all double spaced for ease of readability and editing.

Be sure to use normal indents and consistent spacing between paragraphs. It is not necessary to triple space between paragraphs. All information should be presented in descending order of importance, ending with the last important items in case last-minute editing results in the bottom of your release being lopped off.

Remember to leave at least one-inch margins all around, but resist the urge to leave huge right-hand margins in order to stretch your information.

When you arrive at the bottom of the first page, leave at least a one-inch margin and indicate either the end of your release (-30-) or that more information follows (-more-). If more information follows, try not to break paragraphs or sentences in the middle. Never break a word and complete it on the next page.

- 30 -

Posters and various visual imagery and graphics can capture and influence a large and diverse audience.

Here are some questions that might be asked to determine what makes a good news story: Is the news of interest to the public? Are the facts correct? Is the style direct? Is it written in the third person in nontechnical terms, and is it well organized? Does it include news about individuals or groups who are closely related to the local community, school, college, or other organization? Does the article have a clear goal, theme, or plan of action, and does it play a significant part in describing and interpreting the program to the public?

When a story, news or press release is going to be submitted to a newsprint medium (newspaper, magazine), phone contact should take place prior to the preparation of the manuscript. In some cases, a news advisory is preferable to a story or press release.

The following guidelines (Bevins 1995) should be followed when formulating a press release to promote a program or event:

- Complete the news release; get the message across; use title and summary lead (who, what, when, where, why, and how).
- Use writing style and format of the media outlet to which you are sending the release.
- Be concise, avoid fancy language and adjectives, and deal with the facts; one page should do it.
- Use a lead and present information in decreasing order of importance (reverse pyramid). Most editors take less than thirty seconds to view releases.
- Identify the market segment (target population) that is to be addressed.
- Identify the primary players (e.g., media experts, local feature editors, cable anchor) to whom releases should be mailed, e-mailed, or faxed.
- Contact key media people and explain the importance of the news release, to the program and community as well as to society.
- Target the release to the appropriate audience (e.g., heavy consumer, light consumer, nonconsumer).
- Mail the release in plenty of time (two to three weeks before the event).
- Events like the International Year for Sport and Physical Education, National Physical Education and Sports Week (May 1–7), National Girls and Women in Sports Day (first Thursday in February), National Sportsmanship Day (first week in March), the Great American Workout, or National Employee Health and Fitness Day are just a few of the themes that may be utilized.
- Include any other relevant, controlled materials (e.g., program brochure, annual report, media guide, description, schedule, Web site).

- Follow up the transmitted news release with a call to be sure it is "good-to-go" and to answer any questions.
- Don't forget to include your twenty-four-hour/day contact or cell phone number.
- Send a note of thanks.

There are no guarantees when dealing with the newsprint media. Many times, a supposedly great story may be submitted and will never appear before the public. Some of the most common reasons for rejecting material include limited reader interest, poor writing, inaccuracies, and insufficient information. The discretion and control that the media exercises over the public relations domain can be discouraging. The best bet is to just be persistent; get to know the key media people and learn who can be relied on for the release of important information (e.g., stories, features, events). Mixing up strategies for releasing information may be helpful. Use word of mouth, press releases, personal letters, phone calls, e-mail, and, of course, the Internet. Never give out incorrect information or information based solely on hearsay; memories are long in the media business and serious repercussions often result in subsequent negative publicity or, worse, neglect.

Thousands of popular magazines, professional journals, newsletters, trade publications (e.g., *Sports Market Place, Athletic Business, Fitness Business Pro*), and other periodicals provide another challenging outlet for building sound public relations. National newsprint media such as *Newsweek, Sport Magazine, Sports Illustrated,* and *Sports Business Journal* are excellent for publicity purposes. So are journals such as *JOPERD, AAHPERD's Update,* and *Physical Activity Today, ACSM's Health & Fitness, Americal Journal of Health Education, NIRSA, Aquatic International, Athletic Management Journal of Park and Recreation Administration, Parks and Recreation, Journal of Sport and Social Issues, NATA News, NASPE News, Journal of Sport Management, Sport Marketing Quarterly, Public Relations Quarterly, Strategies, International Sport Studies,* and *Strength and Conditioning Research,* just to name a few. E-journals ranging from the *Journal*

Public relations and marketing campaigns can be very effective in sending messages to targeted populations.

of Management History to *Women and Sport* and *Physical Activity* are readily available as is the World Wide Web virtual library. However, just like breaking into a major daily newspaper, getting manuscripts or notices in these journals and magazines (many now electronic) is difficult because of their rigid requirements. Compared with the cost of other media (local newsprint, PSAs), journal and magazine contact is usually high. Because they are expertly targeted to very specific audiences or members, however, and are now electronic and e-commerce friendly, they may reach more potential "customers" than do other lower cost related media.

Many of the major media outlets like to cover the stories with their own staff writers. Many times, suggesting ideas to these sources is better than submitting a manuscript. The public relations person can attempt to interest the editors in some particular work or project (i.e., "Dare to Play Fair," Target Market Tour, Be Active North Carolina) being done and ask them to send a staff writer to cover the story. It might be possible to get a freelance writer interested in the organization, program, or event and have him or her develop a story. Someone on the department staff with writing skill can also be assigned to write a piece for newsletter, newspaper, magazine, or Webcast consumption and then also submit the story to various periodicals for consideration.

In many cases, however, it is not necessary to get a story in the national media. Many local and community print outlets provide excellent exposure and are geared specifically to one community or a specific topic. Sound public relations must be built and nurtured, and working with the local paper, magazine, cable, radio, or television outlet will provide an extra personalized boost to the physical, education, recreation, or sport program.

The newsprint media can be used effectively by any school or organization. To be most effective, however, the information must be related to the readership of that particular publication and must meet the needs of the target population. To this end, the focal point of public relations is still providing vital information to the target audience at the most opportune time. So whether you are targeting media to promote or cover an event (the opening of a school's youth fitness camp), the parents to have them enroll their children in the camp program, the general public to have them be aware of community fitness levels and the camp program or to try to attract them as sponsors to fund scholarships for inclusion at the camp, public relations and the media and its timing are crucial.

Pictures and Graphics

Pictures represent an effective medium for public relations. Two words should be kept in mind by the persons who take and select the pictures for publication or posting: action and people. Pictures that reflect action are more interesting and appealing than stills. Furthermore, pictures with people in them are more effective than those without people. Usually a few people are better than many. Finally, such considerations as background, accuracy in details, clarity, diversity, taste, and educational significance should be taken into consideration. Some newspaper outlets require that photographs be taken by union or newspaper-employed photographers. Permission should always be secured and rules checked (e.g., NCAA, agents) to ensure that the photo and its use is within all legal and jurisdictional guidelines.

Educational matters such as budgets, statistical and demographic information about growth and diversity of school population, information or participation in various school or college service learning activities, and many other items relating to schools, corporate fitness centers, and other organizations can be made more interesting, intelligible, and appealing if presented through colorful and creative graphics. Pictures, billboards, flowcharts, and graphs should relate specifically, of course, to the age, gender, level of activity, and message that is being publicized. Digital cameras and enhanced software packages have made photos and graphics easier to place on Web sites, transmit, and download for placement in public relations tools ranging from newsletters and media guides to class posters and year-end reports.

Communications

Knowledge and expertise in both mass and interpersonal communications is imperative if sport managers are to affect any public relations or marketing programs. Management, including teachers, coaches, sports information directors (SID) and other personnel, needs to deal effectively with the reporters, columnists, Web masters, and broadcasters who will encode and transmit messages concerning the program or event. Clear, concise, consistent, and accurate messages based on the objectives of both the organization and the program must be articulated. Public speaking can be another effective medium for achieving good public relations. Presentations to schools and civic and social groups in the community as well as at public functions, gatherings, and professional meetings afford good opportunities for interpreting a "message," program, or profession to the public. However, it is important to do a commendable job, or the result can be marginal, rather than good, community relations.

To make an effective presentation or speech, a person should observe many fundamentals, including mastery of the subject, sincere interest and

Public interaction helps promote a positive image for both student-athletes and physical education, recreation, and sport programs.

enthusiasm, concern for putting thoughts rather than the speaker across to the public, directness, straightforwardness, preparation, brevity, and clear and distinct enunciation.

If the educational or sport organization is large enough and has several qualified speakers within it, a speakers' bureau may also be an asset. Various civic, school, college, church, and other leaders within a community can be informed of the services the organization has to offer. Then, when the requests come in, speakers can be assigned on the basis of qualifications and availability. The entire department or organization should set up facilities and make information and technological resources available for the preparation of such presentations. If desired by the members of the organization, in-service training, educational seminars, or courses could be developed in conjunction with the English, communications, or marketing departments, to provide hints for public speaking. Public speaking is not easy, and young professionals and student-athletes should all be exposed to such positive experiences, although only after appropriate planning, preparation, and practice.

Student-athletes in many high schools and colleges are being mobilized to speak and perform community service at local K–12 schools on academics, reading, Just Say No campaigns, sub-stance abuse, and other crucial topics. Communications and public speaking skills are requisite for all people involved in the physical education, recreation, and sport professions. Service learning opportunities ranging from hospitals to environmental cleanup, both at home and abroad, are becoming the norm, and communications, presentation, and representation are important for all involved.

Radio, Television, and Cable

Electronic media such as radio and television are powerful because of their universal appeal. These media are well worth the money spent for public relations. However, the possibilities of obtaining free or bartered time should be thoroughly explored. The idea of public service will influence some radio, television, or cable station managers to grant free time to an organization or school that is a solid citizen within the community. This publicity may be in the nature of an item included in a newscast program, a spot public service announcement (PSA), or a public service program that might range from fifteen to thirty minutes.

Some radio, television, and cable stations reserve, and make available, spots for educational purposes. One example is the "Kids and Arnold" PSA developed by the President's Council on Physical Fitness and Sports, which captured an estimated $2.8 million in comparative advertising value. These possibilities should be investigated. Many local communities, schools, and colleges have stations (e.g., cable, radio, Webcasts, podcasts) of their own and these resources should be fully utilized.

Sometimes a person must take advantage of these media on short notice; therefore it is important for an organization to be prepared with written plans and programs that can be put into operation immediately. The following include some short list items of preparation that might be kept on file:

- Know your message—health, Physical Best, Sport for All, Healthy People 2010, Move to Improve, stop smoking, Jump Rope or Hoops for Heart, National Youth Sports Program (NYSP), Dare to Play Fair

Television and cable have provided positive attention and recognition to sport at all levels.

- Know the program—style, format, audience participation, call-in time
- Know the target audience—seniors, teens, heavy users, upscale, nonconsumers, fans, fenceline community
- Tailor the message—construct and shape according to audience interest
- Tailor the presentation—to the show, time, target audience, and community pulse
- Practice—rehearse, speak in lay terms, be brief and concise, have technology and graphics ready to go and backed up

Being prepared to contribute might make the difference between being invited, accepted, or rejected for a media opportunity. The organization must also be prepared to assume the work involved in rehearsing, gathering research and background materials, full technological support, sequencing graphics, arranging facility availability, preparing the venue, or other factors essential in presenting or producing such a program.

Radio, television, and cable offer some of the best means of reaching a large number of people at one time. Audio and video Webcasts are now "online." What people see and hear has a great impact on them. Organizations concerned with physical

education, recreation, and sport should continually translate their message into material that can be used by the media. This, in turn, will assist in the building and maintaining of quality programs.

Films and Video

Film and video productions can present dramatic and informative stories ranging from an organization's public service to highlights of the training and accomplishments of its student-athletes. Such a production constitutes an effective medium for presenting a program, school, or interest story. A series of visual impressions will remain long in the minds of the viewers.

Because a vast majority of Americans enjoy films, videos, and now, Web presentations, it is important to consider them in any public relations or marketing program. Film and video are not only a form of entertainment, but also an effective medium to use to inform, educate, and motivate. They stimulate attention, create interest, and provide a way of getting across information not inherent in printed material. They can be a powerful tool if effectively incorporated into an organization's public relations campaigns.

Movies, videos, CD-ROM infomercials, DVDs, DVR (TiVo), educational television, Webcasts, and other visual aids have also been used by a number of physical education, recreation, and sports organizations, not only to present their programs to the public, but also to interest and motivate individuals in their message (e.g., health, fitness, wellness, school and community-building, social responsibility).

Information Technology

This form of public relations and marketing is truly coming into its own and ranges from the intranet where the organization can share information, reports, research, and newsletters internally to public Web sites where access to information is free flowing. The Net not only provides information about programs, but it is indeed the electronic version of a visit to your school, center, pool, or gymnasium. Video clips, virtual tours of facilities, and live stats and biographies of those involved play an integral role in public relations initiatives. In addition to Web sites and discussion groups, audio and visual Webcasts will soon bring schools, programs, field trips, games, and publics worldwide into a like arena. This presents a tremendous cultural challenge and responsibility not yet fully realized (Sterne 1999). Online auctions for fund-raising, the establishment of "kids clubs" with 20,000 members, distance education, online personal training and coaching, data mining, and all forms of data exchange ranging from one-on-one personal e-mail and list serves to the establishment of frequently asked questions (FAQ) protocols make the Internet the public relations tool of the future. The future, however, is now since more than 300 million people worldwide use the Internet, and it is estimated that over 80 percent of U.S. households will have broadband Internet access by 2010. Those of us in the profession of physical education, recreation, and sport must vigorously join and master the electronic frontier, not only to keep in touch with our publics, but to ensure their active engagement and health and well-being.

Brochures, Posters, Exhibits, and Demonstrations

Brochures, posters, and exhibits are important in any public relations program concerned with physical education, recreation, and sport. Well-illustrated, brief, and attractive brochures can visually and informatively depict programs, activities, facilities, projects, opportunities, and services that a department or organization has to offer as part of its total program.

Drawings, paintings, charts, graphics, digital pictures, and other aids, when placed on posters and properly packaged and distributed, will illustrate activities, show progress, direction, and concern, and present information visually. These media will attract and interest the public and may also provide give-aways to promote the program.

Exhibits, when properly prepared, placed, timed, and presented, such as in a store window or gymnasium entryway, school foyer, or some other prominent spot, can do much to demonstrate work being done by the school or organization.

Coaching clinics serve as effective community relations builders.

Demonstrations (including virtual demonstration diskettes) that entertain, inform, and present the total program of an organization or profession are a unique aspect of any community public relations program. The main objectives for a physical education or sport demonstration are (1) to inform the public and provide an outlet for interest in physical education and sport programs by community members; (2) to provide an opportunity for members of an organization to work together toward a common goal; (3) to demonstrate the need, value, and benefit of physical education and sport to all participants; (4) to provide opportunities for the general public to see the physical education and sport program in action; (5) to contribute to the objectives of the organization; (6) to include all participants in the activities; (7) to reflect the needs of the consumer in the present and in the future; and (8) to contribute to the education, health, and psychosocial well-being of participants and spectators.

PUBLIC RELATIONS IN ACTION

Many publics play a vital role in the arena of physical education, recreation, and sport. Each demands a personalized public relations agenda, which must be a vibrant part of the profession's creative and coordinated marketing strategy. Effective public rela-

Box 14-2   President's Council on Physical Fitness and Sport Advocacy Checklist

Yes No

☐ ☐ Physical fitness is not a part-time agenda. Does your school provide at least one period per day of instruction in vigorous physical activity?

☐ ☐ Play alone won't develop physical fitness. Is a part of each physical education period devoted to activities like running, calisthenics, agility drills, and strength training?

☐ ☐ Skill in sport is a valuable social and health asset. Does your school program offer instruction in lifetime sports like tennis, swimming, golf, skiing, and jogging?

☐ ☐ Most physical problems can be alleviated if discovered early enough. Does the school give a screening test to identify those students who are weak, inflexible, overweight, or lacking in coordination?

☐ ☐ All children can improve with help. Are there special physical education programs for students with varying disabilities?

☐ ☐ Testing is important to measure achievement. Are all students tested in physical fitness at least twice a year?

What to do to change the "No" answers to "Yes"

First: Make sure you know what your local school code says about physical education and what is specified in state laws or regulations.

Then:

1. Speak to the physical education teacher in your child's school. You will find him or her very cooperative and willing to answer your questions.

2. If the physical education teacher can't help, speak to the school principal.

3. If significant changes are needed in the school's priorities or scheduling, try to encourage your parent/teacher organization to support a regular physical education program with an adequate emphasis on physical fitness.

4. If the problem is one of policy in the entire school district, take up the issue with your local Board of Education.

5. If your school is doing all it can at this time, make certain your child gets at least one-half hour of vigorous physical activity every day before or after school.

For additional information or help in setting up a program of vigorous physical activity for your child, write:

THE PRESIDENT'S COUNCIL ON
PHYSICAL FITNESS & SPORTS
HHH Building, Room 738H
200 Independence Avenue, S.W.
Washington, DC 20201-5211
(202) 690-9000

---

tions and their accompanying marketing programs are an integral aspect of the profession of physical education and sport. AAHPERD, through various public relations efforts such as its Jump Rope for Hoops and Heart Programs or Legislation Action Center (LAC), provides quality programs, training, and resources (e.g., books, manuals, online fact sheets, standards, videos, CD-ROMs, kits, and speakers) for public consumption. NASPE (National Association for Sport and Physical Education) over the years has contributed public relations initiatives ranging from its Physical Education Public Information (PEPI) project, Physical Best, PE-TV, and Move to Improve to the Hershey Youth Project, Sport for All, and Skate in Schools Program. These activities all have served to bring to the public the values and benefits of active participation in physical education and sport programs. NASPE—Talk and NASPE—Forum online discussion groups delve further into physical activity, public relations, and advocacy.

Organizations such as the President's Council on Physical Fitness and Sport (see box 14-2), the Institution for International Sport, the Women's

Sports Foundation, and some institutions of higher education among others have also played crucial roles in not only getting out the message, but also determining through research what the message should be and how the message should be delivered as it makes its way into the global community. Some examples of the profession's public relations initiatives follow.

Jump Rope and Hoops for Heart

One of the most successful public relations activities of AAHPERD is the Jump Rope for Heart (JRFH) program. Since 1977, the American Heart Association (AHA) and AAHPERD have cooperated to sponsor rope-skipping exhibitions, Jump Rope for Heart, and Jump-Rope-a-Thons to raise funds and promote physical education. Student groups who have been involved in demonstrations have been very well received. This project has raised considerable money (over $327 million) to benefit the AHA as well as to augment AAHPERD funds and remains a tremendous public relations vehicle that focuses on community involvement. JRFH has completed over twenty-five years of providing students with jump rope skills as well as knowledge, attitudes, and understanding about the positive effects that cardiovascular fitness can play in prevention of various forms of heart disease and stroke. AAHPERD added a Hoops for Heart Program in 1995 in an effort to reach out to an even greater share of its targeted public (middle school, youth/antitobacco). Each year over 5 million children from all 50 states participate in JRFH and HFH. AAHPERD provides thorough media training supplements (i.e., kits, videos, CD-ROMs, online newsletters, and guides) that are helpful to any educator who wishes to implement these or any other AAHPERD public relations programs.

Kids in Action (NASPE)

Whether it is Kids in Action, Move to Improve, or Fit to Achieve, NASPE's initiatives and themes continue to focus on why children need physical education. Because of the continuing battle that physical education faces in our school systems, NASPE

Jump rope provides a good cardiovascular workout and also serves as an AAHPERD public relations initiative.

provides the professional pertinent information concerning initiatives such as the Physical Education for Progress (PEP) Act and the Surgeon General's Reports on Physical Activity and Sport, including Healthy People 2010, that encourage all K–12 schools to provide quality physical education and sport programs that promote healthy behaviors and lifestyles and individual well-being. The Pep Act, which was introduced in the 106th Congress on May 27, 1999, as Senate Bill 1159 and approved on December 15, 2000 is an omnibus spending bill, originally introduced by Senator Ted Stevens (R-Alaska), authorizing $400 million over a five-year period for grants to local educational agencies and schools to help initiate, expand, enhance, and improve K–12 physical education programs. NASPE recommends the following concerning quality physical education:

- It should be taught daily.
- It should be taught by a certified physical education teacher.

- It provides logical progression, K–12.
- It allows for all children, including those with disabilities, to participate and succeed at their own level.
- It encourages students to use the skills and knowledge acquired in class.

NASPE also provides guidelines, standards, and program appraisal checklists for K–12 physical education programs and coaches as well as materials ranging from brochures and press releases to PowerPoint presentations and PIPEline workshops to inform the public of the value of physical education in schools. Indeed, all K–12 teachers should be familiar with NASPE's initiatives, such as Physical Best, Skate in School, the ProLink Program, the Hershey Youth Project, Sport for All, the Active Start Project (preschool), and the PEP Grant program. NASPE—Forum, NASPE—Talk, and the Academy Action e-newsletter keep members linked (NASPE 2004, 2005).

Institute for International Sport

The Institute for International Sport (IIS) is housed at the University of Rhode Island and for almost two decades has sought to promote and improve relations among nations through the medium of sport. The IIS has brought to the public events such as the World Scholar-Athlete Games and National Sportsmanship Day (Dare to Play Fair programs). The IIS selects and honors outstanding Sports Ethics Fellows (e.g., Lance Armstrong, Bonnie Blair, Joan Benoit Samuelson, Mi Hamm, Grant Hill, March Krotee, Joe Paterno), promotes research into fair play, and provides practical application through its coordinated outreach programs ranging from its International Senior Games to its Center for Sports Parenting.

With the expansion of the Internet in school systems around the world, IIS will expand its public relations initiatives on sportsmanship and fair play, as well as its sportsmanship essay contest via its expanded Web site.

The Tucker Center for Research on Girls & Women in Sport

The vision and pioneering spirit of Dorothy McNeil Tucker led to the establishment of the Tucker Center for Research on Girls & Women in Sport at the University of Minnesota in 1993. Housed in the College of Education and Human Development's School of Kinesiology, the Tucker Center's mission is threefold: (1) to conduct, sponsor, and promote basic and applied research; (2) to support and enhance the education, training, and mentorship of graduate students; and (3) to engage in community outreach and public service by disseminating research findings and educational materials such as "Playing Unfair" and "Throw Like a Girl" to targeted constituencies.

Since its inception, the Tucker Center has provided centralization, organization, scientific excellence, and national leadership on issues of great national and local significance, such as Physical Activity and Sport in the Lives of Girls (PCPFS 1997). Through its direction and leadership, the center encourages researchers, policymakers, educators, parents, and practitioners to work together to better the lives of girls and women in ways that go far beyond the playing fields.

National Girls and Women in Sports Day (NAGWS)

The National Association for Girls and Women in Sports (NAGWS), founded in 1899, began National Girls and Women in Sports Day in 1986 to honor former volleyball great Flo Hyman, who died of Marfan's syndrome while competing overseas. With themes such as "Get in the Game" and with wide support over time from the Girl Scouts of America, the YWCA, the National Women's Law Center, the Women's Sport Foundation, and sponsorship from companies such as State Farm Insurance, NAGWS encourages young girls and women to become active participants and believers not only in the potential of sport but in themselves. NAGWS's mission to develop and deliver equitable and quality sports for ALL women and girls remains constant. NAGWS fosters quality and equality for girls and women by celebrating

National Girls and Women in Sports Day in Minnesota.

Poster used in public relations effort to promote National Physical Education and Sport Week and quality daily physical education.

National Girls and Women in Sport Day (the first Thursday in February) and by sponsoring the Wade Trophy (basketball), Backyards and Beyond, and a series of awards such as the Pathfinder Award. This nonprofit national association among five that comprise AAHPERD publishes the *Women in Sports and Physical Activity Journal,* and offers its 2005 Community Action Kit with important samples of public relations materials ranging from press releases to government proclamations to physical educators and sport professionals. (NAGWS 2005).

National Physical Fitness and Sports Month (PCPFS)

The President's Council on Physical Fitness and Sports (PCPFS) was established by executive order on July 16, 1956, by President Eisenhower as part of a national campaign to help shape up America's younger generation. Through its programs and partnerships with the public and private sectors, the council serves as a catalyst to promote health, physical activity, and fitness for people of all ages. Some of the council's programs include the Presidential Sports Honor Award, the President's Chal-

lenge Awards programs, the President's Active Lifestyle Award, National Physical Fitness and Sports Week and Month, and the Hershey Track and Field Program.

May is usually designated National Physical Fitness and Sports Month. National Physical Fitness and Sports Month was established in 1983 by the President's Council on Physical Fitness and Sports and is endorsed by the President of the United States and supported by AAHPERD. Various partnering and public relations plans are utilized to motivate the public into action. Slogans such as "Shape up America," "Spring Into Action," "Many Faces Many Ways," "Your it. Get fit!," and public relations messages delivered by the president and governors as well as by celebrities such as Arnold Schwarzenegger, Florence Griffith Joyner, Ralph Boston, Pam Shriver, Tom McMillen, Zina Garrison-Jackson,

Lynn Swann, and Dot Richardson among others are used to alert people of all ages that physical education, sport, and fitness remain a top priority and a national concern. As a result of this promotion, many communities, schools, and businesses (e.g., Burger King, Coke, General Mills, Trec Bicycle, Bally's, and the National Dairy Council) across the country sponsor various physical education and sport activities and other health-related fitness events during the month of May. The PCPFS provides posters and its May: National Physical Fitness and Sports Month/Week Kit to serve as a further resource to help promote physical education, health and fitness, and sport programs.

PUBLIC RELATIONS IN SCHOOL AND COMMUNITIES

Research conducted in various school systems concerning the nature and scope of their public relations programs has revealed the following information about physical education and sport.

The policies that govern the programs indicated that the director of physical education and/or athletics and activities was usually directly responsible for public relations press releases. All printed material needed the approval of the director, principal, and/or the superintendent of schools before being released. The coaches of interscholastic sport were responsible for preparing all sport-specific press releases regarding their programs. Each physical educator and coach was urged to recognize that his or her activities were an integral part of the professional and public relations programs of the entire school district.

The most frequently used public relations tools included newspaper, posters, videos, public speaking, school publications, newsletters, letters to parents, demonstrations and exhibits, personal contact, pictures, radio, television, cable, window displays, brochures, sports days, and bulletin boards. Electronic public relations tools (e-mail, Webcasts) are beginning to be utilized. The five media public relations tools found to be the most effective in their professional and pub-

lic relations programs were (1) the total physical education and sport program, (2) personal contact, (3) newspapers, (4) public speaking, and (5) demonstrations and exhibits (see box 14-3).

All the directors of physical education and sport indicated that sport received more publicity than the physical education program. When asked why they thought this was so, some typical comments were: "the public demands it," "because of public interest," and "the newspapers will only accept and print press releases on athletics." This has been slightly modified with the nation's health and fitness status drawing a lot of attention.

When the directors were asked what message they were trying to convey to the public, the following were typical answers: the value of the total physical education and sport programs, the importance of the programs to the student, recognition and achievement of all students in all areas of physical education and sport, efforts and energies being expended to give each person a worthwhile experience in physical education and sport, the role of the physical education and sport programs in enhancing the health, wellness, and welfare of the participant, and the aims and objectives of the total physical education and sport programs.

In summary, the professional and public relations programs in the school districts surveyed were conducted in light of the following principles:

- Each physical education and sport department recognized the importance of an active public relations program.

- Sound policies guided the program.

- Responsibility for public relations was shared by all members of the department and staff, with central authority residing with the director.

- Many different media modes were employed to interpret the program to the numerous publics (i.e., parents, community).

- The total physical education and sport program was recognized as being the most effective medium of professional and community relations.

Box 14-3 Public Relations and Fund-Raising Promotional Ideas

Art and sports memorabilia auction	Exhibitions or shows	Races—10K, 5K, walking
Arts and crafts fair	Fairs (i.e., health, fitness)	Radio marathon
Backgammon tournament	Field days	Raffles (turkey)
Bake sale (cheesecakes)	Fiesta days	Reading marathon
Ballroom dancing	Film festival	Roller-skating marathon
Basketball marathon	Fishing derby	Sailing regatta
Bicycle marathon	Garage sale	Silent or online auction
Bingo	Golf tournament	Skating marathon
Book sale and fair	Greeting card sales	Spaghetti or chili dinners
Bowling contest	Guest speakers	Sponsorships
Candles	"Guiness" risk activities	Sport camps
Candy, coffee, cookie, or fruit sales	Hayrides	Sports clinics
Canoe/kayak race	Historical and/or house tour	Sports tournaments
Car wash	Holding a dance	Superstars competition
Carnivals	Magazine sale	Swimming marathon
Church supper	Monopoly marathon	T-shirt and sweatshirt sales
Club exhibitions	Naming rights	Tailgate party
Concert	Night or mini golf	Talent show
Coupon book sales	Pageant (male or female)	Tennis tournament
Craft fest	Pancake breakfast	Tree/flower wreath sale
Cross-country skiing marathon	Photos	Used equipment swaps
Dedications	Picture taking	Web clubs
	Pins/buttons	Weiner and pig roasts
	Pizza sales	Wrapping paper sales

- Efforts were made to interpret accurate facts about physical education and sport to the public.
- Considerable planning was needed for the effective use of public relations media.
- The Internet plays important role in promoting programs.

Communities have also assisted schools and other public and private sector organizations and associations in the promotion of physical education and sport. Rotary Clubs, Lions Clubs, American Legion Posts, Boys and Girls Clubs, Job Corps, The American Red Cross, Junior Chamber of Commerce, Partners of the Americas, and Special Olympics International, among other service organizations, have a long tradition of assisting in the positive public relations of physical education and sport programs. Publishing houses and sporting goods organizations have also entered the pub-lic relations arena and have established such partnered programs as Active Start, Physical Best, Sport for All, STARS, PE4LIFE, Quality Sports through Quality Coaching, and Skate in School.

MARKETING PHYSICAL EDUCATION, RECREATION, AND SPORT PROGRAMS

In the past, U.S. corporate structures manufactured goods and then made every effort to sell them. Today, management teams adhere to a strict policy of marketing analysis, or identifying the needs and interests of the consumer, and then trying to satisfy these desires. Contemporary management is marketing oriented rather than production oriented. In other words, nothing should be manufactured or supplied unless there is a demand for it. This concept applies to physical education and sport as well as to the corporate arena.

Partners of the Americas in cooperation with the University of Minnesota and Special Olympics International play host to a Uruguyan coach and gold medal winning athlete.

Turn on the television and watch or participate in a fitness show or infomercial, trek down a supermarket aisle and collect a coupon for "diet something" or an entry form for the 5K Turkey Trot, or pick up the phone and answer an opinion survey concerning Healthy People 2010 or your activity preferences for your next vacation—all these situations involve marketing.

According to the American Marketing Association, marketing is the process of planning and executing the conception, pricing, promotion, and distribution of ideas, goods, and services to create exchanges that satisfy individual and organizational goals (Churchill and Peter 2000). Marketing is the dynamic human activity directed toward the analysis, planning, implementation, and control of carefully formulated programs designed to bring about voluntary exchanges of values with target markets for the purpose of achieving organizational objectives. It relies heavily on designing the organization's offering in terms of the target markets' needs and desires (Kotler 2003; Lamb, Hair, and McDaniel 2006). Physical education and sports marketing is the development of exchanges

Box 14-4 Steps in Strategic Marketing Management

Set organizations, mission and objectives
   Include a "positive statement"
Analyze consumer or user group
   Conduct an environmental scan
   Consumer needs, wants, desires
   Consumer demographics, motivations, etc.
   Forecasting data collected and considered
Target consumer group segment or population
   Gather more detailed information, such as psychographics, social patterning and lifestyle, etc.
   Form, consult, and data mine databases and other marketing information systems
   Identify barriers and limitations to promotion plans
   Cost, distribution, competitor groups, culture, technology, etc.
Select plan
   Consider strengths, weaknesses, opportunity, threats, and competition (SWOT)
   Consider all questions, issues, and concerns
   Evaluate alternative plans
   Initiate pilot study or project
Implement plan
   Including internal and external assignments and time constraints and promotion (print, electronic, Internet)
Review and evaluate plan
   Including process, outcome, and consumer satisfaction

Source: Krotee, 1997.

in which the organization (physical education and sport) and customers (participants, users, spectators) voluntarily engage in transactions (activities, programs, events) that are designed to benefit both of them. For example, a customer buys a membership to the YMCA and receives services (health and fitness), whereas the YMCA receives compensation to provide quality programs, facilities, and trained personnel. In physical education and sport programs, the marketing concept is that the organization or school should satisfy the participant's needs and wants as a means to achieve the objectives desired.

Physical education, recreation, and sport marketing is the anticipation, management, and satisfaction of the consumers' wants and needs through the application of marketing principles, processes, and practice. It begins and ends with the consumer, participant, and user. It relates to the various services provided and activities, programs, and events implemented and how well these services meet the needs of the consumer or user group (i.e. students, faculty, alumni, community, and public in general). Marketing is a continuous process by which the objectives of the physical education, recreation, and sport organization or its programs can be achieved (Pitts and Stotlar 2002). It is a process guided by principles and guidelines that facilitate the development of a marketing strategy or plan that enables the organization to accomplish its objectives as efficiently and effectively as possible. This marketing strategy plan should be grounded in the organization's mission and objectives, operated within its financial resources (budget), and based on factors that can be controlled. Although marketing physical education, recreation, and sport is unique, it can help guide the school or organization to accomplish the following:

- Define your unique niche and be sure that you have the right programs, personnel, and services to meet the publics' needs and wants.
- Reach the publics (i.e., preschool, male teens, fenceline, seniors) you want with a clear and consistent message that motivates people to respond.
- Decide what you want to accomplish, go for it, and secure resources and support to meet your objectives.
- Stand out from the crowd and gain the positive attention, support, and enthusiasm needed to sustain the organization's mission.
- Have an impact on the health, wellness, and welfare of your community as well as in the global marketplace.

Successful public relations and marketing campaigns bring championship events, as well as revenue and recognition, to programs, schools, and communities. Target Center, Minneapolis, Minn.

Marketing, if effectively managed, can serve to increase the participant base and numbers of activities and programs, create additional revenue streams, enhance visibility and image, increase the demand for services, and promote the recognition and reputation of the school or program.

Principles of Marketing Physical Education and Sport

Principles are fundamental, comprehensive rules for action. There are several principles that members of the profession should adhere to when marketing physical education and sport programs.

Customer Principle

Physical education and sport marketing should be customer-driven. Customers (i.e., students, participants, user groups) are the "life blood" of the organization. We should know who they are, how they think, and what they feel, so we can strive to deliver superior consumer value in the way of programs and services.

Competition Principle

Value-driven marketing recognizes the competitors' programs, facilities, and perks that influence the participant. Our school programs, activities, instruction, and services must be and should be superior. Sometimes cross-functional partnering (i.e., school district/private sector fitness club) serves to add strength to school or professional programs while neutralizing the competition.

Practice Principle

Managers of physical education, recreation, and sport programs must become more proactive and innovative and not reactive in their marketing and public relations strategies. Physical educators and sport managers must continually and enthusiastically reach out to their respective publics and sell their messages to create more demand for their programs, facilities, and expertise.

Cross-Functional Principle

Marketing is relatively new to many physical education, recreation, and sport programs. It is, however, becoming more and more crucial to the profession as well as many schools' and institutions' programmatic sustainability. We must involve all resources (i.e., teachers, coaches, administrators, parents, community) in order to more effectively fund, support, and deliver school programs and their messages. It is recommended that cross-functional teams or task forces be formed to plan, implement, evaluate, and control marketing initiatives concerning programmatic operation and delivery. This team approach will not only serve to reduce potential conflict but also assist in the development of more successful marketing strategies derived from many input sources and developed from a wide range of ideas and viewpoints.

Continuous Improvement Principle

Managers and all involved in physical education, recreation, and sport programs must continually strive to improve programs, processes, operations, facilities, services, and instructional delivery. Periodic audits, reviews, and opinion surveys with user groups, potential consumers, and nonparticipant groups can help guide marketing and public relations strategies, as well as programmatic adjustments and new initiatives. Further, encouraging

and rewarding staff and other internal team members' ideas and suggestions are requisite to delivering value to the participant.

Stakeholder Principle

Although most of physical education and sport marketing initiatives are focused on a targeted segment of the public, other stakeholders must also be considered. These include the consumer/ user, special interest group, employees, the neighborhood, and society at large. All stakeholders must be fully considered as programs are marketed and delivered, so no one is or believes that he or she is marginalized or left behind.

The Marketing Process in Physical Education, Recreation, and Sport

There are several key ingredients and activities that make up the marketing process. These include the organization's mission and objectives, marketing opportunity analysis, development of market strategy, implementation of the strategy, and evaluation of the marketing efforts. The process is grounded in the various factors that relate to influencing and/or persuading the identified or targeted public to participate in, join, endorse, purchase, support, and/or utilize a service, program, organization, place, person, or cause. Effective marketing makes things happen—classes increase in size, participants are excited, funding increases, the phone rings more often, and human needs are more powerfully met.

Organization Mission and Objectives

The marketing process has its roots embedded in the organization's mission and objectives. The identification and setting of these are one of management's primary responsibilities. An organization's mission statement and objectives are based on careful analysis of the needs and benefits sought by present and potential participants. The organization's mission and objectives, together with its vision of what the organization or program is about, what it strives for (action goals), or wants (image goals) establishes the boundaries for the marketing strategy and plans that must be developed, which in turn will carry more specific marketing objectives.

Marketing Opportunity Analysis

A market analysis identifies for the organization which benefits (i.e., activities, programs, social contact) people want the organization to deliver and satisfy. It provides the organizer with a description and estimation of the number of market segments (e.g., urban male teens, female middle-age tennis players) that may be of interest to the organization. It further scans the environment concerning forces (social, demographic, economic, technological, legal, political), events, and relationships that may affect the organization. It also provides a demographic (age, gender, income, education), psychographic, (lifestyle), and geographical (urban, climate) picture of potential segment participants. It serves to help identify market opportunities on the basis of organizational or programmatic strengths, weaknesses, opportunities, as well as threats or competition (SWOT analysis). Marketing opportunity analysis provides guidelines for the development of market strategy.

Market Strategy

Marketing strategy involves a combination of three integrative activities (1) selection of one or more target markets, (2) setting marketing objectives, and (3) developing and maintaining an appropriate marketing mix (the six Ps).

The first integrative activity serves the organizations' purposes by deciding on which group to focus or target. This permits the manager to move to the second activity or the development of specific marketing objectives or statements of what is to be accomplished through marketing activities. Marketing objectives should be consistent with organizational objectives, be measurable, and specify a timeframe during which they will be achieved. These objectives set the standard so everyone involved can gauge his or her performance; they may also serve as an internal motivational tool.

The third component of market strategy is that of marketing mix. The marketing mix or six Ps refers to the unique blend of product/program, publics, place, pricing, production, and promotion strategies designed to produce mutually satisfying exchanges with the target market. Successful marketing mixes do not occur by chance. They represent fundamental strategies designed by astute professionals who want to achieve success. Effective marketing mixes, such as those that follow, should be carefully tailored to satisfy target market members.

Product/program strategies   The core of any organization is its product (e.g., Minnesota Vikings, New York Yankees, Manchester United) or its programs (e.g., Learn-to-Swim). There is no substitute for a quality product/program. Just the names of quality products/programs can create additional recognition and value if marketed properly. It is difficult to proceed with any other of the six Ps without identifying exactly what product/program is to be marketed in order to meet the public's needs, wants, and preferences.

Publics   The potential user of the product/program must be identified (e.g., elementary school children), targeted, and informed of the benefits of the program (e.g., health, safety, fun, friends, fitness). Programs, in turn, must be malleable and able to fit the ever-changing public preference.

Place or distribution strategies   Products/programs must be available, assessable, and where and how the customers want them. Schools are often used as places for targeted community programs such as Learn-to-Swim or Evening Hoops. Places (e.g., schools, facilities, neighborhoods, educational travel and development destinations) are often employed as critical elements of marketing strategies.

Pricing strategies   Prices are the most visible, flexible, and manipulated of the marketing mix components. Pricing involves, for example, what a parent or participant must give up to obtain entrance into the Learn-to-Swim program or a Minnesota Vikings game. Price is often linked with value and must be marketed with this concept in mind. For the consumer to receive positive satisfaction, the product/program benefits must outweigh the costs. Pricing typically plays an integral role in the organization's ability to meet objectives.

Production strategies Production usually refers to the organization's capability to keep up with the demand for product, programs, or services. For physical education, recreation, and sport this might entail having enough space in programs, enough classes in pilates, tennis, or yoga, or a large enough inventory of sweatshirts to sell at school promotions. Production, demand, and supply are crucial in marketing strategy.

Promotion strategies The final component of the six Ps comprising the marketing mix is promotion strategies. Promotion strategies describe various marketing efforts and interventions to stimulate consumer interest in, awareness of, and "signing on" for the product/program. Promotion includes personal selling, advertising, sales promotions, and the public relations strategies that were discussed earlier in the chapter. Its role is to bring about mutually satisfying exchange with target markets by informing, educating, persuading, and reminding parents, for example, of the benefits of daily physical education or recreational sports programs. A good promotions program involves all parties and when skillfully integrated with the other Ps and implemented can make physical education and sport programs an integral part of all communities. Needless to say, there is much to be done to improve marketing strategy as it is applies to physical education, recreation, and sport.

Not every market strategy and plan calls for the inclusion of each of the six Ps in order to meet its objectives. Some objectives can be reached by simply moving to a new location (place), adding a new program (soccer for girls), changing your name from Blue Ribbon Sports to Nike (promotion), or making facilities more accessible, such as providing free parking or free game day light rail or bus transport (price). Adding new program elements, carefully pricing product/programs or

events, and improving services (e.g., on-line credit card registration and payment), or other such adjustments can greatly influence the emphasis needed on other marketing mix strategy components.

Implementation This is the segment of the marketing process that turns marketing strategy and plans into action and ensures that these actions or assignments are executed in a manner that accomplishes the plans' objectives. If a school were going to increase the Learn-to-Swim enrollment by 10 percent or its recreational sport enrollment for girls by 25 percent, a promotion strategy would need to be implemented. This might include a door-to-door peer recruitment program and Internet follow-up, and if these were not properly implemented, then the marketing strategy may very well be doomed. Many physical education, recreation, and sport programs call upon students and/or volunteers to implement their marketing strategies, plans, and resulting programs. It is imperative that a solid public relations program be in place so that the publics are well aware of this unique situation. It is also vital that all involved in the marketing process be well trained, aware of their important roles, and recognized and rewarded for their efforts.

Evaluation Evaluation is the final link in the continually evolving physical education, recreation, and sport marketing process. Evaluation entails gauging the extent to which marketing objectives were met during specific time periods. Periodic evaluation enables the manager (i.e., teacher, coach, youth sport leader) to adjust programs, objectives (if unrealistic), or marketing mix components to meet, sustain, or exceed customer satisfaction. Informal internal and external participant feedback, formalized product/program audits, and market research are requisite to ensuring that all aspects of programs are current and meet the needs of the customer. The rapidly changing environment evolving in physical education and sport makes evaluation and market research crucial to effectively keep pace with our product/programs.

Marketing and its principles and processes play a significant role in everyday society. We all participate in the marketing process as both consumers and educators. Indeed almost half of every dollar we spend as consumers goes toward public relations and marketing initiatives. By developing a better understanding of marketing and its principles and participant feedback processes, we can become a more sophisticated provider and physical education, recreation, and sport manager who will be better able to meet the health and fitness needs and demands of society.

TAKE IT TO THE NET!

American Marketing Association
www.ama.org

The Association of Fund-Raising Distribution and Suppliers (AFRDS)
www.afrds.org

Gopher Sports Web Site
www.gophersports.com

Institute for International Sport (IIS)
www.internationalsport.com

Jump Rope and Hoops for Heart Programs
www.aahperd.org

National Association for Girls and Women in Sport (NAGWS)
www.nagws.org

National Association of Collegiate Directors of Athletics (NACDA)
www.nacda.collegesports.com

The Physical Education for Progress Act (PEP)
www.pecentral.org

Press Release Writing (PRW)
www.press-release-writing.com

Sports Marketing Quarterly (online)
www.smqonline.com

Tucker Center
www.education.umn.edu/tuckercenter

SUMMARY

Public relations and marketing are important responsibilities for all managers of physical education, recreation, and sport programs. Public support for physical education, recreation, and sport programs is essential if the necessary funds, facilities, human and technical resources, and other support essentials are to be provided. Therefore, sound principles and guidelines should chart the course for public relations and marketing programs in a way that will communicate the mission and objectives of these programs to the various publics who are interested. Furthermore, all the faculty, staff, and members of the organization should be involved in both the public relations and marketing programs to ensure that the content, conduct, and delivery of such programs are of the highest standard.

SELF-ASSESSMENT ACTIVITIES

These activities will assist students in determining if material and competencies presented in this chapter have been mastered.

1. As a manager, you are conducting a staff meeting in your school. Explain to the staff why you believe that an in-service program in public relations would be valuable to staff members and managers alike.

2. What is meant by the term *marketing,* and what are its implications for promoting physical education and sport programs?

3. What is meant by the fact that physical education, recreation, and sport organizations are dealing with not just one but many publics? Identify two different publics and how they differ; indicate what type of public relations program you would employ with each.

4. List the principles that should be observed in a marketing program. Apply five of these principles in communicating the importance of a strong physical education program in your school.

5. Prepare a one-page press release to be published or a thirty-second public service announcement (PSA) for broadcast to the public about some

event or phase of a physical education or sport program. Present these to the class and have the class evaluate them.

6. Present a fund-raising plan that would serve to build public relations in an elementary physical education program.

7. Prepare a five-minute speech to present to a local civic organization about the role of sport in community building and global awareness.

8. Divide the class into groups of four and construct a trifold brochure that will market your school's physical education, recreation, and sport programs to the immediate community.

REFERENCES

1. Appley, L. A.1956. *Management in action.* New York: American Management Association.
2. Bevins, T. 1995. *Handbook for public relations writing.* Lincolnwood, IL: NTC Business Books.
3. Churchill, G. A., and J. P. Peter. 2000. *Marketing: Creating value for customers.* New York: McGraw-Hill.
4. Cutlip, S. M., A. H. Center, and G. M. Broom. 2000. *Effective public relations.* Upper Saddle River, NJ: Pearson Prentice Hall.
5. Frigstad, D. B. 1995. *Know your market.* Grants Pass, OR: Oasis Press.
6. Kotler, P .2003. *Marketing management: Analysis, implementation planning, and control.* Upper Saddle River, NJ: Pearson Prentice Hall.
7. Lamb, C. W., J. F. Hair, and C. McDaniel. 2006. *Essentials of marketing.* Mason, OH: South-Western.
8. McCarthy, E. J. 1960. *Basic marketing: A managerial approach.* Homewood, IL: Richard D. Irwin.
9. M. A. Milne, and McDonald, G. R. 1999. *Sport marketing: Managing the exchange process.* Sudbury, MA: Jones and Bartlett.
10. Meek, A. 1998. An estimate of the size and supported economics of the sports industry in the United States. *Sport Marketing Quarterly* 6(4):15–21.
11. NAGWS. 2005. Community Action Kit. Reston, VA: AAHPERD.
12. NAPSE. 2004. *Moving into the future: National standards for physical education.* Reston, VA: NASPE.
13. ———. 2005. *Quality coaches, quality sports: National standards for sport coaches.* Reston, VA: NASPE.
14. PCPFS. 1997. *Physical activity and sport in the lives of girls.* Washington, DC: U.S. Department of Health and Human Services.
15. Pitts, B. G., and D. K. Stotlar. 2002. *Fundamentals of sport marketing.* Morgantown, WV: Fitness Information Technology.
16. Sterne, J.1999. *World Wide Web marketing: Integrating the Web into your marketing strategy.* New York: Wiley.
17. Williams, J. 2000. Public relations. In *Successful sport management,* edited by G. Lewis and H. Appenzeller. Durham, NC: Carolina Academic Press.

SUGGESTED READINGS

AAHPERD, Jump Rope for Heart, Hoops for Heart, and Sport and Physical Advocacy Publicity Kits, 1900 Association Drive, Reston, VA 22091.

AAHPERD and NASPE provide excellent materials by way of publicity kits that assist in forming vigorous promotion for physical education and sport programs.

Brooks, C. M. 1994. *Sports marketing: Competitive business strategies for sports.* Englewood Cliffs, NJ: Prentice Hall.

Presents an environmental or climate assessment approach to various marketing strategies. Examines topics ranging from priority seating to internal and external sport competitions in order to facilitate better strategic market planning processes.

Cousens, L., and T. Slack. 1996. Using sport sponsorship to penetrate local markets: The case of the fast food industry. *Journal of Sport Management* 10: 169–87.

Frigstad, D. B. 1995. *Know your market.* Grants Pass, OR: Oasis Press.

Presents an overview of the market research process including forecasting, market analysis, and setting up a market information system.

Fullerton, S., and R. Dodge. 1995. An application of market segmentation in a sports marketing arena: We all can't be Greg Norman. *Sport Marketing Quarterly* 4(3):43–47.

Gregory, J. R. 1999. *Marketing corporate image.* Lincolnwood, IL: NTC Business Books.

Hoffman, K. D. 2006. *Marketing Principles & Best Practices.* Mason, OH: South-Western.

Horine, L., and D. Stotlar. 2003. *Administration of physical and education sport programs.* Dubuque, IA: McGraw-Hill.

Jackson, J. J. 1981. *Recreation and Sport.* Springfield IL: Charles C. Thomas.

Presents the theoretical base for various aspects of management, including public relations, then links it with specific situations in physical education, recreation, and sport.

Kaser, K., and D. B. Oelkers. 2001. *Sports and entertainment marketing*. Cincinnati, OH: South-Western.

Marken, G. A. 1987. Thirteen ways to make enemies of the press. *Public Relations Quarterly* 32(Winter):30–31.
Discusses guidelines for management when dealing with the press. Provides information on how to work in cooperative spirit with the media.

Sutton, W. A., and R. Watlington. 1994. Communicating with women in the 1990s: The role of sport marketing. *Sport Marketing Quarterly* 3(2):9–13.

Yiannakis, A. 1989. Some contributions of sport sociology to the marketing of sport and leisure organizations. *Journal of Sport Management* 3:103–15.

Presents a detailed analysis of critical concerns involving sport marketing, consultative assistance, target market identification, and product marketing. Also discusses the marketing mix of product, price, place, promotions, and people.

Yow, D. A., R. H. Migliore, W. W. Bowden, R. E. Stevens, and D. L. Loudon. 2000. *Strategic planning for intercollegiate athletics*. Binghamton, NY: Haworth Press.
Provides insight into strategic and tactical planning for intercollegiate sport marketing, as well as other salient management functions.

CHAPTER 15

Office Management

INSTRUCTIONAL OBJECTIVES AND COMPETENCIES TO BE ACHIEVED

After reading this chapter the student should be able to:

- Appreciate the importance of office management in a physical education and sport program.
- Understand and appreciate the role of information technology and related applications in accomplishing management tasks.
- Justify the need for office staff in the management of a physical education and sport program.
- Identify and describe the role that "boundarylessness" can play in sound office management.

- Identify basic office management procedures that should be used in carrying out the tasks of a physical education and sport program.
- List the records and databases that should be maintained in a physical educator's or athletic and activities director's office.
- Identify the various roles office personnel may play in a physical educator's or athletic and activities director's office.

Managers of physical education and sport programs know that efficient office management determines to a great extent the success and image of their programs. Good organizational skills, solid technological capability, and efficient management of schedules, priorities, and deadlines, as well as how people are treated, separate an outstanding office from a good office. Therefore, along with integrated functions such as fiscal accountability and responsibility, facility management, and public relation, and marketing, office management is a crucial management component.

Office management has often been neglected by physical educators, coaches, directors of athletics and activities, and other sport managers. Efficient and effective office management indicates a well-run department. The main office is the hub of information gathering, distribution and records management. It is the place for first impressions, communication between student and teacher or athlete and coach, the focus of management duties and functions, and a point of contact for the management and staff and, oftentimes, the public.

479

An effective and efficiently managed office provides a place in which teachers, coaches, and sports managers are assisted and relieved of myriad duties that can be overwhelming unless taken on by well-trained and highly competent office managers or personnel. Sound office management enables others (teachers, coaches, department heads) to enhance their productivity. In addition to relieving these employees of responsibility for other tasks, thereby maximizing their efficiency on other assigned tasks and duties, office personnel provide staff with information they need, when they need it, and in the format they desire. Office personnel also provide service to students and other user groups, which serves to engender sound public relations. Whether an organization is large or small, staffed with student workers or volunteers, the office should be properly maintained, possess up-to-date office equipment and technology, be environmentally and ergonomically friendly, and follow a well-established plan of office procedures (Peterson and Patten 1995; Quible 2005). With that accomplished, office tasks can be appropriately assigned and professionally carried out, and "office management trust"—which involves managing the organization's intellectual capitol; human, physical, and technological resources; and strategic relationships—can be maximized.

OFFICE MANAGEMENT TASKS

Although some office management tasks have been moved to a centralized location (e.g., principal's or district business manager's office), today's widespread use of technology has enabled office staff to continue to play a crucial role in the support of human resources, programs, institutions, or other management enterprises. Technology and its related applications and processes allow office personnel to instantly retrieve relevant information (e.g., student medical status, budget, eligibility, equipment inventory, schedule), and continue to be responsible for many important tasks including the following:

Communication

The office is the nerve center of the organization, where information is received, retrieved, and disseminated to staff members, user groups, and others

Offices and office staff serve as hubs for effective communication and management.

by means such as direct or face-to-face, video or teleconferencing, telephone, cell phone, facsimile, or written correspondence, intercom or personal digital assistant (PDA), pager, and electronic mail (e-mail). Communication systems and procedures ranging from personally recorded voice mail and call waiting to instant messaging and spam control should be in place to effectively and promptly service, record, transmit, and distribute messages. With the proliferation of voice mail systems and automated handling of incoming calls, care should be taken to not alienate callers. The option to speak to a live person should always be provided. The word communication comes from the Latin *communicare,* which means "to make common." So the degree the message sender and receiver connect and how a valid and accurate common understanding is reached are crucial. Office personnel should be trained to handle the majority of incoming calls and should know where to route a caller if they cannot assist them directly. Proper office management procedure protocol should be followed and professional courtesy always extended.

The advent of electronic mail systems has replaced some face-to-face and telephone communication. Usually less formal than a written letter, an electronic mail message is beneficial for rapid response and forwarding information to many recipients. Personnel and company policies should be in place regarding the use of electronic messaging. In addition it is recommended that a weekly "brainstorming" meeting be scheduled where program issues and departmental concerns and targets can be addressed to the office management team. Staff development in the form of successful teamwork (conflict resolution, problem solving), communications, leadership, and technology should be a part of all physical education, recreation, and sport offices (Chesla 2000).

Correspondence and Processing of Materials

The office is the setting for preparing and filing written letters and reports for managers and staff members and for handling and sorting incoming and outgoing mail, faxes, and FedEx's.

The office is also the focal point for gathering, retreiving, recording, entering, duplicating, processing and storing data, information, and materials pertinent to the management of the program. It is also where information packets (e.g., schedules, program guides, promotional materials) are distributed.

Record Keeping/Human Resources/Reporting

The office is the place in which records containing information on personnel, students, athletes, and other materials are housed or made available via computer database. Payroll entry, calendar management, schedules, attendance, and medical status reports are typically priorities of well-run offices. Technology has greatly improved the accessibility to centrally located records. These records must be safeguarded and secured (HIPAA) to prohibit unauthorized access. Personnel information that can be accessed by others should not contain medical records. There should be a separate folder and secure location for individual confidential medical records. Generally, the office is not only the gatekeeper but also the watchdog of the organization.

The office is a place for preparing, compiling, and retrieving data and information and for finalizing reports for various faculty and staff members and other personnel to whom the management is required to report. The managing and reporting of information consumes the majority of any offices'

day. Because we are in the technology, information, and knowledge age, we have more information available to us in one day than our previous ancestors could have encountered in one year. Being able to use, organize, and present the information effectively is a goal of a well-run office.

Budget Preparation and Implementation

The office is where budget information is collected and prepared, payrolls are initiated and may be distributed, revenues and expenditures are recorded and reconciled, and financial reports and summaries are compiled and stored or electronically submitted to a central database. A solid financial system such as a CUFS (College and University Financial System) among others should be in place, so the budget can be easily organized for review and auditing.

Supplies and Equipment

The office is the place for requesting, ordering, receiving, and disbursing supplies and equipment needed for conducting the organization's various activities. It should be a place that safeguards programmatic assets. An adequate assignment of duties system should be in place, so one office person is not responsible for the ordering, receiving, and disbursement of payment for supplies and equipment. At the minimum, two people should be involved in the receiving, recording, and disbursement of payment. Office forms, such as purchase orders and receiving slips, should contain proper authorization, usually in the form of initials and budget code number before an invoice is paid. Accurate inventory records should be maintained on all supplies and equipment. Property records, warranty information, date recieved, repaired, and manufactured, and directions should be maintained on all equipment.

Community and Public Relations

The office is a key communications center for the conduct, planning, and management of community-based and professional projects that are closely related and important to the achievement of the

Teleconference by computer assists in building solid networks and informed managers and staff at the University of Maryland, College Park. Copyright Mike Morgan.

mission, objectives, goals, and functions of the organization. It is the place that is contacted, serves as a reference point for, and represents the organization to the public. The office also serves as a primary location for appointments, small conferences, and employment interviews. In many organizations it is also a place for informal meetings and gatherings. Reception and receiving of visitors and guests as well as other personnel is crucial to the program and staff training concerning courtesy, communications, and office environment is highly recommended.

Emergencies

The office is a focal point for meeting day-to-day crisis and emergency situations that call for immediate action. Instant communication and location of personnel, students, and program participants necessitate precise and up-to-date record keeping. All office staff should be trained in emergency plans, and procedures, and the office should have an emergency plan for medical, fire, disaster, hurricane, tornado, and other life-threatening emergencies. Practice drills should be conducted at least twice a year.

IMPORTANCE OF OFFICE MANAGEMENT

Colleagues, community leaders, business contacts, new staff members, potential employees, vendors, students, and other visitors frequently have their initial contacts with physical education, recreation and sport managers and departments in the central office (Timm and Peterson 2000). Their reception, the environment and the courtesies they are promptly shown, the efficiency and attitude with which the office work is conducted, and other covert operational details leave lasting impressions. Friends, alumni, employees, and recruits are often made or lost at this strategic control point.

Communications Center

Office work, broadly defined, is the handling and management of information. The office is usually the place in which schedules are arranged and distributed; telephone calls made and received; fax and electronic mail transmitted; reports and correspondence word processed, duplicated, and electronically or manually distributed and stored; mail received, opened, and sorted; bulletins prepared and issued; conferences arranged and held; appointments made and confirmed; and visitors received and greetings voiced and exchanged. The office represents the hub of activity around which revolves the effective and efficient functioning of the physical education and coaching personnel. Unless these functions are carried out with dispatch, accuracy, and courtesy, with the intent to serve the student, customer, or user group the entire management process begins to break down.

Focus of Management Duties

The chief management personnel (e.g., department chair, athletic and activities director, office manager, etc.), administrative assistants, and office workers help constitute the office staff. The filing system (e.g., computer, manual), key records and files, and reports are usually housed in the office. When inventories need to be examined, budgets audited, letters and reports pulled from files, or the program chair or director consulted

Offices can take on many shapes and forms, but they are always crucial to the management process.

on important matters, the office is frequently the point of contact. Management responsibilities are carried out in the office, making this space a focal point for the entire organization (see box 15-1).

Handbook or Manual of Tasks

Every office and office staff should be well organized, and one way to assist office personnel is to develop a manual or handbook for office procedures (Maslow and Kaplan 1998). This manual will serve as a guide not only for accomplishing office tasks, assignments, and duties but also for all office conduct and behavior. The manual should contain checklists detailing each job assignment and policies related to the terms of employment, as well as emergency and risk management plans and protocol. As new tasks are created and assigned to office staff, the manual should be updated.

Point of Contact for Management and Staff Members

Staff members visit the office regularly. Mailboxes may be located there, and telephone calls, faxes, messages, and electronic mail may be taken and transferred by the office. Conferences and appointments with students and visitors often bring staff members to the office. Constant communication and dialogue take place between the management and staff members in this setting. The atmosphere, culture, and environment in the office can and should create high staff morale, efficiency, a friendly and secure climate, and a feeling of working toward common goals (Chesla 2000).

BUILDING MANAGEMENT AND OFFICE STAFF RELATIONSHIPS

The management should establish a good working relationship with office staff members. To accomplish this, management must be aware of employee needs, desires, interests, and expectancies in order to build confidence, self-respect, esteem, and trust. Job security, professional development opportunity, reward packages, recognition, and attention are keys to relationship building. The office staff should have a feeling of belonging and a recognition that they are an important part of the organization. This form of "boundarylessness" or co-location (that should be practiced throughout the organization) serves as a behavior definer, a way of getting people outside of their organizational boxes and offices, and working together faster. The work each one performs, his or her ideas, and workplace socialization patterns are essential to the achievement of the organization's goals (Susskind, McKarnan, and Thomas-Larmer 1999).

Most managers depend heavily on their office staff members to carry out day-to-day duties and routines efficiently and productively. Well-trained, highly motivated, and satisfied office personnel are a must to effectively accomplish this task. Furthermore, managers (e.g., teachers, athletic and activities directors, coaches) are frequently away from their desks and the office on organization assignments, and in their absence, the office must function in the same manner as when the manager is present. This goal cannot be achieved unless an excellent working relationship exists between the management and office staff members and the staff is empowered to make decisions that fall within their sphere of influence. The greater the empowerment (e.g., sharing of information, continuous learning, trust, respect), the better the training, and the more collaborative the work environment, the more successful the office team will be in meeting the needs of both the organization and its immediate community.

In-Service Education of Office Staff

Management should adopt the learning organization model (Chesla 2000; Peters 1999) and provide the time and resources for office staff development. Management should encourage office staff members to engage in in-service and continuing education and training (knowledge capital accumulation). Areas in which improvement might take place include word processing skills, computer programming and graphics, Web construction, updating the filing system, simplifying record keeping, and human relations skills (e.g., assertiveness, multicultural, diversity, leadership, and self-development training).

Sexual Harassment/Workplace Violence

Sexual harassment is a problem that has been highlighted in recent years. Electronic and print media stories and court cases have described how sexual harassment in educational settings has resulted in dismissals as well as psychological trauma, not to mention the damage to the reputation of the school or institution. Unwanted flirtation, unwelcome sexual advances, obscene jokes or lewd comments, and other verbal or physical contact are all forms of sexual harassment and serve to create a hostile work environment. The United States Census Bureau estimates 146 incidents of violence per every 1,000 teachers each year. Managers must recognize that such conduct and situations occur and cannot be tolerated. Clearly written departmental procedures and policies outlining such behavior and its consequences should be established, and staff should be encouraged to attend workshops and training programs (sexual harassment, nonviolent crisis prevention intervention, chemical abuse) concerning these and other serious workplace problems.

OFFICE AND WORKSTATION SPACE

The central office for physical education, recreation, and sport departments should be readily accessible. This means both in employment, Title I of the ADA prohibits discrimination in employment against people with disabilities, as well as in

Reception areas with viewing windows are popular in health and fitness centers.

Box 15-2	Recommended Space Guidelines	
Individual Room		**Space Requirements**
Department head		350 square feet
Faculty and staff		250 square feet
Supervisors		200 square feet
Office employees		100–125 square feet
Modular workstation		100 square feet
Conference/seminar room		25 square feet per person
Reception room		35 square feet per person
Main corridor		6–8 feet wide
Secondary corridor		4–5 feet wide
Cross aisles (every 25–30 feet)		3–4 feet wide

matters regarding Title II and III of the ADA encompassing public services, use, and accommodations (Colker and Milani 2005). If physically possible, the central office should be near health service and athletic training offices, gymnasiums, arenas, exercise rooms, locker rooms, fields, pools, and other departmental facilities.

Most central offices for physical education and sport should consist of at least three divisions including (1) a general reception area, (2) office staff workstations, and (3) private offices. Other desirable features to be considered are a restroom, storage and multifunction copying room, and conference/seminar room for staff and other meetings and functions.

General Reception Area

The general reception area is used by visitors as a waiting room, reception room, or information center; and for office services in general. The area should be attractive and well maintained, with comfortable chairs, current and attractive message boards, a computer information kiosk, and other items essential to carrying out necessary management routines. The area should create a warm, friendly, professional atmosphere. A counter, railing, or desk divider should separate

the general reception area from the rest of the office facilities and workstations. This division helps ensure greater privacy, ownership, and security and reduces work distractions for more efficient conduct of office responsibilities. (See box 15-2.)

Support Staff Workstations

All work spaces and workstations should meet established environmental health and safety standards. Consideration should be given to designing work areas ergonomically, especially those areas where keyboards are in use and/or staff are seated for long periods of time (Peterson and Patten 1995; Quible 2005). The work space should be separated from the general reception and waiting area. It should be equipped with desktop computer systems, files, tables, telephones, multifunction copying machine (fax, laser printer, scanner), and ample counter or work space. It is often desirable to have a private alcove or office for one or more office staff, depending on the size of the department and office space. Office dividers (voice privacy design) are also effective in providing personalized work stations. Privacy is often needed for word processing, certain phone calls, preparing reports, or for the convenience of visitors and other personnel. Ample lighting and sufficient space for freedom of movement should ensure that duties can be carried out comfortably and with minimal confusion, traffic, and difficulty.

Private Offices

The chairperson or director of the department or program and possibly other staff members, depending on the school size and educational domain (college, university), should have private offices. The offices should be large enough (at least 120 square feet) so that the persons in managerial positions can concentrate on their work without interruptions, conduct private conferences and tutorials with students, interact with staff members or visitors, and in general carry out their duties as efficiently as possible. The offices should be well lighted, wired for cable, climate controlled, and appropriately equipped with intranet and the Internet (see Equipment and Supplies, on pages 487–488), well maintained, and secure. Desks and workstations should be functional, and calendars, schedule pads, and palm pilots for appointments and conferences, and other essential organizational materials should be provided. Filing and storage cabinets, bookshelves, resource material, and other office equipment (e.g., computer, laser printer, Power Point set-up, VCR, etc.) should be provided as needed. Some issues concerning the cost and supervision of private offices versus open, cluster, or neighborhood workstation schemes have been studied and deserve consideration depending on the mission and scope of the organization.

Conference, Seminar, and Resource Room

Because the cost of office space is increasing, many organizations seemingly cannot afford to have such a multidimensional meeting place and workstation. Upon further review, however, and depending on the size and mission of the organization, having such a room (twenty-five square feet per person) is highly recommended. It should be

Private staff offices are necessary for maximal efficiency.

wired and equipped for multimedia presentations, video, and teleconferencing; maintain adequate shelf and display space; and possess limited restroom and kitchen facilities.

OFFICE PERSONNEL

The number of office personnel depends on the size, scope, and mission of the program or department. The staff can consist of an office manager (supervisor), an administrative assistant (i.e., accounts, grants, payroll), and office staff in a large department. However, most offices, especially at the school level, usually consist of one administrative assistant or principal secretary. In some situations, student workers, interns, and volunteers may be the only office personnel available. This is why the selection and qualities of office personnel (sometimes only one person) and the interpersonal relationships established are vital to any physical education, recreation, and sport program.

The following are brief descriptions of the roles of various specialized office personnel, but as mentioned, these duties are usually collapsed into one or, if fortunate, two top-notch office staff.

The office staff position and their accompanying roles will vary with departments and programs. In some programs, office staff serve as receptionist or greeter. In this role it is essential that they be polite, courteous, respectful, and helpful to visitors, guests, members, and callers. They should be knowledgeable about how to deal with routine departmental matters and where to direct inquiries that can be handled better elsewhere.

Office staff must be solid contributors to the chairperson and to the department as a whole. To be most helpful, they should be well versed in one or more computer operation systems, experienced in a variety of office software, be master word processors, public relations representatives, expert computer operators, and be efficient at photocopying, scanning, faxing, and time management. They see that the office runs smoothly. They must know where documents and materials are filed and be able to access them quickly, should assist manage-

ment with minor details (e.g., appointments, calendar, copying, presentations), and should see that accurate records are maintained, databases established, and reports sent out on time.

Other duties and functions of outstanding office staff range from keeping managerial calendars to maintaining public relations, from taking minutes to control and security (e.g., keys, locks), and from completing endless forms to laboring over transcribed reports and manuscripts. The office staff are the backbone of most departments and should both command respect from and show respect for all personnel involved in the managerial process.

Office staff should be selected very carefully. Experience, intelligence, character, personality, honesty, common sense, appearance, and ability should play important roles in the selection process. They should be well educated, experienced, technologically proficient, and possess a solid background in word processing, computer and software applications, bookkeeping and accounting, and English as well as the requisite psychosocial qualities (e.g., discretion, loyalty, integrity). In some small schools, and colleges, the manager may have to rely partially or entirely on students (e.g., work study) to perform much of the office work. In-service and continuing education should take place for all student workers to ensure that acceptable procedures are followed in the conduct of their work. Student help is a necessary part of most office teams and should provide a meaningful experience for the employee. This responsibility usually resides with the office manager, or administrative assistant, but sometimes the manager must also embrace this important duty.

EQUIPMENT AND SUPPLIES

Whether an office is efficient and effective sometimes depends on the equipment, technology, and supplies available. The materials needed vary with the size of the organization. In smaller organizations, equipment such as computers and copying machines might be centrally located rather than in departmental office space. The following are some of the physical resources that should be considered when conducting a functional analysis of office requirements (FAOR):

Bookcases

Bulletin boards or white board

Bursting machine (ticketing)

Cabinets (lockable)

Calendars

Calculator

Camera (digital-MP3)

Cell phone

CD burner

Chairs (ergonomically adjustable)

Clips

Coat racks

Clock

Computer package and desktop system with Internet access and antivirus software installed (laser printer, keyboard tray, mouse or trackball, network interface cards, appropriate software such as Internet browser, spreadsheet, database, word processor, collaboration software, address book, e-mail client, graphics design package, Web programming, etc.)

Copying and reproduction machine

Desk baskets, dividers, lamps, and pads

Desks/workstations (ergonomically fitted)

Dictionaries/thesaurus/atlas

Digital mini disc audio recorder

Digital projector (PowerPoint)

Digital video recorder (TiVo)

Facsimile machine

File cabinet (lockable)

First-aid kit

Folding machine

Keyboard (split with ergonomic waist rest)

Lamination machine

Laser printer

Letter trays

Magazine racks

Paper cutter

Paperweight

Paste, glue, tape

Pencil sharpeners (manual and electric)

Pencils and pens

Personal digital assistant (PDA)

Phone directory

Pictures or posters

Poster printer

Rulers

Safe

Scale for postage

Scanner

Scissors

Scrapbooks

Shredder

Stamps (postage meter, electronic or PC postage)

Stapling machine, three-ring punch

Stationery and paper

Tables

Telephone

Typewriter

Umbrella rack

Video, VCR, and DVD

Wastebaskets

Word processor

Although physical resources (e.g., equipment, supplies, technology, space) are vital for effective and efficient office functioning and/or communicating and for sound records management, the well-trained and committed human resource in the form of competent office staff is still the most crucial commodity and is the key to successful office management.

COMPUTER APPLICATIONS IN OFFICE MANAGEMENT

In 1983, sales of personal computers reached approximately 3.5 million units. By the early 1990s, over $61 billion was spent on computers with the government alone spending over $300 billion over this timeframe to move its information technology systems into the twenty-first century. Today, well over half of United States households are reported to have computers with projected 2006 expenditures to reach $665 billion or almost $3,000 per person aged sixteen and over. It is estimated that 80 percent of all professional, managerial, and administrative jobs depend on computers, and expenditure relating to computer utilization has reached almost 25 percent of our gross national product. Needless to say, the computer, technology, information, and knowledge age is here and will continue to play a significant role not only in office management where it serves to expedite and enhance service for the customer (e.g., student, user group, community) but also in the conduct of all physical education, recreation, and sport programs.

The Lexington, Massachusetts, public schools have used their computer system to link all physical education staff members to an electronic mail system. This link enables physical education teachers and their supervisors to communicate instantaneously within all school buildings through the use of desktop computers linked to the school system's mainframe computer. This system eliminates delays caused by use of interoffice mailing systems and provides for immediate communication to individuals or specified groups on the network.

Technology and well-trained staff play important roles in office management.

The Lexington school system has also developed a computerized program for tracking students in grades 3 through 12 as they participate in AAHPERD's Physical Best. Teachers in each school, upon completion of the testing, enter the raw data from their desktop computer into a user-friendly, menu-driven mainframe program. This program converts entered data instantaneously to national normed percentiles, maintains a progressive student database, and provides an individualized fitness report card. The program also offers predesigned graphics packages to help with presentations at parent conferences, school board meetings, and other public relations ventures.

Another feature of the Lexington program allows each physical education teacher and coach, after being assigned a predetermined budget amount, to enter a computerized catalog of physical education and sport equipment and purchase requirements. These orders are sorted and compiled into a singular bid list and sent to a variety of vendors. When the bids are returned and analyzed, the computer writes the purchase orders automatically. The manager, supervisor, or coach can keep up to date on purchases and budget expenditures and their projected implications through specified procedures and continuous staff input concerning needs (e.g., equipment, travel, tournaments, etc.).

Whether it is signing up for the appropriate physical education, recreation, or distance education class (online registration); taking a virtual tour of school or campus facilities, or programs including staff biographies and scholarship opportunities; designing a curriculum or interactive computer-assisted feedback programs, assessment tools, or individualized exercise programs and report cards; or joining professional listservs (i.e., PE-News, PE-Talk, NASPE-Talk), the computer and its accompanying technology have begun a revolution in the profession. This technology-driven revolution has brought to the fingertips of the professional numerous "instructional and reference" Web camps ranging from K–12 content (i.e., biomechanics, drugs and alcohol, obesity) and resource programs (i.e., message boards, clip art, award maker, Publisher) to those sites dedicated to professional development (i.e., ASCD Education Bulletin, PE-Central, PE-Forum). Online classes, listservs, newsgroups, Blogs TEL or technology-assisted learning and computer-based training (CBT) programs, library resources, and electronic newsletters and journals continue to be developed, expanded, exposed, and explored as the computer and its technological infrastructure become more sophisticated and accessible. Indeed, computer and information management, if expertly applied, can contribute substantially to cost reduction, as well as to increased managerial efficiency and productivity across the entire Physical Activity and Sport Continuum.

Public and private sector physical fitness and wellness organizations have also significantly increased their efficiency as well as reduced their costs by adopting computer technology. Member attendance, activity preferences, entry, control and security, member registration and billing, and market segmentation research all contribute to satisfied customers and good public relations. Many corporate entities maintain a computer systems approach to help achieve the goals of their corporate health and fitness programs. The computer has been particularly helpful in providing demographic, fitness, and health and risk assessment data on employees and in providing exercise and nutritional analyses, in which the employee keeps a daily record of activity workouts including type, duration, and intensity to gain caloric expenditure (see figure 15-1).

Technology is not only useful in physical education, sport, and corporate fitness settings but it also plays a significant role in the conduct of the recreation, parks, and leisure service industry. Computers are regularly employed to examine community needs and interests, and survey respective constituencies, membership, or target populations (i.e., Wilderness Inquiry). From residential usage patterns (i.e., fee structure, loyalty, constraints), and Delphi environmental impact studies to scheduling and personalized therapeutic recreational programming and from Photoshop brochure design for public relations to Quicken, the computer has made an immense contribution to all phases of the recreation, parks, and leisure service profession.

Computer Contributions to Management

Computers are electronic digital machines that can, among other things, perform managerial functions in areas such as physical education, recreation, and sport. The computer possesses a central processing unit (CPU) including memory and will carry out a given set of instructions almost instantaneously. It can process data about physical education and sport programs (e.g., budget, test scores, body mass index, report cards) by performing mathematical and logical operations. The computer can process, store, and instantaneously transfer or move information or output, typically in the form of a letter, report, manuscript, proposal, or budget statement.

The main advantages for management in using a computer include *speed;* it saves a considerable amount of time (e.g., the addition that one person could do in 100 days can be done in a second or less via computer). The speed of a computer is determined by its microprocessor. The first PCs were 8-bit, 4.77 MHz machines while today's PC weighs in at 64 bits, 350–733 MHz and increasing. This means the PC can move 350 million bits of information per second—over 1,000 times faster than its PC predecessor. A second advantage is *accuracy;* the computer does not make errors if the correct data or input are applied. Some programs even identify and correct errors. A third advantage is that it *imposes discipline;* a person must thoroughly understand a problem before programming the computer to arrive at the correct answer. A fourth advantage is *versatility;* the computer can score, add, subtract, multiply, divide, sort, compare, correct, simulate, draw, transfer, and store information as well as perform a variety of other potentially helpful operations. This together with its flexibility, expandability, reliability, and cost effectiveness make the computer a valuable tool limited only by the imagination of the user (Mohnsen 2004).

The computer software most likely to be applied by management includes word processing, database, spreadsheets, desktop publishing including presentation graphics, and networking through the Internet, including accessing the World Wide Web.

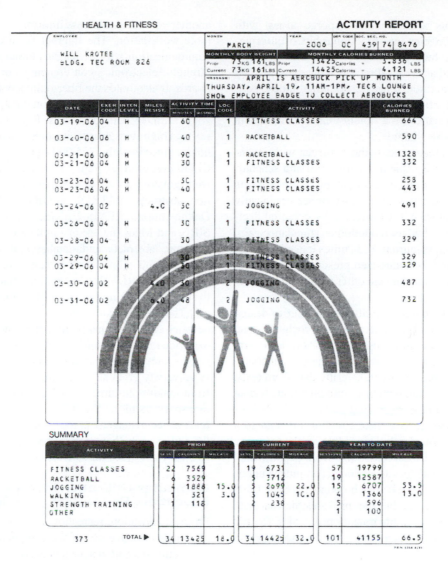

HEALTH & FITNESS   **ACTIVITY REPORT**

EMPLOYEE	MONTH	YEAR	DEP. CODE	SOC. SEC. NO.
WILL KROTEE BLDG. TEC ROOM 826	MARCH	2006	OC	439|74|8476

		MONTHLY BODY WEIGHT		MONTHLY CALORIES BURNED			
	Prior	73 KG 161 LBS	Prior	13425 Calories	=	3.836 LBS
	Current	73 KG 161 LBS	Current	14425 Calories	=	4.121 LBS

MESSAGE: APRIL IS AEROBUCK PICK UP MONTH
THURSDAY, APRIL 19, 11AM-1PM, TEC8 LOUNGE
SHOW EMPLOYEE BADGE TO COLLECT AEROBUCKS

DATE	EXER CODE	INTEN LEVEL	MILES. RESIST.	ACTIVITY TIME MINUTES	SECONDS	LOC CODE	ACTIVITY	CALORIES BURNED
03-19-06	04	H		60		1	FITNESS CLASSES	664
03-20-06	06	H		40		1	RACKETBALL	590
03-21-06	06	H		90		1	RACKETBALL	1328
03-21-06	04	H		30		1	FITNESS CLASSES	332
03-23-06	04	M		30		1	FITNESS CLASSES	258
03-23-06	04	H		40		1	FITNESS CLASSES	443
03-24-06	02		4.0	30		2	JOGGING	491
03-26-06	04	H		30		1	FITNESS CLASSES	332
03-28-06	04	H		30		1	FITNESS CLASSES	329
03-29-06	04	H		30		1	FITNESS CLASSES	329
03-29-06	04	H		30		1	FITNESS CLASSES	329
03-30-06	02		4.0	30		2	JOGGING	487
03-31-06	02		6.0	48		2	JOGGING	732

SUMMARY

ACTIVITY	PRIOR			CURRENT			YEAR TO DATE		
	SESS.	CALORIES	MILEAGE	SESS.	CALORIES	MILEAGE	SESSIONS	CALORIES	MILEAGE
FITNESS CLASSES	22	7569		19	6731		57	19799	
RACKETBALL	6	3529		5	3712		19	12587	
JOGGING	4	1888	15.0	5	2699	22.0	15	6707	53.5
WALKING	1	321	3.0	3	1045	10.0	4	1366	13.0
STRENGTH TRAINING	1	118		2	238		5	596	
OTHER							1	100	
373 TOTAL ▶	34	13425	18.0	34	14425	32.0	101	41155	66.5

7EN 1556 4/81

Figure 15-1. Sample computer activity report used in many corporate fitness program settings.

Word processing is the computer function most called upon by management. Letters, agendas, memos, minutes, and other correspondence; manuscripts; reports; curriculum guides; policy manuals; playbooks; forms; and evaluations; among other items, are common word processing outcomes that can be created, edited, alphabetized, spell checked, stored and manipulated through mail merge, and graphics applications.

Mail merge is a word processing option that saves manager's and office staff's time when writing letters or sending out personalized promotional materials. One standard or boilerplate letter is written and merged with individualized information from other fields or files to create a personalized document.

Database processing or software has transformed worn phone books, old student and personnel records, mailing lists, and past locker assignments and scouting reports, along with other collectibles into functional bits of information for the business manager, teacher, coach, and athletic and activities director. A database permits the user to enter, retrieve, organize, index, sort, link related files and update and manipulate related information in a timely manner. These data can be readily shared.

Spreadsheets assist the manager with inventory, purchasing, facility utilization, and scheduling, budgeting, and other countables. Spreadsheets permit the manager to forecast, or see graphically how the future will be affected by potential decisions such as budget reduction or attendance gain. Grades, fitness journals (i.e., miles logged, calories burned), and individualized prescribed exercise or training program data are other recommended uses for spreadsheets.

Desktop publishing allows the user to design newsletters and produce fliers, brochures, and overhead transparencies as well as curriculum guides and playbooks with graphics. Scanners facilitate this process by transfering data from texts, ledgers, and printed pictures into electronic format for editing and storage.

Networking is a means to link the staff to a centralized data bank. Depending on the software, this communication may range from departmental electronic mail to international computer conferencing and BITNET, which connects about 1,500 organizations. The Internet provides the user with not only e-mail but file transfer protocol (FTP) and remote log-on, which enable the user to log on to

another computer to access information from a remote workstation. The Internet is an enabler for communication with colleagues either directly or through electronic conferencing or message boards. It also holds the fiber-optic key to valuable library resources and information databases.

CD-ROM (Compact Disk–Read Only Memory) is a high storage capacity, optimal disk that can hold approximately 275,000 typewritten pages. CD-ROMs often contain large databases, ranging from government census information to dissertation abstracts. DATRIX, SPORT Discus, Sport Dokumention, LEXIS-NEXIS, ERIC, PsyLIT, SIRC and MedLine are examples of professional literature abstracts and databases that teachers, coaches, and administrators can access. Digital versatile discs (DVDs) are commonplace and able to store endless amounts (4.7 GBs) of information.

The *World Wide Web (WWW)* is a universal network of servers that permits the user to connect to a wide range of resources (over 800 million Web sites)—everything from Supreme Court decisions to university graduate programs' home pages, and from making an airline reservation to purchasing rare sports memorabilia, the WWW is the consummate office management tool. Take It to the Net! at the end of each chapter provides some representative Web resources for consideration.

Computer Utilization in Physical Education, Recreation, and Sport

Physical education, recreation, and sport programs can make effective use of the computer. It can be programmed to aid in management decision making at all levels. The bottom line is recognizing that many management tasks—budgeting, class, contest, and event scheduling, record keeping, assessment and evaluation, direct mail public relations—can be handled by the computer at a far more accurate and efficient pace than manually by the office staff.

The computer can be especially valuable in the areas of budget and finance, human resources, programs and scheduling, and facilities. Budget and finance tasks such as handling payrolls, inventories, budget control and allocation (see figure 15-2), cost analysis, purchasing, billing, and general accounting

Well-trained, courteous, and friendly office staff serve to build sound public relations.

REPT FIN333 16   INSTRUCTIONAL SUPPORT SERVICES
ACCOUNTING PERIOD 12

SORT KEYS: NBR-PRG-EXP

OBJ	DESCRIPTION		YTD-EXPENDED	A YTD-EXPENDED	B YTD-ENCUMBER	C BUDGET	C-(A+B) BUDGET-BALANCE	%EXP
200	DISTRICT CONTEST	TOTAL	0.00	1,315.82	0.00	3,500.00	2,184.18	37.6
220	ATHLETIC DIR OFFICE	TOTAL	18,579.35	72,336.13	0.00	264,540.00	192,203.87	27.3
221	FOOTBALL-BOYS	TOTAL	2,984.03	70,129.30	0.00	90,010.00	19,880.70	77.9
222	BASKETBALL-BOYS	TOTAL	5,131.51	6,139.85	0.00	42,980.00	36,840.15	14.3
223	HOCKEY-BOYS	TOTAL	6,626.46	7,371.31	0.00	49,360.00	41,988.69	14.9
224	BASEBALL-BOYS	TOTAL	0.00	994.00	0.00	34,880.00	33,886.00	2.8
226	SOCCER-BOYS	TOTAL	1,182.73	34,109.46	0.00	37,580.00	3,470.54	90.8
227	GYMNASTICS-BOYS	TOTAL	197.00	12,144.11	0.00	17,480.00	5,335.89	69.5
228	SWIMMING-BOYS	TOTAL	2,883.37	5,987.47	0.00	24,760.00	18,772.53	24.2
229	CC-SKIING-BOYS	TOTAL	797.64	797.64	0.00	5,640.00	4,842.36	14.1
230	WRESTLING-BOYS	TOTAL	2,568.20	3,560.79	0.00	27,960.00	24,399.21	12.7
231	TRACK-BOYS	TOTAL	265.26	1,283.61	0.00	26,570.00	25,286.39	4.8
232	CC-RUNNING-BOYS	TOTAL	5.82	4,219.30	0.00	5,360.00	1,140.70	78.7
233	GOLF-BOYS	TOTAL	373.43	389.48	0.00	9,980.00	9,590.52	3.9
234	TENNIS-BOYS	TOTAL	0.00	82.20	0.00	12,540.00	12,457.80	.7
235	SLALOM/SKIING-BOYS	TOTAL	520.55	520.55	0.00	6,320.00	5,799.45	8.2
240	VOLLEYBALL-GIRLS	TOTAL	803.90	24,915.16	0.00	34,780.00	9,864.84	71.6
241	BASKETBALL-GIRLS	TOTAL	6,303.42	9,886.92	0.00	41,380.00	31,493.08	23.9
242	GYMNASTICS-GIRLS	TOTAL	2,724.62	2,724.94	0.00	16,980.00	14,217.06	16.2
243	CC-SKIING-GIRLS	TOTAL	717.66	717.66	0.00	5,380.00	4,662.34	13.3

Figure 15-2. A school district computer-driven sport budget control document.

are areas that benefit from the computer. In the area of human resources, the computer can save much office staff time and work in tasks like student registration, grade reporting and recording, faculty assignments, and year-end reports. The computer can assist in programming, preparing presentations, designing curricula and instructional strategies, and in scheduling students (e.g., demand analysis) or other clientele for particular classes, space, activities or programs. It can record facts about students and user group interests, faculty and staff availability, facility scheduling, and staff use (Fulton-Calkins 2003).

To be more specific, physical educators and sport managers are interested in having complete demographic records on faculty and staff: names; addresses; phone and fax numbers; e-mail addresses; teaching background; accomplishments; and teaching loads. The computer is a tremendous asset in having such records filed, sorted, and immediately accessible. Registration and billing of students and class scheduling can be better accomplished. The computer can accurately report which gymnasiums, swimming pools, tennis courts, weight rooms, basketball courts, fields, classrooms, and other facilities are in use and by whom at any particular time. The computer can be used to keep physical fitness assessment data, health status, and accident reports on every student or member of an organization.

Support staff can also employ the computer to generate a master file of physical fitness data for each person, compare the data to past performance, state and national norms, and print out, label, and mail a report card. The computer can keep attendance records, compare prices for equipment and supplies, and locate every book and periodical related to physical education and sport in your library (Mohnsen 2004). Additionally, some institutions and systems, such as the Big Ten, the University of Chicago, and the University of North Carolina have formed cooperative information management consortiums so that their library resources are electronically available to each other's members.

For facilities management, the computer can help in configuring the best use of building space, availability of facilities, facility user groups, equipment inventory, cost of building maintenance and energy, and projected future needs of buildings and other facilities. This information is crucial to long-range planning as well as to efficient and effective facility usage.

Uses for the computer in sport programs include scheduling games, travel, and practice facilities, gathering data on players in a school or organization, and identifying team and players' tendencies, weaknesses, and strengths. The computer can also keep individual statistics on every team or position player as well as on the opponents.

Other computer applications called upon in physical education, recreation, and sport may include long-range scheduling, newsletter construction, travel arrangements and transportation schedules, news releases, fitness forms, grade or report cards, locker and lock assignments, access control, media guides, injury reports and rehabilitation schedules, playbooks, ticket generation, eligibility and insurance lists, potential sponsors for fundraising, trend analysis, scoreboard graphics, maintenance inventory, and a host of other applications that can reduce time and increase the efficiency and effectiveness of office and program operation.

Without question, office management and the profession of physical education and sport have been revolutionized by the computer. From local area networks (LAN) to e-mail and e-journals, from computer-assisted instruction and simulation to SPSS and SAS statistical programs, and from the Virtual Library Home Page on the World Wide Web to spell checking and Web cam, the computer and its endless supply of software programs has permeated contemporary society including the arena of physical education, recreation, and sport. The functions described here are only some of the applications of the computer to physical education, recreation, and sport.

Although the computer and its accompanying operating systems and application software have brought about dramatic change for the profession and this "megashift" has been for the most part positive in regard to the consolidation and storage of information, the reduction of error and surprise, the relief of drudgery, and the saving of time and money, it has not come without problems and concerns. These range from literacy apprehension to expense, from repetitive overuse injury and technostress to fiber-optic highway viruses, and from security to intellectual property rights and cybernetics. The psychological cost of always being accessible and the "check in" syndrome also come into play in this arena. Some also have associated the computer to decreasing levels of fitness, increased obesity, and growing psychosocial depersonalization. Regardless, as the result of computerization, the demand for qualified office staff to operate the engines of technology and make decisions about processing information will remain a high priority, so the goals of "enlightened management" to keep as many people as possible in the loop can be accomplished (Maslow and Kaplan 1998). The challenge, as we traverse the twenty-first century, is to become computer literate and conversant in order to function more effectively and to better contribute to society. Computer literacy is requisite for all students and staff and should play an ongoing role in the professional development of all teachers, coaches, athletic and activities directors, and sport managers.

MANAGEMENT ROUTINE

The management routine (Tedesco and Mitchell 1987), or manner in which the day-to-day business of the organization, center, or department is carried out by the organization's office staff, represents the basic reason why such an entity exists. Although technology has reduced labor intensity and time and has even omitted some office procedures, there are still basic aspects of management routine that should continue to receive careful consideration and attention for optimal office efficiency and effectiveness.

Appearance, Dress, and Conduct

The physical education and sport office (or even the "floor") is a professional setting, and those working in the office should look professional. Clothing should be in good taste and reflect the professionalism of the office. If there is uncertainty as to what is appropriate, new staff should take their cues

Office professionalism and conduct are important for all office staff personnel.

from dress worn by other staff or check with their supervisor or immediate manager. Of course each person will want to express his or her own taste and style, but this will be an indication of what is considered appropriate attire for the office and reflect on the department, school, institution, or agency. Office staff are often the first people encountered by the public when making initial contact with the office. Office staff have the responsibility to be professional, thoughtful, considerate, and courteous in manner. First impressions are often lasting impressions! Office staff should be good listeners, accurate, articulate, discrete, and loyal. If excessive demands are made, the staff should be able to communicate their feelings to the manager and keep the lines of communication open.

Office Hours

The office should be open during regular hours. This usually means from 7:30 or 8:00 A.M. to 4:30 or 5:00 P.M. in most school and institutional settings. During this time, someone should always be present to answer the telephone, greet visitors, field questions, and carry out the regular functions of the office. Some exceptions to these hours may be made (e.g., flextime, job sharing), but in all cases, office hours should be posted, publicized as widely as possible, and placed on the departmental Web site. Staff members should post regular office hours indicating when they will be accessible, and these hours should also be posted and placed on file in the central office as well as the Web. Staff members should faithfully observe their office hours and keep office staff informed of their whereabouts. Alternative times should be supplied to the central office if for some circumstance (e.g., attendance at national meeting, professional development seminar), office hours cannot be observed; the result will be that requests for information and assistance can be properly handled or forwarded and staff members can be reached if necessary.

Assignments

All assignments for office staff should be in writing, with job descriptions and tasks clearly outlined and appropriately publicized. Office staff may be required to turn on, check, and audit office machines; process and duplicate materials; prepare weekly bulletins or PowerPoint presentations; order, distribute, and account for supplies; check, update, and prepare the calendar of events; recycle office materials; contact students; sort mail; and assist in general office cleanup. These duties, among others, should be clearly understood and carried out at the proper time. Specific responsibilities should be set, appropriate work priorities established, and a schedule of duties prepared to prevent any misunderstanding. Any misunderstandings should be quickly and amicably resolved because respect, pride, cooperative spirit, motivation, and efficiency of the organization must be maintained.

Correspondence

Correspondence represents a most effective public relations medium. Letters, memos, and messages can be written and transmitted in a cold, impersonal, and inappropriate manner, or they can carry warmth, respect, and courtesy and help interpret what a program reflects and is trying to accomplish for student, staff, faculty, or other user group or organization. Letters, memos, and messages should be prepared carefully, using proper grammar and a format that meets the highest standards of professional practice. If a staff member must prepare his or her own letters, these same standards should be met. All correspondence should convey the feeling that the department is anxious to assist, support, and serve wherever possible. Even with the advent

of computer spell checking, all correspondence should be proofread and all addresses checked. Letters and memos should be distributed promptly, and follow-up memos should be sent in a timely fashion. Copies, both electronic and manual (paper), of all important correspondence should be given a reference number and stored for future retrieval. Creative office personnel should also improve and refine appropriate office forms and management information systems in an effort to reduce turnaround time.

Records Management Systems

For manual, lateral, or vertical filing, the office should contain metal filing cases that can be secured. The filing system employed depends on the number of staff involved and the person doing the filing, but in any case, it should be simple and functional and should be used for storing only the most current information. Other records, data, and information should, when possible, be stored on computer disk or microfiche or in another storage area that is easily accessible. Files usually consist of correspondence and informational material. For ease of retrieving material, some form of alphabetical filing should be applied, although numerical, geographical, and alphanumerical filing may at times be practical. The alphabetical files utilize a name or subject designator (e.g., "Bucher, Charles A.," "Medical Examinations," or "Equipment") and a manila or hanging folder to hold all the material to be filed under that name, subject, number, or "index code." Files can also be scanned to disc or microfilmed. Cross-references (by numbers, dates, classification, or keyword) should be included to facilitate locating material. Guide cards can be used to show which divisions of the file pertain to each letter of the alphabet, thus facilitating the search for material.

Office files should be maintained accurately. Documents should be filed chronologically with the most recent on top. The person responsible for the files should take care to see that any letter or other material borrowed from a file is returned to the proper folder and that the folder is returned to its correct location. Filing should also be kept up to date. A periodic review of the files should be made to cull material that is no longer pertinent to the department. Files that for any reason are removed from the file cabinet should be signed out and signed in on return. If files are stored via computer, backup copies and vital records protection are a must. Document management software can digitize paper documents and index, store and facilitate retrieval, not to mention, recapturing manual storage space. All state and federal requirements for record retention (i.e., Individual Education Plans, equipment specifications and directions, contracts) should be followed. Some documents, such as payroll records, must legally be kept for a specified time period.

Telephone, Facsimile Machine, and E-Mail

The use of the office telephone, fax machine, and e-mail is a major consideration for good departmental and institutional public relations. Here are a few simple rules that should be observed.

Promptness

The telephone and all communications should be prioritized and answered as promptly and courteously as possible. Answering promptly reflects efficient office practice and consideration for the person calling. Answering machines, voice mail, and phone rollover to the central office should be considered, however, there should always be someone on the scene to answer the phone. Every office should have a standardized telephone greeting. In the case of receiving a message, care should be used. Ask questions such as, "When Dr. Bucher returns, may I tell him who called?" Of course messages must be taken accurately and completely!

Professional Purposes

The telephone, fax, and electronic mail are installed in an office for professional purposes. Office staff should not be permitted to talk for long periods of time about personal matters. The telephone and other forms of communication linkages, including copying machines, should be kept clear for business important to the achievement of organizational objectives.

Courtesy, Friendliness, and Helpfulness

The person answering the phone should be pleasant and courteous and should desire to be of assistance to the caller. This manner represents a professional responsibility that should be standard procedure at all times. Often it is helpful to prepare a laminated script strip for the most frequently asked questions, e-mail addresses, or phone numbers. This will ensure expedient handling of all communications. Speak clearly using the caller's name and ask any questions tactfully. Many problem calls have been defused by courteous engagement by professional office staff.

Messages

At times staff members who are being called will not be available. A memo pad should be kept at hand for recording day, time, name, phone number, and e-mail address of a caller in such cases. A definite procedure should be established for receiving and relaying these messages (e.g., phone, e-mail, file transfer, fax, FedEx or UPS, packages, etc.) to the proper persons. Voice and electronic mail have become popular aids in this procedure; however, a central number should be made available that the caller can use to speak to a real live person as opposed to a totally automated voice mail menu.

Calendaring and Appointments

There should be an office calendar to record all appointments. Incoming mail and messaging should be used to continually update and confirm the status of appointments. A tickler system may be employed where important dates and deadlines (e.g., bills, contracts, insurance, meetings, reports) are entered into the computer, generating a master calendar on a weekly basis that includes ticklers or reminders. Tickler cards may also be filed by dates and distributed to the appropriate person close to the meeting or due date as a reminder.

Appointments should not be made unless it is believed they can be kept. Furthermore, all appointments should be kept as close to the time scheduled as possible. Many times, the person making an appointment has arranged his or her day with the understanding that the conference will be at a certain time. If this time is not adhered to, the schedule has to be altered, and complications frequently arise as a result. Office staff should keep an accurate and up-to-date list of appointments. If no staff are available, each person should keep his or her own schedule of appointments and check it regularly to see that all appointments are honored.

Meetings

Meetings—including staff meetings, office personnel meetings, and orientation for new office team members—should be regular and requisite. Regular meetings reaffirm that a line of open communication exists and provide a time for building, monitoring, and assessing interpersonal relationships and evaluating how the management system is functioning. Meetings should begin on time, end on time, have an agenda that has been distributed at least a day before, and stay on task. If minutes are necessary, they should be prepared within twenty-four to forty-eight hours of the meeting. Good meetings are crucial to smooth, efficient, and effective office management as well as to solid departmental functioning.

RECORDS AND REPORTS

At times, records and reports are not prepared and maintained accurately because the directions provided by management to staff members are not clear and definite. When complicated reports are to be prepared, oral instructions alone will usually not be sufficient. Instead, directions (i.e., format, style, computer compatibility, and a prototype or model) should be drawn up and distributed. The preparation of a sample method and preferred style will save time and energy and will also help ensure better results.

Managers are often responsible for poorly kept records, inaccurate reports, and late submissions. Directions and deadlines should be made clear, and managers should receive announcements or "ticklers" at regular intervals and reminders of when re-

ports are due. A timely check of report status on the master calendar will indicate whether the reports have been submitted, or are in process. Any omissions, updates, or other inaccuracies in records and reports should be corrected immediately.

The profession of physical education, recreation, and sport is unique in the number of records (i.e., health status, permission to participate, attendance) and reports (i.e., injury, accident, equipment maintenance) that must be generated, disseminated, and stored. Budgeting and inventory are other crucial management duties that command significant recording and reporting. Research indicates that although many school departments report having access to computers, half have yet to fully engage various emerging technology to these vital tasks. In fact, the profession seems to be in a state of transition, with most departments having access to technology but few fully taking advantage of it, especially to maintain and manage records. Contemporary management must lead the way to build effective, efficient functioning at this crucial management level (see box 15-3).

Office staff employing computer technology facilitate record keeping and report preparation.

Box 15-3   Checklist of Some Important Considerations for Office Management

Space and Working Environment	Yes	No
1. Does the reception area provide ample space for waiting visitors?	_____	_____
2. Is work space separated from the reception room so that office work is not interrupted by the arrival of guests?	_____	_____
3. Are there private offices or cubicles for the director of physical education and athletics and activities and as many staff members as possible?	_____	_____
4. Is there equality in work space assignment?	_____	_____
5. Is there adequate space, equipment, and supplies for all work tasks?	_____	_____
6. Is the office arranged in a "teamed" or quad area for maximum office efficiency?	_____	_____
7. Is the office environment safe and respectful?	_____	_____
8. Have the office space and workstations been ergonomically designed and painted in accordance with the best color dynamics?	_____	_____
9. Have provisions been made so that unnecessary noise is eliminated, distractions are kept to a minimum, and cleanliness and a smoke-free environment prevail?	_____	_____
10. Are there good ventilation, appropriate artificial lighting, and climate control?	_____	_____
11. Is technology being fully integrated?	_____	_____
12. Does recycling take place and are recycled materials (paper) purchased?	_____	_____

Human Resources

	Yes	No
13. Is office staff available to greet guests and answer queries?	_____	_____
14. Is there a recorded job description of the duties of each office staff position?	_____	_____
15. Are channels available for ascertaining causes of dissatisfaction among office staff?	_____	_____
16. Do office staff dress appropriately?	_____	_____
17. Do office staff maintain workstations that have an orderly appearance?	_____	_____
18. Do office staff concern themselves with the efficiency of the office?	_____	_____
19. Are office staff loyal to the department and staff members?	_____	_____
20. Do staff members have and keep regular office hours?	_____	_____
21. Are appointments kept promptly?	_____	_____
22. Is up-to-date and appropriate reading material furnished for waiting guests?	_____	_____
23. Do office staff continually pay attention to maintaining offices so that they are neat, with papers, books, and other materials arranged in an orderly manner?	_____	_____
24. Are the office staff knowledgeable about departmental activities so that they can intelligently answer queries about staff members and activities?	_____	_____
25. Do office staff assist guests promptly and courteously?	_____	_____
26. Is work arranged neatly, free from errors, and presented appropriately?	_____	_____
27. Are correspondence and work assignments handled promptly?	_____	_____
28. Is the filing system easily learned and is the filing done promptly so that the work does not pile up?	_____	_____
29. Does the office routine use human resources efficiently, so office staff is productive and just not busy?	_____	_____
30. Are the most effective and efficient office methods and technology employed?	_____	_____

Procedures

	Yes	No
31. Is the office staff output satisfactory, with work starting promptly in the morning and after lunch, and breaks taken according to schedule?	_____	_____
32. Has a streamlined procedure been developed so that telephones are answered promptly, guests are treated courteously, and personal arguments and gossiping are minimized?	_____	_____
33. Are essential records properly maintained, kept up to date, and secure?	_____	_____

Continued

Box 15-3   Checklist of Some Important Considerations for Office Management—cont'd

Procedures—cont'd	Yes	No
33. Have procedures for word processing and duplicating reports, examinations, bulletins, fliers, letters, and announcements been developed to eliminate uncertainty or confusion on the part of staff members?	_____	_____
34. Are regular office hours for staff posted and known so that office staff members can make appointments as needed?	_____	_____
35. Are office staff acquainted with such details as securing supplies, obtaining reference material, helping in registration and report preparation, duplicating and scanning material, and obtaining and managing appropriate forms and records?	_____	_____
36. Is the office staffed continuously during working hours?	_____	_____
37. Does the office have a personnel policy and an office manual or handbook?	_____	_____

TAKE IT TO THE NET!

American Disabilities Act
www.usdoj.gov/crt/ada

The Association for Information Management
Professionals (ARMA)
www.arma.org

Association for the Advancement of Computing in
Education (AACE)
www.aace.org

Bonnie's Fitware Inc.
www.pesoftware.com

Employee Retention Strategies
www.employeeretentionstrategies.com

HR-Guide.com
www.hr-guide.com

International Association of Administrative
Professionals (IAAP)
www.iaap-hq.org

National Association of Education Office
Professionals (NAEOP)
www.naeop.org

Records Management
www.nara.gov/records

U.S. Equal Employment Opportunity Commission
(EEOC)
www.eeoc.gov

Vital Records Protection (VRP)
www.vitalrecordsprotection.org

SUMMARY

Office management is an important consideration in the management of physical education, recreation, and sport programs. Office management concerns such matters as communication, correspondence, materials processing, records management, budget and report preparation, in-service training, and public relations. The office is the nerve center of the operation; therefore, if the group, center, program, department, or other unit of the organization is to be effectively and efficiently run, much attention must be given to office management. Human resources, human relations, workplace environment, space, workstation upkeep, equipment, computers, technology management routine, evaluations, and reports must receive continual and careful attention. Too often, office management is taken for granted or overlooked; however, this important component of managerial responsibility is requisite and a crucial key to any well-run organization.

SELF-ASSESSMENT ACTIVITIES

These activities will assist students in determining if material and competencies presented in this chapter have been mastered.

1. Form diversified working groups and have each group develop a table of contents for a manual of office procedures.

2. What are some important reasons why "boundarylessness" office management is important to a department of intercollegiate athletics?

3. In what ways can technology be used in physical education, recreation, and sport programs?

4. As a manager of a large high school physical education program, describe the office personnel and equipment you would need and then justify your request.

5. Construct a class or departmental Web site directory, including information about faculty, staff, and programs.

6. Prepare a set of sample forms that you would want to maintain as part of a junior high or middle school physical education program.

7. Form a team and make an appointment with your department head or manager of a community-based physical activity, recreation, or sport setting and conduct an office management audit via observation. Report your findings to the class.

REFERENCES

1. Chesla, E. 2000. *Successful teamwork: How to become a team player.* New York: Learning Press.
2. Colker, R., and A. A. Milani. 2005. *The law of disability discrimination.* Albany, NY: Matthew Berder & Company.
3. Fulton-Calkins, P .2003. *Technology and procedures for administrative professionals.* Mason, OH: South-Western.
4. Maslow, A., and A. R. Kaplan. 1998. *Maslow in management.* New York: Wiley.
5. Mohnsen, B. S. 2004. *Using technology in physical education.* Reston, VA: NASPE.
6. Peters, T.1999. *The professional service firm.* New York: Knopf.
7. Peterson, B., and R. Patten. 1995. *The ergonomic PC: Creating a healthy computing environment.* New York: McGraw-Hill.
8. Porter, M. E., and V. E. Miller. 1985. How information gives you the competitive edge. *Harvard Business Review* July/August, 149–60.
9. Quible, Z. K. 2005. *Administrative office management.* Upper Saddle River, NJ: Pearson Prentice Hall.
10. Susskind, L., S. McKarnan, and J. Thomas-Larmer. 1999. *Consensus building handbook.* Thousand Oaks, CA: Sage.
11. Tedesco, E. H., and R. B. Mitchell. 1987. *Administrative office management systems.* New York: Wiley.
12. Timm, P. R., and B. D. Peterson. 2000. *People at work: Human behavior in organizations.* Cincinnati, OH: South-Western.

SUGGESTED READINGS

Bridges, F. J., and X. Roquemore. 1996. *Management for athletic/sport administration: Theory and practice.* Decatur, GA: Educational Services for Management. Devoted to management procedures and functions with many implications for office management.

Cloke, K. 2000. *Resolving conflicts at work.* San Francisco, CA: Jossey-Bass.

Drucker, P. 1998. *On the profession of management.* Boston: Harvard Business School. Discusses important issues confronting management during workplace shift and social change.

Giom, J. L., and R. E. Herman. 2000. *Workforce stability.* Winchester, VA: Oakhill Press.

Henderson, R. I. 1994. *Compensation management: Rewarding performance.* Englewood Cliffs, NJ: Prentice Hall.

Jones, T. E. 1996. *Breakaway management: Overcoming dysfunction in the workplace.* Fresno, CA: Worx Publishing. Provides managers with insight into human behavior enabling workers and organizations to better facilitate change.

Levine, J. R. 1999. *The Internet for dummies.* Indianapolis, IN: IDG Books.

Ludden, L. L. 1998. *Job savvy: How to be a success at work.* Indianapolis, IN: JIST Works.

Mayer, J. J. 1999. *Time management for dummies.* Foster City, CA: IDG Books. Offers helpful suggestions concerning workstation organization, including filing, hard-drive house cleaning, and the development of a "master list."

Mitchell, M., R. McKethen, and B. S. Mohnsen. 2004. *Integrating technology and physical education.* Cerritos, CA: Bonnie's Fitware.

Robbins, S. P., and M. Coulter. 2005. *Managing today.* Upper Saddle River, NJ: Pearson Prentice Hall. Presents relevant material concerning customer service, reengineering work processes, office work flow, and technology transfer.

Spinello, R. A. 2000. *Cybernetics: Morality and law in cyberspace.* Sudbury, MA: Jones and Bartlett.

Timm, P. R., and B. D. Peterson. 2000. *People at work: Human behavior in organizations.* Cincinnati, OH: South-Western. Presents techniques concerning the establishment of a motivational working environment.

Physical Education and Sport with a Purpose

- International Charter of Physical Education and Sport (UNESCO)
- A Global Vision for School Physical Education and Sport and the Physically Educated Person (AAHPERD/CAHPERD)
- International Year of Sport and Physical Education (UN General Assembly)
- Healthy People 2010 Objectives for the Nation: Physical Activity and Fitness (USDHHS)

INTERNATIONAL CHARTER OF PHYSICAL EDUCATION AND SPORT (UNESCO)

The General Conference of the United Nations Educational, Scientific and Cultural Organization, meeting in Paris at its twentieth session, this twenty-first day of November 1978,

Recalling that in the United Nations Charter the peoples proclaimed their faith in fundamental human rights and in the dignity and worth of the human person, and affirmed their determination to promote social progress and better standards of life,

Recalling that by the terms of the Universal Declaration of Human Rights, everyone is entitled to all the rights and freedoms set forth therein without discrimination of any kind as to race, color, sex, language, religion, political or other opinion, national or social origin, property, birth or other consideration,

Convinced that one of the essential conditions for the effective exercise of human rights is that everyone should be free to develop and preserve his or her physical, intellectual and moral powers, and that access to physical education and sport should consequently be assured and guaranteed for all human beings,

Convinced that to preserve and develop the physical, intellectual and moral powers of the human being improves the quality of life at the national and the international levels,

Believing that physical education and sport should make a more effective contribution to the inculcation of fundamental human values underlying the full development of peoples,

Stressing accordingly that physical education and sport should seek to promote closer communion between peoples and between individuals, together with disinterested emulation, solidarity and fraternity, mutual respect and understanding, and full respect for the integrity and dignity of human beings,

Considering that responsibilities and obligations are incumbent upon the industrialized countries and the developing countries alike for reducing the disparity which continues to exist between them in respect of free and universal access to physical education and sport,

Considering that to integrate physical education and sport in the natural environment is to enrich them and to inspire respect of the earth's resources and a concern to conserve them and use them for the greater good of humanity as a whole,

Taking into account the diversity of the forms of training and education existing in the world, but noting that, notwithstanding the differences between national sports structures, it is clearly evident that physical education and sport are not confined to physical well-being and health but also contribute to the full and well-balanced development of the human being,

Taking into account, furthermore, the enormous efforts that have to be made before the right to physical education and sport can become a reality for all human beings,

Stressing the importance for peace and friendship among peoples of cooperation between the international governmental and non-governmental organizations responsible for physical education and sport,

Proclaims this International Charter for the purpose of placing the development of physical education and sport at the service of human progress, promoting their development, and urging governments, competent non-governmental organizations, educators, families and individuals themselves to be guided thereby, to disseminate it and to put it into practice.

Article 1. The practice of physical education and sport is a fundamental right for all

1.1 Every human being has a fundamental right of access to physical education and sport, which are essential for the full development of his or her personality. The freedom to develop physical, intellectual and moral powers through physical education and sport must be guaranteed both within the educational system and in other aspects of social life.

1.2 Everyone must have full opportunities, in accordance with his or her national tradition of sport, for practicing physical education and sport, developing physical fitness and attaining a level of achievement in sport which corresponds to his or her gifts.

1.3   Special opportunities must be made available for young people, including children of pre-school age, for the aged and for the handicapped to develop their personalities to the fullest through physical education and sport programs suited to their requirements.

Article 2.   Physical education and sport form an essential element of lifelong education in the overall education system

2.1   Physical education and sport, as an essential dimension of education and culture, must develop the abilities, will-power and self-discipline of every human being as a fully integrated member of society. The continuity of physical activity and the practice of sports must be ensured throughout life by means of a global, lifelong and democratized education.

2.2   At the individual level, physical education and sport contribute to the maintenance and improvement of health, provide a wholesome leisure-time occupation and enable man to overcome the drawbacks of modern living. At the community level, they enrich social relations and develop fair play, which is essential not only to sport itself but also to life in society.

2.3   Every overall education system must assign the requisite place and importance to physical education and sport in order to establish a balance and strengthen links between physical activities and other components of education.

Article 3.   Physical education and sport programs must meet individual and social needs

3.1   Physical education and sport programs must be designed to suit the requirements and personal characteristics of those practicing them, as well as the institutional, cultural, socioeconomic and climatic conditions of each country. They must give priority to the requirements of disadvantaged groups in society.

3.2   In the process of education in general, physical education and sport programs must, by virtue of both their content and their timetables, help to create habits and behavior patterns conducive to full development of the human person.

3.3   Even when it has spectacular features, competitive sport must always aim, in accordance with the Olympic Ideal, to serve the purpose of educational sport, of which it represents the crowning epitome. It must in no way be influenced by profit-seeking commercial interests.

Article 4.   Teaching, coaching and administration of physical education and sport should be performed by qualified personnel

4.1   All personnel who assume professional responsibility for physical education and sport must have appropriate qualifications and training. They must be carefully selected in sufficient numbers and given preliminary as well as further training to ensure that they reach adequate levels of specialization.

4.2   Voluntary personnel, given appropriate training and supervision, can make an invaluable contribution to the comprehensive development of sport and encourage the participation of the population in the practice and organization of physical and sport activities.

4.3   Appropriate structures must be established for the training of personnel for physical education and sport. Personnel who have received such training must be given a status in keeping with the duties they perform.

Article 5.   Adequate facilities and equipment are essential to physical education and sport

5.1   Adequate and sufficient facilities and equipment must be provided and installed to meet the needs of intensive and safe participation in both in-school and out-of-school programs concerning physical education and sport.

5.2   It is incumbent on governments, public authorities, schools and appropriate private agencies, at all levels, to join forces and plan together so as to provide and make optimum use of installations, facilities and equipment for physical education and sport.

5.3   It is essential that plans for rural and urban development include provision for long-term needs in the matter of installations, facilities and equipment for physical education and sport, taking into account the opportunities offered by the natural environment.

Article 6.   Research and evaluation are indispensable components of the development of physical education and sport

6.1   Research and evaluation in physical education and sport should make for the progress of all forms of sport and help to bring about an improvement in the health and safety of participants as well as in training methods and organization and management procedures. The education system will thereby benefit from innovations calculated to develop better teaching methods and standards of performance.

6.2   Scientific research whose social implications in this sphere should not be overlooked, must be oriented in such a way that it does not allow for improper applications to physical education and sport.

Article 7.   Protection of the ethical and moral values of physical education and sport must be a constant concern for all

7.1   Top-class sport and sport practiced by all must be protected against any abuse. The serious dangers with which phenomena such as violence, doping and commercial excesses threaten its moral values, image and prestige pervert its very nature and change its educative and health-promoting function. The public authorities, voluntary sports associations, specialized non-governmental organizations, the Olympic Movement, educators, parents, supporters' clubs, trainers, sports managers and the athletes themselves must combine their efforts in order to eliminate these evils. The media have a special role to play, in keeping with Article 8, in supporting and disseminating information about these efforts.

7.2   A prominent place must be assigned in curricula to educational activities based on the values of sport and the consequences of the interactions between sport, society and culture.

7.3   It is important that all sports authorities and sportsmen and women be conscious of the risks to athletes, and more especially to children, of precocious and inappropriate training and psychological pressures of every kind.

7.4   No effort must be spared to highlight the harmful effects of doping, which is both injurious to health and contrary to the sporting ethic, or to protect the physical and mental health of athletes, the virtues of fair play and competition, the integrity of the sporting community and the rights of people participating in it at any level whatsoever. It is crucial that the fight against doping should win the support of national and international authorities at various levels, and of parents, educators, the medical profession, the media, trainers, sports managers and athletes themselves, to ensure that they abide by the principles set out in the existing texts, and more particularly the International Olympic Charter against Doping in Sport. To that end, a harmonized and concerted policy must guide them in the preparation and application of anti-doping measures and of the educational action to be undertaken.

Article 8.   Information and documentation help to promote physical education and sport

8.1   The collection, provision and dissemination of information and documentation on physical education and sport constitute a major necessity. In particular, there is a need to circulate information on the results of research and evaluation studies concerning programs, experiments and activities.

Article 9.   The mass media should exert a positive influence on physical education and sport

9.1   Without prejudice to the right of freedom of information, it is essential that everyone involved in the mass media be fully conscious of his responsibilities having regard to the social importance, the humanistic purpose and the moral values embodied in physical education and sport.

9.2   Relations between those involved in the mass media and specialists in physical education and sport must be close and based on mutual confidence in order to exercise a positive influence on physical education and sport and to ensure objective and well-founded information. Training of personnel for the media may include elements relating to physical education and sport.

Article 10.   National institutions play a major role in physical education and sport

10.1   It is essential that public authorities at all levels and specialized non-governmental bodies encourage those physical education and sport activities whose educational value is most evident. Their action shall consist in enforcing legislation and regulations, providing material assistance and adopting all other measures of encouragement, stimulation and control. The public authorities will also ensure that such fiscal measures are adopted as may encourage these activities.

10.2   It is incumbent on all institutions responsible for physical education and sport to promote a consistent, overall and decentralized plan of action in the framework of lifelong education so as to allow for continuity and co-ordination between compulsory physical activities and those practiced freely and spontaneously.

Article 11.   International cooperation is a prerequisite for the universal and well-balanced promotion of physical education and sport

11.1   It is essential that States and those international and regional intergovernmental and non-governmental organizations in which interested countries are represented and which are responsible for physical education and sport give physical education and sport greater prominence in international bilateral and multilateral cooperation.

11.2   International cooperation must be prompted by wholly disinterested motives in order to promote and stimulate endogenous development in this field.

11.3   Through cooperation and the pursuit of mutual interests in the universal language of physical education and sport, all peoples will contribute to the preservation of lasting peace, mutual respect and friendship and will thus create a propitious climate for solving international problems. Close collaboration between all interested national and international governmental and non-governmental agencies, based on respect for the specific competence of each, will necessarily encourage the development of physical education and sport throughout the world.

A GLOBAL VISION FOR SCHOOL PHYSICAL EDUCATION AND SPORT AND THE PHYSICALLY EDUCATED PERSON (AAHPERD/CAHPERD)

Physical Education—Building on a Valuable Tradition

The need for children and youth to engage in regular physical activity (PA) as one of the prerequisites for achieving optimum health and quality of life has long been recognized. The UNESCO Charter of Physical Education and Sport established in 1978 was one of the first international statements espousing these beliefs.

Although many children and youth, particularly those with concerned parents, learn physical skills and participate in community settings, only the schools can reach and influence all children. Physical education (PE) is vital to all aspects of normal growth and development of children and youth—not only physical but social and emotional growth as well. Enhanced learning, better concentration, improved self-control and self-confidence, as well as promotion of healthy, positive, and lifelong attitudes toward PA are well-documented benefits of quality PE in schools. In addition, school PE establishes the foundation of skills for a lifetime of participation while at the same time building a natural immunizing effect against many sedentary lifestyle diseases.

Rationale for Global Vision

Despite widespread public acceptance of the need for PA, quality PE is not seen as a priority for many policymakers in most school systems. Where PE exists today it is under strong attack. It occupies a tenuous place in the school curriculum, and in some cases it is being replaced and moved out of the curriculum. Budget cutbacks, inadequate and aging facilities, the absence (and continued attrition) of PE specialists, insufficient allocations of time within the school timetable, as well as societal factors, such as impact of a technology-based economy, are contributing to its perilous status.

There is a misconception among the general public that existing school programs have the capacity to meet the PA requirements of our children and youth. However, the average school curriculum does not allot sufficient instructional time to PE for skill acquisition, health related fitness, and the attainment of a positive attitude and appreciation for PA.

The lack of opportunities for daily PE at school, coupled with the continuing decline in PA within the home setting is leading to the development of sedentary lifestyle patterns that will continue into adulthood and throughout life. Furthermore, efforts to recognize PA as a strategy to offset unhealthy behaviors have not been realized.

The need to promote active, healthy lifestyles among children and youth is great. Increasing numbers of children and youth are exposed to [a] wide variety of social ills and behaviors which put their health and lifestyles at risk. This is evidenced by growing reports of poor self-image, inadequate nutrition, family problems, stress, higher drop-out rates, youth violence, early sexual activity, increases in smoking, declining activity levels, increasing obesity, and increasing sedentary health risk factors, alcohol and drug abuse, within our young population.

The North American Regional Forum believes that we must reverse this negative trend if we are to significantly influence the personal well-being of all children and youth as we journey into the 21st century. As a consequence of our beliefs in the importance of quality, daily school PE, the Canadian Association for Health, Physical Education, Recreation and Dance, and the American Alliance for Health, Physical Education, Recreation and Dance have collectively developed the Global Vision for School Physical Education.

Statement of Beliefs

We believe that:

- All students in every grade have the right and the opportunity to experience sustained, vigorous physical activity (PA) and participate in quality, daily physical education (PE) programs;
- All aspects of a quality PE program have a positive impact on the thinking, knowing, and doing (or the cognitive, affective, and physical) domains of the lives of children and youth and that physically educated children and youth will go on to lead active, healthy, and productive lives;
- All teachers responsible for teaching PE must be professionally prepared physical educators. Through their preparation and ongoing professional development, all teachers will have a sound knowledge of the contribution of movement to the total education of children and youth;
- Each school must have at least one professionally prepared PE specialist who can act as the lead resource teacher assisting all teachers in developing the total PE program;
- Quality PE programs are equitable (gender, culture, race, ethnicity, ability, etc.) in all respects;
- Local school officials, school boards, and departments of education have a responsibility to provide appropriate support services to teachers in PE as well as adequate facilities, resource supplies, and equipment.

The Physically Educated Person

Physically educated persons have ACQUIRED skills enabling them to perform a variety of physical activities which can help them maintain health-related fitness levels; they PARTICIPATE regularly in physical activity [PA] because it is enjoyable and exhilarating; they UNDERSTAND and VALUE PA and its contribution to a healthy lifestyle.

1. Acquired Skills

- Physically educated persons move efficiently using body and space awareness and are able to differentiate between personal and general space.
- They have competence in manipulative, transport, and balance skills and can perform each of these skills along or with others; they have ability in a variety of activities; and they have the ability to process new skills.
- They are able to assess personal needs, design a realistic fitness program, and achieve and maintain a level of personal fitness.
- Physically educated persons have acquired culturally normative physical skills that provide a base for ongoing participation throughout life.

2. Participation

- Physically educated persons lead physically active lives and can select and integrate regular PA into their lifestyles through participation with others and/or alone.

3. Understand and Value

- Physically educated persons understand that PA provides lifelong opportunities for enjoyment, self-expression, and social interaction. They understand that there are many reasons to value and enjoy PA: to fulfill their human development potential, adapt and control their physical environment, relate and interact with others, and learn to live in and with the world around them.

- Physically educated persons accept and appreciate the differences and abilities of self and others. They understand risks, safety factors, and appropriate behaviors associated with PA. They value PA and its impact upon physical, emotional, social, and spiritual well-being. They display positive personal and social responsibility.

Solutions Expected from Schools

As families and social institutions become transformed, many people increasingly look to schools for solutions. The educational institution is the agency with the potential to positively impact attitudes and behaviors of all children and youth as a captive audience, regardless of gender, age, ability, ethnicity, or socioeconomic status.

Although there exists mounting concern for health and quality of life, many education policymakers fail to recognize the role of physical activity [PA] and its contribution. A narrow perception exists among some education leaders that the primary role of schools is to educate students only for academic achievement. There is a failure to recognize the important connection between PA, health, and vitality on the one hand and academic performance, productivity, and success in school on the other. With schools expected to teach students to lead productive lives, there should be community commitment to schools as health promoters through quality physical education.

Our Vision for Global School Physical Education—Learner-Centered and Comprehensive

- In our vision, physical education [PE] plays a valued and vital role in providing a quality, balanced education for all students in the world.
- The well-being of the students and the quality of the skills, knowledge and values they will ultimately derive from PE is the driving force of PE principles and practices.
- PE is a planned program of instruction and complementary activities, such as intramurals, interscholastics, and leadership opportunities.

The core instructional component of the program provides the opportunity to develop skills, fitness, knowledge, attitudes, and appreciation, whereas intramural and recreational sports programs provide all students with the opportunity to utilize learned behaviors in a recreational setting. The interscholastic and leadership components represent the enrichment opportunities to those so inclined.

- Students are physically educated in a creative, safe, and caring atmosphere which recognizes the students' individual interests/needs as central factors in curriculum design and program implementation.
- PE is conducted in various environments, including the outdoors, allowing personal growth in environmental citizenship and ethics.
- PE involves students in a variety of activities, including games, sports, gymnastics, dance, outdoor pursuits, fitness, and aquatics.
- PE programs utilize appropriate assessment techniques to enhance the learning of the students.
- PE is actively interfaced with other disciplines such as science, the arts, humanities, and mathematics.
- PE enables students to become responsible decision makers relative to their own physical well-being.
- PE provides the necessary skills, knowledge, and attitudes to integrate physical activity into daily living during the school years and beyond.
- PE programs are designed and implemented by professionally prepared physical educators.
- PE contributes to the promotion of lifelong, active, and healthy lifestyles and the prevention of disease.
- PE is inclusive and equitable. It excludes no students on the basis of gender, race, ability, ethnicity, socioeconomic level, religion, or language.

INTERNATIONAL YEAR OF SPORT AND PHYSICAL EDUCATION (UNITED NATIONS GENERAL ASSEMBLY)

1. Ministers and senior officials responsible for physical education and sport from more than 103 countries met at the headquarters of the United Nations Educational, Scientific and Cultural Organization (UNESCO) on 9 and 10 January 2003. They adopted a communiqué in which they called for according sport its rightful place in educational systems, protecting young athletes against the risks inherent in high-level sport and combating doping.

2. Physical education and sport are powerful factors contributing to peace and development. They provide an experience of solidarity and cooperation that is conducive to inculcating a culture of peace, overcoming social inequalities and fostering dialogue and consensus.

3. Physical education and sport provide excellent opportunities for young people to learn to communicate, cooperate, work in teams, respect others, acquire discipline and accept defeat. All these aspects are becoming increasingly important in a globalized world, in which it is essential to learn to live together in peace while preserving the cultural identities of all parties.

4. Physical education and sport are an integral part of the process of social development. They allow for a positive synergy among the various social partners (family, school, sports clubs and associations, local communities, social partners, the competent authorities, the public and private sectors).

5. In many countries, physical education and sport are facing increasing marginalization within educational systems, even though they are a major tool for promoting health, physical

development and acquisition of the values necessary for social cohesion and intercultural dialogue.

6. The protection of young athletes should be understood in the light of the principles stated in the Convention on the Rights of the Child. Protection of young athletes should be understood as comprising both the physical and psychological aspects of sport and as ensuring quality education that facilitates long-term personal and professional development. Protection of young athletes also covers such areas as child labour, violence, over-training, doping, premature specialization and commercial exploitation.

7. Doping constitutes a breach of sporting ethics and a danger to public health. The scourge must be combated by all means at the international community's disposal. Prevention remains the most effective tool to that end.

There is an urgent need to elaborate an international convention against doping, so that the necessary measures of prevention and control can be introduced into national legislation in a consistent manner.

8. Consequently, Tunisia, being convinced of the importance of physical education and sport as contributors to physical and mental well-being, social advancement, development and peace, proposes that the General Assembly should include in the agenda of its fifty-eighth session a new item dealing with the points raised above and should proclaim an international year of sport and physical education in order to draw attention to the stated goals.

Address by Adolf Ogi (Special Advisor to the UN Secretary-General on Sport for Development and Peace). www.un.org./themes/sport

Healthy People 2010 Objectives for the Nation: Physical Activity and Fitness (USDHHS)

Physical Activity in Adults

22.1   Reduce the proportion of adults who engage in no leisure-time physical activity.
Target: 20 percent
Baseline: 40 percent of adults aged 18 years and older engaged in no leisure-time physical activity in 1997 (age adjusted to the year 2000 standard population).
22.2   Increase the proportion of adults who engage regularly, preferably daily moderate physical activity for at least 30 minutes per day.
Target: 30 percent.
Baseline: 15 percent of adults aged 18 years and older were active for at least 30 minutes 5 or more days per week in 1997 (age adjusted to the year 2000 standard population).
22.3   Increase the proportion of adults who engage in vigorous physical activity that promotes the development and maintenance of cardiorespiratory fitness 3 or more days per week for 20 or more minutes per occasion.
Target: 30 percent.
Baseline: 23 percent of adults aged 18 years and older engaged in vigorous physical activity 3 or more days per week for 20 or more minutes per occasion in 1997 (age adjusted to the year 2000 standard population).

Muscular Strength/Endurance and Flexibility

22.4   Increase the proportion of adults who perform physical activities that enhance and maintain muscular strength and endurance.
Target: 30 percent.
Baseline: 19 percent of adults aged 18 years and older performed physical activities that enhance and maintain strength and endurance 2 or more days per week in 1997 (age adjusted to the year 2000 standard population).
22.5   Increase the proportion of adults who perform physical activities that enhance and maintain flexibility.
Target: 40 percent.
Baseline: 30 percent of adults aged 18 years and older did stretching exercises in the past 2 weeks in 1995 (age adjusted to the year 2000 standard population).

Healthy People 2010 Objectives for the Nation: Physical Activity and Fitness (USDHHS)—cont'd

Physical Activity in Children and Adolescents

22.6   Increase the proportion of adolescents who engage in moderate physical activity for at least 30 minutes on 5 or more of the previous 7 days.

Target: 30 percent.

Baseline: 20 percent of students in grades 9 through 12 engaged in moderate physical activity for at least 30 minutes on 5 or more of the previous 7 days in 1997.

22.7   Increase the proportion of adolescents who engage in vigorous physical activity that promotes cardiorespiratory fitness 3 or more days per week for 20 or more minutes per occasion.

Target: 85 percent.

Baseline: 64 percent of students in grades 9 through 12 engaged in vigorous physical activity 3 or more days per week for 20 or more minutes per occasion in 1997.

22.8   Increase the proportion of the nation's public and private schools that require daily physical education for all students.

Objective: Increase in schools requiring daily physical activity for all students

		1994 Baseline %	2010 Target %
22.8a	Middle and junior	17	25
22.8b	Senior high	2	5

22.9   Increase the proportion of adolescents who participate in daily school physical education.

Target: 50 percent.

Baseline: 27 percent of students in grades 9 through 12 participated in daily school physical education in 1997.

22.10   Increase the proportion of adolescents who spend at least 50 percent of school physical education class time being physically active.

Target: 50 percent.

Baseline: 32 percent of students in grades 9 through 12 were physical activity in physical education class more than 20 minutes 3 to 5 days per week in 1997.

22.11   Increase the proportion of children and adolescents who view television 2 or fewer hours per day.

Target: 75 percent.

Baseline: 60 percent of persons aged 8 to 16 years viewed television 2 or fewer hours per day in 1984–1994.

Access

22.12   (Developmental) Increase the proportion of the nation's public and private schools that provide access to their physical activity spaces and facilities for all persons outside normal school hours (that is, before and after the school day, on weekends, and during summer and other vacations).

22.13   Increase the proportion of work sites offering employer-sponsored physical activity and fitness programs.

Target: 75 percent.

Baseline: In 1998–1999:

Healthy People 2010 Objectives for the Nation: Physical Activity and Fitness (USDHHS)—cont'd

Work Site Size	Work Site %	Health Plan %	Work Site or Health Plan %
50 employees or less		Developmental	
50 to 99 employees	24	21	38
100 to 249 employees	31	20	42
250 to 749 employees	44	25	56
750 + employees	61	27	68
Total (50 +)	36	22	46

22.14   Increase the proportion of trips made by walking.
Target and baseline:

Objective	Increase in Trips Made by Walking	Activity	1995 Baseline %	2010 Target %
22.14a	Adults aged 18 years and older	Trips less than 1 mile	16	25
22.14b	Children and adolescents aged 5 to 15 years	Trips to school less than 1 mile	28	50

22.15   Increase the proportion of trips made by bicycling.
Target and baseline:

Objective	Increase in Trips Made by Bicycling	Activity	1995 Baseline %	2010 Target %
22.15a	Adults aged 18 years and older	Trips less than 5 miles	0.6	2.0
22.15b	Children and adolescents aged 5 to 15 years	Trips to school less than 2 miles	2.2	5.0

From Public Health Service, US Department of Health and Human Services, *Healthy People 2010: Conference edition* (Washington D.C., US Government Printing Office November 30, 1999).

The Role of the Parent

- Notice of an Educational Assessment/Reassessment Plan for Parent's Permission
- Notice of a Team Meeting
- Individualized Education Program (IEP)
- Initial Assessment Summary Report or 3 year Summary Assessment
- Review of Discipline Policy
- Notice of Proposed Special Education Services Presented to Parents for Their Consent
- Notice of Procedural Safeguards: Parental Rights for Special Education

----

Richfield Public Schools 7001 Harriet Avenue South Richfield, MN 55423	TSES #4 Rev. 4-01	**NOTICE OF EDUCATIONAL ASSESSMENT/REASSESSMENT** Page 1 of 3

Student's Full Name _____

Identification Number _____

Birthdate _____ Age _____ Grade _____

School _____

Date _____

Dear _____ :　　　　　(M/D/Y)

We request your permission to assess your child's current educational functioning.

☐ This notice is for an **Initial Assessment.** The school district must receive your signed permission before we can begin the assessment.

☐ This notice is for a **Reassessment.** The school district will begin the reassessment upon receipt of your signed permission. If signed permission is not received following a reasonable number of attempts, the district will begin the reassessment. If you object in writing within 10 school days after receiving this request, the district will not begin the reassessment. If you sign and return this form right away, it will allow us to begin the reassessment without delay.

Reason(s) for this assessment:

Information used by the team in determining the areas to be assessed:

Other **options** and **factors** that were considered, including those identified as **special considerations** (behavior, limited English proficiency, blind or visually impaired, deaf or hard of hearing, or assistive technology):

Student's Name: _____

Richfield Public Schools 7001 Harriet Avenue South Richfield, MN 55423	TSES #4 Rev. 4-01	**NOTICE OF EDUCATIONAL ASSESSMENT/REASSESSMENT** Page 2 of 3

Proposed Assessment/Reassessment Plan:

A. *For children birth to age seven* suspected of having a hearing or
vision disability, the team includes a licensed teacher in each area
of suspected sensory impairment. ☐ Yes   ☐ No

B. The student's language, cultural, economic or environmental
background indicates special adaptations in assessment procedures
need to be made. ☐ Yes   ☐ No
    If yes, special adaptations are included in the plan below.

C. The student's physical or sensory status indicates special adaptations
need to be made in the assessment process. ☐ Yes   ☐ No
    If yes, special adaptations are included in the plan below.

Area to Be Assessed	Personnel Who Will Assess (name and title)	Assessment/Reassessment Plan (tests, procedures, and adaptations)

Student's Name: _____

Richfield Public Schools **7001 Harriet Avenue South** **Richfield, MN 55423**	**TSES #4** **Rev. 4-01**	**NOTICE OF** **EDUCATIONAL** **ASSESSMENT/REASSESSMENT** Page 3 of 3

The assessment will be conducted at _____
and is provided at no cost to you.   (Location)

Note to parent(s): It is important to know your rights. Please read the enclosed **PARENT RIGHTS AND PROCEDURAL SAFEGUARDS** brochure, which includes sources for parental assistance. If you have questions you may contact me.

_____

      Name   Position   Telephone

_____

                          Address

PARENT ACTION

Parent(s): Check one of the options below, sign and date this form, and return the original of this page.

☐ **I give permission** to the school district to proceed with the assessment as proposed.

☐ **I need further information.** Please contact me for further explanation or to schedule a meeting.

☐ **I do not give permission** for the school to proceed with the assessment as proposed. I understand that you will contact me to offer a conciliation conference or mediation where my concerns will be discussed. I also understand that I may choose not to participate in the conciliation conference or mediation and may proceed directly to a due process hearing.

_____

    Parent Signature (Student if age 18 or older)   Date

_____

        Address   Telephone Number

Date received by district		Assessment completion due: (30 school days)
	(for district use only)	

Enclosed: **Parent Rights and Procedural Safeguards** brochure   Copies: Due Process File   IEP Manager
                                                       Parent   IFSP Service Coordinator
                                                       Other Assessment Personnel
This form is available in several languages, Braille, or other format. Contact the director of special education.

Student's Name: _____

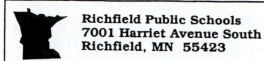

Richfield Public Schools 7001 Harriet Avenue South Richfield, MN 55423	TSES #6 Rev. 4-01	**ASSESSMENT SUMMARY REPORT** (Final Page) (Page ___ of ___)

Based on the information included in this report, the team has made the judgment that the student:

(Check only one of the following boxes.)

A. does not meet eligibility criteria for special education.

☐ does not have a disability (initial assessment)

☐ does not demonstrate a need for special education service at this time

☐ lack of instruction in reading or math or to limited English proficiency (initial assessment)

☐ **no longer qualifies** for special education services (*exit summary included or attached*)

☐ **is graduating,** or has reached **age 22,** and is **no longer eligible** for further special education services

☐ **does not meet** categorical eligibility criteria when transitioning from **early childhood special education** developmental delay category and is not eligible for further special education services (*exit summary included or attached*)

B. does meet eligibility criteria for special education.

☐ **meets criteria** for the following disability(ies) (initial assessment):

☐ **continues** to demonstrate need for special education service (reassessment):

(X) indicates primary disability and (✓) indicates secondary disability(ies)

___ Autism Spectrum Disorders	___ Early Childhood Special Education	___ Physically Impaired
___ Blind/Visually Impaired	___ Emotional/Behavior Disorder	___ Severely Multiply Impaired
___ Deaf/Hard of Hearing	___ Mild-Moderate Mentally Impaired	___ Specific Learning Disability (SLD)*
___ Deafblind	___ Moderate-Severe Mentally Impaired	___ Speech/Language Impairment
	___ Other Health Impaired	___ Traumatic Brain Injury

☐ qualifies through **override*** for the above disability(ies). *Attached rationale explains why the standards and procedures used with the majority of students resulted in **invalid findings** for this pupil, what **objective data** were used, and which data had **greatest importance** in eligibility decision.*

* If a team member disagrees with the override decision, a statement as to the reason is attached and noted below.

Identify team members: (** Team **signatures are required** for override of any criteria and SLD assessments*)

> **For override and SLD, indicate AGREEMENT WITH CONCLUSIONS. Check yes or no.*

NAME	TITLE	YES	NO
_____	Parent _____	☐	☐
_____	Regular Education Teacher (K–12) _____	☐	☐
_____	Special Education Teacher _____	☐	☐
_____	District Representative _____	☐	☐
_____	Student (by grade nine or age 14) _____	☐	☐
_____	_____	☐	☐
_____	_____	☐	☐
_____	_____	☐	☐

A copy of this report is sent to the student's resident district when the student is not a resident of the providing district.

Copies: Due Process File   IEP Manager
Parent   IFSP Service Coordinator

This form is available in several languages, Braille, or other format. Contact the director of special education.

519

Richfield Public Schools **7001 Harriet Avenue South** **Richfield, MN 55423**	**NOTICE OF A TEAM MEETING**

Student Name:__Kevin_____   Date:____10/3/2006_____

School:__Richfield Intermediate_____   Grade:__4__ Birthdate:___12/7/95____

Dear _____&_____:

We would like you to meet with us to plan for your child's education program. It will be at

__6:30 PM__ on __10/17/2006__, at _____Rm #105 7020 12th Ave. S. Richfield, MN 55423_____
    Time   *Date*   *Room Number—Building—Address*

The purpose of this meeting is (*Check all that apply*)
- ☐ to discuss development of an evaluation/reevaluation plan.
- ☐ to discuss evaluation results and determine if your child is eligible for special education and related services.
- ☐ to consider the development of an Individualized Education Program (IEP) or Individualized Family Service Plan (IFSP).
- ☒ to review your child's IEP or IFSP, including consideration of extended school year services, and revise the IEP or IFSP as needed
- ☐ to consider secondary transition needs, services, and development of a transition plan.
- ☐ to discuss a conditional behavioral intervention procedure.
- ☐ to make a manifestation determination.

- ☐ Other: _____

The following people are expected to attend:

Name	Title	Name	Title
_____	Parent	Sharon	Special Ed. Teacher
_____	Parent	John	Adaptive P. E. Teacher
Maribeth	Representative of District		
Leslie	Special Ed Teacher		
Nancy	General Ed Teacher		

Note to Parent: If you want to invite additional people to participate in this meeting, you must notify them. If the time, date, or location is not convenient for you, please contact me as soon as possible so we can make other arrangements. If you do not attend this meeting, you will be notified before any significant changes are made regarding your child's education. Please read the enclosed **NOTICE OF PROCEDURAL SAFEGUARDS** brochure. If you have questions please contact me.

_____Leslie_____	____Special Ed. Teacher____	_____
Name	Position	Telephone

As a parent, you have protections under the procedural safeguards of IDEA.
Resources you may contact for further information about parent rights and procedural safeguards:
PACER (Parent Advisory Coalition for Educational Rights): 612-827-2966 (Voice), 612-827-7770 (TTY), 1-800-53-PACER
MN Disability Law Center: 612-332-1441, 612-332-4668 (TTY), 1-800-292-4250
MN Special Education Mediation Services: 651-297-4635, 651-297-5353, 1-800-627-3529 (TTY)
MN Department of Children, Families & Learning: 651-582-8689, 651-582-8201 (TTY)
ARC Minnesota (advocacy for persons with developmental disabilities): 651-523-0823, 1-800-582-5256

Attached: Notice of Procedural Safeguards Brochure

This form is available in several languages, Braille, or other format. Contact the Director of Special Education.

Richfield Public Schools 7001 Harriet Avenue South Richfield, MN 55423	IEP Meeting Date: 10/17/2006 Last Assessment Summary Report Date: 10/18/2006	Individualized Education Program (IEP)

STUDENT INFORMATION   State ID

Student's Name Kevin,	Grade 4	Sex M	Birthdate 12/7/95	ID Number

Street Address City, State, Zip Richfield MN 55423	Native Language/Primary English Communication Mode

School of Enrollment Richfield Intermediate	School Phone # 612-798-6648	Providing District # 280

Student's Permanent Residence Address (If Different)		Resident District # 280

PARENT/GUARDIAN INFORMATION

Parent Name(s) &	Home Phone #	Daytime Phone # Ext.

Parent's Address (if different)	Native Language/Primary Communication Mode

Parent/Guardian/Surrogate Parent Name(s)	☐ Parent ☐ Guardian(s) ☐ Surrogate Parent(s)	

Parent/Guardian/Surrogate Parent Address (if different)	Home phone #	Daytime phone #

IEP INFORMATION

IEP Manager LESLIE	Special Ed.	Phone #	Federal Setting: I.

Primary Disability Emotional disorders		08	Type of IEP: ○ Initial ● Annual ○ Interim

Secondary Disability 1 Other health impaired	10	Secondary Disability 2

PROGRESS REPORTING

Frequency and method(s) to be used for reporting progress to parents:

Periodic Review on April 30th, one written IEP, and a Verbal Conference.

TRANSFER OF RIGHTS AT AGE OF MAJORITY

Address only in IEPs for students who will reach age 17 during tenure of this IEP.

The student, upon reaching age 17, has been informed the rights which will transfer to him/her upon reaching the age of majority (18), unless legal guardian or conservator had been appointed.   **Date notice was provided:**

IEP PLANNING MEETING

Title	Names of All Team Members	Indicate Attendance
Parent		☒ Yes ☐ No
Parent		☐ Yes ☐ No
School District Representative	Maribeth	☒ Yes ☐ No
Special Education Teacher	Leslie	☒ Yes ☐ No
General Education Teacher (K–12 Only)	Nancy	☒ Yes ☐ No
Special Ed. Teacher	Sharon	☒ Yes ☐ No
Adaptive P.E. Teacher	John	☒ Yes ☐ No
		☐ Yes ☐ No
		☐ Yes ☐ No

This form is available in several languages, Braille, or other format. Contact the Director of Special Education.

Page 2. 1 of 5 **IEP Meeting Date:** 10/17/2006   Student's Name: **Kevin**

E.2	PROGRAM PLANNING

Performance Areas

☐ Intellectual/Cognitive Functioning	☐ Communication	☐ Sensory
☐ Academic Performance	☐ Motor Skills	☐ Health/Physical
☐ Functional Skills	☒ Emotional, Social, and Behavioral Development	

Present Level(s) of Educational Performance and Educational Needs: including how the student's disability affects involvement and progress in the general curriculum (for preschool children, participation in appropriate activities). For students age 14 and above, include transition areas.

Present Level(s) of Educational Performance:

Kevin is currently succeeding in the mainstream setting. His classroom teacher reports that he is excellent at grasping concepts, displays high-level thinking, and is able to think things through carefully. Kevin is reading at a 5th-grade level and demonstrates excellent math skills. He is able to hand in most assignments on time. During class discussions, he contributes good ideas. Kevin's classroom teacher states that Kevin appears to need a lot of one-to-one attention with adults. He will help others, if they will accept his help. Kevin does have some difficulty making friends. Kevin's teacher reports that Kevin can be emotional and sensitive about things that happen at school or at home. Kevin can be distracted by people around him or by changes in the daily schedule. Once he gets an idea in his mind, he has difficulty moving on to the next activity. Kevin is able to state what appropriate social skills are, but at times has difficulty implementing the skills.

Student-Based Need:
Kevin needs to improve his peer relationships and attention-seeking behaviors.

Annual Goal: 1 of 1 Goals	Kevin will improve his peer relationships and classroom behaviors from a level of doing things that may bother others to a level of demonstrating appropriate social skills that will enable Kevin to make friends and seek attention appropriately.

Short-Term Objectives or Benchmarks:	**Progress Notes:**
1. Given a situation when Kevin has a chance to interact with a peer, Kevin will display appropriate social skills by listening to the peer, not dominating the conversation, and choosing activities that are of interest to both on 80 percent of occasions as measured by teacher observation.	
2. Given a situation when Kevin would like attention, he will seek the attention without displaying negative behaviors such as continuous talking, pouting, invading others' personal space on 80 percent of all occasions as measured by teacher observation.	
3. Given a cueing system set up in advance between the teacher and Kevin, Kevin will refrain from interacting with peers who are easily agitated and provoked by Kevin's behavior on 4 of 5 trials as measured by teacher observation.	
4. Given corrective feedback from a teacher or staff member, Kevin will refrain from arguing or engaging in a lengthy discussion with peers or adults on 4 of 5 situations as measured by teacher observation.	
5. Given social skills instruction, Kevin will accept others' point of view and settle minor differences without arguing on 4 of 5 occasions as measured by teacher observation.	
6. Given a situation when Kevin would like to assist another student, Kevin will check to see if the other student would like help before doing so on 4 of 5 situations as measured by teacher observation.	
7. Given a cueing system set up in advance and social skills instruction, Kevin will stop behaviors that are considered bothersome to others and choose more appropriate behaviors on 4 of 5 occasions as measured by teacher observation.	

E.2	PROGRAM PLANNING

Performance Areas

☐ Intellectual/Cognitive Functioning   ☐ Communication   ☐ Sensory
☐ Academic Performance   ☒ Motor Skills   ☐ Health/Physical
☐ Functional Skills   ☐ Emotional, Social, and Behavioral Development

Present Level(s) of Educational Performance and Educational Needs: including how the student's disability affects involvement and progress in the general curriculum (for preschool children, participation in appropriate activities). For students age 14 and above, include transition areas.

Present Level(s) of Educational Performance:
Kevin is a friendly boy who enjoys participating in his physical education class. He is capable of listening to and following directions. However, he has difficulty with activities that involve muscular strength and endurance.

Student-Based Need:
Kevin needs to improve his physical fitness level in the areas of muscular strength and endurance.

Annual Goal: 2 of 2 Goals	Kevin will improve his physical fitness level in the areas of muscular strength and endurance from a level of not being able to perform activities that involve muscular strength and endurance to a level of being able to successfully perform physical activities that involve muscular strength and endurance.

Short-Term Objectives or Benchmarks: **Progress Notes:**

1. Given activities to improve abdominal strength and endurance, Kevin will perform 30 correct curl-ups in 60 seconds as observed and documented by the teacher.	
2. Given activities to improve upper body strength and endurance, Kevin will perform 12 mature push-ups in 30 seconds as observed and documented by the teacher.	
3. Given activities to improve cardiovascular endurance, Kevin will run/walk 1 mile at the 15 percent-level for his age-group norms as observed and documented by the teacher.	

TSES#11

REV. 4-98

| H.1 | MINNESOTA STATEWIDE TESTING |

*Address **only** in IEPs developed for grades 3, 5, 8, 10+.*   Grade level to be covered: _____

(Check the appropriate box.)

A. ☐ If applicable, the team plans for the following **accommodations** for test administration:
   (Test **modifications** are not allowed for Statewide Testing.)

B.☐ Student is **exempt.** The alternate assessment will be used.
   1. Rationale for exemption:

| H.2 | BASIC STANDARDS TESTING |

*Address **only** in the IEP for grade 8 or above.*

Prior to Basic Standards Testing, the team determined the following standards for this student:

Accommodations if appropriate or if needed:

Modifications if appropriate or if needed:

If **exempt,** the reason:

If **exempt,** the alternate assessment(s) to be used:

Check the appropriate box to indicate the level the student will attempt for testing:

	State	Individual*	Exempt**	Passed
Reading:				
Math:				
Writing:				

*If the modification is to alter the district's passing level, **test score expected** to be achieved is entered.

If the student is **exempt, the goals on the IEP will be the criteria for awarding the diploma.

E.3	**TRANSITION PROGRAM PLANNING**

Transition Areas

(All areas must be addressed.)

☐ Employment
☐ Post-Secondary Education & Training
☐ Community Participation

☐ Recreation/Leisure
☐ Home Living/Daily Living Skills

Following the initial evaluation or a reevaluation, the Evaluation Summary Report may be attached to the IEP.

Future Outcome/Goal:

Present Levels of Performance:

Transition Service Needs: *(for instruction, experiences, and related service).* **If no need, provide rationale.**

Activities Planned to Meet Future Outcome/Goals and who is accountable for each activity: (school courses/standards; home, community, and work experienced; and/or related services).

Annual Goal:

0 of 0 Goals

Short-Term Objectives or Benchmarks:

Progress Notes:

Annual Goal:

0 of 0 Goals

Short-Term Objectives or Benchmarks:

Progress Notes:

Page 4 of 5 **IEP Meeting Date:** 10/17/2006   Student's Name: **Kevin**

PROFILES OF LEARNING
See documentation attached to this IEP

ADAPTATIONS IN GENERAL AND SPECIAL EDUCATION

Adaptations and the duration of these adaptations, including 1) supplemental aids and services to be provided to the child or on behalf of the child in general and special education, and 2) program modifications or supports for the school personnel that will be provided to meet the needs of the child:

Kevin is currently succeeding in the mainstream setting. Special Education staff will be available to assist the classroom teacher with behavioral strategies. Kevin is able to access the curriculum and work toward meeting his IEP goals with the strategies and equipment that is currently available.

MINNESOTA COMPREHENSIVE ASSESSMENT	BASIC STANDARDS ASSESSMENT
Address only in IEP's developed for grades 3, 5, 8, 10+	**Address only in the IEP for grade 8 or above**
☒ Will participate without accommodations.	☐ Will participate without accommodations or modifications
☐ Will participate with accommodations below.	☐ Will participate with accommodations stated below.
☐ Exempt: reason and alternative assessments stated below.	☐ Will participate with modifications stated below.
	☐ Exempt: reason and alternative assessments stated below.

Accommodations:

Modifications:

If exempt, **reason** and **alternative assessment:**

Check the appropriate box to indicate the level the student will attempt for testing:

	State	**Individual***	**Exempt****	**Passed**	**Date Passed**
Reading:					
Math:					
Writing:					

*If the modification is to alter the district's passing level, **test score expected** to be achieved is entered.

If the student is **exempt, the goals on the IEP will be the criteria for awarding the diploma.

Page 5 of 5 **IEP meeting date:** 10/17/2006   Student's Name: **Kevin**

I.	SPECIAL EDUCATION AND RELATED SERVICES TO MEET GOALS AND OBJECTIVES						
Instructional Service Provided Provider name	Location		Anticipated Frequency	Total Minutes per Session		Service	
	General Education	Special Education		Indirect	Direct	Start Date	Anticipated Duration
EBD Processing		Rm. 105	1 ×/week	10		10/18/01	1 year
EBD Social Skills		Rm. 104 Resource Room	2 ×/week		30	10/18/01	1 year
15 Adaptive Physical		Gym/Playground	3 ×/week		30	10/18/01	1 year

INTERAGENCY SERVICES	
Agency Name	Interagency/Organization Linkages (*identify services, funding, responsibilities, etc.*)

LRE JUSTIFICATION
Other options considered and why rejected, and **why** this student's disability requires service(s) in this setting: The team agreed that Kevin did not need a behavior chart, because he is succeeding in the mainstream classroom. No other restrictive classroom settings were considered at this time.

J.   **EXTENDED SCHOOL YEAR**

Are extended school year services required for this pupil?   ☐ Yes   ☒ No   ☐ More Data Needed
If yes, reasons are described here or attached:

RICHFIELD PUBLIC SCHOOLS
Special Education Department   TSES #8
7001 Harriet Ave. S. Richfield, MN 55423   9-06

REVIEW OF DISCIPLINE POLICY

School: _____

Name: _____ Date: _____ Related to IEP

Dated: _____

For every student with a disability, the IEP team, including parents, must determine whether the student is able to adhere to the School District's code of discipline. Consideration of the specific rules and procedures needs to be made in the following environments: classroom, hallways, recess, lunchroom, field trips, assemblies, and bus. Some students may require modifications.

Team Participants/Titles:

_____   _____

_____   _____

_____   _____

_____   Parents (s)   _____ Date: _____

_____ I have received the district's discipline policies and understand the content. Any modifications are addressed in the IEP and/or on the Significant Change Form.

Parent Signature: _____ Date: _____

Copies: White - Due Process File
Yellow - Parent

TSES #8A   9-06   ED-01938-06

RICHFIELD PUBLIC SCHOOLS
Special Education Department
7001 Harriet Ave. S. Richfield, MN 55423

REVIEW OF
DISCIPLINE POLICY WORKSHEET
(For Section G & H)

Student Name: _____ Date: _____

The IEP team is required to review the school/district discipline policy at the annual IEP meeting. The team must determine whether the student is able to adhere to the discipline policy. This is a requirement for all students receiving special education services, regardless of their disability.

Consideration of the specific rules and procedures needs to be made in the following environments: classroom, hallways, recess, lunchroom, field trips, assemblies and bus. Discuss specific rules and procedures in the following areas:

a. **STUDENT ATTENDANCE** (Absences, Tardiness & Truancy)
   Policy expectations reasonable for student   ___ yes   ___ no
   If no, describe modifications needed on IEP: _____
   _____
   _____
   _____

b. **DISRUPTIVE BEHAVIOR**
   Policy expectations reasonable for student   ___ yes   ___ no
   If no, describe modifications needed on IEP: _____
   _____
   _____
   _____

c. **NONCOMPLIANCE**
   Policy expectations reasonable for student   ___ yes   ___ no
   If no, describe modifications needed on IEP:_____
   _____
   _____
   _____

d. **TRANSPORTATION**
   Policy expectations reasonable for student   ___ yes   ___ no
   If no, describe modifications needed on IEP:_____
   _____
   _____
   _____

e. **OTHER BEHAVIORAL CONCERNS**
   Policy expectations reasonable for student   ___ yes   ___ no
   If no, describe modifications needed on IEP: _____
   _____
   _____
   _____

White: Due Process File   Yellow: Parent   Pink: District File

<table>
<tr><td rowspan="3">**Richfield Public Schools**
7001 Harriet Avenue South
Richfield, MN 55423</td><td>**NOTICE OF PROPOSED**
SPECIAL EDUCATION
SERVICES</td></tr>
</table>

Student Name: <u>Kevin</u>   Date: <u>10/9/2006</u>

School: _____<u>Richfield Intermediate</u>_____   Grade: <u> 4 </u>   Birthdate: ___<u>12/7/95</u>___

Dear _____&___

This notice is required whether or not you attended the Individual Education Program (IEP) or Individualized Family Service Plan (IFSP) Team meeting on

<u>10/17/06</u>
(Month/day/year)

☐ Your child will begin to receive special education services. The school district will not proceed without your written consent.

☒ Your child's IEP/IFSP will be changed as noted. The school district will proceed with this change unless you object in writing within 10 school days of receiving this notice.

☐ All current special education and related services are discontinued. The school district will proceed with this change unless you object in writing within 10 school days of receiving this notice.

Reason(s) for the above proposal, the basis for this decision, and other options and factors that were considered: It is the required time for the annual IEP. Goals and objectives may be added, deleted, or changed on the IEP.

Note to parent(s): If you have questions you may contact me.
<u>LESLIE</u>   <u>Special Ed. Teacher</u>
Name   *Position*   *Telephone*

As a parent, you have protections under the procedural safeguards of IDEA.
<u>Resources you may contact for further information about parent rights and procedural safeguards:</u>
PACER (Parent Advisory Coalition for Educational Rights): 612-827-2966 (Voice), 612-827-7770 (TTY), 1-800-53-PACER
MN Disability Law Center: 612-332-1441, 612-332-4668 (TTY), 1-800-292-4250
MN Special Education Mediation Service: 651-297-4635, 651-297-5353, 1-800-627-3529 (TTY)
MN Department of Children, Families & Learning: 651-582-8689, 651-582-8201 (TTY)
ARC Minnesota (advocacy for persons with developmental disabilities): 651-523-0823, 1-800-582-5256

PARENT ACTION

Parent(s): Check one of the options below, sign and date this form, and return the original of this page. If you do not return this page or otherwise respond within ten (10) school days, the team will proceed as indicated above.

☐ **I give permission** to the school district to proceed as proposed.

☐ **I need further information.** Please contact me to explain further and/or schedule a team meeting.

☐ **I do not give permission** for the district to proceed as proposed. I understand that you will contact me to offer a conciliation conference or mediation. I understand that I (or the district) have the right to proceed directly to a due process hearing.

Parent Signature (Student if age 18 or older)   *Date*

Date Received by District:

This form is available in several languages, Braille, or other format. Contact the Director of Special Education.

Richfield Public Schools
7001 Harriet Avenue South, Richfield, MN 55423

NOTICE OF PROCEDURAL SAFEGUARDS
PARENTAL RIGHTS FOR SPECIAL EDUCATION

March 2006

INTRODUCTION

This brochure provides an overview of special education rights, sometimes called procedural safeguards. These same procedural safeguards are also available for students with disabilities who have reached the age of 18. This **Notice of Procedural Safeguards** must be given to you when you ask for a copy. It must also be given to you:

1. The first time your child is referred for a special education evaluation;
2. Each time an annual individual education program (IEP) or an annual individual family service plan (IFSP) meeting is scheduled for your child;
3. Each time your child is reevaluated;
4. If you request a due process hearing;
5. If the district suspends your child for more than ten (10) consecutive days; or,
6. If the district places your child in an interim alternative education setting for up to 45 days for certain drug- and weapons-related misconduct.

PRIOR WRITTEN NOTICE

The district must provide you with prior written notice each time it proposes to initiate or change, or refuses to initiate or change the identification, evaluation, or education placement of your child.

This written notice must include:

1. A description of the action proposed or refused;
2. An explanation of why the district proposes or refuses to take the action;
3. A description of any other options the school considered and the reasons why those options were rejected;
4. A description of each evaluation procedure, test, record, or report the school used as a basis for its proposal or refusal;
5. A description of any other factors relevant to the school's proposal or refusal;
6. A statement that your child has protection under these procedural safeguards and information about how you can get a copy of the brochure; and
7. Sources for you to contact to obtain assistance in understanding these procedural safeguards.

FOR MORE INFORMATION

If you need help in understanding any of your procedural rights or anything about your child's education, please contact the principal or the person listed below. This notice must be provided in your native language or other mode of communication you may be using, like a sign language interpreter.

If you have any questions or would like further information, please contact:

Name _____

Phone _____

You may also contact a statewide Minnesota advocacy organization to explain the notice to you:

ARC Minnesota (advocacy for persons with developmental disabilities): 651-523-0823, 1-800-582-5256

Family Service Inc., Learning Disabilities Program: 651-222-0311, 651-222-0175 (TTY), 1-800-982-2303

MN Association for Children's Mental Health: 651-644-7333, 1-800-528-4511

MN Brain Injury Association: 612-378-2742, 1-800-444-6443

MN Department of Children, Families & Learning: 651-582-8689, 651-582-8201 (TTY)

MN Disability Law Center: 612-322-1441, 612-332-4668 (TTY), 1-800-292-4150

MN Special Education Mediation Service: 651-297-4635, 651-297-5353, 1-800-627-3529 (TTY)

PACER (Parent Advocacy Coalition for Educational Rights): 612-827-2966 (Voice), 612-827-7770 (TTY), 1-800-53-PACER

PARENTAL CONSENT

The district must obtain your written consent before conducting its initial evaluation with your child and before the first time it provides special education and related services to your child. Giving consent for an initial evaluation does not mean that you have given consent for an initial placement.

The district can do a reevaluation without your consent if it can show that reasonable steps have been taken to get your written consent. After reasonable efforts have been made to obtain your consent, the district can proceed with the proposed reevaluation if you do not object in writing within ten days.

You have a right **to object in writing** to any action the district proposes. Upon receipt of your written objection, the district will ask you to attend a conciliation conference, mediation, or other mutually agreed upon method of alternative dispute resolution.

If you object to a proposed service or evaluation, the district may not deny your child any other service or activity. The district must continue to provide an appropriate education to your child.

If you do object in writing, the district cannot evaluate your child without your consent unless authorized by a hearing officer. The district can proceed with its proposal if you fail to object in **writing.**

1. Schools cannot give information to a medical agency without parental consent.

2. The district can request but not require you to utilize your private health insurance to help pay for services.

INDEPENDENT EDUCATIONAL EVALUATIONS

An independent educational evaluation (IEE) is an evaluation by a qualified person(s) who is not an employee of your district. You may ask for an IEE at school district expense if you disagree with the district's evaluation. **Your request must be in writing.** A hearing officer may also order an independent evaluation of your child at school district expense during a due process hearing.

Upon request, the district must give you information regarding its criteria for selection of an independent examiner and information about where an independent education evaluation may be obtained.

If the district does not believe an IEE is necessary, the district must ask a hearing officer to determine the appropriateness of its evaluation. If the hearing officer determines the district's evaluation is appropriate, you still have the right to an independent evaluation, but not at public expense.

If you obtain an IEE, the results of the evaluation must be considered by the IEP/IFSP team and may be presented as evidence at a due process hearing regarding your child.

EDUCATION RECORDS

Access to Records

If you want to look at your child's records, ask the principal to provide you with access to those education records you want to review. These records include all information that is collected, maintained, or used by staff. The district must let you review the records without unnecessary delay and before any IEP/IFSP meeting or any hearing about your child. The district has ten (10) business days to respond to your request.

Your right to inspect and review records includes the right to :

1. An explanation or interpretation of your child's records upon request;

2. An opportunity to have someone of your choice inspect and review the records; and

3. Request that the district provide copies of your child's educational records to you. A fee may be charged for the copies.

Record of Access

The district must keep a record of any individual other than authorized district employees who has reviewed your child's education records. This record of access must include the name of the person, the date when he/she reviewed the records, and his/her purpose for reviewing the records.

Consent to Release Records

Parent consent is required before personally identifiable information is released to unauthorized persons or agencies.

Fees for Searching, Retrieving, and Copying Records

The district may not charge a fee to search or retrieve records, but may charge a reasonable fee for making copies of these records, unless you cannot afford to pay the fee.

Amendment of Records at Parent's Request

1. The district is obligated to inform you of the type and location of its education records on your child.

2. If you believe that information in your child's records is inaccurate, misleading, or violates the privacy or other rights of your child, you may request in writing that the district amend or remove the information. The district must decide if it will change the records. If the district decides not to make the changes, the district must inform you in writing that you have the right to a hearing to challenge the district's position. The hearing officer decides whether the information is accurate.

Destruction of Records

Before the district destroys any education records pertaining to your child, you will be informed. However, the school will always maintain permanent information on your child, including: name, address, phone number, and transcripts with grades and classes.

MEDIATION

Mediation is a voluntary process. You or your district may request mediation from the Minnesota Special Education Mediation Service (MNSEMS) at 651.297.4635. Mediation uses a neutral third party trained in mediation techniques. Mediation may not be used to deny or delay your right to a due process hearing. Both you and district staff must agree to try mediation before a mediator can be assigned. At any time during the mediation, you or the district may withdraw.

If your child is age birth to 3, you may request mediation and all public agencies involved in the dispute must participate in the process. Mediations for children birth to 3 must be completed within 30 days. Mediation proceedings for older children have no time restrictions.

WRITTEN COMPLAINTS

Any organization or individual may file a complaint with the Minnesota Department of Children, Families & Learning (CFL). Complaints sent to CFL must:

1. Be **in writing** and be signed by the individual or organization registering the complaint;

2. Allege violations of state or federal special education law or rule which have occurred within the last year unless a longer period is reasonable because the violation is continuing;

3. State the facts upon which the allegation is based; and

4. Include the name, address, and telephone number of the person or organization registering the complaint.

The complaint should be mailed to:
Minnesota Department of Children,
Families, & Learning
Division of Monitoring and Compliance
Complaint System Supervisor
1500 West Highway 36
Roseville, MN 55113-4266
651.582.8689 Phone 651.582.8725 Fax

IMPARTIAL DUE PROCESS HEARING

Both you and the district have a right to request **in writing** an impartial due process hearing. A due process hearing may address any matter related to identification, evaluation, education placement, or provision of a free appropriate public education.

If you request a hearing in writing, the district must inform you of the availability of mediation. The district must provide you with information regarding free or low cost legal services available in your area.

Procedures for Initiation of a Due Process Hearing
Upon your written request to the district for a hearing, the district must give you a copy of your rights. Your **written request** must include:

1. The name of your child;
2. The address of your child;
3. The name of school your child is attending;
4. A description of the problem(s) related to the proposed or refused initiation or change of special education or related services. Include as many facts as possible; and
5. A proposed resolution of the problem to the extent known to you at the time.

The district directly responsible for your child's education must arrange for the hearing to be conducted. The rights list below is an outline and not a complete guide to a due process hearing.

Both you and the district have certain rights in a hearing, including the right to:

1. One opportunity to remove a hearing officer within 48 hours of their appointment (does not apply to "expedited hearings");
2. Have an attorney and one or more individuals who have knowledge or training about children with disabilities represent and advise you prior to and at the hearing;
3. Present evidence, including expert medical, psychological, and education testimony, records, tests, reports and/or other information;
4. Compel the attendance of witnesses and to confront and cross-examine witnesses;
5. Participate in a pre-hearing conference held within ten (10) calendar days of the appointment of the hearing officer;
6. Stop the introduction of any evidence that was not given to either party at least five (5) business days before the hearing;
7. Be told that the hearing officer has the authority to subpoena any person or paper necessary to adequately understand the issues of the hearing;
8. Have your child, who is the subject of the hearing, present at the hearing;
9. A closed hearing unless you specifically request an open hearing; and
10. Receive a written copy or, at your option, an electronic verbatim record of the hearing at no cost to you.

The hearing decision is final unless you or the district appeal the decision.

Disclosure of Additional Evidence before a Hearing
At least five (5) business days before a hearing, you and the district must disclose to each other all evaluations of your child completed by that date and recommendations based on those evaluations that are intended to be used at the hearing. A hearing officer may refuse to allow you to introduce any undisclosed evaluations or recommendations at the hearing without consent of the other party. All evidence must be limited to the specific issues described to the hearing officer.

<u>Administrative Hearing Appeal Process</u>
If you decide to appeal the final decision of a hearing officer, the appeal must be made **in writing** to CFL within 30 calendar days of the receipt of the written decision. CFL will then appoint a hearing review officer and ensure that a final decision is mailed within 30 calendar days after the filing of the appeal, unless the reviewing official has granted an extension at the request of either party. You may appeal the findings and decision made in a hearing review by appealing the decision to state or federal court.

CIVIL ACTION

When either you or the district disagree with the findings or decisions made by a hearing review officer, either party may file a court action. The action may be brought in state or federal district court. In any civil action, the court will:

1. Receive the records of the administrative proceedings;
2. Hear additional evidence at the request of a party;
3. Base its decision on the preponderance of the evidence; and
4. Grant such relief as the court determines is appropriate.

PLACEMENT DURING A HEARING OR CIVIL ACTION

During a hearing or judicial action, unless the district and the parent agree otherwise, your child remains in the education placement where he/she is currently placed, commonly referred to as the "stay-put" rule.

Two exceptions to the "stay-put" rule exist:

1. For students who have been removed from their educational setting to an interim alternative educational placement for certain weapon or drug violations, "stay-put" would be the interim alternative educational placement, not the current educational setting; and

2. After a hearing officer's decision is issued agreeing with the parents that a change in placement is appropriate, the hearing officer's decision would be the "stay-put" placement during subsequent appeals.

EXPEDITED HEARINGS

Hearings must be expedited in the following situations:

1. Whenever you request a hearing to dispute the district's determination that your child's behavior was not a result of his/her disability;
2. Whenever you request a hearing to dispute a 45 day interim alternative education placement order by school personnel; or
3. When a district requests an expedited hearing to establish that it is dangerous for your child to remain in the current placement.

<u>Placement by a Hearing Officer</u>
A hearing officer may decide to move your child to an interim alternative educational setting for up to 45 calendar days:

1. When the district has demonstrated that your child is substantially likely to injure self or others if he/she remains in the current placement; and
2. When the district has made reasonable efforts to minimize the risk of harm in the current placement.

INTERIM ALTERNATIVE EDUCATIONAL PLACEMENT

The district may change your child's educational placement for up to 45 calendar days, if your child:

1. Possesses a weapon at school or a school function; or
2. Knowingly possesses or uses illegal drugs, or sells or solicits the sale of a controlled substance while at school or a school function.

The interim alternative educational setting is determined by the IEP team. Even though this is a temporary change, it must allow your child:

1. To continue to progress in the general curriculum, although in a different setting;
2. To continue to receive those services and modifications, including those described in your child's IEP, that will help your child meet his/her IEP goals; and
3. Include services and modifications designed to prevent the behavior from recurring.

If your child is placed in an interim alternative educational setting, an IEP meeting must be convened within ten (10) school days of the decision. At this meeting, the team must discuss the behavior and its relationship to your child's disability, review evaluation information regarding the behavior, and determine the appropriateness of your child's IEP and behavior plan.

ATTORNEY'S FEES FOR HEARINGS

You may be able to recover attorney fees if you prevail in a due process hearing. A petition for fees must be filed in a court of competent jurisdiction. A judge may make an award of attorney's fees based on prevailing rates in your community. The court may reduce an award of attorney's fees if it finds that you unreasonably delayed the settlement or decision in the case.

PRIVATE SCHOOL PLACEMENT

You may be able to recover tuition expenses for a private school placement if:

1. You inform the district either at an IEP/IFSP meeting or give written notice to the district of at least 10 business days of your intent to enroll your child in the private school; and
2. You state why you disagree with the district's proposed IEP/IFSP or placement;
3. A hearing officer finds that the district failed to provide or is unable to provide your child with an appropriate education and that the private placement is appropriate.

If the district gave you written notice of its intent to evaluate your child before you removed your child from the public school, you must make your child available to the district for evaluation.

Failure to tell the school of your intent to enroll your child in a private school at public expense, failure to make your child available for evaluation, or other unreasonable delay on your part could result in a reduction or denial of reimbursement for the private school placement. If the district prevented you from providing this notice or you cannot write in English, the hearing officer may not reduce the reimbursement.

APPENDIX C

Approaches to Crowd Control

- Approaches to Crowd Control: Summary (AAHPERD)
- Coaches Council Code of Conduct (NASPE)
- Share the Spirit of Fair Play: Be a Good Sport (MSHSL)
- Spectator Behavior (MPRB)
- Junior Olympics Coaches Code of Ethics (USAV)

APPROACHES TO CROWD CONTROL: SUMMARY

The nature and seriousness of the problems in crowd control have recently become more drastic and bizarre as they have occurred with increasing frequency. They take on the collective character of a deliberate attempt to either ignore or confront the system just because they buy a ticket or go through a turnstile. Research, however, suggests that being in an unfriendly territory and in competition for not only the game or contest, but also for space, goods, services, and information (i.e., parking tickets, seating, concessions), and being somewhat anonymous because of the large crowd, can potentially lead to situations that encourage troublemakers to act more irresponsibly than they might in situations where they can be easily identified. This social problem may be impossible to eliminate completely, but an attempt must be made to cope with the immediate symptoms. Our best hope is for imaginative and coordinated efforts by the school, institution, agency, and sport management; the majority of students; and community authorities to promote standards of conduct conducive to continuing spectator sports in comparative tranquility. The alternatives are to allow a disruptive element to completely negate the nature of school and community sport, to play with no spectators, or to abandon this school and community building activity.

The following will present some causes of crowd control problems and some approaches to solutions.

Some Causes of Problems

- Lack of anticipation of, and preventive planning for, possible trouble
- Lack of proper facilities
- Poor communication resulting in lack of information
- Lack of an organizational system concerning parking, tickets, seating, and security
- Lack of involvement of one or more of the following: school administration, faculty, student body, parents, community, press, law enforcement, and security agencies
- Lack of respect for authority and property
- Attendance at games of youth under the influence of illegal substances
- Increased attitude of permissiveness
- School dropouts, recent graduates, and outsiders including gangs

Some Approaches to Solutions

Develop written policy statements, guidelines, and regulations for crowd control

1. Consult the following before writing policy statements or promulgating regulations: school administration, athletic and activities director, conference representatives, coaches, faculty members involved in the school sports program, school youth organizations, parents, community education department, local police, community leaders, and student body.
2. Properly and efficiently administer regulations and provide for good communications.
3. Constantly evaluate regulations and guidelines for their relevance and effectiveness.
4. Make guidelines and regulations so effective that the director of athletics and activities who follows them is secure in knowing he or she has planned with the staff for any eventuality and has sufficient help to cope with any situation that may arise.

Events policy and procedures manual content

1. Welcome and philosophy of sportsmanship and community building.
2. An introduction to the facility (i.e., maps, parking, locker room, phone numbers).
3. Codes of conduct (i.e., coaches, players, spectators).
4. Arrival and departure procedures (i.e., greeting, postgame reception).
5. Seating arrangements (i.e., team, band, visiting spectators).
6. Safety and emergency procedures.

7. Pre- and postgame activities (i.e., parents' reception).

8. Job description and duties of all staff, security, medical team members, volunteers, and all those involved in the event.

Provide adequate facilities

1. Plan and design stadiums, field houses, arenas, and gymnasiums for effective crowd control.

2. Provide for adequate rest room facilities.

3. Establish a no-smoking and drug-free school and promote these policies during contests.

4. Provide for complete preparation of facilities including security before and after the game or event.

5. Meet, greet, and escort the visiting team to and from the game, contest, or event.

6. Have appropriate signage (i.e., directions, warnings, pricing) posted at entrances and gates, as well as in printed programs.

Teach good fair play throughout the school and the community

1. Begin education in good sportspersonship in the earliest grades and continue it throughout the school life.

2. Make frequent approving references to constructive and commendable behavior, especially by the public address announcer.

3. Institute a fair play and sportspersonship award for both teams and fans at events and competitions.

4. Arrange for program appearances by faculty members and students jointly to discuss the true values of sport competition including good sportspersonship.

5. Make use of all news media through frequent and effective television, radio, and press presentations and interviews, commentaries, and frequent announcement of good sportspersonship slogans and awards.

6. Distribute a printed Code of Conduct for Good Sportspersonship.

7. Include the good sportspersonship slogan and logo in all printed programs at sports events.

8. Urge the use of sports events as an example in elementary school citizenship classes, stressing positive values of good conduct at school games and events, during the raising of the flag and singing of the national anthem; also emphasize courtesy toward visitors.

9. Involve teachers and community leaders in school athletic associations, provide them with passes to all sports events, and stress the positive values of their presence and setting an example of good sportspersonship.

Intensify communications before scheduled games

1. Arrange for an exchange of speakers at school assembly programs; the principals, coaches, or team captains could visit the opposing school.

2. Discuss with appropriate personnel of the competing school the procedures for the game (i.e., conduct, safety, security), including method and location of team entry and departure.

3. Provide superintendent or principal, athletic and activities director, and coach with a copy of the written policy statement, guidelines, and regulations.

4. Meet all game officials and request them to stress good sportspersonship before, during, and after all contests.

5. Meet with coaches and instruct them not to question officials during a contest; stress the importance of good sportspersonship and that their conduct sets the tone for spectator reaction to game incidents.

6. Instruct students, parents, fans, coaches, and athletes about what to expect and what behavior is expected of them.

7. Schedule preventive planning conferences with local police and security to be assured of their full cooperation and effectiveness in spectator control.

Inform the community

1. Request coaches and athletic and activities directors to talk to service groups and other community groups.
2. Invite community leaders and their families (nonschool people) to attend sports events on a regular basis.
3. Post on all available notice boards around the community and in businesses, factories, and other public places, posters showing the Sportspersonship Code of Conduct.
4. Release constructive information and positive statements to news media and request publication of brief guidelines on sports pages.
5. Provide news media with pertinent information as to ways in which the community may directly and indirectly render assistance in the crowd control problem.

Involve law enforcement personnel

1. Police and other security personnel should be highly visible and strategically located so as to afford the best possible control.
2. Law enforcement professionals should handle *all* enforcement and disciplining of spectators.
3. Strength in force may be shown by appearance of several police officers, motorcycles, police cars, etc., at and near the site of the game.
4. Police may be stationed in rest rooms.
5. Civil Defense organizations could patrol parking areas.
6. A faculty member from the visiting school may be used as a liaison with police and local faculty in identifying visiting students.
7. Attendants, police, security, EMTs, county sheriffs, and deputies should be in uniform; uniformed authority figures command greater respect.

Use supervisory personnel other than police

1. Carefully select teacher and/or volunteer supervisors who are attentive and alert to signs of possible trouble.
2. Identify faculty members by armbands, T-shirts, or other means.
3. Provide for communication by means of walkie-talkie or cellular phone.
4. Assign some faculty members to sit behind the visiting fans; this reduces verbal harassment of visitors.
5. Employ paid ticket takers and paid chaperones to mingle strategically among the crowd and to remain on duty throughout the game, including halftime.
6. Issue free or complimentary passes to elementary and junior high physical education teachers and coaches and other responsible adult volunteers to provide more adult presence and supervision.

Plan for ticket sales and concession stands

1. Arrange for advance sale of student tickets to avoid congestion at the gate.
2. Sell tickets in advance only to students in their own schools, and avoid if possible the sale of tickets to outsiders and nonstudents.
3. Provide for a thorough security check at the gate or entrance (crowd audit).
4. Arrange for concession stands to be open before the game, during halftime, and after the game.
5. Channel the flow of traffic to and from concession stands using ropes or other means; keep traffic moving and away from the playing area.

Prepare spectators and contestants

1. Encourage as many students as possible to be in the uniforms of the athletic club, pep club, booster clubs, band, majorettes, cheerleaders.
2. Provide transportation for participants to and from the game site.

3. Have participants dressed to play before leaving for a game or contest.

4. Adhere to established seating capacity of stadiums, arenas, and gymnasiums.

5. Try to arrange for a statewide athletic association regulation prohibiting all noisemakers including musical instruments except for the school band or orchestra under professional supervision.

6. Request the assistance of visiting teams and other community organizations and clubs.

7. Educate cheerleaders, student leaders, band captains, pep squads, and faculty supervisors by means of a one-day safety and conduct seminar.

8. Keep spectators buffered from the playing area as much as practical.

9. Request that elementary school children be accompanied by an adult.

10. Have a well-trained public address announcer who assists in crowd control and responsibility and knows the procedures in case of emergency.

11. Make sure that the venue is well marked (i.e., signage), well lighted, accessible, and the flow of traffic avoids the participants of the game (i.e., coach, players, officials, scorekeepers, timers, cheerleaders, band).

Miscellaneous

1. Inform and involve school superintendents when problems arise in connection with sports events.

2. Impose appropriate penalties on faculty, coaches, and students guilty of poor conduct.

3. Identity offenders at games and notify parents if possible; any penalties inflicted should also be noted (Note: If the offense leads to juvenile court action, care should be taken not to contravene laws about publishing names of juvenile offenders).

4. Consistently enforce rules and regulations; this is a necessity.

5. Work toward the assumption of responsibility for strong regulation and enforcement of team behavior on the part of the state athletic leagues and associations.

6. Attempt to work with the courts toward greater cooperation.

7. Avoid overstressing the winning of games.

8. Be sure that a well-trained medical team including a physician, certified athletic trainer, and EMT are at each game and know the procedures to be followed in case of emergency.

9. Remember, people (i.e., spectators) do not surrender their rights because they purchase tickets to an event; sports managers must do all they can to see that their staff and volunteers treat them with courtesy and respect.

10. After-game incidents away from the proximity of the stadium, arena, or gymnasium are out of the control of school officials, but they do cause bad public relations.

Summary

Safety and crowd controls at school sport functions are imperative! Greater concentration on treating the causes of the problem is essential. Preliminary planning and groundwork is the key to good crowd control. Coordination and cooperation of school, community, and law enforcement agencies are keys to success.

Youths should be taught to know what to expect and what is expected of them at sponsored school events. Consistent enforcement of rules and regulations is a necessity if youth are to respect authority. Adult behavior should be such that it may be advantageously and admirably emulated by youth whose actions may result in deserving praise instead of negative criticism and disapproval.

The school sport program is a constructive and valuable educational activity. It should be permitted to function in a favorable, healthful, positive, respectful, and friendly environment.

THE COACHES COUNCIL CODE OF CONDUCT

The effect that a sport coach has on young athletes is apparent in the way the athletes conduct themselves. Although that influence is not always a positive one, the coach-athlete relationship provides an opportunity to help maximize the development of the athlete physically, mentally and social/emotionally.

Sport is such an integral part of our culture yet coaching is not always seen as a true profession. This attitude is gradually changing. Coaching can no longer be perceived as simply a hobby or informal second job; coaching is a profession. It may be necessary for a coach to work as a teacher or in business or other occupations. But this need not and must not diminish the professional responsibilities for executing the coaching role as a professional.

If we are to continue to enhance the cultural perceptions of coaching, then we must strive toward maintaining minimum expectations. At minimum, the role of the coach should include the knowledge and awareness of the competencies within the following eight domains from the *National Standards for Athletic Coaches:*

- Injury: Prevention, Care and Management
- Risk Management
- Growth, Development and Learning
- Training, Conditioning and Nutrition
- Social/Psychological Aspects of Coaching
- Skills, Tactics and Strategies
- Teaching and Administration
- Professional Preparation

The Coaches Council of the National Association for Sport and Physical Education (NASPE) has established the following **Code of Conduct** to which coaches at all levels should be held accountable.

- Coaches have the knowledge and preparation to lead their teams within the parameters outlined in the National Standards for Athletic Coaches (NASPE 2005).
- Coaches are responsible to ensure that the health, well-being and development of athletes take precedence over the win/loss record.
- Coaches accept that they do serve as role models and there must be congruency between their actions and words.
- Coaches provide a physically and emotionally safe environment for practices and competition.
- Coaches exemplify honesty, integrity, fair play, and sportsmanship regardless of the impact that might have upon the outcome of the competition.
- Coaches maintain a professional demeanor in their relationships with athletes, officials, colleagues, administrators and the public and treat them with respect and dignity.
- Coaches maintain confidentiality when appropriate and avoid situations that would potentially create a conflict of interest or exploit the athlete.
- Coaches are committed to the education of their athletes and should encourage academic achievement.
- Coaches are committed to the safety and well-being of each athlete and promote healthy lifestyles by their actions.
- Coaches discourage the use of performance enhancing substances and dietary supplements.
- Coaches prohibit the use of any illegal or recreational drugs.
- Coaches educate athletes about nutrition, safe and healthy weight loss or gain, and healthy eating behaviors.
- Coaches follow current safe training and conditioning techniques.
- Coaches exhibit sound injury and risk management practices.
- Coaches demonstrate an understanding of growth and developmental stages of their athletes.
- Coaches encourage athletes to adopt a physically active lifestyle.
- Coaches place the athlete's needs and interests before their own.
- Coaches remember that competition should be healthy and enjoyable for all.

SHARE THE SPIRIT OF FAIR PLAY: BE A GOOD SPORT

Sharing the Spirit of Fair Play is an important part of any sports program. It teaches young people a valuable life skill that is applicable to far more than sports. That is why organizations such as the Minnesota State High School League and its corporate partner, First Bank, are proud to sponsor a sportsmanship awards program for schools participating in their state tournaments. To earn an award, a school's spectators, coaches, cheerleaders, bands, and players must honor their parts of the Sportsmanship Code of Conduct.

Sportsmanship Code of Conduct
Spectators

1. Take part in cheers with the cheerleaders and applaud good performances.
2. Work cooperatively with game officials and supervisors in keeping order.
3. Refrain from crowd booing, foot stomping, or making negative comments about officials, coaches, and/or participants.
4. Stay off the playing area at all times.
5. Show respect for public property and equipment.

Coaches

1. Follow the rules of the contest at all times.
2. Accept the decisions of game officials.
3. Avoid offensive gestures or language.
4. Display modesty in victory and graciousness in defeat.
5. Avoid public criticism of game officials and/or participants.

Participants

1. Show respect for opponents at all times.
2. Accept the decisions of game officials.
3. Avoid offensive gestures or language.
4. Display modesty in victory and graciousness in defeat.
5. Show respect for public property and equipment.

Cheerleaders

1. Know the contest rules and cheer at proper times.
2. Lead positive cheers which support and uplift your team.
3. Encourage support for any injured participant.
4. Show respect for opposing cheerleaders.
5. Avoid offensive gestures or language.

Bands

1. Choose appropriate music and time for performing.
2. Dress in school-approved uniforms.
3. Show respect at all times for officials, opponents, and spectators.
4. Show respect at all times for public property and equipment.
5. Avoid offensive gestures or language.

SPECTATOR BEHAVIOR

Parents and spectator codes of conduct are becoming common especially at youth sporting events. The following is the Spectator Code of Conduct for Youth Sporting Events for the Minneapolis Park and Recreation Board.

Rules of the Game

1. No profanity, abusive language, or negative personal remarks.
2. Let the officials do their job. Constant criticism detracts from the game.
3. Let the coaches do their job. They need and appreciate your support more than your criticism.
4. Obey rules of the game site: no smoking, no drinking, no drugs, no food in gyms, etc.
5. Stay within your designated area. Entering the field or court is disruptive and disrespectful.
6. Physical confrontations or throwing objects onto the court or field are absolutely forbidden.

7. Treat the game for what it is—a game.
8. If you are remembered as a role model, let it be as a positive one.
9. Protect the rights of young athletes to a safe environment, to be treated with dignity, to have fun through sport and to participate.

Sanctions for Misbehavior

1. Individual will be given a warning.
2. Individual will be asked to leave the game.
3. Individual is banned from all youth sports events.
4. Other sanctions as deemed necessary.

Junior Olympic Coaches Code of Ethics
USA Volleyball/North Country Region

NOTE: For the purposes of this Code, "coaches" includes coaches, team reps, and chaperones of athletes. All coaches, team reps, and chaperones must read the Code of Ethics and sign the commitment form which will be in the team registration packet.

PHILOSOPHY

1. In all cases, what is good for the athlete and the sport of volleyball should guide decisions and choices.
2. All coaches should strive to be positive role models representing volleyball and good sportsmanship.
3. All coaches are expected to conduct themselves in a forthright and honorable manner.
4. It is within each individual's ability to treat each other with dignity and respect. The region expects that all coaches take responsibility for their own actions.

CODE OF ETHICS

1. All coaches are expected to abide by the USA Volleyball (USAV) guidelines, Code of Conduct, and the Junior Olympic Coaches Code of Ethics.
2. Coaches will fully disclose all pertinent information regarding their programs (i.e., total costs, philosophy, coaching personnel) to potential players and will refrain from representing a competing program or coach.
3. Coaches will exhibit standards of good sportsmanship at all times being positive representatives of their team, club, region, and the sport of volleyball. A coach will be in violation of standards for good sportsmanship by:
    a. making degrading or critical remarks about officials during or after a contest, either on the court or from the bench or spectator area.
    b. arguing with officials or going through motions indicating disdain or disagreement with a decision.
    c. physically detaining officials after a contest.
    d. gross misconduct, including physical or verbal intimidation of any individual; or abusive or inappropriate behavior directed toward one's own or opposing team members or coach(es).
4. Coaches may not contact players by phone or personally about playing for their club program from day 1 of their high school practice until after the state tournament (16- and 18-under divisions only). Between the last sanctioned USA Volleyball tournament and the first day of practice for their high school team, a coach may contact players and ask them if they would like to play for their club program. Please respect the high school athlete's privacy during her or his high school season. If a player who was not on the team last year contacts a coach before the state tournament, the coach may get her or his name and address to send information about the club.
5. All forms of sexual abuse or harassment with players are unethical, even when a player invites or consents to such behavior or involvement. Sexual abuse/harassment is defined as, but not limited to, repeated comments, gestures, or physical contacts of a sexual nature.
6. All coaches must be adults (under 21 they need a waiver, must be 18) and registered members of North Country Region.
7. All coaches must inform both their players and the players' parents or guardians that they must sign a Release and Waiver of Liability form before they can become USAV members.
8. All coaches must inform both their players and their players' parents or guardians of the USAV transfer policy during a season. This policy prohibits a player from transferring teams during the season once that player has represented a team in a USAV sanctioned tournament.
9. Coaches will provide a positive role model and atmosphere in practices and matches acting courteously, respectfully, and politely to all players, parents, other coaches, and officials.
10. Coaches will work with and develop every member of your team, not just the starters.
11. No coach will supply or condone the use of drugs, alcohol, or tobacco.
12. No coach will participate, require, or condone any action by the players which is illegal under either the civil or criminal code.

13. A registered adult coach must be present at all practices, during team-supervised travel and during competition.
14. No coach shall allow, encourage, condone, or require any behavior that threatens a player's high school association, USAV, or NCAA eligibility.
15. Once a player has committed to a team or club for the season, either verbally or in writing, no coach from another team or club, players under the direction of another team or club coach, or parents under the direction of another coach, may contact that player for the purpose of persuading her or him to leave the club to which she or he has committed. This does not prohibit anyone from talking to another player or giving the player or his/her parents or guardians information about their club tryouts, practices, organization, etc., if it is requested by the player or her or his parents or guardians, and the information must not relate to any promises of future considerations or inducements to leave her or his present club or team.
16. All coaches must read this Code, sign the Junior Coaches Code of Ethics Commitment Form and be IMPACT or CAP certified to coach in the North Country Region. Violations of the Code or certification requirements may result in sanctions against either or both the coach and/or the club involved.

REPORTING

Actions that are in violation of this Code should be reported to the Executive Director of North Country Region, who will refer them to the Hearing Board Chair.

SANCTIONS

1. According to the USAV Participant Code of Conduct, which is signed by each member at the time of registration.
2. Penalties may include, but are not limited to, reprimand, censure, suspension, expulsion, fines, and/or other actions deemed appropriate by the regional Hearing Board Chair.
3. The North Country Region Board of Directors will serve as a court of appeals and has the authority to modify any penalty to exceed these guidelines in any situation as it deems appropriate.

NOTE: Although parents may not necessarily be USAV members, it may be appropriate to extend responsibility for the actions of some parents representing a club to the coach or administrator of that club.

(PLEASE CUT ALONG DOTTED LINE AND STAPLE TO COACHES', TEAM REPS', OR CHAPERONES' MEMBERSHIP FORM) (MAKE A COPY OF THIS DOCUMENT BEFORE YOU CUT FOR EACH COACH, TEAM REP, OR CHAPERONE TO KEEP)

- -

**USA VOLLEYBALL/NORTH COUNTRY REGION
JUNIOR COACHES CODE OF ETHICS**

COMMITMENT FORM
MUST BE SIGNED BY ALL COACHES, TEAM REPS, & CHAPERONES

NAME OF CLUB _____

I, _____ HAVE READ THE NCR JUNIOR OLYMPIC COACHES CODE OF ETHICS AND FULLY UNDERSTAND BY COMMITMENT TO THE USAV NORTH COUNTRY REGION'S JUNIOR OLYMPIC PROGRAMS.

_____   _____
            (Signature)   (Month, Day, Year)

ARE YOU IMPACT CERTIFIED? ___ YES ___ NO; CAP CERTIFIED? ___ YES ___ NO; LEVEL I OR II?

SITE OF CERTIFICATION _____

Drugs and Alcohol

- Intercollegiate Drug and Alcohol Education, Testing, and Rehabilitation Program
- NCAA Division I Intercollegiate Consent to Participate Statement
- High School Pledge of Honor
- Junior High School Rules Concerning Mood-Altering Chemicals and Informed Consent
- National Athletic Trainers' Association Code of Ethics
- TARGET Minnesota (Courtesy of the Minnesota State High School League)
- NCAA Banned-Drug Classes

U OF M INTERCOLLEGIATE ATHLETICS DRUG AND ALCOHOL EDUCATION, TESTING, AND REHABILITATION PROGRAM

Illicit drug use and alcohol abuse are major problems in America today, and they are present on all college and university campuses. Student-athletes are as prone to the ills of drug use and alcohol abuse as anybody else and the Department of Intercollegiate Athletics believes it is their responsibility to do everything possible to protect the health and welfare of the student-athletes and to eradicate the problem. Drug testing is appropriate to help ensure the safety of student-athletes while they participate in athletic contests. In addition, a program to prevent the use of performance-enhancing drugs promotes fair competition in intercollegiate athletics. The NCAA has established a drug testing program for student-athletes and the University of Minnesota program serves the same purposes. It is reasonable for the University to require a student to submit to drug testing as a condition of the privilege of participating in intercollegiate athletics. Toward that end, the Athletic Department has formulated a comprehensive drug and alcohol program that focuses on Education, Testing, and Rehabilitation.

Purposes of the Intercollegiate Athletic Drug Program

1. To adhere to NCAA, Big Ten, and University of Minnesota rules and procedures regarding licit or illicit drug use by student-athletes.
2. To disseminate information and educate student-athletes about problems associated with drug and alcohol abuse.
3. To identify student-athletes who are using illicit drugs or abusing alcohol or other illicit drugs and provide avenues for remediation.
4. To assure all athletes, parents, and University officials that the University of Minnesota Intercollegiate Athletic Department is committed to providing a drug-free environment for the conduct of all athletic programs.
5. To protect the reputation and integrity of the University of Minnesota Intercollegiate Athletic Program.

Drug Education

At least once a year, all student-athletes will be required to participate in an Alcohol Drug Education Seminar to discuss drug and alcohol use and to review the Intercollegiate Athletics Drug Program including all policies and procedures. This program will be administered through the Center for Student-Athletic Development. Behavioral responsibilities and disciplinary expectations will also be fully discussed at that time.

Additionally, a resource pool of educational materials, films, and speakers will be made available for use by the coaches and student-athletes at any time throughout the year.

Each fall, a copy of the drug and alcohol program will be provided for all newly entering student-athletes. Parents or guardians will be encouraged to contact the athletic department regarding any questions they might have.

Finally, each student-athlete will be asked to sign, and return to the Head Athletic Trainer, a "Consent to Participate" form relative to the Athletic Drug Testing Program. A sample of the form follows this Drug Education and Testing policy statement.

Voluntary Participation

Any student-athlete who feels that he/she has a problem with alcohol or other drugs may request assistance through the Athletic Medicine Staff, Team Physician, Coach, or other staff member. Such a request *shall not* be treated as a positive test, and the student-athlete shall be treated/counseled in a manner appropriate to his/her problem. Any positive test (or equivalent) occurring after such voluntary participation shall be treated as a first positive test.

Student-Athlete Responsibility

As a member of any University of Minnesota Athletics Department team participating in any events or activities authorized by the department, you are required to provide proof of compliance with the U of M Drug and Alcohol Education, Testing, and Rehabilitation Program. It is your responsibility to present a urine specimen free from banned substances or evidence of inappropriate use of alcohol or illicit medications. Any urine sample testing positive will be considered valid and that of an active user.

Selection of the student-athlete or team for testing will be determined by the Athletic Director of the University of Minnesota Intercollegiate Athletics Department or designee.

Alcohol and Prescription (Licit) Medication

The University recognizes that alcohol and prescription medications are the most commonly used and abused drugs in our society. For this reason, any use of alcohol and/or prescription medications that results in harmful consequences (i.e., assault, theft, public intoxication, property destruction, underage drinking, and others) to the student-athlete or others shall be treated as a positive drug test and dealt with according to the conditions of this drug program. *Student-athletes are reminded that the legal age for consumption of alcohol in the State of Minnesota is 21.*

Drug Counseling Staff

The drug counseling staff shall consist of

Team Physician
Alcohol/Drug Education Counselor
Sport Administrator
Head Coach
Head Athletic Trainer

The Team Physician and the Alcohol/Drug Education Counselor shall be the overall coordinators for the counseling staff. Physicians and counselors who are responsible for direct patient care shall be qualified in their respective fields in accordance with community standards and regulations. All members of the counseling staff are expected to have training in the field of alcohol and other drug use/abuse appropriate to their job description.

Screening for Illicit Drug Use

At unannounced dates throughout the academic year, student-athletes will be asked to give urine samples as part of the drug testing program. *Refusal to provide a urine specimen will be considered a positive test.*

Each student-athlete should be expected to be tested at least once a year for selected drugs including, but not limited to

alcohol
amphetamines
anabolic steroids
barbiturates
cocaine
diuretics
heroin
LSD
marijuana
PCP
quaaludes

Use of any of the above drugs by a student-athlete at the University of Minnesota is prohibited, except as may be prescribed by a licensed physician to treat specific medical conditions. All student-athletes should declare all medications routinely taken, prescription or nonprescription, to their team Athletic Medicine Staff prior to the beginning of their season.

Testing Procedures

All urine samples for testing will be collected under direct observation to eliminate substitutions. Procedures will be designed to preserve the integrity, accuracy, and confidentiality of the testing process.

Containers and samples will remain under constant supervision of Athletic Training Staff members until they are delivered to the Hennepin County Medical Center (HCMC) Toxicology Laboratory or another appropriate facility for testing. Identification signature sheets will remain under constant supervision until delivered to the Head Athletic Trainer.

Upon completion of the testing, the Supervisor/Lab Manager of the HCMC Toxicology Lab will telephone the Head Athletic Trainer to report the results *regardless of whether or not all specimens were found to be negative, or if positive samples were found.* The Head Athletic Trainer will then notify the respective Head Coach of the laboratory's findings. If positive specimens are identified, the Head Athletic Trainer will also notify the Senior Associate Athletic Director, the Head Team General Physician, and the Alcohol/Drug Education Counselor of any positive samples.

The Supervisor/Lab Manager of the HCMC Toxicology Lab will also submit a *written* report of *all* test results to the Head Team General Physician, who will review all measurements and data listed on the report. The Team Physician will identify samples below the minimum specific gravity threshold, or those whose measurements are suspect. These student-athletes will produce another sample as instructed until they have provided a sample approved by the Head Team Physician. It is the student-athlete's responsibility to report as instructed at the proper place and time until cleared by the medical staff. The student-athlete's coach will be notified of any delinquencies in this regard, and the coach will impose appropriate discipline. The Head Athletic Trainer will submit summary statistical reports to the Athletic Director upon his/her request.

Policy Regarding Positive Tests

All positive results will be retested from a reserve sample for verification. If the positive test is verified, the Head Coach, Athletic Medicine Staff, or Team Physician will notify the student-athlete of the results and explain the procedure to be followed.

1. First Positive Test

The student-athlete will arrange an appointment with the Team Physician or Alcohol/Drug Education Counselor for the purposes of evaluation, education, and if necessary, treatment or counseling. The evaluation will include a diagnosis using standard diagnostic instruments, history, and if necessary, physical examination. Information from other sources will be solicited for the purposes of the evaluation. These sources include, but are not limited to, coaches, academic counselors, Athletic Medicine Staff, residence hall personnel, other student-athletes, and members of the athletic department staff. Such information shall be used for the purposes of obtaining the clearest view possible of the student-athlete's clinical picture. Upon completion of the interview, a diagnosis will be formulated, which will characterize the student-athlete in one of five general categories with respect to alcohol/drug use. These categories include experimental use, social use, chemical abuse, chemical dependency, and an indeterminate category. In the case of the chemical abuse and dependency categories, diagnosis shall be made in accordance with the Diagnostic and Statistical Manual (current edition) or the criteria of the National Council on Alcoholism.

In some cases disposition may include simple education and limit-setting techniques. In the case of chemical dependency, structured treatment will be a prerequisite to the student-athlete's continued participation in athletics. When problems other than chemical use/abuse are uncovered, the physician/counselor may refer the student-athlete to other appropriate resources. The student-athlete will also be subject to periodic retests on any given date. These tests will be done under the supervision of the Alcohol/Drug Counselor, Athletic Medicine Staff and/or Team Physician. Although a first positive test may warrant no specific sanctions, other than referral to a Alcohol/Drug Education Counselor for guidance, it does not preclude a coach from enforcing a team policy or team rule.

In addition to the evaluation process, the student-athlete will be required to participate in a conference call with his/her parents, guardian, or spouse, the Athletic Director (or designee), Head Coach, Physician, or Counselor.

Refusal or failure of the student-athlete to meaningfully participate in the evaluation/counseling process, as defined by the counselors, shall result in immediate suspension from the team until such time as the student-athlete shall cooperate with counseling and evaluation measures.

Prior to implementation of any suspension, or as soon thereafter as is practical, the student-athlete will have the opportunity to fully discuss the matter with the drug counseling staff and present evidence contesting the accuracy of the test or any mitigating circumstances the student-athlete believes important.

2. Second Positive Test

A second positive test, by its very nature, indicates a more serious problem requiring more formal intervention. Upon confirmation of the second positive test the student-athlete will be suspended from all competition for a period equivalent to 10 percent of his/her regular season games. The suspension shall be served starting with the next scheduled game and will be in effect for both regular and playoff competition. If the infraction occurs at the end of the season or during the off-season, the suspension will be served in the next season. If the infraction occurs at the end of the regular season but before a playoff, it shall be served during the playoff.

In addition, the player will be reevaluated by the Team Physician or Alcohol/Drug Counselor Education and will be referred to appropriate treatment on or off campus. Student-athletes who receive treatment for chemical dependency will be required to attend weekly meetings of an appropriate self-help group such as Alcoholics Anonymous (AA), Cocaine Anonymous (CA) etc. In addition, the student-athlete will be responsible for carrying out the discharge plans of the treatment facility. Student-athletes will sign appropriate authorization forms to ensure that results of treatment, treatment plans, etc., are available to the Team Physician, Alcohol/Drug Education Counselor, and Athletic Director. Failure to comply with Athletic Department Drug Policy or treatment program recommendations will result in immediate suspension from all competition, practice, and training until compliance is achieved. A second positive test could result in the suspension of the student-athlete from related financial aid.

The student-athlete will also be subject to periodic retests on any given date. These tests will be done under the supervision of the Drug Counselor, Athletic Medicine Staff, and/or Team Physician.

Prior to implementation of the treatment/penalties, or as soon thereafter as is practical, the student-athlete will have the opportunity to fully discuss the matter with the Alcohol/Drug Counseling staff and present evidence contesting the accuracy of the test or any mitigating circumstances that they feel are important.

In addition to the evaluation process, the student-athlete will be required to participate in a conference call with his/her parents, guardian, or spouse, the Athletic Director (or designee), Head Coach, Physician, or Alcohol/Drug Counselor.

3. Third Positive Test

Upon confirmation of a third positive test, the student-athlete will be suspended from all competition, practice, and training for one year. In addition, athletic financial aid will be revoked for the same period. The student-athlete's parents, guardian, or spouse will be notified by the Athletic Director or designee concerning said suspension.

After appropriate treatment and aftercare (including regular attendance at AA, CA, etc.), and at the end of the suspension, the student-athlete shall be eligible to apply for reinstatement to the athletic program. Reinstatement will not be considered automatic. A panel including the Athletic Director (or designee), Team Physician, Alcohol/Drug Counselor, Head Athletic Trainer, Head Coach, and others deemed appropriate by the Athletics Director shall review and determine the outcome of the petition for reinstatement. Participation in and cooperation with treatment goals, maintenance of sobriety, academic performance, and social functioning shall be considered requirements for reinstatement. During this conference, the student-athlete will have appropriate opportunity to present his/her case for reinstatement.

Prior to implementation of the suspension, or as soon thereafter as is practical, the student-athlete will have the opportunity to fully discuss the matter with the Alcohol/Drug Counseling staff and present evidence contesting the accuracy of the test or any mitigating circumstances he/she feels are important.

In addition to the evaluation process, the student-athlete will be required to participate in a conference call with his/her parents, guardian, or spouse, the Athletic Director (or designee), Head Coach, Physician, or Counselor.

Relapse

The University of Minnesota recognizes that chemical dependence (as opposed to chemical use or abuse) is a chronic disease requiring abstinence from all mood-altering chemicals (including alcohol) and is associated with the possibility of relapse. Any student-athlete having been diagnosed as having the disease of chemical dependency, and having cooperated with appropriate treatment, who sustains a relapse, may not be treated as having a third positive test if the student-athlete reacquires his/her sobriety, cooperates with relapse treatment recommendations, or if necessary, reenters treatment and aftercare. If a second relapse occurs, the student-athlete will be subject to the consequences of a third positive test.

Appeal Process

After an appeal or presentation of mitigating circumstances to the Drug Education Committee, any student-athlete who is found to test positive for a banned substance has the right to register an appeal to the Athletic Director. The Athletic Director will implement appropriate procedures to review the appeal. This procedure involves discussions with the student-athlete involved, the Alcohol/Drug Counseling Staff, the student-athlete's Head Coach and appropriate Assistant Coaches, and any other person the Athletic Director believes has relevant bearing on the appeal.

Reinstatement

Reinstatement of the student-athlete to athletic participation would be made possible only after the provision of proof of successful completion of appropriate Certified Drug Education and/or Rehabilitation Program (on or off campus), drug testing results, and approval by the counseling staff and athletic department.

Refusal of the student-athlete to meaningfully participate and cooperate in the evaluation and counseling program will result in *immediate suspension from the team, immediate revocation of aid, and ineligibility for athletic aid for the subsequent year.*

Reinstatement may involve a behavioral contract with the Athletic Director (or designee), Physician, Counselor, or Head Coach, outlining their expectations.

Conclusion

It is believed and hoped that the implementation of this University of Minnesota Intercollegiate Athletic Drug Education and Testing Program will serve to benefit all connected with intercollegiate athletics at the University of Minnesota.

NCAA DIVISION I, BIG TEN U OF M INTERCOLLEGIATE ATHLETICS CONSENT TO PARTICIPATE STATEMENT

Consent to Participate

I certify by my signature below that I have read and reviewed the University of Minnesota Intercollegiate Athletics Drug Program. I recognize and understand that I will be asked to provide urine for drug analysis. I consent to any such testing conducted as a part of the University of Minnesota Intercollegiate Athletics' Program and agree that I will not refuse to take any such test or otherwise dispute the University's right to perform such tests. Likewise, I hereby agree to abide by the treatment program and guidelines set forth in the University of Minnesota Intercollegiate Athletics' Drug Program for a *First Positive Test,* a *Second Positive Test,* and a *Third Positive Test.*

I understand that the University will abide by State and Federal Laws and the Data Privacy Act to maintain the confidentiality of all matters related to drug tests and other information to be performed pursuant to this policy.

I further agree to inform the Team Physician or Head Athletic Trainer of any and all medications I may take from time to time, either under prescription or self-administered. I recognize that this information is necessary to assist my Team Physician and Athletic Medicine Staff in providing me with the best possible care, should such care be needed.

I also authorize the Team Physician to make a confidential release to the Athletic Director, Head Coach, and Head Athletic Trainer, and to contact my parents, legal guardian, or spouse with information relating to positive test results, in accordance with terms of the University of Minnesota Intercollegiate Athletics Drug Program.

I understand that the University of Minnesota's Counseling Center and other help is available to me should I have any difficulty with drugs, alcohol, or any other personal matter, or with any questions regarding the University of Minnesota Intercollegiate Athletics Drug Program.

To the extent set forth in this document and the University of Minnesota Intercollegiate Athletics' Drug Program, I waive any privileges I may have in connection therewith.

The Regents of the University of Minnesota, its officers, employees, and agents are hereby released from legal responsibility or liability and the release of such information and records as authorized by this form.

_____

Print Full Name

_____   _____

Signature   Date

Signature of legal guardian if student-athlete is not 18 by September 1.

_____   _____

Signature   Date

OLSON JUNIOR HIGH SCHOOL ELIGIBILITY INFORMATION BULLETIN FOR INTERSCHOLASTIC ATHLETICS

Scholarship Rules

1. First semester 7th graders must have been promoted from the 6th grade.
2. Second semester 7th graders and 8th graders must be making satisfactory progress in completing course work toward promotion.

Mood-Altering Chemicals

1. Philosophy and Purpose

The Bloomington Schools recognize the use of mood-altering chemicals as a significant health problem for many adolescents, resulting in negative effects on behavior, learning, and the total development of each individual. The misuse and abuse of mood-altering chemicals for some adolescents affect extracurricular participation and devel-opment of related skills. Others are affected by misuse and abuse by family, team members, or other significant persons in their lives.

2. Rule

During the school year, regardless of the quantity, a student shall not (1) use a beverage containing alcohol, (2) use tobacco, or (3) use or consume, possess, buy, sell, or give away any other controlled substance (including steroids).

A. The rule applies to the entire school year and any portion of an activity season that occurs before the start of the school year or after the close of the school year.

B. It is not a violation for a student to be in possession of a controlled substance specifically prescribed for the student's own use by her/his physician.

3. Penalties Affecting Participation in Athletic Activities

A. First Violation

Penalty: After confirmation of the first violation, the student shall lose eligibility for the next two (2) consecutive interscholastic contests or two (2) weeks of a season in which the student is a participant, whichever is greater. No exception is permitted for a student who becomes a participant in a treatment program.

B. Second Violation

Penalty: After confirmation of the second violation, the student shall lose eligibility for the next six (6) consecutive interscholastic contests or two (2) weeks of a season in which the student is a participant, whichever is greater. No exception is permitted for a student who becomes a participant in a treatment program.

C. Third and Subsequent Violations

Penalty: After confirmation of the third or subsequent violation, the student shall lose eligibility for the next twelve (12) consecutive interscholastic contests in which the student is a participant. If after the third or subsequent violations, the student on his/her own volition becomes a participant in a chemical dependency program or treatment program, the student may be certified for reinstatement in MSHSL activities after a minimum period of six (6) weeks. Such certification must be

TROJAN HOCKEY
PLEDGE OF HONOR

I, _Rob Krotee_ , as a member of Wayzata High School's hockey team, recognize my responsibility to my teammates and coaches to follow the training rules set forth by the Minnesota State High School League and any other rules set by my coaches for the 2000–2001 hockey season. By signing this contract, I pledge and promise not to use or possess alcoholic beverages, illegal drugs, or tobacco products during the 2000–2001 hockey season.

If I am tempted to break training, I will gain the strength to abstain by remembering the trust my teammates and coaches have in me, my own self respect, and the pride I take in being a member of the Wayzata Trojan hockey team.

Robert L. Krotee   _11/23/01_
Player's Signature   Date

Derek Schwach
Rick Etzel
Chris Ysaacson   Team Captains

I have read this contract signed by my son.

Leslie Krotee
Parent's Signature

issued by the director or a counselor of a chemical dependency treatment center.

D. Penalties shall be accumulative beginning with and throughout the student's participation on Junior High and Senior High athletic teams.

E. A student shall be disqualified from all interscholastic athletics for nine additional weeks beyond the student's original period of ineligibility when the student denies violation of the rule, is allowed to participate, and is subsequently found guilty of the violation.

Statements to Be Signed by Participant and Parent or Guardian

I have read, understand, and acknowledge receiving the Athletic Eligibility Information, which contains a summary of the eligibility rules for interscholastic athletics at Olson Junior High School.

Informed Consent for Student-Athletes
By its nature, participation in interscholastic athletics includes risk of injury, which may range in severity. Although serious injuries are not common in supervised school athletic programs, it is impossible to eliminate the risk. Participants can and have the responsibility to help reduce the chance of injury. Players must obey all safety rules, report all physical problems to their coaches, follow a proper conditioning program, and inspect their own equipment daily.

_____
Student's Signature

_____
Grade in School

_____
Date

_____
Parent or Guardian's Signature

_____
Date

Tear off and return signed statement to the school office prior to practice or participation

NATIONAL ATHLETIC TRAINERS' ASSOCIATION CODE OF ETHICS

PRINCIPLE 1:

Members Shall Respect the Rights, Welfare, and Dignity of All Individuals

1.1   Members shall not discriminate against any legally protected class.

1.2   Members shall be committed to providing competent care consistent with both the requirements and the limitations of their profession.

1.3   Members shall preserve the confidentiality of privileged information and shall not release such information to a third party not involved in the patient's care unless the person consents to such release or release is permitted or required by law.

PRINCIPLE 2:

Members Shall Comply with the Laws and Regulations Governing the Practice of Athletic Training

2.1   Members shall comply with applicable local, state, and federal laws and institutional guidelines.

2.2   Members shall be familiar with and adhere to all National Athletic Trainers' Association guidelines and ethical standards.

2.3   Members are encouraged to report illegal or unethical practice pertaining to athletic training to the appropriate person or authority.

2.4   Members shall avoid substance abuse and, when necessary, seek rehabilitation for chemical dependency.

PRINCIPLE 3:

Members Shall Accept Responsibility for the Exercise of Sound Judgment

3.1   Members shall not misrepresent in any manner, either directly or indirectly, their skills, training, professional credentials, identity or services.

3.2   Members shall provide only those services for which they are qualified via education and/ or experience and by pertinent legal regulatory process.

3.3   Members shall provide services, make referrals, and seek compensation only for those services that are necessary.

PRINCIPLE 4:

Members Shall Maintain and Promote High Standards in the Provision of Services

4.1   Members shall recognize the need for continuing education and participate in various types of educational activities that enhance their skills and knowledge.

4.2   Members who have the responsibility for employing and evaluating the performance of other staff members shall fulfill such responsibility in a fair, considerate, and equitable manner, on the basis of clearly enunciated criteria.

4.3   Members who have the responsibility for evaluating the performance of employees, supervisees, or students, are encouraged to share evaluations with them and allow them the opportunity to respond to those evaluations.

4.4   Members shall educate those whom they supervise in the practice of athletic training with regard to the Code of Ethics and encourage their adherence to it.

4.5   Whenever possible, members are encouraged to participate and support others in the conduct and communication of research and educational activities that may contribute knowledge for improved patient care, patient or student education, and the growth of athletic training as a profession.

4.6   When members are researchers or educators, they are responsible for maintaining and promoting ethical conduct in research and educational activities.

PRINCIPLE 5:

Members Shall Not Engage in Any Form of Conduct that Constitutes a Conflict of Interest or That Adversely Reflects on the Profession

5.1   The private conduct of the member is a personal matter to the same degree as is any other person's except when such conduct compromises the fulfillment of professional responsibilities.

5.2   Members of the National Athletic Trainers' Association and others serving on the Association's committees or acting as consultants shall not use, directly or by implication, the Association's name or logo or their affiliation with the Association in the endorsement of products or services.

5.3   Members shall not place financial gain above the welfare of the patient being treated and shall not participate in any arrangement that exploits the patient.

5.4   Members may seek remuneration for their services that is commensurate with their services and in compliance with applicable law.

Ethics violations may be reported to:

NATA
Ethics Investigations
2952 Stemmons Freeway
Dallas, TX 75247-6196
(214) 637-6282

TARGET MINNESOTA

It's Cool to Be Chemically Free

Whereas adults can only imagine it, teenagers know what it's like for high schoolers in today's pressure-packed society where drugs and alcohol can be easy to get and hard to resist.

TARGET Minnesota, a League service program, taps that teen knowledge of their times to lead the way into a new era. It puts student leaders out front, showing their peers in League activities that it's "cool" to be chemically free.

TARGET is about responsibility. Students taking responsibility for themselves. Parents for their children. Schools for training student leaders and communicating with parents. Communities for supporting all three in their efforts to teach and foster healthy, chemically free lifestyles.

Students Lead the Way

TARGET Minnesota training teaches student leaders how to recognize chemical-use behavior, to listen, to express concern, to say:

"I care" and tell a friend or teammate why she/he is concerned;

"I see" and describe the actions that have caused concern;

"I feel" and talk about feelings of disappointment, anger, hurt, or fear;

"I want" and express her/his expectations for a behavior change;

"I will" and express how, as a student leader, she/he will support a student's efforts and commitment to change.

Parent Responsibility

Parents should attend the preseason meeting(s) their schools offer, with their teenagers, to openly and clearly express how they feel about the use of alcohol, drugs, or tobacco. They should then follow through by verifying their teens' whereabouts. (Most drinking goes on at parties where there is no supervision.)

Communicating with other parents; getting to know their sons' and daughters' friends; praising their teen's efforts as well as their accomplishments; supporting coaches/advisors, their rules and principles, shows support for teen attempts to free their schools of chemical use.

Parents should know about the "691 reporting law," which states that any adolescent whom the police apprehend for possession of alcohol, drugs, or paraphernalia will have the police report forwarded to the school. Parents should understand their liability for consequences that occur as a result of having served alcohol to minors in their homes.

Region Responsibility

Grassroots support of TARGET Minnesota comes from the Minnesota State High School League's sixteen regions. Each has a TARGET TEAM, which supports the program with information and annual training workshops/meetings held in schools, hotels, conference centers, or outdoor camps. Here, school personnel and students share their successes and lessons learned from their TARGET-affiliated program.

Each school's TARGET coordinator gets information through TARGETalk, a special section in the *League Bulletin,* and from special mailings.

The League office stands ready to help with resources and information. TARGET banners, pins, T-shirts, and sweatshirts are available by calling the League office at 612/569-0491.

School Responsibility

TARGET Minnesota helps member schools to identify, train, support, and recognize chemically free students and to put the program to work for their students, in just six steps.

Step One: Select Student Leaders

Schools determine a selection process which defines student leaders (i.e., students who show the qualities of good leaders, who have demonstrated leadership, or whose peers have selected them as leaders).

Coaches, advisors, counselors, and teachers help by recommending students for the program.

Step Two: Provide Leadership Training

Training teaches potential leaders about the qualities of motivational, positive leaders and

- how to learn from those leaders
- how to learn from their own personal mistakes
- how to recognize the needs of their group
- how to focus on issues important to their group
- how to intervene with peers who experience/create problems for the group

Regularly held TARGET leadership support group meetings also provide an outlet for pressures and a place to mutually discuss and resolve problems.

Step Three: Present Role Modeling Opportunities

Student leaders can become role models for elementary and middle school students, carrying the message of

- personal and team consequences of chemical use
- effects of chemical use on school performance
- how to refuse when pressured to use mind-altering chemicals
- the importance of telling someone when they are facing a problem(s)

Step Four: Recognize Commitment

Emblems/pins for TARGET student leaders to wear recognize the commitment they bring to the program. Articles that profile individual students in school and local newspapers give deserved recognition.

Other recognition can come through public service announcements promoting students' choices to be chemically free and through special awards to chemically free student leaders at awards ceremonies.

Opportunities for students in the TARGET program to speak to community organizations publicly rewards students' efforts and broadens their leadership experience.

Step Five: Support Student Leaders with Coach/Advisory Training

Student leaders can be most effective when working with adult coaches or advisors who know how to lend their support. Students learn from them how to recognize the signs and symptoms of chemical use as it affects an individual or team activity.

Coaches/advisors have to examine their own attitudes about the use of mood-altering chemicals; clarify their roles in establishing team/group standards about use; and develop their skills for "care-fronting" use by team/activity member.

They have to be ready for student expectations that they will be role models concerned with individuals, not just with winning. Students will look for them to have a "we can do this" attitude and to show respect for students.

Students will expect them, as coaches/advisors, to avoid showing favoritism; to be knowledgeable about their activities; to be good listeners; to give constructive criticism; to be able to have fun; to motivate team unity; and to relate to students.

Step Six: Bring Parents into the Circle

Schools can give parents a chance to speak out, to state their positions on chemical use, to communicate their feelings, and to show their support for the TARGET program. They do this by including TARGET in at least one preseason parent-student meeting each year where schools introduce and discuss Minnesota State High School League athletic and fine arts activities.

Or schools may choose to schedule a separate meeting for TARGET and for each League activity to promote communication, cooperation, and mutual support among parents, coaches/advisors, and school administrators.

Meetings provide a setting for signing the League *Eligibility Information Brochure* indicating an understanding of and support for League and school rules. They are an opportunity to inform parents and the general public of the school's leadership program and the expectations and goals for the year.

Meetings also send a community-wide message about chemical usage among teens and about interscholastic activities available to students.

Putting TARGET to Work

Here is a step-by-step checklist for schools to follow as they put the TARGET program to work for their students.

Identify TARGET program goals.

Develop a committee to define programs (i.e., identify the student selection process, membership requirements, consequences for rules violations, and other necessary elements for the program).

Develop clear, consistent, and enforceable rules, and define the roles of school personnel.

Conduct a training session for athletic coaches, fine arts advisors, and other activity directors.

Establish support groups for student leaders and trained group facilitators.

Conduct leadership training for identified students.

Conduct a preseason meeting to develop communication, cooperation and support between students, coaches/advisors, school administrators, and parents.

Develop strategies for providing regular communication to students, administrators, coaches/advisors, and parents.

Conduct chemically free activities for students with the involvement of parents in the school's community.

Develop an evaluation procedure to compare and monitor the TARGET program and its activities.

NCAA Banned–Drug Classes

The problems with drugs are pervasive in all facets of society. The arena of sport and its participants of all ages are not immune. Indeed there seems to be an increase in anxiety disorder, depression, disordered eating (especially in female athletes) and a preoccupation with body image especially in aesthetic or "thin-build-sports" (gymnastics, diving, cheerleading, distance running, figure skating, swimming, wrestling, light weight rowing). The following provides a valuable resource concerning various banned drug classes.

NCAA Banned-Drug Classes

Drugs banned by both NCAA and USOC
Anabolic steroids
Diuretics
Beta blockers (used to lower blood pressure, decrease heart rate, decrease cardiac arrhythmias)
Peptide hormones (human growth hormone, corticotropin, erythropoietin, human chorionic gonadotropin, etc.)
Stimulants* (amphetamines, cocaine, and anorexiants)
Caffeine (limited ingestion permits up to 12 µg/ml USOC and 15 µg/ml (NCAA)
Blood doping

Drugs banned by USOC only
Narcotic analgesics (codeine is permitted)
Skeletal muscle relaxants (banned for modern pentathlon and biathlon events only)
Cough and cold decongestants (sympathomimetic drugs)
Injectable anesthetics (acceptable with prior written permission)
Corticosteroids (intramuscular, intravenous, rectal, and oral use is banned; most topical and inhaled use is permitted with written permission)

Drugs banned by NCAA only†
Substances that contain alcohol (banned for riflery)
Street drugs (heroin and marijuana)

* USOC permits inhaled albuterol and terbutaline with prior written permission; NCAA permits all inhalants.

† USOC reserves the right to test for alcohol and street drugs with possible sanctions for positive tests.

NCAA Banned-Drug Classes—cont'd

(a) Stimulants:
amiphenazole
amphetamine
bemigride
benzphetamine
bromantan
caffeine[1]
chlorphentermine
cocaine
cropropamide
crothetamide
diethylpropion
dimethylamphetamine
doxapram
ephedrine
ethamivan
ethylamphetamine
fencamfamine
meclofenoxate
methamphetamine
methylene-dioxymethamphetamine
 (MDMA) (Ecstasy)
methylphenidate
nikethamide
pemoline
pentetrazol
phendimetrazine
phenmetrazine
phentermine
picrotoxine
pipradol
prolintane
strychnine and related compounds*

(b) Anabolic Agents:
anabolic steroids
androstenediol
androstenedione
boldenone
clenbuterol
clostebol
dehydrochlormethyl-testosterone
dehydroepiandrosterone (DHEA)
dihydrotestosterone (DHT)
dromostanolone
fluoxymesterone
mesterolone
methandienone
methenolone
methyltestosterone
nandrolone
norandrostenediol
norandrostenedione
norethandrolone
oxandrolone
oxymesterone
oxymetholone
stanozolol
testosterone[2] and related compounds*
other anabolic agents

(c) Substances Banned for Rifle Sports:
alcohol
atenolol
metoprolol
nadolol
pindolol
propranolol
timolol and related compounds*

(d) Diuretics:
acetazolamide
bendroflumethiazide
benzthiazide
bumetanide
chlorothiazide
chlorthalidone
ethacrynic acid
flumethiazide
furosemide
hydrochlorothiazide
hydroflumethiazide
methyclothiazide
metolazone
polythiazide
quinethazone
spironolactone
triamterene
trichlormethiazide and related
 compounds*

(e) Street Drugs:
heroin
marijuana[3]
THC (tetrahydrocannabinol)[3]

(f) Peptide Hormones and Analogues:
chorionic gonadotrophin (HCG—
 human chorionic gonadotrophin)
corticotrophin (ACTH)
growth hormone (HGH,
 somatotrophin)
All the respective releasing factors
 of the above-mentioned
 substances also are banned.
erythropoietin (EPO)
sermorelin

Definitions of positive depends on the following:

[1]For caffeine—if the concentration in urine exceeds 15 micrograms/ml.

[2] For testosterone—if the administration of testosterone or the use of any other manipulation has the result of increasing the ratio of the total concentration of testosterone to that of epitestosterone in the urine to greater than 6:1, unless there is evidence that this ratio is due to a physiological or pathological condition.

[3] For marijuana and THC—if the concentration in the urine of THC metabolite exceeds 15 nanograms/ml.

* The term "related compounds" comprises substances that are included in the class by their pharmacological action and/or chemical structure. No substance belonging to the prohibited class may be used, regardless of whether it is specifically listed as an example.

Supplements

Nutritional supplements are not strictly regulated and may contain substances banned by the NCAA. For questions regarding nutritional supplements, contact the National Center for Drug Free Sport Resource Exchange Center (REC) at 877/202-0769.

Prentice, W. E. 2003, Arnheim's Principles of Athletic Training, Dubuque, IA: McGraw-Hill.

Selected Associations for Athletes with Disabilities

American Hearing Impaired Hockey Association
Irvin G. Tiahnybik
1143 West Lake St.
Chicago, IL 60607
(312) 226-5880
www.ahiha.org

American Wheelchair Bowling Association
P.O. Box 69
Clover, VA 24534-0069
(434) 454-2269
www.awba.org

Canadian Wheelchair Sports Association
2460 Lancaster Road, Suite 200
Ottawa, Ontario, Canada K1B 4S5
(613) 523-0004
www.cwsa.ca

Courage Center
3915 Golden Valley Road
Golden Valley, MN 55422
(800) 846-8253
www.courage.org

Disabled Sport USA
Kirk Bauer, Executive Director
451 Hungerford Dr., Suite 100
Rockville, MD 20850
(301) 217-0960
www.dsusa.org

Eastern Amputee Athletic Association
Jack Graff, President
2080 Ennabrock Rd.
North Bellmore, NY 11710
(516) 826-8340

Handicapped Scuba Association International
1104 El Prado
San Clemente, CA 92672-436
(949) 498-4540
www.hsascuba.com

International Foundation for Wheelchair
Tennis
Peter Burwash
2203 Timberlock Place, Suite 126
The Woodlands, TX 77380
(713) 363-4707

International Paralympic Committee
Adenauer Allee 212-214
53113 Bonn
Germany
(49) 228-2097-200
www.paralympic.org

International Wheelchair Road Racers Club, Inc.
Joseph M. Dowling, President
30 Mayano Lane
Stamford, CT 06902
(203) 967-2231

National Beep Baseball Association
4427 Knottynold
Houston, TX 77053
www.nbba.org

National Foundation of Wheelchair Tennis
Brad Parks, Executive Director
940 Calle Amancer, Suite B
San Clemente, CA 92673
(714) 361-3663
www.nfwt.org

National Wheelchair Basketball Association
6165 Lehman Drive, Suite 101
Colorado Springs, CO 80918
(719) 266-4082
www.nwba.org

National Wheelchair Softball Association
Jon Speake, Commissioner
1616 Todd Court
Hastings, MN 55033
(651) 437-1792
www.wheelchairsoftball.com

North American Riding for the Handicapped
Association
P.O. Box 33150
Denver, CO 80233
(800) 369-7433
www.narha.org

Ski for Light, Inc.
1455 West Lake Street
Minneapolis, MN 55408
(612) 827-3232
www.sfl.org

Special Olympics International
1133 19th St. NW
Washington, DC 20036
(202) 628-3630
www.specialolympics.org

United States Association for Blind Athletes
Charlie Huebner, Executive Director
33 North Institute
Colorado Springs, CO 80903
(719) 630-0422
www.usaba.org

National Disability Sports Alliance
25 West Independence Way
Kingston, RI 02881
(401) 792-7130
www.ndsaonline.org

Wheelchair Sports, USA
1668 320th Way
Earlham, IA 50072
(515) 833-2450
www.wsusa.org

Wilderness Inquiry
808 14th Ave. SE
Minneapolis, MN 55414-1516
(800) 728-0719
www.wildernessinquiry.org

Your State's Special Olympics
North Carolina Special Olympics
2200 Gateway Centre Blvd., Suite 201
Morrisville, NC 27560-9122
(800) 843-6276
(919) 719-7662
www.sonc.net

USADEAF Sports Federation
102 North Krohn Place
Sioux Falls, SD 57103-1800
(605) 367-5760
www.usadsf.org

Checklist for Facility Planners

	Yes	No

General

1. A clear-cut statement has been prepared concerning the nature and scope of the program and the special requirements for space, equipment, fixtures, climate control, lighting, safety and risk management, and facilities dictated by the activities to be conducted.

2. The facility has been planned to meet the total requirements of the program as well as the special needs of those who are to be served, including those with disabilities.

3. The plans and specifications have been checked by all governmental agencies (city, county, state, and federal) whose approval is required by law.

4. Plans for areas and facilities conform to local, state, and federal regulations and to accepted standards, codes, and practices.

5. The areas and facilities planned make possible the programs that serve the interests and needs of all people.

6. Every available source of property or funds has been explored, evaluated, and utilized whenever appropriate.

7. All interested persons and organizations concerned with the facility have had an opportunity to share in its planning (professional educators, users, consultants, administrators, engineers, architects, city planners, environmental experts, program specialists, building managers, and builder—a team approach).

8. The facility and its appurtenances will fulfill the maximal demands of the program. The program has not been curtailed to fit the facility.

9. The facility has been functionally planned to meet the present and anticipated needs of specific programs, situations, and publics.

10. Future additions and phases are included in present plans to promote economy of future expansion and construction.

Checklist for Facility Planners—cont'd

	Yes	No
11. Instructional venues, work stations, and offices are isolated and insulated from sources of distracting noises and motion.	____	____
12. Storage areas for indoor and outdoor equipment are adequately sized, well ventilated, and located adjacent to the gymnasiums.	____	____
13. Shelves in storage rooms are secure and slanted toward the wall.	____	____
14. All passageways are accessible, free of obstructions, and have recessed fixtures.	____	____
15. Facilities for health services, athletic training, health assessment and instruction, and the first-aid and emergency-isolation rooms are suitably interrelated.	____	____
16. Buildings, specific areas, and facilities are clearly identified, with hazards noted by appropriate warning signage.	____	____
17. Locker rooms are arranged for accessibility, ease of traffic flow, and supervision.	____	____
18. Offices, teaching stations, and service facilities are properly interrelated.	____	____
19. ADA and ABA standards are fully met, including a ramp into the building at a major entrance and accessibility to all floors and areas.	____	____
20. All "dead space" is used.	____	____
21. The building is compatible in design and comparable in quality and accommodation to other organizational structures.	____	____
22. Storage rooms are accessible to the play area and free of doorway center mullions or thresholds.	____	____
23. Workrooms, conference rooms, and staff and administrative offices are interrelated.	____	____
24. Shower and dressing facilities are provided for professional staff members and are private and conveniently located.	____	____
25. Thought and attention have been given to making facilities and equipment as durable, safe, and risk free and vandalproof as possible.	____	____
26. Low-cost maintenance and energy conservation features have been adequately considered.	____	____
27. This facility is a part of a well-integrated master plan.	____	____
28. All areas, courts, facilities, equipment, climate control, lighting security, etc., conform rigidly to detailed standards, codes, laws, and specifications.	____	____
29. Shelves are recessed and safety mirrors are supplied in appropriate places in rest rooms and dressing rooms.	____	____
30. Dressing space between locker rows is adjusted to the size and age of multiple user groups.	____	____
31. Drinking fountains are conveniently and safely placed in locker room and activity areas or immediately adjacent thereto.	____	____
32. Special attention is given to provision for the locking of service windows, doors, and counters, supply bins, carts, shelves, and equipment racks.	____	____
33. Provision is made for the repair, maintenance, replacement, and off-season storage of equipment and uniforms.	____	____
34. A well-defined program for laundering and cleaning of towels, uniforms, and equipment is included in the plan.	____	____
35. Noncorrosive metal is used in dressing, drying, and shower areas except for enameled lockers.	____	____
36. Antipanic hardware is used where required by fire regulations.	____	____
37. Properly placed hose bibbs and drains are sufficient in size and quantity to permit flushing and cleaning the entire area with a water hose.	____	____
38. A water-resistant, coved base is used under the locker base and floor mat, and where the floor and wall join.	____	____

Checklist for Facility Planners—cont'd

	Yes	No
39. Whiteboards and/or tackboards and electronic message boards with map tracks, including evacuation paths, are located in appropriate places in dressing rooms, hallways, and classrooms.	___	___
40. Bookshelves, hooks, and storage space are provided in toilet areas.	___	___
41. Space and equipment are planned in accordance with the types and number of participants.	___	___
42. Basement rooms, because they are undesirable for dressing, drying, and showering, are not planned for those purposes.	___	___
43. Spectator seating (permanent) in areas that are basically instructional is kept at a minimum. Portable risk-free code rollaway bleachers are used primarily. Balcony seating is considered as a possibility.	___	___
44. Well-lighted and effectively displayed trophy cases or walls of fame enhance the interest and appearance of the lobby.	___	___
45. The space under the stairs is used for storage.	___	___
46. Department heads' offices are located near the central administrative office, which includes a well-planned and fully wired conference/seminar room.	___	___
47. Workrooms are located near the central office and serve as a repository for department materials and records.	___	___
48. The conference area includes a cloakroom, lavatory, and toilet.	___	___
49. In addition to regular administrative assistants' offices established in the central and department chairperson's offices, a special room arranged in teamed quads for office personnel and staff members should be provided.	___	___
50. Staff dressing facilities are provided. These private facilities may also serve game officials.	___	___
51. The community and/or neighborhood has a planning and programming "round table."	___	___
52. All those (persons and agencies) who should be a party to planning and development are invited and actively engaged in the planning process.	___	___
53. Space and area relationships are important. They have been carefully considered.	___	___
54. Both long-range plans and immediate plans, including alternatives, have been made.	___	___
55. The safety and physical comfort of the student and other participants, a major factor in securing optimal learning, has been considered in the plans.	___	___
56. Plans for quiet areas and time-out space have been made.	___	___
57. In the planning, consideration has been given to the need for adequate recreation areas and facilities, both near and distant from the homes of targeted publics.	___	___
58. Security cameras, monitors, and consoles have been strategically integrated into key access and information control points.	___	___
59. Every effort has been exercised to eliminate hazards and risk.	___	___
60. The installation of low-hanging door closers, light fixtures, signs, and other objects in traffic areas has been avoided.	___	___
61. Warning signals, visible, tactile, and audible, are included in the plans.	___	___
62. Ramps have a slope equal to or less than a 1-foot rise in 12 feet.	___	___
63. Minimum landings for ramps are 5 feet × 5 feet, they extend at least 1 foot beyond the swinging arc of a door, have at least 6-foot clearance at the bottom, and have level platforms at 30-foot intervals on every turn.	___	___
64. Adequate, safe, and secure locker and dressing spaces are provided.	___	___

Checklist for Facility Planners—cont'd

	Yes	No
65. The design of dressing, drying, shower, and sauna areas reduces foot traffic to a minimum and establishes clean, dry aisles for bare feet.	____	____
66. Teaching stations are properly wired and equipped and are related to service facilities.	____	____
67. Toilet facilities are adequate and equal in number. They are accessible and serve all user groups.	____	____
68. Mail and delivery services, outgoing and incoming, are included in the plans.	____	____
69. Hallways, ramps, doorways, and elevators are designed to permit equipment to be moved easily and quickly.	____	____
70. A keying card swipe design suited to management and instructional needs is planned.	____	____
71. Toilets used by large groups have circulating (in and out) entrances and exits.	____	____
72. Standard and official measurements for all facilities and venues (i.e., courts, doors, fields, pools, standards, etc.) are called for.	____	____
73. Vents on handball, racquetball, and squash courts should be in the back one-third section of the ceiling.	____	____
74. Storage space design has been integrated for all classrooms, specialty rooms, and activity areas.	____	____
75. All work and instructional stations have been ergonomically designed and meet OSHA standards. They are also wired and equipped with the latest technology.	____	____

Climate Control

	Yes	No
1. Provision is made throughout the building for climate control—heating, ventilating, humidity control, and air conditioning.	____	____
2. Special ventilation is provided for locker, dressing, shower, drying, toilet, and equipment storage rooms.	____	____
3. Heating, humidity, ventilation, and air-conditioning plans permit both area and individual room control.	____	____
4. Research areas where animals are kept and where chemicals are used have been provided with special climate control and safety equipment.	____	____
5. The heating and ventilating of the wrestling, combatives, and dance gymnasiums have been given special attention.	____	____
6. Thermostats are centrally controlled, computerized, zoned, and secure.	____	____
7. There has been a thorough energy cost analysis study in the planning process (i.e., best lighting options for outdoor or indoor facilities).	____	____

Electrical

	Yes	No
1. Shielded, vaporproof lights are used in moisture prevalent areas.	____	____
2. Lights in strategic areas are key controlled.	____	____
3. Lighting intensity conforms to approved standards.	____	____
4. An adequate number of electrical outlets are strategically placed.	____	____
5. Gymnasium lights are controlled by dimmer or user capacity units.	____	____
6. Locker room lights are mounted above the space between lockers.	____	____
7. Natural light is controlled properly for purposes of visual aids and to avoid glare.	____	____
8. Electrical outlet plates are installed 3 feet above the floor unless special use dictates otherwise.	____	____
9. Controls for light switches, phone, cable, computer, VCR, and projection equipment are suitably located, recessed, and interrelated.	____	____
10. All lights are shielded. Special protection is provided in gymnasiums, arenas, court areas, pools, and shower rooms.	____	____

Checklist for Facility Planners—cont'd

	Yes	No

11. Lights are placed to shine between rows of lockers.
12. Lights are easily accessible for replacement and maintenance.
13. Indirect lighting has been used or integrated whenever possible.
14. All lighting options and energy costs over time have been explored.

Walls

1. Movable and folding partitions are power operated and controlled by keyed switches.
2. Wall plates are located where needed and are firmly attached.
3. Hooks and rings for nets are placed (and recessed in walls) according to court locations and net heights.
4. Materials that clean easily and are impervious to moisture are used where moisture is prevalent.
5. Showerheads are placed at varying and appropriate heights—four feet (elementary) to seven feet (high school, university)—for each school level and special situation (ADA).
6. Protective matting is placed permanently on the walls in the wrestling room, at the ends of basketball courts, and in other areas in which such protection is needed.
7. An adequate number of drinking fountains is provided. They are properly placed (recessed in wall).
8. One wall (at least) of the dance studio and strength-training room has full-length mirrors.
9. All corners in locker rooms are rounded.
10. All walls and surfaces of gymnasiums and court sports (e.g., handball, racquetball, wallyball, squash) are flush, flat, have juts or exposed columns.
11. The lower parts of walls are glazed for ease of maintenance.
12. Walls should be acoustically treated and pastel colored if feasible.
13. Handball, racquetball, and squash courts should have a tempered glass back wall and/or observation deck.
14. Flat wall space is planned for target and rebounding usage, not to mention creative climbing and strength areas, which may require wall reinforcement.
15. Windows should be kept to a minimum in gymnasium and pool areas where glare is a problem, however, windows and natural lighting should be fully considered in office space and other appropriate creative facility design concepts.

Ceilings

1. Overhead-supported apparatus is secured to beams engineered to withstand stress.
2. The ceiling height is adequate for the activities to be housed.
3. Acoustical materials impervious to moisture are used in moisture prevalent areas.
4. Skylights, being impractical, are seldom used because of problems in waterproofing roofs and controlling sun rays (gyms, pools).
5. All ceilings except those in storage areas are acoustically treated with sound-absorbent materials.
6. Most ceilings are painted off-white.

Floors

1. Floor plates are placed where needed and are flush-mounted.
2. Floor design and materials conform to recommended standards and specifications.

Checklist for Facility Planners—cont'd

	Yes	No

3. Lines and markings are painted on floors before sealing is completed (when synthetic tape is not used). _____ _____

4. A coved base (around lockers and where wall and floor meet) or the same water-resistant material used on floors is found in all dressing and shower rooms. _____ _____

5. Abrasive, nonskid, slip-resistant flooring that is impervious to moisture is provided on all areas where water is used—laundry, swimming pool, and shower, sauna, dressing, and drying rooms. _____ _____

6. Floor drains are properly located, and the slope of the floor is adequate for rapid drainage. _____ _____

7. Appropriate hardwood flooring is used in courts, gymnasium, and dance areas. _____ _____

Gymnasiums and Special Rooms

1. Gymnasiums are planned so as to provide safety zones (between courts, end lines, and walls) and for best use of space. _____ _____

2. One gymnasium wall is free of obstructions and is finished with a smooth, glazed, hard surface for target and ball-rebounding activities. _____ _____

3. The elementary school gymnasium has one wall free of obstructions, a minimum ceiling height of 18 feet, a minimum of 4,000 square feet of teaching area, and a recessed area for housing appropriate equipment and teaching aids. _____ _____

4. Secondary school gymnasiums have a minimum ceiling height of 22 feet; a scoreboard; electrical outlets placed to fit with bleacher installation; wall attachments for apparatus and nets; and a power-operated, sound-insulated, and movable partition with a small pass-through door at one end. _____ _____

5. A small spectator alcove adjoins the wrestling and combatives room and contains a drinking fountain (recessed in the wall). _____ _____

6. Cabinets, storage closets, supply windows, and service areas have locks. _____ _____

7. Provisions have been made for the cleaning, storing, and issuing of physical education and sport equipment and uniforms. _____ _____

8. Weight rooms/fitness centers have safety racks for all free weights and dumbbells. _____ _____

9. Special equipment is provided for use by persons with disabilities. _____ _____

10. Special provision has been made for audio and visual aids, including intercommunication systems, cable, radio, television, computer, and interactive videodisk linkage. _____ _____

11. Team dressing rooms have provision for the following:
    a. Hosing down and disinfecting the room _____ _____
    b. Floors pitched to drain easily _____ _____
    c. Hot- and cold-water hose bibbs _____ _____
    d. Windows safe, secure, and located above locker heights _____ _____
    e. White, chalk, tack, and bulletin boards, and movie, video, and *PowerPoint* projection _____ _____
    f. Lockers for each team member _____ _____
    g. Drying facility for uniforms or bathing suits _____ _____

12. The target archery range includes the following:
    a. Targets located 20–50 yards from the firing line _____ _____
    b. Three to eight feet of space between targets _____ _____
    c. Twelve or more feet of space behind firing line _____ _____
    d. Video feedback area and white board lecture space _____ _____
    e. Secure storage cabinets and repair space _____ _____

Checklist for Facility Planners—cont'd

	Yes	No

13. The indoor rifle range includes the following:
    a. Targets located 54 inches apart and 50 feet from the firing line
    b. Three feet to 8 feet of space behind targets
    c. Twelve feet of space behind firing line
    d. Ceilings at least 8 feet high
    e. Width adjusted to number of firing lines needed (1 line for each 3 students)
    f. A pulley device for target placement and return
    g. Secure storage and repair space
14. Dance facilities include the following:
    a. One hundred square feet per student (4,500–5,400 square feet recommended)
    b. A minimum length of 60 linear feet for modern dance
    c. Full-height viewing mirrors on one wall (at least) of 30 feet; also a 20-foot mirror on an additional wall if possible
    d. Acoustical drapery or leaf-fold bulletin board to cover mirrors when not used and for protection if other activities are permitted nearby.
    e. Dispersed electrical outlets, microphone jacks, and appropriate wiring for cable, computer, and speaker installation for music and instruction
    f. Built-in cabinets for record, tape, computer simulation, video and, CD players, microphones, and amplifiers, with space for equipment and technology carts
    g. An exercise bar (34 inches to 42 inches above floor) on one wall
    h. Appropriate floor surface (hardwood maple) and maintenance for type of dance (ballet, ballroom, clogging, modern, tap, etc.)
    i. Location near dressing rooms and outside entrances
15. Athletic training rooms include the following:
    a. Rooms large enough to adequately administer proper injury prevention protocol, and assess, evaluate, treat, counsel, and rehabilitate those needing sports medicine services
    b. Office space of 120 square feet for certified athletic trainer, team physician, and the various support services of sports medicine.
    c. Secure storage cabinets for medical supplies and records (HIPPA)
    d. Installation of drains for whirlpool, hydrotherapy tubs, etc.
    e. Installation of GFI-rated electrical outlets at each treatment site and throughout room
    f. High stools for use of equipment such as whirlpool, ice tubs, etc.
    g. Deep double-basin stainless steel sink, a toilet, sauna, and shower
    h. Extra sink, freezer, and refrigerator in the athletic trainer's room proper
    i. Direct fluorescent lighting
    j. Biohazard waste containers
    k. Adjoining dressing rooms
    l. Installation and use of hydrotherapy, diathermy, and rehabilitation equipment in separate areas
    m. Rehabilitative exercise laboratories located conveniently and adapted to the needs of persons with injuries or disabilities
    n. Double doors for access to the area

Checklist for Facility Planners—cont'd

	Yes	No

16. Coaches room should provide the following:
    a. A sufficient number of dressing lockers for coaching staff and officials
    b. A security closet or cabinet for valuables and athletic equipment such as timing devices
    c. A sufficient number of showers, toilet facilities, and storage
    d. Drains and faucets for hosing down the rooms where this method of cleaning is desirable and possible
    e. Whiteboard, scheduling chart, tackboard, and computer workstation
    f. A movie screen, video monitor, VCR, cable connection, and projection table for coaches to review films and videos and view multiple games

Persons with Disabilities (www.access-by-design.com)

Have you included those considerations that would make the facility fully accessible?
These considerations include the following:

1. The knowledge that persons with disabilities (17 percent of the U.S. population) will be participants in almost all activities, not merely spectators. The facility must conform to the Americans With Disabilities Act (ADA) and Architectural Barriers Act (ABA). It must be fully accessible and barrier free.
2. Ground-level entrance(s) or stair-free entrance(s) using inclined walks(s) or inclined ramp(s).
3. Uninterrupted walk surface; no abrupt changes in levels leading to the facility.
4. Approach walks and connecting walks no less than 4 feet wide.
5. Walks with gradient no greater than 5 percent and smooth and free of cracks.
6. A ramp with handrail and with rise no greater than 1 foot in 12 feet.
7. Flat or level surface inside and outside of all exterior doors, extending 5 feet from the door in the direction that the door swings, and extending 1 foot to each side of the door.
8. Automatically activated doors with flush thresholds.
9. Appropriate door widths, heights, and mechanical features.
10. At least 6 feet between vestibule doors in series, i.e., inside and outside doors.
11. Access and proximity to parking areas (at least 12 feet wide).
12. No obstructions by curbs at crosswalks, parking areas, etc.
13. Proper precautions (handrails, etc.) at basement window areas, open stairways, porches, ledges, and platforms.
14. Handrails on all steps, ramps, and rest rooms.
15. Precautions against the placement of utility covers or barriers in primary or major sidewalks.
16. Corridors that are at least 60 inches wide and without abrupt pillars or protrusions.
17. Floors and ramps that are nonskid and have no abrupt changes or interruptions in level.
18. Proper design of steps and accompanying railings.
19. Access to rest rooms, water coolers (33-inch level), telephones (48-inch level), food-service areas, lounges, toilets (20-inch level), dressing rooms, play area, elevators (48-inch level), and auxiliary services and areas.
20. Elevators in multiple-story buildings.
21. Appropriate placement of controls to permit and prohibit use as desired.
22. Sound and braille signals for the blind, and visual signals for the deaf as counterparts to regular sound and sight signals and signage throughout.

Checklist for Facility Planners—cont'd

	Yes	No
23. Proper placement, concealment, or insulation of radiators, heat pipes, hot water pipes, drain pipes, etc.	____	____
24. All operational devices (e.g., locker locks, wall controls) should be no more than 48 inches above floor level.	____	____
25. Persons in wheelchairs have an average vertical reach of 60 inches, horizontal reach of 30 inches, and need 63 inches by 56 inches to negotiate a turn.	____	____
26. All public places in the facility (e.g., bathroom, toilet, shower, lockers, meeting rooms, etc.) should be fully accessible.	____	____

Swimming Pools

	Yes	No
1. Has a clear-cut statement been prepared on the nature and scope of the design program and the special requirements for space, equipment, safety and emergency plan, and facilities dictated by the activities to be conducted?	____	____
2. Has the swimming pool been planned to meet the total requirements of the program to be conducted, as well as any special needs of the clientele to be served?	____	____
3. Have all plans and specifications been checked and approved by groups such as the state local boards of health or USA Swimming and USA Diving?	____	____
4. Is the pool the proper depth to accommodate the various age-groups and types of activities it is intended to serve (e.g., wet classroom ADA)?	____	____
5. Does the design of the pool incorporate the most current knowledge and best experience and practice available regarding the technical aspects (depth, length, width, bottom profile, overflow system, touchpad, tiling, color, bulkhead adjustments, etc.) of swimming pools?	____	____
6. If a local architect or engineer who is inexperienced in pool construction is employed, has an experienced pool consultant, architect, or engineer been called in to advise on design, maintenance, and equipment?	____	____
7. Is there adequate deep water for diving (minimum of 12 feet for 1-meter boards and 3-meter boards, 18 feet for 10-meter towers and 5 feet for starting blocks)?	____	____
8. Have the requirements for competitive swimming been met (7-foot lanes; 12-inch black or brown lines on the bottom; pool 1 inch longer than official measurement for touch pads; depth and distance markings)?	____	____
9. Is there adequate deck space around the pool? Has more space been provided than that indicated by the minimum recommended deck-pool ratio?	____	____
10. Does the aquatic director's or swimming instructor's office face the pool? And is there a window through which the instructor may view the entire pool area? Is there a toilet-shower-dressing area next to the office for instructors?	____	____
11. Are recessed steps or removable ladders located on the walls so as not to interfere with competitive swimming turns?	____	____
12. Does a properly constructed overflow gutter extend around the pool perimeter?	____	____
13. Where skimmers are used, have they been properly located so that they are not on walls where competitive swimming is to be conducted?	____	____
14. Have separate ventilated storage spaces been allocated for maintenance and instructional equipment?	____	____
15. Has the area for spectators been properly separated from the pool and diving area?	____	____
16. Have all diving standards and lifeguard stands been properly spaced, equipped, and anchored?	____	____

Checklist for Facility Planners—cont'd

	Yes	No
17. Does the pool layout provide the most efficient control of traffic from showers and locker rooms to the pool and wet classrooms? Are toilet facilities provided for wet swimmers separate from the dry area?	_____	_____
18. Is the recirculation pump located below the water level?	_____	_____
19. Is there easy vertical access to the filter room for both people and materials (stairway if required)?	_____	_____
20. Has the proper pitch to drains been allowed in the pool, on the pool deck, in the overflow gutter, and on the floor of shower and dressing rooms?	_____	_____
21. Has adequate space been allowed between diving boards and between the diving boards and ceiling and side walls?	_____	_____
22. Is there adequate provision for lifesaving equipment (backboard, oxygen, AED)? Pool-cleaning equipment?	_____	_____
23. Are inlets and outlets adequate in number and located so as to ensure effective circulation of water in the pool?	_____	_____
24. Has consideration been given to underwater lights, observation windows, and sound and video systems?	_____	_____
25. Is there a coping around the edge of the pool?	_____	_____
26. Has a pool heater been considered in northern climates in order to raise the temperature of the water?	_____	_____
27. Have underwater lights in end racing walls been located deep enough and directly below surface lane anchors, and are they on a separate circuit?	_____	_____
28. Has the plan been considered from the standpoint of persons with disabilities?	_____	_____
29. Is seating for swimmers and spectators provided on the deck?	_____	_____
30. Has the recirculation-filtration system been designed to meet the anticipated future user load?	_____	_____
31. Have chemical feed systems been placed in a separate room accessible from and vented to the outside?	_____	_____
32. Has the gutter wastewater been valved to return to the filters, and also for direct waste?	_____	_____
33. Can a computer be used to control chemical balance?	_____	_____
34. Are bottom drain covers secure?	_____	_____
35. Are proper warning signs placed where appropriate?	_____	_____
36. Are depth markers (4 or more inches in height) conspicuously placed both in the pool and on the pool deck?	_____	_____
37. Are starting blocks placed in the deep end or in at least 5 feet of water?	_____	_____
38. Are proper safety equipment and emergency plans and procedures kept current and practiced?	_____	_____
39. Are rules and warning signs properly posted?	_____	_____
40. Are telephone, cell phone, computer, 2-way radios, emergency phone numbers, member tracking, and instant communication readily available?	_____	_____

Indoor Pools

	Yes	No
1. Is there proper mechanical ventilation (HVAC-dehumidification)?	_____	_____
2. Is there adequate acoustical treatment of walls and ceilings?	_____	_____
3. Is there adequate overhead clearance for diving (20 feet above low springboards and 3-meter boards, and 15 feet for 10-meter platforms)?	_____	_____

Checklist for Facility Planners—cont'd

	Yes	No

4. Is there adequate lighting (50 foot-candles minimum)?
5. Has reflection of light from the outside been minimized by proper location of windows or skylights (windows on side walls are not desirable)?
6. Are all wall bases coved to facilitate cleaning?
7. Is there provision for proper temperature control in the pool room for both water and air?
8. Are all surfaces nonslip?
9. Is the wall and ceiling insulation adequate to prevent "sweating"?
10. Are all metal fittings of noncorrosive material?
11. Is there a tunnel around the outside of the pool, or a trench on the deck that permits ready access to pipes?
12. Are in-pool lights 3 ½ feet below the surface lane line anchors?

Outdoor Pools

1. Is the site for the pool in the best possible location (away from railroad tracks, heavy industry, trees, and dusty open fields)?
2. Have sand and grass been kept the proper distance away from the pool to prevent them from being transmitted to the pool?
3. Has a fence been placed around the pool to ensure safety when not in use?
4. Has proper subsurface drainage been provided?
5. Is there adequate deck space for sunbathing?
6. Are the outdoor lights placed far enough from the pool to prevent insects from dropping into the pool?
7. Are the deck and pool bottom made of nonslip material?
8. Is there an area set aside for eating, separate from the pool deck?
9. Is the bathhouse properly located with the entrance to the pool leading to the shallow end?
10. If the pool shell contains a concrete or tile finish, has the length of the pool been increased by 3 inches over the official competitive size in order to permit eventual tiling of the basin without making the pool too short?
11. Are there other recreational facilities nearby for the convenience and enjoyment of swimmers?
12. Do diving boards or platforms face north or northeast?
13. Are enough lifeguard stands provided and properly equipped and located?
14. Has adequate parking space been provided and properly located?
15. Is the pool oriented correctly in relation to the sun?
16. Have windscreens been provided in situations where heavy winds prevail?
17. Is there appropriate aboveground and underwater lighting?
18. Are ladders recessed?
19. Does pool design allow an additional inch for electrical timing pads (more space is needed if movable bulkheads are part of the aquatic plan)?
20. Are first aid and emergency equipment readily available and staffed by well trained and certified staff?

Adapted and updated from National Facilities Conference, Planning Areas and Facilities for Health, Physical Education, and Recreation, Washington, DC, 1965, AAHPER.

Sample Budgets

- Typical Suburban School District Budget and Funding Sources
- Typical High School Varsity Sport Budgets
- Typical Middle School Sport Budget
- Intercollegiate Recreational Sport Budget Management
- Community-Based Youth Sport Budget
- Community-Based Youth Club Sport Budget Report
- Sample YMCA Revenue and Expenditures

Typical suburban school district budget and funding*
(1 High School and 2 Junior High Schools)

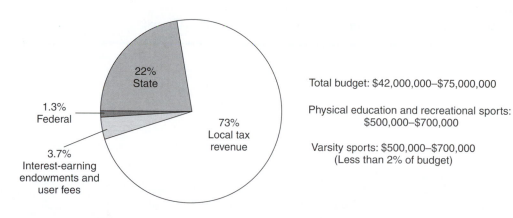

Total budget: $42,000,000–$75,000,000

Physical education and recreational sports:
$500,000–$700,000

Varsity sports: $500,000–$700,000
(Less than 2% of budget)

* Dependent on commercial and residential tax base of the school district

Typical High School Varsity Sport Budget (Boys)

	Fall Sports			Winter Sports		
Revenues	**653** **Cross Cty.**	**654** **Football**	**663** **Soccer**	**651** **Basketball**	**657** **Ice Hockey**	**660** **Nordic Ski**
070 Entry Fees						
071 Gate Receipts		26,622	2,292	6,407	6,500	
072 Miscellaneous Income						
073 User Fees	3,780	10,900	4,425	2,175	3,600	1,450
Total Revenue	3,780	37,522	6,717	8,582	10,100	1,450
Expenses						
Salaries	6,872	46,432	16,436	15,600	20,141	4,805
Benefits—12.65%	869	6,965	2,079	1,973	2,548	608
182 Game Workers-Employees		1,200	350	700	800	—
313 Subscriptions						
365 District Transportation	1,440	2,740	3,000	2,640	5,000	1,080
371 Entry Fees	250					200
372 Game Workers-Nonemployees		3,800	600	2,600	1,200	
373 Officials		2,100	1,950	1,800	2,200	275
374 Supplies, Training		1,500	—	300	300	—
376 Uniforms	500	4,000	—	1,000	3,300	400
431 Supplies, Equipment	100	5,200	1,200	700	2,800	340
505 Rent						75
899 Miscellaneous Expense						
902 Professional Development	110	900	100	160	240	150
370 Ice Time						
Total Expenses	10,141	74,837	25,715	27,473	38,529	7,933
Net Cost	6,361	37,315	18,998	18,891	28,429	6,483
# of Participants	64	112	62	29	36	30
Net Cost/Participant	99	333	306	651	790	216

	Winter Sports				Spring Sports				
661 **Alpine**	**664** **Swimming**	**670*** **Wrestling**	**650** **Baseball**	**655** **Golf**	**666** **Tennis**	**667** **Track**	**659** **I-M**	**Total**
								—
								41,821
								—
1,420	2,100	—	3,375	1,250	1,600	4,575	—	40,650
1,420	2,100	—	3,375	1,250	1,600	4,575	—	82,471
3,549	13,263	2,257	16,637	5,547	7,113	17,811	1,700	178,163
449	1,678	286	2,105	702	900	2,253	215	23,629
—	—	—	—	—	—	600	—	3,650
								—
1,500	2,200	1,000	2,100	1,200	840	2,640	—	27,380
350	350	200	500	375		400	—	2,625
						2,400	—	10,600
200	550	200	1,900	—	—	250	—	11,425
—	—	—	—	—	—	—	—	2,100
—	900	500	600	—	—	900	—	12,100
250	400	500	2,500	800	800	800	150	16,540
1,000								1,075
								—
125	185	85	230	120		260	—	2,665
								—
7,423	19,526	5,028	26,572	8,744	9,653	28,314	2,065	291,952
6,003	17,426	5,028	23,197	7,494	8,053	23,739	2,065	209,481
28	35	19	40	25	32	61	—	573
214	498	—	580	300	252	389	—	366

*coop-Richfield.

Typical High School Varsity Sport Budget (Girls)

Revenues	Fall Sports				Winter Sports					
	653 Cross Cty.	663 Soccer	664 Swimming	666 Tennis	669 Volleyball	651 Basketball	656 Gymnastics	657 Ice Hockey	660 Nordic Ski	661 Alpine Ski
070 Entry Fees										
071 Gate Receipts		2,292	—	—	2,273	5,379	392	1,000	—	—
072 Miscellaneous Income										
072 User Fees	5,250	4,800	4,190	1,675	2,250	1,950	720	1,700	4,160	1,010
Total Revenue	5,250	7,092	4,190	1,675	4,523	7,329	1,112	2,700	4,160	1,010
Expenses										
Salaries	8,179	16,306	21,051	7,347	11,843	15,600	13,391	16,614	4,805	3,549
Benefits—12.65%	1,035	2,446	2,663	929	1,498	1,973	1,694	2,102	608	449
182 Game Workers-Employees		350	—	—	380	700	200	200	—	—
313 Subscriptions										
365 District Transportation	1,440	3,000	2,640	1,700	1,700	3,200	960	4,500	1,080	1,500
371 Entry Fees	250	—	200	85	400	350	250	235	200	350
372 Game Workers-Nonemployees		600	—	—	820	2,600	500	800	—	—
373 Officials		2,100	620	—	800	1,800	630	2,200	275	200
374 Supplies, Training						300	—	—	—	—
375 Transportation, Other										
376 Uniforms	500	—	520	—	1,200	3,000	—	—	400	—
431 Supplies, Equipment	100	1,200	250	900	1,100	700	1,200	500	340	250
505 Rent									75	1,000
899 Miscellaneous Expense										
902 Professional Development	110	100	180		90	160	65	180	150	125
370 Ice Time										
Total Expenses	11,614	26,102	28,124	10,961	19,831	30,383	18,890	27,331	7,933	7,423
Net Cost	6,364	19,010	23,934	9,286	15,308	23,054	17,778	24,631	3,773	6,413
# of Participants	85	66	69	33	33	25	12	17	83	20
Net Cost/Participant	75	288	347	281	464	922	1,481	1,449	45	321

	Spring Sports				Other			
655 Golf	662 Softball	665 Syn. Swim	667 Track	652 Cheerldg.	658/671 Dance	659 Intra	Total
—	—	—	—	—	778	—	12,114
1,150	2,025	1,680	9,600	3,110	1,475	—	46,745
1,150	2,025	1,680	9,600	3,110	2,253	—	58,859
5,497	11,323	10,096	21,325	7,190	8,040	1,700	183,856
695	1,432	1,277	2,698	910	1,017	215	23,641
—	—	—	600	—	—	—	2,430
—	1,800	1,440	2,640	900	900	—	29,400
375	100	200	400	780	200	—	4,375
—	—	—	2,400	—	200	—	7,920
—	950	800	250	—	250	—	10,875
—	—	—	—	—	—	—	300
1,200	—	—	—	—	—	—	1,200
—	200	300	900	2,000	1,500	—	10,520
800	900	200	800	200	200	150	9,790
—	—	—	—	—	—	—	1,075
120	150	75	260	150	85	—	2,000
8,687	16,855	14,388	32,273	12,130	12,392	2,065	287,382
7,537	14,830	12,708	22,673	9,020	10,139	2,065	228,523
23	27	28	128	62	40	25	776
328	549	454	177	145	253	—	294

Typical Middle School Sport Budget

Report	Boys' Athletics					
Revenues	650 **Baseball**	651 **Basketball**	654 **Football**	663 **Soccer**	667 **Track**	**Total**
070 Entry Fees						
071 Gate Receipts						
072 Miscellaneous Income						
073 User Fees	1,080	585	3,150	780	2,400	7,995
Total Revenue	1,080	585	3,150	780	2,400	7,995
Expenses						
Salaries	5,493	8,640	8,969	2,506	7,557	33,165
Benefits 12.65%	695	1,093	1,135	317	956	4,195
182 Game Workers-Employees						
365 District Transportation	1,440	875	780	450	780	4,325
371 Entry Fees						
372 Game Workers-Nonemployees		200	—	—	400	600
373 Officials	540	640	480	160	—	1,820
374 Supplies-Training						
376 Uniforms					400	400
431 Supplies-Equipment	170	200	2,200	160	200	2,930
902 Professional Development						
Total Expenses	8,338	11,648	13,564	3,593	10,293	47,435
Net Cost	7,258	11,063	10,414	2,813	7,893	39,440
# of Participants	36	24	56	24	80	220
Net Cost/Participant	202	461	186	117	99	179

| | Girls' Athletics | | | | | | |
651 Basketball	663 Soccer	662 Softball	667 Track	669 Volleyball	Total	Admin	Total
						—	
							—
615	600	450	3,750	1,230	6,645	—	14,640
615	600	450	3,750	1,230	6,645	—	14,640
8,474	2,317	2,359	7,554	4,822	25,526	5,518	64,209
1,072	293	298	956	610	3,229	698	8,122
							—
780	450	660	780	1,440	4,110	—	8,435
				220	220	—	220
200	—	—	400	—	—	—	600
640	160	160	—	240	1,200	—	3,020
							—
—	—	—	400	—	400	—	800
200	160	160	200	100	820	—	3,750
							—
11,366	3,380	3,637	10,290	7,432	35,505	6,216	89,156
10,751	2,780	3,187	6,540	6,202	28,860	6,216	74,516
24	24	18	100	36	178	—	820
448	116	177	65	172	162	—	91

Intercollegiate Recreational Sport Budget Management

Expense Budget Summary

Component	Organization Number	Year 1 (Actual) FTE	Year 1 (Actual) Amount	Year 2 (Budgeted) FTE	Year 2 (Budgeted) Amount	Change FTE	Change Amount	Year 3 (Proposed) FTE	Year 3 (Proposed) Amount	% Change Years 1-2	% Change Years 2-3
General Administration		10.81	557,353	10.95	604,860	(0.35)	53,768	10.60	658,628	18.17	8.89
Youth & Community Programs		5.12	132,978	6.78	183,088	1.86	33,080	8.64	216,168	62.56	18.07
Professional Development		0.00	28,373	0.00	25,000	0.00	0	0.00	25,000	(11.89)	0.00
Intramurals		11.21	236,155	11.40	204,021	(0.50)	21,000	10.90	225,021	(4.71)	10.29
Fitness		13.89	312,863	14.53	392,184	0.02	3,831	14.55	396,015	26.58	0.98
Open Rec./Court Sports		0.88	15,699	4.06	78,210	(0.39)	12,715	3.67	90,925	479.18	16.26
Membership/Marketing		1.08	66,723	1.30	75,345	0.24	2,787	1.54	78,132	17.10	3.70
Aquatics		13.07	325,277	13.87	345,900	0.45	19,834	14.32	365,734	12.44	5.73
Twin Cities Swim Club		1.00	37,421	1.00	37,817	0.00	208	1.00	38,025	1.61	0.55
Sport Clubs		4.20	167,519	2.57	130,734	(0.02)	41,068	2.55	171,802	2.56	31.41
Vehicle Leasing		0.00	60,385	0.00	65,978	0.00	662	0.00	66,640	10.36	1.00
Facilities Operation		16.55	483,675	13.93	458,098	(1.52)	0	12.41	458,098	(5.29)	0.00
Equip. Room/Bldg. Maint.		0.00	0	5.12	105,000	(0.42)	0	4.70	105,000	0.00	0.00
Other Programs & Operations		7.49	249,626	7.40	250,377	5.73	116,893	13.13	367,270	47.13	46.69
Total		85.30	2,674,047	92.91	2,956,612	5.10	305,846	98.01	3,262,458	22.00	10.34
Income			1,532,208		1,402,903		305,846		1,708,749	11.52	21.80
Student Fee Component			1,747,713		1,553,709		0		1,553,709	(11.10)	0.00

Intercollegiate Recreational Sport Budget Management

Income Budget Summary

Component	Organization Number	Year 1 (Actual) Amount	Year 2 (Budgeted) Amount	Change Amount	Year 3 Amount	Years 1–2	% Change Years 2–3
General Administration		0	0	0	0	n/a	n/a
Youth & Community Programs		169,895	201,500	39,500	241,000	41.85	19.60
Professional Development		0	0	0	0	n/a	n/a
Intramurals		78,228	81,630	(380)	81,250	3.86	(0.47)
Fitness		78,224	82,500	54,000	136,500	74.50	65.45
Open Rec./Court Sports		10,753	8,000	20,000	28,000	160.39	250.00
Membership/Marketing		1,190	0	2,000	2,000	40.50	n/a
Aquatics		123,957	85,000	39,000	124,000	0.03	45.88
Twin Cities Swim Club		37,510	46,895	1,838	48,733	29.92	3.92
Sport Clubs		31,471	9,000	6,000	15,000	(52.34)	66.67
Vehicle Leasing		62,085	65,978	662	66,640	7.34	1.00
Facilities Operation		840,999	750,500	74,426	824,926	(1.91)	9.92
Equip. Room/Bldg. Maint.		0	0	0	0	0.00	0.00
Other Programs & Operation		97,896	71,900	68,800	140,700	43.72	95.69
Total		1,532,208	1,402,903	305,846	1,708,749	11.52	21.80

585

Community-based Youth Sport Budget

Wayzata Youth Hockey Association

Gross Receipts/Sales

Registrations (726)	$17,170.00	
Sponsors	5,750.00	
Blue Line Boosters	31,138.19	
Ice time	10,699.07	
Wayzata Tournament (2)	10,607.12	
General donations	250.00	$75,614.38

Expenses and Cost of Sales

League fees, referees, and ice time	$13,523.38	
Registration expense	1,269.50	
Equipment	14,462.21	
Rink and arena maintenance	5,260.58	
Outside tournaments and playoffs	3,265.00	
Wayzata tournament costs	3,892.68	
Insurance	694.00	
Interest on loan	347.59	
Loan payment	2,000.00	
Blue Line Boosters	20,525.41	
Concession commission to school district	1,732.18	
Travel team coaches' expense	1,487.30	
Miscellaneous administrative expense	517.35	68,977.18
Net results of operations—gain		$ 6,637.20
Beginning cash: Association Checking Account	$11,113.53	
Blue Line Boosters Accounts	1,804.39	
Savings Account (Capital Improvement)	7,072.34	$19,990.26
Plus Interest on Savings		478.56
		$20,468.82
Ending cash: Association Checking Account	$18,043.81	
Blue Line Boosters Accounts	1,511.31	
Savings Account (Capital Improvement)	7,550.90	27,106.02
Net cash increase		$ 6,637.20

NOTE: The savings account is held as collateral for the $3,000 loan at Anchor Bank.

The Association Account and Blue Line Account are held for capital improvements and season start-up costs.

Community-based Youth Club Sport Budget Report

Subcategory	Total		
	Actual	Budget	Difference
Income categories			
Challenger Camp			
	13,774.00	$0.00	$ 13,774.00
Fall			
Recreational	3,450.00	7,000.00	(3,550.00)
Traveling	22,267.50	12,960.00	9,307.50
Total Fall	25,717.50	19,960.00	5,757.50
Merchandise			
Apparel	23,819.55	0.00	23,819.55
Merchandise—Unassigned		5,000.00	(5,000.00)
Total Merchandise	23,819.55	5,000.00	18,819.55
MYSA District Tournament	2,553.00	2,000.00	553.00
Referee Clinic	1,050.00	0.00	1,050.00
Scholarship 2006	1,399.51	0.00	1,399.51
Summer			
Jamboree	1,093.23	0.00	1,093.23
Recreational	18,898.50	19,200.00	(301.50)
Traveling	112,952.68	97,920.00	15,032.68
Summer—Unassigned	(20.00)	0.00	(20.00)
Total Summer	132,924.41	117,120.00	15,804.41
Summer 2006			
Recreational	384.00	0.00	384.00
Scholarship	216.10	0.00	216.10
Traveling	15,605.40	0.00	15,605.40
Total Summer 2006	16,205.50	0.00	16,205.50
Training			
Augsburg Dome	8,905.00	5,200.00	3,705.00
Plymouth Dome	4,188.00	5,200.00	(1,012.00)
Total Training	13,093.00	10,400.00	2,693.00
U15B Premier	10,000.00	0.00	10,000.00
Wings Invitational			
Advertising	925.00	0.00	925.00
Concessions	2,771.10	0.00	2,771.10
T-shirt	2,080.00	0.00	2,080.00
Team fees	11,390.00	0.00	11,390.00
Wings Invitational—Unassigned		13,500.00	(13,500.00)
Total Wings Invitational	17,166.10	13,500.00	3,666.10
Income—Unassigned	0.00	0.00	0.00
Total Income Categories	$257,702.57	$167,980.00	$ 89,722.57

Community-based Youth Club Sport Budget Report—cont'd

Subcategory	Actual	Total Budget	Difference
Expense categories			
2006			
Facility rental	$ 1,097.14	$0.00	$ (1,097.14)
Fall tournament	125.00	0.00	(125.00)
Total 2006	1,222.14	0.00	(1,222.14)
Administrative			
Advertising	1,854.09	500.00	(1,354.09)
General copy	2,441.92	500.00	(1,941.92)
General postage	155.65	350.00	194.35
Internet Web page	900.00	1500.00	600.00
Legal	1,137.50	500.00	(637.50)
Newsletter: other	51.10	0.00	(51.10)
Newsletters: copy	2,114.76	1,450.00	(664.76)
Newsletters: postage	303.38	3,050.00	2,746.62
Office equipment	1,450.67	2,500.00	1,049.33
Office lease	2,318.16	0.00	(2,318.16)
Office supplies	4,137.65	500.00	(3,637.65)
Promotional	3,279.28	500.00	(2,779.28)
Registration refund	1,549.50	0.00	(1,549.50)
Risk management		800.00	800.00
Uniform refund	144.00	0.00	(144.00)
Voice mail	443.79	900.00	456.21
Wings Club Handbook		1,000.00	1,000.00
Administrative—Unassigned	448.12	0.00	(448.12)
Total Administrative	22,729.57	14,050.00	(8,679.57)
Augsburg			
Rental	6,215.50	3,510.00	(2,705.50)
Trainers	2,768.25	1,687.00	(1,081.25)
Total Augsburg	8,983.75	5,197.00	(3,786.75)
Challenger Day Camp	10,729.00	0.00	(10,729.00)

Community-based Youth Club Sport Budget Report—cont'd

Subcategory	Total		
	Actual	Budget	Difference
Income categories			
Coaching			
Apparel	952.00	1,250.00	298.00
Director of Coaching	26,380.36	20,000.00	(6,380.36)
DOC Expense Account	1,219.11	2,000.00	780.89
Fall reimbursement	4,590.00	3,600.00	(990.00)
General/miscellaneous	250.00	500.00	250.00
Licensing	4,475.00	2,500.00	(1,975.00)
Summer reimbursement	29,470.00	26,910.00	(2,560.00)
Total Coaching	67,336.47	56,760.00	(10,576.47)
Equipment			
Storage	3,050.24	1,500.00	(1,550.24)
Equipment—Unassigned	2,675.83	8,500.00	5,824.17
Total Equipment	5,726.07	10,000.00	4,273.93
Financial Assistance	4,070.00	3,480.00	(590.00)
Logo			
Apparel	1,779.00	0.00	(1,779.00)
Magnet	366.03	0.00	(366.03)
Pins/patches	2,369.50	0.00	(2,369.50)
Total Logo	4,514.53	0.00	(4,514.53)
MYSA (Fall)			
Adult		375.00	375.00
Player	4,926.00	1,620.00	(3,306.00)
Recreational		1,000.00	1,000.00
State tournament		1,400.00	1,400.00
Team	1,230.00	1,800.00	570.00
Total MYSA (Fall)	6,156.00	6,195.00	39.00
MYSA (Summer)			
Adult	1,340.00	1,400.00	60.00
Player	7,709.00	3,552.00	(4,157.00)
Recreational	2,415.00	2,400.00	(15.00)
State tournament	1,725.00	1,600.00	(125.00)
Team	5,610.00	5,280.00	(330.00)
Total MYSA (Summer)	18,799.00	14,232.00	(4,567.00)
MYSA 2006	1,705.00	0.00	(1,705.00)

Community-based Youth Club Sport Budget Report—cont'd

Subcategory	Actual	Total Budget	Difference
Income categories			
Recreational (Fall)			
T-shirt	588.00	1,200.00	612.00
Recreational (Fall)—Unassigned	550.00	0.00	(550.00)
Total Recreational (Fall)	1,138.00	1,200.00	62.00
Recreational (Summer)			
Coach shirt	438.75	0.00	(438.75)
Coaches' refund	825.00	1,200.00	375.00
Jamboree	2,336.97	1,000.00	(1,336.97)
T-shirts	2,058.00	2,400.00	342.00
Total Recreational (Summer)	5,658.72	4,600.00	(1,058.72)
Recreational Merchandise		5,000.00	5,000.00
Referee (Fall)			
Assignor	180.00	162.00	(18.00)
Payment	3,386.00	2,700.00	(686.00)
Total Referee (Fall)	3,566.00	2,862.00	(704.00)
Referee (Summer)			
Assignor	495.00	576.00	81.00
Clinic	344.00	800.00	456.00
Payment	9,000.00	9,600.00	600.00
Total Referee (Summer)	9,839.00	10,976.00	1,137.00
Team Uniform			
Fall	4,549.50	0.00	(4,549.50)
Refund	55.00	0.00	(55.00)
Team Uniform—Unassigned	12,602.00	0.00	(12,602.00)
Total Team Uniform	17,206.50	0.00	(17,206.50)
Tournament			
District	411.49	0.00	(411.49)
u11/u19	11,485.00	10,000.00	(1,485.00)
u9/u10	2,250.00	3,000.00	750.00
Wings invitational	85.00	13,000.00	12,915.00
Total Tournament	14,231.49	26,000.00	11,768.51

Community-based Youth Club Sport Budget Report—cont'd

Subcategory	Actual	Total Budget	Difference
Income categories			
Tryouts/Training			
Facility rental	11,064.76	4,080.00	(6,984.76)
Specialized training	200.00	750.00	550.00
Trainers	6,561.31	5,100.00	(1,461.31)
u6/u8	3,982.50	4,000.00	17.50
Tryouts/Training—Unassigned	150.00	0.00	(150.00)
Total Tryouts/Training	21,958.57	13,930.00	(8,028.57)
U15B Premier Travel	10,000.00	0.00	(10,000.00)
Wings Tournament			
Administration	690.05	0.00	(690.05)
Awards	3,319.00	0.00	(3,319.00)
Book	1,919.79	0.00	(1,919.79)
Concessions	2,420.26	0.00	(2,420.26)
Fields	1,800.00	0.00	(1,800.00)
Referees	5,307.50	0.00	(5,307.50)
Refund	1,038.30	0.00	(1,038.30)
Wings Tournament—Unassigned	157.00	0.00	(157.00)
Total Wings Tournament	16,651.90	0.00	(16,651.90)
Expense—Unassigned	2,848.96	0.00	(2,848.96)
Total Expense Categories	$255,070.67	$174,482.00	$(80,588.67)
Grand Total	$2,631.90	(6,502.00)	$9,133.90

Sample YMCA Revenue and Expenditures

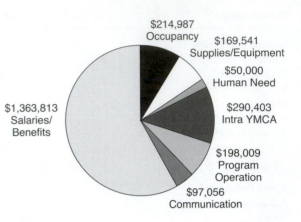

Revenue - $2,383,912

$113,747 Contributions

$52,821 United Way

$126,031 Other

$489,313 Program

$1,602,000 Membership

Expenditures - $2,383,809

$214,987 Occupancy

$169,541 Supplies/Equipment

$50,000 Human Need

$290,403 Intra YMCA

$198,009 Program Operation

$97,056 Communication

$1,363,813 Salaries/ Benefits